Canadian POLITICS

Canadian POLITICS

Critical approaches

2nd Edition

Rand Dyck
Laurentian University

Nelson Canada

I(T)P An International Thomson Publishing Company

Toronto • Albany • Bonn • Boston • Cincinnati • Detroit • London • Madrid • Melbourne
Mexico City • New York • Pacific Grove • Paris • San Francisco • Singapore • Tokyo • Washington

I(T)P⁻

International Thomson Publishing
The ITP logo is a trademark under licence

© Nelson Canada
A division of Thomson Canada Limited, 1996

Published in 1996 by
Nelson Canada
A division of Thomson Canada Limited
1120 Birchmount Road
Scarborough, Ontario M1K 5G4

Cover design and interior design: Steve MacEachern
Page composition: VISU*TronX*

Canadian Cataloguing in Publication Data

Dyck, Perry Rand, 1943–
    Canadian politics

2nd ed.
Includes bibliographical references and index.
ISBN 0-17-604930-4

1. Canada – Politics and government. I. Title.

JL75.D93 1996   320.971   C95-933150-6

Team Leader and Publisher	Michael Young
Acquisitions Editor	Andrew Livingston
Senior Production Editor	Bob Kohlmeier
Projects Coordinator	Joanne Scattolon
Art Director	Liz Harasymczuk
Production Coordinator	Brad Horning
Input Operator	June Reynolds

Printed and bound in Canada
1 2 3 4 (BBM) 99 98 97 96

To Jackie and Timmie,
two great sisters

Contents in Brief

Contents

x   **Contents**

Preface

This book presents the reality of Canadian government and politics in a concise but comprehensive manner. In its aim to be comprehensive, it includes all the traditional aspects of the subject—federalism, Parliament, cabinet, elections, political parties, pressure groups, political culture, etc.—as well as those of more recent origin or interest, such as the mass media and public opinion polls and the judiciary, especially in its interpretation of the Charter of Rights and Freedoms. At the same time, the object is to present a lean account of the subject and to avoid unnecessary tangents or detail.

Compared to the first edition, this book gives greater emphasis to the constitutional setting of Canadian government and politics. It includes a new chapter on the historical, constitutional, and institutional underpinnings of the system, and it also moves this section to the beginning. In dealing with the societal setting of the political system, it recognizes the significance of women, aboriginal peoples, and other ethnic groups by giving each its own chapter, while according less attention to questions of religion and age. On the other hand, this edition integrates the chapter on the Crown into the larger chapter on the Executive, and contains one chapter on Parliament, including both the House of Commons and the Senate. A glossary of key terms and definitions has been added, as has an appendix containing important constitutional documents. The book went to press in January 1996, and thus includes the 1993 federal election and the 1995 Quebec referendum on sovereignty.

If the underlying analytical framework of the book is the systems approach, it supplements that neutral model with a variety of other analytical approaches, drawing from public choice theory, pluralism, class analysis, and statism. In this way the book seeks to enliven the subject with a plurality of perspectives. The text refers to these four supplementary approaches wherever most appropriate and sets up an amalgamated analytical framework in which they all play a part. This framework takes from public choice theory the constant priority of those in power to enhance their chances of re-election; from class analysis, the inequality of political influence and the pervasive influence of capitalist values; from pluralism, the predominant influence, in a contest of floating coalitions of groups and interests, of business pressure groups; and from the state-centred model, the persistent influence of the bureaucracy.

As the troubled Canadian political system approaches the turn of the century, no text could be completely satisfied with the status quo. This book therefore points out aspects of the political and governmental operations of the country that are not working as well as they might, and suggests possible reforms and alternative arrangements, sometimes drawing on the experiences of other countries. Without being rigidly ideological, the book is a critical account, and seeks to make informed critics of its readers.

The preparation of this second edition gave me the opportunity to renew acquaintances with many of those who assisted me in writing the initial book three years ago. That included officials in many government departments and agencies, political parties, interest groups, research organizations, the media, and publishers. I thank all of them again.

Those who particularly stood out in the production of this edition include James Hurley and Iain Klugman in the Privy Council Office, Robert Marleau, Barbara Whittaker, and Claude Emery in the service of the House of Commons, John A. Chenier of ARC Publications, and three leading party officials: Darrell Reid (Reform), Michael Allen (PC), and Aurèle Gervais (Liberal). Also very helpful were public servants in the Finance Department, the CRTC, Elections Canada, Statistics Canada, Indian Affairs, Status of Women Canada, Treasury Board, and the office of the Information Commissioner. So too were officials at the Canadian Tax Foundation, the Canadian Council on Social Development, the National Council of Welfare, and the Caledon Institute.

I especially enjoyed talking to the cartoonists whose illustrative work adds spice to written words herein: Guy Badeaux (Bado), (whose drawing from *Le Droit*, Ottawa, appears on page 446); Susan Dewar (whose work appears with permission from the Ottawa *Sun* on 159, 181, and 225); Andy Donato (four of whose Toronto *Sun* drawings appear on 86, 484, 546, and 578); Paul Lachine (whose drawing from the *Chatham Daily News* appears on 33); Bruce MacKinnon (whose work appears with permission from the *Halifax Chronicle-Herald* on 244); Steve Nease (two of whose cartoons from the *Oakville Beaver* are reproduced on 108 and 410); Roy Peterson (who is represented by a *Maclean's* drawing on 257 and a Vancouver *Sun* drawing on 384); freelancer Dennis Pritchard (whose work appears on 303); Dan Murphy (whose work from the Vancouver *Province* is reprinted on 354); Adrian Raeside (whose work appears, with permission from Doubleday Canada, on 8, 129, and 530 and, from the Victoria *Times-Colonist*, on 58 and 321); and Merle Tingley (from the *London Free Press*, on page 200).

The shifts in focus between the first and second editions are largely the result of suggestions from academics that Nelson Canada contacted, including Maria Peluso, Concordia University; Richard Sigurdson, University College of the Cariboo; and reviewers at the University of Toronto, the University of Western Ontario, and Wilfrid Laurier University, all of whom I thank but do not hold responsible for the results.

At Nelson Canada I worked closely and congenially with Andrew Livingston, Joanne Scattolon, and Bob Kohlmeier, but I would also like to thank others there that had a hand in producing the book. Encouraging colleagues at Laurentian University assisted on specific points, Keith Sinclair being indispensable; student assistants included Samuel Bottomley, Michael Freeze, David Middleton, and Peter Dinsdale; and Karin Bell was invaluable in a host of different ways. As usual, my wife, Joan, provided the most supportive home environment that it is possible to imagine.

PART 1

Introduction

The introductory part of the book consists of two chapters. The first provides a general framework on which the rest of the book is built, as well as outlining how the book approaches the study of politics. It points out that the subject matter of political science is not all cut-and-dried factual material, and that the same substance can be viewed from different perspectives. The second chapter explores the historical context of Canadian politics and sketches its institutional foundations. In particular, it deals with the aspects of the British and U.S. models that Canada chose to be a base for its own, and establishes the institutional differences between the Canadian and U.S. systems of government.

Chapter 1

Approaching
THE STUDY OF
politics

Where does one start in the study of Canadian politics? How can the material be organized? How much of the material is of a factual nature, and how much is a matter of opinion? What different perspectives can be adopted in this study? These are the central questions addressed in this introductory chapter.

THE POLITICAL SYSTEM

Perhaps it is best to begin with the 30 million individuals who inhabit the territory called Canada. All of these individuals have an array of needs that they attempt to satisfy, ranging from water and food through security and friendship to self-esteem and self-fulfilment. These needs have been ranked by the psychologist Abraham Maslow into a hierarchy, some being more basic than others.[1] Political science lumps such needs together with interests, preferences, opinions, motivations, expectations, and beliefs and sometimes calls them "wants." It is quite obvious that most of us spend much of our time trying to satisfy such needs or wants.

Most of us do so, in the first instance, by our own efforts, in pairs, in families, in organizations of all kinds, at work and at play, and do not automatically call for government help. At some point, however, we may begin to feel that the satisfaction of such needs or wants is beyond such personal, interpersonal, family, or group capacity, and come to the conclusion that the government should step in to help us. When we express the opinion that the government should take some action, we are converting a want into a "demand" and crossing the threshold between the **private** and **public sectors**.

We are thus introduced to the concept of *government*, which can be defined as the set of institutions that make and enforce collective, public decisions for a society. We must also deal with the concept of *power*, which is often defined in political science as the ability of one actor to impose its will on another, whether through force of personality or material inducement.

Government, backed up by armed forces, police, and punishments, if necessary, possesses a particular kind of power called **coercion**. That is, the government has the ability to impose its will upon us by means of sanctions or penalties. Indeed, as a general rule, *only* the government is allowed to use force or coercive power in society. But if we (or our ancestors) had a hand in the creation of such a government apparatus, as well as in the selection of the current governors, then we have in a sense agreed to be bound by its decisions, and we have cloaked it with *legitimacy*. Such legitimate power is often called *authority*, and a synonym for government is "the authorities." To some extent we obey the government because of the threat or expectation of penalties if we do not, but we also obey because we accept government decisions to be binding upon us and necessary for the general good. Think of stopping at a red light as an example.

Coming back to the definition of demands, therefore, we can say that a demand is the expression of opinion that some authoritative action be taken. What governments do is make and execute decisions for a society or formulate and enforce social or public policies.

Who are these authorities? As can be seen in the diagram of the political system in Figure 1.1, we usually divide them into four branches of government: the *legislature*, the *executive*, the *bureaucracy*, and the *judiciary*. The authoritative decision that a demand seeks can sometimes be made by a single branch of government. If the demand requires the adoption of a private bill, for example, then action of the legislative branch will be necessary. If the demand can be satisfied by a patronage appointment or large monetary grant, then the political executive or cabinet can respond to it. If the demand is for the provision of routine government services or for changes in regulations, then bureaucratic action will probably suffice. Finally, if the demand can only be settled by judicial interpretation or adjudication, then it should be addressed to the courts.

Figure 1.1 **A Model of the Political System**

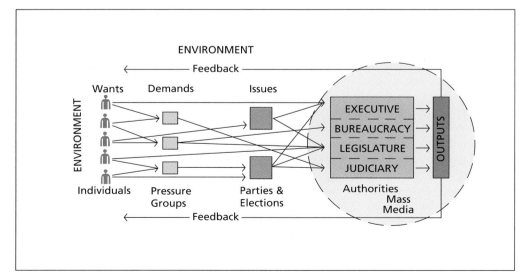

In many instances, however, the demand will require combined actions of any two of the executive, legislative, and bureaucratic branches, or even all three working together, such as in the formulation, passage, and implementation of a new law. The courts normally stand somewhat apart from the other three organs of government, operating on the principle of the independence of the judiciary. Judicial decisions usually follow authoritative actions in other branches of government, such as when the Supreme Court threw out the abortion provisions of the Criminal Code. But they may also lead to subsequent legislative action, as when the government sought to overturn a Supreme Court decision by introducing a revised law that did not permit an extreme state of intoxication to serve as an excuse for committing a sexual assault.

Authoritative decisions take many forms—laws, regulations, appointments, grants, contracts, services, and judgments—and are collectively referred to as the "outputs" of the political system. Authoritative decisions are also made in the provinces and in an assortment of regional and local councils and boards, and often require the agreement of two or more levels of government. Federal and provincial outputs can sometimes be in conflict, such as when the two levels pursue different strategies in dealing with government deficits during a recession.

Having encountered demands and authorities as two main parts of the political system, we must now discover how demands are transmitted from individuals to the government, as indicated in the model of the political system. This can be done on a personal basis, by means of a letter, fax, telephone call, or face-to-face encounter. Sometimes such directly transmitted demands will achieve their desired result, but very often they will not. When they do not, it may be time to consider some kind of group action. Canadian society is replete with groups, and it is quite likely that a group already exists to articulate the demand an individual decides to transmit. If such a group does not already exist, it may be worthwhile to create one since, as a general rule, the authorities are more likely to respond to a demand coming from a group than one from a single individual. Such groups are usually called *interest groups* or *pressure groups* and constitute an important part of Canadian political activity. The Canadian Chamber of Commerce and the Canadian Labour Congress are two prominent examples. Corporations and other institutions also make demands, either individually or in groups.

A special kind of group that is even more overtly political is the *political party*, and this instrument can also be used to transmit demands to the authorities. People join a political party or support it financially, and try to get it to recognize their concerns in its platform or policies. If the party forms the government, it can incorporate the demand into its decisions and government policy; if the party is in opposition, it may be able to bring the problem to national media attention. Parties are particularly responsive to such demands in an election campaign, seeking to attract the support of large numbers of individuals and groups by promising them the action they seek. Those dissatisfied with the manner in which existing parties are responding to their demands can create new parties, such as the Reform Party and the Bloc Québécois.

Another means of transmitting the demand to the authorities is, as suggested above, via the *mass media* of communication. The media are usually eager to publicize controversial issues and often delight in pointing out problems that the government has failed to resolve. The media give attention to individual and interest group concerns on a regular basis, cover political party activities, and are especially active in election campaigns. But the media are much more important than that. They shape the whole nature and quality of political discourse of Canadian politics in their constant search for the dramatic, the conflictive, and the colourful, and provide the electorate with most of its information about politics and government.

We have assumed thus far that any and all demands expressed actually reach the authorities. In fact, however, relatively few demands have any impact. Demands that do not concern very many people or demands for action that is contrary to the values of the authorities of the day may be ignored. Governments have historically been much more sensitive to demands from the business community, for example, than to the concerns of Native peoples. Since the number of demands under serious consideration at any given time is such a small proportion of the total number being made, it is sometimes useful to distinguish between demands and "issues," the latter including only those demands that the authorities have taken under serious consideration or that have "registered."

The authorities are thus bombarded by demands, no matter what means are used to transmit them. What is more striking than the vast quantity of demands, however, is that there is usually intense conflict among them. The essence of politics and government, therefore, is not only making and executing decisions for society, but in having to choose among competing demands, in trying to resolve conflict or in making social choices in the midst of social conflict. *Politics*, therefore, is said to originate in conflict, and is often defined as the struggle for power and the management of conflict. Here let us say it is activity in which conflicting interests struggle for advantage. It should also be added that the authorities can make their own demands (sometimes called "withinputs"), which may carry more weight than those arising from the wider society.

Demands are only one of two kinds of "inputs" in the system. The other is the concept of "support." This is not as concrete a phenomenon, but it is fairly evident as well. Support can be defined as a positive orientation toward something, and as used in this context, three different parts of the system can be objects of support. First, one can support the government of the day, that is, the party and cabinet that currently occupy the authoritative political positions (for example, the Chrétien Liberal government). Second, one can support the whole decision-making apparatus, or the constitutional principles and arrangements according to which decisions are being made. In this case, one might not support the government of the day, but still feel positively about the whole decision-making process. Most Canadians fall into this category most of the time. Third, one can support the political community called Canada. Again, one can do so without supporting the current government, or even without supporting the institutions it occupies. For example, an Albertan obsessed with Senate reform to articulate regional interests in federal institutions might support the political community without supporting the existing policy-making structures. On the other hand, a Quebec separatist would not support the political community of Canada.

Support is a more passive concept than demands, and usually exists in the realm of feelings and orientations rather than in action. Of course, action is involved in voting for one party or another on election day—in demonstrating support for the incumbent government or an opposition party. The act of voting is also a subtle indication of support for the decision-making structure and for the political community. But apart from voting (or standing at attention for the national anthem), support is mostly demonstrable in terms of such feelings as trust, efficacy, pride, and patriotism.

Whatever the type of output, it usually sparks a reaction in the rest of the system. This leads us to the concept of "feedback," that is, a communication of the outputs back into the system, in response to which the pattern of demands and support is altered. If an output satisfies a particular demand, then that demand will no longer have to be articulated. Think of the federal Official Languages Act silencing the demands for bilingualism. But the bilingualism issue also shows that the satisfaction of one demand may lead those involved to expect even more along the same lines: French-language services at the provincial as well as the federal level. On the other hand, a backlash may result, and the Official Languages Act also promoted the articulation of contrary demands. Similarly, outputs affect support. Gratitude for the satisfaction of a demand will likely lead to increased levels of support, as shown by the relationship between the Mulroney government's Free Trade Agreement and the business community. On the other hand, those opposed to such an output will probably have less confidence in the authorities and the system, and their level of support will decline. The authorities will then respond in one way or another to this new pattern of demands and support, in the second stage of the feedback process.

By now we have established that the political system is a dynamic, circular process in which the authorities react to demands and support, convert some of the demands into outputs, and then respond in turn to whatever changes in the pattern of inputs have resulted from the feedback from such outputs. Individuals and groups raise conflicting demands, but because there is a consensus on the legitimacy of the government, people generally abide by its authoritative decisions, even when they disagree with them. It is sometimes said, therefore, that politics and government are characterized by both conflict and consensus. While the conflict is more evident, it normally operates within an underlying consensus about the decision-making apparatus and about remaining together as part of a united political community. Moreover, the authorities usually seek to develop some kind of consensus out of the conflicting demands.

One more part that must be added to the model we are constructing is the "environment" of the political system. This is an even more abstract concept than those encountered thus far, and can be defined as everything surrounding the political system. If the political system within a society is made up of all those actions and interactions concerned with the making of public policy, there also exist within the same society an economic system, a social system, and perhaps many others. These other systems constitute the internal environment of the Canadian political system.

Most of these systems are characterized by internal divisions, and from these divisions springs the concept of *cleavages*. A cleavage in political science terms is a deep, persistent division in society that has significant implications for the political system. The cleavages in Canadian society that most readily come to mind are between the geographic regions, between English, French, aboriginal, and other ethnic and linguistic groups, and between various socioeconomic classes, as well as those related to gender, religion, and age. The relative importance and nature of these cleavages changes over time.[2] While such cleavages are part of the environment of the political system, they can also be seen as the source of many of the demands expressed. In other words, demands can be said to originate from cleavages in the internal environment.

But there is also an external environment consisting of a huge number of international, multinational, transnational, and supranational factors, such as other states, international organizations, and transnational corporations. In fact, such actors in the external environment serve increasingly as the source of demands on national political systems and as constraints upon domestic policy-making.

The model of the political system just described and illustrated in Figure 1.1 is designed to provide a framework for the study of government and politics in Canada. It is a simplified version of systems analysis, largely the work of Canadian political scientist David Easton,[3] which many of his colleagues find useful for organizing and explaining political phenomena.

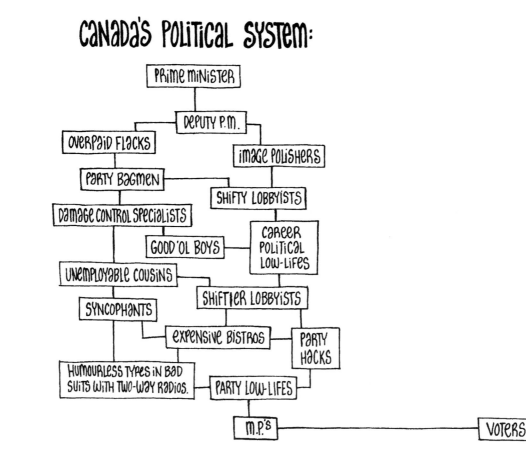

Reproduced with permission of Doubleday Canada.

Systems theory is closely related to a line of analysis called structural-functionalism.[4] This approach begins with the identification of the "functions" that are or must be performed in any political system, and then searches for the "structures" that perform them. Gabriel Almond postulated that seven basic functions are performed in any political system: interest articulation, interest aggregation, political socialization and recruitment, political communication, *rule making, rule application*, and *rule adjudication*. The last three of these generally correspond to the traditional functions of government as performed by the legislature, executive, and judiciary, but it may be useful to express such functions in less specific terms. *Interest articulation* consists essentially of making demands, while *interest aggregation* refers to the process of combining, consolidating, and narrowing the demands that are being expressed into manageable proportions or issues. *Political socialization* is the process of acquiring, teaching, or inculcating political values, attitudes, and opinions, a function that goes on in every political system and is necessary for its continued operation; *political recruitment* is the process of selecting political leaders, another obvious necessity. *Political communication* is a more general function of transmitting information among the various participants within the political system and between the system and its environment. Such a simple version of structural-functionalism will be useful here in order to identify the structures that perform these basic functions. Once such structures have been discovered, however, it may well be found that they perform other functions as well. Since the political system and structural-functionalism are straightforward and widely utilized approaches in political science, they are used together to provide a subtle framework for this book.

ALMOND'S SEVEN FUNCTIONS PERFORMED IN THE POLITICAL SYSTEM

(1) Political socialization and recruitment

(2) Interest articulation

(3) Interest aggregation

(4) Political communication

(5) Rule making

(6) Rule application

(7) Rule adjudication

APPROACHES TO THE STUDY OF POLITICS

The political system and structural-functionalism do not exhaust the possible analytical models that can be applied to Canadian politics. Any one of a number of other theoretical approaches can be used alongside them. Such models and approaches provide a guide in the selection of significant and relevant facts, as well as in putting the facts together in a meaningful way. Before getting into the substance of our subject, therefore, we will outline four other approaches that political scientists have found useful and that will illuminate aspects of the Canadian political system from time to time in the remainder of the book: the pluralist, public choice, class analysis, and state-centred approaches.[5] They focus on such crucial questions as how widely power and influence are shared, which political actors in society are most important, which government institutions are most powerful, and how politicians seek and maintain power. As seen in Figure 1.2, the four approaches can be divided into two groups, one emphasizing elites and the other incorporating the influence of the masses. Figure 1.3 shows that they can also be categorized as those that are society-centred and those that focus on the autonomy of the state.

Figure 1.2 **Mass and Elite Approaches**

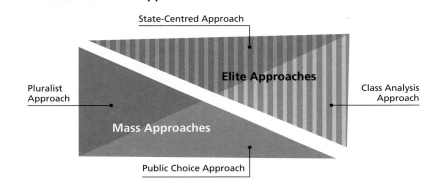

Figure 1.3 **Society-Centred and State-Centred Approaches**

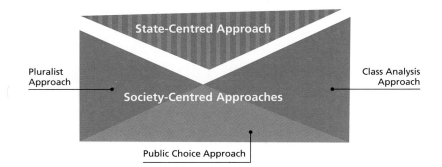

The Pluralist Approach

Pluralism is the analytical framework closest to the democratic ideal. It postulates that power is widely dispersed among many interests in society rather than being tightly controlled by one or more groups or elites, and that the political system is characterized by much openness or "slack." In particular, pluralism suggests that individuals can make use of many different resources in their political participation; that those sharing a demand are free to join together to seek a governmental response; that such group action is the norm of political activity; and that the authorities are open to pressure from a wide variety of such interests. Pluralism does not necessarily expect everyone to be equally interested and involved, or everyone or all groups to be equally influential; indeed, it makes much of most individuals' political "inertia." But the theory argues that the authorities can be moved by the articulation of demands by different groups in different policy areas, and that the policies adopted are usually the result of compromises among competing group demands. The term "brokerage politics" is sometimes used in this connection because in a pluralist system the authorities engage in wheeling and dealing with the various groups in an effort to keep them all content. Pioneers of the pluralist approach include Robert Dahl, particularly in his book *Pluralist Democracy in the United States*. Many accounts of Canadian politics assume a basic pluralist perspective, even if they do not say so.

While pluralism assumes that group action is more common and effective than individual political activity, a more explicit "group" approach can also be identified. It puts particular stress on the role of pressure groups in both the making and execution of public policy. Political scientists are generally agreed that as society becomes increasingly specialized, the number of groups gets more numerous, and as political issues become more complex, political parties and politicians may be less and less capable of dealing with them. In these ways, at least, the significance of pressure groups increases, and no one doubts their contemporary importance. Paul Pross has explicitly emphasized the group approach in his work on Canadian politics, such as *Group Politics and Public Policy*. Business-oriented groups in particular have attracted much scholarly attention in recent years, including William Coleman's *Business and Politics*, Stephen Brooks and Andrew Stritch's *Business and Government in Canada*, and W.T. Stanbury's *Business–Government Relations in Canada*.[6]

In point form, the pluralist approach can be summarized as follows:

1. Power is widely dispersed in the political system and not monopolized by any state or corporate elite.

2. Individuals are free to employ a variety of resources at their disposal and to organize whatever groups they wish in order to back their demands to the authorities.

3. The authorities make decisions that are basically compromises among the various competing interests that articulate their demands.

4. Different policy areas are characterized by different individuals and groups making demands on different authorities.

5. Pressure group activity is increasingly replacing individual and party activity in the political system.

An overview of the evidence supporting this approach suggests that Canada has always been a pluralistic society, given its regional, provincial, ethnic, class, religious, gender, age, and other divisions. But approaching the year 2000, it will be even more pluralistic, especially in terms of ethnic diversity. Pluralism is also of growing relevance because various groups and interests are becoming more self-conscious and self-confident. Women, French, aboriginal, "other ethnic," and non-Christian religious groups are challenging the elitism of the past. Whether elected or appointed, all the institutions of government are characterized by a new pluralism. Such interests, in the form of various subcultures, are part of the very political culture of the country and are even succeeding in changing provisions in the Constitution to protect themselves.

Certain aspects of the Canadian political system are particularly appropriate to pluralism. The broker system used by political parties as they design their election platforms is certainly one; so are the efforts of those who seek to strengthen the provinces in the operation of Canadian federalism. Pluralism welcomes the limitation of authority that is provided when political institutions have checks upon each other. In that sense, federal–provincial conflict and the power of the courts to overrule both federal and provincial governments by means of the Charter of Rights and Freedoms are relevant. On the other hand, the original centralized framework of Canadian federalism has proved to be inappropriate in such a pluralistic society, and rigid party discipline in the House of Commons has sometimes been identified as dysfunctional.

Canadians have not lived up to the pluralist model of being active political participants, although whether the electorate wants to be heard or not, all manner of organizations are asking for their views in public opinion polls. Thus, focusing on groups rather than on individuals leads to greater resonance for the pluralist approach in this country. Canada has hundreds of interest groups, and many are active in the political process. But if pluralism expects any degree of equality in influence or resources among such pressure groups, it is badly mistaken. Only a handful of groups speak for the poor and the working class, and the middle class has no collective voice. Every imaginable business interest has organized a pressure group, however, and several peak business associations are better endowed than national political parties. If pluralism means that much government activity is a response to the influence of pressure groups and that they are displacing parties in many respects, then it is certainly correct, as it is in emphasizing that government decisions are made in a diversity of specialized policy communities.

The Public Choice Approach

The public choice approach also begins with the assumption that Canada is a democracy. It postulates that rational, self-interested voters support the party whose policies are of greatest utility to themselves, and that politicians seeking re-election adopt policies that will most likely keep them in power. The pioneer of this approach was Anthony Downs in his book *An Economic Theory of Democracy*.[7]

At first sight, in a democracy, the largest groups are most influential because they represent the greatest numbers of voters. This is only true, however, if members of such groups are conscious of their common interests. Furthermore, since the authorities do not have to worry about the support of their committed voters, and since they are unlikely to win over those who are hostile, the usual recipe for political success is to concentrate on marginal, undecided voters or voters in strategically located constituencies, rather than on the will of the electorate as a whole.

Public choice theory argues that politicians will do almost anything to keep themselves in power. They take credit for popular policies or the strength of the economy, but blame others (international forces, provincial governments, the courts, and so on) for unpopular policies or economic decline. They give popular policies maximum publicity, but try to conceal those that are bound to be unpopular; they exaggerate the benefits of their policies and understate the costs. They take disagreeable decisions early in their term and unveil popular programs just before the next election. It would therefore take an alert, informed, and sceptical electorate to be able to see through the attempts at manipulation of the "public choice" by the authorities. Public choice theory thus has to acknowledge that individuals in the political marketplace are not always as rational and well informed as they may be in their economic transactions.

Public choice often extends its bargaining model to other aspects of the political system. Similar rational, self-serving exchanges take place at three other principal points in the system: between politicians and bureaucrats, between the authorities and pressure groups, and between the authorities and the media. The public choice approach can be summarized as follows:

1. Politicians and voters act in a rational, self-interested fashion in which politicians make promises in return for votes.

2. Politicians and parties generally adopt policies that will get themselves elected, and, other things being equal, they respond to those interests representing the largest number of votes.

3. Since it is a waste of effort to appeal to committed supporters or opponents, politicians concentrate on marginal, undecided, or strategically located voters.

4. Politicians try to maximize publicity of their successes and minimize their failures, take credit for good things and blame others for the bad, and manipulate the timing of positive and negative decisions.

5. A similar bargaining process goes on at other points in the political system, such as between politicians and the bureaucracy, the authorities and pressure groups, and the authorities and the media.

In practice, the public choice approach can be seen at many points in the system, especially in the relationship between politicians and voters in the formulation of election platforms and in the decision of how to vote. The operation of the House of Commons is also central to this approach because observing the partisan exchanges in that chamber helps voters make up their minds about which party will best satisfy their demands. Public choice is also relevant to the operations of the cabinet as that body calculates which interests it will have to placate in order to ensure re-election. In this calculation, the role of public opinion polls is crucial, as governments, parties, the media, and other organizations seek to identify the basic concerns of different groups within the electorate. Governments rarely do what is in the long-term interest of the country if it conflicts with short-term electoral advantage.

The public choice approach gives particular attention to marginal voters. For a long time, the party preferences of a majority of Quebeckers and Westerners could be taken for granted so that parties focused their campaigns in Ontario, which had the largest number of flexible voters. Since 1984, Quebec has also provided a great pool of marginal voters, so that most parties have put new emphasis on that region in their campaigns. The threat of separation has only heightened the attention that parties and politicians pay to that province.

The public choice approach is confirmed on a daily basis when it emphasizes the ways in which the authorities portray their performance in the most favourable light, such as in timing, packaging, exaggerating benefits, and downplaying of costs. When it comes to manipulating their message, however, the level of sophistication of the authorities far exceeds that of the average voter, and the public choice model probably overstates the extent to which voters are rational and well informed. The lack of class consciousness among all but the upper classes and the delayed political consciousness of women and other groups in society all attest to the skill of authorities and parties in persuading voters to support platforms that were not truly in their own interests.

Class Analysis

A third approach to the study of Canadian government and politics emphasizes socio-economic classes or *class analysis*.[8] This approach is sometimes called neo-Marxism because to some extent it is based on the writings of Karl Marx. It is neither possible nor appropriate to deal with that analysis in any depth here, but the demise of Marxist-Leninism as a state-sponsored ideology in Eastern Europe does not necessarily make this critique obsolete. Suffice it to say that in Marxist eyes political activity is determined by economic relationships, particularly in the production process. In a capitalist system, Marx saw these relationships primarily in terms of a class struggle between the "proletariat" (the working class) and the "bourgeoisie" (the capitalist class). He emphasized that the latter would exploit the former until the proletariat engaged in an eventual revolution. Many modern observers see much truth in what Marx wrote over 100 years ago, but most would modify his analysis to some extent in the light of subsequent developments, which is why "class analysis" is a preferable label.

In this approach, the political elite takes orders from the capitalist elite, and the state is an instrument of bourgeois domination. While capitalism may generally prefer to minimize the role of the state in order to allow "free market forces" to have full play, class analysts point out that the bourgeoisie will tolerate public activity to some extent, but only to further its own interests in the accumulation of capital. Public policies advocated by the capitalist elite include, for example, the assumption by the public purse of many of the costs of capitalist development, called social capital, such as education, health care, electricity, and transportation. While a degree of fragmentation may exist within the bourgeoisie, such as between manufacturers and resource industries, this approach sees the state pursuing policies that seek to create or maintain the conditions in which capitalists can maximize their wealth, in what is called the "accumulation" function. Given today's universal franchise, however, most modern, democratic governments find it politically advantageous to disguise much of this activity on behalf of capital.

Many political observers who do not claim the validity of a class analysis would nevertheless agree that the state gives priority to the demands of big business.[9] In part this is because the bourgeoisie provides personnel for public offices, organizes powerful pressure groups, finances political parties, and generally shapes societal values. Another reason for the predominance of the corporate elite is that the state depends on the capitalist system for the provision of jobs, economic growth, and a portion of tax revenues.

Class analysis recognizes that modern society is composed of more than just the bourgeoisie and the proletariat, and generally inserts between them the traditional "petite bourgeoisie" (farmers, small business people, and self-employed professionals) and the "new middle class" (civil servants, teachers, and other salaried professionals). The increasing size of this latter group as well as the enfranchisement of the working class give both groups considerable significance today. Class analysts refer to the use of the state to benefit the middle or working classes as "legitimation." They still emphasize, however, that by humanizing and legitimizing the capitalist system and by disguising support for it, the bourgeoisie is able to continue its pursuit of the basic accumulation function.

If legitimation is not effective in facilitating capital accumulation, the government may have to resort to a third function, that of coercion. This involves adopting penalizing measures or measures to impose order, such as legislation to end strikes, or the intervention of the police to end demonstrations. Coercion is more often imposed on labour and other subordinate groups than on those with greater political and economic clout.[10]

Another central theme of class analysis is the influence of the external environment of the political system. The role of transnational corporations as sources of investment in Canada and the policies of dominant capitalist countries, especially the United States, are particularly important in this regard. So too are the actions of such organizations as the International Monetary Fund and the World Bank.

The class analysis literature in Canadian politics and economics is voluminous. Indeed, the whole political economy school of scholarship that goes back many decades and emphasizes the connection between politics and economics has been taken over by such writers. A list of such sources is contained at the end of Chapter 10, but two leading books in the field are *The Canadian Corporate Elite*, by Wallace Clement, and *The Canadian State*, edited by Leo Panitch.

The class analysis approach can be summarized in the following five points:

1. The corporate elite or bourgeoisie not only controls the private sector of the economy, but also largely determines the shape of public policies that are designed to facilitate their accumulation of wealth.

2. This predominant influence is the result of the bourgeoisie's providing personnel for public offices and funds for political parties, shaping societal values, and organizing pressure groups, as well as of the dependence of the state on the capitalist system for the provision of jobs and economic growth.

3. The petite bourgeoisie, the new middle class, and even the working class must be accommodated to some extent by public policies that legitimate the capitalist system.

4. If these classes are not satisfied by such legitimation, the government may have to resort to coercion.

5. Modern states must also contend with powerful transnational corporations.

Class analysts find practical confirmation of their approach in the widespread definition of politics—by the media, politicians, pressure groups, and other participants and observers—in terms of regionalism, ethnicity, and gender, rather than class. Such definitions serve the interests of these apologists of capitalism, as does the current obsession with government deficits and debts at the expense of essential public services to the have-not segments of society. The Liberal and Conservative parties are heavily financed by major corporations, and reward such contributions in their general policies as well as in specific favours once in power. The most prominent pressure groups are those representing big business, while individual companies also lobby for government handouts. Prominent individuals frequently serve as cabinet ministers between stints in the corporate sector, and many senators blatantly represent corporate interests in their parliamentary work. Large corporations control most of the media and influence public opinion with carefully selected images.

Class analysts point out that a close scrutiny of policy instruments reveals how the authorities choose more intrusive instruments and apply them more coercively when dealing with the working class than with the corporate elite. They demonstate how governments disguise their routine servitude to the corporate sector with occasional legitimating measures for the working class. "Snitch lines" send welfare recipients to jail while corporate income tax evasion is rampant. And they remind us of incidents in which the full force of the law and the police has been brought down upon those on strike or demonstrating against unemployment, in contrast to corporate executives who allow pollution of the environment or who make employees work in hazardous conditions. As critical as they are of politicians' actions, such analysts are even more suspicious of the courts. Given the expense and elitist personnel involved, they do not expect judicially imposed limitations on the other branches of government to benefit the working classes. Moreover, as much as they lack confidence in Canadian authorities and corporations, class analysts are even more critical of U.S. transnationals operating in Canada, to say nothing of efforts by the United States government to have Canada follow its lead.

The State-Centred Approach

While public choice theory and class analysis are, in sequence, increasingly critical reactions to the idealistic aspects of democratic pluralism, all three see the state responding to societal forces. The state-centred approach, on the other hand, views the state—those individuals endowed with the authority to formulate and implement public policies—as basically automomous from the rest of society. Public policies are made by the authorities without much reference to the demands flowing in from the public, and often despite them. Since the authorities try to direct the development of society, the French word *dirigiste* is sometimes used to describe their activity. The executive and bureaucracy do what *they* think is best for the country or act in pursuit of their own preferences and priorities, regardless of anyone else's interests or opinions. Such state actors seek to enhance their autonomy by generating internally the information needed to pursue their objectives, and by maximizing their jurisdiction, discretionary power, and fiscal resources. It is possible to single out either the political executive or the bureaucracy in this approach, or to see them as acting together in making such decisions. Individually or in tandem, they try to persuade the public of their wisdom, or, failing that, resort to coercion, the main point being that government operations are quite divorced from public input. The originator of this approach was Eric Nordlinger, who in his book *On the Anatomy of the Democratic State* wrote that "the preferences of the state are at least as important as those of civil society in accounting for what the democratic state does and does not do."[11]

While the political executive (the prime minister and cabinet in Canada) have the right to make major governmental decisions subject to some kind of accountability to Parliament, some theorists prefer to emphasize the influence of the bureaucracy within the apparatus of the state.[12] They see the bureaucracy as the most important part of the policy-making process because neither legislators nor cabinet ministers can possibly understand the details of complex modern issues, and are therefore content to be advised by their experts. Politicians may still have a role to play in identifying problems and determining priorities, but once that is done, they are in the hands of their advisers in finding ways to proceed.

It should be added that the state, as large as it is, is not without internal conflicts, and in order to maximize their influence and protect themselves, state forces are often wiser to develop functional links with certain private interests, especially pressure groups, than to try to act in total isolation. Thus, in a combination of state-centred and pluralist approaches, the concept of "policy communities" is often useful.[13] The state is composed of a conglomeration of specialized policy processes, each of which nurtures support from the most relevant interest in society.

The following points summarize the state-centred approach:

1. The state is largely autonomous from societal forces.

2. The authorities decide what is good for society and design policies to fulfil their vision of the public interest.

3. The politicians rely heavily on the bureaucracy for advice.

4. The authorities seek to enhance their autonomy by the internal generation of information and by maximizing their discretion, jurisdiction, and financial resources.

5. If necessary, the authorities resort to the manipulation of information or coercion in order to persuade the public of their wisdom, or seek the support of the most relevant societal interest.

A variant of the state-centred approach is that of institutionalism or neo-institutionalism. This approach essentially argues that the institutions that make up the state should be the principal focus of attention in political science. Like the state-centred approach, institutionalism downplays the importance of societal forces, and contends that institutions affect societal forces as much as the reverse. Institutionalism is particularly relevant to Canada because so much of our political debate is about governmental institutions, and because many societal forces—French, English, aboriginal, and so on—are actually in conflict over institutional change. Institutionalism has always been an integral part of the political science discipline in this country, but neo-institutionalism is a reaction to an emphasis on broader social, cultural, and economic forces in recent years. In the book *Parameters of Power*, Archer et al. argue that institutions help determine who has standing in the political process, structure the interactions of the players, are often the very things at stake in politics, and shape the interests at play in the political system. Institutionalism therefore seeks to discover each institution's basic principles and then to examine any contestation among such principles.[14]

The state-centred approach is anchored in the Canadian political culture—in the values of deference to authority, elitism, and collectivism—and, at least in the past, Canadians have generally welcomed state intervention and trusted the authorities who intervened. Politicians and bureaucrats naturally took advantage of this invitation to function in such an autonomous fashion. This approach is related to the low level of political participation in Canada, to the minimal effort of most political parties to develop policy within their own ranks, and to the consequent lack of policy differences among the parties in election campaigns. Governing parties have changed policy directions so frequently after achieving power that to do so no longer causes particular criticism.

The state is not equally autonomous from societal forces in all policy areas. Foreign policy is one traditionally autonomous field because relatively few citizens feel deeply about it; in the past, the constitution and federalism were other such state-centred sectors. Pierre Trudeau's policy of national bilingualism and Brian Mulroney's policies of privatization, deregulation, and deficit reduction were all imposed from the top rather than being demanded by the grassroots at the time. So, too, were the Goods and Services Tax (GST) and the Canada–U.S. Free Trade Agreement. These latter cases are good examples of what the authorities do when they encounter public criticism of state-centred policies: they resort to public relations campaigns and manipulation of public opinion via the media at public expense.

Other state-centred policies bear the mark of bureaucratic inspiration, although the bureaucracy contributes a great deal even to those that do originate with the political executive. In this advisory capacity, the bureaucracy does not always act in its own interest alone; sometimes bureaucrats promote policies that they genuinely believe are in the public interest. Cases of government (both politicians and bureaucrats) actually creating advocacy organizations to demand or support what the authorities themselves want to do have also been documented.[15]

Figure 1.4 **A General Framework from the Four Approaches**

An Amalgam Model

This book suggests that each of the approaches outlined above offers perspectives that enhance our understanding of Canadian government and politics. Accordingly, the approaches have been applied to the subject matter of each chapter wherever relevant. It should be added that these approaches do not necessarily constitute competitive explanations, and in fact often overlap. They point to the multidimensional character of politics, and are useful whenever they add insight to the explanation of aspects of the political system. While the book takes the position that the Canadian political system is too variable and complex to be explained in any single, simple fashion, we can in fact extract and combine aspects of these four approaches in order to construct a coherent, general framework. The predominant influence of business pressure groups can be taken from pluralism and put together with the government's attempt to present itself to the electorate in the most favourable light from public choice theory, the pervasive influence of capitalist values from class analysis, and the persistent influence of the bureaucracy from the state-centred approach. The exercise of extracting and combining these aspects of the four approaches is demonstrated in Figure 1.4.

Canadian politics is characterized by a tremendous amount of pressure group activity, and conflicting group demands regularly confront the authorities. From among this plethora of group demands, however, the authorities most frequently single out business groups for special treatment. Business groups and individual corporations know where and how to apply pressure and have the resources to hire professional lobbyists to make their case. Since the authorities share many of their values and social background characteristics, the meeting of such forces is normally quite congenial.

While public choice theory may generally overrate the rationality of the average voter, it is quite correct in emphasizing the extent to which the authorities use public funds and the media to manage and manipulate messages to the electorate so as to portray its performance most favourably and therefore obtain re-election. If it must make unpopular decisions from time to time, the government will give careful attention to their timing and packaging, and try to find some other target on which it can pin the blame.

If there is one value that pervades Canadian policy-making more than any other, it is undoubtedly the capitalist ethic: allowing the economic elite to maximize its accumulation of wealth. Government policy can foster capital accumulation in many ways, such as with tax breaks, government grants and loans, lack of regulation, and impediments to unionization. This objective, of course, is often disguised as contributing to economic growth and the creation of employment and diluted by a certain amount of taxation and regulation. It is also accompanied by the provision of social services and a limited degree of income redistribution. Now that all adults have the vote, the authorities must promise enough to the middle and lower classes to get themselves re-elected. But such promises are regularly unfulfilled, and those legitimation measures that are adopted are often overblown. Thus, while in the perspective of this book it is too extreme to say that accumulation and coercion tempered by legitimation explain everything political, the value that governments put on accumulation does explain a great deal of Canadian political activity.

Finally, while some authoritative decisions are taken by the political executive (and others by the courts), the bureaucracy advises on almost all ministerial and cabinet decisions and then makes many others on its own. The decisions that governments are called on to make nowadays are so numerous and so technical that ministers have neither the time nor the expertise to get personally involved in more than a fraction of them. The rest get delegated to the bureaucrats who often pursue their own conception of the public interest.

It is not the intention of this discussion to claim that individual and nonbusiness group demands are never satisfied, that the public is totally at the mercy of the government's manipulative media management, that the authorities are never moved by values other than capital accumulation, or that the bureaucracy is the only branch of government that matters. But in an effort to portray a coherent and realistic picture of the national political system, it must be said that Canada does have a political elite that listens primarily to business pressure groups, whose concern with re-election leads it to manage the message that the electorate receives about its performance, that is imbued with capitalist values, and that is guided to a large extent by the bureaucracy. The amalgam model explains more about Canadian government and politics than any other.

Two variations on the amalgam model should also be mentioned. The first is the concept of **elite accommodation**. This refers to the interaction of various elites, either within government circles or in both the public and private sectors, in order to work out policies in their own mutual interests. Although they are seriously divided in some ways, the elites of various ethnic, regional, and other groupings have certain background characteristics and values in common that enable them to come to agreement. Specific individuals have often come to know each other before occupying elite positions or have shared educational and social institutions and experiences in their youth. It is sometimes argued that the mass members of any group have such confidence in their own group leaders that they will abide by whatever decisions have been arrived at in the interaction of their group leaders with other elites. It is even hypothesized that elite accommodation is a means of contributing to national unity in a country like Canada that is characterized by so many cleavages. In other words, the mass members of various ethnic, religious, regional, or class groupings may find themselves in conflict with the mass members of other groups, but if their leaders can arrive at compromises with the leaders of other groups, the mass members will accept them.[16] The foremost advocate of elite accommodation, however, applies it primarily to interaction among the political, bureaucratic, and economic elites, an approach that is quite compatible with what is outlined above.

Another variation on the approaches outlined is that of the **embedded state**.[17] This is the idea that while the political and bureaucratic elites can sometimes function quite independently of societal forces, the state is so embedded in society that they cannot operate with total autonomy. Instead, because of this fusion of state and society or web of state–society interdependence, they interact with whatever societal elites are most relevant to their operations. In a sense, this is a variation on pluralism, with close interaction between specialized governmental elites and the pressure groups who constitute their principal clienteles.

CONCLUSION

This book will study Canadian government and politics using the basic framework of the "political system" and examine the functions performed by various institutions. It also claims that the subject matter can be illuminated by applying a number of other theoretical approaches.

DISCUSSION QUESTIONS

1. Does the use of theories, perspectives, approaches, and models add to the study of the "facts" of the political system? Why or why not?

2. How close to the democratic ideal of pluralism do you feel Canada comes?

3. What pressure groups are you aware of or do you belong to?

4. Do you agree with the public choice approach? Why or why not?

5. Do you agree with class analysis? Why or why not?

6. Do you agree that business pressure groups have more influence than others? Why or why not?

7. Do you agree with the state-centred approach? Why or why not?

8. Do you agree that the bureaucracy is the most significant part of the government apparatus? Why or why not?

9. Do you agree that the amalgam model provides a useful general approach? Why or why not?

NOTES

1. See Ronald Manzer, *Canada: A Socio-Political Report* (Toronto: McGraw-Hill Ryerson, 1974), ch. 1. Manzer has linked these needs to the traditional political science concerns about security, liberty, equality, and fraternity.
2. For example, language is now more divisive than religion, but this was not always the case, and the class cleavage has changed to some extent from a conflict over material issues to quality-of-life issues.
3. David Easton, *A Systems Analysis of Political Life* (New York: John Wiley & Sons, 1965).
4. Gabriel Almond, "A Developmental Approach to Political Systems," *World Politics* 17, no. 2 (January 1965), pp. 183–214.
5. Other books to outline similar approaches are Stephen Brooks, *Public Policy in Canada: An Introduction* (Toronto: McClelland and Stewart, 1989); Stephen Brooks and Andrew Stritch, *Business and Government in Canada* (Scarborough: Prentice-Hall Canada, 1991); and Kenneth Kernaghan and David Siegel, *Public Administration in Canada* (Scarborough: Nelson Canada, 2nd ed., 1991; 3rd ed., 1995). The summaries are necessarily simplified here. For greater elaboration, see references below and in subsequent chapters.
6. Pluralism and the group approach are increasingly viewed in combination with the state-centred approach in terms of "policy communities." See William Coleman and Grace Skogstad, eds., *Policy Communities and Public Policy in Canada* (Mississauga: Copp Clark Pitman, 1991).
7. Canadian applications include D.G. Hartle, *A Theory of the Expenditure Budgetary Process* (Toronto: University of Toronto Press, 1976); M.J. Trebilcock et al., *The Choice of Governing Instrument* (Ottawa: Economic Council of Canada, 1982); W.T. Stanbury, *Business–Government Relations in Canada* (Toronto: Methuen, 1986), ch. 4; Mark Sproule-Jones, "Institutions, Constitutions, and Public Policies: A Public Choice Overview," in Michael Atkinson and Marsha Chandler, eds., *The Politics of Canadian Public Policy* (Toronto: University of Toronto Press, 1983); and Réjean Landry, "Biases in the Supply of Public Policies to Organized Interests," in Coleman and Skogstad, *Policy Communities and Public Policy in Canada.*
8. Leo Panitch, "Elites, Classes, and Power in Canada," in Michael Whittington and Glen Williams, eds., *Canadian Politics in the 1990s*, 4th ed. (Scarborough: Nelson Canada, 1995).
9. Coleman, *Business and Politics*; Brooks and Stritch, *Business and Government in Canada*; and Robert Dahl and Charles Lindblom, *Politics, Economics and Welfare* (Chicago: University of Chicago Press, 1976).
10. Nicholas Baxter-Moore, "Policy Implementation and the Role of the State: A Revised Approach to the Study of Policy Instruments," in Robert Jackson et al., eds., *Contemporary Canadian Politics* (Scarborough: Prentice-Hall Canada, 1987).
11. Canadian applications include Elizabeth Riddell-Dixon, "State Autonomy and Canadian Foreign Policy: The Case of Deep Seabed Mining," *Canadian Journal of Political Science* (June 1988), pp. 297–317; Leslie Pal, "Relative Autonomy Revisited: The Origins of Canadian Unemployment Insurance," *Canadian Journal of Political Science* (March 1986), pp. 71–102; Leslie Pal, *State, Class and Bureaucracy: Canadian Unemployment Insurance and Public Policy* (Montreal: McGill–Queen's University Press, 1987); K.R. Nossal, *The Politics of Canadian Foreign Policy*, 2nd ed. (Scarborough: Prentice-Hall Canada, 1989); and R. Brian Howe and David Johnson, "Variations in Enforcing Equality: A Study of Provincial Human Rights Funding," *Canadian Public Administration* (Summer 1995).
12. Two of the leading books on the Canadian bureaucracy are Kenneth Kernaghan and David Siegel, *Public Administration in Canada*, and Robert Adie and Paul Thomas, *Canadian Public Administration*, 2nd ed. (Scarborough: Prentice-Hall Canada, 1987).
13. Pross, *Group Politics and Public Policy*; Coleman and Skogstad, *Policy Communities and Public Policy in Canada.*
14. Keith Archer et al., *Parameters of Power: Canada's Political Institutions* (Scarborough: Nelson Canada, 1995).
15. Leslie Pal, *Interests of State: The Politics of Language, Multiculturalism, and Feminism in Canada* (Montreal: McGill–Queen's University Press, 1993).

16. This phenomenon is close to the concept of "consociationalism." See Kenneth McRae, ed., *Consociational Democracy* (Toronto: McClelland and Stewart, 1974).
17. Alan C. Cairns, "The Embedded State: State–Society Relations in Canada," in Keith Banting, ed., *State and Society: Canada in Comparative Perspective*, Vol. 31 of the Research Studies for the Royal Commission on the Economic Union and Development Prospects for Canada (Toronto, 1986) and reprinted in Alan C. Cairns, *Reconfigurations: Canadian Citizenship and Constitutional Change* (Toronto: McClelland and Stewart, 1995).

FURTHER READING

Archer, Keith, et al. *Parameters of Power: Canada's Political Institutions*. Scarborough: Nelson Canada, 1995.

Brooks, Stephen, and Andrew Stritch. *Business and Government in Canada*. Scarborough: Prentice-Hall Canada, 1991.

Cairns, Alan C. "The Embedded State: State–Society Relations in Canada." In Keith Banting, ed. *State and Society: Canada in Comparative Perspective*. Research Studies for the Royal Commission on the Economic Union and Development Prospects for Canada. Toronto, 1986.

Clement, Wallace. *The Canadian Corporate Elite*. Toronto: McClelland and Stewart, 1975.

Coleman, William. *Business and Politics*. Montreal: McGill–Queen's University Press, 1988.

Coleman, William, and Grace Skogstad. *Policy Communities and Public Policy in Canada*. Mississauga: Copp Clark Pitman, 1991.

Easton, David. *A Systems Analysis of Political Life*. New York: John Wiley & Sons, 1965.

Pal, Leslie. *Interests of State: The Politics of Language, Multiculturalism, and Feminism in Canada*. Montreal: McGill–Queen's University Press, 1993.

Panitch, Leo. *The Canadian State*. Toronto: University of Toronto Press, 1977.

———. "Elites, Classes, and Power in Canada." In Michael Whittington and Glen Williams, eds. *Canadian Politics in the 1990s*, 4th ed. Scarborough: Nelson Canada, 1995.

Presthus, Robert. *Elite Accommodation in Canada*. Toronto: Macmillan, 1973.

Pross, Paul. *Group Politics and Public Policy*. Toronto: Oxford University Press, 1986.

Stanbury, W.T. *Business–Government Relations in Canada*. Toronto: Methuen, 1986.

Chapter 2

The Historical Context
AND INSTITUTIONAL
foundations

How much violence occurred in Canada's constitutional development? How did the new British conquerors treat the almost completely French colony of Quebec? How much of the new government structure in 1867 was based on that of Britain, and how much on that of the United States? What were the key points in the move toward democracy and the achievement of Canadian sovereignty?

This chapter sketches the historical context within which the Canadian political system operates and outlines the basic institutional foundations of that system. It surveys the institutions established in the colonial period, focuses on the great fusion in 1867 of the British parliamentary system with a variation on American federalism, and discusses the evolution of Canada from a British colony to a sovereign state.

EARLY SETTLEMENT AND POLITICAL INSTITUTIONS

The territory that is now called Canada was first occupied by aboriginal peoples. France and Britain colonized parts of this territory in the 1500s and 1600s and periodically fought over them and others for nearly 200 years. The British Hudson's Bay Company took possession of Rupert's Land around Hudson Bay, and Nova Scotia and Newfoundland came under permanent British control by the 1713 Treaty of Utrecht. Then, after the 1759 Battle of the Plains of Abraham, which was part of the Seven Years' War between these traditional European rivals, Quebec, Prince Edward Island, Cape Breton, and New Brunswick all became British colonies by the 1763 Treaty of Paris. This left France with only the islands of St. Pierre and Miquelon. Interaction between the new British power and the aboriginal peoples is discussed in Chapter 7.

The **Royal Proclamation of 1763**, the first distinctively Canadian constitutional document, created the colony of Quebec.[1] In the long term, it was more significant in terms of aboriginal peoples than of Québécois, but as far as ex-Europeans were concerned, Quebec was largely made up of French-speaking farmers, clergy, and seigneurs. The British-appointed government was English-speaking, and the nonagricultural economy increasingly came under British control. On the other hand, British governors resisted the idea of imposing the English language and Protestant religion on such a homogeneous French-Catholic population.

In 1774, the **Quebec Act** provided for a new set of government institutions. It established a Council in the colony, but no assembly. Roman Catholics were allowed freedom of religion and could be appointed to the Council, and the colony combined British criminal law with French civil law. Meanwhile, the first elected assembly in the "Canadian" part of British North America was summoned in Nova Scotia in 1758, followed by Prince Edward Island in 1773.

At this point, the residents of the thirteen "American" colonies revolted against British rule. French Canadians essentially remained neutral in this dispute, and because little anti-British sentiment existed in the "Canadian" colonies, thousands of ex-Americans loyal to Britain—the United Empire Loyalists—migrated to "Canada." This migration led to the severing of New Brunswick from Nova Scotia in 1784, together with the creation of its own assembly. Then, in response to pressure from those Loyalists who migrated to Quebec and who were already accustomed to operating with an elected assembly, as well as to reward the loyalty of the French for not joining in the American Revolution, Britain passed the **Constitutional Act of 1791**. It divided the colony into two—Upper and Lower Canada— each with a governor, an appointed executive council, an appointed legislative council, and a locally elected assembly. In the case of Lower Canada, the appointed councils were primarily composed of anglophones, and the assembly, of francophones. In Upper Canada, which was almost exclusively English, the Constitutional Act provided for British civil law. The executive council gradually evolved into the cabinet, while the legislative council was the forerunner of the Senate. Thus, by 1791, all the colonies had achieved **representative government**, that is, a set of political institutions including an elected legislative assembly.

Subsequent discord in the Canadian colonies was not so much between them and Britain as between the local assembly and the executive composed of the governor and his appointed advisory executive council. The elected assembly represented the people and could articulate their views but had no real power over the appointed councils. This situation was complicated by the cultural division in Lower Canada, where Lord Durham found "two nations warring in the bosom of a single state."[2] Reformers demanded **responsible government**, in which advisers to the governor would reflect the views of the elected assembly. That would mean that the members of the executive council came from the assembly and had its support. This presented a problem in the colonies, however, because on many subjects Britain wanted the governor to do *its* will, not that of the local assembly. This problem eventually erupted into the rebellions of 1837 in both Upper and Lower Canada, led by William Lyon Mackenzie and Louis-Joseph Papineau respectively, and forced the British government to appoint Lord Durham to investigate the situation. The 1839 **Durham Report** provided a blueprint for solving the problems of assembly–executive relations, recommending that the principle of responsible government be implemented with respect to local affairs, so that the executive branch would govern only as long as it retained the confidence of the assembly. Durham outlined a division of powers between local and imperial authorities such that in local matters the governor would follow the advice of colonial authorities, but in matters of imperial concern he would act as an agent of the British government. Responsible government came to Nova Scotia, New Brunswick, and the colony of Canada in 1848, and three years later to Prince Edward Island. Thus, by 1851, all these pre-Confederation British colonies operated on the basis that the cabinet or executive council had to resign if it lost the confidence of the elected legislative assembly. Manitoba and British Columbia would acquire responsible government when they joined Confederation.

Durham also recommended that Upper and Lower Canada be united into a single colony of Canada, partly as one last attempt to submerge and assimilate the French. The colonies were amalgamated by the 1840 **Act of Union**, but English did not remain the sole language of government operations for long. When it became clear that assimilation of the French Canadians would not be achieved, French was also recognized as an official language of the legislature. Moreover, most governments of the period were headed by one English and one French leader.

Figure 2.1 Evolution of Canadian Pre-Confederation Political Institutions

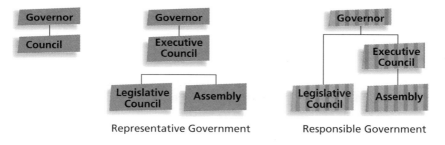

THE ROAD TO CONFEDERATION

The British North American colonies were driven to consider uniting due to economic, political, and military factors.[3] Because the British had discontinued colonial trading preferences, and because a reciprocity treaty with the United States had expired, the colonies hoped to establish a new, large tariff-free trading area among themselves. Confederation offered the hope of economic prosperity; this large internal market would be enhanced by a railway link between the Maritimes and central Canada, which in turn would provide the latter with a winter Atlantic port. The future prospect of annexing and developing the West was also seen as a source of economic prosperity.

Meanwhile, the colony of Canada had experienced political deadlock between its two parts, then called Canada East (Quebec) and Canada West (Ontario), as well as between French and English component groups. Public decisions had to be made in one large, combined set of governmental institutions, yet the needs and demands of the two parts were often quite different. This led to the practice of requiring a "double majority" (a majority of members from each part of the colony) for the passage of bills. Confederation would allow greater autonomy to the two parts because it would entail a central government to deal with problems that all the colonies had in common, but would also provide for provincial governments to handle distinctive internal matters on their own. Such a two-tier structure also appealed to the Maritime provinces, which did not feel like turning all decisions over to a distant central government.

The individual colonies also felt vulnerable in a military sense. The United States had a powerful army on their doorstep, and prominent Americans could be heard advocating the takeover of the existing colonies and/or the vast territories to the west. Moreover, the British government no longer seemed interested in providing military protection to the colonies. By joining together, the colonies would make American military aggression more difficult and provide a stronger force to resist its appetite for the "Canadian" West.

Confederation was thus precipitated by economic, political, and military problems and seemed to most colonial leaders to be a means of solving them. But it also held out the hope that the new country would one day become a prosperous, transcontinental nation similar to its southern neighbour.

In the 1860s, Nova Scotia, New Brunswick, and Prince Edward Island began to consider forming a Maritime union, and called the Charlottetown Conference of 1864 for this purpose. When delegates from the colony of Canada arrived, however, the idea of a larger union was put up for debate. Discussions continued at the Quebec Conference later that year, and the essentials of the Confederation scheme were agreed upon. The London Conference of 1866 fine-tuned the agreement, leaving Prince Edward Island (and Newfoundland) temporarily on the sidelines. The four provinces—Nova Scotia, New Brunswick, Quebec, and Ontario—were officially united on July 1, 1867, by the **British North America Act**, later renamed the **Constitution Act, 1867**.

FUSING THE BRITISH PARLIAMENTARY SYSTEM WITH AMERICAN FEDERALISM

Canadian Confederation was the first attempt to fuse the principles of the British parliamentary system with those of federalism, although Australia would make a similar move shortly afterwards. Since the United States was the leading federal state of the day, and the one closest to Canada, the federal aspects of the new constitution were directly related to those next door.

Within the new central government (often called the "federal government," only to make things more confusing), and within each of the governments of the new provinces, the British parliamentary system provided the institutional foundations. This system is based on the periodic popular election of the members of the House of Commons. Parliament also has a second or "upper" chamber, which in Britain was the hereditary House of Lords. Canada lacked the historic landed nobility found in Britain, however, so it was decided that the members of the Canadian Senate would be appointed by the prime minister. The third part of British Parliament is the monarch or the Crown, and approval of all three parts is necessary for the passage of legislation and certain other authoritative decisions. Canada would, of course, continue to be a monarchy, and automatically shared the widely esteemed British monarch of the day, Queen Victoria. On a practical daily basis, however, the governor general would exercise the functions of the Crown.

Although the British system is called parliamentary government, and although it is said that Parliament is sovereign or supreme, such labels and descriptions are somewhat misleading. The core of the parliamentary system, even in 1867, was the prime minister and the cabinet. While they must be members of Parliament, they are such an important part of Parliament that they often relegate both the monarch and other members of the House of Commons and Senate (or House of Lords) to a position of insignificance. To the prime minister and cabinet are conferred the powers to lead the country and make the most important decisions in the political system. But the principle of responsible government holds that they retain their position and their powers only as long as they are supported by a majority in Parliament. If the House of Commons declares a lack of confidence in the prime minister and cabinet, they must either resign and make way for another group to take their place, or else call an election, the latter option being most common. Because the prime minister and cabinet ministers have seats in the legislative branch, mostly the House of Commons, the system is often termed a *fusion of powers*—that is, it involves a combination of legislative and executive powers.

In the British parliamentary system, then, the prime minister and cabinet ministers, who have seats in Parliament, are given the power to introduce most legislation and the right to control most of the time of the legislature. They are given the exclusive power to introduce legislation of a financial nature—laws either to raise or to spend money. They are given wide powers of appointment, broad powers to draft subordinate legislation under the authority of laws, wide powers in international affairs, and essentially all powers necessary to provide effective political leadership for the country. The parliamentary system is executive-dominated, and because the British Parliament operates in the Palace of Westminster, this system is sometimes called the **Westminster model**. Other members of Parliament (MPs) may criticize and propose amendments, the monarch (or governor general) may advise and warn, but the prime minister and cabinet almost always get their way. This is because a majority of the members of Parliament normally belong to the same political party as the prime minister and cabinet, and together they constitute a *majority government*. Even more in Canada than contemporary Britain, the cabinet imposes rigid party discipline on its MPs to support its every move. It should be added that while government was small and simple at the time of Confederation, it has gradually developed another important branch: the bureaucracy or public service. The bureaucracy essentially advises the prime minister and cabinet on their decisions and then carries out whatever government programs have been authorized.

The significance of the Senate has declined since Confederation because arriving there by appointment rather than election diminishes its members' legitimacy in a democratic age. The powers of the Senate have remained virtually equal to those of the House of Commons (unlike those of the British House of Lords, which have been curtailed), but senators have rarely felt it proper to exercise them. Moreover, independent behaviour has usually been discouraged by the fact that the party with a majority in the Senate has usually been the same one as has a majority in the Commons. If for any reason the Senate should ultimately defeat a government bill, it does not affect the constitutional standing of the prime minister and cabinet. The principle of responsible government in the Westminster model, whether in Britain or Canada, does not apply to upper chambers. The model outlined above is also operational in each of the provinces, except that they all possess one-chamber or unicameral legislatures.

The British parliamentary system also incorporates the principle of the independence of the judiciary. Although courts are established by acts of Parliament and judges are appointed by the prime minister and cabinet, the whole judicial system is then expected to operate independently of the executive and legislative branches of government. In the case of Britain itself, the judges have considerable discretion in interpreting laws, but lack the power of judicial review, that is, the power to declare them invalid. The Canadian judiciary soon appropriated to itself the power to invalidate laws that violated the federal–provincial division of powers, but were otherwise quite restrained.

The British parliamentary system is distinct in many ways from the U.S. presidental-congressional system. There, the president and the two houses of the legislature are independently elected, and no one is permitted to sit in more than one branch of government. The *separation of powers* means that executive, legislative, and judicial powers are distributed to three separate branches of government: president, congress, and the courts respectively. Moreover, the U.S. system is also characterized by "checks and balances" designed to ensure that the actions of any one branch of government are subject to veto by another. Members of the House of Representatives and the Senate have much more legislative power than their counterparts in the British parliamentary system in terms of both initiating bills and amending or vetoing those emanating from the president. Party discipline is also much looser, so that even if a majority of the members of Congress belong to the same party as the president,

Figure 2.2 An Outline of Canadian Political Institutions

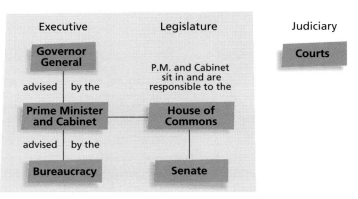

there is no guarantee that the president's initiatives will be passed. The Supreme Court also has the power of *judicial review* and can overturn any legislation it feels is in violation of the Constitution. Apart from the name of the upper chamber, the Senate, the Fathers of Canadian Confederation adopted virtually nothing from the U.S. system with respect to the internal operation of the federal and provincial governments.

On the other hand, the Fathers were dealing with a large piece of territory, one they hoped would soon become larger, someday equalling or exceeding that of the United States. They were also dealing with colonies that had separate identities and a previous semi-autonomous existence. In this respect, the model of American federalism could not help but influence the design of the new country they were establishing. It would have to be a *federation* of some kind, with a division of powers between the central and provincial governments.

Confederation was to a large extent the work of John A. Macdonald, who went on to become the first Canadian prime minister. Macdonald preferred a unitary state or legislative union in which the new central government would have almost all the powers and the provinces would be little more than municipalities. But Quebec and the Maritimes were not prepared to join such a system. Quebec in particular demanded an autonomous provincial government so that its cultural concerns, such as education and civil law, would be placed in the hands of a French-speaking majority. The Maritimes, too, insisted on provincial govern-ments because they did not want to lose their previously established identities, they had little in the way of municipal government to handle local problems, and they were so far removed from the new capital in Ottawa. Hence, the logical compromise was a system that contained a central government to deal with common purposes, and provincial governments to look after local concerns. Although this principle was essentially that of American federalism, it was also consistent with the existing British colonial tradition of having two levels of gov-ernment (Britain and local), and the Fathers of Confederation were accustomed to such divided jurisdiction.

Macdonald accepted a federal form of government, then, to allow the former colonies to retain some of their political and economic independence, but he intended the new country to be a highly centralized federation. He felt that its economic and defensive objectives required a strong central government, a conviction reinforced by the conclusion among most of the participants that the American Civil War (which had just ended as they began their deliberations) had been the result of too much power at the state level. Some historians have added that most of the Fathers of Confederation had links to banks and to railway and man-ufacturing companies, which looked upon the Confederation project primarily as a source of profit. By controlling the development of the country at the centre, they would be free to exploit the hinterland.[4]

In many ways the Confederation settlement was not consistent with the modern defini-tion of federalism because in certain respects the provinces were made subordinate to the central government. Some observers thus prefer to label the arrangement at its creation as "quasi-federal."[5] Ironically, however, the Fathers used the word "Confederation," which in political science indicates a loose, decentralized federation, the opposite of what Macdonald intended. In the U.S. federal system, for example, the central government was given only certain delegated powers, while the residual powers remained at the level of the states.

Macdonald was determined to reverse this pattern; he essentially gave the provinces 16 enumerated powers and left the residual powers at the centre. He was also careful to give Ottawa unlimited powers of taxation, the broadest powers to regulate trade and commerce, and power over such other important fields as defence and criminal law.

Besides dividing powers between the two levels of government, constitutional architects in both the United States and Canada had to decide how the provinces or states would be represented at the national level. In both cases, the lower house of the legislature would be based on the principle of representation by population, so that the most populous provinces or states would have the largest number of members in that chamber. To counterbalance this, and to protect the interests of the smaller states, the United States decided that each state, regardless of population, would have two senators at the national level. Some Fathers of Confederation preferred this idea, but others wanted representation by population in both houses of Parliament. The Canadian compromise was to base the Senate on the principle of equal *regional* representation rather than equal *provincial* representation.

Since Canadian politicians were already familiar with divided authority, it might seem that a fusion of the British parliamentary system and American federalism was not such a constitutional innovation. The colonial division of powers was a somewhat different kind, however, and more importantly, the whole ethos underlying the Canadian and U.S. systems was different. In the British parliamentary system, everything is designed to *facilitate* government action by concentrating power in the hands of the executive, whether in terms of its relationship with other institutions of government such as Parliament or the courts, or with territorial units such as local governments. In the American system, everything is designed to *inhibit* government action by preventing the concentration of power in the hands of any government. Institutions of the national government—president, House of Representatives, Senate, and Supreme Court—should be able to veto each other, and they should collectively be kept in line by a division of powers that gives most authority to the states. It is largely because the British system is designed to facilitate government action and because the American system is designed to inhibit it that the fusion of the two systems in Canadian confederation was such a distinctive phenomenon. John A. Macdonald saw the contradiction and therefore tried to establish a federal system that was much more centralized than that next door.

The major change in the institutional structure established in Canada in 1867 was the adoption of the Charter of Rights and Freedoms in 1982. It added to the scope of judicial review, which the Canadian courts had appropriated with respect to the federal–provincial division of powers by importing American-style judicial activism in the area of protecting civil liberties. Henceforth, the courts could disallow federal or provincial legislation that violated the Constitution either in terms of the division of powers or the Charter of Rights.

PRINCIPLES OF THE CANADIAN CONSTITUTION

The preceding discussion has identified three basic principles of the Canadian constitution: responsible government, which is the essence of the British parliamentary system; federalism; and limited judicial review, especially since 1982. At least three other fundamental principles are also embedded in the Canadian Constitution, however, these being constitutional monarchy, the rule of law, and democracy.[6]

PRINCIPLES OF THE CANADIAN CONSTITUTION

- Responsible government
- Federalism
- Limited judicial review
- Constitutional monarchy
- Rule of law
- Democracy

In terms of its head of state, Canada is a *constitutional monarchy*. This is not a principle that attracts much attention, largely because the monarch herself lives in another country and because her actual power, as well as that of her Canadian representative, the governor general, is not extensive. Nevertheless, as outlined in Chapter 20, the monarchical system underlies a great deal of the operation of government in Canada, largely in the form of the

Reproduced with permission.

Crown. The Crown can be defined as the sum total of residual or discretionary powers still left in the hands of the monarch. The term constitutional monarchy basically means that the monarch reigns according to the Constitution and that the Constitution has put most of the powers of government into someone else's hands. Almost all of the powers once exercised by the monarch have been whittled away either by legislation or constitutional convention.

The *rule of law* is another constitutional principle inherited from Great Britain that rests largely on convention and judicial precedent. In essence, it means that all government action must be based on law and that governments and government officials must obey the law. In other words, the law is supreme, and no one, including the lawmakers, is above it.[7] Courts in Canada as well as Britain have had occasion to overturn government decisions and actions that were not based on law.[8]

Finally, Canada is a *democracy*. This term, which is related to responsible government, constitutional monarchy, and the rule of law, will be analyzed more fully in Chapter 13. In Canadian terms, democracy has four components: popular sovereignty, meaning that the people ultimately rule, primarily through periodic elections; political equality, meaning that everyone has one vote on election day; political freedom, meaning that during and between elections people are free to organize and advocate for political purposes; and majority rule, meaning that except in defined situations designed to protect minority rights, the will of the majority prevails.

THE ROAD TO CANADIAN SOVEREIGNTY

Having outlined the development of the basic institutions and the fundamental constitutional principles of the Canadian political system, let us trace the evolution of Canada from British colony to sovereign state. Contrary to popular belief, the British North America (BNA) Act of 1867 (that is, the Constitution Act, 1867) did not directly advance the cause of Canadian independence. That act simply divided the powers that were already being exercised in Canada between a new central government and the provincial governments. British control still existed in many forms: British appointment of the governor general; the power of the governor general to reserve Canadian legislation for the approval of the British cabinet; the power of the British government to disallow Canadian legislation; the power of the British Parliament to amend the BNA Act; the arbitrary extension to Canada of imperial legislation; the paramountcy of any British legislation in conflict with Canadian statutes; Canadian incapacity to pass legislation with extra-territorial effect; the authority of the Judicial Committee of the Privy Council as Canada's final court of appeal; and British control of Canadian foreign and trade policy. The act of confederation made Canada a more respectable and viable entity and ultimately strengthened its case for greater autonomy, but it did not fundamentally alter the British–Canadian relationship.

Canada had succeeded in claiming the right to control its own tariffs even before Confederation, and between 1867 and 1914 it became increasingly autonomous in making commercial treaties with other countries. The same was true in terms of political treaties, although progress in this area came more slowly. One modest advance was the inclusion of

Prime Minister Macdonald as a member of the British team that negotiated the 1871 Treaty of Washington. Relations with Britain were handled through the governor general, the Colonial Office, the Canadian High Commissioner in London after 1879, and in periodic Imperial Conferences after 1887.

By the turn of the century Canadian autonomy had progressed to the point that when Canada sent an official contingent to the South African (Boer) War, it was done more in response to Canadian public opinion than to British pressure. In the Alaska Boundary dispute of 1903, however, the British representative on the Anglo-Canadian half of the judicial tribunal voted with the three American representatives to award the United States a long strip of the northern British Columbia coastline. In defending Canadian interests, Britain was apparently not prepared to jeopardize its relations with the United States.

The ultimate independence of Canada and several other British colonies is usually attributed to developments connected to the First World War. Although Canada was automatically at war in 1914 as a result of British action, the Canadian government did determine the extent of its own commitments. A series of conferences of Dominion prime ministers called the Imperial War Cabinet began in 1917 as Canada and the other dominions—Australia, New Zealand, and South Africa—demanded a role in policy-making in return for their wartime contributions. Prime Minister Robert Borden and his counterparts took part in the Paris Peace Conference and signed the peace treaties, and the dominions became individual members of the League of Nations. Thus, by 1919, Canada had gained new international status as a result of both accomplishments on the battlefield and subsequent demands for recognition at the conference table.

Postwar attempts to forge a unified Empire foreign policy broke down as various dominions sought to flex their fledgling muscles, and Canada insisted on signing alone the 1923 Halibut Treaty with the United States. The Imperial Conference of 1926 ended with a proclamation of the complete equality in status of the United Kingdom and the dominions in internal, international, and imperial affairs. They were described in the proclamation as

> autonomous Communities within the British Empire, equal in status, in no way subordinate one to another in any aspect of their domestic or external affairs, though united by a common allegiance to the Crown, and freely associated as members of the British Commonwealth of Nations.

Besides giving Canada complete autonomy in all policy fields, the 1926 Balfour Report had implications for the position of the governor general. This official would no longer be an agent of the British government, but rather only a representative of the Crown. Disallowance of Canadian legislation by the British cabinet and reservation of Canadian legislation by the governor general would now be obsolete. These arrangements were refined at another conference in 1930 and then constitutionalized in the **Statute of Westminster** of 1931. That statute provided

> that the Colonial Laws Validity Act (under which dominion statutes were void if they conflicted with statutes of the Imperial Parliament) was no longer to

apply to the dominions, that in the future no dominion statute was to be declared void because it was repugnant to the law of the United Kingdom, and that no act of the Imperial Parliament was to extend to a dominion unless it declared that the dominion had requested and consented to its enactment. The Statute also declared that a dominion Parliament had the power to enact laws having extra-territorial operation.[9]

After 1931, therefore, Canada was completely independent of Britain, but a number of anomalies continued to disguise this fact. First, Canada continued to share a head of state with Britain, although from the Canadian perspective, that person was King or Queen of Canada. Even though the Canadian government now had the power to select the governor general, prime ministers continued to make British appointments (aristocrats, diplomats, and war heroes) until 1952. Of more importance, since Canada had not been able to decide how to amend the BNA Act within Canada, such amendments still had to be passed by the British Parliament, albeit only at Canadian request. In 1949 a procedure was developed to make constitutional amendments in Canada if they affected only the federal government, but it was not until 1982 that a comprehensive domestic formula for making constitutional amendments was agreed to. Also of great significance, the Judicial Committee of the Privy Council remained Canada's final court of appeal in criminal cases until 1933 and in all other cases, notably constitutional, until 1949. Other British legacies included the fact that, until 1965, the Union Jack and the Red Ensign, combining a smaller Union Jack in the corner with a Canadian crest, continued to serve as Canadian flags. In 1967 the government recognized "O Canada" rather than "God Save the Queen" as the Canadian national anthem, but it was not until 1980 that the former was designated officially.

Once Canada made an autonomous decision to take part, the Second World War saw the Canadian armed forces integrated with the allied powers. Afterwards, however, British–Canadian ties declined as Canada's population became more diversified in its ethnic origins, as Britain occupied a diminished role in world affairs, and as both Britain and Canada drew closer and closer to the United States.[10] While the definitive break occurred between 1914 and 1940, perhaps the final realization did not dawn until the Suez Crisis of 1956 when Canada refused to support British action.[11]

In the 1990s, Canada continues to share the Queen with Britain and several other countries and is part of the Commonwealth; nationals of both Canada and Britain have invested in each other's economies; the Canadian parliamentary and legal systems are based on those of Britain; a majority of Canadians speak a variant of the English language; and many are still linked to Britain by family ties. Otherwise, however, both Canada and Britain see each other as just another friendly, foreign country, with minimal influence and no control.

. . . .

CONCLUSION

This chapter has shown how Canada developed from a British colony to a sovereign state. It also traced the evolution of government institutions along the way, focusing primarily on the foundations established in 1867. Those foundations consisted of the grafting of the British parliamentary and American federal systems, although certain aspects of the latter were deliberately avoided. The discussion has also revealed the fact that the question of French–English relations has been integral to Canadian constitutional development from the very beginning.

(SC) Canadian constitutional development has usually resulted from the decisions of a small political elite sitting around a table, whether this elite was British (1763–1864), colonial (1864–1867), Canadian (1980–1982), or some combination thereof (1926–1931). In this sense, of the different approaches outlined in Chapter 1, the state-centred approach is most appropriate for our discussion here. Canada became more democratic within its own government structures in a gradual progression of statist decisions. Moreover, the drive to loosen links with Britain was largely engineered by prime ministers Laurier, Borden, and King, without much apparent public pressure. Reducing British control would automatically increase the power of the Canadian state that these politicians controlled. O.D. Skelton, the trusted adviser of Liberal prime ministers in the early years of this century, has also been identified as a leading advocate of breaking the British bonds in behind-the-scenes discussions with Laurier and King.[12]

(P) In some cases, however, such as in the establishment of colonial assemblies and then in the recognition of responsible government, pluralists would emphasize that such authorities were forced to respond to public pressure. It was only in the 1837 rebellions in both Upper and Lower Canada that such pressure took on violent proportions and only for a short period of time.

(C) In some cases, too, class analysts can identify the economic elites that had a hand in guiding constitutional developments. The influence of the corporate elite can be seen both in the move toward confederation and in the design of the confederation scheme: to some extent Canada was formed to maximize the profits of railway promoters.

DISCUSSION QUESTIONS

1. Did the British treat French Canadians well? Explain.

2. Why did French Canadians remain loyal to Britain during the American Revolution?

3. How did the United Empire Loyalists change the face of Canada?

4. What aspects of the French–English political relationship were established before or at Confederation?

5. What is meant by the "Westminster model," and how does it differ from the U.S. system of government?

6. What aspects of American federalism did Canada adopt, and what aspects did we reject?

7. Is there an inherent contradiction between the British parliamentary system and the American federal system? Explain.

8. Why did Canada fall into the U.S. sphere of influence so soon after emerging from British domination?

9. How does the state-centred approach apply to Canadian constitutional development?

10. What other approaches are relevant to this development?

....

NOTES

1. Some of the key sources on Canada's constitutional evolution are W.P.M. Kennedy, ed., *Documents of the Canadian Constitution, 1759–1915* (Toronto: Oxford University Press, 1918); R. MacGregor Dawson, *The Government of Canada*, 5th ed., revised by Norman Ward (Toronto: University of Toronto Press, 1970); and Bayard Reesor, *The Canadian Constitution in Historical Perspective* (Scarborough: Prentice-Hall Canada, 1992).

2. Lord Durham, *Report of the Affairs of British North America*, ed. Gerald M. Craig (Toronto: McClelland and Stewart, 1963).

3. Some of the basic sources on Confederation include P.B. Waite, *The Confederation Debates in the Province of Canada/1865* (Toronto: McClelland and Stewart, 1963); P.B. Waite, *The Life and Times of Confederation, 1864–1867*, 2nd ed. (Toronto: University of Toronto Press, 1962); and Donald Creighton, *The Road to Confederation* (Toronto: Macmillan, 1964).

4. Stanley B. Ryerson, *Unequal Union: Confederation and the Roots of Conflict in the Canadas, 1815–1873*, 2nd ed. (Toronto: Progress Books, 1973).

5. K.C. Wheare, *Federal Government*, 4th ed. (London: Oxford University Press, 1963).

6. Reesor, *The Canadian Constitution in Historical Perspective*, ch. 4.

7. Ibid., pp. 66–71.

8. The most famous case probably being *Roncarelli v. Duplessis*, in which the courts found the premier of Quebec personally guilty of cancelling Roncarelli's liquor licence merely because he had provided bail for Jehovah's Witnesses.

9. Dawson, *The Government of Canada*, p. 54. See also his *The Development of Dominion Status, 1900–1936* (London: F. Cass, 1955), and *Constitutional Issues in Canada, 1900–1931* (London: Oxford University Press, 1933).

10. Many observers and historians saw the King and St. Laurent governments as the villains in the Americanization of Canada after the Second World War, although J.L. Granatstein argues that British weakness was of greater significance in this regard than any deliberate Canadian government objective. See Donald Creighton, *Canada's First Century* (Toronto: Macmillan, 1970); George Grant, *Lament for a Nation: The Defeat of Canadian Nationalism* (Toronto: McClelland and Stewart, 1965); and J.L. Granatstein, *How Britain's Weakness Forced Canada into the Arms of the United States* (Toronto: University of Toronto Press, 1989).

11. The question of British and French bombardment of Egypt in defence of the Suez Canal in 1956 represented the first major international incident in which Canada found itself at odds with Britain.

12. John Hilliker, *Canada's Department of External Affairs: The Early Years, 1909–1926* (Montreal: McGill–Queen's University Press, 1990).

FURTHER READING

Creighton, Donald. *The Road to Confederation*. Toronto: Macmillan, 1964.

———. *Canada's First Century*. Toronto: Macmillan, 1970.

Dawson, R. MacGregor. *The Government of Canada*, 5th ed., revised by Norman Ward. Toronto: University of Toronto Press, 1970.

Durham, Lord. *Report of the Affairs of British North America*, ed. Gerald M. Craig. Toronto: McClelland and Stewart, 1963.

Granatstein, J.L. *How Britain's Weakness Forced Canada into the Arms of the United States*. Toronto: University of Toronto Press, 1989.

Hilliker, John. *Canada's Department of External Affairs: The Early Years, 1909–1926*. Montreal: McGill–Queen's University Press, 1990.

Kennedy, W.P.M., ed. *Documents of the Canadian Constitution, 1759–1915*. Toronto: Oxford University Press, 1918.

Reesor, Bayard. *The Canadian Constitution in Historical Perspective*. Scarborough: Prentice-Hall Canada, 1992.

Ryerson, Stanley B. *Unequal Union: Confederation and the Roots of Conflict in the Canadas, 1815–1873*, 2nd ed. Toronto: Progress Books, 1973.

Waite. P.B. *The Life and Times of Confederation, 1864–1867*, 2nd ed. Toronto: University of Toronto Press, 1962.

———. *The Confederation Debates in the Province of Canada/1865*. Toronto: McClelland and Stewart, 1963.

PART 2

The Constitutional Context

The constitutional context of Canadian government and politics forms the framework of the whole political system and is analyzed in the three following chapters. Chapter 3 outlines the ingredients of the Canadian Constitution and the succession of attempts to make major changes to it. One of the most important aspects of the Constitution is the relationship between the federal and provincial governments. Thus, Chapter 4 examines all aspects of Canadian federalism. The other central aspect of the Constitution since 1982 is the Charter of Rights and Freedoms. How it has been interpreted and how it has affected the operation of the Canadian political system are discussed in Chapter 5.

Chapter 3

The
CANADIAN
CONSTITUTION
and Constitutional Change

What is the Canadian Constitution? What formula should be used to amend it? Should a Charter of Rights be incorporated into the Constitution? Should the distribution of powers between Ottawa and the provinces be altered? Should Quebec be given constitutional recognition as a distinct society? Should the inherent right to aboriginal self-government be enshrined in the Constitution? Should it be given a new, inspiring preamble? These and related constitutional questions have obsessed Canadian policy-makers and scholars for many years, yet many remain unresolved. Canada has gone through several attempts at constitutional review since 1960, and at least some of the issues involved are expected to be settled before the turn of the century.

The Canadian Constitution would be easier to comprehend if it consisted of a single piece of paper by that name. In the absence of such a document, we can define a **constitution** as "the whole body of fundamental rules and principles according to which a state is governed." To be more specific, the Constitution provides for the basic institutions of government and the relations between them, the relations between national and provincial governments, and the relations between governments and citizens.[1] Such a comprehensive definition suggests that the final product will not be neat and tidy, and that some of its ingredients may not be written down at all. In structural-functional terms, the Constitution outlines how the rule-making, rule-application, and rule-adjudication functions will be performed and by what political structures.

This chapter begins by examining the ingredients of the Canadian Constitution and then considers successive attempts at constitutional change. These include the search for a domestic amending formula, the quest for a constitutional Charter of Rights, and the pressures for constitutional change arising from the Quiet Revolution in Quebec: the 1971 Victoria Charter, the Constitution Act, 1982, the 1987 Meech Lake Accord, and the 1992 Charlottetown Accord, all attempting to resolve the "Quebec problem."

COMPONENTS OF THE CANADIAN CONSTITUTION

In the search for the components that fit the definition of a constitution provided above, it will be seen that the Canadian Constitution is a great hodge-podge. Some parts of it are written and other parts are unwritten.

COMPONENTS OF THE CANADIAN CONSTITUTION

- Constitution Act, 1867
- Amendments to the Constitution Act, 1867
- British statutes and orders-in-council
- Canadian statutes
- Constitution Act, 1982
- Judicial decisions
- Constitutional conventions

The Constitution Act, 1867

We turn first to the formal, legal documents, the most important of which is the **British North America (BNA) Act**, 1867, which in 1982 was officially renamed the **Constitution Act, 1867**.[2] This was the law passed by the British Parliament that joined Nova Scotia, New Brunswick, Ontario, and Quebec together as the new Dominion of Canada, as mentioned in Chapter 2. The act contained many components that would be expected in a constitution, providing much of the basic machinery and institutions of government and establishing a federal system.

The act lacks an inspirational introduction, and its preamble is seriously out of date. It merely states that the four original provinces have expressed their desire "to be federally united with a constitution similar in principle to that of the United Kingdom." Many of the subsequent 147 clauses are also obsolete, and several have actually been repealed.

Part III deals with the executive power, and section 9 declares that the executive authority over Canada is vested in the Queen. Subsequent clauses refer to the governor general and to the Canadian Privy Council, which is "to aid and advise in the Government of Canada." Section 13 observes that the governor in council refers to the governor general acting by and with the advice of the Canadian Privy Council. Note that the prime minister and cabinet are not explicitly mentioned.

Part IV establishes the legislative power, the Senate and House of Commons. The Senate (sections 21–36) is based on the principle of equal regional representation, and the act details the qualifications for appointment. Section 26 allows for the appointment of four or eight extra senators, the power used by Prime Minister Brian Mulroney in 1990 to get the Goods and Services Tax passed. Sections 37 to 57 deal with the House of Commons. Many of these provisions have been superseded by other legislation, but sections 53 and 54 require that money bills originate in the House of Commons, and within it, from members of the executive branch.

Part V concerns the constitutions of the provinces, including the position of lieutenant governor. Since the 1867 act created the provinces of Ontario and Quebec, sections 69 to 87 establish their legislatures, whereas the legislatures of Nova Scotia and New Brunswick continued in their pre-Confederation form.

Part VI, the "Distribution of Legislative Powers" between the central and provincial governments, is probably the most important part of the document. This includes section 91, the federal powers; section 92, provincial powers; section 93, education; and section 95, concurrent powers.

Part VII is concerned with the judiciary. It is a short section that, in section 96, allows the governor general to appoint superior, district, and county judges. It also provides for judges' retirement and removal, and allows Parliament to set up a general court of appeal. Note that the 1867 act does not explicitly establish the Supreme Court of Canada.

Part VIII deals with the division of provincial revenues, debts, assets, and taxation at the time of Confederation. It makes clear that the provinces have possession of their own lands, mines, and minerals. Part IX is a miscellaneous collection, including section 132, the treaty power, and section 133, regarding the use of the English and French languages. The last section provides for the admission of other colonies.

The Constitution Act, 1867, was thus very brief on the executive and judicial branches of government. It included virtually nothing about limiting the powers of government in relation to the people. The act also lacked any mention of the means to amend it; since it was a statute of the British Parliament, most formal changes to the act have been made by the British Parliament at Canadian request.

Amendments to the Constitution Act, 1867

Formal amendments to the 1867 act are indeed the second ingredient of the Canadian Constitution. Some of these are more important than others, and some did not have to be made in London, so that the exact number of such amendments is not easy to determine. The Constitution Act, 1982, sought to make a definitive list, however, and Schedule I to that act lists 17 amendments to the 1867 act made by the British Parliament and another eight made by the Canadian Parliament that are still operative. The former were often termed "British North America Acts" of whatever year in which they were passed, but in 1982, they were mostly renamed "Constitution Act" of the appropriate year. The most important of the 17 British amendments to the 1867 act are as follows:

Constitution Act, 1907 – established a new regime of federal–provincial grants
Constitution Act, 1915 – established a new distribution of Senate seats
Constitution Act, 1930 – transferred ownership of natural resources to Western provinces
Constitution Act, 1940 – added unemployment insurance to the list of federal powers
Newfoundland Act, 1949 – joined that province to Canada
Constitution Act, 1960 – made it mandatory for provincial superior court judges to retire at age 75
Constitution Act, 1964 – extended federal power in the field of old age pensions, superseding an amendment in 1951

British Statutes and Orders-in-Council

The third major component of the Canadian Constitution is a collection of British statutes and orders-in-council. Chief among these is the Statute of Westminster, 1931, which declared Canada to be totally independent of Britain. The Northwest Territories, British Columbia, and Prince Edward Island were British colonies added to Canada by means of British orders-in-council, that is, decisions of the British cabinet. These, along with the 1949 amendment that added Newfoundland, completed the territorial dimensions of what we now know as Canada and are included in the Constitution for that reason. The four British orders-in-council in question are now known as follows:

Rupert's Land and North-Western   – transferred Hudson's Bay Company lands
    Territory Order (1870)   to Canada
British Columbia Terms of Union (1871)   – joined that province to Canada
Prince Edward Island Terms of Union (1873) – joined that province to Canada
Adjacent Territories Order (1880)   – added Arctic Islands to Canada

Canadian Statutes

If the British order-in-council that transferred the Northwest Territories to Canada is considered part of the Canadian Constitution, so must the Canadian statutes that carved provinces out of those territories, that is, the Manitoba Act of 1870 and the Saskatchewan and Alberta Acts of 1905. Although it may seem strange to consider ordinary Canadian statutes as part of the Constitution, this must be done when they are of such constitutional significance.

Constitution Act, 1982

Although the Constitution Act, 1982, was in a sense the last amendment to the Constitution Act, 1867, to be passed by the British Parliament, it is worthy of separate mention. While Canada was completely self-governing after 1931, amendments to the 1867 act still had to be made by the British Parliament because no formula had been developed to do so in Canada. The Constitution Act, 1982, contained such a domestic constitution-amending formula, and the **Canada Act** passed by the British Parliament at the same time finally terminated all British authority over Canada.[3] It thus provided Canada at long last with a domestic constitutional amending formula (outlined below). As noted in Chapter 20, however, the constitutional documents of 1982 did not alter the position of the monarchy in Canada. The same person continues to be recognized as Queen of Canada as is claimed by several other countries, including Britain.

     The second main aspect of the Constitution Act, 1982, was the Charter of Rights and Freedoms. The Charter guaranteed fundamental, democratic, legal, egalitarian, and linguistic rights and freedoms against government intrusion. In other words, the Charter of Rights and Freedoms imposed formal new limitations on the government in interaction with its citizens. In addition, it changed the manner in which such civil liberties were protected, now relying more on judicial interpretation than parliamentary restraint. The Charter is examined in depth in Chapter 5.

The 1982 act also contained statements on equalization payments to have-not provinces, multiculturalism, and aboriginal rights. As far as the division of powers was concerned, a new section 92A was added that clarified and extended provincial powers over natural resources.

According to the Constitution Act, 1982, the Constitution of Canada consists of the British statutes and orders-in-council and Canadian statutes mentioned above. These 26 formal, legal documents comprise the Constitution in the narrow sense of being subject to the constitutional amending formula adopted in 1982. Important as they are, these documents are silent on so many vital aspects of the fundamental rules and principles according to which Canada is governed that they cannot possibly constitute the entirety of the Canadian Constitution. Most authorities would therefore cast a much wider net in selecting the ingredients of the Constitution in its broader sense.

Other Canadian Statutes

The fourth ingredient that most authorities would include are certain other basic Canadian statutes. For example, many aspects of the Supreme Court are provided for only in the Supreme Court Act, an ordinary law that fleshes out the provisions of the 1867 act with respect to the judicial branch of government, along with the Federal Court Act. It could be argued that certain other fundamental Canadian statutes should also be included, such as the Parliament of Canada Act, the Bill of Rights, the Canada Elections Act, the Citizenship Act, the Emergencies Act, the Canadian Human Rights Act, the Yukon Act, and the Nunavut Act. Where to stop in formulating such a list is not crystal clear.

Judicial Decisions

The fifth ingredient of the Canadian Constitution consists of judicial decisions that have clarified or altered provisions of the 1867 act or other parts of the Constitution. The largest body of such decisions are the judgments of the British Judicial Committee of the Privy Council, Canada's final court of appeal until 1949, which significantly affected the division of powers between the federal and provincial governments. As discussed in Chapter 4 on Canadian federalism, it was John A. Macdonald's intention to create a strong central government, but the Judicial Committee interpreted the 1867 act in such a way as to minimize federal powers and maximize those of the provinces. The court decisions that effected such a wholesale transformation of the federal nature of the country must be considered as part of the Constitution alongside the actual provisions of the original act.

A number of earlier court decisions also imposed restrictions on government power vis-à-vis its citizens—that is, in the area of civil liberties—and many such decisions have been made since the Charter of Rights was adopted in 1982. These "civil liberties" decisions are part of the Constitution along with the "division of powers" decisions mentioned.

Constitutional Conventions

Thus far, all the ingredients listed can actually be found in written form, however difficult it would be to collect them all together. The final component of the Constitution, on the other hand, has never been confined to writing. It consists of **constitutional conventions**, that is, unwritten rules of constitutional behaviour that are considered to be binding by and upon those who operate the Constitution, but that are not enforceable by the courts.[4] Conventions develop from traditions, and through constant recognition and observance become as established, rigid, and sacrosanct as if they were written down. Many of these informal rules have been inherited from Britain, some have been modified in the Canadian environment, and others are unique to Canada. Some conventions are more important than others, and some may be *recognized* by judges even if they cannot be *enforced* by the courts. But, as in Britain, conventions are no less real for being in an unwritten state. Many of them relate to the executive branch of government, which is given slight attention in the 1867 act. The dominant position of the prime minister and cabinet, the subordinate place of the governor general, and the principle of responsible government (i.e., that the cabinet must resign or call an election if it loses the confidence of the House of Commons) are three of many conventions that are part of the Constitution. Such conventions will be discussed at relevant points in subsequent chapters.[5]

The Constitution of Canada, therefore, is a rather complex phenomenon. It has two central documents—the Constitution Act, 1867, with its amendments, and the Constitution Act, 1982; it contains other written documents including other British statutes and orders-in-council, Canadian statutes, and British and Canadian court decisions; and, in its unwritten part, it incorporates a whole series of constitutional conventions that fill in gaps or alter the way in which written provisions are implemented. Many observers would prefer a neater Constitution; some want it to be up-dated; and others would like it to be more inspirational so that it could function more satisfactorily as a symbol of unity. Thus far, however, attempts to recast the Canadian Constitution in any of these ways have foundered.

THE QUEST FOR CONSTITUTIONAL CHANGE

In the early years of Confederation, one principal concern for constitutional change involved completing the territorial integrity of Canada with the eventual creation of ten provinces and two territories. Another early constitutional issue was complete autonomy from Britain by means of the Statute of Westminster and the abolition of court appeals to the Judicial Committee of the Privy Council. Two other persistent constitutional questions also arose prior to 1960: the search for a formula by which the 1867 act and the Constitution generally could be formally amended in Canada, and the proposal that civil liberties be given constitutional protection. These two issues then became enmeshed in constitutional issues inspired by the Quiet Revolution in Quebec, leading to the 1970 Victoria Charter, the Constitution Act, 1982, the 1987 Meech Lake Accord, and the 1992 Charlottetown Accord.

THE QUEST FOR CONSTITUTIONAL CHANGE

- A domestic constitutional amending formula
- A constitutional charter of rights
- The Victoria Charter
- The Constitution Act, 1982
- The Meech Lake Accord
- The Charlottetown Accord

A Domestic Constitutional Amending Formula

As the final thrust toward full Canadian independence took place after the Balfour Declaration of 1926, it became clear that Canadians would have to find a way to amend the 1867 act in Canada. For over 50 years federal and provincial governments wrestled with the problem without being able to agree on an acceptable balance between rigidity and flexibility.

Attempts to find a domestic **constitutional amending formula** began in 1927, but since no success was achieved before 1931, the Statute of Westminster contained a clause allowing the British Parliament to amend the 1867 act at Canadian request. Further attempts were made in 1935–36, and in 1949 a partial domestic amending formula was adopted that became the BNA Act Amendment (#1) of 1949. That act added a clause to section 91 to the effect that in matters of concern to the national government alone, the federal Parliament could make constitutional amendments in Canada, without reference either to the provinces or to Britain. However, five exceptions remained, the most important being that any amendment affecting the provinces would still have to be made by the British Parliament. The basic question was whether such amendments should require the unanimous approval of the provincial governments (as demanded particularly by Quebec in order to protect its rights and powers) or whether the approval of a lesser number of provinces would be sufficient. In the absence of a resolution of this problem, a constitutional convention developed such that the federal government would not request an amendment to the federal–provincial division of powers without the prior unanimous consent of the provinces. Thus, in the case of the transfer of unemployment insurance from provincial to federal jurisdiction in 1940, the designation of pensions and supplementary benefits as concurrent powers in 1951 and 1964 respectively, and the imposition of a retirement age of 75 years for judges in 1960, Ottawa did not request British action until it had obtained the agreement of all the provinces.[6]

Further attempts to find a complete domestic formula were made around 1950 and 1960, after which federal–provincial agreement was reached on the Fulton–Favreau formula in 1964. This procedure provided that unanimous federal and provincial consent be required for changes to the division of powers (ss. 91, 92, and 93) and language provisions (s. 133), but on other matters affecting the whole country, the agreement of the federal government plus two-thirds of the provinces representing at least 50 percent of the population would be sufficient. After having agreed to this formula, the Jean Lesage government of Quebec rescinded its approval—ironically now fearing that the unanimity requirement would prevent making certain changes that Quebec wanted—and the formula died.

As discussed above, a domestic constitutional amending formula was finally adopted as part of the Constitution Act, 1982. Part V of the act actually provided for a series of such formulas, depending on the subject matter of the amendment.

FIVE CONSTITUTIONAL AMENDING FORMULAS

(1) Unanimous consent of federal and provincial legislatures

(2) Consent of Parliament and seven provincial legislatures representing 50 percent of the population

(3) Consent of Parliament and one or more provinces affected

(4) Consent of Parliament alone

(5) Consent of provincial legislature alone

First, as set out in s. 41, unanimous federal and provincial consent was required to amend any of the following items:

(a) the office of the Queen, the Governor General and the Lieutenant Governor of a province;

(b) the right of a province to a number of members in the House of Commons not less than [its] number of Senators ...;

(c) the use of the English or the French language [at the federal level];

(d) the composition of the Supreme Court of Canada; and

(e) changes to this list of subjects requiring unanimous consent.

Second, for other matters affecting both levels of government, the 1982 document required the approval of the federal Parliament and the legislatures of two-thirds of the provinces representing at least 50 percent of the Canadian population. However, no amendment that reduced provincial powers, rights, or privileges could affect a province that did not agree to it. This clause effectively meant that if seven provinces (representing at least 50 percent of the population) wished to transfer one of their powers to a willing federal government but the three other provinces did not, the change would only affect the seven that agreed to it. The document went on to say that if such an amendment related to education or culture, Canada would provide compensation to any province to which the amendment did not apply. Thus, if nine provinces and the federal government agreed to transfer education from provincial to federal jurisdiction, Ottawa would pay compensation to the province that continued to operate its own education system.

For greater clarity, section 42 listed certain subjects to which the two-thirds and 50 percent formula applied, but on which no opting-out of dissenting provinces was permitted. These include

(a) the principle of proportionate representation of the provinces in the House of Commons ...;

(b) the powers of the Senate and the method of selecting Senators;

(c) the number of members by which a province is entitled to be represented in the Senate and the residence qualifications of Senators;

(d) the Supreme Court of Canada [other than its composition];

(e) the extension of existing provinces into the territories; and

(f) the establishment of new provinces.

In the third place, constitutional matters that applied to one or more but not all provinces, including boundary alterations and changes to the use of the English or French languages within a province, could be amended with the approval of the federal Parliament and the legislative assembly of each province to which the amendment applied. Fourth, those provisions relating to the executive government of Canada or the Senate and House of Commons could be amended by the federal Parliament alone. This clause allowed the partial formula adopted in 1949 to be repealed. Finally, each province could amend its own constitution in matters not affecting any other jurisdiction (or the position of lieutenant governor), as had been recognized as early as 1867.

In general, the rigidity and opting-out provisions of the 1982 amending formula were considered a victory for the provinces, and a trade-off for accepting the federal government's Charter of Rights.[7] The formula required that the federal Parliament and provincial legislatures approve such amendments, not just cabinets, as had often sufficed in the past. This innovation had later implications for the Meech Lake Accord, for while it was initially adopted by all ten provincial premiers, it ran into trouble when it came before certain provincial legislatures. Thus, the 1982 amending formula was not a simple one and was not designed to approve amendments easily. It did, however, put an end to requests to the British Parliament to make Canadian constitutional amendments.

A Constitutional Charter of Rights

Given the lack of a constitutional charter of rights in Britain and that country's generally impressive record of civil liberties based on parliamentary restraint, the common law, public opinion, and political culture, Canadians were not originally concerned about the absence of a bill of rights in their Constitution. After federal mistreatment of Japanese Canadians in the Second World War, however, and after provincial discrimination against Asians (B.C.), Jehovah's Witnesses and Communists (Quebec), and violations of freedom of the press (Alberta), some Canadians began to advocate a constitutional bill of rights along the lines of that of the United States. One person who felt very strongly about this question was John Diefenbaker, and when he became prime minister he had Parliament pass a Bill of Rights in 1960. Although the wording of the Bill of Rights was generally adequate, the bill had major structural weaknesses, as discussed in Chapter 5. Such deficiencies led many observers to recommend constitutionalizing the bill, which was part of the rationale for the Charter of Rights and Freedoms, another part of the Constitution Act, 1982.

The Victoria Charter

The unresolved issues of a domestic amending formula and a constitutional charter of rights then became part of the third main thrust of constitutional change, that which emanated from the Quiet Revolution in Quebec. This was primarily related to Quebec's place in the Canadian federation as well as to the general division of powers between the two levels of government. Such demands have been the essence of Canadian politics for the past 30 years,[8] and at the time of writing threaten the continued existence of the country as we know it. Table 3.1 lists the significant constitutional developments over the period 1960–1995.

TABLE 3.1 Constitutional Developments, 1960–1995

1. Quiet Revolution, 1960–1966
2. John Robarts's Confederation of Tomorrow Conference, 1967
3. Federal–Provincial constitutional conferences, 1968–1971
4. Victoria Charter, June 1971
5. Trudeau proposal for patriation & amending formula, 1975
6. Trudeau revival of Victoria Charter proposal, 1976
7. Election of Parti Québécois, 1976
8. Trudeau Bill C-60, Phase I, 1978
9. Federal–provincial conferences, October 1978 and February 1979
10. Task Force on Canadian Unity, January 1979
11. René Lévesque sovereignty-association proposal, November 1979
12. Claude Ryan Beige Paper proposal, 1980
13. Quebec referendum, May 1980
14. Federal–Provincial constitutional conferences, June and September 1980
15. Federal unilateral package, October 1980
16. Supreme Court decision on unilateral package, September 1981
17. Federal–provincial conference, November 1981
18. Proclamation of Constitution Act, 1982, April 17, 1982
19. Bourassa government's five demands, 1985
20. Meech Lake conferences, April and June 1987
21. Legislative ratification of Meech Lake Accord, 1987–1990
22. Federal–Provincial Conference on Meech Lake Accord, May 1990
23. Death of Meech Lake Accord, June 1990
24. Quebec's Post–Meech Lake proposals (Allaire and Bélanger-Campeau Reports), 1991
25. Citizens' Forum, November 1990–June 1991
26. Beaudoin-Edwards Committee on amending formula, June 1991
27. New federal constitutional reform package, September 1991

---

28. Dobbie-Beaudoin Committee, February 1992
29. Federal–provincial–aboriginal negotiations, April–August 1992
30. Charlottetown Accord, Ottawa and Charlottetown, August 1992
31. National referendum, October 26, 1992
32. Election of PQ government in Quebec, 1994
33. Tabling of Quebec sovereignty question, 1994
34. Quebec vote on sovereignty, October 30, 1995

As noted in Chapters 4 and 8, many of Quebec's demands could be and were addressed by bureaucratic, legislative, and judicial decisions, at the federal level, in Quebec, or in other provinces, and did not require formal constitutional changes. By the end of the 1960s, however, the government of Quebec was demanding changes of a constitutional nature, demands often echoed by certain other provinces. Following the initiative of Ontario premier John Robarts's Confederation of Tomorrow Conference in 1967, a series of federal–provincial conferences over the 1968–1971 period led to agreement on the Victoria Charter in June 1971.

The **Victoria Charter** contained an amending formula that required unanimity for some amendments and the approval of Ontario, Quebec, two Atlantic provinces, and two Western provinces for others. This regionalized formula would have given Ontario and Quebec a constitutional veto. The Pearson and Trudeau governments also sought to constitutionalize the Bill of Rights in the Victoria Charter and to add provisions dealing with language rights. Besides containing an amending formula and a constitutional bill of rights, the Victoria Charter provided for provincial consultation on Supreme Court appointments and would have inserted a clause in the Constitution guaranteeing equalization payments to redress regional disparities. It also represented some progress on changes to language rights and to the federal–provincial division of powers. But, after endorsing the document in Victoria, the Bourassa government later responded to nationalist public opinion in the province and vetoed the package because Quebec had not received sufficient additional powers in the field of social policy.

The Constitution Act, 1982

The 1970s and early 1980s thus saw a tug-of-war between Ottawa and Quebec, with the other provinces arrayed in between, over the amending formula, the Charter of Rights, the Supreme Court, the Senate, language rights, and the division of powers. The Trudeau strategy continued to be based on the extension of French-language services from coast to coast to coast in order to undermine Quebec's claim to be linguistically distinctive and therefore to require additional powers.[9] Increasingly, he had to fight the other provinces, too, as most of them also demanded greater decentralization.

After the collapse of the Victoria Charter, Trudeau tried a number of devices to pre-empt the election of a separatist government in Quebec and, after its success in 1976, to convince Quebeckers to follow his lead. These are outlined in Table 3.1—proposals for patriation with an amending formula in 1975–76 and for institutional reform in 1978. The Pépin–Robarts Task Force on Canadian Unity might have been a fruitful basis on which to approach the problem, but because its recommendations differed from Trudeau's own principles of centralization and national bilingualism, he immediately dismissed them. In May 1980, four years after its election, the Parti Québécois government asked the people of Quebec for a mandate to negotiate **sovereignty-association** with the federal government—that is, Quebec would be a sovereign state, but with continued economic links to the rest of Canada. Quebec Liberal leader Claude Ryan published his alternative proposals, while Trudeau and other federal ministers entered the referendum campaign, promising that if Quebeckers rejected the PQ plan, Ottawa would immediately initiate a process of constitutional renewal. When Quebec rejected Lévesque's proposal by a margin of 60 percent to 40 percent, Trudeau immediately embarked on a new round of federal–provincial constitutional discussions.

By October of that year, however, Trudeau gave up on trying to come to federal–provincial agreement and issued his own package of constitutional reform proposals, which he intended to have adopted by the British Parliament without provincial consent. This package was particularly provocative to the Quebec government and a large proportion of Quebeckers because it reflected Trudeau's version of a centralized, bilingual country, rather than the kind of constitutional reform—a distinct status and increased powers for Quebec—they assumed he had promised in the referendum debate. Upset at both the substantive and the procedural aspects of the Trudeau initiative, several other provinces also challenged it in the courts. The provinces claimed that Trudeau's unilateral action in securing significant constitutional amendments was a violation of constitutional convention. In one of its most famous decisions, the Supreme Court of Canada ruled that nothing *in law* prevented the federal government from unilaterally requesting that such an amendment be made by Britain. On the other hand, unilateral federal action would violate the constitutional *convention* that provincial consent should be secured beforehand. In a rare example of judicial recognition of conventions, the Court went on to interpret the convention as requiring a "substantial degree of provincial consent" but not necessarily unanimity. A majority of the Court argued that the federal nature of Canada would be greatly changed if Ottawa could unilaterally alter the powers of the provincial governments in this way.[10] This prompted Trudeau to sit down with the premiers again, and in October 1981 they came up with compromises on all sides in the package that became the Constitution Act, 1982. Ironically, Quebec, which had been the inspiration of it all, was the one dissenter.[11]

The act itself had already been extensively discussed. It contained a domestic constitutional amending formula and a Charter of Rights. Also included was the constitutional entrenchment of equalization payments to have-not provinces and an amendment to the division of powers that enhanced provincial control over natural resources. The Charter essentially constitutionalized the federal and New Brunswick Official Languages acts to guarantee the rights of official language minorities to government services, trials, and so on. It also established the rights of official language minorities to schools in their own language wherever numbers warranted. The clear objective of these provisions was to entrench official bilingualism across the country to the extent that Prime Minister Trudeau could persuade provincial premiers to do so. On the other hand, the Constitution Act, 1982, did not respond to any of the demands for constitutional change emanating from Quebec. It is not surprising that Quebec Premier René Lévesque refused to sign it, but it is doubtful that even a federalist premier of that province would have reacted any differently. Nevertheless, Quebec was legally bound by the document in almost all respects. This imposition created much hostility within Quebec toward Trudeau, his Justice Minister Jean Chrétien, the other provinces, and the Charter itself.

The Meech Lake Accord

Although the 1982 act was operative in Quebec, Brian Mulroney was determined that Quebec should symbolically rejoin the Canadian constitutional family "with honour and enthusiasm." Upon coming to power in 1984, he asked the new federalist Quebec premier, Robert Bourassa, to outline his conditions for such a reunion. The Quebec government proceeded to make five demands: constitutional recognition of Quebec as a "distinct society" within Canada; a veto on constitutional amendments; increased jurisdiction over immigration; participation in Supreme Court appointments; and financial compensation when Quebec opted out of national programs set up by Ottawa within provincial jurisdiction.

....

QUEBEC'S CONDITIONS FOR REJOINING THE CONSTITUTIONAL FOLD

- recognition as a distinct society within Canada
- increased jurisdiction over immigration
- participation in Supreme Court appointments
- veto on constitutional amendments
- opting out, with compensation, of national programs within provincial jurisdiction

After considerable preparation, Mulroney called the premiers together at Meech Lake in April 1987 and they unexpectedly agreed to a document that addressed Quebec's demands and became known as the **Meech Lake Accord**. The prime minister secured unanimous provincial consent by extending to the other provinces most of the same rights as were demanded by Quebec. The document also contained clauses that constitutionalized the Supreme Court of Canada, provided for provincial participation in Senate appointments, and guaranteed annual first ministers' conferences on the Constitution and on the economy.[12]

Despite the relative ease with which it was drafted, the Meech Lake Accord generated much controversy. On the negative side, many critics did not approve of the designation of Quebec as a distinct society within Canada, and especially objected to the phrase that it was the role of the government and legislature of Quebec to "preserve and promote" that distinctiveness. No one was sure what implications the **distinct society clause** would have for the federal–provincial division of powers, leaving it for judicial clarification on an issue-by-issue basis. Some felt that in a federation all provinces had to have exactly equal status, and many argued that, armed with the distinct society clause, Quebec would immediately begin to challenge federal powers in a variety of fields. Others worried about the status of the English and aboriginal minorities within Quebec, as well as the francophone minorities in other provinces, and some women's groups argued that the distinct society clause might be used to override the gender equality provisions of section 28 of the Charter of Rights and Freedoms.

A second objection to the Accord was that it enlarged the list of subjects that required unanimous provincial consent in the constitutional amending formula, especially the list contained in section 42, such as changes to most aspects of the Senate and the creation of new provinces. Many critics felt that Senate reform and the transformation of the Northern territories into provinces would be virtually impossible if they required agreement of all ten provinces instead of only seven.

Objections to Quebec's expanded role in immigration and to provincial involvement in the nomination of judges to the Supreme Court of Canada were also raised by those opposed to increases in provincial power. But these concerns were not expressed as vehemently as those relating to the provisions allowing provinces to opt out of national programs within provincial jurisdiction and be compensated by Ottawa. Fears were expressed that satisfactory new national social programs (such as day care or a guaranteed annual income) would never materialize because provinces would be compensated for programs that merely met national *objectives*, not national *standards*. Apart from criticizing what was in the Accord, many opponents faulted it for what was left out. The North was not allowed to nominate senators or Supreme Court judges; aboriginal rights were not strengthened; and multiculturalism was ignored.

Others condemned the process through which the Accord had emerged—a behind-the-scenes gathering of (male) first ministers. In the post-Charter era, individual Canadians in all parts of the country insisted on being part of the constitutional amendment process; moreover, the primacy of Quebec's concerns was rejected by those given constitutional standing by the Charter—women, aboriginals, and multicultural and other minorities.[13] The public now demanded more meaningful participation in the process of constitutional change.

The leading opponents of Meech Lake were former prime minister Pierre Trudeau, whose vision of a centralized, bilingual federation was at odds with the document, and Clyde Wells, elected as premier of Newfoundland in April 1989, two years after the Accord had been drafted. Other opponents took a more moderate stance. The federal Liberal and New Democratic parties were both split on the Accord, but generally managed to agree on a number of proposed amendments to address the concerns of various groups: aboriginals, the North, linguistic minorities, women, and those concerned about multiculturalism and the opting-out provisions. The federal government took the position, however, that no changes could be made because they might destroy the fragility of the compromises contained in the Accord.

Those who defended Meech Lake argued that it would symbolically bring Quebec back into the constitutional fold and would overcome the isolation and betrayal that many residents of that province felt after 1982. They called this the "Quebec round," and argued that aboriginal, Northern, Western, and other concerns would be next on the constitutional agenda. Rather than promote incremental separatism, they felt that the Accord would give Quebec the flexibility to remain satisfied within Confederation. Quebec's involvement would also permit certain constitutional amendments to be made (e.g., with respect to aboriginal self-government) that had been delayed by its boycott of constitutional conferences.

Supporters contended that in demographic, linguistic, and cultural terms, the distinctiveness of Quebec society could not be denied. Those who felt that Trudeau's concept of official bilingualism was unrealistic for certain parts of the country thought that the Accord, in noting that French-speaking Canadians are centred in Quebec, might lessen linguistic tensions and the pressure for bilingualism.

Many political scientists and others had long argued that the provinces should have a say in the appointment of senators and Supreme Court judges. In the former case, this was because the Senate was intended to represent the provinces within Ottawa's decision-making structure; in the latter, because the Supreme Court rules on federal–provincial disputes. Many true federalists also contended that Ottawa should not be able to invade provincial jurisdiction with its spending power and set up national programs without provincial consent, as had often happened in the past. In addition, many felt that Quebec had a legitimate interest in immigration, given its low birth rate and its isolation in an English-speaking North American environment.

Supporters pointed out that multicultural and aboriginal rights in Quebec were protected against the distinct society clause, and that most Quebec women did not feel threatened by it. Defenders of Meech Lake also welcomed the constitutionalization of the Supreme Court and of annual federal–provincial first ministers' conferences on the economy and the Constitution.

According to the constitutional amending formula adopted in 1982, the Accord then had to be approved by the federal and all provincial legislatures within three years, that is, before June 23, 1990.[14] In most cases such legislative approval came rather easily, but governments changed in New Brunswick and Manitoba before the Accord could be ratified by the legislatures of those two provinces, and their new governments had reservations about the Accord. Both provinces set up legislative committees that held extensive public hearings and delayed ratification. In the case of Manitoba, the new Gary Filmon government was in a minority position, dependent upon Liberal and/or NDP support. Later, the new Wells government in Newfoundland rescinded the legislative approval that had previously been given to the Accord in that province.

Thus, with three provinces left to ratify the Accord, Prime Minister Mulroney convened a first ministers' conference in Ottawa in May 1990. After a week of protracted, behind-the-scenes negotiations, the participants emerged with a modest companion resolution, adopted to the satisfaction of Manitoba and New Brunswick. Still with his substantive and procedural reservations, Clyde Wells would only agree to put it before the Newfoundland legislature, not to endorse it. Amid a bitter public exchange between Wells and the federal government, Newfoundland did not vote on the Accord a second time before the deadline. Meanwhile, the Accord also ran into difficulty in the Manitoba legislature, where aboriginal MLA Elijah Harper delayed passage because of the absence of any advance for Native peoples.

The Charlottetown Accord

With the death of the Meech Lake Accord, many observers felt that Quebec was destined to leave Confederation, given that the demands incorporated in the Accord were the province's basic minimum. Sure enough, nationalist and separatist sentiment in Quebec mushroomed

Reproduced with the permission of The Times–Colonist, Victoria.

over the next year or so as the Quebec Liberals and Parti Québécois issued new constitutional proposals. The Liberal position first appeared as the **Allaire Report**, which called for a highly decentralized federation in which Quebec and the other provinces would have almost all powers. According to the Report, Quebec would insist on exercising its full sovereignty in the areas of jurisdiction already exclusive to it according to the present Constitution, notably social affairs, urban affairs, culture, education, housing, recreation, family policy, manpower policy, natural resources, health, and tourism. It would do the same in other fields that it somewhat dubiously claimed were currently either shared with Ottawa or not mentioned in the Constitution, such as agriculture, unemployment insurance, communications, regional development, energy, environment, language, research and development, and public security. Ottawa and Quebec would share jurisdiction over aboriginal affairs, revenue and taxation, immigration, financial institutions, justice, fisheries, foreign policy, post office, telecommunications and transportation, and the federal government would have exclusive power over only defence, customs and excise, and management of the national debt.

Quebec's **Bélanger–Campeau Committee** report, representing both major parties as well as other interests in the province, was less specific than the Allaire report with respect to the division of powers, but no less demanding in terms of general constitutional reform. It argued that unless a satisfactory proposal for a new constitutional arrangement was forthcoming from the rest of Canada, Quebec should separate. It therefore recommended that a referendum on Quebec sovereignty be held in June or October 1992 and that if the referendum was positive, Quebec would acquire the status of a sovereign state within one year of the date it was held. Bélanger-Campeau anticipated that in the interim, the rest of Canada would offer Quebec some kind of new partnership, perhaps along the lines of the Allaire Report, so that Quebeckers would essentially have two alternatives before them when they cast their vote.

After being psychologically immobilized for several months by the death of Meech Lake, the Mulroney government finally acted in November 1990 with the appointment of the **Citizens' Forum** on Canada's Future headed by CRTC Chairman Keith Spicer. Responding to the criticism that the public had been shut out of the Meech Lake negotiations, the Citizens' Forum was a unique, costly, and controversial exercise in encouraging ordinary Canadians to discuss constitutional issues and transmit their views to the committee, which would write the Forum's report. Although many were growing weary of the subject by this time, a large proportion of Canadians engaged in angry exchanges, the Constitution becoming a lightning rod for every conceivable grievance in the country. After listening to some 400 000 Canadians over an eight-month period, the Forum's June 1991 report supported recognition of Quebec's distinctiveness (even if the anglophone public did not agree), aboriginal self-government, and settlement of Native land claims. On the other hand, the Forum suggested that official bilingualism was a divisive issue and government funding for multiculturalism should be cut.

Meanwhile, in response to another problem central to the defeat of Meech Lake, the federal government set up a joint House of Commons–Senate Committee to study the constitutional amending formula. This Beaudoin-Edwards Committee also reported in June 1991 and endorsed a change in the formula that would restrict the requirement for unanimous provincial consent and replace it with regional vetoes, as well as allow national referenda on a new Constitution.

Just before the presentation of these reports, the Prime Minister appointed Joe Clark as the Minister Responsible for Constitutional Affairs and set up a special cabinet committee on Canadian Unity and Constitutional Negotiations. After lengthy, emotional discussions, the committee agreed on a 28-point package of constitutional proposals in September 1991 called *Shaping Canada's Future Together*. Yet another joint Commons–Senate committee was set up to gather public reaction to the package and other reports on the subject. This Dobbie-Beaudoin Committee on the Renewal of Canada ran into innumerable problems, such that the government decided to supplement its hearings with a series of specialized public forums on specific constitutional issues. These were almost akin to the constituent assembly that many observers were calling for. The committee issued its report in February 1992.

Meanwhile, Joe Clark was persuaded to try to develop a collective federal–provincial–territorial–aboriginal response to offer to Quebec before the fall.[15] After several rounds of negotiations, the nine premiers, territorial and aboriginal leaders, and Clark all agreed on a comprehensive constitutional proposal in July. Quebec Premier Bourassa considered that it was promising enough to return to the bargaining table for the first time since the demise of the Meech Lake Accord, and a full-fledged constitutional conference took place in Ottawa in mid-August. After nearly a week of hard bargaining, the leaders unanimously signed a new constitutional accord upon which they put the final touches in Charlottetown a week later. It had four main parts.[16]

· ·

PRINCIPAL COMPONENTS OF THE CHARLOTTETOWN ACCORD

- Canada clause
- Triple-E Senate
- Aboriginal self-government
- Changes to the division of powers

THE CANADA CLAUSE

The 1992 Charlottetown Accord began with a new **Canada clause** that would recognize Quebec as a distinct society within Canada as well as enumerate the other fundamental values and characteristics of the country: democracy, the rule of law, a parliamentary and federal system, the aboriginal peoples of Canada and their enhanced rights, official language minorities, cultural and racial diversity, individual and collective rights, gender equality, and the equality and diversity of the provinces.

THE TRIPLE-E SENATE

A new **Triple-E Senate** would give each province six representatives and each territory one, for a total of 62. It would be popularly elected, except for Quebec members who would be chosen by the National Assembly. The institution would have a veto over federal laws that taxed natural resources but virtually no power over government money bills. For other legislation a defeat in the Senate would trigger a joint sitting of both houses in which MPs would outnumber senators by 337 to 62. Defeat of a government bill in the Senate would not be considered a vote of nonconfidence, but bills dealing with the French language and culture would have to be approved by a majority of francophone members. To enhance their independence, senators would not be eligible to sit in the cabinet, but they would have the power to ratify or veto key government appointments.

To compensate Ontario and Quebec for their loss of 18 senators, these two provinces would each be given 18 additional seats in the House of Commons. In an effort to maintain the general principle of representation by population, British Columbia would gain four MPs and Alberta two, and it was agreed that a supplementary redistribution of Commons seats would be held after the 1996 census to reflect B.C.'s rapidly increasing population. Quebec was also guaranteed a mimimum of 25 percent of the Commons seats.

ABORIGINAL SELF-GOVERNMENT

Native peoples would have their inherent right to **aboriginal self-government** enshrined in the Constitution but with no access to the courts to enforce it for five years. Aboriginal governments would constitute a third order of government, analogous to Ottawa and the provinces. Federal and provincial governments committed themselves to negotiate aboriginal self-government agreements and their laws would continue to apply until displaced. New aboriginal laws could not be inconsistent with laws essential to the preservation of peace, order, and good government in Canada and would also have to comply with the Charter of Rights and Freedoms, subject to the use of the notwithstanding clause. The Accord would entrench treaty rights in the Constitution but not result in any new land rights. Sections 25 and 35 of the 1982 Constitution Act were strengthened, and Métis rights, especially in Alberta, were also given recognition.

THE DIVISION OF POWERS

The fourth main issue was the federal–provincial division of powers. As in the Meech Lake Accord, provinces could opt out of new national shared-cost programs set up within provincial jurisdiction and receive federal financial compensation if the programs met national objectives. In addition, Ottawa offered to withdraw from six fields at provincial request: forestry, mining, tourism, recreation, housing, and municipal and urban affairs, again with financial compensation. Culture and labour market training would essentially become provincial powers, and the two levels would share jurisdiction in immigration, telecommunications, and regional development. Thus, beyond the immigration power in Meech Lake, provinces would now have full or partial power over ten additional fields of public policy. In return for this increased decentralization of powers, Ottawa hoped to strengthen the economic union by eliminating interprovincial trade barriers, but had to settle for agreement in principle, with the issue to be negotiated later.

OTHER

Provisions of Meech Lake with respect to the Supreme Court of Canada were included in the Accord, along with those concerning an annual meeting of first ministers, and changes in the constitutional amending formula, except that the creation of new provinces would no longer require unanimous consent. Ontario premier Bob Rae was successful in having a social charter added to the Constitution to guarantee rights to health care, social services, and education, workers' rights, and protection for the environment. The guarantee of equalization payments was strengthened, and the federal reservation, disallowance, and declaratory powers were essentially removed.

The Accord would be of no effect until ratified by Parliament and the ten provincial legislatures. Before ratification, however, the federal government announced that a national referendum would be held on the new constitutional deal on October 26, the same date selected by Quebec. The decision to hold such a referendum was based on three main considerations: Alberta and B.C. laws required a referendum on constitutional amendments, so that three provinces would be voting on the Accord in any case; Meech Lake had been criticized for lack of public input; and public approval would lend legitimacy to the agreement and spur the 11 legislatures into speedy affirmative action.

On a national basis the referendum result was 55 percent no and 45 percent yes. As shown in Table 3.2, majorities voted no in Quebec, Nova Scotia, the four Western provinces, and the Yukon. Even though the referendum was not legally binding, there was no point in bringing the constitutional package before legislatures for ratification: the Charlottetown Accord was dead.

Public opinion polls showed that rather than base their decision on the contents of the Accord as such, many people who voted no did so to vent their anger and frustration with Prime Minister Mulroney, the premiers, and politicians and governments in general. Such was the problem of holding the vote during a period of severe recession and at a time when respect for incumbent politicians was at an all-time low. Voters were not in a generous frame of mind, and rather than seeing it as a multi-sided compromise, they generally felt that the Accord gave too much to others and not enough to themselves. Thus, the negative vote in Quebec was largely based on the view that the Accord did not give Quebec sufficient new powers, but many outside Quebec argued that that province got too much. Many westerners did not see the proposed reforms to the Senate as sufficient protection of their interests in

TABLE 3.2 **Results of the National Referendum on the Charlottetown Accord, in Percentages**

	Yes	**No**
Newfoundland	63.2	36.8
Prince Edward Island	73.9	26.1
Nova Scotia	48.8	51.2
New Brunswick	61.8	38.2
Quebec	43.3	56.7
Ontario	50.1	49.9
Manitoba	38.4	61.6
Saskatchewan	44.7	55.3
Alberta	39.8	60.2
British Columbia	31.7	68.3
Northwest Territories	61.3	38.7
Yukon	43.7	56.3
TOTAL	45.0	55.0

Ottawa, and many aboriginal Canadians were dissatisfied with the provisions on aboriginal self-government. Indeed, while the Accord was primarily designed to address the constitutional insecurity of Quebec, aboriginal Canadians, and Western and smaller provinces, a majority in all three groups believed that their elites had not bargained hard enough.

The Chrétien Liberals were elected in 1993 on the promise that they would concentrate on improving the economy and put constitutional issues aside. On the other hand, the Parti Québécois returned to power in Quebec in 1994 on the exact opposite platform—that it would move quickly to take Quebec outside Confederation. With Ottawa largely ignoring the issue, the Parti Québécois thrashed around for about a year looking for a formula for sovereignty that would attract a majority of Quebeckers' consent. Premier Jacques Parizeau wanted a quick vote on a clear-cut question, but others, including Bloc Québécois leader Lucien Bouchard, preferred a delayed vote on a scheme that retained significant ties to Canada. When the polls showed that Parizeau could not achieve a majority of Quebec voters on the question of his choice, he succumbed to the pressure of public opinion and Bouchard, and agreed to an extensive list of continuing links to Canada. This wrenching *virage* was ratified in an agreement between the PQ, the BQ, and Mario Dumont's small party, Action démocratique du Québec, in June, and a bill respecting the future of Quebec set the referendum date for October 30, 1995. The convoluted question put to the people of Quebec was as follows:

> Do you agree that Quebec should become sovereign, after having made a formal offer to Canada for a new economic and political partnership, within the scope of the bill respecting the future of Quebec and of the agreement signed on June 12, 1995?

The bill in question would allow a sovereign Quebec to use the Canadian dollar as its currency and its residents to retain concurrent Canadian citizenship. It anticipated the adoption of a new Quebec constitution and retention of Quebec's existing boundaries. The government of Quebec was then to propose a treaty of economic and political partnership to the rest of Canada. The treaty would set up a joint Council (executive), Secretariat (bureaucracy), Assembly (legislature), and Tribunal (court); establish rules for the division of assets and debt; and provide for the free movement of goods, individuals, services, and capital. If agreement with the rest of Canada on such a treaty was not achieved within a year, Quebec would unilaterally declare its sovereignty and expect recognition by other states, anticipating continued membership in the North American Free Trade Agreement. Premier Parizeau even had to vacate the leadership of the "Yes" campaign when it became obvious that the cause had a chance only if the much more popular Bouchard became leader.

On the "No" side, the federal government stuck to its position that if Quebeckers could be persuaded that "Yes" meant separation, a majority would vote "No." Ottawa thus made no counter-offers until polls showed that such a strategy was seriously flawed and could lead to defeat. In the final week of the campaign, Prime Minister Chrétien promised change—constitutional, if necessary, but not necessarily constitutional—if Quebeckers voted No. The three principal changes he alluded to were some kind of recognition of Quebec as a distinct society, some kind of veto over constitutional amendments, and some kind of decentralization of powers from Ottawa. The other dramatic development of the last few days was a gigantic No rally in Montreal, made up primarily of Canadians from coast to coast who "invaded" the city in order to tell Quebeckers how much the rest of Canada wanted them to stay.

The result of the referendum could not have been closer: 50.6 percent voted No, while 49.4 percent voted Yes. The turnout rate was a record 92 percent. Considerable controversy surrounded the high number of rejected ballots (most of them favouring the No side), but it was clear that nearly 60 percent of the francophones in the province had voted Yes. Parizeau promptly resigned the premiership in favour of Bouchard, who led observers to expect a provincial election in 1996 and another referendum in 1997.

CONCLUSION

Canada has one of the oldest constitutions in the world. Although it has been altered incrementally over its 125-year existence by formal amendments, judicial interpretation, and conventions, its basic provisions remain intact. Since the Quiet Revolution, the issue of constitutional amendment has never been far from the top of the Canadian political agenda, and in the mid-1990s the country faced a constitutional crisis that threatened to split it apart.

(SC) Of the approaches outlined in Chapter 1, the state-centred theory is most relevant to the Constitution and constitutional change. These questions have historically been the preserve of federal and provincial political and bureaucratic elites. Before 1982, constitutional accommodations could be made among first ministers and their advisers at federal–provincial conferences and only needed to be ratified by federal and provincial cabinets. After 1982, legislative approval was also required, but that did not necessarily involve the wider society. Elite theorists would add to the picture a small number of representatives from the intellectual elite—constitutional law professors, political scientists, historians, economists, and journalists.

P Pluralists, on the other hand, point to the increasing public interest in such matters. They emphasize that several elite-designed proposals have foundered once exposed to public opinion: the Fulton–Favreau formula and the Victoria Charter in Quebec, and Meech Lake in other parts of the country. The public now demands more meaningful participation in the process of constitutional change. This participation was provided for in the public hearings of legislative committees on Meech Lake and the subsequent Citizens' Forum, but some pluralist critics go further and advocate the convening of constituent assemblies on the subject. When three provinces decided to hold a referendum on the Charlottetown Accord, a national referendum was held, and it is commonly thought that if the issue is revisited, a referendum will be required again even though it is not required by the constitutional amending formula.

© Class analysts see the Constitution as legitimizing arrangements for the capitalist elite to control the political system. They also consider constitutional issues as a device used by politicians to distract the public from the real issues of unemployment, the exploitation of workers, and the unfair distribution of wealth.

DISCUSSION QUESTIONS

1. Would it be possible or advisable to incorporate all ingredients of the Canadian Constitution into a single document? Why or why not?

2. If the 1982 constitutional amending formula is too rigid, how should it be changed?

3. What do you think of the Trudeau strategy to extend French-language services across the country so that Quebec could not justify demands for special powers?

4. What do you think of the alternative Mulroney strategy embodied in the Meech Lake Accord?

5. What do you think of the Allaire and Bélanger–Campeau reports?

6. Was the effort and expense of the Spicer Report justified in the symbolic sense of offering Canadians a chance to participate in constitutional reform?

7. To what extent would you give special powers to Quebec if that was necessary to prevent it from separating?

8. To what extent do politicians use constitutional issues to distract public attention from the basic social and economic problems facing the country?

9. To what extent should politicians be guided by popular referenda on constitutional matters?

10. How do the approaches outlined in Chapter 1 relate to the material in this chapter?

NOTES

1. One of Canada's leading constitutional scholars, Alan C. Cairns, has defined the Constitution in similar terms as follows: "[it] is the body of understandings defining the basic institutions of government and the relations between them, plus the relationships between governments in the federal system, and between the citizens and those governments." See *Constitution, Government, and Society in Canada* (Toronto: McClelland and Stewart, 1988), p. 31.

2. The act has not been included in this book in its entirety, but the crucial sections are listed in the Appendix.

3. Theoretically, the Constitution Act, 1982, is an appendix to the Canada Act, and the Charter of Rights and Freedoms is part of the Constitution Act.

4. Many definitions of conventions exist and are discussed by Andrew Heard in *Canadian Constitutional Conventions* (Toronto: Oxford University Press, 1991). My definition is an amalgam of those he cites.

5. Even a legal text such as *Constitutional Law of Canada*, 2nd ed., by Peter Hogg (Toronto: Carswell, 1985) includes conventions as part of the Constitution. The question of judicial recognition of such conventions will be addressed below.

6. On about ten other occasions constitutional amendments were made without prior consultation with the provinces because Ottawa considered they were of exclusive federal concern. These included repeated redistributions of seats in the House of Commons and the entry of Newfoundland into Confederation. See Guy Favreau, *The Amendment of the Constitution of Canada* (Ottawa: Queen's Printer, 1965), and Paul Gérin-Lajoie, *Constitutional Amendment in Canada* (Toronto: University of Toronto Press, 1950).

7. Among other sources on this subject, see Alan C. Cairns, *Constitution, Government and Society in Canada* (Toronto: McClelland and Stewart, 1988).

8. See, for example, Edward McWhinney, *Quebec and the Constitution 1960–1978* (University of Toronto Press, 1979); Edward McWhinney, *Canada and the Constitution 1979–1982* (University of Toronto Press, 1982); and Peter Russell, *Constitutional Odyssey* (Toronto: University of Toronto Press, 1992).

9. For their comments on this point, see Ian Greene, *The Charter of Rights* (Toronto: Lorimer, 1989), pp. 37–38, and Michael Mandel, *The Charter of Rights and the Legalization of Politics in Canada* (Toronto: Wall and Thompson, 1989), pp. 17, 20, 22, and 111.

10. *Reference re Amendment of the Constitution of Canada* [1981] 125 DLR (3rd) 1. See Heard, *Canadian Constitutional Conventions*, and Mandel, *The Charter of Rights*, pp. 22, 24–34, 111. In another political decision, the Court decided that Quebec had never had a veto on constitutional amendments. See Marc Gold, "The Mask of Objectivity: Politics and Rhetoric in the Supreme Court of Canada," *The Supreme Court Law Review* 7 (1985).

11. See, for example, Keith Banting and Richard Simeon, eds., *And No One Cheered: Federalism, Democracy and the Constitution Act* (Toronto: Methuen, 1983); Roy Romanow, J. Whyte, and H. Leeson, *Canada … Notwithstanding: The Making of the Constitution 1976–1982* (Toronto: Methuen, 1984); and Ross Sheppard and M. Valpy, *The National Deal: The Fight for a Canadian Constitution* (Toronto: Macmillan, 1984).

12. Michael Behiels, ed., *The Meech Lake Primer: Conflicting Views of the 1987 Constitutional Accord* (Ottawa: University of Ottawa Press, 1989); *Canadian Public Policy* (September 1988); Roger Gibbins, ed., *Meech Lake and Canada: Perspectives from the West* (Edmonton: Academic Printing and Publishing, 1988); Peter Hogg, *Meech Lake Constitutional Accord Annotated* (Toronto: Carswell, 1988); Bryan Schwartz, *Fathoming Meech Lake* (Winnipeg: Legal Research Institute, University of Manitoba, 1987); K.E. Swinton and C.J. Rogerson, *Competing Constitutional Visions: The Meech Lake Accord* (Toronto: Carswell, 1988); and David Milne, *The Canadian Constitution* (Toronto: Lorimer, 1991).

13. Alan C. Cairns has written extensively on these themes. See his *Constitution, Government, and Society in Canada*, and his *Disruptions: Constitutional Struggles, from the Charter to Meech Lake* (Toronto: McClelland and Stewart, 1991).

14. The former cabinet secretary and clerk of the Privy Council, Gordon Robertson, argued strenuously that no such deadline existed, but to no avail.

15. Two other proposals issued about the same time were Ronald L. Watts and Douglas M. Brown, eds., *Options for a New Canada* (Toronto: University of Toronto Press, 1991), and Thomas J. Courchene, *In Praise of Renewed Federalism* (Toronto: C.D. Howe Institute, 1991).

16. Alan C. Cairns, *Reconfigurations: Canadian Citizenship and Constitutional Change* (Toronto: McClelland and Stewart, 1995); Duncan Cameron and Miriam Smith, *Constitutional Politics: The Canadian Forum Book on the Federal Constitutional Proposals* (Toronto: Lorimer, 1992); Curtis Cook, ed., *Constitutional Predicament: Canada after the Referendum of 1992* (Montreal: McGill–Queen's University Press, 1994); Kenneth McRoberts and Patrick Monahan, eds., *The Charlottetown Accord, the Referendum and the Future of Canada* (Toronto: University of Toronto Press, 1993); Peter Russell, *Constitutional Odyssey*, 2nd ed. (Toronto: University of Toronto Press, 1993).

FURTHER READING

Banting, Keith, and Richard Simeon, eds. *And No One Cheered: Federalism, Democracy and the Constitution Act.* Toronto: Methuen, 1983.

Behiels, Michael, ed. *The Meech Lake Primer: Conflicting Views of the 1987 Constitutional Accord.* Ottawa: University of Ottawa Press, 1989.

Bell, David V.J. *The Roots of Disunity.* Rev. ed. Toronto: Oxford University Press, 1992.

Cairns, Alan C. *Constitution, Government and Society in Canada.* Toronto: McClelland and Stewart, 1988.

———. *Disruptions: Constitutional Struggles, from the Charter to Meech Lake.* Toronto: McClelland and Stewart, 1991.

———. *Reconfigurations: Canadian Citizenship and Constitutional Change.* Toronto: McClelland and Stewart, 1995.

Cameron, Duncan, and Miriam Smith. *Constitutional Politics: The Canadian Forum Book on the Federal Constitutional Proposals.* Toronto: Lorimer, 1992.

Cohen, Andrew. *A Deal Undone: The Making and Breaking of the Meech Lake Accord.* Vancouver: Douglas & McIntyre, 1990.

Cook, Curtis, ed. *Constitutional Predicament: Canada after the Referendum of 1992.* Montreal: McGill–Queen's University Press, 1994.

Courchene, Thomas J. *In Praise of Renewed Federalism.* Toronto: C.D. Howe Institute, 1991.

Favreau, Guy. *The Amendment of the Constitution of Canada.* Ottawa: Queen's Printer, 1965.

Freeman, Alan, and Patrick Grady. *Dividing the House: Planning for a Canada without Quebec.* Toronto: HarperCollins, 1995.

Gérin-Lajoie, Paul. *Constitutional Amendment in Canada.* Toronto: University of Toronto Press, 1950.

Gibbins, Roger, ed. *Meech Lake and Canada: Perspectives from the West.* Edmonton: Academic Printing and Publishing, 1988.

Gibson, Gordon. *Plan B: The Future of the Rest of Canada.* Vancouver: Fraser Institute, 1994.

Greene, Ian. *The Charter of Rights.* Toronto: Lorimer, 1989.

Heard, Andrew. *Canadian Constitutional Conventions.* Toronto: Oxford University Press, 1991.

Hogg, Peter. *Canada Act Annotated.* Toronto: Carswell, 1982.

———. *Constitutional Law of Canada,* 2nd ed. Toronto: Carswell, 1985.

———. *Meech Lake Constitutional Accord Annotated.* Toronto: Carswell, 1988.

McRoberts, Kenneth, and Patrick Monahan, eds. *The Charlottetown Accord, the Referendum and the Future of Canada.* Toronto: University of Toronto Press, 1993.

McWhinney, Edward. *Quebec and the Constitution 1960–1978.* Toronto: University of Toronto Press, 1979.

———. *Canada and the Constitution 1979–82: Patriation and the Charter of Rights.* Toronto: University of Toronto Press, 1982.

Mandel, Michael. *The Charter of Rights and the Legalization of Politics in Canada.* Toronto: Wall and Thompson, 1989.

Milne, David. *The Canadian Constitution.* Toronto: Lorimer, 1991.

Monahan, Patrick J. *Meech Lake: The Inside Story.* Toronto: University of Toronto Press, 1991.

Parti Québécois. *Quebec in a New World.* Toronto: Lorimer, 1994.

Reesor, Bayard. *The Canadian Constitution in Historical Perspective.* Scarborough: Prentice-Hall Canada, 1992.

Romanow, Roy, J. Whyte, and H. Leeson. *Canada ... Notwithstanding: The Making of the Constitution 1976–1982.* Toronto: Methuen, 1984.

Russell, Peter. *Constitutional Odyssey.* 2nd. ed. Toronto: University of Toronto Press, 1993.

Schwartz, Bryan. *Fathoming Meech Lake.* Winnipeg: Legal Research Institute, University of Manitoba, 1987.

Sheppard, Ross, and M. Valpy. *The National Deal: The Fight for a Canadian Constitution.* Toronto: Macmillan, 1984.

Swinton, K.E., and C.J. Rogerson. *Competing Constitutional Visions: The Meech Lake Accord.* Toronto: Carswell, 1988.

Task Force on Canadian Unity. Hull: Canadian Government Publishing Centre, 1979.

Watts, Ronald L., and Douglas M. Brown. *Options for a New Canada.* Toronto: University of Toronto Press, 1991.

Chapter 4

The FEDERAL system

Prime Minister Mackenzie King once said that he would not give "one red cent" to a Tory provincial government. Provincial governments often centre election campaigns on complaints about Ottawa. The courts threw out federal legislation that aimed at alleviating the Depression, ruling that only the provinces could pass such laws. In the postwar period, Ottawa introduced a multitude of national programs within provincial jurisdiction—especially postsecondary education, health insurance, and social assistance—and through financial inducements persuaded the provinces to join them. The federal government now pays over $30 billion a year to provincial governments, but since 1990 and especially since 1995 has cut back on such transfers, to considerable provincial complaint.

The federal character of Canada is designated in the Canadian Constitution and its impact is seen in almost every aspect of governance and society. The federal system is closely related to regional economic cleavages, is important for ethnic cleavages, influences the Canadian political culture, and affects the operation of the electoral system, political parties, and pressure groups. Federalism also has a major impact on the institutions of the national government.

In a formal sense, **federalism** can be defined as a division of powers between central and regional governments such that neither is subordinate to the other. This definition distinguishes the relationship between municipal and provincial governments from that between provincial and national governments, for in the former case the municipalities are clearly subordinate entities while in the latter, provinces are "coordinate" or equal in status to the central government. This equality of status is provided for in the constitutional division of powers between the two levels of government, which is found primarily in sections 91 and 92 of the Constitution Act, 1867. Other aspects of federalism are also important, however, such as federal–provincial financial relations (taxing and spending) and joint policy-making mechanisms.

This chapter begins by outlining the federal system in Canada at its creation, and then traces the evolution of that system, especially through changes in the division of powers and federal–provincial financial relationships. In the following section this evolution is depicted in chronological phases, as the federal system veered between centralization and decentralization. The chapter concludes with a discussion of Canadian federalism today.

THE CONFEDERATION SETTLEMENT

The fundamentals of Canadian federalism, often called the **Confederation Settlement**,[1] were incorporated into the 1867 British North America Act, which in 1982 was renamed the Constitution Act, 1867. As noted in Chapter 2, the principal architect of Confederation was Sir John A. Macdonald, who intended the new country to be a highly centralized federation. In many ways, in fact, the Confederation Settlement was not consistent with the modern definition of federalism because in certain respects the provinces were made subordinate to the central government.[2]

The Confederation Settlement consisted of five principal components: first, the division of powers between the central and provincial governments; second, the division of financial resources; third, federal controls imposed upon the provinces; fourth, provincial representation in the central institutions; and fifth, certain cultural guarantees.

COMPONENTS OF THE CONFEDERATION SETTLEMENT

- Division of powers
- Division of financial resources
- Federal controls over the provinces
- Provincial representation in central institutions
- Cultural guarantees

As far as the division of powers between the central and provincial governments was concerned, the Fathers of Confederation gave the provinces 16 specific **enumerated powers** in section 92 (e.g., hospitals and municipal institutions) and then left everything else—the **residual powers**—to Ottawa in section 91. For greater certainty, however, they also included 29 enumerations of federal powers such as trade and commerce and national defence. Two **concurrent powers**—agriculture and immigration—were listed in section 95, and the treaty power in section 132 gave the federal government the power to implement Empire treaties, regardless of their subject matter.

In the division of financial resources, federal dominance was even more apparent. The Fathers gave Ottawa the power to levy any mode or system of taxation, which included both **direct and indirect taxes**. Since the only tax widely used at the time was the customs duty, an indirect tax, provincial power over direct taxation was not considered to be very significant. Instead, the provinces were expected to raise their revenues from the sale of shop, saloon, tavern, and auctioneer licenses, as well as to rely on federal subsidies. The federal government was to pay each province an annual per capita grant of 80 cents plus a small subsidy to support its government and legislature. The Constitution Act also stated that the federal government would assist the provinces by assuming their pre-Confederation debts. It should be added that the provinces were authorized to raise revenues from their natural resources, but this source was not taken very seriously at the time because few such resources (except trees) had yet been discovered.

In the third place, in a clear departure from what is now regarded as the federal principle, Ottawa was given several means of controlling the provinces. The lieutenant governor, a federal appointee, was permitted by section 90 to reserve provincial legislation for the consideration of the federal cabinet, which could then approve or reject it. Even if the lieutenant governor gave assent to a piece of provincial legislation, however, the federal cabinet could subsequently disallow it. Then, under section 92-10 (c), the federal government could declare any local work or undertaking to be for the general advantage of Canada and thus place it within federal jurisdiction. These three controls are respectively referred to as **reservation**, **disallowance**, and the **declaratory power**.

Given the highly centralized nature of the division of powers, the limited financial resources of the provinces, and the federal controls, it is clear that the Confederation Settlement of 1867 placed the provinces in a subordinate position, somewhat akin to municipalities, rather than giving them the equal or coordinate status provided for in the modern definition of federalism.

In the light of the federal government's dominant position, it is not surprising that the smaller provinces were concerned with their representation in Ottawa. The fourth aspect of the Settlement, therefore, was agreement on provincial representation in the House of Commons and the Senate, a question of much more concern at the time than the division of powers. The great compromise that allowed Confederation to go forward was that the provinces would be represented according to population in the Commons but that regional equality would prevail in the Senate. Thus each of the three original regions—the Maritimes, Quebec, and Ontario—was to receive 24 senators, appeasing smaller provinces that could be easily out-voted in the lower chamber.

Such concern about provincial representation *within* the institutions of the national government has come to be called "intrastate federalism" as opposed to an emphasis on relations between federal and provincial governments, or what is sometimes termed "interstate federalism."[3] Beyond the House of Commons and the Senate, interests of the various provinces can be represented within the cabinet and, perhaps less explicitly, within the bureaucracy and Supreme Court, an issue that arises in the discussion of these institutions later in the book. To some extent, federal–provincial (or interstate) tensions can be reduced if "intrastate" mechanisms are working effectively so that the people of all provinces feel adequately represented within the national government's policy-making process. But rigid party discipline and representation by population in the House of Commons and unilateral federal appointment of senators and Supreme Court judges may diminish such confidence, and as a result provincial premiers often come to be the principal articulators of provincial interests.

Confederation was more than just a union of provinces; it was also a uniting of two cultural groups, English and French. Thus, the fifth aspect of the Confederation Settlement might be called *cultural guarantees*. Considering the anxiety of French Canadians about the preservation of their language and culture, these guarantees were surprisingly minor. Section 133 of the 1867 Act made French and English official languages in the federal Parliament and federal courts as well as in the Quebec legislature and Quebec courts—but nowhere else. At the time, religion was probably of greater concern than language, so existing separate school systems in the provinces (especially Ontario and Quebec) were guaranteed by allowing the federal government to step in to restore them, if necessary, according to section 93. French Canada was also protected by giving power over property and civil rights to the provinces so that Quebec could maintain certain cultural particularisms, including its civil law system.

Since the evolution of French language rights is discussed in Chapter 8 and since the question of representation is addressed in Chapter 22, this chapter will proceed to track the development of the Confederation Settlement in its other three aspects, the division of powers, financial resources, and federal controls.

EVOLUTION OF CANADIAN FEDERALISM

In a discussion of the evolution of Canadian federalism, a key concern will be to explain how the very centralized federation created in 1867 became the highly decentralized Canada of today. In all three areas—the division of powers, financial resources, and federal controls—this trend is apparent.

Division of Powers

The evolution of the **division of powers** between federal and provincial governments can be examined in two respects: formal constitutional amendments that altered the division of powers, and judicial decisions that interpreted sections 91, 92, and 132 of the Constitution Act of 1867. It will be seen that the latter development was by far the more important.

CONSTITUTIONAL AMENDMENTS

Since 1867, only five formal constitutional amendments have been adopted that directly affected the division of powers. In 1940, unemployment insurance was added to the list of federal powers in section 91 after the courts had earlier declared it to belong to the provinces. In 1951, old age pensions were made a concurrent power, allowing the federal government into this area as well, and in 1964 its jurisdiction was enlarged to include widows' and survivors' benefits and disability pensions. In 1949, the federal Parliament was allowed to amend the Constitution unilaterally in areas of purely federal concern, a power previously held by Britain. This amendment was repealed in 1982 with the adoption of a more general amending formula. Also in 1982, the new section 92A increased provincial jurisdiction over natural resources, while the Charter of Rights and Freedoms generally reduced the powers of both levels of government. Thus, in the first three cases, the net result was a slight increase in federal powers, but, as pointed out in Chapter 3, this increase was accomplished with the unanimous consent of the provinces. Some provinces complained about the 1949 amendment, but it did not directly affect their powers. The 1982 amendment was the only formal constitutional amendment that in any way increased provincial powers at the expense of Ottawa.

JUDICIAL INTERPRETATION

Judicial interpretation of the federal and provincial powers in the 1867 act is a much more complicated subject. Before 1949, the **Judicial Committee of the Privy Council** (JCPC) in London was Canada's final court of appeal, and most constitutional decisions were rendered by that body. There is no doubt that its decisions had a major impact in transforming the nature of Canadian federalism from a centralized to a decentralized system, whether it acted out of ignorance or by deliberate design. The JCPC decisions can be examined primarily in terms of the **Peace, Order, and Good Government clause**, the **Trade and Commerce power**, and the **Treaty power**.

THE PEACE, ORDER, AND GOOD GOVERNMENT CLAUSE

It shall be lawful for the Queen, by and with the Advice and Consent of the Senate and House of Commons, to make laws for the Peace, Order, and good Government of Canada, in relation to all matters not coming within the Classes of Subjects by this Act assigned exclusively to the Legislatures of the Provinces; and for greater Certainty, but not so as to restrict the Generality of the foregoing Terms of this Section, it is hereby declared that (notwithstanding anything in this Act) the exclusive Legislative Authority of the Parliament of Canada extends to all Matters coming within the Classes of Subjects next hereinafter enumerated ...

Section 91 of the 1867 act has two parts. First, the "Peace, Order, and Good Government" clause says that all powers not given to the provinces in section 92 are left with the federal government. This is also known as "POGG" or the residual clause. Then, for greater certainty, a list of 29 examples of federal powers is included, a clause that was logically unnecessary and eventually became counterproductive. In a nutshell, in the course of its judgments, the Judicial Committee drove a wedge between these two parts of section 91, decided that the 29 enumerations were the *real* federal powers rather than just examples, and ignored the Peace, Order, and Good Government clause except in time of national emergency. How it managed to transform the residual clause into an emergency power is very difficult to fathom and is the subject of much scholarly discussion and whole courses in Canadian constitutional law. On the other hand, the JCPC gave an extremely broad interpretation to section 92-13, property and civil rights in the province, finding that almost any matter that was the subject of a federal–provincial constitutional dispute could be incorporated within this provincial power. That is why so little was left over for the federal residual clause. The full text of sections 91 and 92 is included in Appendix A.

Let us briefly summarize some of the leading POGG cases to see how this strange development took place.[4] In *Russell v. the Queen*, 1882, the federal Temperance Act was challenged. This law routinely provided the means by which the people of a local community could vote to outlaw the sale of alcohol. The JCPC ruled that the regulation of liquor was not mentioned explicitly in sections 91 and 92, and that while it affected property and civil rights (Mr. Russell's tavern and his right to operate it), the main purpose of the act was the promotion of public order and safety throughout the Dominion. Thus the federal act was a valid exercise of the Peace, Order and Good Government power. However, in an 1883 case, *Hodge v. the Queen*, the Judicial Committee ruled that there was a double aspect to the regulation of liquor— "subjects which in one aspect and for one purpose fall within s. 92, may in another aspect and for another purpose fall within s. 91." This decision opened the door for provincial action in the liquor field as well. Then, in the *Local Prohibition* case of 1896, the JCPC said that the Peace, Order, and Good Government clause was merely supplementary to the enumerations in section 91, and that POGG would come into play only if a subject could not be found in either list of enumerations in sections 91 and 92, and if the subject had attained such dimensions as to affect the body politic of the country as a whole. From this point, at which the POGG clause was divorced from the rest of section 91 and at which the list of enumerations effectively became federal powers, matters in dispute were increasingly found to fit into property and civil rights in the provinces.

POGG was then transformed into an **emergency clause** in a series of cases in the 1920s. In the *Board of Commerce* case, 1922, the Privy Council said that the regulation of prices and profiteering would normally fall within section 92-13, and only in special circumstances such as war or famine could such matters become of national importance. In the *Fort Frances* case, 1924, federal regulation of the price and supply of newsprint was upheld because it had been done in wartime, an emergency that justified federal action in a field that would ordinarily be provincial. Finally, in the 1925 *Toronto Electric Commissioners v. Snider* case, federal legislation to deal with serious strikes was ruled unconstitutional since labour–management relations were normally matters of property and civil rights in the province, and could only be the subject of federal action in an emergency. Faced with the disparity between this line of interpretation (that POGG was only an emergency clause), and that used in the *Russell* case (that POGG was a simple residual clause), the JCPC resorted to a reinterpretation of the earlier case: the evil of drunkenness at the time must have amounted to a national emergency!

A series of "New Deal" cases followed in the 1930s in which federal laws in the fields of unemployment insurance, labour standards, and the marketing of farm products were ruled invalid since the legislation was intended to be permanent rather than deal only with the temporary emergency of the Depression. These highly controversial decisions rendered Ottawa impotent in dealing with the human devastation the Depression wrought. Strangely enough, however, when the *Russell* case was duplicated in the 1946 *Canada Temperance Federation* case, the JCPC disavowed the emergency doctrine and reverted to the simple residual basis of POGG.

When appeals to the Privy Council were abolished in 1949, all eyes were on the Supreme Court to see which line of interpretation it would take with respect to POGG—emergency power or residual clause? The record has been unclear, but in general the federal level has won more cases than it did before 1949. Perhaps this reflects a better understanding of the Canadian situation, or a reaction to the excessive provincial orientation of the JCPC. Some of these federal victories have been based on POGG as a simple residual clause (with an issue having national but not emergency dimensions), such as the *Johannesson* case, which reaffirmed federal control over aviation and airports, the *B.C. Off-Shore Minerals* case, which gave Ottawa jurisdiction over the area beyond the B.C. coast, and *Munro v. National Capital*

Commission, which permitted federal regulation of property in the National Capital Region. But in the leading decision, the *Anti-Inflation Board* case of 1976, the Court was badly split. One group ruled against the federal legislation, but even the majority that upheld it did so for different reasons: some adhered to the emergency doctrine while others were prepared to accept a broader interpretation of POGG. Later environmental cases such as *The Queen v. Crown Zellerbach Canada Ltd.* in 1988 and the *Oldman River* decision in 1992 have strengthened federal jurisdiction over pollution control with extra-provincial implications. Ottawa's control over telephones and telecommunications has also been recently enhanced.[5] Even if a recent pro-Ottawa stance can be detected, however, the net effect of judicial interpretation of Peace, Order, and Good Government since 1867 is to have greatly increased provincial powers at federal expense.

A similar fate awaited the federal trade and commerce clause, section 91-2. The Fathers of Confederation deliberately expressed this clause in wide, general, unlimited terms, "the regulation of trade and commerce," but as early as the *Parsons* case, 1881, the JCPC restricted federal power to international and interprovincial trade. Besides drawing this unanticipated but rigid line between interprovincial trade (federal) and intraprovincial trade (provincial), the courts created a no-man's-land wherever the two kinds of trade were unavoidably combined. The general result of this line of interpretation was to enhance the provincial power over property and civil rights, and to downgrade the federal commerce power. Since 1949, the Supreme Court has rendered more realistic judgments in this area, recognizing the complexity of the situation, and often, but not always, favouring the federal side.

The Treaty power, section 132, effectively says that in cases of Empire treaties, the division of powers becomes inoperative and the federal government can implement them regardless of subject matter. Such was the decision of the *Aeronautics* case of 1932; the *Radio* case of the same year applied this rule to non-Empire treaties as well. However, in the 1937 *Labour Conventions* case, the JCPC reversed itself and said that Ottawa could only implement treaties the subject matter of which was within federal jurisdiction. In this particular case, the subject matter fell instead into property and civil rights.

The combined effect of the judicial interpretation of the Peace, Order, and Good Government, Trade and Commerce, and the Treaty powers has been to reduce significantly the intended dominance of the federal government, and to increase substantially the scope of provincial powers, especially given the broad interpretation given to property and civil rights. This influence has been very controversial in political, judicial, and academic circles because it was clearly contrary to John A. Macdonald's conception of Canadian federalism and because it did not permit Ottawa to take many initiatives that centralist advocates often wished it would.[6] Some observers give the JCPC the benefit of the doubt and think it operated in ignorance; others feel that it chose to adopt a narrow, literal line of interpretation, rather than the "aspect doctrine," a competing legal approach. Still other commentators argue that the British judges deliberately imposed their own decentralized conception of federalism on Canada or supported the provinces out of personal conservative ideological motives. The JCPC could only deal with the cases brought before it, of course, so that the decentralized results of its interpretation also depended on who challenged federal laws. Several such cases were initiated by corporations that expected to be given a freer hand in their pursuit of profits if power remained at the provincial level. Other cases were started by provincial premiers with the support of their cabinets and advisers, which followed naturally from the legitimation in a federal constitution of subnational elites.

On the other hand, many observers contend that the Judicial Committee's line of interpretation was consistent with the increasing size and distances that characterized the country as time went on, as well as with societal forces and public orientations at least outside Ontario. They argue that Canada has a federal, decentralized, diversified society, and the provincial bias pervading so many of the JCPC's decisions was "in fundamental harmony with the regional pluralism" of that society. However desirable centralization may have seemed at the outset, it was inappropriate in the long run "for the regional diversities of a land of vast extent and a large, geographically concentrated, minority culture."[7] Most French-Canadian observers, for example, were quite happy with the line of interpretation taken by the JCPC. Thus, Alan Cairns finds it impossible "to believe that a few elderly men in London deciding two or three constitutional cases a year precipitated, sustained, and caused the development of Canada in a federalist direction the country would otherwise not have taken."[8] Moreover, he observes,

> the discovery and amplification of an emergency power in Section 91 may have done an injustice to the intentions of Macdonald for the residual power, but it did allow Canada to conduct herself virtually as a unitary state in the two world wars in which centralized government authority was both required and supported.[9]

Federal–Provincial Finance[10]

In the Confederation Settlement, the federal government was given the power to levy any kind of tax, while the provinces were restricted to direct taxation.[11] Ottawa assumed provincial debts (also paying debt allowances to those provinces with smaller debts) and paid unconditional grants to the provinces based on 80 cents per capita and in support of governments and legislatures. While the intention was thus to create a highly centralized federation, the financial factor also ultimately contributed to the increased power of the provinces. This situation came about because some provincial revenues, such as those from natural resources, turned out to be more significant than anticipated; because the provinces levied direct taxes, such as income taxes, which they were not expected to use; and because the provinces successfully lobbied for larger federal grants, mostly unconditional in nature, than were set out in 1867.

Provincial revenues proved to be inadequate from the beginning, and special grants and arrangements had to be made immediately. A wholesale change in the grant system followed in 1907. By this time, too, the provinces had begun to levy their own direct personal and corporate income taxes, a situation complicated by the federal entry into the same fields during the First World War. About the same time, the **conditional grant** made its appearance. This was a grant paid by the federal government to the provinces in an area of provincial jurisdiction but for which provincial revenues were jointly deemed to be inadequate. The provinces usually had to match the federal share of 50 per cent, as well as adhering to whatever conditions or standards Ottawa imposed. The most important conditional grant in the early years was the old age pension, which started in 1927.

With both levels of government taxing the same personal and corporate incomes, but in a totally uncoordinated fashion, and with the two levels increasingly intertwined in conditional grant programs, the federal–provincial financial situation became very complicated. This muddied state of affairs worsened with the advent of the Depression, when even fewer funds were available to go around. The result was the appointment of the **Rowell–Sirois Commission**, officially the Royal Commission on Dominion–Provincial Relations, in 1937. Its 1940 Report recommended that the costly responsibility for unemployment insurance be transferred to the federal government, that Ottawa again assume provincial debts, that the provinces give up the fields of personal and corporate income taxes and succession duties to the federal government. In return, the federal level should pay the provinces an annual unconditional grant based on need. The first recommendation was quickly implemented, as was a temporary Wartime Taxation Agreement, but the Report's other suggestions were shelved.

Before 1940, therefore, the two levels of government were relatively independent on both the taxation and expenditure sides of public finance. Since the Second World War, on the other hand, they have become intimately intertwined, and Ottawa has taken the lead (sometimes with provincial encouragement) in coordinating the various ingredients of the federal–provincial financial relationship. The complicated federal–provincial financial situation since 1940 might be simplified somewhat by taking three aspects separately: **taxation agreements**, **conditional** and **block grants**, and **equalization payments**.

MAIN FEATURES OF POST-1940 FEDERAL–PROVINCIAL FINANCE

* Taxation agreements
* Conditional and block grants
* Equalization payments

FEDERAL–PROVINCIAL TAXATION AGREEMENTS

Since 1942 the taxation side has been characterized by a series of five-year federal–provincial agreements. The name and terms of the agreements have changed over the years—tax rental, tax sharing, tax collection, and so on—but the basic objective has been the same: to effect a degree of coordination in the field of federal–provincial taxation. The main taxes in question were personal and corporate income taxes and succession duties, although the latter are no longer applied in any province. Since 1962 the provincial portion of personal income tax has been allowed to vary, and today, while the federal tax is standard across the country (except for Quebec), the provincial portion varies widely. Table 4.1 indicates how much of an individual's personal income tax is extracted by each province as a percent of his or her basic federal tax. Except for Quebec, all personal income taxes are collected by Ottawa in the first instance, after which the provincial portion is transferred back, an arrangement

TABLE 4.1	Provincial Personal Income Rates, 1994, as Percent of Basic Federal Tax	
Newfoundland	69.0
New Brunswick	64.0
Nova Scotia	59.5
Prince Edward Island	59.5
Ontario	58.0
British Columbia	52.5
Manitoba	52.0
Saskatchewan	50.0
Alberta	45.5

Source: Canadian Tax Foundation, The National Finances, 1994. Used with permission.

found generally satisfactory to all concerned. Quebec collects its own personal income tax, so that its residents complete two separate income tax forms. The federal income tax return in Quebec reflects the fact that that province receives a "tax abatement" of 8.5 personal income tax points to cover the financing of those conditional grant programs from which it has opted out. A tax abatement is a transfer of "tax room" from the federal to the provincial level. All provinces except Ontario, Quebec, and Alberta also have tax collection arrangements with Ottawa with respect to provincial corporate income taxes.

CONDITIONAL AND BLOCK GRANTS

The Rowell–Sirois Report frowned on **shared-cost programs**, preferring that each level of government operate independently. Such joint programs expanded considerably after 1940, however, as pressure from the CCF, industrial unions, and other newly articulated interests on the left forced federal and provincial governments into the joint development of a welfare state. The most important shared-cost social programs were postsecondary education (1952), hospital insurance (1957), the **Canada Assistance Plan** (CAP) (1966), and medical insurance (1968). Health insurance later replaced the two earlier measures in this field.

Federal grants for postsecondary education have always been of a **block grant** variety, that is, a sum of money given to each province for the operating costs of postsecondary educational institutions but without any detailed conditions or strings attached. Between 1967 and 1977 they were based on a formula of providing 50 percent of such expenditures.

The other three major shared-cost programs originally fell into the conditional grant category. The usual pattern here was that after it laid down certain conditions, the federal government paid approximately 50 percent of the cost of each program. In the case of hospital insurance, Ottawa would pay half the cost of provincial programs that provided their residents with basic hospital care without charge. The provinces could finance their half of the program costs from premiums or general tax revenues. Medical insurance was an extension of the prior program to cover basic doctors' services. Ottawa would fund half of any provincial health care program that was comprehensive (covering all necessary health services provided by hospitals and medical practitioners), universal (covering the whole population), portable (covering the costs of provincial residents while temporarily absent from the province), accessible (not impeding or precluding reasonable access to services by extra charges), and publicly administered. Under the Canada Assistance Plan, Ottawa similarly provided half the funding for almost any provincial or municipal program that provided social assistance and welfare services to persons in need.

Most of these programs fell constitutionally within provincial jurisdiction, but Ottawa always maintained that its **spending power** allowed it to make payments to individuals, institutions, and other governments in fields over which Parliament did not necessarily have the power to regulate. The federal government even claimed that it could attach conditions to such spending and has often done so. The constitutional status of this argument has never been settled authoritatively, although it was addressed by the courts in several cases.[12]

While a combination of provincial pressure and federal political and bureaucratic expansionism inspired most of these programs, the provinces often criticized the federal conditions attached as being out of place in areas of provincial jurisdiction. Quebec in particular took this point of view in the early 1960s. The Pearson government responded in 1965 with the Established Programs (Interim Arrangements) Act, which allowed provinces to opt out of certain conditional grant programs and continue to receive federal funding as long as they maintained an equivalent program. Then, in the 1970s, Ottawa became upset at the rapidly escalating costs of many of these programs and its commitment to finance 50 percent of whatever the provinces spent on them. In 1977 the federal government transferred health insurance from the conditional to the block grant category, under the **Established Programs Financing Act**. This transformation had two major implications. First, Ottawa removed the detailed conditions attached to the health insurance programs, as many provinces wished, but in return, the federal government no longer felt obliged to pay 50 percent of the provincial program costs. The federal grants now took the form of tax transfers as well as cash, and henceforth, Ottawa would only increase its funding of such programs by a certain annual percentage, which would not necessarily cover one-half of their overall costs. The tax transfers represent federal tax revenue forgone as a result of a coordinated reduction of federal taxes and increase in provincial taxes such that the position of the taxpayer is left unchanged. Removing the conditions from health insurance grants, however, led to problems with hospital user fees, doctors' double-billing, and provinces using health care funds for other purposes. The second implication, therefore, was the passage of the **Canada Health Act** in 1984, to much provincial condemnation. This law penalized provinces that permitted user fees and double-billing in the health field.

Especially after 1982, the federal share of such programs fell below 50 percent, and the 1990s saw a progression of freezes and cuts in such funding. For a time, the Canada Assistance Plan remained a conditional grant program, with Ottawa continuing its 50 percent contribution, but the Mulroney government put a ceiling on its CAP contributions to the three richest provinces in the early 1990s, and the Liberals later repealed it. It should be added that these four shared-cost programs are only the most expensive of many joint endeavours. Others are discussed later in this chapter. See also Table 4.4.

FEDERAL CONDITIONS UNDER THE CANADA HEALTH ACT

- Comprehensiveness
- Universality
- Portability
- Accessibility
- Public administration

The 1994 federal budget brought in by Finance Minister Paul Martin announced a freeze on all major federal transfers except equalization, and the 1995 budget inaugurated a major transformation of federal–provincial transfer payments. Established Program Funding (post-secondary education and health insurance) and the Canada Assistance Plan (social assistance and welfare services) would be combined into one block grant beginning in 1996–97 called the Canada Health and Social Transfer (CHST). It would be a combination of cash payments and tax points, but would represent a significant reduction in previous amounts. As a block grant, the CHST would not contain the conditions of CAP, nor would Ottawa's expenditures be driven by provincial costs. The only condition on welfare transfers would be that provinces not impose a minimum residency requirement. Despite the protests of almost all social reformers, who did not trust provincial governments, Ottawa felt it could not retain such conditions when it was reducing its contributions, and was particularly loath to provoke the PQ government of Quebec immediately before the 1995 referendum. On the other hand, the federal Liberal government intended to continue to enforce the principles of the Canada Health Act and fought with Alberta over the funding of private health clinics that charged "facility fees."

EQUALIZATION PAYMENTS

The third aspect of federal–provincial finance consists of **equalization payments**.[13] Picking up on the Rowell–Sirois Report's recommendation, but not until 1957, the federal government began to pay unconditional grants to have-not provinces based on provincial need, so that all could offer a relatively equal standard of services. The basic idea behind equalization payments was to bring the have-not provinces up to the national average tax yield per capita. At first only three sources of provincial revenue were considered in the equalization formula, but in 1967 the number was increased to 16, in 1972 to 19, in 1977 to 29, and now to 32—including almost every conceivable source of provincial revenue. Typically, Ontario, British Columbia, and Alberta have been above the national average and have not received equalization payments, but Alberta petroleum revenues raised the national average so high that Ontario began to qualify in 1980, and an adjustment to the formula had to be made to remove natural resource revenue. Such revenues were later added back, but Alberta was removed along with the Atlantic provinces in the calculation of the national average. The current formula uses as a base the average of per capita revenue of five representative provinces (Quebec, Ontario, Manitoba, Saskatchewan, and British Columbia). Any province whose total per capita revenue is below this average receives a payment based on the per capita shortfall multiplied by the province's population. Equalization payments were not touched by the federal reforms of 1995.

Combining these three (or, after 1996–97, two) major federal contributions to the provinces, Table 4.2 shows that in 1995–96 Ottawa paid the provinces $8.87 billion in equalization payments, $21.7 billion in health and postsecondary education block grants, and $7.95 billion under CAP, for a total of $37.745 billion. Even so, these figures do not include smaller conditional and unconditional federal grants or federal contributions to economic development such as the Atlantic Canada Opportunities Agency and Western Economic Diversification programs. In contrast, unadjusted for inflation, the federal grant of 80 cents per capita in 1867 would amount to about $24 million today!

TABLE 4.2 **Federal Transfers to Provinces and Territories**

	($ Millions)				
	1993–94	**1994–95**	**1995–96**	**1996–97**	**1997–98**
Current Arrangements					
CAP	7 719	7 952	7 952	—	—
EPF	21 236	21 476	21 734	—	—
TOTAL	28 956	29 428	29 686	—	—
Canada Health and Social Transfer	—	—	—	26 900	25 100
Equalization	8 034	8 332	8 870	9 270	9 618
Total Major Transfers *	36 212	36 975	37 745	35 351	33 889
Territorial Formula Financing	1 141	1 164	1 164	1 127	1 163
Total Transfers **	37 353	38 138	38 909	36 478	35 052

* Equalization associated with tax point transfers under EPF (CHST after 1995–96) appears in both the Equalization and EPP/CHST figures. Totals are adjusted to avoid double counting.

** Does not include other federal transfers to provinces totalling: $2.7 billion in 1993–94, $3.5 billion in 1994–95 and $3.0 billion in 1995–96. Figures for these other transfers are not available beyond 1995–96.

Source: Figures provided by the Department of Finance as of February 1995. Used with permission.

OTHER PROVINCIAL REVENUES

The provinces have discovered and levied over 30 forms of direct taxation that were unanticipated in 1867.[14] The enormous natural resource revenues that some provinces receive on top of direct taxation and federal contributions are also significant.[15] Over and above the natural resource revenue that is collected in the form of corporate income taxes, provinces obtain specific natural resource revenues from forests, including taxes on logging operations; leases and rentals of Crown lands; and royalties, rentals, and stumpage fees from timber and forest management. They also obtain revenues from mines, including taxes on mining operations, acreage taxes, licence and permit fees, rentals and lease payments, and royalties on mineral production. In addition, the petroleum-producing provinces collect revenue from oil and gas, including proceeds from the sale of Crown oil and gas leases, taxes on oil and gas production, royalties, freehold taxes, lease rentals, and fees and permits.[16] Some idea of the balance among federal transfers, natural resources, and provincial taxes and other provincial revenues can be gathered from Table 4.3.

Thus, the combination of unanticipated federal grants, direct taxes, and natural resource revenues has contributed significantly to the enhanced status of the provinces in the Canadian federal system. It should be added that pressure for decentralization and for turn-

TABLE 4.3	Estimated Federal Transfers, Natural Resource Revenues, Provincial Taxes and Other Revenues, and Total Revenue, 1994–95			
	(millions of dollars)			
	Federal Transfers	*Provincial Taxes & Other Provincial Revenues*	*Natural Resource Revenues*	*Total Provincial Revenues*
Newfoundland	$1 507.4	$1 943.0	$ 31.2	$ 3 481.6
P.E.I.	301.3	506.5	0.6	808.4
Nova Scotia	1 750.8	2 780.7	10.5	4 542.0
New Brunswick	1 588.2	2 830.8	50.2	4 469.2
Quebec	7 751.6	33 691.5	96.0	41 539.1
Ontario	7 186.5	41 836.7	364.6	49 387.8
Manitoba	1 830.4	4 590.7	63.2	6 484.3
Saskatchewan	1 642.2	4 216.0	407.7	6 265.9
Alberta	2 455.5	9 254.1	2 687.8	14 397.4
B.C.	2 336.5	17 204.6	1 687.0	21 228.1
Total	$28 350.4	$118 854.6	$5 398.8	$152 603.8

Source: Statistics Canada, Public Sector Finance 1994–95, Financial Management System, cat. no. 68-212 (March 1995), adapted by author. Reproduced with the permission of the Minister of Supply and Services Canada, 1995.

ing taxation power over to the provinces comes from those provinces that have substantial personal and corporate incomes to tax. The Atlantic provinces sometimes fight against decentralization because they would not benefit if their taxation powers were expanded while Ottawa's were lessened. They want to keep Ottawa strong so that it can redistribute revenues at least by means of equalization payments. It should also be reiterated that the two levels of government began by operating more or less independently of each other, taxing and spending in different areas, with federal grants being unconditional in nature. Now, the federal and provincial governments are closely intertwined by taxation agreements on the revenue side and by conditional and block grant programs in terms of expenditures.

Federal Controls

The 1867 Constitution Act contained three specific federal controls over the provinces: reservation, disallowance, and the declaratory power. The decline in the use of these powers has also increased the stature of the provinces today. In the first 30 years after Confederation all three controls were actively used, and this had the effect of keeping the provinces subordinate to Ottawa.[17] Their use has gradually declined since then, the two major exceptions being the combatting of anti-Asian legislation in B.C. around 1900, and the throwing out of Social Credit legislation in Alberta in the 1930s. Overall, reservation has been used 70 times, but on 14 occasions the federal government assented to the provincial legislation the lieutenant governor had reserved, and it was last exercised in 1961. The federal cabinet used its disallowance power 112 times, most recently in 1943. The declaratory power has been used 470 times, mostly to put local railroads into federal jurisdiction in the early years, but not since 1961. It is now a convention of the Constitution, superseding the written words of the 1867 act, that Ottawa not use these federal controls.[18] As these were the federal powers that originally precluded Canada from being classified as a true federation, their disuse has meant that the provinces have shrugged off their subordinate status. Canada is now a genuine federation, and a highly decentralized one at that.

PHASES OF CANADIAN FEDERALISM

Putting these three aspects of the Confederation settlement together and examining their simultaneous operation, we can now divide the years since 1867 into a number of eras of Canadian federalism,[19] as illustrated in Figure 4.1. These divisions demonstrate pendulum-like swings between centralization and decentralization so that the evolution from a centralized to a decentralized federal system has not been a unilinear process.

The period 1867–96 can be classified as **quasi-federalism**, in which the provinces were subordinate to Ottawa. The courts gave the intended broad interpretation to federal powers, especially Peace, Order, and Good Government; the federal level was still predominant in finance; and John A. Macdonald made widespread use of the federal controls of reservation, disallowance, and the declaratory power.

Figure 4.1 Centralization and Decentralization in Canadian Federalsm

The period 1896–1914 can be termed one of **classical federalism**. During these years the two levels were coordinate and independent. By now, the courts generally favoured the provinces, the provinces had more money to spend, and the federal government made little use of its controls, so that the provinces were no longer subordinate. This was also the period before taxation agreements and conditional grants; that is, there was little connection between federal and provincial operations—they were independent.

Classical federalism was displaced by **emergency federalism** during the war years, 1914–20. In this era the courts permitted the federal government virtually unlimited powers under the emergency doctrine and the War Measures Act. The federal government also increased its financial resources in this period with the imposition of personal and corporate income taxes. Ironically, in this most centralized phase of Canadian federalism—more centralized even than in the first 30 years—the use of the federal controls was unnecessary because of the courts' emergency interpretation of Peace, Order, and Good Government.

Between the wars, from 1920 to 1939, Canada reverted to another period of classical federalism. In these years, again, the two levels of government were coordinate (neither subordinate to the other) and operated more or less independently. Only a handful of conditional grants, for example, was developed during this time.

In the Second World War, from 1939 to 1945, Canada entered another period of emergency federalism. Once again, the courts allowed Ottawa to operate almost like a unitary government under the emergency interpretation of POGG and the War Measures Act. Public finance was also highly centralized with the development of the Wartime Taxation Agreements, under which the federal government took complete control over personal and corporate income taxes and succession duties. As in the First World War, any additional use of the federal controls was unnecessary.

The postwar world brought with it a completely new phase—**cooperative federalism**. The essence of this concept is that while neither level is subordinate to the other (the same as in classical federalism), they are closely intertwined rather than operating independently. Here the crucial variable is financial relations. As noted in that connection earlier, the post-1945 period has been marked by federal–provincial taxation agreements on the revenue side and a host of conditional grant and other shared-cost programs in terms of expenditures.

Cooperative federalism results from several developments.[20] First, federal and provincial objectives must often be harmonized if public policy is to be effective, such as in the case of countercyclical fiscal policy. Second, public pressure forces the federal government to establish minimum standards throughout the country in certain public services within provincial jurisdiction such as health care. In the third place, the two levels of government compete for tax revenues and end up needing to coordinate these efforts to some extent, at least for the convenience of taxpayers. Fourth, given a generally vague division of powers, federal and provincial ministers and bureaucrats all seek to maximize their jurisdiction and eventually overlap with the other level of government.

Cooperative federalism is made operational by hundreds of **federal–provincial conferences** at all levels—first ministers, departmental ministers, deputy ministers, and even lesser officials, who engage in almost continuous consultation, coordination, and cooperation. Cooperative federalism can be conducted on a multilateral basis, involving the federal government and several or all provinces, or, alternatively, on a bilateral basis in which Ottawa interacts with individual provinces. Since the ministers and bureaucrats involved are all part of the executive branch of government, cooperative federalism is sometimes called **executive federalism**. Two main implications of executive federalism are that legislatures, political parties, and the public at large are not given much role to play in decisions that emerge from the secrecy of such meetings, and that federal–provincial conflicts are worked out in conferences rather than referred to the courts.

Executive federalism can therefore be defined as "relations between elected and appointed officials of the two levels of government."[21] When it is practised at the level of first ministers, it is often called "federal–provincial summitry." The **first ministers' conference**, that is, a federal–provincial conference of premiers and the prime minister, is nowhere provided for in the written Constitution and rests on a conventional base.[22] Nevertheless, since 1945 this institution has made many significant Canadian policy decisions, especially with respect to constitutional issues, shared-cost programs, and taxation and fiscal arrangements. Some of these had to be ratified later by federal and provincial legislatures, but legislative ratification was usually a formality. Such agreements could rarely be altered in any legislature because they would then have to be changed in all eleven. First ministers' conferences have become more elaborate and institutionalized as time goes on. They are usually held in the Government Conference Centre in Ottawa, the refurbished old train station across from

Reproduced with permission.

Parliament Hill. They can be televised, in whole or in part, but it is generally agreed that any serious negotiation has to take place behind closed doors. They are only called by the federal government, which also determines the agenda, although it is customary to consult the provinces on dates and agenda items.[23] The prime minister functions as chair, in addition to representing the federal government (roles that are often in conflict), and individual ministers from either level of government are usually allowed to speak as well. Every delegation brings along a host of advisers, who quickly fill up the room.

Successful federal–provincial summitry depends on the mutual respect of its participants and a willingness to engage in negotiation. Hence, this form of executive federalism was practised more successfully by Lester Pearson (1963–68) and in the first term of the Mulroney government (1984–88) than by Pierre Trudeau (1968–84) or in the second Mulroney term (1988–92).

Executive federalism conducted at the level of departmental ministers and leading bureaucrats is sometimes labelled "functional" or "bureaucratic" federalism. This form of executive federalism is frequently more successful than federal–provincial summitry, partly because the officials involved often share certain professional norms, and once they reach a consensus, these experts may be able to "sell" it to their departmental ministers. Functional federalism works best with "departmentalized cabinets" in which individual federal and provincial ministers and deputy ministers have considerable autonomy so that they can interact productively with their counterparts at the other level of government. Such interaction was therefore hampered by the trend between the mid-1960s and 1993 toward "institutionalized cabinets" in which decisions were made in cabinet committees and under the guidance of powerful central agencies such as finance departments, treasury boards, and cabinet offices, as discussed in Chapter 20.[24]

Canadian federalism between 1945 and 1960 may have been "cooperative" in the sense that the two levels of government were closely intertwined, but it continued to be highly centralized in the postwar period. The ministers and bureaucrats in Ottawa who had almost single-handedly run the country during the Second World War were reluctant to shed their enormous power. Moreover, they had discovered **Keynesian economics**, which prescribed a leading role for the central government in guiding the economy.[25]

The Diefenbaker government after 1957 was more sensitive to provincial demands, and the whole picture was increasingly complicated from about 1960 onward by the Quiet Revolution in Quebec. Thus, for about a decade, Canada experienced cooperative federalism with a French (or bilingual) twist, which has been called "double-image federalism."[26] This period still witnessed an intertwined, nonsubordinate relationship between the two levels of government, but cooperation was sometimes harder to come by, with Quebec regularly rejecting federal initiatives. Moreover, for the first time since 1890 or so, language and culture became important again in a constitutional sense. An extension of official bilingualism and the concept of opting-out were hallmarks of this phase of Canadian federalism, which saw a significant degree of decentralization take place.

Then, between about 1970 and 1984, federal–provincial relations became less cooperative, and the period might best be described as one of "conflictual federalism." Quebec and the other provinces were more aggressive than ever, but the Trudeau government was not prepared for any further decentralization. Thus, the taxation agreements were now accompanied by more provincial unhappiness, and block funding replaced conditional grants in important areas, leaving the two levels less intertwined than before. Moreover, especially at the level of first ministers, federal–provincial conferences frequently failed to come to any agreement, and Ottawa often chose to act unilaterally. Issues in this period were also considered too serious to leave to bureaucrats alone. Another factor involved after 1970 was the attempt at both levels to engage in more rational decision-making, so that departmental ministers and their officials no longer operated with the same autonomy. Besides politicians displacing bureaucrats in this phase, federal–provincial conflicts were more frequently referred to the courts, resulting in a renewed emphasis on the division of powers.

The Trudeau era was characterized by years of federal–provincial discord over resource and energy policies, especially the National Energy Program, federal–Newfoundland conflict over offshore oil, and federal–Saskatchewan conflict over the regulation and taxation of that province's oil and potash industries. When these disputes coincided with Trudeau's unilateral attempt to amend the Constitution and to entrench official bilingualism as a national policy, many Western Canadians began to re-examine their place in the federation. Some of the heat was reduced when Trudeau conceded the new section 92A, which recognized enhanced provincial jurisdiction over natural resources, in order to secure federal NDP support for the 1982 constitutional package and as a peace offering to the West.

CANADIAN FEDERALISM SINCE 1984

When Brian Mulroney came to power in 1984, he was determined to improve federal–provincial relations and embark on another period of decentralized, Pearsonian cooperative federalism. During his first term many would say he succeeded, for much of the federal–provincial animosity of the Trudeau years seemed to dissipate. Western and Eastern concerns about energy resources were respectively resolved to a large extent in the 1985 Western and Atlantic Accords. The highlight of the Mulroney approach, of course, was the 1987 Meech Lake Accord, which was designed to bring Quebec symbolically into the new constitutional framework and which would have generally increased provincial powers at Ottawa's expense.[27] Trudeau was the leading dissenter, feeling that Mulroney had given too much away. During the second term, however, the Mulroney government increasingly aroused provincial anger, especially as it became obsessed with deficit reduction and cut back on grants to the provinces. To the surprise of many observers, the Mulroney government enforced the Liberals' Canada Health Act, which imposed penalties on provinces that allowed doctors to extra-bill or permitted hospitals to charge user fees. Ontario, Alberta, and B.C. objected to the 1990 policy of reducing their grants under the Canada Assistance Plan, and several provinces, especially Ontario, were opposed to the Canada–U.S. and North American Free Trade Agreements. The major federal–provincial dispute of the Mulroney years concerned the Goods and Services Tax (GST). To some extent it was just "good politics" for provincial premiers to jump on the anti-GST bandwagon because of widespread popular opposition. Most provinces refused to integrate their sales taxes with the new federal tax, even though many mutual advantages would have accrued from doing so.

The Chrétien Liberals began by appointing a specific minister, Marcel Massé, to be in charge of federal–provincial relations. They were initially popular with provincial governments in offering funds under the national infrastructure program, and were somewhat successful in negotiating a reduction in barriers that provinces imposed to the free movement of people, goods, services, and capital across the country. They had no initial success in implementing their promise to replace the GST, however, and made the provinces angry with reductions in their transfers to the provinces. The principal complaints included severe reductions in health, postsecondary education, and welfare transfers, although provinces also joined in to protest the cuts to almost every other aspect of federal government operations, such as a wide range of transportation subsidies. At the same time, most provinces were realistic enough to recognize the desirability of reducing the federal deficit. Ottawa did not cut equalization payments, however, and even the centralist foe of the Meech Lake Accord, Newfoundland's Clyde Wells, was content that Ottawa reduced other targeted federal transfers. Given the mixture of harmony and discord since 1988, it is difficult to find an appropriate label for the federal–provincial relations of the period.[28]

On a whole range of issues, federal and provincial governments practise executive federalism involving cooperation at the political and bureaucratic levels. These routine arrangements used to be coordinated to some extent by the Federal–Provincial Relations Office in Ottawa, then a semi-independent part of the Privy Council Office (PCO).[29] It has since been reintegrated into the PCO, but still publishes an annual catalogue of *Federal–Provincial Programs and Activities: A Descriptive Inventory*, which demonstrates that cooperative arrangements exist with the provinces in many fields and within almost every federal department and agency. Table 4.4 provides a statistical picture of such federal–provincial programs.

A representative selection of examples of these cooperative federal–provincial ventures includes the following: Human Resources Development cooperates with the provinces in the Canadian Student Loans Program; Canada Mortgage and Housing Corporation subsidizes the construction and operation of public, Native, and nonprofit housing programs in the provinces; Parks Canada shares with the provinces the cost of the acquisition, restoration, and preservation of national historic sites; and Natural Resources Canada has signed forest resource development agreements with most provinces to improve the management of forests and increase the supply of wood. The Department of Finance collects income taxes for all provinces except Quebec; the Office of Infrastructure began to share the cost of upgrading community infrastructure across the country in 1994, a program extended to 1999; Tourism Canada shares the cost of a biennial travel survey with the provinces; the Department of Justice contributes to provincial legal aid programs; the Canadian Heritage department subsidizes official language programs such as French immersion in the provinces; and the RCMP provides general policing services under contract to all provinces except Ontario and Quebec and to 199 municipalities. As of 1995, executive or bureaucratic federalism was evident in over 400 cooperative federal–provincial programs.

Canada has passed the apex of such cooperative efforts, however. For many reasons both levels of government increasingly want to extract themselves from such programs. Since duplication probably increases program costs, federal and provincial governments' strained fiscal positions are largely responsible. If Ottawa is no longer funding programs so generously, for example, it cannot impose standards on them. In other cases, each side simply wants to do things in its own way. In addition to the likely decentralization of about ten federal powers in the Charlottetown Accord, a list of potential areas in which the two levels of government are seeking to reduce duplication follows on page 91:

TABLE 4.4   **Federal–Provincial Programs, by Federal Department or Agency, 1995**

Department/Agency	Multilateral	Bilateral
Agriculture and Agri-Food Canada	14	40
Atlantic Canada Opportunities Agency	2	4
Canada Mortgage & Housing Corporation	10	
Canadian Dairy Commission	1	
Canadian Heritage	17	17
Canadian International Development Agency	2	
Citizenship and Immigration Canada	3	1
Environment Canada	31	45
Federal Office of Regional Development—Quebec		8
Finance	10	
Fisheries and Oceans	3	33
Foreign Affairs and International Trade Canada	1	
Health	11	
Human Resources Development Canada	21	2
Indian and Northern Affairs Canada	12	36
Industry Canada	7	4
Office of Infrastructure	1	
Department of Justice Canada	3	
National Capital Commission	1	1
National Defence	5	
Natural Resources Canada	9	41
Public Works and Government Services Canada	6	1
Revenue Canada	10	2
Solicitor General Canada	7	2
Statistics Canada	2	
Transport Canada	6	10
Veterans Affairs	1	
Western Economic Diversification Canada	1	4
Total	197	251

Source: Privy Council Office, Federal–Provincial Programs and Activities: A Descriptive Inventory, 1993–1994 and 1994–1995, *cat. no. CP41-1/1995W (April 1995), adapted by author.*

AREAS OF POTENTIAL TO REDUCE FEDERAL–PROVINCIAL DUPLICATION

* enforcement of retail tobacco laws
* tax evasion, smuggling, and underground economy
* providing information on federal and provincial business programs
* drug prosecutions (turning some over to provinces)
* student loans (single program by 1996–97)
* international trade promotion
* food inspection
* environmental assessment processes
* pension and securities regulation
* wildlife management
* federal and provincial rail safety rules
* map drawing

CONCLUSION

Federalism in Canada is both based on and intensifies regional, economic, and ethnic cleavages. In the beginning, the Canadian federal system was highly centralized, but this original design was soon found to be inappropriate for the society in which it operated. When the cleavages became difficult to overcome, and as "province-builders" competed with "nation-builders," Canada gradually became a very decentralized federation. Both in the courts and in negotiations with Ottawa, the provinces successfully fought for more powers and more financial resources. While federalism often seems to be an unending source of intergovernmental discord, as well as a convenient excuse at both levels of government for not responding to demands, the maze of cooperative federal–provincial interaction should not be ignored.

(SC) As in the case of the Constitution, the state-centred approach is most relevant to the Canadian federal system. It maintains that federal and provincial governments act in their own interests or in accordance with their own conception of the public interest, without much regard for the wishes of the general public. Ministers and bureaucrats usually want to maximize their own power and responsibility, so that both levels of government have expanded operations to the point of considerable overlap. Federal authorities argue for federal jurisdiction, revenue, conditions, standards, and controls, while provincial authorities fight for maximum provincial revenue, flexibility, and freedom. Some state-centred theorists contend that much of the federal–provincial discord is an artificial competition among federal and provincial politicians and bureaucrats, rather than a *real* fight reflecting public opinion. Provincial governments demand powers, money, and constitutional vetoes in the name of their residents, but the residents themselves may be indifferent as to whether they are taxed, regulated, or provided for by federal or provincial governments. The cooperative mechanisms of executive federalism and the central role of the public service in bureaucratic federalism can also be seen as evidence of the state-centred approach, for the public can do little but accept whatever arrangements are worked out among federal and provincial bureaucrats and then sold to their ministers. The federal–provincial conference is one of the prime venues in which elite accommodation takes place. If provincial electorates have confidence in their own political leaders, the voters will accept whatever promises are negotiated between the two sets of elites as they grapple with the problems of overlapping jurisdiction.

The centralist and decentralist swings, which have been identified above, are sometimes analyzed in terms of the concepts of "nation-building" as opposed to "province-building." The overarching concern of the national political elite—prime ministers, federal cabinets, and leading bureaucrats—has been to construct a strong central government. But the creation of provinces produced counterbalancing provincial political elites—premiers, provincial cabinets, and bureaucrats—who were more interested in building strong provinces. Province-building is usually related to post–Second World War increases in provincial revenues and in the size of provincial bureaucracies, the creation of provincial Crown corporations and central planning agencies, and a willingness and capacity for provincial governments to intervene in the process of industrial development and diversification. In short, province-building means that the provincial state plays a significant role within the confines of the provincial society. Strong provincial governments want more powers, autonomy, and money, which explains much of the pressure for decentralization in the Canadian federal system since 1960 or so.

Nation-building and province-building are not confined to government elites. In each case, they have been supported by certain societal forces. At the national level, these include elements of the business community (banking, transportation, communications, manufacturing) and by most of the anglophone intellectual elite. Provincial political elites also had support within their societies, primarily including natural resource companies, professionals, and others concerned with property.

P Pluralists argue that provincial political and bureaucratic elites genuinely represent diversified provincial societies. They oppose a highly centralized federation, since it was in response to the scattered and diverse population with its different interests and regional loyalties that a federation was originally established. Pluralist theorists contend that the Judicial Committee of the Privy Council was remarkably far-sighted in interpreting the division of powers in a decentralist direction. Contrary to the intentions of John A. Macdonald, its decisions were entirely consistent with the "federal society" into which Canada evolved. Federalism allows provincial governments to take action in the interests of their own cultural majorities or distinctive industries that would generate much controversy at the national level. It permits experimentation in social policies, such that those that prove successful at the provincial level (e.g., medicare) can later be adopted in other provinces and/or at the national level.[30] Federalism also maximizes the number of organized groups that can make their voices heard, some at the national level and others in the provinces.

(C) Most class analysts decry decentralization of the federal system for its stifling of creative, national programs.[31] They would prefer new and stronger national social programs and labour and environmental standards, which are not possible because of broad provincial jurisdiction. Generally speaking, such analysts assume that the federal government is more likely than the provinces to produce "progressive" policies. They want high and uniform national standards and are suspicious of what provincial governments would do with federal health or welfare grants without conditions attached. While arguing for greater centralization, class analysts point out how frequently private corporate interests have taken the opposite position. The corporate elite has often used its influence with friendly provincial governments to frustrate national initiatives and challenged the federal government in court in order to enhance provincial jurisdiction in places where it has been more influential at that level.[32] Corporate preference for decentralization is not absolute, however; it depends on what actions provincial governments try to take. In Saskatchewan in the 1970s, mining and petroleum companies challenged the constitutionality of provincial NDP legislation they opposed, and in Alberta in the 1930s and 1940s, the banks took oppressive Social Credit banking legislation to the courts.

PC Finally, public choice theorists see Ottawa's relations with the provinces in electoral terms. If Ontario and Quebec have the largest number of marginal seats at stake, for example, federal authorities will be most responsive to the demands articulated by their governments. This can be seen in the case of the National Energy Program (supported by Ontario) or in awarding Quebec the CF-18 maintenance contract. On the other hand, it is often productive for provincial governments to base their election campaigns on opposition to Ottawa.

DISCUSSION QUESTIONS

1. Are you a centralist or a decentralist? Why?

2. Why has Ontario usually preferred a highly centralized federal system? Do the residents of other provinces want a decentralized federal system or is it just the politicians and bureaucrats in such provinces who do?

3. Is it possible to have a clear-cut division of powers between federal and provincial governments in the modern era of such extensive government activity?

4. Why do you think the Judicial Committee of the Privy Council generally favoured the provinces over the federal government in its decisions?

5. How can we simultaneously achieve federal–provincial coordination and autonomy in the field of taxation?

6. Should the federal government be able to spend money for any purpose, even within provincial jurisdiction? Should it be able to set conditions on provincial medicare programs?

7. Should federal grants to the provinces take the form of conditional, block, or unconditional grants? Why?

8. What are the advantages and disadvantages of executive federalism?

9. Why is it that provincial premiers have come to speak for provincial interests? Is it because of the impotence of the Senate and the rigid party discipline in the House of Commons?

10. How do the approaches outlined in Chapter 1 relate to the material in this chapter?

·····················

NOTES

1. Donald Smiley, *The Canadian Political Nationality* (Toronto: Methuen, 1967).
2. K.C. Wheare, *Federal Government*, 4th ed. (London: Oxford University Press,1963).
3. These terms are derived from Donald Smiley. See D.V. Smiley and R.L. Watts, *Intrastate Federalism in Canada* (Toronto: University of Toronto Press, 1985).
4. Among the leading sources on this subject are Peter Russell et al., *Federalism and the Charter* (Ottawa: Carleton University Press, 1989), and Peter Hogg, *Constitutional Law of Canada*, 2nd ed. (Toronto: Carswell, 1985).
5. Recent division of powers cases include *R. v. Crown Zellerbach Ltd.*, [1988] I.S.C.R. 401; *Friends of the Oldman River Society v. Canada (Minister of Transport)*, [1992] 1 S.C.R. 3; *Alberta Government Telephones v. Canada (Canadian Radio-television and Telecommunications Commission)*, [1989] 2 S.C.R. 225; and *Téléphone Guèvremont Inc. v. Quebec (Régis des télécommunications)*, [1994] 1 S.C.R. 878.
6. Some of the leading criticisms include V.C. MacDonald, "Judicial Interpretation of the Canadian Constitution," *University of Toronto Law Journal* 1 (1935–36), pp. 260–85, and the *O'Connor Report*, Senate of Canada, 1939. It is ironic that judicial interpretation contributed to decentralizing a centralized Canadian federation but centralized a decentralized federation in the United States. See Roger Gibbins, *Regionalism* (Toronto: Butterworths, 1982), ch. 4.
7. Alan C. Cairns, "The Governments and Societies of Canadian Federalism," *Canadian Journal of Political Science* (December 1977), pp. 695–725.
8. Alan C. Cairns, "The Judicial Committee and Its Critics," *Canadian Journal of Political Science* (September 1971), pp. 301–45, and reprinted in Cairns, *Constitution, Government and Society in Canada* (Toronto: McClelland and Stewart, 1988).
9. *Constitution, Government, and Society in Canada*, p. 63.
10. Some of the leading sources on this subject include House of Commons Task Force on Federal–Provincial Fiscal Arrangements, *Fiscal Federalism in Canada* (Ottawa: Supply and Services, 1981); the annual publications of the Canadian Tax Foundation, *The National Finances and Provincial and Municipal Finances*; and D.V. Smiley's many works on Canadian federalism.
11. The distinction is usually expressed as follows: direct taxes are derived from the very people who are intended to pay them, while indirect taxes are extracted from one person in the expectation that they will be passed on to someone else.
12. On this point, see Keith Banting, *The Welfare State and Canadian Federalism* (Kingston: McGill–Queen's University Press, 1982), pp. 52–54; Canada, *Federal–Provincial Grants and the Spending Power of Parliament: Working Paper on the Constitution* (Ottawa: Queen's Printer, 1970); Canada, *Income Security and Social Services* (Ottawa: Queen's Printer, 1969); D.V. Smiley and R.M. Burns, "Canadian Federalism and the Spending Power: Is Constitutional Restriction Necessary?" *Canadian Tax Journal* 17 (1969), pp. 468–82; and Andrew Petter, "Federalism and the Myth of the Federal Spending Power," *Canadian Bar Review* (September 1989), pp. 448–79.

13. T.J. Courchene, *Equalization Payments: Past, Present and Future* (Toronto: Ontario Economic Council, 1984).

14. G.V. La Forest, *The Allocation of Taxing Powers Under the Canadian Constitution*, 2nd ed. (Toronto: Canadian Tax Foundation, 1981).

15. Richard Simeon, *Natural Resource Revenues and Canadian Federalism: A Survey of the Issues* (Kingston: Institute of Intergovernmental Relations, 1980).

16. Canadian Tax Foundation, *Provincial and Municipal Finances*, 1989, p. 12:1.

17. G.V. La Forest, *Disallowance and Reservation of Provincial Legislation* (Ottawa: Queen's Printer, 1965).

18. Andrew Heard, *Canadian Constitutional Conventions* (Toronto: Oxford University Press, 1991).

19. This discussion is loosely based on J.R. Mallory, "The Five Faces of Canadian Federalism," in P.-A. Crépeau and C.B. Macpherson, eds., *The Future of Canadian Federalism* (Toronto: University of Toronto Press, 1965) and reproduced in the various editions of Peter Meekison's *Canadian Federalism: Myth or Reality* (Toronto: Methuen, 1977). See also E.R. Black, *Divided Loyalties: Canadian Concepts of Federalism* (Montreal: McGill–Queen's University Press, 1975).

20. Donald Smiley, *Canada in Question: Federalism in the Seventies* (Toronto: McGraw-Hill Ryerson, 1972), p. 56.

21. Ibid.

22. Heard, *Canadian Constitutional Conventions*, pp. 110–16.

23. In his *Federal–Provincial Diplomacy* (Toronto: University of Toronto Press, 1972), Richard Simeon outlines many of the informal practices that have grown up around this institution.

24. J. Stefan Dupré, "Reflections on the Workability of Executive Federalism," in Richard Simeon, ed., *Intergovernmental Relations* (Toronto: University of Toronto Press, 1985), and D.V. Smiley, *The Federal Condition in Canada* (Toronto: McGraw-Hill Ryerson, 1987), pp. 87–89.

25. Much has been written on the wartime and postwar influence of the "mandarins." See especially J.L. Granatstein, *The Ottawa Men: The Civil Service Mandarins 1935–1957* (Toronto: Oxford University Press, 1982).

26. Mallory, "The Five Faces of Canadian Federalism."

27. The Meech Lake Accord is addressed in Chapter 3.

28. Among the best sources on this subject are the annual reviews published by the Queen's University Institute of Intergovernmental Relations since 1980. Some of them are listed in the sources at the end of this chapter by name of author. See also David Milne, *Tug of War: Ottawa and the Provinces under Trudeau and Mulroney* (Toronto: Lorimer, 1986); R.O. Olling and M.W. Westmacott, eds., *Perspectives on Canadian Federalism* (Scarborough: Prentice-Hall Canada, 1988); Bruce Pollard, *Managing the Interface: Intergovernmental Affairs Agencies in Canada* (Kingston: Institute of Intergovernmental Affairs, 1986); Garth Stevenson, *Unfulfilled Union*, 3rd. ed. (Toronto: Gage, 1989); and Garth Stevenson, ed., *Federalism in Canada: Selected Essays* (Toronto: McClelland and Stewart, 1989); François Rocher and Miriam Smith, *New Trends in Canadian Federalism* (Peterborough: Broadview, 1995); Garth Stevenson, "Federalism and Intergovernmental Relations," in Michael Whittington and Glen Williams, eds., *Canadian Politics in the 1990s*, 4th ed. (Scarborough: Nelson Canada, 1995); and Ian Robinson and Richard Simeon, "The Dynamics of Canadian Federalism," in James Bickerton and Alain Gagnon, eds., *Canadian Politics*, 2nd ed. (Peterborough: Broadview, 1994).

29. Privy Council Office, *Federal–Provincial Programs and Activities: A Descriptive Inventory 1993–1994 and 1994–1995* (Ottawa: 1995).

30. Ironically, it was Pierre Trudeau who told the socialist academic community in 1961 that they should not be so obsessed with centralization; that progressive social policies could sometimes be pioneered more successfully at the provincial level. "The Practice and Theory of Federalism," in Michael Oliver, ed., *Social Purpose for Canada* (Toronto: University of Toronto Press, 1961).

31. See, for example, John Porter, *The Vertical Mosaic* (Toronto: University of Toronto Press, 1965).

32. J.R. Mallory, *Social Credit and the Federal Power in Canada* (Toronto: University of Toronto Press, 1954).

FURTHER READING

Banting, Keith. *The Welfare State and Canadian Federalism*. Kingston: McGill–Queen's University Press, 1982; 2nd ed., 1987.

Black, E.R. *Divided Loyalties: Canadian Concepts of Federalism*. Montreal: McGill–Queen's University Press, 1975.

Brown, Douglas M., ed. *Canada: The State of the Federation*. Kingston: Institute of Intergovernmental Relations, Queen's University, annual.

Cairns, Alan C. "The Judicial Committee and Its Critics." *Canadian Journal of Political Science* (September 1971), pp. 301–45.

———. "The Governments and Societies of Canadian Federalism," *Canadian Journal of Political Science* (December 1977), pp. 695–725.

———. *Constitution, Government, and Society in Canada*. Toronto: McClelland and Stewart, 1988.

Canadian Tax Foundation. *The National Finances*. Toronto, biennial.

Heard, Andrew. *Canadian Constitutional Conventions*. Toronto: Oxford University Press, 1991.

Hogg, Peter. *Constitutional Law of Canada*, 2nd ed. Toronto: Carswell, 1985.

La Forest, G.V. *Disallowance and Reservation of Provincial Legislation*. Ottawa: Queen's Printer, 1965.

———. *The Allocation of Taxing Powers under the Canadian Constitution*, 2nd ed. Toronto: Canadian Tax Foundation, 1981.

MacDonald, V.C. "Judicial Interpretation of the Canadian Constitution." *University of Toronto Law Journal* 1 (1935–36), pp. 260–85.

Mallory, J.R. "The Five Faces of Canadian Federalism." In P.-A. Crépeau and C.B. Macpherson, eds. *The Future of Canadian Federalism*. Toronto: University of Toronto Press, 1965.

Meekison, J. Peter, ed. *Canadian Federalism: Myth or Reality*, 3rd ed. Toronto: Methuen, 1977.

Milne, David. *Tug of War: Ottawa and the Provinces under Trudeau and Mulroney*. Toronto: Lorimer, 1986.

Norrie, K., et al. *Federalism and Economic Union in Canada*. Toronto: University of Toronto Press, 1985.

Olling, R.O., and M.W. Westmacott, eds. *Perspectives on Canadian Federalism*. Scarborough: Prentice-Hall, 1988.

Petter, Andrew. "Federalism and the Myth of the Federal Spending Power." *Canadian Bar Review* (September 1989), pp. 448–79.

Pollard, Bruce. *Managing the Interface: Intergovernmental Affairs Agencies in Canada*. Kingston: Institute of Intergovernmental Affairs, 1986.

Privy Council Office. *Federal–Provincial Programs and Activities: A Descriptive Inventory, 1993–1994 and 1994–1995*. Ottawa: Supply and Services, 1995.

Rocher, François, and Miriam Smith, eds. *New Trends in Canadian Federalism*. Peterborough: Broadview, 1995.

Russell, Peter, et al. *Federalism and the Charter*. Ottawa: Carleton University Press, 1989.

Seidle, Leslie. *Seeking a New Canadian Partnership: Asymmetrical and Confederal Options*. Montreal: Institute for Research on Public Policy, 1994.

Shugarman, David, and Reg Whitaker, eds. *Federalism and Political Community*. Peterborough: Broadview Press, 1989.

Simeon, Richard. *The Political Economy of Canadian Federalism: 1940–1984*. Toronto: University of Toronto Press, 1985.

———, ed. *Division of Powers and Public Policy*. Toronto: University of Toronto Press, 1985.

———, ed. *Intergovernmental Relations*. Toronto: University of Toronto Press, 1985.

Smiley, D.V. *The Canadian Political Nationality*. Toronto: Methuen, 1967.

———, *The Federal Condition in Canada*. Toronto: McGraw-Hill Ryerson, 1987.

Smiley, D.V., and R.L. Watts. *Intrastate Federalism in Canada*. Toronto: University of Toronto Press, 1985.

Stevenson, Garth. *Unfulfilled Union*. 3rd ed. Toronto: Gage, 1989.

———, ed. *Federalism in Canada: Selected Essays*. Toronto: McClelland and Stewart, 1989.

Swinton, Katherine. *The Supreme Court and Canadian Federalism: The Laskin–Dickson Years*. Toronto: Carswell, 1990.

Trudeau, Pierre Elliott. "The Practice and Theory of Federalism." In Michael Oliver, ed. *Social Purpose for Canada*. Toronto: University of Toronto Press, 1961.

Watts, R.L., and D.M. Brown, eds. *Canada: The State of the Federation*, 1990. Kingston: Institute of Intergovernmental Relations, 1990.

Wheare, K.C. *Federal Government*, 4th ed. London: Oxford University Press, 1963.

Chapter 5

The CHARTER OF RIGHTS *and freedoms*

Does freedom of association guarantee the right to strike? Does freedom of expression prohibit restrictions on pornography and prostitution? Is restriction of Sunday shopping a violation of freedom of religion? Does a person have the right to counsel when stopped by a police officer to take a breath test? Should terminally ill people be allowed to end their own lives? Should tobacco companies be allowed to advertise cigarettes? Is extreme drunkenness an excuse for committing rape or murder?

Civil liberties consist of rights and freedoms that individuals enjoy beyond the reach of the government or the state. Such rights and freedoms are an integral part of a democratic political system and represent territory into which the government is not allowed to enter as it makes and enforces public policy for a society. They have recently been entrenched in the Canadian Constitution in the form of the Charter of Rights and Freedoms, and it is increasingly the task of the judiciary to determine if and when governments have encroached upon them.

This chapter begins by defining civil liberties and discussing the means of protecting them in Canada before 1982. The central part of the chapter examines the provisions of the Charter of Rights and Freedoms and the principal court cases that interpreted each clause up to mid-1995. It concludes by discussing the implications of the Charter for the overall political system.

DEFINING AND PROTECTING CIVIL LIBERTIES

Civil liberties are commonly classified into four categories.[1] The first relates to political liberty, including the **fundamental freedoms** of speech, press, assembly, and religion. The second, **legal rights**, includes the procedural rights of a person suspected or accused of committing a crime, a liberty encompassing that person's right to legal counsel, a presumption of innocence, bail, and a fair trial. The third aspect of civil liberty involves **equality rights**, that is, freedom from discrimination on such bases as gender, race, religion, or age. Canadians almost universally support these three categories of civil liberties, and they are therefore embedded and expanded on in the Charter of Rights and Freedoms. The fourth category of civil liberties, economic rights, is more controversial. While the right to own property, for example, is widely adhered to and recognized in law as well as in the Bill of Rights, it has not been enshrined in the Charter.[2]

Political systems that value civil liberties have adopted two principal methods to protect them. The British approach is to make Parliament supreme, but on the presumption that neither the legislature nor the executive would infringe civil liberties because both are held in check by public opinion, tradition, the political culture, and self-restraint. Civil liberties are so deeply engrained in the values of the people and politicians alike that the latter would never think of infringing them, even though, in theory, Parliament could do so. While the courts cannot overturn legislation in Britain—that is, they do not have the power of **judicial review**—they have wide **judicial discretion** in the interpretation of laws, and many civil libertarian values have been introduced into the law as canons of interpretation.[3] Thus, even in the British system, judicial precedents accumulated into the **common law** offer some protection against arbitrary government action. So does the basic constitutional principle, the rule of law, which requires that every official act be based on law.

The American approach, derived in reaction to an imperial government that *did* encroach on colonial liberties, is to provide for a written statement of civil liberties (usually called "civil rights") in the Constitution or in a constitutional Bill of Rights. Then, if legislation is passed or the executive takes action that is felt to violate a person's rights, such acts can be challenged in the courts. It is up to the courts to determine whether the government has infringed civil liberties as defined in the Constitution. The courts thus have the power of judicial review and can overturn offensive legislation or executive acts.

Before we explore the role of judicial review in greater detail, it should be added that while bills and charters of rights restrict the actions of *governments*, they do not extend in most cases to private, interpersonal relationships. Prohibitions against private discrimination, such as in employment and accommodation, are instead generally covered by human rights codes. Each province has such a Code, as does the federal government, and they are enforced by human rights commissions through investigation, conciliation, and, if necessary, adjudication of disputes.[4]

. . . .

EN ROUTE TO THE CHARTER

A discussion of protecting civil liberties in Canada can be divided into three eras. In the first place, Canada inherited the British system based on parliamentary restraint within parliamentary supremacy, but the Canadian situation was complicated by the adoption of federalism. Hence, Canada possessed two supreme legislatures, one in Ottawa and another in the provinces, each operating within its own constitutional jurisdiction. Federalism allowed the courts to engage in judicial review in the sense of invalidating federal or provincial legislation that violated the division of powers. In so doing, federalism opened the door to judicial review in the protection of civil liberties. That is, if the courts could show that either level of government infringed civil liberties in the process of exceeding its jurisdiction in terms of the division of powers, then the courts could strike down the law.

Thus, even before the adoption of a constitutional bill or charter of rights, the Canadian courts were able to intervene to a limited extent to overturn legislation that violated civil liberties. The simultaneous violation of the division of powers and civil liberties most often took place at the provincial level, where the courts found provincial legislation infringing federal power in the realm of criminal law.

Because a division of powers case would still allow the other level of government to pass legislation offensive to civil liberties, the courts sometimes supplemented this ground for their decisions by citing the preamble to the 1867 Constitution Act. It speaks of Canada's desire to have "a constitution similar in principle to that of Great Britain." Since Britain recognized civil liberties (albeit without judicial review), Canadians should enjoy them too. This interpretation, sometimes called an **implied bill of rights**, would have allowed the courts to go beyond the division of powers in striking down legislation that violated civil liberties, but it was rarely and inconsistently applied.[5]

Three principal cases of judicial protection of civil liberties arose in the period before 1960. First, freedom of the press was at issue in the 1938 *Alberta Press Bill* case. Among other things, Alberta legislation allowed the government to order newspapers to reveal the sources of unfavourable comment and gave it the right to respond to criticism. The courts found this legislation invalid because it was an infringement of the federal criminal law power.[6] In 1953, the freedom of religion of Jehovah's Witnesses in Quebec was at stake, this time in requiring them to obtain permission from the chief of police before they could distribute their literature on the sidewalk. Once again the federal criminal law power and the preamble proved to be useful in overturning a provincial law.[7] In 1957 the Supreme Court disposed of Premier Maurice Duplessis's **Padlock Law** on the same grounds. This law had given the premier and the attorney general the power to padlock any building that Duplessis considered was being used for the propagation of communism and bolshevism, but left these terms undefined and was used against opposition groups of any kind.[8]

Another means of protecting civil liberties even in the pre-1960 period was to find executive actions to be contrary to the rule of law. This ground was used successfully on three occasions with respect to police and government treatment of Jehovah's Witnesses in the Duplessis period in Quebec. In the most famous case, the court found the premier himself had acted contrary to the rule of law: that is, he took action not based on law, when he personally cancelled Roncarelli's liquor licence because of his dislike of Jehovah's Witnesses.[9]

Violations of civil liberties that did not also violate the division of powers gave the courts little discretion. For example, in a 1903 case that concerned denial of the vote to Asians in British Columbia provincial elections, the courts ruled that such electoral matters were entirely within the jurisdiction of provincial politicians.[10] Neither did Canadian blacks find any satisfaction in the courts when they challenged discriminatory practices.[11] While the federal government was generally more sensitive to the civil liberties than the provinces, its record was not unblemished, especially in the case of the Winnipeg General Strike and in its treatment of citizens of certain ethnic groups during the two world wars. Ottawa's outrageous internment of Canadian citizens of Japanese extraction during the Second World War proved both that the federal government was not above reproach and that the courts could do nothing about it.[12]

The fact that both federal and provincial politicians would stoop to such violations of civil liberties and the realization that the courts could not be counted on to invalidate them unless they also contained a division of powers problem persuaded John Diefenbaker to enact the **Canadian Bill of Rights** in 1960.[13] This document inaugurated the second era in the protection of civil liberties in Canada. The bill's apparent aim was to allow the courts to invalidate legislation that they found to conflict with the Bill of Rights, but if so, this aim was not clearly articulated. The courts were never completely certain if they had been given this power or not. Other serious gaps in the bill were that it only applied to the federal government, not to the provinces; that it allowed legislation to be passed that overrode the bill, as long as this was acknowledged (that is, a notwithstanding clause); that as an ordinary piece of legislation, the bill could be amended in the routine way; and that it was superseded by the **War Measures Act**, at the very time when it might be needed most.

Not surprisingly, the courts made very limited use of the Bill of Rights. In only one case, the *Drybones* case of 1970, did they decide that a clause of an act violated the Bill of Rights and was therefore inoperative.[14] The Bill was more useful in clarifying legal rights and was referred to in several cases to fill in gaps in such definitions as what was meant by the "right to counsel," the "right to an interpreter," and the "right to a fair hearing."[15]

Several other cases arose regarding violations of civil liberties within federal jurisdiction, but in each case the Court found a way around applying the Bill of Rights.[16] At the same time, provinces continued to violate civil liberties, but the Bill of Rights was of even less assistance in these cases.[17]

THE CHARTER OF RIGHTS AND FREEDOMS

Recognizing the limitations and ambiguities of the Canadian Bill of Rights, and wanting to incorporate new kinds of rights into the Constitution, several politicians, most notably Pierre Trudeau, attempted to improve it. Ironically, in the midst of this quest, Trudeau invoked the War Measures Act in 1970 and used it to encroach on freedom of speech as well as to throw innocent, nonviolent Quebec separatists in jail. Finally, in 1982, with the adoption of the **Canadian Charter of Rights and Freedoms**, he accomplished his objective. The Charter essentially replaced the Bill of Rights, using much of its language in the sections on fundamental freedoms and legal rights, but going beyond it to include democratic, linguistic, mobility, egalitarian, and limited aboriginal rights.

CATEGORIES OF RIGHTS IN THE CHARTER OF RIGHTS & FREEDOMS

- fundamental freedoms
- democratic rights
- mobility rights
- legal rights
- equality rights
- language rights
- aboriginal rights

Trudeau not only wanted to remedy the deficiencies in the Bill of Rights; he was also determined to protect official minority language rights across the country in an effort to undercut Quebec's claim that it represented French Canada. Moreover, Trudeau hoped to counter centrifugal forces throughout the land and pressures for general decentralization to the provinces by creating an instrument that the courts could use to cut down self-serving provincial laws. As a new national symbol, the Charter would increase the allegiance of all citizens to the national government.

The Charter is generally a much stronger document than its predecessor. Besides being broader in scope, the Charter applies equally to both federal and provincial governments, and being entrenched into the Constitution, it is difficult to amend. It also states very clearly that the courts are to invalidate any legislation that they feel conflicts with the provisions of the Charter.

On the other hand, the rights articulated in the Charter are not absolute. In the first place, section 1 indicates that such rights are subject to "such reasonable limits, defined by law, as can be demonstrably justified in a free and democratic society." The courts are thus allowed to find that, while a piece of legislation does violate certain rights, it is still acceptable according to their definition of **reasonable limits**. Second, in the areas of fundamental freedoms, legal rights, and equality rights, either level of government is allowed to pass legislation contrary to the Charter by means of the notwithstanding clause, section 33. Governments were not expected to acknowledge in advance that legislation was contrary to the Charter, so the **notwithstanding clause** would normally come into play when legislation was introduced to override a judicial decision regarding a Charter right. Such a bill can only be exempted from the provisions of the Charter for a five-year period, after which it becomes inoperative if not repassed for another five years.

The Charter of Rights and Freedoms with its concomitant politicization of the judiciary has profoundly affected the operation of the Canadian political system.[18] Let us now examine the provisions of the Charter and see how they have been interpreted by the courts, especially the Supreme Court of Canada. The following discussion only sketches the broad lines of Charter interpretation during its first 13 years of operation, and is not intended to be a definitive statement of the law.

The Reasonable Limits Clause

Section 1 is often called the "reasonable limits" clause. It reads as follows:

> The Canadian Charter of Rights and Freedoms guarantees the rights and freedoms set out in it subject only to such reasonable limits prescribed by law as can be demonstrably justified in a free and democratic society.

The Supreme Court has made extensive use of section 1, upholding many laws that it considered to be in violation of Charter rights but that were saved by being reasonable limits upon them. At the very least, restrictions on Charter rights must be "prescribed by law." For example, after striking down Ontario's first film censorship law because the statute did not stipulate any standards for cutting or banning films, the Supreme Court approved of a revised statute in which the criteria were more clearly articulated in the law. In other words, film censorship is a reasonable limit on freedom of expression as long as the criteria of the censors were "prescribed by law."[19]

As for restrictions that can be "demonstrably justified in a free and democratic society," the Court developed guidelines in the *Oakes* case, which have come to be called the **Oakes test**.[20] First, the objective of the government in limiting a right must be pressing and substantial; second, the means must be proportional to that objective. Three criteria are attached to this second point: the limit must be rationally connected to the government objective; it should impair the right as little as is necessary in order to achieve the objective; and the costs must be proportional to their benefits. The Oakes test has been applied in subsequent interpretations of the reasonable limits clause in a large proportion of Charter cases.

Fundamental Freedoms

Section 2 lists the following **fundamental freedoms**:

> (a) freedom of conscience and religion;
> (b) freedom of thought, belief, opinion and expression, including freedom of the press and other media of communication;
> (c) freedom of peaceful assembly; and
> (d) freedom of association.

FREEDOM OF RELIGION

With respect to freedom of religion, the Supreme Court threw out the Lord's Day Act as an infringement of freedom of religion because its restrictions on Sunday activities were clearly related to the Christian sabbath and discriminated against other religions. When Ontario passed the Retail Business Holidays Act, designed to prevent Sunday shopping with certain exceptions and to preserve Sunday as a day of rest but on a secular rather than a religious foundation, the Court found this to be valid. The Court also ruled that a father could not use freedom of religion to justify teaching his children in the basement of his church rather than sending them to the public school system. A number of cases have taken the view that a child welfare authority may approve of a blood transfusion for a child despite the parents' religious beliefs to the contrary. Public schools may no longer hold a compulsory and exclusively Christian school prayer or religious studies classes. On the other hand, while Ontario's publicly funded Roman Catholic separate school system has been upheld as a pre-Charter constitutional right, public funding for other private religious schools is not guaranteed.[21]

FREEDOM OF EXPRESSION

With respect to freedom of expression, a wide range of issues has been brought before the courts. Perhaps most controversial was the Supreme Court's rejection of the French-only sign provision of Quebec's Bill 101, which was actually a violation of Quebec's own Charter of Rights as well. The Court decided that freedom of expression not only included the freedom to express ideas, but also the freedom to choose the language in which to express them. Moreover, the concept of freedom of expression incorporated commercial expression. In this case, the Court hinted that it would be a reasonable limit on freedom of commercial expression in Quebec if the law were amended to provide for the *predominant* rather than the *exclusive* use of French on commercial signs.[22] Freedom of commercial expression also justified the negation of the federal prohibition of cigarette advertising.

In cases involving anti-Semitic denials of the Holocaust, the Court threw out the Criminal Code provision prohibiting the spreading of false news, but a majority turned around and concluded that the section prohibiting the dissemination of hate literature was a reasonable limit on freedom of expression.[23]

Several freedom of expression cases have involved the labour movement. The Court ruled that freedom of expression includes the freedom of trade unions to engage in picketing, even secondary picketing, but it is a reasonable limit on that right to prohibit the picketing of courthouses by court employees.[24]

Other cases have arisen in connection with election campaigns. Attaching posters on public property including utility poles was protected by freedom of expression, and paying a portion of the campaign expenses of candidates and parties from the public purse does not infringe a taxpayer's right to freedom of expression. On the other hand, limits on third-party advertising during election campaigns have thus far been invalidated. Federal legislation prohibiting public servants from engaging in electoral work for a political party or candidate was found to be invalid, but the more balanced Ontario legislation on the subject was upheld.[25]

Freedom of expression encompasses freedom of the press, and several cases have dealt with this issue. The Court found it a reasonable limit that the Criminal Code requires judges to prohibit the publication of the name of the victim of sexual assault if the victim so requests, but not to prohibit the public from attending a trial under the Juvenile Delinquents Act. Compelling journalists to reveal their sources of information, prohibiting the CBC from showing the mini-series *The Boys of St. Vincent*, and restricting media coverage of the Paul Bernardo case before his trial are other issues that have been addressed by judicial decisions. The Nova Scotia legislature was even allowed to limit media access to its proceedings, and Quebec was allowed to restrict advertising aimed at children.[26]

Obscenity also falls into this category, where one main case stands out, *R. v. Butler*. The Court divided pornography into different categories, saying that portrayals of sex with violence and sex that is degrading or dehumanizing can be restricted by the authorities, but that a portrayal of explicit sex that is neither violent nor degrading is generally acceptable unless it depicts children. In a later case, an artist's depiction of children in various sexual activities was deemed to be art rather than pornography.[27] As for prostitution, the Supreme Court upheld the prohibition on communicating for the purposes of sidewalk solicitation, Chief Justice Brian Dickson feeling that this was a reasonable limit on freedom of expression.[28] Interestingly, the two women on the Court dissented, finding that the Code infringed both freedom of expression and association and was not a reasonable limit on them.

FREEDOM OF PEACEFUL ASSEMBLY AND ASSOCIATION

In another controversial decision, the Supreme Court ruled that freedom of association does not guarantee the right of trade unions to strike. Thus freedom of association does not prevent federal or provincial legislatures from passing back-to-work legislation or otherwise interfering in the collective bargaining process. Justices Dickson and Wilson dissented on this decision, arguing that the freedom to belong to a union is of little value if the union cannot engage in a strike as a last resort. Labour was happier with the ultimate disposition of the *Lavigne* case in which the Court rejected Mr. Lavigne's objection to part of his union dues going to support causes with which he did not agree.[29]

Democratic Rights

Under **Democratic Rights** in sections 3 to 5, the Charter guarantees that every citizen of Canada has the right to vote in federal and provincial elections; that no parliament can continue for more than five years from the previous election, except in time of real or apprehended war, invasion, or insurrection; and that each parliament must sit at least once every year. Section 3 has been used in several cases dealing with federal and provincial electoral laws that deny the vote to certain categories of people. At the national level, it was used in the course of the 1988 election to invalidate two provisions in the Canada Elections Act that denied the vote to federally appointed judges and patients in mental institutions. Many similar cases have arisen in connection with provincial electoral laws, especially relating to prisoners, persons on parole, and those remanded but not yet charged. In 1993 the Supreme Court agreed with the Federal Court of Canada that denying prisoners the right to vote violated section 3, but in the meantime, the law had been amended to allow those serving less than two years to vote.[30]

Another interesting application of section 3 arose in cases involving the drawing of provincial constituency boundaries, especially in B.C. and Saskatchewan. Indeed, the courts surprised many observers by ruling that such a matter came within the scope of section 3. In the 1989 *Dixon* case in British Columbia, the electoral map was thrown out because constituency boundaries did not approach equality of voting power and such disparities could not be justified on any other grounds. In Saskatchewan, the Court of Appeal invalidated that province's electoral map in 1991 primarily because of disparities between the size of urban and rural ridings, but on a quick appeal a divided Supreme Court of Canada re-established it. Even though the electoral map systematically overrepresented rural voters, a majority of the Court decided that they would not insist on greater equality in the size of constituencies because "effective representation" had been achieved. Other cases have not gone as far as the Supreme Court of Canada, but the P.E.I. electoral map was disallowed by the courts of that province, while the Alberta map was upheld.[31]

Mobility Rights

Under section 6, **Mobility Rights**, every citizen of Canada has the right to enter, remain in, and leave Canada, and every citizen or permanent resident has the right to take up residence and pursue the gaining of a livelihood in any province. On the other hand, laws providing for reasonable residency requirements for receiving public services are acceptable, as are laws that give preference to local residents if the unemployment rate in that province is higher than the national rate. Mobility rights were included in the Charter because of Pierre Trudeau's concern that some provinces were restricting the entry of residents of other provinces, as in the case of cross-border employment. Mobility rights have not featured frequently in judicial interpretation, but have arisen in unanticipated ways. It is often professionals—usually lawyers—denied permission to practise in a particular province who have tried to use mobility rights to their advantage. They have generally been unsuccessful because the Court has said that section 6 does not guarantee the "right to work." But while it has upheld the right of each province to establish its own professional qualifications, these cannot be based on provincial boundaries. On the other hand, P.E.I. legislation that taxed non-residents at a higher level than residents did not violate section 6.[32]

Legal Rights

Legal rights are contained in sections 7 to 14. In section 7, everyone has the right to life, liberty, and security of the person and the right not to be deprived thereof except in accordance with the principles of fundamental justice. "Security of the person" was used as the main basis for throwing out the abortion provision of the Criminal Code in the famous *Morgentaler* case in 1988. A majority of the Court ruled that that law, with all its arbitrary and bureaucratic procedures, violated the security of the person of the woman concerned and constituted a "profound interference with a woman's body." Having invalidated the abortion law in the *Morgentaler* case, the Court declined to rule in the absence of any legislation in the *Borowski* case on whether the "right to life" included any fetal rights. But in the *Daigle* case, the Court found no fetal right to life in the Quebec Charter of Rights, the Canadian Criminal Code or the common law, and ruled that the "father" has no right to prevent an abortion.[33] Sue Rodriguez was not so fortunate in persuading the Court that security of the person provided her with the right to an assisted suicide—only a minority of judges agreed with her.[34]

Security of the person was also involved in the *Operation Dismantle* case. The Supreme Court ruled that the causal link between American Cruise missile testing in Canada and the threat to the security of the person because of the potential escalation of the international arms race was uncertain, speculative, and hypothetical.[35]

"Security of the person" and "fundamental justice" combined in the *Singh* case to require the Immigration Department to provide an oral hearing for refugee claimants when their life could be in danger if deported. Fundamental justice necessitated giving such claimants an opportunity to state their case and to know the case against them. This case was the cause of much of the subsequent backlog in the Immigration Department. Fundamental justice was also violated, the Court ruled, in connection with B.C. legislation that could suspend a person's driving privileges without his or her knowledge and then fine or imprison the person when caught.[36]

Section 8 establishes the right to be secure against unreasonable search and seizure. In the case of collusion between the Southam and Thomson newspaper chains, the Court decided in the *Southam* case that a reasonable search by the police or other government authorities

Reprinted with permission.

had to be authorized by statute and conducted after a search warrant was issued by an impartial arbiter who had reasonable and probable grounds to believe that an offence had been committed and that the evidence was located in the place to be searched. This decision did nothing to remedy the feebleness of the Combines Investigation Act. Many cases in this realm have arisen with respect to drug seizures, with the general rule being that a search will not be wrongful if authorized by law, if the law itself is reasonable, and if the search is conducted in a reasonable manner. Similarly, a police officer's demand to see a person's driver's licence and insurance card during a spot check is not an unreasonable search. But taking blood samples without legal authorization and strip searches at Canadian border points without the opportunity to contact counsel were outlawed.[37]

Section 9 grants the right not to be arbitrarily detained or imprisoned, and section 10 reads that on arrest or detention, everyone has the right to be informed promptly of the reasons, and the right to contact a lawyer without delay and to be informed of that right. A huge number of Charter cases have arisen in this connection; the Court has ruled that random police spot checks are a reasonable limit on the right not to be arbitrarily detained, and that roadside breath tests do not include the right to retain counsel. However, if a person fails that test and is asked to accompany the police officer to a police station, the individual has a right to retain counsel before the police station breathalyzer test. In the *Clarkson* case, an intoxicated woman who voluntarily waived her right to counsel and then proceeded to confess to the murder of her husband was acquitted because she was not aware of the consequences of not having counsel present, and the double-murder confessions of a man with an I.Q. of less than 80 were not admitted as evidence because he did not understand his rights. Moreover, the Court has ruled that a person has the right to be told of his or her right not only to a lawyer but also to legal aid, and must have a reasonable opportunity to exercise these rights. In a 1995 case, for example, a man convicted of rape and murder was granted a new trial because he had been subjected to an "intensive and manipulative interrogation by police" during which his repeated request to consult a lawyer was ignored.[38]

Section 11 includes a variety of rights available to a person charged with an offence. "To be tried within a reasonable time" has been extremely controversial after the *Askov* decision, which found that a delay of almost two years between a preliminary hearing and a trial had been excessive. The lower courts took this to mean that everyone had a right to a trial within six to eight months of being charged, and some 34 500 cases were thrown out in Ontario alone. The Supreme Court then took the unprecedented initiative to point out in a speech by one of its members that this was not what the *Askov* decision intended.[39]

Persons charged cannot be compelled to testify against themselves, cannot be denied reasonable bail without just cause, and are presumed innocent until proven guilty according to law in a fair and public hearing by an independent and impartial tribunal. The "impartial tribunal" was addressed in the *Valente* case, cited again in Chapter 23. In this connection, the Supreme Court also found that before 1992, the Crown had an unfair advantage in naming stand-by prospective jurors and in having a greater number of peremptory challenges in the jury selection process. The presumption of innocence was addressed in the *Oakes* case. Under the "reverse onus" clause of the Narcotics Control Act, a person proved to be in possession of a narcotic was also presumed to be guilty of trafficking and it was up to the person charged with possession to prove his or her innocence on the trafficking charge. Although many observers find this to be a perfectly acceptable requirement, the *Oakes* case invalidated this clause as an unreasonable limit on the presumption of innocence. On the other hand, a person occupying the driver's seat of a vehicle is presumed to have "care and control" of the vehicle unless he or she can prove otherwise. Thus, even if the vehicle is not in motion, an intoxicated person in the driver's seat can be convicted of impaired driving. The Court has also ruled that indiscreet remarks by politicians about a case before the courts, however regrettable, cannot be used as a defence to throw the case out. Persons charged are guaranteed trial by jury where the maximum punishment for the offence is imprisonment for five years or more, and, whether finally acquitted of the offence or found guilty and punished, cannot to be tried for it again.[40]

Everyone has the right not to be subjected to any cruel and unusual treatment or punishment. In this connection, the Court ruled that a minimum sentence of seven years for illegally importing any quantity of narcotic into Canada was excessive. Indeterminate sentences for dangerous offenders have, however, been upheld.[41]

The final clause of section 11 provides that a party or witness in any proceedings who does not understand or speak the language in which the proceedings are conducted or who is deaf has the right to the assistance of an interpreter.

Equality Rights

Equality rights are contained in section 15, which reads as follows:

(1) Every individual is equal before and under the law and has the right to the equal protection and equal benefit of the law without discrimination and, in particular, without discrimination based on race, national or ethnic origin, colour, religion, sex, age or mental or physical disability.

(2) Subsection (1) does not preclude any law, program or activity that has as its object the amelioration of conditions of disadvantaged individuals or groups including those that are disadvantaged because of race, national or ethnic origin, colour, religion, sex, age or mental or physical disability.

In the *Andrews* case the Supreme Court laid down a two-step process for interpreting equality rights.[42] The Court first determines if there has been a violation of the equality rights listed in section 15 (or of others analogous to them), and then whether there has been a discrimination, that is, a harmful or prejudicial effect. In other words, inequalities and distinctions are permitted if no negative discrimination is involved. The Court overturned the 1978 Bill of Rights decision that allowed the Unemployment Insurance Commission to discriminate against pregnant women because they were pregnant, not because they were women. In addition, the Court ruled that provincial human rights codes must not prevent girls from playing on boys' athletic teams. In 1995, the Supreme Court ruled unanimously that the Charter prohibited discrimination on the basis of sexual orientation, even though this was not explicitly listed in section 15, but a majority then found that the case in question (old age spousal benefits for a same-sex couple) was subject to reasonable limits. Reasonable limits has been used to justify certain other kinds of discrimination as well. In the case of mandatory retirement, for example, the Court ruled that while such a policy was a violation of equality rights and did involve discrimination, it was reasonable for laws to require retirement at age 65.[43] According to Ian Greene, the Court made it clear that "it intends to interpret section 15 to help clearly disadvantaged groups in society."[44] Whether or not this has always been the case, subsection (b) does permit **affirmative action** programs that give preference to those who have been discriminated against in the past.

Official Languages of Canada

Sections 16 to 22 of the Charter constitutionalize the federal and New Brunswick official languages acts and reaffirm the limited official bilingualism of Quebec and Manitoba. These sections guarantee that certain government agencies will operate on a bilingual basis, as discussed in Chapter 8. Although judicial interpretation of linguistic rights has been extensive, it related almost exclusively to the original provisions of the 1867 Constitution Act as well as the 1870 Manitoba Act rather than to the 1982 Charter. The extension of official bilingualism in the federal and New Brunswick official languages acts was ruled valid; several aspects of Quebec's Bill 101 were invalidated because they conflicted with section 133 of the BNA Act; the 1890 Official Language Act of Manitoba, which removed French as an official language in the province, was thrown out as a violation of the Manitoba Act; and the Supreme Court then required Manitoba to translate all its laws into French.[45] As noted above, the unilingual sign provisions of Bill 101 were challenged in terms of freedom of expression rather than on the basis of sections 16 to 23.

Minority Language Education Rights

Section 23 deals with constitutional **minority language education rights**, and some would argue that they were the only part of the Charter with which Pierre Trudeau was truly concerned.[46] Section 23 has come before the courts in two main contexts. First, the Supreme Court struck down the provision in Bill 101 that allowed only the children of parents who were themselves products of the English school system in Quebec to go to that system, essentially those who were already there (the "Quebec clause"). Indeed, section 23 (the "Canada clause") was deliberately drafted so that it would conflict with this clause, in order that Canadian citizens who moved to Quebec could also send their children to the English schools. The clause limits such access in all provinces to areas "where numbers warrant." The Supreme Court decided not only that the number of francophone students in Edmonton warranted a French-language school, for example, but also that it must have a "distinct physical setting" and that French-language parents must have a say in the "management and control" of it.[47]

Enforcement

Section 24 makes clear, where the Bill of Rights did not, that the courts have the power to interpret the Charter and to invalidate laws that conflict with it. It also moves in the American direction with regard to the admissibility of evidence. The Charter does not actually bar illegally obtained evidence, as in the United States; the admission of such evidence is acceptable as long as it does not bring the administration of justice into disrepute. The Supreme Court laid the basis for interpreting this section in the *Collins* case.[48] First, evidence should be excluded if it would prejudice the fairness of the trial, and second, the more seriously the obtainment of the evidence violated the Charter, the more compelling was the need to exclude it. In the third place, however, if to *exclude* the evidence would bring the judicial system into disrepute, the evidence should *not* be excluded. Such questionable evidence usually related to a violation of the right to counsel or to an unreasonable search or seizure.

General Provisions

Sections 25 through 30 relate to specific groups in society, and will be discussed in relevant chapters later in the book. Section 25 says that the rights and freedoms in the Charter shall not be construed so as to abrogate or derogate from any aboriginal, treaty, or other rights or freedoms that pertain to the aboriginal peoples of Canada including any rights or freedoms that have been recognized by the Royal Proclamation of October 7, 1763, and any rights or freedoms that may be acquired by the aboriginal peoples of Canada by way of land claims settlement. The potential of the Charter to advance aboriginal rights has never been clear, but an encouraging sign emerged from the *Sparrow* case. In acquitting an Indian from the offence of using a bigger fishing net than authorized by law, the Supreme Court asserted that governments must bear the burden of proving laws are necessary if they have a negative effect on any aboriginal right. In another early case on the subject of treaty rights, the Court ruled that an ancient treaty-based fishing right took precedence over a Quebec law that prohibited fishing in provincial parks. On the other hand, Native land claims have not yet received much judicial support.[49]

Section 27 asserts that the Charter shall be interpreted in a manner consistent with the preservation and enhancement of the multicultural heritage of Canadians, and section 28 reads that notwithstanding anything in the Charter, the rights and freedoms referred to in it are guaranteed equally to male and female persons. The women's movement considered the addition of section 28 essential so that governments would not be able to use the notwithstanding clause (section 33) to override the gender equality provision of section 15. According to section 29, nothing in the Charter abrogates or derogates from any rights or privileges guaranteed by or under the Constitution of Canada in respect of denominational, separate, or dissentient schools. Section 29 protects section 93 of the 1867 Constitution Act, which guaranteed existing Protestant and Roman Catholic separate schools. Although section 93 clearly discriminates against other religions, the drafters of the Charter did not want to take responsibility for altering rights established in the original Constitution.[50]

Application of the Charter

Section 32 clarifies that the Charter applies to the Parliament and government of Canada, including the Yukon and Northwest Territories, and to the legislature and government of each province. By implication, it also applies to the municipal level of government. Thus all legislation in Canada must be consistent with the Charter, as must all actions of government executives—ministers, public servants, police officers, and so on. It is not intended to apply to the private sector, but certain institutions occupy an ambiguous position. While the courts interpret the Charter, for example, it is not certain whether their own actions are governed by it.[51] The Charter has been applied to law societies because they have been delegated governmental powers, and community colleges, but more autonomous semi-public institutions such as hospitals and universities are exempt.[52] As mentioned earlier, federal and provincial human rights codes rather than the Charter regulate certain aspects of the private sector. But since such codes take the form of laws, they must also remain consistent with the Charter.[53]

The Notwithstanding Clause

Section 33 is the famous "notwithstanding" clause. Parliament or legislatures may override three parts of the Charter—fundamental freedoms (section 2), legal rights (sections 7–14), and equality rights (section 15)—but not democratic rights, mobility rights, or linguistic rights. This provision was a compromise between provincial premiers, who wanted the clause to apply to the whole Charter, and Pierre Trudeau, who was adamant that it could not be used to circumvent the three sections about which he cared most. For the sections it covers, all that a federal or provincial legislature has to do is expressly declare in a statute that the act or a provision thereof shall operate notwithstanding what the Charter says. If such action is taken, however, it is only good for five years, after which it lapses or must be re-enacted.

Despite the number of times the Supreme Court has thrown out federal or provincial legislation since 1982, governments have rarely re-enacted such provisions under section 33. Over the first 13 years, it was used only in Saskatchewan and Quebec. The government of Grant Devine used section 33 even before a court interpretation of its back-to-work legislation to settle a public-service strike in 1986 and before the Alberta Labour reference made such use of the notwithstanding clause unnecessary. During the first Parti Québécois period in Quebec, up to 1985, the notwithstanding clause was routinely applied, as a matter of principle, to all new legislation passed in that province as well as to all pre-1982 laws. The government of Robert Bourassa discontinued that practice, but used the notwithstanding clause to get around the Supreme Court decision with respect to bilingual signs in the province. As mentioned, when the Supreme Court ruled that French-only store signs violated their owners' freedom of expression, Bourassa invoked section 33 (and the equivalent clause in the Quebec Charter of Rights) and then passed what he considered to be a compromise law that allowed certain English signs *inside* the store. While this incident in particular gave the notwithstanding clause a negative reception in most of English Canada, section 33 is often defended as a general principle. It allows democratically elected legislators to have the final say in many areas and takes pressure off judges to solve political crises because they know that politicians can, if necessary, override their strictly legal decisions.[54]

IMPLICATIONS OF JUDICIAL INTERPRETATION OF THE CHARTER

Both before its adoption and after 13 years of experience, the Charter of Rights and Freedoms attracted passionate support and opposition. Supporters and opponents alike agree, however, that the adoption of the Charter has significantly changed the operation of the Canadian political system. The courts have become involved in almost all of the most difficult political issues that have arisen over the past 13 years: aboriginal rights, abortion, assisted suicide, French-only signs, gender equality, impaired driving, mandatory retirement, minority language schools, official bilingualism, political rights of public servants, prostitution, redistribution of constituency boundaries, the right to strike, same-sex spousal benefits, separate schools, Sunday shopping, tobacco advertising and testing the Cruise missile.[55] Such cases have enmeshed the courts in considerable political controversy and, as Russell says, the Charter has "judicialized politics and politicized the judiciary."[56]

As for the politicization of the judiciary, the new political role of the courts is sometimes exploited by the politicians. After the *Morgentaler* decision, for example, the Mulroney government pressured the Supreme Court to delay the Borowski hearing until after new abortion legislation had been passed by Parliament. According to Greene, this "was obviously a strategy to keep the abortion issue out of the public spotlight until after the imminent federal election."[57] On the other hand, politicians are "often quite relieved to have controversial and unpredictable issues transformed into 'nonpartisan' questions about rights and about the correct interpretation of the Constitution so they can be taken off their hands and resolved in the courts."[58] The Supreme Court itself has made some very political moves, and members of the Court make little effort to divorce themselves from the hurly-burly of daily political developments in Ottawa.[59]

One main implication of the Charter is that public consciousness of the policy-making role of the courts has created greater interest in the quality of judicial appointments. In some ways this is advantageous, for that quality has not been overly impressive in the past. On the other hand, to begin selecting judges on the basis of their ideological orientation would be another regrettable element in the Americanization of the Canadian system.

The most scathing attack on the "legalization of politics" in Canada has been made by law professor Michael Mandel. He mounts five main arguments. First, an enormous "leeway" exists within which the courts make highly political decisions, but judges disguise their work through legal interpretations and abstract principles that are unintelligible to the general public. Mandel challenges the generally accepted view that while politicians make popular, political, self-serving decisions, judges' decisions are impartial, objective, technical, rational, and in the public interest. Marc Gold supports Mandel in this view in writing that "judicial rhetoric functions both to obscure the true basis for the decision reached and to sensitize the audience into accepting the result as both legitimate and appropriate."[60] Especially given the reasonable limits clause, almost every Charter case could have been decided differently, and the content of Canadians' rights has "depended to a large extent upon which judges happened to sit on the panels that heard the cases." Canadian scholars are thus beginning to examine the records of individual Supreme Court judges and to categorize them ideologically.[61]

Mandel's second argument is that while the Charter has been sold as enhancing democracy and the power of the people, it has really reduced the degree of popular control over government by transferring power from representative, accountable legislatures and politicians to unrepresentative, unaccountable, and unrestrained judges, courts, and an elitist legal profession. "It is both simpler and cheaper to get to see your MP than to get to see a judge."[62]

In the third place, legalized politics enhances individual and corporate rights against the collective welfare of the community (as in the tobacco advertising decision) and is therefore part of the Americanization of Canada. The adoption of individualistic American values in the Charter, as opposed to traditional Canadian collectivism, is strengthened by the tendency of the courts to cite American precedents when making their decisions.[63]

Mandel's fourth point is that legalized politics is conservative, class-based politics that defends existing social arrangements and undermines popular movements. For a variety of reasons including the cost of litigation, the background and attitudes of judges, the biases in the law and the Charter, the socially disadvantaged and labour unions were better off without it. "The Charter is capable of opposing every kind of discrimination but class discrimination."[64]

Finally, Mandel argues that Canadians have come to attribute such significance to Charter rights that we are in danger of forgetting the much more important social rights about which it is silent. Is the right to have one's child educated in a certain language more important than to educate children at public expense? Is the distribution of trade union funds more important than the basic right of collective bargaining with the possibility of a strike? Is the right of a doctor to work in a hospital after 65 years of age more important than a basic right to public health services? In making these points, Mandel at least offers a reminder to question the face value of court decisions, to refrain from glorifying the Charter, judges, lawyers, and courts, and to remember traditional ways of making public decisions.

Another implication of the adoption of the Charter, as Mandel and others have pointed out, is that minority groups increasingly ignore the usual political processes—legislatures, cabinets, and bureaucracies—and take their demands to the courts instead.[65] To some extent this has happened when such groups were unable to accomplish their goals through traditional political activity, in which case this alternative avenue is advantageous. However, groups may simply believe it is less trouble to go to court rather than to engage in the struggle of mobilizing popular support for their cause. Few observers, even in the legal profession, would welcome a general transformation of political activity into legal activity with the attendant loss of political skills and organization that traditionally characterize a democracy. Seymour Martin Lipset fears that the Charter will remove one of the last traits that distinguish Canadians from Americans by increasing the litigious character of citizen–state relations and bring about a "rights-centred" political culture.[66]

While reflecting the fact that it was born of political compromise, the Charter nonetheless retains one main limitation on judicial interpretation. As long as they say so explicitly, legislatures may pass an act violating certain aspects of the Charter or pass a law in spite of a judicial decision that it is unconstitutional. Canadians are left with a strange system under which the courts can overrule the legislatures but the legislatures can overrule the courts. Rank Canadian political compromise that it is, this system of protecting civil liberties may turn out to be superior to either total legislative supremacy or exclusive judicial review. Some observers advocate the abolition of the notwithstanding clause, but others (including the author), not wanting to entrust their fate entirely either to legislatures or to courts, prefer the check and balance that they provide to each other.

A final implication of the Charter has to do with its effects on the federal–provincial relationship. Some researchers have found that the Supreme Court has constructed principles of interpretation that accommodated provincial policy diversities, but others discovered a centralist thrust to its interpretation, much as Trudeau intended. In its first ten years of operation, the Supreme Court invalidated 41 statutes, 23 federal and 18 provincial. But most of the federal nullifications involved procedural, legal questions rather than salient issues. On the other hand, 13 of the provincial statutes invalidated were more substantive in nature, eight of them involving minority language rights, and most frequently in Quebec. In this and other policy fields, the Charter has "transferred authority ... out of provincial legislatures and into the federal courts." Morton and Knopff have coined the term "court party" to describe the link between "Charter groups" such as official language minorities, feminists, civil libertarians, aboriginals, visible minorities, people with disabilities, and gay men and lesbians, and the ascendancy of judicial power in Canadian politics. "Ottawa has been able to forge a strategic alliance with select, non–territorial-based interest groups and with sympathetic federally-appointed judges" at the expense of the provinces.[67] In this respect the Charter is working even better than Trudeau anticipated.

CONCLUSION

The protection of civil liberties in Canada has always occupied an intermediate position between the parliamentary sovereignty of Britain and the judicial review of the United States. The adoption of the Charter of Rights and Freedoms moved the country considerably closer to the U.S. model. As time goes on, its unconscious influence on the Canadian political culture and the use of U.S. precedents by the Supreme Court of Canada will probably enhance this southward pull. On the other hand, the reasonable limits and notwithstanding clauses in the Charter are unique Canadian responses to the question.

P Of the approaches outlined in Chapter 1, pluralists are most enthusiastic about the addition of the Charter of Rights in the protection of civil liberties in Canada. In defending individualist values and lauding the Charter in protecting them, pluralists draw their inspiration from the ideology of liberalism as articulated by such philosophers as John Locke and John Stuart Mill. Liberalism emphasizes the basic rationality of all people and advocates equality and liberty as embodied in the fundamental freedoms—of speech, press, religion, and association—and in the rule of law. Pluralists thus point out how often very ordinary people have gained from Charter restraints on police and from such decisions as the right to be informed of the right to legal aid. Pluralists expect that equality rights together with affirmative action programs will help to remove various kinds of discrimination. They also believe that judicial decisions have been ideologically balanced, citing the *Lavigne* case, which ultimately ended in a pro-labour decision even if many previous ones were anti-labour. Rather than be concerned that the legalization of politics has discouraged groups and popular movements from engaging in traditional political organization, pluralists welcome an additional means by which such demands can be advanced, and point to special programs to fund certain kinds of Charter challenges.

C Class analysts have a less positive view of the Charter, which follows the general line of argument made by Mandel above. Charter rights have often been used to benefit corporations rather than individuals, such as in the *Big M Drug Mart*, tobacco advertising, and *Southam* cases. The stringent search requirements laid down in the latter case constituted another blow to the already weak laws restricting corporate collusion in Canada.[68] On the other hand, the Court denied unions a constitutional right to strike, and showed more sympathy to nonunionized workers (in the *Edwards* case) than to organized workers because the former were much less of "a threat to the social status quo."[69] Mandel cites the *Singh* and *Morgentaler* cases as two of the few where the socially disadvantaged appeared to have benefited from a Charter decision, but he reminds us to look at subsequent attempts by governments to dilute these victories through legislation and regulation. Moreover, the costs of taking cases to the courts are generally prohibitive except to wealthy individuals and corporations, and in 1992 the Mulroney government cancelled the Court Challenges Program that had funded many Charter cases, although the Liberals later resurrected it. Mandel also stresses the Charter's preference for individualism over collectivism, adding that it "unites people against the state but the result is to leave them at the mercy of private power."[70]

Class analysts also emphasize the elitist background of judges and question whether they can make fair decisions for the ordinary mortals who appear in court. For example, Andrew Petter writes,

> there is nothing about the Canadian judiciary to suggest that they possess the experience, the training or the disposition to comprehend the social impact of claims made to them under the Charter, let alone to resolve those claims in ways that promote, or even protect, the interests of lower income Canadians.[71]

(SC) In one sense, a Charter of Rights or other means of restraining government action is contrary to the view of state-centred theorists. The *Singh* decision, for example, necessitated a complete overhaul of the refugee admission system, and the *Askov* decision created chaos in the Ontario court system. On the other hand, state-centred theorists emphasize the frequency with which the Supreme Court has used the "reasonable limits" clause to justify state infringement of Charter rights, such as on film censorship, soliciting, Holocaust deniers, and some kinds of picketing. In addition, they point out that the Charter has been used far more often to restrict individual police actions than to overturn major government policies, such as in Operation Dismantle.

DISCUSSION QUESTIONS

1. What are the advantages and disadvantages of the "reasonable limits" clause in the Charter?

2. What are the advantages and disadvantages of the "notwithstanding" clause in the Charter?

3. What is your opinion of court decisions with respect to:
   (a) section 2?
   (b) section 3?
   (c) section 7?
   (d) section 10?
   (e) section 11?
   (f) section 15?
   (g) section 24?

4. Are Supreme Court decisions impartial and technical or biased and political?

5. Does the Charter enhance democracy or restrain it?

6. Does legalized Charter politics inherently discriminate against the socially disadvantaged?

7. Does the Charter discourage traditional political activity?

8. How do the approaches outlined in Chapter 1 relate to the material in this chapter?

NOTES

1. For example, Peter Hogg, *Constitutional Law of Canada*, 2nd ed. (Toronto: Carswell, 1985), ch. 28.
2. Alexander Alvaro, "Why Property Rights Were Excluded from the Canadian Charter of Rights and Freedoms," *Canadian Journal of Political Science* (June 1991), pp. 309–29.
3. While the British courts do not have such power, the European Court of Justice, part of the European Union, can make nonbinding decisions on whether British acts violate civil liberties.
4. On the other hand, the Supreme Court has occasionally found violations of Charter rights *within* provincial human rights codes, and, unless protected by the reasonable limits clause, has expunged them.
5. It was first articulated in the *Alberta Press Bill* case and used as a supplementary argument to criminal law in several cases, but never on its own.
6. *Reference Re Alberta Statutes*, [1938] S.C.R. 100.
7. *Saumer v. City of Quebec*, [1953] S.C.R. 299.
8. *Switzman v. Elbling and Attorney-General of Quebec*, [1957] S.C.R. 285.
9. *Roncarelli v. Duplessis*, [1959] S.C.R. 121. In *Chaput v. Romain*, [1955], S.C.R. 834 police had broken up a private meeting of Jehovah's Witnesses, and in *Lamb v. Benoit*, [1959], S.C.R. 321 the police arrested Jehovah's Witnesses for distributing their literature. In all three cases, action of the authorities was ruled contrary to the rule of law.
10. *Cunningham v. Tomey Homma*, [1903] A.C. 151. On the other hand, the federal power over naturalization and aliens had allowed the Court to overturn an earlier anti-Asian law in B.C. in *Union Colliery Co. of B.C. Ltd. v. Bryden*, [1899] A.C. 580.
11. Ian Greene, *The Charter of Rights* (Toronto: Lorimer, 1989), p. 18.
12. Thomas Berger, *Fragile Freedoms*, rev. ed. (Toronto: Clarke Irwin, 1982). Greene also refers to the secret trials held in connection with the Gouzenko spy affair in 1945, in *The Charter of Rights*, p. 21.
13. Walter Tarnopolsky, *The Canadian Bill of Rights*, 2nd rev. ed. (Toronto: McClelland and Stewart, 1975). Saskatchewan had an earlier provincial Bill of Rights, while Alberta and Quebec each passed one later. These provincial bills of rights could not be constitutionally entrenched any more than the federal one was.
14. *R. v. Drybones*, [1970] S.C.R. 282. The Indian Act created a liquor offence that had harsher penalties for Indians than the equivalent offence for non-Indians.
15. These respective cases are *Brownridge v. The Queen*, [1972] S.C.R. 926; *A.-G. Ont. v. Reale*, [1975] 2 S.C.R. 624; and *Lowry and Lepper v. The Queen*, [1974] 26 D.L.R. (3rd) 224.
16. *Robertson and Rosetanni v. The Queen*, [1963] S.C.R. 651 (upholding the regulation of operating hours of a bowling alley based on the Lord's Day Act); *A.G. Can. v. Lavell and Isaac v. Bédard*, [1974] S.C.R. 1349 (upholding a distinction in the Indian Act between men and women marrying whites); *Hogan v. The Queen*, [1975] 2 S.C.R. 574 (denying the right to counsel before taking a breathalyzer test, after the *Brownridge* case had upheld such a right).
17. *Oil, Chemical and Atomic Workers International Union v. Imperial Oil Ltd. and A.-G. B.C.*, [1963] S.C.R. 584 (denying unions the right to contribute to the NDP via a check-off procedure); *Walter v. A.-G. Alta.*, [1969] S.C.R. 383 (upholding Alberta legislation restricting the settlement of Hutterites); *Morgan v. A.-G. P.E.I.*, [1976] 2 S.C.R. 349 (upholding P.E.I. legislation restricting the ownership of land in the province to P.E.I. residents); *A.-G. Can. and Dupond v. Montreal*, [1978] 2 S.C.R. 770 (upholding a Montreal bylaw prohibiting parades and public gatherings); and *Nova Scotia Board of Censors v. McNeil*, [1978] 2 S.C.R. 662 (upholding provincial film censorship boards).
18. See, for example, Rainer Knopff and F.L. Morton, *Charter Politics* (Scarborough: Nelson Canada, 1992).
19. *Re Ontario Film and Video Appreciation Society and Ontario Board of Censors*, [1984] 45 O.R. (2d) 80.
20. *R. v. Oakes*, [1986] 1 S.C.R. 103.
21. *R. v. Big M Drug Mart Ltd.*, [1985] 1 S.C.R. 295. Of course, Big M itself had no religion, but "worshipped only the Almighty Dollar." Michael Mandel, *The Charter of Rights and the Legalization of Politics in Canada* (Toronto: Wall & Thompson, 1989), p. 225. *R. v. Edwards Books and Art Ltd.*, [1986] 2 S.C.R. 713. Chief Justice Dickson's famous passage about a restful, recreational Sunday is located on

p. 770. *R. v. Jones*, [1986] 2 S.C.R. 284. *Zylberberg et al. v. The Director of Education of the Sudbury Board of Education* (1988), 65 O.R. 641 (Ont. C.A.); *Alder v. Ontario*, [1994] 116 D.L.R. (4th) 1 (Ont. C.A.); and *Re Davis* (1982), Can. Charter of Rights Ann. 9.1-1 (Alta. Prov. Ct.—Fam. Div.).

22. *Ford v. Quebec* (Attorney General), [1988] 2 S.C.R. 712; *Devine v. Quebec* (Attorney General), [1988] 2 S.C.R. 790.

23. *R. v. Keegstra*, [1990] 3 S.C.R. 697; *R. v. Zundel*, [1992] S.C.R. 731.

24. *RWDSU v. Dolphin Delivery Ltd.*, [1986] 2 S.C.R. 573; *B.C.G.E.U. v. British Columbia (Attorney General)*, [1988] 2 S.C.R. 214.

25. *Osborne v. Canada* (Treasury Board), [1991] 2 S.C.R. 69.

26. *Her Majesty the Queen v. Canadian Newspapers*, [1988] 2 S.C.R. 122; *Canadian Broadcasting Corp. v. New Brunswick (Attorney General)*, [1994], 116 D.L.R. (4th) 506 (N.B.C.A.); *Irwin Toy Ltd. v. Quebec (Attorney General)*, [1989] 1 S.C.R. 927; and *Dagenais v. Canadian Broadcasting Corp*.

27. *R. v. Butler*, [1992] 1 S.C.R. 452.

28. *R. v. Skinner*, [1990] 1 S.C.R. 1235.

29. *Reference re Public Service Employee Relations Act, Labour Relations Act, and Police Officers Collective Bargaining Act of Alberta*, [1987] 1 S.C.R. 313. Two other simultaneous cases made up the "labour trilogy": *Public Service Alliance of Canada v. The Queen*, [1987] 1 S.C.R. 424, and *Saskatchewan v. Retail, Wholesale and Department Store Union*, [1987] 1 S.C.R. 460. According to Mandel, however, Dickson "always had section 1 in the back of his mind," *The Charter of Rights*, p. 194. *Lavigne v. Ontario Public Service Employees Union*, [1991] 81 D.L.R. (4th) 545 (S.C.C.).

30. *Canadian Disability Rights Council v. Canada*, [1988] 21 F.T.R. 268 (T.D.); *Belczowski v. Canada* [1993] 2 S.C.R. 438.

31. *Dixon v. British Columbia (Attorney General)*, [1989] 59 D.L.R. (4th) 247 (B.C.S.C.); *Reference Re Provincial Electoral Boundaries (Sask.)*, [1991] 2 S.C.R. 158.

32. *Law Society of Upper Canada v. Skapinker*, [1984] 1 S.C.R. 357; *Black v. Law Society of Alberta*, [1989] 1 S.C.R. 591; *Basile v. Attorney-General of Nova Scotia*, [1984] 11 D.L.R. (4th) 219 (N.S.C.A.).

33. *R. v. Morgentaler*, [1988] 1 S.C.R. 30; *Borowski v. Canada (Attorney General)*, [1989] 1 S.C.R. 342.

34. *Rodriguez v. British Columbia (Attorney General)*, [1993] 24 C.R. (4th) 281 (S.C.C.).

35. *Operation Dismantle Inc. v. The Queen*, [1985] 1 S.C.R. 441.

36. *Singh v. Minister of Employment and Immigration*, [1985] 1 S.C.R. 177; *Re B.C. Motor Vehicle Act*, [1985] 2 S.C.R. 486. For other uses of section 7, see *R. v. Beare*; *R. v. Higgins*, [1988] 2 S.C.R. 387.

37. *Hunter v. Southam Inc.*, [1984] 2 S.C.R. 145; *R. v. Dyment*, [1988] 2 S.C.R. 417; *R. v. Simmons*, [1988] 2 S.C.R. 495; *R. v. Hufsky*, [1988] 1 S.C.R. 621; *R. v. Thomson*, [1988] 1 S.C.R. 640; and *R. v. Ladouceur*, [1990] 1 S.C.R. 957.

38. *R. v. Therens*, [1985] 1 S.C.R. 613; *Clarkson v. The Queen*, [1986] 1 S.C.R. 383; *R. v. Manninen*, [1987] 1 S.C.R. 1233; *R. v. Brydges*, [1990] 1 S.C.R. 190; Terrence Burlingham case.

39. *R. v. Askov*, [1990] 2 S.C.R. 1199; *R. v. Rahey*, [1987] 1 S.C.R. 588.

40. *R. v. Whyte*, [1988] 2 S.C.R. 3. A person in possession of house-breaking instruments can also be required to prove they were intended for another purpose. *R. v. Holmes*, [1988] 1 S.C.R. 914; *R. v. Vermette*, [1988] 1 S.C.R. 985.

41. *R. v. Smith (Edward Dewey)*, [1987] 1 S.C.R. 1045; *R. v. Lyons*, [1987] 2 S.C.R. 309; *R. v. Milne*, [1987] 2 S.C.R. 512.

42. *Andrews v. Law Society of British Columbia*, [1989] 1 S.C.R. 143.

43. The Bill of Rights case was *Bliss v. A.-G. Can.*, [1979] S.C.R. 183; the Charter case which overturned it was *Brooks v. Canada Safeway Ltd.*, [1989] 1 S.C.R. 1219; the Supreme Court refused to review the Ontario Court of Appeal ruling in the *Blainey* case, which found that this was not a case of reasonable limits; *McKinney v. University of Guelph*, [1990] 3 S.C.R. 229. The Court would defer to legislatures in this area, so that the latter were free to abolish or retain mandatory retirement, as they wished. The 1995 sexual orientation case involved James Egan and Jack Nesbit.

44. Greene, *The Charter of Rights*, p. 172.

45. *Jones v. A.G. New Brunswick*, [1975] 2 S.C.R. 182; *Attorney General of Quebec v. Blaikie*, [1979] 2 S.C.R. 1016; *A.G. Manitoba v. Forest*, [1979] 2 S.C.R. 1032; *Reference Re Manitoba Language Rights*,

[1985] 1 S.C.R. 721; *Order Re Manitoba Language Rights*, [1985] 2 S.C.R. 347; *Bilodeau v. Attorney General Manitoba*, [1986] 1 S.C.R. 449; and *Reference Re Manitoba Language Rights*, [1992] 1 S.C.R. 272.

46. Both Mandel and Greene support my contention here.

47. *Attorney General of Quebec v. Quebec Association of Protestant School Boards*, [1984] 2 S.C.R. 66; *Mahe v. Alberta*, [1990] 1 S.C.R. 342.

48. *R. v. Collins*, [1987] 1 S.C.R. 265.

49. *R. v. Sparrow*, [1990] 1 S.C.R. 1075; *R. v. Sioui*, [1990] 1 S.C.R. 1025; *Ontario (Attorney General) v. Bear Island Foundation*, 1991, on the Native land claim in the Temagami area.

50. *Reference Re Bill 30, An Act to Amend the Education Act (Ont.)*, [1987] 1 S.C.R. 1148. The Ontario Court of Appeal made greater use of this section than did the Supreme Court of Canada.

51. This was addressed in the *Dolphin Delivery* case. In a complicated decision it was determined that a court order enforcing the common law in a private litigation (a court injunction to prevent secondary picketing) did not constitute government action and was not covered by the Charter. Thus, in order to invoke the Charter, either the government had to be a party or some statute or regulation had to infringe a right. Mandel, *The Charter of Rights*, p. 205.

52. *McKinney v. University of Guelph*. But the *Lavigne* case treated community colleges as part of government.

53. The *Blainey* case found that a clause in the Ontario Human Rights Code allowed discrimination against women in sports organizations, and since this was inconsistent with the Charter, it was held to be of no force or effect and was later repealed. This case demonstrates how the Charter can indirectly affect the private sector.

54. Greene, *The Charter of Rights*, p. 107.

55. While these cases are of greatest interest to political science, the largest number of Charter cases involved legal rights. See F.L. Morton, Peter Russell, and Michael Withey, "Judging the Judges: The Supreme Court's First One Hundred Charter Decisions," in Paul Fox and Graham White, eds., *Politics: Canada*, 7th ed. (Toronto: McGraw-Hill Ryerson, 1991).

56. Peter Russell, "The Political Purposes of the Canadian Charter of Rights and Freedoms," *Canadian Bar Review* (March 1983).

57. Marc Gold, "The Mask of Objectivity: Politics and Rhetoric in the Supreme Court of Canada," *The Supreme Court Law Review 7* (1985), p. 458.

58. Andrew Heard, "The Charter in the Supreme Court of Canada: The Importance of Which Judges Hear an Appeal," *Canadian Journal of Political Science* (June 1991); Morton, Russell, and Withey, "Judging the Judges."

59. The Court repeatedly linked Quebec and Manitoba language cases, for example, to balance pro-French with pro-English cases, and backtracked on language rights after the Parti Québécois was safely out of power. Even more political were the Court decisions that paved the way for the adoption of the Charter in the *Patriation Reference* of 1981 and the *Quebec Veto Reference* of 1982. Marc Gold writes, for example, that "however much a judicial opinion may reflect how the court actually reached its decision, it is clear that the opinion should be viewed primarily as a portrayal of how the court wanted itself to be viewed in reaching that decision," p. 457.

60. Gold, "The Mask of Objectivity," p. 458.

61. Heard, "The Charter in the Supreme Court of Canada: The Importance of Which Judges Hear an Appeal," pp. 289–307; Morton, Russell, and Withey, "Judging the Judges."

62. Mandel, *The Charter of Rights*, p. 59.

63. Christopher Manfredi, "The Use of United States Decisions by the Supreme Court of Canada under the Charter of Rights and Freedoms," *Canadian Journal of Political Science* (September 1990), pp. 499–518.

64. Mandel, *The Charter of Rights*, p. 300. Mandel ridicules David Beatty's *Putting the Charter to Work: Designing a Constitutional Labour Code* (Kingston: McGill–Queen's University Press, 1987), which argues that labour should welcome the adoption of the Charter, pp. 199–202.

65. See Russell, "The Political Purposes of the Charter of Rights and Freedoms."

66. Seymour Martin Lipset, *Continental Divide* (New York: Routledge, 1990).

67. F.L. Morton and Reiner Knopff, "The Charter Revolution and the Court Party," *Osgoode Hall Law Journal* (Fall 1992); F.L. Morton, "Federalism and the Charter of Rights: Empowering the Centre," Canadian Political Science Association, June 1995.

68. Ontario Attorney General Roy McMurtry, one of the authors of the Charter, actually foresaw this possibility and referred to it in an address to a group of corporate lawyers in which he emphasized the value of the Charter for big business. He is now Chief Justice of Ontario. See Mandel, *The Charter of Rights*, p. 168–69.

69. Mandel, *The Charter of Rights*, p. 229.

70. Ibid., p. 301.

71. Quoted in Mandel, *The Charter of Rights*, p. 43.

FURTHER READING

Alvaro, Alexander. "Why Property Rights Were Excluded from the Canadian Charter of Rights and Freedoms." *Canadian Journal of Political Science* (June 1991).

Beatty, David. *Putting the Charter to Work.* Montreal: McGill–Queen's University Press, 1987.

Berger, Thomas. *Fragile Freedoms*, rev. and updated. Toronto: Clarke Irwin, 1982.

Borovoy, Alan. *When Freedoms Collide: The Case for Our Civil Liberties.* Toronto: Lester & Orpen Dennys, 1988.

Gold, Marc. "The Mask of Objectivity: Politics and Rhetoric in the Supreme Court of Canada." *The Supreme Court Law Review* 7 (1985).

Greene, Ian. *The Charter of Rights.* Toronto: Lorimer, 1989.

Heard, Andrew. "The Charter in the Supreme Court of Canada: The Importance of Which Judges Hear an Appeal." *Canadian Journal of Political Science* (June 1991).

Hiebert, Janet. "Fair Elections and Freedom of Expression under the Charter." *Journal of Canadian Studies* (Winter, 1989–90).

———. "The Evolution of the Limitation Clause." *Osgoode Hall Law Journal* (Spring 1990).

Knoff, Rainer, and F.L. Morton. *Charter Politics.* Scarborough: Nelson Canada, 1992.

Mandel, Michael. *The Charter of Rights and the Legalization of Politics in Canada.* Toronto: Wall and Thompson, 1989; rev. ed., 1994.

Manfredi, Christopher. "The Use of United States Decisions by the Supreme Court of Canada under the Charter of Rights and Freedoms." *Canadian Journal of Political Science* (September 1990).

———. *Judicial Power and the Charter.* Toronto: McClelland & Stewart, 1993.

Morton, F.L. "The Political Impact of the Canadian Charter of Rights and Freedoms." *Canadian Journal of Political Science* (March 1987).

Morton, F.L., Peter Russell, and Michael Withey. "Judging the Judges: The Supreme Court's First One Hundred Charter Decisions." In Paul Fox and Graham White, eds. *Politics: Canada*, 7th ed. Toronto: McGraw-Hill Ryerson, 1991.

Romanow, Roy. "Shortcomings and Dangers in the Charter." *Canadian Parliamentary Review* (Spring 1986).

Russell, Peter. "The Effect of a Charter of Rights on the Policy-Making Role of Canadian Courts." *Canadian Public Administration* (Spring 1982).

Russell, Peter. "The Political Purposes of the Canadian Charter of Rights and Freedoms." *Canadian Bar Review* (March 1983).

Russell, Peter, Rainer Knopff, and Ted Morton, eds. *Federalism and the Charter*. Ottawa: Carleton University Press, 1989.

Schmeiser, D.A. *Civil Liberties in Canada*. London: Oxford University Press, 1964.

Tarnopolsky, Walter. *The Canadian Bill of Rights*, 2nd, rev. ed. Toronto: McClelland and Stewart, 1975.

Tarnopolsky, Walter, and G.A. Beaudoin, eds. *The Canadian Charter of Rights and Freedoms: Commentary*. Toronto: Carswell, 1982.

PART 3

The Societal Context

The next seven chapters deal with the main elements of the societal or socioeconomic context of the Canadian political system. It is widely held that the aspects of Canadian society most relevant to politics are its regional–economic, ethnic, and class features, primarily because they represent deep, persistent divisions that are called cleavages. Hence we begin with chapters on regional–economic, ethnic/linguistic/cultural, and class cleavages. Many of the demands with which the authorities have to contend, or many of the interests that the authorities represent, originate from such cleavages.

Regionalism and conflicting regional–economic claims have been a constant of Canadian politics since the beginning and continue to be animating agents. The ethnic/linguistic/cultural policy field was traditionally dominated by the French–English question, but recent political developments justify separate chapters on aboriginal peoples and other ethnic groups and multiculturalism. The claims of the Native, French, English, and new Canadian communities have been legitimated in policy, law, and the

Constitution, such as in the recognition of aboriginal rights, official bilingualism, and multiculturalism, but the achievement of such recognition did not end ethnic conflict. That is partly because of the contrasting perceptions that each group has of its own history and current status. The class factor is not as obvious to many observers as some of the other cleavages, but it will become increasingly evident as governments curtail social programs as they approach the turn of the century.

It is now also common to point to the increasing importance of gender in the political system, making it time for a separate chapter on that question. Since other cleavages such as religion and age do not achieve the same political salience as those identified above, they are mentioned only in passing.

If the six factors mentioned constitute the principal components of the internal environment of the Canadian political system, they must be accompanied by a discussion of the external environment. The world has become a "global village," and international, multinational, transnational, and supranational factors are important elements of any national political system. This is especially true of Canada, which has always been open to such external influences.

Chapter 6

Regional–
ECONOMIC
cleavages

Manitoba was up in arms that the maintenance contract for the CF-18 military aircraft went to Quebec. Alberta was enraged at the National Energy Program. Quebec wants increased, if not exclusive, jurisdiction over social and economic policy. The Atlantic groundfish industry has collapsed, the Saskatchewan wheat industry has fallen on hard times, and both regions demand federal assistance. Ontario argues that the free trade deal, demanded by generations of Westerners, has caused thousands of layoffs in its manufacturing industry. Many Albertans question federal support for the Hibernia project in Newfoundland.

Regional–economic cleavages are a basic fact of Canadian life. Many government decisions are direct responses to such cleavages, and most policies at least have to take them into account. Regions usually have some concrete, physical foundation, and are more powerful when they correspond to explicit political divisions. But to some extent regions are also a state of mind. In any case, regional–economic cleavages can be most usefully discussed in terms of distance and division, regional–economic differences, regional–economic conflicts, and regional–economic disparities. These topics thus constitute the four parts of this chapter in its examination of the geography and economy of Canada.

DISTANCE AND DIVISION
Physiographic Regions

In terms of size, Canada's 9 922 000 km^2 pale beside Russia's 17 075 000 km^2, but exceed China's 9 597 000 km^2 and the United States's 9 363 000 km^2. From east to west Canada is 5 050 km long, and from southern to northern tip it stretches 4 600 km. The territory involved is vast, even the part below the 60th parallel, which has traditionally been of most interest to politicians because it is more densely populated and is organized into provinces. Prime Minister Mackenzie King once remarked that if some countries had too much history, Canada had too much geography.[1] In fact, St. John's, Newfoundland, is closer to London, England, than to Victoria, B.C., and many Canadians feel closer to adjacent U.S. states than to other Canadian regions. Such tremendous distances have always had a crucial influence on the Canadian political system, both in generating regional–economic demands and influencing patterns of support.

Distance would be difficult enough to cope with even if the territory involved was one level, undifferentiated plain, but the problem is immensely complicated by divisions caused by physical barriers. Canada is usually divided into five basic physiographic regions, as shown in Figure 6.1. The Atlantic provinces are in the rocky Appalachian region, while British Columbia and the Yukon are composed of the even more mountainous Western Cordillera. Extending in a great sweep around Hudson Bay is the rocky Canadian or Precambrian Shield. It encompasses most of Quebec and Ontario, northern parts of the Prairies, and melds into Arctic tundra above the 60th parallel. This leaves only two level plains regions, the Interior Plains of the Prairie provinces, and the Great Lakes–St. Lawrence Lowlands of southern Ontario and Quebec. In other words, the vast territory is divided into five main regions by natural barriers running in a north–south direction. In many ways it is simpler to travel from any of these regions southward to the United States than it is to cross the barriers into another part of Canada.

One aspect of Canadian geography that counterbalances these north–south forces is the river and lake system. In this respect, the central historical role of the St. Lawrence River and the Great Lakes has often been noted.[2] Since this natural east–west flow was enhanced by the construction of the St. Lawrence Seaway, ships have been able to go halfway across the country, a fact that improves Canada's capacity to engage in international trade.

Transportation and Communications Systems

Apart from the Great Lakes–St. Lawrence water route, transportation and communications systems in Canada had to be constructed across the natural barriers. The establishment of each of these great transportation and communications projects dominated successive eras in Canadian politics, and even on their completion demands continued to be expressed with respect to viability, maintenance, rates, and service.

Railways were the stuff of Canadian politics throughout the nineteenth and early twentieth centuries. In particular, they formed a crucial part of the Confederation Settlement of the 1860s and 1870s. The Maritimes agreed to enter Confederation only if they were linked to central Canada by the Intercolonial Railway, and British Columbia was persuaded to join in 1871 with the promise of a transcontinental rail link within ten years.[3] Political scandal involving railways then led to the defeat of Sir John A. Macdonald in 1872, but after his re-election in 1878 the construction of the Canadian Pacific Railway (CPR) to Vancouver became one of his lasting monuments. Macdonald brought the project to completion in 1885, only four years behind schedule.[4] Although it was a private company, the CPR received enormous government assistance in the form of cash and land grants that later became prime real estate in the centre of many Canadian cities. While the building of the CPR was one of the great heroic events in Canadian history, it was also a classic example of the state's being used for the advantage of private capital.[5]

Figure 6.1 **Canada's Physiographic Regions**

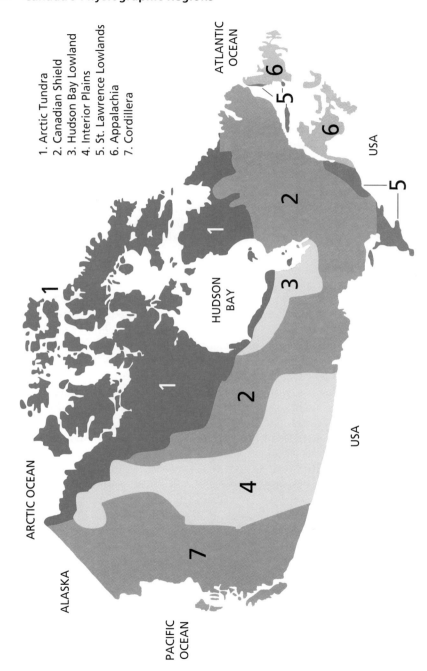

1. Arctic Tundra
2. Canadian Shield
3. Hudson Bay Lowland
4. Interior Plains
5. St. Lawrence Lowlands
6. Appalachia
7. Cordillera

Since the CPR served the southern part of Western Canada, demands immediately arose for other, more northerly routes. This was especially so because the Prairies chafed under the CPR monopoly clause that, in the absence of competition, allowed it to charge high rates. Indeed, freight rates have been a constant complaint of Western Canadians since the day the CPR was completed. Eventually other railways were built, but even with government assistance they went into receivership, and in the 1919–23 period they were bailed out by the federal government in the creation of the Canadian National (CN) system. Thus, the establishment of CN as a Crown corporation was a benefit to bankrupt capitalist interests.

When both CP and CN wanted out of the passenger side of the railroad business, a separate Crown corporation, VIA Rail, was created in 1977–78. Although politicians made initial promises about improving Canada's rail passenger service, the system was starved for funds and steadily declined until, because of large annual subsidies, the Mulroney government discontinued half the routes in 1990. Train enthusiasts howled in protest and argued that the extent of government subsidization of highway, marine and air transport should be taken into consideration when railway deficits were discussed. Nevertheless, rationalization of the country's railway system continued to be a major issue throughout the 1990s, with CP and CN both trying to buy each other out and with the Chrétien government's announcement in 1995 that it would privatize Canadian National by selling shares to the public.

The early twentieth century was almost as obsessed with automobiles as the previous era was with railways. Since roads are primarily a responsibility of the provinces, however, their political significance was and continues to be greatest at that level. The federal government was mainly called on to ensure that a decent highway existed across the whole country for commercial, recreational, and symbolic purposes. Thus, in 1949, the federal government signed the Trans-Canada Highway agreement with the provinces under which Ottawa paid one-half the cost of bringing a transcontinental highway up to a national standard. It was eventually completed in 1962, but not before some provinces demanded more than 50 percent, and Newfoundland in particular managed to secure some 90 percent of the funding from the federal government. Most provinces continue to demand that Ottawa help them finance the upgrading of their portion of the highway.

Given the distances involved, it is not surprising that demands also arose for a coordinated nation-wide airline service, passenger as well as freight. Transport Minister C.D. Howe negotiated a deal to create Trans-Canada Airlines (now Air Canada) as a joint private–public corporation, but when the private backers withdrew at the last minute, TCA was created in 1937 as a Crown corporation. Air Canada was later one of the Mulroney government's first candidates for privatization. Official thinking in the late 1980s was that the country was now well served by a variety of private carriers and that the government airline no longer served a **public policy purpose**. The federal government is thus substantially evacuating the transportation industry, a field in which it was historically very active. The Mulroney government privatized the Vancouver airport and tried to privatize Pearson International in Toronto, while the Chrétien government hoped to withdraw from the airport and harbour business more generally. This follows a deregulation of the whole transportation system as well, although the industry is still subject to some regulation by the National Transportation Agency. Demands from one region or another are constantly on the agenda of that agency too.

The weather map of canada:

Reprinted with the permission of Doubleday Canada.

MAJOR TRANSPORTATION AND COMMUNICATIONS LINKS AND AGENCIES WITH WHICH THE GOVERNMENT HAS BEEN ASSOCIATED

* Canadian Pacific
* Canadian National
* VIA Rail
* National Transportation Agency
* Trans-Canada Pipeline
* Canadian Radio-television and Telecommunications Commission (CRTC)
* Canadian Broadcasting Corporation (CBC)
* National Film Board
* Telesat
* Teleglobe

Oil and natural gas pipelines, a newer means of transportation, have figured prominently in Canadian politics since 1950. Sometimes the desire of Western provinces to sell petroleum coincided with that of Eastern Canadians' wish to buy it, but at other times inter-regional conflicts arose with respect to pricing, exportation, and importation of these resources. In any case, although privately owned, pipelines have sought considerable government support in one form or another. The construction of the main natural gas line to Eastern Canada, the **Trans-Canada Pipeline**, was probably the most controversial issue on the Canadian political agenda in the mid-1950s and had a major role to play in the defeat of the St. Laurent government in 1957.

Transportation presents special challenges in the North. Roads and railways were virtually nonexistent there until the Diefenbaker government sponsored its "Roads to Resources" program, and the Yellowknife region of the Northwest Territories became linked to Edmonton. The Alaska Highway, which passes through the Yukon on its way from British Columbia, has been a crucial part of that territory's development. Various pipeline proposals have also been significant to the North. The proposed Mackenzie Valley Gas Pipeline of the 1970s and the Berger Commission, which was appointed to assess it, had a major effect on Northern and Southern attitudes alike. Berger recommended that the pipeline be put on hold for ten years while Native land claims were settled, as well as for environmental reasons. Few such pipelines have yet been constructed in the North, although that is more a matter of economics than of concern about Natives or the environment.

Turning to communications, telegraph, telephone, radio, and television usually developed first in the private sector. But because some of these systems were natural monopolies or because of the limited number of frequencies available, they soon led to government regulation, now primarily done by the **Canadian Radio-television and Telecommunications Commission, the CRTC**. That agency issues radio and television licences and Canadian content regulations and reviews telephone rates. In most of these sectors demands also arose for public ownership, such as in the Prairie provinces' telephone systems and in the **Canadian Broadcasting Corporation, the CBC**. Amid great controversy, CBC radio began in 1932 in response to pressure for more Canadian content and more enlightened programming than was usually provided on local private stations, many of which carried U.S. programs. It became operational in English and French with its own stations as well as affiliated private stations in 1936. The same motives led to the establishment of the National Film Board, the NFB, in 1939, and of CBC television in 1952. In 1977, the CBC also began to televise proceedings of the House of Commons on a second channel, and in 1989 it was given the green light to establish a third, English-language all-news channel, Newsworld. Meanwhile, certain provinces also became involved in educational television. To supplement the country's terrestrial microwave system, the government took the initiative in 1969 to launch Telesat, a joint public–private supplier of domestic communications satellite services. Intercontinental communications via submarine cables and satellites are handled by Teleglobe Canada, which was a Crown corporation until the Mulroney government privatized it in 1987. Financial constraints led the Chrétien Liberals to further reduce the budgets of the CBC and the National Film Board.

Thus, in the field of transportation and communications, demands to overcome distances and divisions have been dominant features of Canadian politics. Governments have primarily responded with assistance to private corporations, the establishment of Crown corporations, and the creation of regulatory agencies. In the neoconservative 1980s and cash-starved 1990s, however, both the Mulroney and Chrétien governments privatized a number of government operations in this field, reduced support for others, especially the CBC, and generally deregulated the transportation industry.

Population Distribution

Geographic barriers are only one complication to the distances that characterize Canada; the distribution of population is another, for the people are not spread uniformly throughout this gigantic territory. It is commonly emphasized that the overall density of the Canadian population is one of the lowest in the world, some 2.5 people per km². But it is really more significant that there is no permanent settlement in nearly 90 percent of the country and that 72 percent of the population is huddled together within 150 km of the U.S. border.[6] The population of the various provinces can be seen in Table 6.1.

Geographers frequently speak of the *core*, *heartland*, or *metropolis* on the one hand, and the *periphery* or *hinterland* on the other, concepts that can be usefully applied to political science. The Toronto–Ottawa–Montreal triangle obviously constitutes the core of Canada, and Ontario and Quebec combined contain over 62 percent of its people. While central Canada constitutes the political core of the country, it is also the economic heartland, containing more large corporate head offices, especially in the Toronto area, than in the rest of the country put together. Moreover, it is the communications and cultural core, containing the headquarters of French and English CBC, CTV, Global, and private French television, many other Canadian cultural institutions, and most of the Canadian computer industry. The rest of the country, the hinterland or periphery, with its smaller population base, regularly complains that it is overlooked by both public and private decision-makers. It is not surprising that many Westerners advocate a reformed Senate that would be based on equal representation for each province. Quebec is also extremely sensitive to its proportion of the total Canadian population, which by January 1995 had fallen below a symbolic 25 percent.

The distribution of the Canadian population is even more complicated. In addition to this national core–periphery system, a series of regional core–periphery systems exists across the country. Several metropolitan centres dominate their own regional hinterlands: Vancouver in British Columbia; Edmonton and Calgary in Alberta; Regina and Saskatoon in Saskatchewan; Winnipeg in Manitoba; Toronto in Ontario; Montreal in Quebec; and Halifax and to a lesser extent St. John's in Atlantic Canada. The same could be said of Whitehorse in the Yukon and Yellowknife in the Northwest Territories. The interior of B.C. and northern Ontario are two examples of regions within a province that feel isolated from and exploited by their own economic cores, Vancouver and Toronto respectively. Figure 6.2 is an isodemographic map depicting Canada in terms of population (1971) rather than area, and highlighting these national and regional core–periphery systems.

Such regional cores are heavily urbanized, of course, and constitute *census metropolitan areas* (CMAs) in Statistics Canada terms. The 25 largest metropolitan centres in Canada (see Table 6.2) constituted 61.1 percent of the total population in 1991. More than one politician has calculated that the support of only these highly urbanized areas would be enough to form a government. Overall, Statistics Canada categorized 76.6 percent of the population as urban in 1991.

TABLE 6.1   **Population of Provinces and Territories**

	1991 Census		*January 1995*	
Ontario	10 084 885	(36.9%)	11 004 800	(37.4%)
Quebec	6 895 963	(25.3%)	7 300 000	(24.8%)
British Columbia	3 282 061	(12.0%)	3 719 400	(12.6%)
Alberta	2 545 553	(9.3%)	2 726 900	(9.3%)
Manitoba	1 091 942	(4.0%)	1,132,800	(3.9%)
Saskatchewan	988 928	(3.6%)	1 017 200	(3.5%)
Nova Scotia	899 942	(3.3%)	938 300	(3.2%)
New Brunswick	723 900	(2.7%)	760 600	(2.4%)
Newfoundland	568 474	(2.1%)	579 500	(2.0%)
Prince Edward Island	129 765	(0.5%)	130 100	(0.4%)
Northwest Territories	57 649	(0.2%)	65 000	(0.2%)
Yukon	27 797	(0.1%)	30 100	(0.1%)
Canada	27 296 859		29,409,900	

Sources: Statistics Canada, 1991 Census, A National Overview—Population and Dwelling Counts, cat. no. 93-301, and Statistics Canada, "Quarterly Demographic Statistics," January 1995, cat. no. 91-002 (May 1995). Reproduced with the permission of the Minister of Supply and Services Canada, 1995.

Provinces and Territories

In speaking of regionalism in Canada, then, we begin with great distances complicated by geographic barriers and concentrations of population that cause variations in political and economic power. In addition, it was partly because of such distances and divisions that provinces and territories were created. Whether originally separate colonies of Britain or later carved out of the Western territories, the provinces were granted considerable power by the Constitution. The political–legal–constitutional basis of such units is quite different from the natural, physiographic basis of regions, and the fit between regionalism and provincialism is not perfect. Feelings of regionalism can exist within a province, such as in the northern parts of many provinces; regional sentiment can cut across provinces, as in the case of people in northwestern Ontario feeling psychologically closer to Manitoba than to southern Ontario; and provinces can be lumped together into regions, such as the Maritimes or the Prairies. Nevertheless, the connection between regionalism and provincialism is a compelling relationship. In discussing the question of regionalism, the 1979 Task Force on Canadian Unity had this to say:

> Regional communities require an institutional framework if they are to become viable units which can express themselves and organize their collective life in an effective manner. For that reason, it seems to us that the provinces and the

Figure 6.2 Isodemographic Map of Canada

Source: David Taras, Beverly Rasporich, and Eli Mandel, eds., *A Passion for Identity: An Introduction to Canadian Studies* (Scarborough: Nelson Canada, 1993), p. 354

TABLE 6.2 **Population of Census Metropolitan Areas, 1991**

Toronto	3 893 046	Victoria	287 897
Montreal	3 127 242	Windsor	262 075
Vancouver	1 602 502	Oshawa	240 104
Ottawa–Hull	920 857	Saskatoon	210 023
Edmonton	839 924	Regina	191 692
Calgary	754 033	St. John's	171 859
Winnipeg	652 354	Chicoutimi	160 928
Quebec	654 550	Sudbury	157 613
Hamilton	599 760	Sherbrooke	139 194
London	381 522	Trois-Rivières	136 194
St. Catharines–Niagara	364 522	Saint John	124 981
Kitchener	356 421	Thunder Bay	124 427
Halifax	320 501		

Source: Statistics Canada, 1991 Census, Census Metropolitan Areas and Census Agglomerations, cat. no. 93-303. Reproduced with the permission of the Minister of Supply and Services Canada, 1995.

northern territories are the basic building blocks of Canadian society and the logical units on which to focus a discussion of Canadian regionalism, even though they may not be the most "natural" regions from an economic point of view.[7]

The creation of provinces and territories has two primary effects as far as regional–economic demands are concerned. On the one hand, if a region is identified with a political unit, that unit can become a persuasive transmitter of regional demands to Ottawa. Regional demands articulated by a provincial premier or territorial government are harder to ignore than those that come from less authoritative sources. In fact, to politicize such regional demands in this way may well serve to magnify them, since premiers and bureaucrats can use such diversity to justify an increase in their power. On the other hand, provinces and territories may be able to facilitate the decision-making process by handling local problems that are not controversial at the provincial or territorial level but that would cause great difficulty in Ottawa. The basic quest in the establishment of a federal system of government is to find the most appropriate division of powers and responsibilities between the national and provincial levels. This issue, the degree of centralization and decentralization in Canada, has never been settled to everyone's satisfaction, as demonstrated by the debate over the Meech Lake and Charlottetown Accords from 1987 to 1992 and subsequent constitutional questions that threaten the continued existence of the country. Canadians still raise demands about the design of the federal system as well as about policies within it.

In the 1990s, Quebec came closer than ever before to separating from the rest of Canada. If this were to happen, Quebec would take almost one-quarter of the Canadian population with it, about 16 percent of its territory, nearly 23 percent of Canada's gross domestic product.

Among many other complications, from a strictly geographic point of view the separation of Quebec would raise the question of continuing transportation links between Atlantic Canada and Ontario, border-crossing impediments, and jurisdiction over the St. Lawrence Seaway.[8]

In terms of distance, natural barriers, population distribution and political divisions, then, it is most common to speak of the following principal Canadian regions: Ontario, Quebec, the Prairies, the Atlantic region, British Columbia, and the North. Ontario and Quebec qualify as separate regions because of their size and provincial status. The Prairie provinces and the Atlantic provinces are sufficiently small and similar in character to be grouped together for many purposes as two regional units. British Columbia's claim to regional status is less well established, but it has gained increasing recognition because of its size and its geographic division and distinctiveness from the Prairie provinces. Newfoundland often makes a claim for similar status at the eastern end of the country, but primarily because of its much smaller size, is usually lumped with the three Maritime provinces to form the Atlantic region. The North has traditionally been ignored, but is increasingly regarded as a separate region worthy of mention. On the other hand, to those on the periphery, Ontario and Quebec seem to constitute a single central core.

REGIONAL–ECONOMIC DIFFERENCES

Having identified the regions of Canada, we may now proceed to examine their economies. Such a discussion, utilizing the distinctions among *primary*, *secondary*, and *tertiary* sectors, reveals striking regional–economic differences that serve to reinforce their geographic distinctiveness and create another pattern of demands on the Canadian political system.[9]

Regional–economic differences begin with primary industries, that is, the natural resource and energy base of the various provinces. The importance of natural resources to the national economy has been a central tenet of Canadian political economy for generations; it is usually termed the **staples theory** and is identified with the famous economic historian Harold Innis.[10] It postulates that Canadian economic development has relied on a succession of resource exports—furs, fish, timber, wheat, minerals, and energy—rather than manufacturing; Canadians are mere "hewers of wood and drawers of water." The staples theory also includes the notions of dependence on one or more foreign industrial centres as well as of an economy that remains underdeveloped and that is subject to the rise and fall of international markets. In international trade, Canada continues to this day to rely primarily on exports of natural resources. Sometimes an element of interregional exploitation is involved as well, especially in the relationship between inner and outer Canada.

To economists, secondary industry consists of manufacturing, construction, and utilities. Manufacturing includes the initial processing and refining of primary products as well as the making of finished goods, and generally produces more revenue and more jobs than primary industry, is less seasonal, and commands higher wages. Many observers have criticized the economic policy of almost all Canadian governments for having fostered the exploitation and exportation of raw natural resources rather than having developed an industrial policy that would give priority to manufacturing. They also blame the banks for preferring resource

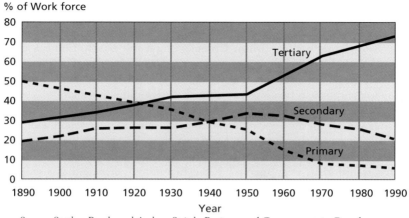

Figure 6.3 **Employment in Canada by Sector**

% of Work force

Source: Stephen Brooks and Andrew Stritch, Business and Government in Canada (Scarborough: Prentice-Hall Canada, 1991), p. 96. Reproduced with permission.

companies and foreign-owned manufacturers in their lending policies.[11] Furthermore, the fact that both governments and corporations in Canada spend so little money on *research and development (R & D)* does not augur well for the future when "high tech" will be so important.

Economists then put transportation and communications, trade, finance, insurance and real estate, private services, and public administration into the tertiary or services category. While the Canadian economy was never strong on manufacturing, much political attention in this "post-industrial" era is focused on the services sector. Figure 6.3 demonstrates the contemporary importance of the tertiary sector in outlining the trends in the Canadian labour force among the three divisions of the economy. By 1995, the tertiary sector had risen to 75 percent, compared with 5.2 percent for primary and 20 percent for secondary.

Atlantic Provinces

How do the provinces differ in their economic bases?[12] The Atlantic provinces have a distinctive and heavy reliance on fishing, which has rarely been a very prosperous industry. In the 1990s, however, the Atlantic fishery has been in deeper trouble than ever before, primarily due to a dramatic reduction in groundfish stocks, especially cod, and an oversupply of fishermen, plant workers, and trawlers. The three Maritime provinces have a substantial agricultural base, which has provided prosperity for a few large firms but generally poor returns for most farmers. New Brunswick, Newfoundland, and Nova Scotia also engage in forestry and mining. Newfoundland possesses great quantities of hydroelectric power in Labrador, and looks forward to the day when its offshore petroleum will be developed. None of these resources has led to much general prosperity in any of the Atlantic provinces, however, and most of the larger projects have been developed by central Canadian or foreign firms. Some processing and refining of natural resources takes place in the region, but among other factors, the small local market and the distance from major population centres have left the region in a state of underdevelopment. Led by New Brunswick, however, a new emphasis on communications technology has revitalized the Atlantic provinces' economies to some extent, for in the modern techological world, physical distance is not the hindrance it was in the past.

Quebec

The Quebec economy is more diversified than that of the Atlantic region and somewhat more prosperous. Quebec's primary industries include farming in the St. Lawrence Lowlands, along with mining and forestry in the Canadian Shield. That Shield is also traversed by numerous powerful rivers, making hydroelectricity Quebec's most valuable resource. Huge dams have been built on many of its rivers including the controversial James Bay hydroelectric project. Hydro is the basis of Quebec's aluminum industry, for example, as well as of much other secondary industry. Quebec also stands out in the production of pulp and paper, especially newsprint. In addition, Quebec is much stronger than the Atlantic region in the more sophisticated aspects of manufacturing. Thus, in addition to the refining and processing of metals, oil, and the production of textiles, food and beverages, and chemicals, Quebec produces clothing, aeronautics, electronics, pharmaceuticals, and cars and other transportation equipment. It also houses a large financial sector. The fact that economic power in Quebec used to rest largely in English-Canadian and foreign hands fuelled the nationalist debate in that province. But since 1960 a major transformation has occurred, and both the public and francophone private sectors in Quebec have repatriated a great deal of industrial ownership. One means of doing so was the Caisse de Dépôt et Placement, which primarily invested Quebec Pension Plan premiums in domestic firms.

Ontario

Ontario has always had the most diversified and strongest economy of any region. The province has an abundance of natural resources, including a great expanse of prime agricultural land in the Great Lakes Lowlands, and vast stretches of trees and almost every conceivable mineral in the Canadian Shield. The province also contains several powerful rivers for the production of hydroelectricity, although it is increasingly dependent on nuclear power in this regard. Ontario's early development of hydroelectricity and of a steel industry gave it a head start over other regions. A skilled labour force, a large domestic market, proximity to the United States, and the advantage of federal tariff and banking policies also helped to make it the manufacturing heartland of the country. It now produces over half of the Canadian total, including automobiles, electronic products, machinery, and publishing, in addition to steel, food and beverages, smelting and refining, metal fabrication, and pulp and paper, although many of these industries were hit hard by the 1990–92 recession. In addition,

Ontario leads the country in the tertiary sector, such as finance, trade, and services, and the seats of the two largest governments in the country, in Ottawa and Toronto, also provide considerable employment, although less than in the past.

The Prairie Provinces

The Prairie provinces are historically associated with agriculture, especially wheat, other grain, and livestock, and this industry continues to be very important. Saskatchewan in particular suffered from a dramatic decline in the grain industry in the 1980s, however, and the high value of primary industry in the Prairies is due largely to Alberta's oil and natural gas production. Alberta is Canada's petroleum province and has become the richest part of the country by many measures. Petroleum is also of increasing significance in Saskatchewan, in concert with that province's other mineral resources, potash and uranium. In addition, Alberta possesses large amounts of coal, and Manitoba, of nickel, copper and zinc. Forestry has been an important industry in Manitoba and is just beginning to make a major breakthrough in Alberta, while Manitoba's hydroelectricity complements the petroleum of the other two Prairie provinces. Thus, while the Prairies can be compared to the Atlantic region to some extent in their relatively heavy dependence on primary industry, a contrast is readily apparent: resource extraction on the Prairies is usually a much more profitable venture. The Prairies are also engaged in a certain amount of manufacturing, including food and beverages, transportation equipment, machinery, metal fabrication, chemicals, petrochemicals, and fertilizer. With the new wealth of the Western provinces, especially since 1960, the finance, trade, and service industries have expanded rapidly, and the Prairies are less dependent on Ontario in this respect than they used to be.

British Columbia

Mountainous British Columbia is the leading forestry province and also specializes in mining, including natural gas, copper, and coal. Several fertile river and lake valleys provide for farming, and, being a coastal province, B.C. also possesses a significant fishing industry. The mountains are the source of several large rivers that have been dammed for the production of hydroelectricity, and, as in Quebec, the abundant electricity is used to produce aluminum as well as being exported. Manufacturing is primarily related to the forestry, mining, and agricultural bases of the B.C. economy: assorted wood products such as shakes and shingles and pulp and paper; food and beverages; and the processing and refining of metals, petroleum, chemicals, and coal.

The North

The North has very limited agriculture and forestry, given its frigid climate, short growing season, and lack of soil. Mining has inspired many southerners to venture north over the years, especially in the gold rushes of the 1890s in Dawson City, Yukon, and the 1930s in

Yellowknife, N.W.T. Other isolated mineral deposits have been found, but most proceeded with artificially high levels of government support, and many have since been abandoned. The prospects of oil and natural gas are more promising, especially in the Mackenzie River delta and the Beaufort Sea. Government policy has encouraged Northern petroleum exploration at public expense, but it awaits full-scale development. The unstable world price, the uncertain supply in Southern Canada and the United States, the outstanding Native land claims, and the cost and difficulty of transporting the petroleum southward have all combined to limit such a flow. Northern Natives used to be self-sufficient in hunting, fishing and trapping, activities that continue to occupy them to some extent, while tourism is on the increase. In general, however, the inhospitable climate, the isolation, the small and transient labour force, and the poor transportation facilities conspire to retard economic development of the region. But a positive recent sign is the settlement of some Native land claims, and increased autonomy from Ottawa should better allow the territories to respond to local needs.

Regional Demands

Since most natural resources fall within provincial jurisdiction, demands arising from the primary sector are often first addressed to the respective provincial government. Every primary industry has also sought federal government support of one kind or another over the years, however, and most other regional–economic demands are primarily directed to Ottawa. In response, its outputs have often benefited a certain industry throughout the country. At other times, its support of one region has also been in the national interest, such as in the creation of the **Canadian Wheat Board** to help Prairie farmers export more grain. Because these farmers could then pay higher federal taxes and buy more goods produced in other provinces, such a policy generally made the whole country more prosperous. Similarly, if Ottawa protects or promotes the Atlantic fishing industry, the rest of the country will pay less in unemployment insurance and equalization payments to that region.

Thus, as a result of regional–economic differences, the national government regularly faces demands to assist the economy of a single province, region, or industry. Many such demands have elicited a positive response, especially when the case was desperate, popular, or articulated by the right interest. Such outputs do not necessarily involve conflict between one region and another, and sometimes benefit them all.

REGIONAL–ECONOMIC CONFLICTS

More often than not, however, demands from one region *do* conflict with those from another. The most pervasive expression of such regional–economic conflict has undoubtedly been between the Prairie and Ontario regions. Since Ontario's regional interests have historically been persuasive with the federal government, the analysis is usually put in terms of the central core versus the periphery of the country.[13]

- Ownership of public lands and natural resources
- Tariffs
- The transportation system, especially freight rates
- The banking system
- Taxation and regulation of natural resources

Ownership of Natural Resources

The problem began in 1870 with the creation of the province of Manitoba. While the Eastern provinces and British Columbia had jurisdiction over their own natural resources, Ottawa decided to retain such control in the case of Manitoba, and when Saskatchewan and Alberta were created in 1905, these provinces were placed in the same subordinate position. The logic of prime ministers Macdonald in 1870 and Wilfrid Laurier in 1905 was that the federal government (i.e., central Canada) should control such resources in the national interest, allowing Ottawa to guide the development of the West. The Prairie provinces fought vehemently against this discrimination, and were finally successful in gaining control of their natural resources in 1930.

Tariffs

In the second place, the West complained for generations that Canadian **tariff** policy was designed in the interest of Ontario (and to a lesser extent Quebec) at the expense of the Prairies. This was because as early as the 1879 **National Policy**, Macdonald saw the tariff as a means of promoting and protecting the industrial heartland of central Canada. Adding a tariff (an import tax) to the price of imported manufactured goods would raise their price above that of goods manufactured in Canada, even if Canadian production costs were slightly higher, and allow domestic goods to be sold more cheaply than imports. In practice, it was largely foreign firms that established themselves in central Canada behind this tariff wall, but the tariff at least had the beneficial effect of creating jobs in Canada rather than in Britain or the United States. Ontario thus gained employment in producing tractors for Western Canada, for example, but Western Canadians felt that this was contrary to their interests because, in the absence of such a tariff, they would have been able to buy a cheaper tractor from abroad. Furthermore, when Canada resorted to tariff protection of its manufacturing industry, other countries were likely to respond by restricting their imports of Canadian grain. The West demanded lower tariffs at every opportunity, and especially in the 1920s sent its own farmer representatives to the House of Commons to fight on this front. Tariffs among all countries have gradually come down since 1945, but the issue took on a new life in the 1980s with the Western demand for a free trade agreement between Canada and the United States. Thus, the controversial Free Trade Agreement between the two countries, which took effect in 1989, can be seen as a response to 110 years of Western discontent with the tariff aspect of the National Policy.[14]

Transportation

Another aspect of Macdonald's National Policy that displeased the West was transportation and especially railways. Here the Western case was not quite as convincing, because in choosing to live so far from the central core of the country, Westerners should have expected to pay additional transportation costs. Some acknowledged this, although others demanded that railway freight rates be subsidized by Ottawa. Indeed, the Crow's Nest Pass Act (or **Crow rate**) of 1897 was an attempt to do just that, and provided a low rate for transporting Prairie grain to eastern ports. About 80 years later, the Trudeau government's decision to increase these rates greatly upset many Westerners, as did the Chrétien government's decision in 1995 to abolish the Crow rate entirely. But a more legitimate complaint was about peculiar inequities within the freight rate structure, including higher rates for finished goods than for raw materials (which discouraged manufacturing in the West), discrimination against short hauls, and deviations from the principle of distance determining price.

Banking

The West was probably on more solid ground in protesting against national banking policy. In contrast to community-based unit banks as in the United States, Canada deliberately developed a centralized branch banking system. This policy was in part an attempt to construct a sound, stable banking community which would avoid frequent local collapses, but the lack of competition it involved was also favoured by the established banking interests themselves, providing evidence of corporate pressure on government policy. The result was a handful of large national banks, usually with headquarters in Montreal or Toronto, and with local branches spread across the country. From a hinterland perspective, money deposited in the local branch of a national bank would not remain in the community to be lent out for local purposes, but was sent to headquarters in central Canada to be used in the economic development of Ontario or Quebec. Moreover, decisions to lend money were largely centralized at the head office so that Western entrepreneurs would have to travel east in order to borrow substantial sums. This was another reason for the farmers' revolt of the 1920s, and displeasure with the Canadian banking system had much to do with the rise of Social Credit in Alberta in the 1930s. For many decades Ottawa refused to make any changes to this policy, but in the 1970s, when the West became stronger in spite of it, the federal government finally responded. On the one hand, Ottawa eased restrictions on chartering regional banks, and several new Western banks were established. On the other hand, the existing national banks saw the merit in decentralizing decision-making within their own operations, so that larger decisions could be made on location. Unfortunately, several of these new Western financial institutions faltered in the 1980s, largely because of a downturn in the Western economy that Westerners blamed on Trudeau's National Energy Program.

Taxation and Regulation of Natural Resources

By that time, the original conflict over natural resources had re-emerged, especially with respect to petroleum pricing. National energy policy in the 1950s and 1960s had actually favoured the West, for Alberta was guaranteed a market for its oil and natural gas as far east as Ontario. But the West quickly forgot that fact after the OPEC (Organization of Petroleum Exporting Countries) cartel agreed on an artificial rise in the international price of oil in 1973. At this point, federal policy began to favour the consumer/manufacturing interest of central Canada at the expense of the producer interest of the West. The height of the regional–economic conflict occurred in 1980 with the Trudeau government's **National Energy Program**, which imposed new federal taxes, retained a larger share of petroleum revenues for Ottawa, kept the national price below the world level, encouraged frontier—largely off-shore—development, and promoted Canadianization of the industry, all objectives inimical to most Westerners. Eventually a partial compromise between central and Western interests was reached in 1981, and the Mulroney government later scrapped the NEP entirely. Nevertheless, the NEP had a profound effect on the Western Canadian psyche, especially when combined with the West's simultaneous opposition to Ottawa's constitutional initiatives and bilingualism policy.

Metropolitan Exploitation of the Hinterland

These four policy areas—tariffs, transportation, banking, and resources—represent the most serious regional–economic conflicts in Canadian history, but they can be seen in a broader context. The metropolitan–hinterland thesis suggests that the West was created as a colony of central Canada and was intended to be held in a subordinate and dependent relationship.[15] Western feeling about its situation was captured in a famous cartoon in the *Grain Growers' Guide* as early as 1915, and while it is depicted in agricultural terms, the image provided in Figure 6.4 is still appropriate some 80 years later. Dissatisfaction with both the Liberal and Conservative parties' focus on Quebec issues in the 1980s and early 1990s led to the formation of the Reform Party, whose initial slogan was "The West Wants In." Although it broadened its focus by the time of the 1993 federal election, the Reform Party won the majority of seats west of Ontario, and almost all of them in British Columbia and Alberta.

The Atlantic Provinces

Many of the Western economic conflicts with central Canada have been echoed by the Atlantic provinces. This was especially true of post-Confederation tariff policy, which also appeared to do the Maritimes more harm than good. Nova Scotia and New Brunswick entered Confederation in 1867 as proud and prosperous colonies, and while changes in marine technology (from wooden sailing ships to steel steamships) were probably the principal factor responsible, their economies quickly declined. Whatever the reason, Maritimers preferred to blame federal economic policy for much of their difficulty. The Atlantic provinces shared the West's concerns about federal freight rates, although they received sub-

Figure 6.4 **The Canadian Economy According to Many Westerners**

"The Milch Cow," by Arch. Dale (1882–1962), from the Grain Growers Guide, *15 December 1915. Reproduced courtesy of the Glenbow Archives, Calgary, Alberta.*

sidization in this area, too, and they opposed federal resource policy in the 1980s, prompting them to fight for provincial ownership of offshore petroleum. They differed from the West to some extent on the Canada–U.S. Free Trade Agreement, fearing that it would eliminate many of their subsidy programs. They also complained of an insufficiently aggressive federal government when it came to protecting Atlantic fish stocks from foreign overfishing. Another common complaint of the Atlantic and Western regions is that the federal government does most of its purchasing or procuring in central Canada. While the economic complaints of the two outlying regions have thus generally coincided, they have occasionally been at odds, such as in the relative decline of Maritime representation in federal political institutions as the West's population expanded.

Routine Regional Conflicts

Smaller-scale regional–economic disputes are also a routine occurrence in Canadian politics. Attempts to support the steel plant in Sydney, Nova Scotia, arouse opposition in Sault Ste. Marie, Ontario; awarding the CF-18 maintenance contract to Canadair of Montreal infuriates supporters of Bristol Aerospace of Winnipeg (and further reinforces Western alienation);[16] extending drug patent protection for multinational pharmaceutical firms in Quebec offends Canadian generic drug producers in Ontario; promoting frontier petroleum exploration (including federal assistance to Newfoundland's Hibernia project) upsets conventional oil and gas producers in Alberta; assisting foreign automobile plants in Ontario raises the ire of

Quebec; and the attempt to fight inflation in Toronto with high interest rates angers those in almost every other part of the country who wish to see such rates lowered. The list of regional economic conflicts is almost endless, and most readers can probably add their own examples. Even subsidizing Western grain farmers or Atlantic fishermen, which could be seen to be of indirect benefit to central Canada, is increasingly opposed by those in Ontario who feel that they are paying most of the cost. Besides these regional–economic conflicts that engaged the attention of Ottawa, interprovincial conflicts may also develop. The most serious of these was probably the fight between Quebec and Newfoundland over the Churchill Falls hydroelectric project in Labrador.

··

REGIONAL–ECONOMIC DISPARITIES

Conflicts between regions are exacerbated in Canada because of regional–economic inequalities or disparities. As mentioned, some have-not regions blame federal economic policies for their fate, but even if this charge has some truth to it, no observer can overlook other factors: Canada's primary resources are not evenly distributed and the regions have different sizes, different populations, and variable distances from key export markets.

Among the available measures of regional–economic disparity are provincial gross domestic product (GDP) (the total value of all goods and services produced), per capita personal income, provincial unemployment rates, and provincial sales taxes. These measures are shown in Table 6.3.

TABLE 6.3	Provincial Gross Domestic Product, GDP Per Capita, Per Capita Personal Income, Unemployment Rate, and Retail Sales Tax				
	Gross Domestic Product 1992 (millions)	1992 GDP Per Capita	Per Capita Income 1992	Unemployment Rate 1994	PST 1995
Newfoundland	$9 232	$16 240	$17 227	20.6%	12%
Prince Edward Island	2 151	16 576	17 915	17.0%	10%
Nova Scotia	17 987	19 987	18 680	13.3%	10%
New Brunswick	13 878	19 171	17 724	12.5%	11%
Quebec	157 067	22 777	20 648	12.1%	6.5%
Ontario	277 454	27 512	23 593	9.6%	8%
Manitoba	23 969	21 951	19 862	9.1%	7%
Saskatchewan	20 239	20 466	18 448	7.0%	9%
Alberta	72 942	28 655	22 389	8.4%	0
British Columbia	86 669	26 407	22 662	9.3%	6%

Sources: Statistics Canada, Provincial Economic Accounts 1992 (cat. no. 13-213), March 1994, adapted by author (column two divides by 1991 Census population), and The Labour Force December 1994, cat. no. 71-001, January 1995. Reproduced with the permission of the Minister of Supply and Services Canada, 1995.

The table generally indicates three categories of provinces: three rich ones, Ontario, Alberta, and British Columbia; four poor ones, the Atlantic provinces; and three intermediate provinces, Quebec, Manitoba, and Saskatchewan. Quebec has a larger economy than any province other than Ontario, of course, but this figure is not so impressive when expressed on a per capita basis. Per capita income statistics show that the average Ontarian received about $6000 more than the average Newfoundlander, with the other provinces arrayed in between. It is also true as a general rule that the provinces with the highest unemployment rates have the highest provincial taxes, while Alberta's petroleum revenue allows it to get by without a provincial sales tax at all. Needless to say, provinces and regions select whichever figures put them in the worst possible light when they demand that Ottawa do something to reduce such disparities.[17]

In addition to developing national social programs and assisting various industries in a uniform national policy, successive governments have focused on two principal means to deal with the specific question of regional–economic disparities. One is to give federal funding to have-not provincial *governments*, and the other is to provide grants to individual *firms* in designated have-not regions of the country.

Equalization Payments

In 1957 Ottawa finally responded to repeated demands and began to make **equalization payments**. These annual cash grants to the have-not provinces are designed to allow them to raise their services to an acceptable national level but can be spent for any purpose. In other words, they are unconditional grants, with no strings attached. The formula according to which provincial eligibility is calculated is extremely complex, now taking into account over 30 sources of provincial income, and designed to equalize the per capita yield of such provincial revenues across the country. Ever since 1957, of course, all four Atlantic provinces have qualified on an annual basis, as have Quebec and Manitoba. Saskatchewan has usually qualified, Alberta and British Columbia did so for a few years, but Ontario has never received a cent from this source. (The formula had to be changed in 1981 in order to exclude Ontario, at its own request.) The equalization formula has been renegotiated every five years since 1957 at federal–provincial conferences, but in recent times Ottawa has unilaterally altered the formula in order to curtail its obligations in this sphere. Nevertheless, the sums involved are astronomical, as Table 6.4 reveals.

TABLE 6.4	Equalization Payments, 1995–1996		
Quebec	$3 857 000 000	New Brunswick	$988 000 000
Nova Scotia	$1 116 000 000	Saskatchewan	646 000 000
Manitoba	1 040 000 000	P.E.I.	207 000 000
Newfoundland	1 016 000 000		

Source: Statistics provided by Department of Finance, as of February 1995. Used with permission.

Equalization payments were entrenched in the Constitution in 1982, so that while the federal government may change the formula at any time, it cannot withdraw from its responsibility in this regard. Section 36 reads as follows:

> Parliament and the government of Canada are committed to the principle of making equalization payments to ensure that provincial governments have sufficient revenues to provide reasonably comparable levels of public services at reasonably comparable levels of taxation.

Many find it puzzling that Quebec should qualify as a have-not province, and indeed, that when its revenue shortfall is multiplied by its large population, it should receive almost as much in equalization payments as all the other have-not provinces combined. The explanation seems to rest with the following facts: Quebec has less natural resource wealth than is commonly assumed, its industry was historically small-scale, business profits were often taken out of the province and sent to corporate headquarters elsewhere, its steel industry was slow to get started, and it did not enjoy the proximity to the U.S. automobile industry that Ontario did. Moreover, until 1960 its labour force was not well trained and the Roman Catholic Church in the province discouraged entrepreneurial activity among its deferential flock. Whatever the reasons, Quebec does well by these federal payments, to which people in all provinces contribute via their federal taxes.

Many attempts have been made to identify the overall "winners" and "losers" of Confederation, that is, which provinces have a net gain or loss when all their federal taxes and benefits have been totalled. This debate has been particularly centred on Quebec, but the results of federalist and sovereignist studies have often been contradictory. Two University of Calgary economists concluded, for example, that between 1961 and 1992 Quebec received $168 billion more in federal spending than it contributed in tax and other revenues to Ottawa, but Parti Québécois studies (somewhat suspect in many eyes) show that Quebec is a net loser in this respect. On a per capita basis, at least, there is no question that the Atlantic provinces are the largest beneficiaries.[18]

Regional Economic Development Programs

The second means of trying to reduce regional–economic disparities is to establish federal **regional economic development programs**.[19] Among the early versions of such policy were the Prairie Farm Rehabilitation Administration (PFRA) of 1935; the Maritime Farm Rehabilitation Act of 1948; the Agricultural Rehabilitation and Development Act of 1961, renamed the Agricultural and Rural Development Act (ARDA) in 1966; the Atlantic Development Board of 1962–63; the Area Development Agency of 1963; and the Fund for Rural Economic Development (FRED) of 1966. These payments and programs culminated in the establishment of the Department of Regional Economic Expansion (DREE) in 1969, which was later renamed the Department of Regional Industrial Expansion (DRIE) and has undergone many changes of organization and emphasis since. The basic thrust of this program was to designate those parts of the country that needed economic assistance (essentially the whole country except Ontario's Golden Horseshoe, that is, Toronto and westward around the head of Lake Ontario), and then to provide grants to firms that would locate or expand existing operations in such areas. An element of federal–provincial cooperation was usually involved, primarily through *economic and regional development agreements*. Even before the 1994 national infrastructure program, some grants also went to provinces or municipalities in order to provide the basic infrastructure that might attract industry, such as highways, water and sewage systems, and industrial parks. In 1987 another reorganization created several separate regional economic development agencies, principally the **Atlantic Canada Opportunities Agency** (ACOA), Federal Economic Development in Northern Ontario (FEDNOR), the Department of **Western Economic Diversification** (WED), and the Federal Offices of Regional Development for Quebec and Ontario (FORD-Q and FORD-O). What remained of DRIE became the Department of Industry, Science and Technology, later Industry Canada. The 1995 budget reduced funding for these agencies and directed them to focus their assistance on small and medium-sized enterprises, to make more extensive use of loans instead of grants, to establish investment pools run jointly with private-sector lending institutions, and to work with the provinces to reduce overlap and duplication in assistance to business.

DISMEMBERMENT OF DRIE INTO SEPARATE REGIONAL ECONOMIC DEVELOPMENT AGENCIES

* Atlantic Canada Opportunities Agency (ACOA)
* Federal Economic Development in Northern Ontario (FEDNOR)
* Department of Western Economic Diversification (WD)
* Federal Office of Regional Development—Quebec (FORD-Q)
* Federal Office of Regional Development—Ontario (FORD-O)

This is not the place to analyze the overall results of the attempts to reduce regional–economic disparities in Canada. Suffice it to say that the many rearrangements of economic development programs are an indication of their recognized deficiencies. Many cases could be documented of corporations receiving money without being in need of it, or taking the money and not living up to their commitments to create jobs. On the other hand, some positive results have also occurred. In any case, whatever the policies and programs in place, federal politicians face a never-ending stream of appeals from have-not communities, have-not provinces, and companies in difficulty (as well as have-provinces and companies not in difficulty) to use the federal power of the purse to make their lives a little easier. Such appeals increasingly fall on deaf ears.

CONCLUSION

The Canadian physical environment is primarily characterized by regionalism, and many demands stemming from such regions can be identified. Some demands seek improved transportation and communications links to bind the country more closely together. Others desire increased provincial or territorial autonomy in order to deal locally with their distinctive problems. A third category of demands concerns federal assistance to one region or another at no expense to other regions, while a fourth involves federal policy that does result from conflicting regional demands. Finally, regional–economic disparities lead have-not regions and provinces to demand further assistance from Ottawa. While such patterns of regional and provincial demands are a constant of Canadian politics, their intensity in the 1990s reached levels that threatened the continued integrity of the political system, at the very time that the federal government's financial capacity forced it to cut spending and privatize Crown corporations designed to hold the country together.

P Of the approaches outlined in Chapter 1, pluralism is most relevant here. Pluralists point to the obvious geographic and economic diversities in Canada and to the interplay of many such forces at the federal level. They remind us that national policies must allow for regional variations. Pluralists claim that a plethora of examples can be found to demonstrate that government policies have stemmed from vociferously articulated regional–economic demands. Pluralists also emphasize that it is this diversity that led to the creation of provinces in the first place. Power has been dispersed to the provincial political units because many of the diversities can be better accommodated at that level.

PC The other three approaches generally take the opposite point of view. Public choice theory, for example, emphasizes the voting power of central Canada in the design of most government policies in this field. Moreover, during the Pearson and Trudeau eras, when Quebec could be counted on to vote Liberal and the West went predominately Conservative, elections were essentially fought out in Ontario, the province with the largest number of marginal voters. This partly explains the thrust of Trudeau's constitutional and energy policies—especially the National Energy Program—which were strongly supported in Ontario but raised great anguish in the West.

SC The state-centred approach comes to much the same conclusion but for different reasons. It concentrates on the predominance of people from central Canada in such authoritative positions as the cabinet and bureaucracy and the ability of these authorities to operate autonomously, without public pressure. If 60 percent of members of parliament and cabinet ministers come from Ontario and Quebec, it is only to be expected that many federal policies will benefit the central part of the country. If the bureaucratic elite has similar geographic origins, this tendency will only be reinforced. In some periods in Canadian history, Western or Atlantic regional demands were more satisfactorily addressed, usually when powerful regional ministers or strong provincial premiers engaged in a process of elite accommodation. But in the case of the 1980 National Energy Program, a combination of an unrepresentative cabinet and an autonomous bureaucracy produced a policy to which the

West reacted with hostility.[20] Partly in response to the NEP, Senate reform became a key point in constitutional discussions because the outlying provinces saw equal and effective provincial representation in that body as their only counterweight at the federal level to the predominance of central Canada in the House of Commons and cabinet.

© Class analysts also see a centralist thrust to most federal policies, but one that primarily facilitates the accumulation of capital among central Canadian corporations. Early railway policy, national tariff and banking policies, the bailout of the predecessors of CN, legislative support of private pipelines, corporate grants under DREE and DRIE, the reliance on natural resource exploitation, reluctance to develop a Canadian industrial policy, and the attempted privatization of the Pearson Airport were all designed to benefit capitalist interests, most of which were headquartered in central Canada. Some such analysts argue that parties have encouraged voters to think of Canadian politics in terms of conflict that "revolves around the allocation of power and resources across geographic units rather than, for example, among social classes." In this perception, regions are largely the creation of government policies or propaganda.[21]

DISCUSSION QUESTIONS

1. What are the traditional demands and/or complaints of each region in Canadian federal politics?

2. To what extent are traditional Western and Atlantic regional complaints justified?

3. To what extent is the Reform Party a product of Western alienation?

4. To what extent can federal policies be taken to help one region without upsetting another?

5. To what extent can the federal government address all regional demands simultaneously, especially in an era of government restraint?

6. Is decentralization of the federal system an answer to conflicting regional demands? Why or why not?

7. To what extent are regional disparities a result of natural endowments of provinces and regions?

8. What can be done to lessen the problem of regional–economic disparities?

9. Have federal government policies with respect to regional–economic cleavages been fair to all regions, as pluralists suggest? Explain.

10. If not, which of the other approaches outlined in Chapter 1 best explains the preference provided for central Canada in public policies?

....

NOTES

1. House of Commons, *Debates*, June 19, 1936.
2. See, for example, Donald Creighton, *The Empire of the St. Lawrence* (Toronto: Macmillan, 1956).
3. Railways figured in Confederation deals as recently as 1949, when Newfoundland joined Canada.
4. The whole romantic story is told in Pierre Berton, *The National Dream* and *The Last Spike* (Toronto: McClelland and Stewart, 1970 and 1971).
5. For an analysis along these lines, see Robert Chodos, *The CPR: A Century of Corporate Welfare* (Toronto: Lorimer, 1973).
6. Statistics Canada, *Canada's Population from Ocean to Ocean* (cat. no. 98-120, January 1989), p. 16.
7. Task Force on Canadian Unity, *A Future Together* (Ottawa: Supply and Services, 1979), pp. 26–27. The "provincialism" of this report was rejected by its government sponsor (Prime Minister Trudeau), but it may have inspired his successors.
8. Several recent books speculate on this question. From a specifically geographic point of view, see Scott Reid, *Canada Remapped* (Vancouver: Pulp Press, 1992).
9. Stephen Brooks and Andrew Stritch, *Business and Government in Canada* (Scarborough: Prentice-Hall Canada, 1991), ch. 4.
10. Among the many discussions of the staples theory, see Wallace Clement and Daniel Drache, *A Practical Guide to Canadian Political Economy* (Toronto: Lorimer, 1978), pp. 9–14. See also their *New Practical Guide to Canadian Political Economy*, 1985.
11. Ibid., pp. 32–35, where R.T. Naylor's perspective on the role of the banks is briefly summarized.
12. One convenient source on the provinces is Rand Dyck, *Provincial Politics in Canada*, 3rd ed. (Scarborough: Prentice-Hall, 1995).
13. For recent discussions of the Western point of view, see David Kilgour, *Uneasy Patriots: Western Canadians in Confederation* (Edmonton: Lone Pine Publishers, 1988); *Inside Outer Canada* (Lone Pine, 1990); Don Braid and Sydney Sharpe, *Breakup: Why the West Feels Left Out of Canada* (Toronto: Key Porter Books, 1990); and Roger Gibbins, Keith Archer, and Stan Drabek, eds., *Canadian Political Life: An Alberta Perspective* (Dubuque, IA: Kendall Hunt, 1990).
14. By this time many large central Canadian corporations also saw advantages for themselves in such a policy.
15. For an excellent summary of this position, see Donald Smiley, *The Federal Condition in Canada* (Toronto: McGraw-Hill Ryerson, 1987), p. 159.
16. Robert Campbell and Leslie Pal, *The Real Worlds of Canadian Politics* (Peterborough: Broadview Press, 1989).
17. In this connection, Donald Savoie argues that earned per capita income provides a better measure of a region's economic performance than total per capita income because the former excludes gains made through interregional transfer payments. See Donald J. Savoie, *The Canadian Economy: A Regional Perspective* (Toronto: Carswell, 1986). Saskatchewan fell below Nova Scotia in terms of per capita income for the first time in 1991 due to a decade of difficulty in the wheat industry.
18. Robert Mansell and Ronald Schlenker, "The Provincial Distribution of Federal Fiscal Balances," *Canadian Business Economics* (Winter 1995), pp. 3–22, which also showed that Alberta lost $139 billion while Ontario lost $45 billion. See also a study by the Fraser Institute, *Government Spending Facts* (Vancouver, 1990); Phil Hartling, *Federal Expenditures as a Tool for Regional Development* (Halifax: Council of Maritime Premiers, 1990); and studies done for the PQ government prior to the Referendum of 1995. A fuller account of federal-provincial finance is contained in Chapter 4.
19. See Anthony Careless, *Initiative and Response: The Adaptation of Canadian Federalism to Regional Economic Development* (Montreal: McGill–Queen's University Press, 1977); Economic Council of Canada, *Living Together: A Study of Regional Disparities* (Ottawa, 1977); and Donald J. Savoie, *Federal–Provincial Collaboration: The Canada–New Brunswick General Development Agreement* (Montreal: McGill–Queen's University Press, 1981).
20. See, for example, Peter Foster, *The Sorcerer's Apprentices: Canada's Super-Bureaucrats and the Energy Mess* (Don Mills: Collins, 1982).

21. See Janine Brodie, "The Concept of Region in Canadian Politics," in David Shugarman and Reg Whitaker, eds., *Federalism and Political Community* (Peterborough: Broadview Press, 1989), p. 36, and Brodie, *The Political Economy of Canadian Regionalism* (Toronto: Harcourt, Brace, Jovanovich, 1990).

FURTHER READING

Alberta Report (weekly).

Berger, Thomas. *Northern Frontier, Northern Homeland: The Report of the Mackenzie Valley Pipeline Inquiry.* Ottawa: Supply and Services Canada, 1977, republished by Douglas and McIntyre, Vancouver, 1988.

Braid, Don, and Sydney Sharpe. *Breakup: Why the West Feels Left Out of Canada.* Toronto: Key Porter Books, 1990.

Brodie, Janine. *The Political Economy of Canadian Regionalism.* Toronto: Harcourt, Brace, Jovanovich, 1990.

Clement, Wallace, and Daniel Drache. *The New Practical Guide to Canadian Political Economy.* Toronto: Lorimer, 1985.

Coates, Kenneth, and Judith Powell. *The Modern North.* Toronto: Lorimer, 1989.

Dyck, Rand. *Provincial Politics in Canada*, 3rd ed. Scarborough: Prentice-Hall Canada, 1995.

Gibbins, Roger. *Conflict and Unity*, 3rd ed. Scarborough: Nelson Canada, 1994.

Gibbins, Roger, Keith Archer, and Stan Drabek, eds. *Canadian Political Life: An Alberta Perspective.* Dubuque, IA.: Kendall Hunt, 1990.

Kilgour, David. *Inside Outer Canada.* Edmonton: Lone Pine Publishers, 1990.

———. *Uneasy Patriots: Western Canadians in Confederation.* Edmonton: Lone Pine Publishers, 1988.

Reid, Scott. *Canada Remapped.* Vancouver: Pulp Press, 1992.

Savoie, Donald J. *The Canadian Economy: A Regional Perspective.* Toronto: Carswell, 1986.

———. *Regional Economic Development: Canada's Search for Solutions.* 2nd ed. Toronto: University of Toronto Press, 1992.

Task Force on Canadian Unity. *A Future Together.* Ottawa: Supply and Services, 1979.

Tomblin, Stephen. *Ottawa and the Outer Provinces.* Halifax: Lorimer, 1995.

Western Economic Opportunities Conference. *Documents and Verbatim Record.* Calgary, July 1973.

Whebell, C.E.J. "Geography and Politics in Canada: Selected Aspects." In John H. Redekop, ed. *Approaches to Canadian Politics*, 2nd ed. Scarborough: Prentice-Hall Canada, 1983.

Wonders, William C. "Canadian Regions and Regionalisms: National Enrichment or National Disintegration?" In Eli Mandel and David Taras, eds. *A Passion for Identity.* Toronto: Methuen, 1987.

Chapter 7

Canada's
ABORIGINAL
peoples

Canada's aboriginal peoples responded angrily to the Trudeau–Chrétien White Paper on Indians of 1969. Elijah Harper helped to veto the Meech Lake Accord in the Manitoba legislature because it did not advance the cause of aboriginal self-government. To what extent are those who arrived during the last 500 years responsible for the deplorable condition in which a majority of aboriginals find themselves? Should Native peoples be allowed to hunt and fish at will? How can their land claims be dealt with fairly? While the way in which they have been governed over the past 150 years is obviously a failure, is aboriginal self-government a realistic alternative? What does it mean?

Suddenly, since about 1970, a host of issues dealing with Canada's aboriginal peoples have been on the political agenda. Partly because of this new consciousness and the character of these demands, and partly out of feelings of guilt, such aboriginal issues have attracted widespread interest even among nonaboriginals in recent years. Opinion is divided on how to deal with such issues, but there has never been such widespread concern to improve the living conditions of aboriginal Canadians.

This chapter will examine the historical evolution of Canada's aboriginal peoples, detail their demographic profile today, and outline the principal political issues they have raised, especially with respect to land and governance. These issues are so unprecedented in official Canadian political experience that they are neither easily explained nor likely to be speedily resolved. Much hope has been placed in the recommendations of the Royal Commission on Aboriginal Peoples, but even before it published its final report, concrete action was taking place at an unprecedented rate.

HISTORICAL EVOLUTION

Native or aboriginal peoples have inhabited Canada for perhaps as long as 40 000 years, most experts linking their origins to Asia. They are an extremely varied group. Those who settled in the southern part of what is now Canada, as well as those in the Yukon and Mackenzie Valley of the north, can be termed *North American Indians*, however erroneous the origin of the label, while those located in the eastern Arctic and northern islands used to be called Eskimo and are now referred to as *Inuit*. Before Europeans came to the continent, most aboriginals functioned as nomadic hunters but some were more permanent fishermen, carvers, or farmers. They were self-sufficient and self-governing. They generally made decisions on the basis of consensus rather than by voting, and in many cases women (sometimes called clan mothers) played a significant role. In their close attachment to the land, they did not think in terms of private ownership; instead, they believed in the shared use of land and saw themselves as trustees of the land for future generations.

It was the fur trade more than anything that led to the invasion by Europeans and to wars between the British and the French in North America. The fur trade was devastating for the aboriginal peoples, totally disrupting their way of life and introducing new diseases that severely reduced their population.

In the **Royal Proclamation of 1763**, which divided up the territory acquired by Britain, Indian rights were clearly defined, however much they have since been ignored.[1] In a large area called Indian Territory, the purchase or settlement of land was forbidden without Crown approval, that is, without a treaty between the Crown and the Indian people concerned. This is sometimes called the principle of "voluntary cession." Shortly afterwards, the Crown concluded land-cession agreements with Indians in what is now southern Ontario in order to provide for the United Empire Loyalists moving in from the United States. Indians originally received a lump-sum payment and, later, annuities.

From about 1830 onward the system changed, and the Crown set aside reserves in exchange for the cession of Indian land, in addition to providing benefits such as the right to hunt and fish on unoccupied Crown land. The first major treaties of this kind were the Robinson Treaties of 1850 in northern Ontario and the Douglas Treaties on Vancouver Island.

The 1867 Constitution Act gave jurisdiction over Indians and lands reserved for the Indians to the federal government. Parliament soon passed the **Indian Act**, which was consolidated in 1876 and provided for federal government control of almost every aspect of Indian life. One of its provisions allowed for "enfranchisement," which encouraged Indians to give up their Indian status. Thus began the distinction between **status Indians**, those registered with the federal government according to the terms of the Indian Act, and *nonstatus Indians*, those not so registered.

Meanwhile, the treaty-making process continued apace, with treaties numbered 1 to 11 covering most of northern Ontario and the Prairie provinces, and parts of British Columbia, the Yukon, and the Mackenzie Valley of the Northwest Territories. These treaties were primarily designed to clear aboriginal title so that the transcontinental railway could be built and western immigrant settlement could begin. Such treaties contained an extinguishment clause, such that aboriginal rights were given up in exchange for treaty rights. In return for surrendering title to the lands involved, Indians received tracts of land for reserves as well as other benefits such as small annuities, gratuities, schools, hunting and fishing rights, agricultural implements, cattle, and ammunition. In retrospect, almost everyone agrees that the Natives were taken advantage of in these negotiations and recognizes that the land given them for reserves was usually small, remote, and lacking in resources.[2] Even worse off, however, were those Indians in much of British Columbia and the Arctic with whom no treaties were signed at all.

By this time another identifiable group existed besides status, nonstatus, treaty, and nontreaty Indians. These were the Métis, essentially the descendants of white fur traders and Indian women. Found largely on the Prairies, the **Métis** combined nomadic hunting with farming. They were not covered by the Indian Act or by treaties, and were therefore left to the mercy of new white settlers and provincial and territorial governments. It is not surprising, therefore, that **Louis Riel** took up their cause in 1885 in the second Riel Rebellion in Saskatchewan. After having been crushed, they remained in an even weaker position to fend for themselves.

The one group of aboriginals that was left untouched by government, although not by fur traders, missionaries, and other whites, was the Eskimo or Inuit of the far north and northeastern Arctic. A 1939 Supreme Court ruling declared that the Eskimo came within the meaning of Indians in the 1867 Constitution Act (but not under the Indian Act), but it was not until the 1950s that the federal government began to deliver health and educational services to them and later to relocate them into about 40 permanent settlements, largely on the coast of the Arctic mainland, Hudson Bay, and northern Quebec.[3] This disruption of their traditional lifestyle based on hunting and trapping caused them to depend increasingly on social assistance and intermittent wages.

ABORIGINAL DEMOGRAPHIC PROFILE TODAY

Partly because there is such diversity among aboriginal Canadians and partly because they were not always easy to find, census and other demographic statistics in this area are not considered as definitive as for other groups. A special supplementary aboriginal survey was conducted after the 1991 census, although exact numbers are still difficult to come by. In 1991, some 1 002 675 Canadians, or 3.7 percent of the total Canadian population, reported aboriginal origins, but only 626 000 (2.3 percent of the total population) identified with an aboriginal group. Moreover, of the slightly more than one million who reported aboriginal origins, over half (53 percent) reported multiple ancestries, almost all of them in combination with nonaboriginal origins. Both those who reported aboriginal origins and those who identified with an aboriginal group can then be broken down into three categories, as outlined above: North American Indian, Métis, and Inuit. The basic 1991 statistics on these variations are provided in Table 7.1.

Whether we are speaking of aboriginal origin or identification, then, Canada's aboriginal population breaks down as follows: about 75 percent North American Indians, about 20 percent Métis, and about five percent Inuit. Aboriginal Canadians are not spread uniformly across the country; Table 7.2 shows the distribution of component groups by province and territory for those reporting Aboriginal origins. It reveals the heavy concentration of aboriginal Canadians in the western half of the country.

TABLE 7.1 Canadians of Aboriginal Origin and Identifying with an Aboriginal Group, 1991

	North American Indian	Métis	Inuit	Total
Aboriginal origin	783 980	212 650	49 260	1 002 675
Identifying as aboriginal	460 680	135 265	36 215	626 000

Source: Statistics Canada, 1991 Census, Profile of Canada's Aboriginal Population, cat. no. 94–325 (1995), and Language, Tradition, Health, Lifestyle and Social Issues, cat no. 89–533 (1993). Reproduced with the permission of the Minister of Supply and Services Canada, 1995.

TABLE 7.2 Distribution by Province and Territory of Those Reporting Aboriginal Origins

	North American Indian	Métis	Inuit	Total	Percent of Provincial Population	Percent of Aboriginal Canadians
Newfoundland	5 840	1 605	6 455	13 110	2.3%	1.3%
P.E.I.	1 670	190	80	1 885	1.5%	0.2%
Nova Scotia	19 950	1 590	770	21 885	2.4%	2.2%
New Brunswick	11 830	980	445	12 820	1.8%	1.3%
Quebec	112 590	19 475	8 485	137 615	2.0%	13.7%
Ontario	220 140	26 905	5 245	243 555	2.4%	24.3%
Manitoba	76 370	45 575	900	116 195	10.6%	11.6%
Saskatchewan	69 385	32 840	540	96 580	9.8%	9.6%
Alberta	99 655	56 310	2 820	148 220	5.8%	14.8%
British Columbia	149 565	22 295	1 990	169 035	5.2%	16.9%
Yukon	5 870	565	170	6 385	23.0%	0.6%
N.W.T.	11 100	4 315	21 355	35 390	61.4%	3.5%
Total	783 980	212 650	49 260	1 002 675	3.7%	100%

Source: Statistics Canada, 1991 Census, Profile of Canada's Aboriginal Population, cat. no. 94–325 (1995). Reproduced with the permission of the Minister of Supply and Services Canada, 1995.

The Department of Indian and Northern Affairs reported a slightly higher number of aboriginal people in 1993: approximately 1.2 million, or 4.3 percent of the population. These were broken down as follows: status Indians on reserve, 326 444; status Indians off reserve, 226 872; non-status Indians, 405 000; Métis, 192 100; and Inuit, 50 800.[4] A rough estimate would therefore be about four percent of the total population, with over a half-million status Indians (now often called **First Nations**), 60 percent of whom reside on reserves. There were 2370 reserves in Canada in 1994, with an average size of about 1160 hectares. They are distributed among some 600 bands, with an average band population of about 650 persons.

Besides these legal distinctions, there are 11 major aboriginal linguistic families, the largest being Cree, Ojibway, Micmac, Montagnais-Naskapi, and Blackfoot, but more than 50 aboriginal languages exist. In terms of mother tongue, on-reserve Indians are about equally divided between those using English and those using an aboriginal language; off-reserve Indians and Métis are mostly urbanized and English-speaking. Among urban areas, Regina, Saskatoon, Winnipeg, and Edmonton have the highest concentrations of such groups. The Inuit are least assimilated, linguistically and geographically, and most speak the Inuktitut language.

These basic statistics present only part of the picture. At least of equal significance are the distressing statistics on aboriginal poverty. Even the Department of Indian Affairs reports that "poverty is very widespread on reserves with about half (47.2 percent) of Indian families falling below the poverty line. This is more than three times the rate for Canada overall."[5] Moreover, many reserve families have incomes *far* below the poverty line, and apart from a few aboriginal urban professionals, the same is true for most of those who live off-reserve. Related to this level of poverty are alarming rates of aboriginal alcoholism, violence, suicide, mortality, low educational attainment, and unemployment. Aboriginal Canadians are four times as likely as non-Natives to be murdered, Native youth are five times as likely to commit suicide, and 35 percent of Native deaths are from accidents and violence. The overall life expectancy of aboriginal Canadians is ten years shorter than that of non-Natives, which is largely due to poor health services and housing on reserves. Twice as many Native infants die before they are one year old and twice as many Native adults die from respiratory diseases. No less than 20 percent of aboriginal Canadians over 40 years of age suffer from diabetes, and Natives suffer ten times as much from tuberculosis as non-Natives. Other diseases that are common on reserves are pneumonia, gastroenteritis, rheumatic fever, ear infections, meningitis, hepatitis, intestinal infections, skin diseases, and disorders of the nervous system. Native children constitute 20 percent of those in the child welfare system, and housing is often sadly deficient, being overcrowded, lacking in running water, indoor toilets, and central heating.[6] Given these deplorable living conditions and the high suicide rate, which is illustrated in Figure 7.1, it is not surprising that so many aboriginal Canadians die before reaching 55 years of age.

In essence, the typical Native scenario runs as follows: having lost their land, original livelihood and culture, and being placed on unproductive reserves, many Indians find themselves with little to do. The resulting unemployment, idleness, and reliance on welfare often leads them to seek solace in alcohol and drugs. In this intoxicated state, many Natives resort to family and other violence, which in turn brings them into trouble with the law. Not being able to pay their fines, and subject to discrimination at the hands the police, the courts, and other aspects of the justice system, they then go to jail where they become even more alienated, depressed, and abused. Aboriginal Canadians have suffered from untold discrimination and indignity at every turn. The Indian Act requires non-Native bureaucratic approval for almost any band decision. In the past, Indian babies were frequently removed from the reserves to be adopted by non-Native parents, and Indian children were forced to go to residential schools where they were punished, sometimes to the point of assault, for speaking their Native language or engaging in Native customs. Native languages and cultures have been systematically discouraged, and traditional forms of government and medicine have been outlawed. Indians living on reserves did not even have the right to vote in federal elections until 1960.

Figure 7.1 **Suicide Rate for Registered Indians and the Total Population, Canada, 1979–1991**

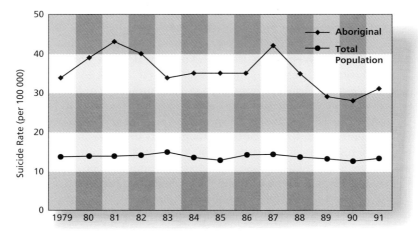

The data for the Pacific region cover only the years 1979–1984 and for the N.W.T. only the years 1979–1986.
Source: Privy Council Office, Choosing Life: Special Report on Suicide among Aboriginal People, *1995.*
Reproduced with the permission of the Minister of Supply and Services Canada, 1995.

One of the most tragic examples of government mistreatment of Native peoples in recent times is that found in Davis Inlet in Labrador. In 1966 the government of Newfoundland moved a group of Innu people to an island off the Labrador mainland, where they developed even worse social and health problems and had even fewer economic opportunities than elsewhere. In January 1993 these conditions and the high incidence of solvent abuse among children alarmed many Canadians. The federal government's attempts to rectify the problems were complicated by the community's expulsion of a provincial judge and police because the Innu did not feel these officials respected their traditions. Clyde Wells's government paternalistically insisted that the issues of the administration of justice and policing be resolved before discussing other problems.

Part of the reason for so little progress in improving the condition of aboriginal life in Canada is the relatively small number of people involved and hence the invisibility of the problem. The dispersion of aboriginal peoples has also made it difficult for them to get elected to federal or provincial governments and has recently generated demands for guaranteed aboriginal seats in Canadian legislatures. Another reason is the stereotype of Native people as lazy, drunken Indians who have brought all these difficulties upon themselves: "Are they not exempt from federal and provincial taxation? Is their post-secondary education not generously funded? Is their housing not heavily subsidized? Do they not have a problem with alcohol? Are there really enough well-educated Indians that they could govern themselves?" There is just enough truth in these stereotypes to allow them to retard understanding of the real causes of the problems faced by aboriginal people. The Department of Indian Affairs is anxious to point out, however, that in many ways considerable improvement has been recorded in on-reserve living conditions since 1960, such as in infant and other mortality

Reprinted with the permission of the Ottawa Sun.

rates, water supply and sewage disposal systems, housing conditions, and postsecondary education participation rates.[7]

ABORIGINAL POLITICAL ISSUES SINCE 1970

For a variety of reasons, Canadian Native peoples and their problems have become a major concern of Canadian politics in the 1990s. In part they were insulted by the terms of the 1963 Royal Commission on Bilingualism and Biculturalism, which spoke of English and French as being Canada's two "founding races," and offended by the Trudeau–Chrétien **White Paper on Indians** of 1969, which called for their complete integration into the wider Canadian society. Another factor was the sympathetic Berger Inquiry into the proposed Mackenzie Valley gas pipeline,[8] as well as an increased awareness of aboriginal issues worldwide. In part, the problems had become so serious that they simply could no longer be ignored by either side, and the incidence of sit-ins, roadblocks and other blockades, rallies, court cases, hunger strikes, and international protests increased. Indeed, at the 1989 Annual Meeting of the **Assembly of First Nations**, a mutual defence pact based on the NATO agreement was signed to the effect that bands would support each other and send reinforcements when requested.

In 1990 two developments helped place aboriginal concerns in the public consciousness: Native MLA Elijah Harper was instrumental in defeating the Meech Lake Accord, and the Mohawks of Oka, Quebec, took the law into their own hands to protect what they considered their land from the expansion of a golf course.

Since 1970, then, the crowded Canadian political agenda has had to find room for a variety of aboriginal issues made all the more complex because of the diversity within the aboriginal community. No better catalogue of such issues has been collected than that of former Chief Justice Brian Dickson, which formed the basis for the mandate of the **Royal Commission on Aboriginal Peoples** appointed in 1991. The following is a summary of his terms of reference:

····································

TERMS OF REFERENCE, ROYAL COMMISSION ON ABORIGINAL PEOPLES

1. The history of relations between aboriginal peoples, the Canadian government and Canadian society as a whole.

2. The recognition and affirmation of aboriginal self-government; its origin, content and a strategy for progressive implementation.

3. The land base for aboriginal peoples, including the process for resolving comprehensive and specific claims, whether rooted in Canadian constitutional instruments, treaties or in aboriginal title.

4. The historical interpretation and application, and potential future scope, of s. 91(24) of the Constitution Act, 1867 and the responsibilities of the Canadian Crown.

5. The legal status, implementation and future evolution of aboriginal treaties, including modern-day agreements.

6. The constitutional and legal position of the Métis and off-reserve Indians.

7. The special difficulties of aboriginal people who live in the North.

8. The Indian Act and the role, responsibilities and policies of the Department of Indian Affairs and Northern Development.

9. Social issues of concern to aboriginal peoples.

10. Economic issues of concern to aboriginal peoples.

11. Cultural issues concerning aboriginal peoples.

12. The position and role of aboriginal elders.

13. The position and role of aboriginal women under existing social conditions and legal arrangements, and in the future.

14. The situation of aboriginal youth.

15. Educational issues of concern to aboriginal peoples.

16. Justice issues of concern to aboriginal peoples.

Source: Royal Commission on Aboriginal Peoples, "Terms of Reference."

The Royal Commission conducted four rounds of public hearings between 1992 and 1993, commissioned extensive research, and proceeded to identify four "touchstones" as a framework for its eventual recommendations. These were a *new relationship* between aboriginal and nonaboriginal people based on equality, respect, and reconciliation; *self-determination* for aboriginal peoples within Canada through self-government, that is, the right to control their collective futures; economic *self-sufficiency* for aboriginal peoples, including breaking the cycle of poverty and dependency on government transfers and creating meaningful employment opportunities; and personal and collective *healing* for aboriginal peoples and communities, to remedy the effects of decades of mistreatment and neglect.[9] The final report was delayed until 1996, but much of its value consisted of its interim educational impact, and many of its recommendations could be anticipated. Here the issues will be discussed under the broad headings of Land Issues and Governance Issues. Although it is easier to visualize aboriginal self-government when it is based on a specific piece of territory, the issues of land claims and governance have usually proceeded independently of each other.

Land Issues

In most of the country, North American Indians signed treaties with the Crown under which they ceded the land to the government in return for protected reserves. But, especially in British Columbia and the North, few such treaties were signed, leaving North American Indians and Inuit in these regions without a land base. The Métis have never possessed any land, with the result that only about one-third of aboriginal peoples have a land base. This gives rise to the issue of **aboriginal title**, that is, a claim to the land on the basis of traditional occupancy and use rather than treaty. The existence of such aboriginal title was first recognized in the *Calder* case in 1973 in connection with the Nisga'a band in British Columbia, but the Supreme Court of Canada was split on the question of whether such title had been subsequently extinguished. In response, the government of Canada announced its intention to negotiate aboriginal title but only where treaties did not exist, and only six at a time. This policy was not satisfactory, because even where treaties were signed, Indians are increasingly challenging their terms and implementation. Moreover, some Métis have also raised the land issue, so the federal government eventually removed earlier restrictions. A great variety of aboriginal land claims have therefore been launched in the past 20 years. They fall into two categories: **comprehensive claims** based on aboriginal title (that is, traditional use and occupancy of land) that have not been dealt with by treaty or other legal means; and **specific claims** arising from alleged nonfulfilment of Indian treaties and other lawful obligations.

NORTHERN LAND CLAIMS

Such claims have moved relatively faster in the North than in the south, since north of the 60th parallel the federal government is in charge of the land as well as of aboriginals. In fact, agreement in principle has been achieved in three comprehensive land claims in the North: the Council of Yukon Indians (later broken down into smaller parts), the Inuvialuit, and the Tungavik Federation of Nunavut. The Dene-Métis claim in the western Arctic was approved in principle but then rejected, and has subsequently been divided into smaller claims, with success reported in the case of the Gwich'in and Sahtu Dene and Métis. Besides providing land and money, such comprehensive claims clarify Native hunting, fishing, and trapping rights and clear obstacles to future economic development.[10] These claims are illustrated in Figure 7.2; however, it should be noted that the rights of current property owners have been protected and that in many cases the specific land boundaries have yet to be designated. In 1993 the federal government announced that it would no longer require blanket extinguishment clauses as a condition for settling comprehensive land claims.

Figure 7.2 **Northern Aboriginal Land Claims**

Source: Indian and Northern Affairs Canada. Comprehensive Land Claims in Canada, 1992. Reproduced with the permission of the Minister of Supply and Services Canada, 1995.

SOUTHERN LAND CLAIMS

In the south, where Ottawa has responsibility for "Indians and lands reserved for the Indians" but where the provinces have jurisdiction over public lands, such claims have moved more slowly. Aboriginals have generally found provincial governments even less sympathetic to Native issues than Ottawa, and conflict has often developed between Indian bands and large natural resource companies as well as other nonaboriginals who now live on the land in question. Ottawa insists that provinces be party to such settlements and contribute to their costs, arguing that it is in the provinces' interests to establish certainty of title to lands and resources. Thus far, relatively few comprehensive land claim successes can be reported below the 60th parallel.

The main provincial comprehensive land claim settlement was the 1975 **James Bay and Northern Quebec Agreement** between the Cree and Inuit and the government of Quebec, supplemented by several subsequent agreements. The James Bay Agreement gave the Natives exclusive use of 13 700 km^2 of land and an additional 450 000 km^2 of exclusive hunting, fishing, and trapping rights, along with $225 million in cash in return for allowing Quebec to construct a giant hydro development project in the area. While the deal was unprecedented and widely heralded in many quarters, one terrible side effect was the mercury poisoning of fish, due to an unanticipated chemical reaction between water and rock in the flooded land, and the Natives who ate them. This problem and the growing perception that the deal may have been less generous to the Native community than originally thought made the Cree of Quebec hesitant to agree to the second, "Great Whale," phase of the James Bay project. Other comprehensive claims negotiations in Eastern Canada are proceeding with the Conseil des Atikamekw et des Montagnais and the Innu Nation and the Labrador Inuit Association in northern Quebec and Labrador.

Since the province of British Columbia contains a large proportion of North American Indians and few treaties, the land claims issue has been particularly significant there. The provincial government was reluctant to begin such negotiations, however, and a 1991 B.C. Supreme Court decision was a major setback for such land claims.[11] The Nisga'a tribe in northwest B.C., which has been seeking recognition of their aboriginal title for over 100 years, took their claim to court in the 1973 *Calder* case, and has been negotiating with Ottawa ever since. Once the province entered the negotiations in 1990, however, prospects of a settlement improved. In 1992, the governments of Canada and British Columbia signed a B.C. Treaty Commission Agreement with the First Nations of that province, and by the end of 1994 the commission had received over 40 statements of intent to negotiate, representing over two-thirds of the status Indians in the province. That, however, was the easy part.

Specific land claims resulting from dissatisfaction with treaties—especially the fact that bands did not receive the full amount of land that the treaties promised—have arisen in most other provinces, but until 1991 Ottawa did not want to hear them. By mid-1993, 584 specific claims had been filed, and by the end of 1994, 312 of these had been resolved, although not always to First Nations' satisfaction. The greatest progress has been reported in Saskatchewan.

OTHER LAND ISSUES

Another dimension of land issues concerns what aboriginals are allowed by treaties to do on public lands. Aboriginal treaty rights, especially hunting and fishing rights, frequently conflict with provincial law. Some progress has been made on this front, especially in two Supreme Court of Canada decisions in 1990. The Court ruled that a 1760 Huron treaty was valid, and its provision that Indians be allowed "the free exercise of their Religion [and] their Customs" prevented Quebec from prosecuting Hurons for practising Native customs and fishing in provincial parks.[12] The Court also gave Indians new hope in a B.C. decision that stated that s. 35(1) of the Charter of Rights affords aboriginal people constitutional protection against provincial legislative power and that the clause should be given a generous, liberal interpretation. In this case the Court said that the aboriginals' right to fish could override provincial regulations regarding the size of a net.[13]

The Innu of Labrador protested for several years against low-level NATO military training flights around Canadian Forces Base Goose Bay, which they claimed were a hazard to human health and the environment. Both federal and Newfoundland governments rejected their arguments, however, and encouraged even more countries to take advantage of the location.

Yet another aspect of the land question arose in the conflict at Oka, Quebec, in the summer of 1990, the most serious conflict between Indians and authorities of modern times.[14] The municipal council's decision to expand a golf course on land claimed by resident Mohawks as sacred ground (a claim of traditional occupancy but not guaranteed by treaty) led to an armed standoff between Mohawk warriors and the Quebec provincial police; one police officer was killed. The Mohawks were supported by the nearby Kahnawake reserve, which also set up barriers and blockaded the Mercier Bridge to Montreal. The Canadian Armed Forces were later brought in, and aboriginal demonstrations took place across the country. While some local nonaboriginal residents stoned vehicles carrying Mohawk families, most Canadians hoped that the incident would speed up the process of settling hundreds of outstanding aboriginal land claims before any worse violence occurred. Unfortunately, violence did erupt again—in a land dispute at Ipperwash, Ontario, in 1995, in which one Native was killed.

Governance Issues

Aboriginal Canadians have long demanded improvements in government health, social, and educational services, and some minor improvements have been made over the years. Natives began to feel, however, that they were too constrained by the Indian Act and that Native problems required Native solutions. They were tired of living at the mercy of politicians and bureaucrats, a fact highlighted by the Mulroney government's reduction in Native postsecondary education support in 1989 and cuts to Native newspapers, broadcasting, organizations and subsidized housing in 1990.[15] Yet most aboriginals did not want to gut the Indian Act and existing government programs until they had something better to put in their place.

The first positive official response to aboriginal discontent was the Hawthorn Report of 1966, *Survey of the Contemporary Indians of Canada*. It took the position that aboriginal Canadians needed a greater degree of local autonomy and deserved a higher level of government services to compensate for everything that had happened in the past. Because non-aboriginal Canadians had built a prosperous society on the lands and resources originally owned by aboriginals, aboriginals should be considered "citizens plus." Nothing much came of this report at the time, and indeed, the next initiative, the 1969 White Paper, took the opposite approach—that aboriginal Canadians should be treated exactly as other Canadians, and that even the Indian Act should be repealed. It was the angry aboriginal response to the White Paper that finally sparked the beginning of changes in the issue of governance.

Aboriginal Canadians argued that they should be able to choose their own decision-making processes, for they could hardly be expected to support the apparatus that created their current problems. Before the passage of the Indian Act, they had sophisticated and distinctive forms of government and many wanted to return to such traditional ways, feeling that the system of elected band councils was an alien imposition. Going well beyond such decision-making machinery, they also wanted aboriginal self-government. Natives want more control over their own affairs, but the specific structures of such proposed self-government are not clear-cut. Some advocates would accept a kind of super-municipality, but others have more ambitious plans that would be harder to fit into the Canadian constitutional framework. For the moment, the demand is for a "two-track" approach: constitutional recognition of the **inherent right of aboriginal self-government** stemming from their unique history as Canada's original inhabitants, plus concurrent progress toward greater *community-based control* at the local level. In this way, an array of self-government arrangements and institutional models can be developed within the existing constitutional set-up. Self-government would also help them take action to preserve aboriginal languages, which are in danger of becoming extinct.

THE CONSTITUTION ACT, 1982, TO MEECH LAKE

The first improvement in the constitutional recognition of aboriginal rights occurred after widespread protests in connection with the constitutional negotiations in 1981–82. The Constitution Act, 1982, ultimately contained two clauses of interest here. Section 25 guaranteed that Charter rights would not be construed so as to abrogate or derogate from any aboriginal, treaty, or other rights or freedoms pertaining to the aboriginal peoples of Canada, including any rights recognized by the Royal Proclamation of 1763, and any rights or freedoms "that now exist by way of land claims agreements or may be so acquired." Section 35 recognized and affirmed the existing aboriginal and treaty rights of the aboriginal peoples of Canada, including the Indian, Inuit, and Métis peoples. To conform with the equality rights clause in the Charter, the Indian Act was amended to remove the clause that had previously taken away Indian status from aboriginal women who married white men but granted such status to white women who married Indian men. Bill C-32 (1985) led to the reinstatement of nearly 100 000 aboriginal women and their children, but since bands were allowed to control their own membership, a high proportion of those reinstated in status were not allowed to return to the reserve.

Based in part on the recommendations of the 1983 Penner Report (Report of the Special Committee of the House of Commons on Indian Self-Government), Section 35 of the 1982 Constitution Act was temporarily amended to provide for a series of federal–provincial first ministers' conferences on aboriginal rights between 1983 and 1987. Prime Ministers Trudeau and Mulroney, in turn, tried unsuccessfully to get provincial premiers and Native leaders to agree to the terms of a constitutional amendment recognizing the principle of aboriginal self-government. Several premiers insisted that the concept be clarified before they would agree even in principle, while aboriginal leaders wanted the principle recognized as an *inherent* right. At the 1987 Conference, Georges Erasmus, national Chief of the Assembly of First Nations, spoke as follows:

> Nothing short of aboriginal self-government will achieve our aspirations for survival as distinct peoples. Attempts by governments at integration and assimilation over the years have failed and we have rejected them. We must be able to control our lives on our own lands and using our own resources.[16]

Although the constitutional talks broke down, two pieces of legislation were passed to provide for self-government in specific localities. The 1984 Cree-Naskapi (of Quebec) Act set in place self-government arrangements for the Indians of Quebec who were parties to the James Bay land claim agreement, and the 1986 Sechelt Indian Band Self-Government Act allowed the Sechelt band in British Columbia to assume control over their lands, resources, health and social services, education, and local taxation in what is usually called the "municipal model." Given the absence of constitutional advance, however, Canadian Natives were understandably opposed to the Meech Lake Accord, which addressed Quebec's constitutional demands but completely overlooked their own. Even supporters of the Accord found it hard to blame Elijah Harper for withholding unanimous consent when it came before the Manitoba legislature for approval.

THE CHARLOTTETOWN ACCORD

Harper's stand, together with the Oka affair, precipitated a dramatic breakthrough of constitutional concern with aboriginal issues and in the participation of Native leaders in constitutional negotiations. As mentioned in Chapter 3, aboriginal leaders were given the same status as premiers in the talks leading up to the 1992 Charlottetown Accord, and that document addressed aboriginal concerns in a more extensive and satisfactory way than it did the demands of Quebec. Before the negotiations, the Royal Commission on Aboriginal Peoples issued a summary of the six criteria it felt were essential to the right of aboriginal self-government:

·······································

THE RIGHT TO ABORIGINAL SELF-GOVERNMENT:

- is inherent in nature,
- is circumscribed in extent, and
- is sovereign within its sphere

The constitutional provision should:
- be adopted with the consent of the aboriginal peoples,
- be consistent with the view that section 35 of the Constitution may already recognize a right to self-government; and,

- be justiciable immediately, though self-government agreements resulting from a constitutional obligation to negotiate will obviously be the normal and desirable vehicle for implementing the right of self-government.

The Charlottetown Accord recognized the inherent right of aboriginal peoples to self-government and agreed that such First Nations governments would constitute a third order of government in Canada, analogous to the provinces. The document provided for self-government agreements to be negotiated among the three levels of government, with access to the courts to enforce such rights delayed for a five-year period. Federal and provincial laws would remain in place until superseded by aboriginal laws, but the latter would have to be consistent with the preservation of peace, order, and good government in Canada. The Charlottetown Accord would also have established a series of ongoing first ministers' conferences on aboriginal constitutional issues. In addition to provisions for aboriginal self-government, Native peoples were to have a new role of one kind or another in the House of Commons, Senate, Supreme Court, first ministers' conferences, and the constitutional amending formula.

Despite the enormous leap in official thinking that this section of the Accord represented, a majority of aboriginal voters opposed it in the referendum. Some found the provisions lacking in detail, and many aboriginal women felt that their individual (Charter) rights were being sacrificed for new group rights. On the other hand, it would appear that nonaboriginals who voted against the Accord did not do so because of the aboriginal provisions.[17] Alan Cairns suggests that it was possible to make such progress on aboriginal matters partly because of the guilt felt by nonaboriginal participants and partly because the first ministers and aboriginal leaders were dealing in unchartered territory. In contrast a huge amount of historical, official, and academic "baggage"—including the notion of the equality of the provinces—hampered advances on the Quebec question.[18]

POST-1992 PROGRESS

After the rejection of the Charlottetown Accord, and in anticipation of future constitutional talks and the results of the Royal Commission on Aboriginal Peoples, activity in the area of aboriginal governance was limited to legislative and administrative changes such as experiments in delegating federal or provincial government powers to First Nations bands. Considerable progress has been made on this second, *community-based* (as distinct from constitutional), track of aboriginal self-government. Aboriginal people have increased their control over how federal funding is spent, and have assumed responsibility for delivering many social and health care services. At the same time, some 50 First Nations are involved in developing legislated self-government along the lines of the Cree Naskapi and Sechelt models.

Another interesting initiative is the experimental dismantling in Manitoba of the Department of Indian Affairs as it affects First Nations. A framework agreement to this effect was signed in December 1994 by the Minister of Indian Affairs and the Grand Chief of the Assembly of Manitoba Chiefs. The Department will essentially withdraw from exercising its functions at the request of local First Nations governments. In mid-1995, the minister announced that Ottawa was launching new negotiations to give Indians in all provinces much wider powers.

Two special cases in which land claims and self-government agreements were negotiated simultaneously should also be mentioned. In the Northwest Territories, a 1992 plebiscite ratified the boundary divisions for the creation, in 1999, of a new territory called **Nunavut**, an area inhabited almost solely by Inuit. It will have all the government institutions associated with a province or territory, while being characterized by a form of aboriginal self-government.

The other case in which self-government and land claims have been linked is in the Yukon. The four Yukon First Nations land claim agreements ratified in 1993 included self-government agreements. The agreements require that each First Nation have a constitution and a citizenship code; they also outline how First Nation powers relate to territorial and federal powers.[19]

THE ABORIGINAL JUSTICE QUESTION

Because of the high proportion of Natives in Canada's correctional system, one important aspect of self-government is the concept of a parallel aboriginal justice system. Native cases would be diverted from the regular judicial process to allow convictions and sentences based on Native values and community traditions. Support for this concept has come from the Canadian Bar Association and the Law Reform Commission of Canada, as well as from many provincial inquiries into the treatment of Natives in the regular judicial system—especially the Donald Marshall Inquiry in Nova Scotia and the Aboriginal Justice Inquiry in Manitoba. Marshall was a Nova Scotia Micmac imprisoned for over ten years for a crime he did not commit. The Manitoba inquiry centred on the rape and murder of Helen Betty Osborne, an Indian girl in The Pas, and on the shooting of a Native leader by a Winnipeg police officer. Both of these inquiries as well as those in other provinces documented incidents of the brutalization of Native peoples by the criminal justice system.

While governments have generally ruled out a wholesale parallel aboriginal justice system, several provinces have allowed experimental judicial processes involving aboriginal input. More aboriginals have been hired as police officers; some reserves have their own aboriginal police forces; and a few even maintain their own correctional facilities.

Many other aboriginal political issues have arisen in recent years. One is the extent to which Indians have a right to operate gambling facilities on their reserves, casinos becoming a leading source of revenue for both Indian bands and provincial governments. Another is the question of tax exemption. In 1995, the federal government began to enforce its Indian Remission Order so that status Indians who earn employment income for duties performed off-reserve would have to pay income tax. This led to the occupation of Revenue Canada buildings in December 1994. A third issue was cigarette smuggling based on Indian reserves that straddle the Canada–U.S. border, especially in Quebec. Rather than deal with the problem head-on, given the risk of armed violence, Ottawa and Quebec decided to reduce their respective cigarette taxes so that the profitability of smuggling would be reduced. Many other provinces were forced to follow suit. The fate of aboriginals in a separate Quebec was also widely discussed.

Two of the traditional weaknesses of the aboriginal cause have been a general attitude of passivity and a lack of effective organization of Native groups. Recent years, however, have witnessed the emergence of strong pressure groups, such as the Assembly of First Nations (status Indians), the Native Council of Canada (nonstatus Indians), the Métis National Council, and the Inuit Tapirisat. Many other aboriginal groups exist at the provincial or territorial level, such as the Council of Yukon Indians, and the Native Women's Association is also vocal.

CONCLUSION

The multidimensional aboriginal problem in Canada will be very hard to solve. In some respects Natives are treated more generously than other groups in society, and some non-Natives resent it, holding aboriginal peoples responsible for most of their own problems. But the momentum of opinion generally blames government policies and corporate practices rather than the Natives for their plight and supports efforts to improve the conditions of aboriginal life. Most thoughtful observers want to maintain or improve existing government programs; enlarge and strengthen reserves, attempting to make them more economically viable; respect treaty rights; recognize land claims (as long as they do not interfere with non-Native economic development); move toward the principle and practice of aboriginal self-government; and treat Native peoples more fairly in the justice system. Although progress has so far been slight, a new generation of well-educated, articulate, and insistent aboriginal leaders has arrived on the scene,[20] and the Canadian public is finally listening.

P Historically, the pluralist approach was irrelevant to the aboriginal question because Native Canadians did not even try to exert any influence on the authorities and their organizations were weak if not nonexistent. But in recent years, pluralism has become much more applicable for a variety of reasons. Aboriginals clearly add to the pluralistic nature of the country; they contain great diversity among themselves, and their organizations have functioned as effective pressure groups in recent years. Indeed, in an almost corporatist manner, aboriginal leaders have been integrated into the policy-making process since 1992, and the delegation of powers of self-government (and recognition of the inherent right to self-government) goes well beyond the pluralist–corporatist concept of delegating self-regulating powers to professional groups.

SC The state-centred approach is also particularly appropriate. At first, almost every decision with respect to Canadian aboriginals was made by the bureaucrats in the Department of Indian Affairs. In most cases, what the politicians and bureaucrats thought was in the interests of the aboriginal peoples clearly was not. The relocation of the Inuit to the high Arctic was one of many such authoritative fiascoes. The relocation of the Innu of Davis Inlet is a more recent manifestation of the same approach, and the disciplinary attitude of Clyde Wells's Newfoundland government is evidence that some political authorities continue to treat aboriginals like children.

Ⓒ Class analysts would fault large corporations as well as governmental elites for the sorry state of aboriginal life in Canada. The corporate elite did its best to preserve the most productive land for itself, even to the point of denying Native peoples reserve land in British Columbia and the North. Corporations have frequently challenged aboriginal rights when valuable supplies of trees, minerals, or petroleum were found on reserve land or land that Indians had claimed as theirs by aboriginal title. Confrontations between forestry companies and aboriginals have occurred at Temagami in Ontario and Clayoquot Sound in British Columbia. Interestingly enough, and contrary to some class-based expectations, the forestry workers involved tended to side with their employers in these disputes.

DISCUSSION QUESTIONS

1. What are the causes of the generally poor condition of aboriginal life in Canada?

2. What are the distinctive features of the values and methods of decision-making of aboriginal communities?

3. What are the principal aboriginal demands on the political agenda?

4. What is the difference between comprehensive and specific land claims?

5. What is meant by aboriginal self-government?

6. What is the difference between constitutional and community-based self-government?

7. If aboriginal societies do not have the resources to operate their own governments, how much financial support from federal and provincial governments is appropriate?

8. What can be done to make First Nations reserves more economically viable?

9. How would an aboriginal justice system interact with Canada's traditional justice system?

10. How do the approaches outlined in Chapter 1 relate to the material in this chapter?

NOTES

1. The Royal Proclamation was a strong statement on Indian rights, and today's aboriginal Canadians point to the significance of its inclusion in the 1982 Charter of Rights. It can be found, among other places, in Michael Asch, *Home and Native Land* (Toronto: Methuen, 1984). See Darlene Johnston, *The Taking of Indian Lands: Consent or Coercion?* (Saskatoon: University of Saskatchewan Native Law Centre, 1989).

2. Thomas R. Berger, *A Long and Terrible Shadow: White Values, Native Rights in the Americas* (Vancouver: Douglas & McIntyre, 1991).

3. A subsequent and controversial relocation occurred in 1953–55. See Royal Commission on Aboriginal Peoples, *The High Arctic Relocation* (Ottawa: Supply and Services Canada, 1994, cat. no. Z1-1991/1-41-3-1E).

4. See, for example, *Building a New Partnership* (March 1995), and *Basic Departmental Data, 1994* (January 1995).

5. Peter R. Oberle, *The Incidence of Family Poverty on Canadian Indian Reserves* (Ottawa: Indian and Northern Affairs Canada, 1993).

6. See, among other sources, Geoffrey York, *The Dispossessed: Life and Death in Native Canada* (Toronto: Lester & Orpen Dennys, 1989); Pauline Comeau and Aldo Santin, *The First Canadians* (Toronto: Lorimer, 1990); Ellen Bobet, "Indian Mortality," *Canadian Social Trends* (Statistics Canada, Winter 1989); and a series in the *Globe and Mail* by Thomas Walkom in April 1990. One-third of on-reserve households have no indoor bathroom.

7. Department of Indian Affairs and Northern Development, *Basic Departmental Data*, 1994 (Ottawa, 1995).

8. Thomas Berger, *Northern Frontier, Northern Homeland: The Report of the Mackenzie Valley Inquiry* (Ottawa: Supply and Services Canada, 1977, republished by Douglas & McIntyre, Vancouver, 1988).

9. Royal Commission on Aboriginal Peoples.

10. The Inuvialuit agreed to 91 000 km^2 and subsurface rights in the western Arctic Islands as early as 1984. The Yukon Indians agreed to 41 439 km^2 and \$248 million in 1990. The Dene-Métis claim in the western Arctic, which includes title to 180 000 km^2 of land and subsurface mineral rights to 10 000 km^2, along with \$500 million, was approved in principle but then rejected. The Inuit of the eastern Arctic have agreed in principle to the creation of a separate territory, Nunavut, and to receiving title to 350 000 km^2 and \$580 million in compensation for renouncing all other land claims.

11. On judicial treatment of land claims, see *Calder v. Attorney General of B.C.*, [1973] S.C.R. 313; *Guerin v. The Queen*, [1984] 2 S.C.R. 335; and *Ontario (Attorney General) v. Bear Island Foundation*, 1991. The decision in the B.C. Supreme Court was *Delgamuukw et al. v. The Queen*, for a discussion of which see Hamar Foster, "It Goes Without Saying: Precedent and the Doctrine of Extinguishment by Implication in Delgamuukw et al. v. The Queen," *The Advocate* 49, (3) (May 1991). See also Paul Tennant, *Aboriginal Peoples and Politics* (Vancouver: University of British Columbia Press, 1990).

12. *R. v. Sioui*, [1990] 1 S.C.R. 1025.

13. *R. v. Sparrow*, 1990 [SCR] 1075.

14. Geoffrey York and Loreen Pindera, *People of the Pines: The Warriors and the Legacy of Oka* (Toronto: Little Brown, 1991); Craig MacLaine and Michael Baxendale, *This Land Is Our Land* (Toronto: Optimum, 1990); and Robert Campbell and Leslie Pal, *The Real Worlds of Canadian Politics*, 2nd ed. (Peterborough: Broadview Press, 1991), ch.4.

15. Murray Angus, *"and the last shall be first": Native policy in an era of cutbacks* (Toronto: NC Press, 1991).

16. Georges Erasmus, "Opening Remarks," First Ministers' Conference on Aboriginal Constitutional Affairs, Ottawa, March 26, 1987. See also Frank Cassidy, ed., *Aboriginal Self-Government* (Halifax: Institute for Research on Public Policy, 1991).

17. Richard Johnston et al., "The People and the Charlottetown Accord," in R.L. Watts and D.M. Brown, eds., *Canada: The State of the Federation 1993* (Kingston: Institute of Intergovernmental Relations, Queen's University, 1993).

18. Alan C. Cairns, "Aboriginal Canadians, Citizenship and the Constitution," in Paul Fox and Graham White, eds., *Politics: Canada*, 8th ed. (Oshawa: McGraw-Hill Ryerson, 1995), p. 31.

19. Michael S. Whittington, "Aboriginal Self-Government in Canada," in Michael S. Whittington and Glen Williams, eds., *Canadian Politics in the 1990s*, 4th ed. (Scarborough: Nelson Canada, 1995).

20. Kathy Brock, "Consensual Politics: Political Leadership in the Aboriginal Community," in Maureen Mancuso et al., eds., *Leaders and Leadership in Canada* (Toronto: Oxford University Press, 1994).

FURTHER READING

Angus, Murray. *"and the last shall be first": Native policy in an era of cutbacks*. Toronto: NC Press, 1991.

Berger, Thomas. *Northern Frontier, Northern Homeland: The Report of the Mackenzie Valley Pipeline Inquiry*. Ottawa: Supply and Services Canada, 1977, republished by Douglas & McIntyre, Vancouver, 1988.

———. *A Long and Terrible Shadow: White Values, Native Rights in the Americas*. Vancouver: Douglas & McIntyre, 1991.

Boldt, Menno. *Surviving as Indians: The Challenge of Self-Government.* Toronto: University of Toronto Press, 1993.

Cairns, Alan C. "Aboriginal Canadians, Citizenship and the Constitution." In Paul Fox and Graham White, eds. *Politics: Canada*, 8th ed. Oshawa: McGraw-Hill Ryerson, 1995.

Campbell, Robert, and Leslie Pal. *The Real Worlds of Canadian Politics*, 2nd ed. Peterborough: Broadview Press, 1991.

Cassidy, Frank, ed. *Aboriginal Self-Government.* Halifax: Institute for Research on Public Policy, 1991.

Comeau, Pauline, and Aldo Santin. *The First Canadians.* Toronto: James Lorimer, 1990.

Elliott, J.L., and Augie Fleras. *The "Nations Within": Aboriginal State Relations in Canada, the United* States and *New Zealand.* Toronto: Oxford University Press, 1992.

Engelstad, Diane, and John Bird, eds. *Nation to Nation: Aboriginal Sovereignty and the Future of Canada.* Concord, ON: Anansi, 1992.

Frideres, James S. *Native People in Canada: Contemporary Conflicts*, 4th ed. Scarborough: Prentice-Hall Canada, 1993.

Long, J. Anthony, Menno Bolt, and Leroy Little Bear. *Governments in Conflict? Provinces and Indian Nations in Canada.* Toronto: University of Toronto Press, 1988.

MacLaine, Craig, and Michael Baxendale. *This Land Is Our Land.* Toronto: Optimum, 1990.

Mawhiney, Anne-Marie. *Towards Aboriginal Self-Government: Relations between Status Indian Peoples and the Government of Canada, 1969–1984.* New York: Garland, 1994.

Mercredi, Ovid. *In the Rapids: Navigating the Future of First Nations.* Toronto: Viking, 1993.

Morse, B. *Aboriginal Peoples and the Law: Indian, Métis and Inuit Rights in Canada.* Don Mills: Oxford, 1984.

Royal Commission on Aboriginal Peoples. Final Report and other documents. In press.

Smith, Dan. *The Seventh Fire: The Struggle for Aboriginal Government.* Toronto: Key Porter, 1993.

Whittington, Michael S. "Aboriginal Self-Government in Canada." In M.S. Whittington and Glen Williams, eds. *Canadian Politics in the 1990s*, 4th ed. Scarborough: Nelson Canada, 1995.

Tennant, Paul. *Aboriginal Peoples and Politics.* Vancouver: University of British Columbia Press, 1990.

York, Geoffrey. *The Dispossessed: Life and Death in Native Canada.* Toronto: Lester & Orpen Dennys, 1989.

York, Geoffrey and Loreen Pindera. *People of the Pines: The Warriors and the Legacy of Oka.* Toronto: Little, Brown, 1991.

Chapter 8

The FRENCH–ENGLISH *cleavage*

Both world wars were marked by French–English conscription crises in Canada. The Trudeau regime enacted the Official Languages Act and made the federal government officially bilingual. Quebec introduced a French-only sign law and demanded constitutional recognition as a distinct society. The increasing unilingualism of Quebec and the expansion of bilingualism in the rest of the country seemed unfair to many Canadians. This issue was exacerbated by the feeling that Ottawa was also giving preferential treatment to Quebec in government policy and spending in order to persuade it to stay within Confederation. That feeling played a part in the success of the Reform Party in the 1993 election.

The French–English cleavage is at least as problematic as the regional–economic one in Canadian politics, and the two reinforce each other in the question of Quebec's place in Confederation. Among all ethnic/cultural/linguistic issues in Canadian politics, the English–French cleavage has always had the greatest significance, primarily reflecting the numbers of people involved, the historical dimensions of the question, and the territorial base of French Canada.[1]

This chapter begins by examining French–English relations up to 1960. It then discusses the Quiet Revolution in Quebec, developments in the relationship between Quebec and the rest of Canada up to the end of 1995, and, finally, French–English relations in the other provinces.

HISTORICAL OVERVIEW OF FRENCH–ENGLISH RELATIONS

Pre-Confederation Developments

Almost every Canadian political decision since 1759 has reflected the French–English relationship to some extent, and the tensions that currently threaten the continued existence of the country can probably best be understood in historical context. As outlined in Chapter 2, the French first colonized what is now the province of Quebec, but when the British defeated them on the Plains of Abraham, many changes occurred in the colony. Except for the clergy and the seigneurs, the French elite retreated to France, leaving the British to take control of the economy. The British also formed the government, and the conquerors assumed that the population would soon become "English."

Certain things did not change, however. The people continued to speak French and attend the Roman Catholic Church, which became a highly influential and autonomous organization. It would probably have been impossible to make Quebec an Anglo-Protestant colony—at least without a great deal of coercion and/or immigration—and the British soon exhibited a policy of tolerance and accommodation. By the time of the Quebec Act of 1774, the British recognized the inevitable, and guaranteed the French their religious rights and their own system of civil law.

As "English" immigrants moved into what is now Ontario in the 1780s, especially the United Empire Loyalists from the new United States, it became logical to divide the colony into two: Lower Canada (Quebec) would be essentially French Catholic, and Upper Canada (Ontario) would be Anglo Protestant. This separation was recognized in the Constitutional Act of 1791.

Difficulties between the popular assembly and the appointed executive and legislative councils became increasingly serious after 1800, culminating in the armed revolts in both colonies in 1837. The battle for democracy in Lower Canada was complicated by the ethnic factor, as French Canadians were predominant in the Assembly alone. Lord Durham felt that the ethnic problem could only be solved by another attempt to assimilate the French. Hence, he recommended that the two colonies be reunited into the colony of Canada, in which English would be the official language and the population of the rapidly expanding western portion (Ontario) would soon outnumber the French.

This final attempt at assimilation was to no avail. In recognition of its failure, the French language was increasingly used along with English in the government, cabinets were usually alliances between English and French leaders, and the legislature operated on the informal principle of the double majority—legislation had to have the approval of a majority of representatives from both sections of the colony.

Given this historical evolution, the logic of Confederation and the cultural guarantees of section 133 of the Constitution Act, 1867, are perfectly understandable. Both French and English could be used in all aspects of the federal Parliament, and laws would be passed in both languages. Both could also be used in whatever federal courts were later established. The francophone minorities in Ontario, Nova Scotia, and New Brunswick were inarticulate and ignored, even though the Acadian minority in New Brunswick constituted 16 percent of the provincial population, as seen in Table 8.1. However, the anglophone minority in Quebec, at 20 percent and centred in Montreal, was well organized and in control of the economy of the province. This ensured that English could be used along with French in the legislature and courts of Quebec. None of these constitutional provisions was particularly controversial in 1867, and protection of the Protestant school system in Quebec and the Roman Catholic system in Ontario attracted greater interest. No constitutional right was granted to minority language schools: religious rights were seen in educational terms; language rights only applied in legislatures and courts.

TABLE 8.1	Provincial Population by Ethnic Origin, 1871 (Percentage)		
	British	*French*	*Other*
Quebec	20	78	2
Ontario	82	4.7	13.3
Nova Scotia	79	8.5	12.5
New Brunswick	79	16	5

Source: 1871 Census. Reproduced with the permission of the Minister of Supply and Services Canada, 1995.

OFFICIAL BILINGUALISM IN THE CONSTITUTION ACT, 1867

Federal Parliament, Proceedings and Laws
Federal Courts
Quebec Parliament, Proceedings and Laws
Quebec Courts

Post-Confederation Ethnic/Linguistic Conflicts

THE RIEL REBELLIONS

Although the two language groups have been regularly accommodated in government circles since 1867, five serious linguistic conflicts erupted from the time of Confederation to the Second World War. The first was the Riel Rebellion, which precipitated the creation in 1870 of the province of Manitoba. The French-Catholic Métis Louis Riel led the fight for provincial status. During that uprising, and in a situation of uncertain government authority, an Ontario Orangeman was executed by a Métis court-martial. Riel maintained a fairly low profile afterward, but in 1885 he re-emerged in what is now Saskatchewan to lead the second Riel Rebellion on behalf of western Natives and Métis who had been treated shamefully by the government. After quelling the rebellion, the federal government charged Riel with treason and found him guilty in a famous trial in Regina. All of this raised ethnic and religious tensions across the country to a fever pitch, for while English Protestants regarded Riel as a murderer, traitor, and madman, French Catholics believed he was a patriot and a saint. To Prime Minister John A. Macdonald fell the unenviable decision of whether to let Riel hang or to use the executive power of mercy to spare him. Caught in the middle of this heated confrontation, Macdonald followed the will of the majority and had Riel hanged. This exacerbated the level of French Catholic outrage across the country, especially in Quebec. As a result, Honoré Mercier and his Parti National were elected in that province in 1886, and the close attachment of the people of Quebec to Macdonald's Conservative Party was permanently damaged. Moreover, Mercier argued that the Riel affair had demonstrated the lack of French-Canadian influence in Ottawa, leading him to demand greater provincial autonomy for Quebec.[2]

BILINGUALISM IN MANITOBA

The second linguistic conflict occurred in Manitoba in 1890. Since the small settlement was about equally divided between French and English, the 1870 Manitoba Act followed the Quebec precedent of giving the two languages official status in the new province's legislature and courts. (Since the province was equally divided between Protestants and Roman Catholics, the separate school system was also guaranteed.) After its creation, however, Manitoba attracted thousands of English-speaking immigrants and others who chose to identify with the anglophone community. Hence, in 1890, the anglophone majority passed the Official Language Act, which removed the official status of French in the province's legislature and courts. To solidify its control of the province, the same group abolished the separate school system.

BILINGUALISM IN ONTARIO: REGULATION 17

The third linguistic conflict concerned minority French-language education rights. Although minority-language schools had not been constitutionally guaranteed, the Protestant schools in Quebec, mostly in Montreal, naturally operated in English, and it was only logical that French-language schools be established in francophone parts of New Brunswick and Ontario. In 1913 the Whitney government issued *Regulation 17*, which virtually abolished the use of French in the Ontario school system; English was to become the sole language of instruction after the third year, and the study of French as a subject was limited to one hour a day. Whitney claimed that he was doing Franco-Ontarian citizens a favour by forcing them to learn English in an English-speaking province, but Franco-Ontarians denounced the regulation and challenged it in court. The 1917 Mackell case confirmed, however, that constitutional protection in educational matters applied only to religious minorities, not linguistic ones.[3]

THE FIRST CONSCRIPTION CRISIS

The Regulation 17 incident in Ontario had its greatest implications in Quebec during the **conscription crisis** of the First World War, the fourth major French–English confrontation. As a British colony, Canada was automatically at war, but could determine its own degree of involvement. Despite small standing armed forces, the Conservative government of Robert Borden made excessive commitments. Appeals for volunteers initially had promising results, but as reinforcements were needed later in the war, few recruits came forward. The government therefore decided to resort to conscription—compulsory military service—in 1917. Borden knew that French Canada generally felt indifferent to the conflict and that conscription would divide the country along linguistic lines. Having few French Canadians in his cabinet to start with, the prime minister appealed to Liberal leader Wilfrid Laurier to join him in a coalition government. Laurier refused the offer, although most of the English-speaking Liberal MPs did join in a **Union government** in 1917, and the subsequent enforcement of conscription entailed considerable violence. A conscription-inspired riot in Quebec City in the spring of 1918, which the federal government sought to quell by sending in the army, left four people dead and many others injured. This confrontation destroyed what little French-Canadian support for the Conservative Party was left after the execution of Louis Riel.

THE SECOND CONSCRIPTION CRISIS

Ontario repealed Regulation 17 in 1927 and French–English tensions returned to a normal, controllable level until they were inflamed by the fifth ethnic conflict, another conscription crisis during the Second World War. In 1939 the Liberal Prime Minister Mackenzie King was in power with a strong contingent of ministers and MPs from Quebec. Although still closely allied with Britain, Canada entered the war as an independent country, and its leader was extremely cautious in determining its degree of involvement. King knew that conscription would be resisted in French Canada, so he was even more reluctant than Borden to adopt it. After first promising not to impose it, he held a national plebiscite to let himself off the hook. While 80 percent of voters outside Quebec agreed to release King from his promise, Quebec voted 73 percent against. On the basis of the slogan "conscription if necessary, but not necessarily conscription," King managed to postpone the adoption of compulsory military service until almost the end of the war. Given the sensitivity with which conscription was imposed on this occasion, King is credited by most observers with having skilfully kept the country together in the circumstances.

THE QUIET REVOLUTION: QUEBEC IN THE 1960s
Changes in Quebec

The Quebec of the past 35 years is quite a different province and society from that which existed before 1960. After that date, the province underwent a **Quiet Revolution**, consisting of a dramatic change of values and attitudes, especially toward the state, a new collective self-confidence, and a new brand of nationalism. These features of the new Quebec had many implications for French–English relations in both the Quebec and Canadian political systems.

The government of Jean Lesage (1960–1966) took over many functions previously administered by the Church.[4] The most important of these was education, which was radically modernized, but health and welfare programs were also made public rather than charitable responsibilities. With the nationalization of private power companies, Hydro-Québec became a huge Crown corporation supplying all the electricity in the province. Lesage also reformed almost every piece of legislation on the books, especially labour and electoral laws, added reams of new ones, and created many government agencies. All these new and expanded public responsibilities required substantial additional revenues, and Lesage put immense pressure on Ottawa to expand federal-provincial grants, to allow Quebec to opt out of the conditions attached to them, and to give the province a greater share of joint taxation. In areas of provincial jurisdiction, Quebec began to move toward distinctive programs, designing its own pension plan, which was then used as a model for the Canada Pension Plan. As time went on, the province began to demand ever larger jurisdiction, including international francophone links, leading to further federal–provincial discord. As far as the Quebec private sector was concerned, francophones had lower incomes and lower-status jobs than anglophones, but the Lesage government did little of substance to rectify this situation, probably for fear of driving out Anglo-Canadian and foreign investment.

Much of the subsequent analysis of the Quiet Revolution centres on the concept of the **new middle class**—civil servants, teachers, professors, and other salaried professionals. Since upward mobility was still difficult in the English-dominated private sector, this new class used Quebec nationalism in order to further its own aspirations in the expansion of the Quebec state.[5] They sponsored an enormous increase in provincial government programs and agencies.

Federally oriented Quebec francophones such as future prime minister Pierre Trudeau began to demand that French be used as a language equal to English in the corridors of power in Ottawa. Since the federal Parliament and courts were already theoretically bilingual, the main gap in official bilingualism at the national level was in the executive branch, where English was the working language of the public service, at least at policy-making levels. Such federally oriented Quebec francophones were also concerned about the fate of francophone minorities in the other provinces. The new self-confidence of the Québécois inspired these dwindling minorities to greater self-assertiveness.

Federal Responses

During the 1960s, the federal government grappled somewhat haphazardly with Quebec's demands. The Diefenbaker government (1957–1963) introduced simultaneous English/French interpretation into Parliament, began printing federal government cheques in a bilingual format, and appointed a French-Canadian governor general. Immediately on taking office, the Pearson government (1963–1968) appointed the **Royal Commission on Bilingualism and Biculturalism**

> to inquire into and report upon the existing state of bilingualism and biculturalism in Canada and to recommend what steps should be taken to develop the Canadian Confederation on the basis of an equal partnership between the two founding races.

Even before the Commission reported, however, Pearson felt obliged to act on Quebec's demands. He gave Quebec and the other provinces more federal funds and taxation power, removed conditions from many shared-cost programs, and permitted Quebec to make international arrangements with France. At the same time, Pearson and Trudeau introduced an **Official Languages** bill to make the Canadian public service bilingual, much to the consternation of those unilingual public servants who were now pressured to learn French and of aspiring applicants for public service positions who had not had the opportunity to learn French in school. The Official Languages Act passed in 1969, and since that time Canada has been officially bilingual in its federal institutions. Ottawa also began to support French immersion educational programs as well as to assist francophone minorities in other provinces.

The question of French–English relations, or "national unity," was the principal political issue throughout the Trudeau era (1968–79, 1980–84). At that point it became clear that two models existed to deal with the problem. The first—the territorial principle—recognized Quebec as the homeland of French Canada and gave the province powers and resources to protect and promote its linguistic and cultural distinctiveness. Quebec would essentially be "French" and the rest of Canada primarily "English."[6] The second option—the personality principle—was to treat Quebec as "une province comme les autres" (a province like the others) and to promote bilingualism at the federal level and in the other provinces so that each person could use either language anywhere in the country. English Canadians had difficulty accepting these demands, which seemed excessive and contradictory: making Quebec more French and more autonomous at the same time as promoting French in Ottawa and the other provinces. They did not understand that the two demands came largely from two different groups of francophones, with contrary conceptions of French Canada. Trudeau fought against recognition of Quebec as the homeland of French Canada and opposed giving that province any special recognition or power. He argued that any kind of special status would be the first step toward separation; he feared that a nationalistic French Quebec would be inward-looking and intolerant; and he felt that francophone Quebeckers would have more opportunity if they followed his example, became bilingual, and participated in the life of a larger country. Part of Trudeau's popularity in English Canada stemmed from the perception that he was "anti-Quebec," but he was passionately "pro-French" in promoting bilingualism in Ottawa and across the country.

The Separatist Option

During the 1960s, advocates of Quebec separatism began to emerge. Because of their conviction that the normal political process was not responding quickly enough to the demands of the Quiet Revolution, one wing of the separatist movement, the **Front de Libération du Québec (FLQ)** resorted to violence—periodic bombings killed two people and injured 27. In October 1970, two small cells of the FLQ kidnapped a British diplomat and abducted and murdered Quebec cabinet minister Pierre Laporte. Trudeau invoked the coercive **War Measures Act**, giving the police and armed forces special powers to quell the violence; over 400 innocent, peaceful separatist supporters were arrested in the process. By crushing the FLQ, by giving French Canadians more clout in Ottawa, and by guaranteeing pan-Canadian bilingualism in the Constitution in 1982, Trudeau hoped to undercut any Quebec demand for special status or separatism.

QUEBEC IN THE 1970s, 1980s, AND 1990s
The 1970s

In spite of the fact that a centralist Trudeau government was in power, the first Robert Bourassa government in Quebec (1970–1976) gained a degree of autonomy from Ottawa in the fields of family allowances and immigration. It also passed **Bill 22** to give primacy to the French language in many spheres in the province, such as in the operations and documents of public and para-public authorities. As far as education was concerned, immigrant children had to show "sufficient knowledge" of English before being allowed to go to an English-language school. This was an attempt to have such children join the majority French linguistic group in the province rather than become "English," as so many previous immigrants had done. Relying on immigration to bolster the francophone segment of the population became a vital issue after the French-Canadian birthrate plummeted in the 1960s. Bill 22 also aimed at the francization of the private sector by pressuring companies to use French as the language of internal corporate operations. The more Quebec moved in the direction of French unilingualism, the more English Canada resisted Trudeau's national policy of bilingualism, and the larger the number of anglophones who left Quebec.

The Parti Québécois was elected to office in 1976 under René Lévesque with an even more nationalistic program. Faced with a hostile Trudeau government in Ottawa, the PQ made few gains in provincial autonomy. But it did pass **Bill 101**, the Charter of the French Language, which extended Bill 22 by making French the predominant language in the province. It generally turned the persuasive and optional aspects of Bill 22 into coercive and mandatory ones, and English Quebeckers and English Canadians generally who could live with Bill 22 were strongly opposed to many aspects of Bill 101. It made French the only official language of the legislature (although laws continued to be translated unofficially into English); only individuals (not corporations) could use English in Quebec courts; the only children who could go to English schools in the province were those whose parents had done so; and all commercial signs had to be in French only.[7] All four of these clauses were subsequently ruled unconstitutional by the courts, but in other ways Bill 101 still stands, and French continues to be the official language of the province.

The 1980s

In 1980 the PQ government held a referendum on the question of pursuing a more independent relationship with Canada called "sovereignty-association." Many federal politicians, including Trudeau, Justice Minister Jean Chrétien, and several provincial premiers, encouraged Quebeckers to defeat the PQ proposal, promising them "renewed federalism" if they did so. When sovereignty-association was turned down by a vote of 60 percent to 40 percent, new federal–provincial constitutional negotiations began, culminating in the Constitution Act, 1982. Ironically, even though the whole effort was supposed to appeal to the residents of that province, Quebec alone objected to the act. That was because it reflected the Trudeau vision of a bilingual Canada rather than recognizing the distinctive French character of Quebec. Nevertheless, it became law in all parts of the country. As far as language was concerned, the act reinforced official bilingualism at the federal level and in New Brunswick, and guaranteed minority official language education in the provinces where numbers warranted. Many Quebeckers never forgave Trudeau and Chrétien for adopting such a significant constitutional document without Quebec's consent.

The second Bourassa government, elected in 1985, was first able to convince the more receptive Mulroney government to allow Quebec to play a fuller part in the **Francophonie**, the international French-speaking community. Then, in 1989, the Supreme Court of Canada declared the sign provision of Bill 101 to be unconstitutional as a violation of freedom of expression, even "commercial expression."[8] Bourassa responded by using the "notwithstanding clause" in the federal and Quebec charters of rights to pass **Bill 178**, which provided for French-only outdoor signs but allowed some English signs indoors. Violating a constitutional right and giving preference to French collective rights over (English) individual rights produced a vehement reaction among English Quebeckers and an anti-Quebec, anti-French response in the rest of the country. New anglophone parties contested the 1989 Quebec provincial election, and the Equality Party won four seats in the predominantly English parts of Montreal. On the other hand, it should be noted that in 1983 some aspects of Bill 101 were voluntarily relaxed, and in 1986 Quebec ensured the provision of social and health services in English to its anglophone minority. Moreover, when the five-year limit on Bill 178 ran out in 1993, Bourassa replaced it with **Bill 86**, which allowed bilingual signs outside as well as inside stores.

Reprinted with the permission of the Ottawa Sun.

The main item on the Bourassa–Mulroney agenda was the Meech Lake Accord, which was designed to bring Quebec back of its own free will into the Canadian constitutional fold. The Accord, discussed in Chapter 3, provided for the recognition of Quebec as a distinct society within Canada, provincial nomination of senators and Supreme Court judges, provincial vetoes on a wider range of constitutional amendments, constitutionalization of Quebec's rights in immigration, and provincial opting-out, with compensation, of federal programs set up within their jurisdiction. In many respects Meech Lake reflected the approach of the 1979 Task Force on Canadian Unity, which had been promptly shelved when its recommendations were contrary to Trudeau's vision of Canada. English-Canadian reaction against Meech Lake stiffened after Bill 178 and in the end, the Newfoundland and Manitoba legislatures failed to approve it before the deadline. Many Quebeckers felt betrayed again, Quebec began a much more aggressive campaign to wrest powers from Ottawa, and several Quebec members of Parliament quit the Conservative and Liberal parties to sit as Quebec indépendantistes in the Bloc Québécois led by Lucien Bouchard.

The 1990s

After intense post-Meech discussions taking the form of the all-party Bélanger–Campeau Committee and the Quebec Liberal Party's Allaire Report, the Quebec legislature decided that a referendum on sovereignty would be held in the province in 1992. Those opposed to independence hoped that the rest of Canada would offer Quebec a model of a new federation before that time so that the voters would have an acceptable federalist option. Such a vision was embodied in the Charlottetown Accord, discussed in Chapter 3. In the end, 56.7 percent of Quebeckers voted against the Accord, just slightly more than did so in the rest of Canada. Had it been ratified, Quebec would essentially have achieved fulfilment of its Meech Lake demands, including recognition as a distinct society within Canada based on its French-language majority, unique culture, and civil law tradition. All provinces would have received increased power over immigration, an enlarged veto over constitutional amendments, and compensation when opting out of national programs. Quebec and the other provinces would have secured some nine powers in addition to immigration if they chose to use them, but this fell far short of the Allaire Report's demands.

After the disheartening, if not traumatic, experience of the Charlottetown Accord, all federal parties decided to put constitutional issues on the back burner, especially the Chrétien Liberals, elected a year later. In 1994, however, the Parti Québécois was elected in Quebec. As in 1976, the PQ argued that it was "safe" to elect it to government, because sovereignty would be decided in a separate, subsequent referendum. For the next two years it concentrated on the sovereignty issue, but more from the standpoint of public opinion polls than party principle. It kept adjusting its concept of sovereignty and delaying the date of the vote until it thought it had a version that would be accepted.

As mentioned in Chapter 3, the referendum on Quebec sovereignty was held in October 1995. While the PQ government proposed a kind of sovereignty that retained significant links to the rest of Canada, its proposal was turned down by a vote of 50.6 percent to 49.4 percent. Such a close result was not particularly comforting, however, to those who wanted to keep the country together, especially when the charismatic Lucien Bouchard succeeded Jacques Parizeau as Quebec premier and promised another referendum within a few years' time.

FRENCH–ENGLISH RELATIONS IN THE OTHER PROVINCES

The distribution of French and English communities in the various provinces is shown in Table 8.2. Statistics Canada gathers figures on ethnic origin, mother tongue, and language spoken at home. It is difficult to use the statistics on ethnic origin, however, because so many Canadians are now an ethnic mixture, and because an increasing number prefer to call themselves "Canadians." It is more reliable to use figures for mother tongue, even though this does not exactly measure the same thing. In absolute numbers, francophone minorities, defined by mother tongue, were located primarily in Ontario (484 265) and New Brunswick (237 570); as percentages, they were largest in New Brunswick (34 percent), Ontario (5.3 percent), Manitoba (4.9 percent), Prince Edward Island (4.7 percent), and Nova Scotia (4.1 percent).

The Quebec government and most Quebeckers have been more concerned about internal linguistic matters than about what happens to French minorities in other provinces. Nevertheless, the Quiet Revolution led "francophones outside Quebec" to seek to preserve their language and culture. Often under pressure from Prime Minister Trudeau, some provincial premiers hoped that by extending rights or services to their francophone minorities, they would help to forestall separatism in Quebec. Thus, considerable improvement has been made in minority francophone rights in many provinces since 1965. As mentioned, all provinces were bound by the Constitution Act, 1982, to provide education in the minority

TABLE 8.2 Mother Tongue and Home Language by Province, 1991 (Percentages)

	Mother Tongue		Home Language	
	English	French	English	French
Newfoundland	98.6	0.5	99.2	0.2
Prince Edward Island	94.2	4.5	97.3	2.3
Nova Scotia	93.6	4.1	96.3	2.5
New Brunswick	65.1	33.6	68.2	31.2
Quebec	9.7	82.2	11.2	83.0
Ontario	76.6	5.0	85.2	3.2
Manitoba	75.0	4.7	87.7	2.3
Saskatchewan	84.2	2.2	94.4	0.7
Alberta	82.5	2.3	91.5	0.8
British Columbia	80.5	1.6	89.6	0.4
North	66.1	2.7	76.5	1.3
Total	62.1	25.1	68.9	24.0

Source: Statistics Canada, 1991 Census, Home Language and Mother Tongue, cat. no. 93-317; adapted by author. Reproduced with the permission of the Minister of Supply and Services Canada, 1995.

official language where numbers warranted. In addition, the Supreme Court ruled in a 1989 case from Alberta that francophone parents must have some control over their children's French-language education.[9] All provinces were also committed to providing for criminal trials in French if demanded by the accused.

Much has been written about the Trudeau government's creation of minority official-language education rights across the country. It has been widely said, as noted in Chapter 5, that this was the real reason he pushed the concept of a Charter of Rights and Freedoms. Moreover, Ottawa helped to create the demand for French-language schools in the nine anglophone provinces. The federal government sought to create advocacy organizations that would promote its own agenda,[10] and then pressured such official-language minority groups to demand and establish French-language schools and gave the provinces the money to finance them. All this was designed to undercut Quebec's claim that it was the homeland of French Canada, and was a classic case of a government's not waiting for societal forces to demand what it wanted to do.

New Brunswick

New Brunswick implemented its own Official Languages Act in 1969, which was constitutionalized at provincial request in 1982.[11] New Brunswick also improved the Acadian educational system at all levels and provided provincial government services in both languages. Under the Richard Hatfield government, it embarked on a policy of cultural equality based on a "separate but equal" strategy rather than individual or institutional bilingualism, with parallel unilingual school boards and other public bodies. The adoption of official bilingualism in New Brunswick was facilitated by all-party support, but many years later, in 1991, the anti-bilingual Confederation of Regions (COR) Party elected several members to the provincial legislature.

Ontario

Ontario began to provide French-language secondary schools in 1968, and later established the right of every Franco-Ontarian to go to French-language school, whether or not warranted by numbers. Ontario then guaranteed French trials in the provincial courts and gradually extended French-language provincial services. In 1986, under David Peterson, the province passed Bill 8, which became effective in 1989 and provided for translation of laws as well as for provincial government services in French in 22 designated regions of the province. Meanwhile, simultaneous French–English interpretation in the legislature began in 1987, and Franco-Ontarians were granted the right to have French-language schools run by trustees elected by the francophone population. As in New Brunswick, the considerable voting power of the Franco-Ontarian community encouraged all parties to support such initiatives, but the combination of Quebec's Bill 178 and Ontario's Bill 8 was too much for some Ontarians to bear. COR did well in parts of the province in the 1988 federal election and some 70 municipalities symbolically declared themselves officially unilingual in 1989–90.

Manitoba

Manitoba moved very slowly on French-language initiatives, but was pushed by a series of Supreme Court of Canada decisions beginning in 1979. The 1890 Official Language Act was declared unconstitutional (a violation of the 1870 Manitoba Act), all laws had to be passed in both languages, trials had to be available in French, and most government documents had to be bilingual.[12] In the 1981–88 period the NDP government tried unenthusiastically to implement the Supreme Court decision while the opposition Conservatives inflamed the issue with an all-out attack. Once in office, however, the Filmon PC government continued the NDP approach, and the Supreme Court refined the guidelines on which government documents had to be translated.

Other Provinces

Given their small francophone minorities, Saskatchewan and Alberta took very little action on French-language issues. Indeed, even asking a question in French in the Alberta legislature created quite a controversy. In the 1988 *Mercure* case, however, the Supreme Court of Canada ruled that Saskatchewan (and by implication, Alberta) was bound by an 1886 territorial statute to pass laws in both French and English and to provide for court cases in French.[13] The Court allowed the province to opt out of these requirements by repealing the territorial law by means of a bilingual provincial statute. Both provinces proceeded to do so, but did allow French to be spoken in their legislatures and courts. With federal arm-twisting and financial incentives, Saskatchewan also began to translate some of its English-only laws into French. Meanwhile, advances for francophone minorities in other provinces have been minimal.

Linguistic minorities at the provincial level find it necessary to organize in order to pursue their objectives. Such groups include the Association canadienne-française de l'Ontario (ACFO), the Société franco-manitobaine, and the Société des acadiens du Nouveau-Brunswick. These provincial French groups have also joined together in the Fédération des francophones hors Québec. Meanwhile, the English minority in Quebec has also formed its own pressure group, Alliance Quebec.

FRENCH–ENGLISH RELATIONS IN THE LATE 1990s

Given that francophones constitute about 25 percent of the Canadian electorate, given their historic constitutional rights, given their geographic concentration in Quebec and majority control of such a large province, and given their modern-day self-consciousness and self-confidence, the French fact in Canada cannot be ignored. If English Canada wants Quebec to remain part of the country, it cannot go back to the easy days of pre-1960 unilingualism.

As outlined earlier, two basic approaches to accommodating this French presence persist. Given that 85 percent of the French are located in Quebec and that 83 percent of Quebeckers are French-speaking, the first is to recognize that Quebec is the heartland of

French Canada; in shorthand form, French Canada equals Quebec. This approach would give that province special recognition and responsibility to protect itself in the North American English linguistic environment. Whether or not it is justified, Quebec has a "siege mentality" with respect to its language and culture, and language has replaced the Church as the focus of French-Canadian identity.[14] The Quebec corporate elite is now a francophone group, and they, along with the new middle class in the Quebec public sector, see themselves benefiting from greatly increased provincial autonomy.

The second approach is to promote the bilingual character of the whole country and most or all of the provinces—that is, the idealistic Trudeau vision that contends that French Canada does not equal Quebec. According to the 1986 census, over four million Canadians claimed that they could conduct a conversation in both English and French. They made up 16.2 percent of the total population, of which 34.5 percent are in Quebec and 29.1 percent in New Brunswick. The policy of official bilingualism is primarily supported by politically active social, economic, and cultural elites, including "new anglophone bilinguals who have invested heavily in their own bilingualism or that of their children."[15] Given the tiny proportion of residents who speak French in many provinces and in the North, however, and given the hostility to the imposition of bilingualism in many parts of the country (as evidenced by the popularity of the Reform Party and COR), it appears that the limits of national bilingualism have been reached.

There is, however, a synthesis option lying between the separatist or quasi-separatist and Trudeau extremes. As advocated by Bourassa and Mulroney (and possibly after 1995 by Chrétien), it sees Quebec as a distinct French society within Canada, but the country as a whole retains a bilingual character. It is the option long supported by a majority of Quebeckers, who reject both the separatist and Trudeau positions and want to remain in Canada—but in a Canada that recognizes their distinctiveness. Many observers (including the author) feel that the only hope of keeping the country intact in a recognizable form is to find a formula along these lines that would be supported by a majority of Canadians both inside and outside Quebec.

It may, however, be too late for compromise. In the early 1990s, especially in the wake of the Bill 178 controversy, many observers detected a visible decline in the will of both French and English to live together. Quebeckers felt increasingly self-confident about going it alone, and many English Canadians invited them to do so. The death of the Meech Lake Accord in 1990 caused many Quebeckers to feel rejected by English Canada, and support for the existing political community and partnership fell to a new low on both sides. Quebec awaited the response of the rest of Canada after its Allaire Report proposed that Ottawa turn almost all its powers over to the province in a relationship not far removed from sovereignty-association. English-Canadian public opinion generally hoped that Quebec would remain in Canada, but it was not prepared to grant that province much in the way of special powers or to eviscerate the federal government in appeasement. A whole array of books began to be written about a Canada without Quebec,[16] although a few people wrote more hopefully about a reconciliation.

The results of the 1995 Quebec referendum on sovereignty were not encouraging. While a slim overall majority of Quebeckers voted No, nearly 60 percent of francophones in Quebec favoured the PQ proposal. Many of these did not necessarily support an independent Quebec, but in the absence of an encouraging response from the rest of Canada it is reasonable to assume that the results could be different in another referendum a few years later.

CONCLUSION

The ethnic cleavages that are such a prominent feature of the Canadian political system are based in part on the number and variety of groups involved, but also on the contrasting perceptions each group has of its own history and current status. The French remember when they were the dominant group in the country and are acutely conscious of their current minority status. They desperately want to preserve their language and culture against the pervasive forces of Anglo-American television and other media. The French of Quebec want to enlarge their capacity to govern themselves, and those outside Quebec want to maximize opportunities to use their own language. English-speaking Canadians, on the other hand, are still by far the largest single group in the land, and resent the number of jobs, mostly in the public sector, that now require fluency in English and French.

P Of the approaches outlined in Chapter 1, pluralism is probably most relevant to our discussion of the French–English cleavage. The French–English relationship in Canadian society is the very essence of pluralism; it is a basic fact of Canadian political life and animates much of the political activity in the country. Pluralists cannot claim that the two groups have operated historically on a level playing field, nor even that their political interaction has always involved organized pressure groups. But the fundamental co-existence of two dominant ethnic groups establishes an underlying pluralism and also provides the foundation for most of the other pluralistic aspects of Canadian government and society.

SC The state-centred approach begins with the fact that the British and French "charter groups" have historically dominated positions of political power, although the British usually prevailed over the French.[17] Apart from two prime ministers, French Canadians generally occupied minor positions in the federal cabinet until 1968, when Pierre Trudeau drew his principal ministers from Quebec. A similar imbalance existed until recently in the public service, but under the Official Languages Act, hiring and promotion preferences have given the French language and francophone public servants a more equitable, if not superior, position. The state-centred approach takes the perspective that many policies in this field reflect the interests or prejudices of the political elite rather than the demands articulated by the wider society. In particular, Trudeau's imposition of official bilingualism was carried out in spite of the opposition of a majority of the anglophone population and the indifference of a majority of francophones in Quebec. Moreover, his dirigiste approach is evident in his creation and financing of official-language minority advocacy groups throughout the country, his determination to guarantee their rights in the Charter, and his funding of whatever official bilingualism he could persuade provincial governments to offer.

PC In terms of the public choice approach, French Quebec voted Liberal so often that it did not figure prominently in any party's electoral calculations until 1960. The neglect of bilingualism at the federal level was one result, although the delayed implementation of conscription in the Second World War is an indication that French Canada could not be completely taken for granted. After the Quiet Revolution, when their demands increased and were backed by the threat of separation, and especially after 1984 when their voting preferences became more volatile, the French became the most courted group in the country.

C Class analysts are interested in socioeconomic rather than ethnic cleavages, but find certain links between the two.[18] They are particularly interested in the relationship between class and ethnicity in Quebec. In the pre-1960 period the titans of big business in Quebec reflected the dominance of British, Anglo-Canadian, and Anglo-American backgrounds. They took little interest in promoting francophone concerns and made English the language of business. Premier Maurice Duplessis welcomed "English" capital into Quebec and did not object to prejudice against or exploitation of French-speaking workers. Then, in the Quiet Revolution, a new middle class of francophone Quebeckers made itself felt in the province's public sector and passed laws to improve the lot of francophones in the private sector as well. These developments fostered the emergence of a new entrepreneurial class in the province, and the economic elite in Quebec today is francophone in character. Class analysts also cite the use of the War Measures Act in 1970 as an unnecessary resort to coercion by the state. They argue that ethnic politics are a reflection of underlying economic, class-based forces. They also suggest that the capitalist-controlled political elite has chosen to emphasize the ethnic factor in Canadian politics in order to distract the population from any consciousness of class divisions.

· · · · · · · · · · · · · · · · · · · ·
DISCUSSION QUESTIONS

1. How would you characterize the manner in which the English majority in Canada has treated the French minority?

2. What are their respective visions of their place in Confederation?

3. How has the French–English relationship within Quebec changed over time?

4. Should the French minorities outside Quebec have the same rights and services as the English minority in Quebec? Explain.

5. Is the territorial or the personality principle a more realistic basis for language policy in Canada? Explain.

6. Why do most Quebeckers insist on constitutional recognition that Quebec is a distinct society within Canada?

7. Why do many Quebeckers argue that Quebec requires additional powers?

8. What is likely to happen to official bilingualism if Quebec ever separates?

9. Contrast the pluralist and state-centred approaches to the French–English cleavage in Canada.

10. Which of the other approaches outlined in Chapter 1 are most relevant to the politics of the French–English cleavage in Canada?

· ·

NOTES

1. Although the label "English" is sometimes used in this chapter to refer to language, as opposed to ethnic origin, special mention should be made of the Scots, who historically controlled the fur trade, the banks and other financial institutions, the major universities, and much of the government. Many prime ministers were of Scottish background, for example. See Pierre Berton, *Why We Act Like Canadians* (Toronto: McClelland and Stewart, 1982), pp. 77–78.
2. Canada's involvement in the British Boer War also complicated French–English relations to a limited extent.
3. *Ontario Roman Catholic Separate School Trustees v. Mackell*, [1917] A.C. 62.
4. Graham Fraser, *René Lévesque and the Parti Québécois in Power* (Toronto: Macmillan, 1984).
5. Kenneth McRoberts, *Quebec: Social Change and Political Crisis*, 3rd ed. (Toronto: McClelland and Stewart, 1993).
6. Kenneth McRoberts, "Making Canada Bilingual: Illusions and Delusions of Federal Language Policy," in David Shugarman and Reg Whitaker, eds., *Federalism and Political Community* (Peterborough: Broadview Press, 1989).
7. See, for example, William Coleman, "From Bill 22 to Bill 101: The Politics of Language under the Parti Québécois," *Canadian Journal of Political Science* (September 1981), pp. 459–85.
8. *Ford v. Quebec* (Attorney General), [1988] 2 S.C.R. 712.
9. *Mahe v. Alberta*, [1990] 1 S.C.R. 342.
10. Leslie Pal, *Interests of State: The Politics of Language, Multiculturalism, and Feminism in Canada* (Montreal: McGill–Queen's University Press, 1993).
11. New Brunswick court cases include *Jones v. A.G. New Brunswick*, [1975] 2 S.C.R. 1982 and *Société des Acadiens v. Association of Parents*, [1986] 1 S.C.R. 549.
12. Manitoba cases include *A.G. Manitoba v. Forest*, [1979] 2 S.C.R. 1032; *Reference Re Manitoba Language Rights*, [1985] 1 S.C.R. 721; *Order Re Manitoba Language Rights*, [1985] 2 S.C.R. 347; *Bilodeau v. Attorney General Manitoba*, [1986] 1 S.C.R. 449; and *Reference re Manitoba Language Rights*, [1992] 1 S.C.R. 212. Parallel Quebec cases include *Attorney General of Quebec v. Blaikie*, [1979] 2 S.C.R. 1016, and *MacDonald v. City of Montreal*, [1988] 1 S.C.R. 460.
13. *Mercure v. Attorney General Saskatchewan*, [1988] 1 S.C.R. 234.
14. See, for example, Dominique Clift, *The Secret Kingdom: Interpretations of the Canadian Character* (Toronto: McClelland and Stewart, 1989), pp. 116–23.
15. Kenneth McRoberts, "Making Canada Bilingual," p. 90.
16. These include the following: David J. Bercuson and Barry Cooper, *Deconfederation: Canada without Quebec* (Toronto: Key Porter, 1991); Alan Freeman and Patrick Grady, *Dividing the House: Planning for a Canada without Quebec* (Toronto: HarperCollins, 1995); Gordon Gibson, *Plan B: The Future of the Rest of Canada* (Vancouver: Fraser Institute, 1994); Daniel Drache and R. Perin, *Negotiating with a Sovereign Quebec* (Toronto: Lorimer, 1992); and Phillip Resnick, *Toward a Canada–Quebec Union* (Montreal: McGill–Queen's University Press). A more positive analysis was Jeremy Webber's *Reimagining Canada: Language, Culture, Community, and the Canadian Constitution* (Montreal: McGill–Queen's University Press, 1994).
17. John Porter, *The Vertical Mosaic* (Toronto: University of Toronto Press, 1965).

18. Janine Brodie and Jane Jenson, *Challenge, Crisis and Change: Politics and Class in Canada Revisited*, 2nd ed. (Ottawa: Carleton University Press, 1990).

FURTHER READING

Bothwell, Robert. *Canada and Quebec: One Country, Two Histories*. Vancouver: University of British Columbia Press, 1995.

Coleman, William. "From Bill 22 to Bill 101: The Politics of Language under the Parti Québécois." *Canadian Journal of Political Science* (September 1981), pp. 459–85.

———. *The Independence Movement in Quebec 1945–1980*. Toronto: University of Toronto Press, 1985.

Cook, Ramsay. *Canada, Quebec and the Uses of Nationalism*. Toronto, McClelland and Stewart, 1995.

Fraser, Graham. *René Lévesque and the Parti Québécois in Power*. Toronto: Macmillan, 1984.

Gagnon, Alain-G. *Quebec: State and Society*, 2nd ed. Toronto: Nelson Canada, 1993.

Gibbins, Roger. *Conflict and Unity*, 3rd ed. Scarborough: Nelson Canada, 1994.

Joy, Richard. *Canada's Official Languages*. Toronto: University of Toronto Press, 1992.

McRoberts, Kenneth. "Making Canada Bilingual: Illusions and Delusions of Federal Language Policy." In David Shugarman and Reg Whitaker, eds. *Federalism and Political Community*. Peterborough: Broadview Press, 1989.

———. *Quebec: Social Change and Political Crisis*, 3rd ed. Toronto: McClelland and Stewart, 1993.

Pal, Leslie. *Interests of State: The Politics of Language, Multiculturalism, and Feminism in Canada*. Montreal: McGill–Queen's University Press, 1993.

Resnick, Philip. *Thinking English Canada*. Toronto: Stoddart, 1994.

Royal Commission on Bilingualism and Biculturalism, *Report*. Ottawa: Queen's Printer, 1967.

Thomson, Dale. *Jean Lesage and the Quiet Revolution*. Toronto: Macmillan, 1984.

Webber, Jeremy. *Reimagining Canada: Language, Culture, Community, and the Canadian Constitution*. Montreal: McGill–Queen's University Press, 1994.

Chapter 9

Other ETHNIC *groups*

The Liberal Party is sometimes accused of entrenching multiculturalism in the Constitution in order to attract immigrant votes. The Reform Party opposes public funding of multiculturalism and high levels of immigration. The black communities of Toronto and Montreal accuse the police of racism. Employment equity and affirmative action programs designed to assist "visible minorities" have generated much controversy.

This third aspect of ethnic cleavage, involving other ethnic groups and multiculturalism, increasingly vies with aboriginal and French–English issues on the political agenda. The three principal topics that arise in this area are immigration, preserving and promoting the identity of ethnic groups, and ensuring that individuals belonging to such groups are treated equitably in law and society. This chapter begins with an examination of Canadian immigration patterns. It then discusses the historic pattern of discrimination that new Canadians experienced and their demands to end such treatment. The third part deals with responses to such demands in the 1970s and 1980s, especially the development of the policy of multiculturalism. The chapter ends with an account of recent opposition to large-scale immigration, publicly funded multiculturalism, and employment equity.

CANADIAN IMMIGRATION PATTERNS

Following the aboriginals, the French, and the British, people from many other lands began to immigrate to Canada. By 1867, a sizable German contingent had already arrived, and, shortly afterwards, the wide, open spaces of northern Ontario, the Prairies, and British Columbia attracted large numbers of immigrants from continental Europe as well as from Britain and the United States. Railway construction and western settlement were two key objectives of the Macdonald government's 1879 National Policy (incorporating the 1872 Dominion Lands Act), and the first dramatic surge of immigrants arrived during the 1880s. These included Danes, Dutch, Icelanders, Poles, Ukrainians, Finns, Norwegians, and Swedes.

In British Columbia, between 1881 and 1884, nearly 16 000 Chinese were brought in as contract labourers to work on the CPR. Nova Scotia and Ontario also received a substantial number of blacks escaping from slavery in the United States.

Between 1910 and 1913, the largest number of immigrants in the country's history arrived in Canada. The prosperous 1920s were another active decade, but immigration declined significantly during the Depression and the Second World War. After the war, another huge wave of immigrants came to Canada, largely from southern Europe. They were supplemented by postwar refugees from around the world, one of the largest groups being from Hungary after the 1956 revolution. Table 9.1 indicates the fluctuation in numbers of immigrants arriving in Canada by decade.

Overall, Britain was the leading source of immigrants between 1900 and 1965, but in certain years the largest number came from the United States. Before 1967, immigration policy favoured British, American, and European newcomers, since they were considered well educated and skilled, and, being predominantly Caucasian, better able to assimilate.

After the Immigration Act was significantly amended in 1967, Canadian immigration patterns changed radically, as Table 9.2 shows. In 1957, over 90 percent of the immigrants were from Britain or continental Europe, a figure that fell to 72 percent in 1967, 33 percent in 1977, 25 percent in 1987, and 17 percent in 1992. In contrast, Asian and Caribbean immigrants accounted for less than two percent of total immigrants in 1957, up to 13 percent in 1967, 30 percent in 1977, over 50 percent in 1987, and over 60 percent in 1992. Immigration statistics for the 1978–1992 period can be seen graphically in Figure 9.1, and the sources of such immigrants in Figure 9.2.

The 1991 Census asked respondents for their ethnic origin, but these statistics are increasingly difficult to interpret because so many Canadians now have multiple ethnic origins and because a large proportion simply answer "Canadian." Statistics on ethnic origin seem to indicate, however, that nearly half the population west of Quebec is of non-British or non-French origin, compared with an average of about 10 percent east of Ontario, as seen in Figure 9.3. In Ontario, the French are the second-largest language group, followed by Italians,

TABLE 9.1	Immigrant Arrivals in Canada by Decade		
1861–1871	183 000	1931–1941	150 000
1871–1881	353 000	1941–1951	548 000
1881–1891	824 000	1951–1961	1 543 000
1891–1901	828 000	1961–1971	1 429 000
1901–1911	1 759 000	1971–1981	1 447 000
1911–1921	1 612 000	1981–1991	1 374 000
1921–1931	1 203 000		

Source: Employment and Immigration Canada, "Immigration Statistics," 1992, cat. no. MP22-1/1992. Reproduced with the permission of the Minister of Supply and Services Canada, 1995.

TABLE 9.2	Principal Sources of Immigrants to Canada, Selected Years (Percentage)			
	Britain	*Europe*	*Asia*	*Caribbean*
1957	38.6	52.6	1.3	0.4
1967	28.0	43.8	9.3	3.9
1977	15.7	19.8	21.0	10.4
1987	5.6	19.1	44.3	7.4
1992	2.8	14.9	55.1	5.9

Source: Employment and Immigration Canada, "Immigration Statistics," Annual. Reproduced with the permission of the Minister of Supply and Services Canada, 1995.

Figure 9.1   Immigration by Calendar Year, 1978–1992

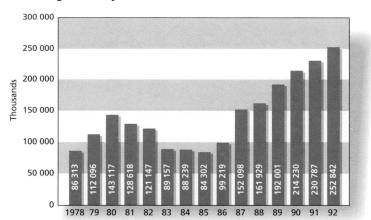

Source: Employment and Immigration Canada, "Immigration Statistics, 1992." Reproduced with the permission of the Minister of Supply and Services Canada, 1995.

Germans, and Chinese. In each of the three Prairie provinces, Germans and Ukrainians out-number the French, as do aboriginals in Manitoba and Saskatchewan. In British Columbia, Chinese, Germans, East Indians, and aboriginals all outnumber the French.

These ethnic groups can be further classified as **visible minorities**—that is, those from Asia, Africa, the Caribbean, South America, and the Middle East—and the invisible minorities—those who have come from southern or eastern Europe. Some recently adopted public policies such as multiculturalism apply to both groups, while others, such as employment equity, apply only to visible minorities.

Recent immigration patterns have changed the face of Canada.

Figure 9.2 Sources of 1992 Immigrants, by Region

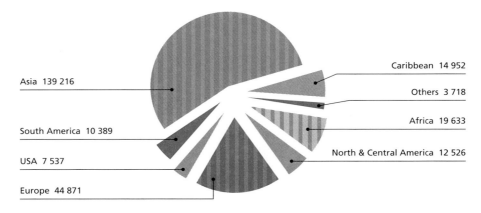

Asia 139 216

Caribbean 14 952

Others 3 718

Africa 19 633

North & Central America 12 526

South America 10 389

USA 7 537

Europe 44 871

Source: Employment and Immigration Canada, "Immigration Statistics, 1992." Reproduced with the permission of the Minister of Supply and Services Canada, 1995.

Figure 9.3 Proportion of Population Reporting Origins Other Than British or French, 1991

Source: Statistics Canada, Canadian Social Trends (Autumn 1993), cat. no. 11-008. Reproduced with the permission of the Minister of Supply and Services Canada, 1995.

DISCRIMINATION AGAINST IMMIGRANTS

Many immigrants settled in ethnic communities and started their own social and cultural organizations such as clubs, choirs, folk dance troupes, and newspapers. Many families spoke the ethnic language at home, but the children generally became proficient in English at school, and the second generation often assimilated into the Anglo-Canadian way of life, as intended. Such ethnic groups maintained a low public profile and made few demands. Once arrived, they were largely ignored by federal and provincial governments, although the occasional privilege was granted, such as promises to Mennonites and Hutterites to leave them alone. In Manitoba between 1896 and 1916 it was legal to establish bilingual English and other-language schools in areas of concentrated ethnic settlement.

As noted above, for 100 years, Canadian immigration policy gave preference to Caucasians. As time went on, however, Canada moved further and further from its British origins, and a growing number of Canadians began to realize the bias in the country's immigration policy. International and domestic pressure thus forced the Pearson government to revise the **Immigration Act** in 1967 to remove its preference for Anglo-Europeans. The great bulk of immigrants in recent years have been visible minorities, although some observers have noted that immigration policy is designed to skim the cream of the crop from Third World countries, to attract doctors and other professionals.

The worst case of federal government mistreatment of visible minorities was that of Japanese Canadians in the Second World War. When Japan entered the war, Canadian citizens of Japanese origin were automatically suspected of being loyal to Japan, a suspicion without any foundation. Canadian citizens of Japanese background were uprooted from the west coast, interned in "relocation centres," and had their property confiscated. At the end of the war, about 4000 were deported.[1]

PRINCIPAL BARRIERS TO IMMIGRANT CANADIANS

- Immigration Act
- Wartime discrimination and internment
- Franchise
- Employment
- Media portrayal
- Political parties

Immigrants have also faced a number of barriers that made it difficult for them to play an active part in mainstream politics, government, and in society in general. These barriers included discrimination in voting rights, employment, media depictions, and political participation.

At the provincial level, the principal example of discrimination was that against Asians in British Columbia; because the federal franchise was sometimes based on provincial franchises, this bias carried over to federal elections. At the federal level, Canadian citizens who came from countries with which Canada was at war (principally Germany and Austria) had their right to vote taken away in 1917. Then, until after the Second World War, Canadians of Chinese, Japanese, and East Indian descent had no vote unless they had served in the armed forces. On the other hand, until 1975, British subjects resident in Canada could vote in federal elections even without becoming Canadian citizens.

Untold cases of discrimination against both visible and invisible ethnic minorities in the area of employment have occurred throughout Canadian history. Blacks and Asians probably suffered most, but so did Caucasians with accents and Canadian citizens who had come from countries with which Canada was at war. Such discrimination extended to government employment and was sometimes even authorized by law. In British Columbia, provincial labour laws in the early part of this century prohibited the employment of Asians in order to preserve jobs for whites.

Canadians of "other" ethnic origins are also sensitive to the way in which the media has portrayed them in a discriminatory manner. In many cases, the complaint is that they are not portrayed at all, and that the media present a picture of a homogeneous white Canadian society. When those of other ethnic origins were included, it was often in a disparaging way. While television stations now hire a number of visible minority anchors and reporters, media stories about new Canadians are often of a negative character.[2]

A final barrier to the equality of those of other ethnic origins was discrimination within political parties. They were generally not welcomed into mainstream parties, and when they did find entry, they were usually given only subordinate roles. They had a hard time winning party nominations, and when they did, it was usually in hopeless or clear-cut "ethnic" constituencies. It was not until the Diefenbaker era, around 1960, that Canadians of Ukrainian background started to make inroads into the Conservative Party. Visible minorities progressed much more slowly, in recent years being most welcome in the Liberal Party.

DEVELOPMENT OF MULTICULTURALISM

It has already been discussed how changes to the Immigration Act in 1967 altered the ethnic composition of the Canadian population over the following 25 years. This increase in the numbers of people of other ethnic origin gave them more leverage to demand improvements in their status as citizens. Changes in the 1970s and 1980s were largely positive for such groups, and started with the adoption of the policy of multiculturalism.

The original mandate of the 1963 Royal Commission on Bilingualism and Biculturalism was to concentrate on the English and French languages and cultures and to make recommendations in the wake of the Quiet Revolution in Quebec. By that time, however, the number of "other" ethnic groups in the country was sufficient to force a change in the Commission's terms of reference. Largely due to pressure from Ukrainian Canadians, the Royal Commission was also asked to examine "the contribution made by other ethnic groups to the cultural enrichment of Canada and the measures which should be taken to safeguard that contribution." The term **multiculturalism** came into increasing use at about this time, and the Commission recommended that increased government attention be given to other ethnic groups including public funding in certain areas. With this encouragement, such groups began to demand public financial assistance as well as verbal and moral support.

In 1971, partly due to the Royal Commission recommendations, group pressure, and politicians hoping to win votes, the Trudeau government announced a new official Canadian policy of multiculturalism within a bilingual framework. Multiculturalism is the official recognition of the diverse cultures in a plural society; it involves encouraging immigrants to retain their linguistic heritages and ethnic cultures instead of abandoning them and assimilating with the dominant group. The government felt that it was "overdue for the people of

Canada to become more aware of the rich tradition of the many cultures"[3] in the country. It argued that the Canadian identity would not be undermined by multiculturalism, that, indeed, cultural pluralism was the very essence of the Canadian identity. Ottawa established a number of new programs to implement the multicultural policy and government department to administer them. To some people of other ethnic origins, however, the policy did not provide for complete ethnic equality because the policy of official bilingualism preserved the historic dominance of the British and French groups. Others saw it as more of a symbolic than substantive policy that was primarily aimed at preserving ethnic folklore. Some Quebeckers viewed multiculturalism as an attempt to diminish their claim of being a distinct society within Canada.

BASIC OBJECTIVES OF MULTICULTURALISM POLICY

* To assist cultural groups to retain and foster their identity
* To assist cultural groups to overcome barriers to their full participation in Canadian society
* To promote creative exchanges among all Canadian cultural groups
* To assist immigrants in acquiring at least one official language[4]

One of the fascinating aspects of multiculturalism policy was the role of the Citizenship Branch of the Secretary of State Department in funding advocacy groups in order to demand services, legislation, recognition, and rights from the government. This was done at the direction of the Trudeau Liberal government and served to help it implement its campaign commitments and advance its own vision of the country.[5] Besides its support of individual ethnic groups, in 1973 the government established the Canadian Consultative Council on Multiculturalism, which was later renamed the Canadian Ethnocultural Council.

Once in place, the policy of multiculturalism legitimized demands for many other changes both in terms of promoting ethnic identities and removing barriers to equity. The next stage was the government's creation of the Canadian Human Rights Commission in 1978. Most provinces already had such bodies to deal with complaints of discrimination in the private sector and to promote anti-discrimination educational programs, but the new Commission closed certain loopholes within federal jurisdiction.

Another major advance was the Charter of Rights and Freedoms in 1982, which provided constitutional protection against discrimination by federal and provincial governments in the equality rights clause, section 15. Moreover, the Charter endorsed affirmative action programs in order to overcome past discrimination. After intense pressure from various ethnic groups, another section was added to the Charter to the effect that it would be interpreted "in a manner consistent with the preservation and enhancement of the multicultural heritage of Canadians" (section 27).

The Multiculturalism ministry that began to take form in the 1970s gradually increased in status, and 1988 saw the passage of a new Canadian Multiculturalism Act. The act gave multiculturalism a stronger legal base by consolidating existing policies and practices into legislation, provided a more detailed policy statement on multiculturalism, and created the

Canadian Multicultural Advisory Committee. In 1991 the Mulroney government created a new Department of Multiculturalism and Citizenship.

As part of a massive reorganization of government departments and functions in 1993, immigration was lumped under Public Security, giving everyone the impression that immigration had become a problem of national security. It was later resurrected to a separate ministry, combined with Citizenship, but at the same time, multiculturalism became part of the Canadian Heritage Department, which reduced it in status, although it also shared a junior minister with the Status of Women.

In 1986 the federal **Employment Equity Act** designated visible minorities, women, people with disabilities, and aboriginals as groups that could benefit from affirmative action programs with respect to hiring in the public service. While those not included complained about reverse discrimination, some ethnic leaders criticized the lack of specific goals and timetables in the legislation.[6]

The treatment of Japanese Canadians during the Second World War nagged at the Canadian conscience for nearly 45 years until the Mulroney government announced a settlement package in the 1988 **Japanese Redress Agreement**, which provided, among other things, $21 000 for each of the surviving internees. This led to demands from other ethnic groups that they be similarly compensated for wartime discrimination in Canada.

Some provinces also support the concept of multiculturalism. Ontario has instituted a heritage language policy in its school system; in 1993 it passed what has been called the strongest employment equity legislation in the country, but the law did not survive the new provincial government elected in 1995. In Quebec, on the other hand, while French-speaking immigrants are welcomed in order to bolster the francophone population, other immigrants are required to attend the French-language school system and are otherwise encouraged to assimilate into the majority French culture.

On the partisan front, the Liberal Party began to welcome those of other ethnic origins into its ranks. Such groups were naturally inclined toward the Liberal Party anyway, seeing that it had usually been in power when they arrived in the country, and that it was the party that initiated the policy of multiculturalism. On the other hand, the practice in many large cities of packing Liberal party nomination and leadership delegate selection meetings with "instant Liberals" from various ethnic groups—primarily Sikh, Italian, Greek, Portuguese, Croatian, Korean, Macedonian, and Chinese—has come under attack. While it has the advantage of integrating these immigrants into the Canadian political process and of giving them political influence which they previously lacked, it alienates those who have been members and worked hard for the party for many years. Such conflict also provides much fodder for the media.

Taking their cue from aboriginal, francophone, and anglophone minority pressure groups, nearly every other ethnic group has established a national organization to promote its culture and to function as a pressure group from time to time. Examples include the Italian National Congress, the German Canadian Congress, and the National Association of Japanese Canadians. As noted above, many such groups were actively encouraged to organize by the government itself, and they were to find common ground in the Canadian Ethnocultural Council. It receives considerable government funding, a fact that some critics feel was responsible for its low-key opposition to the

Charlottetown Accord that did not advance the multiculturalism cause.[7] It now consists of a coalition of 37 national ethnic organizations representing over 100 groups.[8] Ethnic groups have demonstrated a periodic influence on Canadian foreign policy, as well as on internal matters.

REACTION AGAINST MULTICULTURALISM AND IMMIGRATION

If the responses to demands from the multicultural community were largely positive in the 1970s and 1980s, such has not entirely been the case in the 1990s. Opposition has surfaced toward immigration in general, visible minority immigration in particular, as well as multiculturalism, employment equity, and other policies and practices.[9]

This opposition was partly in response to the recession of the early 1990s and the continuing high unemployment rate afterwards. Most economists agree that immigration has little effect on the unemployment rate, that immigration causes as many jobs to be created as immigrants actually fill, and that with a low birth rate and an aging population, Canada needs a relatively high annual intake of immigrants for economic reasons alone. Such views, however, are increasingly rejected by voters, who see recent immigrants taking jobs away from long-time residents. The Reform Party was the first to break rank with an all-party consensus on this issue, calling for a severe cut in annual immigration levels. Other parties resisted to some extent, but the Chrétien government did reduce the level from about 250 000 to about 200 000 in 1994 and imposed a $975 right-of-landing fee. It also announced that it would withdraw from the direct delivery of immigrant integration services and indicated that beginning in 1996, "the balance between economic, family and other immigrant components would place greater emphasis on attracting those with the capacity to settle quickly and contribute to Canada's economy."

After a number of crimes were committed by immigrants who had been ordered deported but who had legally or illegally remained in the country, the Liberals passed a bill in 1995 to remove from the jurisdiction of the controversial Immigration and Refugee Board appeals on humanitarian grounds by criminals declared a danger to the public. Even this did not satisfy critics, who complained about the numerous illegal immigrants and bogus refugee claimants who continued to make a new home in Canada.

The policy of official multiculturalism is also increasingly under attack. In an era of government fiscal restraint, more and more Canadians are reluctant to provide public funding for multicultural purposes, a sentiment first given official voice by the Spicer Commission in 1991.[10] Even some members of the multicultural community have spoken out against the policy, especially Liberal MP John Nunziata and writer Neil Bissoondath. They maintain that official multiculturalism is divisive, that it ghettoizes visible minorities, fosters racial animosity, and detracts from national unity.[11] They argue that multiculturalism emphasizes our differences rather than our similarities as Canadians. A 1995 survey found that 66 percent of respondents disagreed with the statement that "the government should provide funding to ethnic groups so they can protect their traditions and language"; 20 percent agreed, and 14 percent were not sure of their opinion.

The 1990 decision of the RCMP to allow Sikh mounties to wear turbans as a religious symbol produced considerable opposition. So did the wearing of turbans in halls of the Royal

"HE'S AN ARABIAN!"

Reprinted with permission.

Canadian Legion. (On the other hand, the House of Commons, with a similar rule, lost no time in waiving it when the first turbaned Sikh MP was elected in 1993.)

Since most newcomers to Canada settle in Toronto, Montreal, and Vancouver, an increase in racial tensions in these three cities has become apparent. Relations between the black community and the Montreal and Toronto police forces have been strained, while ethnic gangs and inter-ethnic gang wars are becoming more common.

Many multicultural leaders were also dissatisfied with the Charlottetown Accord. When the framers wrote that "Canadians are committed to racial and ethnic equality in a society that includes citizens from many lands who have contributed, and continue to contribute, to the building of a strong Canada that reflects its cultural and racial diversity," they thought such ethnic leaders would be happy. Nevertheless, some of the latter complained that this clause was only a statement of equality, building on s. 15 of the Charter, and not an enhancement of the principle of multiculturalism, as contained in s. 27. In other words, for some multicultural advocates, guaranteeing *equity* is not enough; they also want government to protect and promote *identity*, although they detect greater public opposition to the latter.[12]

CONCLUSION

Immigration is necessary for Canada's economic expansion. More and more immigrants will be coming from Third World countries and will be demanding their share of political influence in the future. In poor economic times, however, established Canadians are resistant to visible minority immigration and publicly financed multiculturalism programs. Increased racial problems can be anticipated over the next decades, particularly in Canada's largest metropolitan centres. When the political agenda is preoccupied with questions of Quebec, Western Canadian influence, debts and deficits, and unemployment, ethnic issues are not likely to receive positive attention.

P Ethnic diversity is the essence of the pluralist approach. Combined with the diversity of the aboriginal, British, and French elements of the population, the recent influx of other ethnic groups makes Canada one of the most heterogeneous societies on the face of the earth. Even before the official policy of multiculturalism was enunciated, many Canadians of all origins celebrated this diversity as a key component of the Canadian national identity: a cultural mosaic in contrast to the American melting pot. Pluralism also relates to the interaction of many ethnic pressure groups as they seek to promote increased immigration (especially from their home country), good relations between Canada and the country of origin, multiculturalism, employment equity, constitutional status, and changes in traditional Canadian ways.

PC The public choice approach is also relevant to developments in multiculturalism in the last 25 years. When ethnic groups began to constitute significant numbers of voters, the Liberal Party could adopt policies fostering even higher levels of immigration as well as multiculturalism. It promised policy changes in return for votes and participation, especially at its nomination meetings. After 1990, however, it had to be more circumspect. At first, it tried to retain the support of the ethnic community with high immigration levels, but for a variety of reasons outlined above, it faced the wrath of other voters and diluted its enthusiasm for both immigration and state-supported multiculturalism. That politicians could to some extent abandon the multicultural constituency reflects the fact that it was weakened by geographical dispersion and internal diversity.

SC The state-centred approach is most applicable to the pre-1970 period in which politicians and bureaucrats formulated policies in this field isolated from societal pressures. Until recently, the state elite contained very few people of non-British or non-French origin, and most were not only insensitive to ethnic concerns, but were actually determined to keep the country as white as possible. John Porter found such a "vertical mosaic" in the political elite as well as in all the other societal elites he studied.[13] Cabinets and bureaucracies in Ottawa, Ontario, Manitoba, and Saskatchewan have reflected more varied hues in recent years, but policy changes are probably more related to voting power and public opinion than to actual changes within the state elite.

In another sense, the state-centred approach was particularly relevant to the Trudeau era as well. Around the time that the policy of official multiculturalism was adopted, the government sought to create advocacy organizations that would promote its own agenda. The politicians and bureaucrats justified their actions by arguing that such interests were inherently difficult to organize on their own. Fledgling ethnic groups (which just happened to represent large numbers of new voters) therefore required government support.[14]

© Class analysts emphasize the class nature of ethnicity in Canada; for them, ethnic inequalities are merely an aspect of economic and class inequalities in society and result from the capitalist pursuit of profit. Domestic and multinational companies often exploited immigrant labour, for example, indentured Chinese immigrants who built the CPR, workers in the garment trade in Toronto or Montreal, or seasonal agricultural workers. Individual affluent Canadian families may also have taken advantage of foreign domestics. Traditional political parties supported by such corporations tried to co-opt ethnic leaders and disguise the real interests of ethnic groups by promising recognition of their cultural identities rather than genuine economic equality.[15] Class analysts point out that one influential group of immigrants, recent arrivals from Hong Kong, have demonstrated considerable influence only because of their vast quantities of capital.[16]

....

DISCUSSION QUESTIONS

1. What annual levels of immigration are appropriate as we approach the year 2000? Does the state of the economy matter?

2. What kinds of immigrants should Canada seek out?

3. What sources of immigrants should Canada concentrate on?

4. To what extent should multiculturalism be constitutionalized?

5. Should the government redress discriminatory policies of the past? Explain.

6. Is there evidence that governmental or other institutional racism still exists? Explain.

7. To what extent should immigrants be encouraged to retain their languages, cultures, and customs?

8. Should such retention be supported from the public purse?

9. To what extent should established Canadian practices and customs be modified in order to accommodate recent immigrants?

10. Which approaches from Chapter 1 are most appropriate to the subject of ethnic groups and multiculturalism?

....

NOTES

1. Department of Canadian Heritage, *Annual Report on the Operation of the Canadian Multiculturalism Act, 1993–1994* (Ottawa: Supply and Services, 1995), p. 1.
2. Daiva Stasiulis, "Deep Diversity: Race and Ethnicity in Canadian Politics," in M.S. Whittington and G. Williams, eds., *Canadian Politics in the 1990s*, 4th ed. (Scarborough: Nelson Canada, 1995), pp.

196–98. Even in more enlightened times, Prime Minister Mulroney telephoned the President of India to offer Canada's condolences for India's loss when an Air India airplane crashed in 1985, even though more than 90 percent of the victims were Canadian citizens (p. 191).

3. Ann Gomer Sunahara, *The Politics of Racism: The Uprooting of Japanese Canadians during the Second World War* (Toronto: Lorimer, 1981).

4. Stasiulis, "Deep Diversity," pp. 195, 202.

5. Prime Minister's Statement in the House of Commons, October 8, 1971.

6. Marc Leman, "Canadian Multiculturalism" (Ottawa: Library of Parliament Research Branch, 1995), p. 4.

7. Leslie Pal, *Interests of State: The Politics of Language, Multiculturalism, and Feminism in Canada* (Montreal: McGill–Queen's University Press, 1993).

8. Stasiulis, "Deep Diversity," p. 209.

9. Yasmeen Abu-Laban, "The Politics of Race and Ethnicity: Multiculturalism as a Contested Arena," in James P. Bickerton and Alain-G. Gagnon, eds., *Canadian Politics*, 2nd ed. (Peterborough: Broadview Press, 1994), p. 255.

10. Leman, "Canadian Multiculturalism," p. 5.

11. Jean Leonard Elliott and Augie Fleras, *Multiculturalism in Canada: The Challenge of Diversity* (Scarborough: Nelson Canada, 1991); Elliott and Fleras, *Unequal Relations: An Introduction to Race and Ethnic Dynamics in Canada* (Scarborough: Prentice-Hall Canada, 1991).

12. Citizens' Forum on Canada's Future, *Report to the People and Government of Canada* (Ottawa: Supply and Services, 1991).

13. Neil Bissoondath, *Selling Illusions: The Cult of Multiculturalism in Canada* (Toronto: Penguin, 1994), and "A Question of Belonging: Multiculturalism and Citizenship," in William Kaplan, ed., *Belonging: The Meaning and Future of Canadian Citizenship* (Montreal: McGill–Queen's University Press, 1993); John Nunziata, "Multiculturalism Policy Feeds Discrimination," *Toronto Star*, October 31, 1989.

14. Abu-Laban, "The Politics of Race and Ethnicity," p. 251.

15. John Porter, *The Vertical Mosaic* (Toronto: University of Toronto Press, 1965).

16. Pal, *Interests of State*.

17. Karl Peter, "The Myth of Multiculturalism and Other Political Fables," in Jorgen Dahlie and Tissa Fernando, eds., *Ethnicity, Power and Politics in Canada* (Toronto: Methuen, 1981); Kogila Moodley, "Canadian Multiculturalism as Ideology," *Ethnic and Racial Studies* (July 1983).

18. Stasiulis, "Deep Diversity," pp. 209–12.

FURTHER READING

Abu-Laban, Yasmeen. "The Politics of Race and Ethnicity: Multiculturalism as a Contested Arena." In James P. Bickerton and Alain-G. Gagnon, eds. *Canadian Politics*, 2nd ed. Peterborough: Broadview Press, 1994.

Abu-Laban, Yasmeen, and Daiva Stasiulis, "Ethnic Pluralism Under Siege: Popular and Partisan Opposition to Multiculturalism." *Canadian Public Policy*, December 1992.

Adelman, Howard, et al. *Immigration and Refugee Policy: Australia and Canada Compared*. Toronto: University of Toronto Press, 1994.

Bissoondath, Neil, "A Question of Belonging: Multiculturalism and Citizenship." In William Kaplan, ed., *Belonging: The Meaning and Future of Canadian Citizenship*. Montreal: McGill–Queen's University Press, 1993.

———. *Selling Illusions: The Cult of Multiculturalism in Canada*. Toronto: Penguin, 1994.

Elliott, Jean Leonard, and Augie Fleras. *Multiculturalism in Canada: The Challenge of Diversity*. Scarborough: Nelson Canada, 1991.

———. *Unequal Relations: An Introduction to Race and Ethnic Dynamics in Canada*. Scarborough: Prentice-Hall Canada, 1991.

Megyery, Kathy, ed. *Ethnocultural Groups and Visible Minorities in Canadian Politics: The Question of Access.* Toronto: Dundurn Press, 1991.

Minister Responsible for Multiculturalism. *Non-Official Languages: A Study in Canadian Multiculturalism.* Ottawa: Supply and Services, 1976.

Minister of State for Multiculturalism. *Multiculturalism and the Government of Canada.* Ottawa: Supply and Services, 1978.

Multiculturalism and Citizenship Canada. *Multiculturalism … Being Canadian.* Ottawa: Supply and Services Canada, 1987.

Pal, Leslie. *Interests of State: The Politics of Language, Multiculturalism, and Feminism in Canada.* Montreal: McGill–Queen's University Press, 1993.

Palmer, Howard. "Mosaic versus Melting Pot?: Immigration and Ethnicity in Canada and the United States." In Eli Mandel and David Taras, eds. *A Passion for Identity.* Toronto: Methuen, 1987.

Ponting, Rick. "Racial Conflict: Turning the Heat Up." In Dan Glenday and Ann Duffy, eds., *Canadian Society: Understanding and Surviving in the 1990s.* Toronto: McClelland and Stewart, 1994.

Stasiulis, Daiva. "Deep Diversity: Race and Ethnicity in Canadian Politics." In M.S. Whittington and G. Williams, eds. *Canadian Politics in the 1990s,* 4th ed. Scarborough: Nelson Canada, 1995.

Sunahara, Ann Gomer. *The Politics of Racism: The Uprooting of Japanese Canadians during the Second World War.* Toronto: Lorimer, 1981.

Wilson, V. Seymour. "The Tapestry Vision of Canadian Multiculturalism." *Canadian Journal of Political Science,* December 1993.

Chapter 10

Class
CLEAVAGES

A few Canadian families are among the richest people in the world, while an increasing number of others line up at soup kitchens and food banks because they cannot afford to buy food. Federal and provincial governments are obsessed with their debts and deficits, commonly blame the costs of social programs for their fiscal woes, and are cutting back on social assistance. No adult can make ends meet on the minimum wage, but small businesses claim they will go bankrupt if it is raised. Canadian history is replete with examples of workers being fired for trying to form unions and of being clubbed by police when they went on strike.[1]

The concept of class is not as clear-cut as that of region or ethnicity, and Canadians are generally more conscious of their regional and ethnic cleavages. Nevertheless, class is an important generator of political activity in most countries, and Canada has its deep-seated class cleavages as well. A discussion of class cleavages in Canada must therefore not only clarify the concept, but also explain why it is not a more significant factor in Canadian politics. This chapter will begin by discussing various definitions of class, then examine the political role of the upper, middle, and working classes, and conclude with an examination of the poor and the social security safety net.

DEFINING CLASS

When dealing with the concept of class, it is customary to start with Karl Marx, who predicted that every capitalist economy would produce a class system consisting primarily of the **bourgeoisie**, the owners of the means of production, and the **proletariat**, the workers. The proletariat would sell their labour for a price; the bourgeoisie would pay them as little as possible (and less than they were worth), thereby accumulating profit or surplus value. While religion and the prospect of a pleasant after-life might keep them content for awhile, the workers would eventually come to resent their low wages and exploitation, and finally engage in a violent revolt.

Capitalist societies have not evolved exactly as Marx predicted, and today's neo-Marxists, while adhering to the essence of their mentor, usually make certain alterations in his analysis. Marx did provide for a small **petite bourgeoisie** of farmers, small business people and self-employed professionals, but this class has become more significant than he expected. Furthermore, the **new middle class** of civil servants, teachers, and other salaried professionals was almost unforeseen in the mid-1800s, and it has become another large and important force. Thus, as mentioned in Chapter 1, those who analyze politics in terms of class speak of the bourgeoisie (the economic elite), the petite bourgeoisie, the new middle class, and the proletariat (the "working class"). They often speak as well of "fractions" within each class.

On the other hand, those social scientists who are not neo-Marxists commonly divide individuals and families into the upper, middle, and working classes, based on such interrelated factors as income, occupation, and education. With these measures, the divisions between the classes are less clear-cut than in the neo-Marxist analysis. Dennis Forcese, for example, defines classes as "aggregates of persons distinguished principally by wealth and income."[2] Although such inequalities both produce and result from inequalities in other characteristics such as education and occupation, income is the simplest measure to use.

One means of measuring income inequality is to divide the population into five equal groups, or quintiles, from highest to lowest income and to indicate the share of total income received by each group. Table 10.1 and Figure 10.1 present such proportions for the year 1992; they also show how the income shares before transfers were even more inequitable, and how the tax system takes a little away from the rich to redistribute to the poor. Thus, even after taxes and transfers, the highest 20 percent of the population receive over 40 percent of the total income, while the lowest 20 percent receive just 5.5 percent. These figures are remarkably constant over time.

A second measure of income distribution is shown in Figure 10.2. It takes the median income in the country as a base and then calculates the proportion of the population that falls within plus or minus 25 percent of that figure. In other words, it shows the percentage of the population that is in the "middle income" group. The chart reveals an increasing polarization in the distribution of earnings in Canada. Workers in the middle-income range accounted for 21.5 percent of the work force in 1986, down from 27.4 percent in 1967. Over

TABLE 10.1	Income Shares of Quintiles before and after Transfers, and after Tax, 1992		
	Income before Transfers	Total Money Income	Income after Tax
Lowest	0.7	4.6	5.5
Second	7.5	10.3	11.5
Middle	16.4	16.7	17.5
Fourth	26.5	24.8	24.7
Highest	49.0	43.6	40.8

Source: Statistics Canada, Income after Tax, Distributions by Size in Canada, 1992, cat. no. 13-210, March 1994. Reproduced with the permission of the Minister of Supply and Services Canada, 1995.

Figure 10.1 **Distribution of Income, Families, by Type of Income and Quintile, 1992**

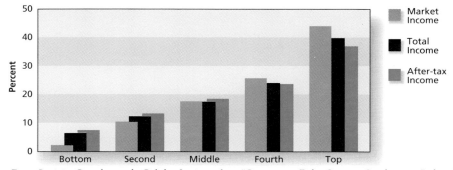

Data: Statistics Canada; graph: Caledon Institute, from "Government Fights Growing Gap between Rich and Poor" (February 1995). Used with permission.

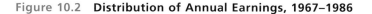

Figure 10.2 **Distribution of Annual Earnings, 1967–1986**

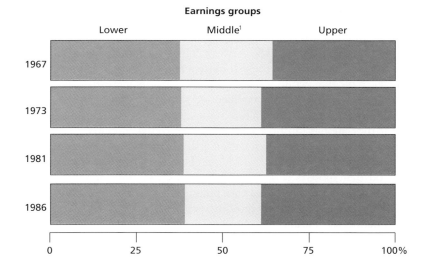

Source: Industry Canada, Economic Council of Canada's Twenty-sixth Annual Review: Legacies, 1989. Reproduced with the permission of the Minister of Supply and Services Canada, 1995.

the same period, the proportion of workers in both the upper and lower earnings groups increased, so that the employment market contains more jobs in the high- and low-paying ranges with fewer jobs in the middle. It is commonly observed that the population is increasingly divided between those holding "good jobs" and those holding "bad jobs."[3]

TABLE 10.2	Level of Educational Attainment, Population 15 Years and Over, March 1994 (Percentage)
0–8 years	13.0
Some secondary	20.2
High-school graduation	19.1
Some postsecondary	9.3
Postsecondary certificate/diploma	25.4
University degree	12.8

Source: Statistics Canada, The Labour Force, cat. no. 71-001, April 1995. Reproduced with the permission of the Minister of Supply and Services Canada, 1995.

The related distribution of educational attainment in Canada in March 1990 is indicated in Table 10.2. The 1986 census was the first to report that the average level of educational attainment in Canada exceeded 12 years of school. In terms of class, potential students from poor and working-class families are still sometimes prevented from undertaking postsecondary education for financial reasons, and even when government assistance helps them overcome the costs involved, attitudinal barriers may persist. Tuition fees have increased dramatically in recent years.

Regardless of whether one uses the neo-Marxist or non-Marxist approach to analyzing social class, a distinction must be made between "objective" and "subjective" class. Objective class refers to the class into which analysts place a person, according to criteria such as type of work or level of income, while subjective class means the class to which people think or feel they belong, even if it contradicts objective standards. Marx himself foresaw the phenomenon of "false consciousness," and that some members of the working class, for example, might feel that they are part of the middle class. Somewhat similarly, people may see themselves as working class but adopt a deferential attitude toward their "betters."

Another qualification that should be added relates to the changing nature of class. Some analysts contend that those born after 1945 have distinctive "postmaterialist" orientations that are less concerned with traditional class polarization than with "quality of life" questions such as environmental, women's, and minority issues.[4]

Relying on neo-Marxist and other class-based analyses, Table 10.3 divides the Canadian population into classes and attempts to estimate the approximate number and percentage of voters (that is, people over 18 years of age) in each class. These objective figures are obviously not as definitive as those on region, ethnicity, or gender, and must also be hedged by considerations of subjective class.[5]

TABLE 10.3   **The Class Structure in Canadian Society**

	Voters	Percent of Electorate
Upper class	500 000	2.5
Middle class	3 000 000	15.0
Petite bourgeoisie	1 500 000	7.5
New middle class	1 500 000	7.5
Working class	13 500 000	67.5
Unionized	4 500 000	22.5
Not unionized	9 000 000	45.0
Poor	3 000 000	15.0
Working	1 500 000	7.5
Welfare	1 500 000	7.5

Source: Devised by author. See explanations in note 5.

THE UPPER CLASS
Identifying the Corporate Elite

It is not difficult to identify those who comprise the upper class. Canada possesses many fabulously rich entrepreneurs and some of the wealthiest families in the world. In 1989, the *Financial Post* estimated the worth of the Irving family at $8 billion, and Ken Thomson at $6.4 billion.[6] The Irving family owns most of New Brunswick, including large tracts of woodlands, pulp mills, all the English-language daily newspapers in the province, oil refineries, gas stations, shipbuilding, trucking, bus lines, railways, and potato operations. Thomson owns over a hundred newspapers in Canada and abroad, the huge Hudson's Bay Co. and Zellers retail chains, and many other firms in the energy, real estate, and publishing fields, including Nelson Canada, the publisher of this book.

The next tier of wealthy Canadian families includes the two branches of the Bronfman family, Galen Weston, and the Eatons, each of whose worth was estimated in 1989 at over one billion dollars. Seagrams is the largest asset of the Montreal Bronfmans (Charles and Phyllis, and Edgar in New York), and in 1995 they took over MCA Universal Studios in Hollywood. Their Toronto cousins, Edward and Peter Bronfman, own or control Trizec, Bramalea, and Carena development companies, London Life, Brascan, Noranda, and MacMillan Bloedel. Galen Weston concentrates on Loblaws, in addition to many other food enterprises including Weston, Zehrs, Neilson Cadbury Canada, and nonfood assets such as Eddy Paper Co. and Holt Renfrew. The Eaton family owns the Toronto Eaton Centre and about 120 other department stores across the country, in addition to Baton Broadcasting.

Beyond these top five, 28 others were worth over $200 million each in 1989, and with one or two unfortunate exceptions (the Reichmanns and Robert Campeau), most are probably worth much more today. Those particularly prominent in the mid-1990s include Ted Rogers (Rogers Communications), Jimmy Pattison (Jim Pattison Group), Paul Desmarais (Power Corp.), Frank Stronach (Magna International), the warring factions of the McCain family (McCain Foods), Conrad Black (Hollinger), the Jodrey family (Crownx Inc.), the Richardson family (James Richardson & Sons), André Chagnon (Le Groupe Vidéotron), and the Sobey family (Empire Company). Stronach received $40 700 000 from his company in 1994, Rogers paid himself $4 375 434, Black got $2 527 237, and Desmarais $1 664 950.

Another category of wealthy Canadians are the corporate chief executive officers (CEOs) who do not actually own their own firms, as do those mentioned above. Various financial publications publish incomes of top CEOs, and some examples from 1994 are listed in Table 10.4, which includes the total value of salary, bonus, incentives, shares, and other benefits.[7]

As indicated, those individuals and families of great wealth and/or income control many of the large corporations operating in Canada. Many firms are owned in whole or in part by the same family, and the extent of intercorporate connections is great. In 1989, for example, the Toronto Bronfmans controlled more than 360 companies; Weston, 126; the Montreal Bronfmans, 118; Irving, 113; and Desmarais, 69.[8] Bell Canada Enterprises, whose ownership is more diversified, controlled 131 corporations including Bell Canada, Northern Telecom, and NewTel, while Canadian Pacific's extensive holdings included Laidlaw, PanCanadian Petroleum, Fording Coal, and Marathon Realty. The corporate scene in the late 1980s was characterized by numerous mergers and acquisitions, but the early 1990s were less active in this respect, being marked especially by Ted Rogers's takeover of the Maclean-Hunter media empire. The great economic families are frequently joint owners of corporations, one of the most prominent recent examples being Paul Desmarais and Conrad Black's joining up to take an increasing share of the ownership of Southam Corp.

It was partly because their companies did well financially that such corporate executives were paid so handsomely. The operating profits of Canadian enterprises increased to $78.4 billion in 1994, returning to the previous peak of profit levels of 1988–89. Of this nearly $80 billion, the small number of large chartered banks garnered a full $5 billion.[9] The degree of corporate concentration is also revealed in the fact that in 1992 the leading 25 enterprises (ranked by assets) controlled 16.1 percent of the operating revenue and 45.8 percent of the assets of all corporations.[10]

Distinct from this "indigenous elite" is the "comprador elite," which is made up of the executives of branches of foreign-owned firms[11] (see also Chapter 12). The comprador elite take orders from the corporate headquarters abroad, a good example being Brian Mulroney when he was president of the Iron Ore Company of Canada, in which Hanna Mining of Cleveland had a controlling interest.[12] On the other hand, many Canadian firms have now become multinationals. Irving, Thomson, Weston and the Bronfmans all have many foreign assets, as do such others as Bata, McCain, Black and such companies as Northern Telecom and the Laurentian Group.

A final point here concerns the vital part which Canadian banks play in the operations of the **corporate elite**. That they do is because so much corporate activity is financed by large

TABLE 10.4 **A Sample of Well-Paid Corporate Executives, 1994–1995**		
Brian Hannan	Methanex	$12 922 579
William Holland	United Dominion	6 379 785
John Doddridge	Magna International	4 671 749
Clayton Woitas	Renaissance Energy	4 226 800
Charles Childers	Potash Corporation	3 918 120
Richard Currie	Loblaw	3 306 309
Jean Monty	Northern Telecom	2 701 806
Allan Taylor	Royal Bank of Canada	2 651 162
Richard Thomson	Toronto-Dominion Bank	2 627 898
Frederick Telmer	Stelco	2 219 272
Purdy Crawford	Imasco	2 030 576
Lynton Wilson	BCE	1 936 069
Matthew Barrett	Bank of Montreal	1 915 716
Peter Godsoe	Bank of Nova Scotia	1 900 095
Al Flood	CIBC	1 826 845
Reto Braun	Moore	1 641 641
Edward Newall	Nova of Alberta	1 640 414
Michael Sopko	INCO	1 559 072
Barry Cochrane	Norcen Energy	1 548 548
Rowland Fleming	National Trustco	1 538 000
W.E. Stinson	Canadian Pacific	1 496 164
Hollis Harris	Air Canada	1 429 149
Jacques Bougie	Alcan Aluminum	1 392 631
James Stanford	Petro-Canada	1 254 443
David Galloway	Torstar	1 236 759
Ronald Oberlander	Abitibi-Price	1 128 940
Israel Asper	Canwest Global	1 058 948
Robert Peterson	Imperial Oil	1 024 747

Source: Globe and Mail, *April 10, 1995, and* Report on Business Magazine, *July 1995; see slightly different figures in the* Toronto Star, *June 19, 1995. Reproduced with the permission of the* Globe and Mail.

bank loans. Thus, many of the individuals named above sit on the board of directors of major Canadian banks, where their presence assures their company or companies of preferential banking treatment.[13] Indeed, a whole theory has been advanced regarding the manner in which the banks have directed the development of the Canadian economy. They have contributed to the widespread foreign ownership in Canada because of their preference for financing foreign branch plants in Canada rather than domestic manufacturers; they have exacerbated regional disparities in their preference for central Canadian clients; and they have encouraged a resource-based economy by preferring export-oriented resource companies to manufacturing.[14]

As far as the social background of the corporate elite is concerned, John Porter found a near Anglo-Protestant monopoly in the l960s, as did Wallace Clement in the 1970s, but this is beginning to change. Several of the largest corporate families are of Jewish background, and French Canadians are increasingly prominent in such circles now, including Paul Desmarais (originally from Sudbury), Claude Castonguay (Laurentian Group), Pierre Péladeau (Quebecor), Bernard Lemaire (Cascades paper), Philippe de Gaspé Beaubien (Télémédia), Laurent Beaudoin (Bombardier), Bertin Nadeau (Unigesco), André Chagnon (Groupe Vidéotron), and Jean Coutu (pharmacies). Those of other ethnic backgrounds are also joining the corporate elite, such as the Batas, Frank Stronach, the Ghermezian brothers, and Li Ka-shing (Husky Oil). While Toronto remains the financial capital of the country, the economic elite is also increasingly diverse in terms of geography, with a new Western flavour.

Demands of the Corporate Elite

While the social homogeneity of the members of the corporate elite has started to decline as the original establishment is being joined or challenged by individuals from more diverse backgrounds,[15] the upper class is no less unified in its basic values. One value that still characterizes the members of this group is the desire to maximize their ownership and control of the private sector and to press the public sector to adopt such policies as will allow them to go about their business of "accumulation."

It is not difficult, therefore, to draw the general lines of the public policy demands of the economic elite. Essentially, they want to be left alone: cut government spending on social programs so that their taxes can be minimized, and reduce the annual government deficit and the accumulated national debt. If taxes are necessary, do not levy estate or wealth taxes. Avoid corporate and progressive individual taxes as much as possible, and provide generous loopholes, write-offs, and tax shelters.[16] Minimize government regulation, labour legislation, and environmental protection, as well as anti-combines laws and other restrictions on corporate takeovers. As Peter Newman says, "What unites [the capitalist elite] is common resentment of the multiplying intrusions of politicians and bureaucrats into the once-sacrosanct ground of Canadian capitalism."[17]

Governments have normally responded positively to such demands, none more so than the Mulroney government between 1984 and 1993. A minimum tax on rich individuals was finally passed in 1986, but significant numbers continue to avoid it; a minimum tax on large corporations was adopted in 1989 after being held up in the Senate. As is argued in Chapter 22, the Senate, especially its influential Banking Committee, functions as a lobby for big business within the apparatus of government.[18] The progressive nature of the personal income tax was reduced when ten tax brackets were reduced to three, and a $500 000 lifetime capital gains tax exemption was introduced, though this was subsequently lowered to $100 000. In her book *Behind Closed Doors*, Linda McQuaig shows how the rich use their political influence to obtain tax breaks that are paid for by those with lesser incomes. While Canada's personal and corporate income tax system is riddled with loopholes, it is one of the few countries in the world without a tax on wealth or inheritance. Moreover, Canadian anti-combines laws are laughable and represent one of the few fields where American regulation of the private sector is more stringent.

Mulroney's finance minister Michael Wilson allowed the corporate elite to continue to deduct 80 percent of the cost of business meals and entertainment, causing the government to lose about $1 billion in tax revenues every year.[19] Other losses to the treasury occur because investors can deduct interest paid on loans used to buy shares, and because only 80 percent of dividends from Canadian corporations are taxable. Wilson completed his tax reform package with the Goods and Services Tax (GST), which most observers believed would benefit the rich by shifting the burden from income to sales taxes. Liberal Finance Minister Paul Martin reduced the entertainment deduction to 50 percent and discontinued the $100 000 capital gains exemption, but at the same time slashed federal contributions to provincial social programs, discussed in more detail later in this chapter. When the Chrétien cabinet overturned a CRTC decision and gave Paul Desmarais's Power Corp. subsidiary Power DirecTV a share of the direct-to-home satellite TV market, many observers raised their eyebrows, given the close connection between Power Corp. and the federal Liberal government.

··

THE POLITICAL CONNECTIONS OF PAUL DESMARAIS'S POWER CORP.

* Close friends of Pierre Trudeau, Brian Mulroney, and Jean Chrétien; both Trudeau and Mulroney associated with Power Corp. in post-PM period
* Son André married to Chrétien's daughter France
* Finance Minister Paul Martin and Quebec Liberal leader Daniel Johnson both former Power Corp. executives
* John Rae, Power Corp. vice-president and Chrétien campaign manager
* Senator Michael Pitfield and former CBC president Gerald Veilleux, now Power Corp. executives

Three principal exceptions to this pressure to minimize the role of government must be noted. First, while the economic elite demands that government minimize spending on others, it often expects sizable chunks of public funds for itself. The new "acquisitors," for example, have "exploited to [the] utmost the Canadian tradition of government subsidies in every-thing from offshore oil to horror films."[20] This tradition goes back as far as the turn of the century when railway companies were given generous amounts of public funds and public lands; it has continued in a wide range of fields at the federal level ever since, especially in terms of regional economic development, and is carried on in give-aways to resource companies at the provincial level. The extent of actual government contributions to business was first made common knowledge by David Lewis, then leader of the New Democratic Party (NDP), in the 1972 election campaign and in his book, *Louder Voices: Corporate Welfare Bums*.[21] Very often, as subsequent NDP leaders have reiterated, the public money involved takes the form of capital cost allowances, deferred taxes, or "tax expenditures" (taxes fore-gone by the government), which are essentially the same thing as a cash grant.

A second exception to the general pattern of corporate demands is the rare occasion on which the economic elite has actually favoured new social programs. Motives here include increasing the purchasing power of the poor and working class, reducing the amounts that companies themselves have to pay in employee benefits, improving their corporate image, and ensuring the basic stability of society so that the upper classes do not have to worry about violent protests from the poor or unemployed. Alvin Finkel writes of the reform measures adopted in the Depression of the 1930s:

> The actions taken were those that businessmen-politicians and other pro-capitalist politicians believed would placate working-class and farmer demands while being assured at the same time that business power within the overall system would be preserved.[22]

In the third place, business leaders sometimes favour an expansion of government activity, usually in the provision of basic utilities or infrastructure, that will decrease their costs or increase their profits. For example, businesspeople in Ontario shortly after 1900 encouraged the provincial government to create a Crown corporation to provide a cheap, reliable supply of electricity, and resource companies have often demanded that governments build roads and railways to save them the trouble.[23]

As noted in Chapter 1, the Canadian state gives priority to big business demands because it depends on the private sector to a large extent to create jobs. Beyond that, politicians respond to the demands of the economic elite for three main reasons. First, corporate executives and politicians often come from the same ranks, including prime ministers and ministers of finance. Brian Mulroney, Michael Wilson, John Turner, and Paul Martin are good examples. Second, companies have many avenues of influence available: making a direct, personal pitch, using professional lobby firms to help them make contact with public decision-makers for a fee, and taking advantage of their membership in pressure groups. Among the hundreds of business pressure groups in existence, the **Business Council on National Issues** is probably the most powerful, representing as it does the chief executive officers of the 150 largest firms in the country. Its executive director, Tom d'Aquino, is a household name in Ottawa. Third, throughout their history both the Conservative and Liberal parties have largely been financed by large corporate contributions. This has changed somewhat in recent years (see Chapter 15), but a link between corporate contributions and general public policy, if not to specific corporate favours, is not difficult to establish. In addition, in the 1988 election, Canadians witnessed an unprecedented parallel campaign in which the country's major corporations spent millions of dollars on top of their party donations to persuade Canadian voters of the merits of free trade. In short, even a non-Marxist admirer of the corporate elite like Peter Newman could write that "the combined power exercised by ... the new Canadian Establishment has seldom been exceeded in any nation that dares call itself a functioning democracy."[24]

THE MIDDLE CLASS

As outlined earlier, the traditional middle class or "petite bourgeoisie" consisted of farmers, small-business people, and self-employed professionals, including doctors and lawyers. This group could also be called the upper middle class. The "new middle class" consists of civil servants, teachers, and other salaried professionals such as nurses, social workers, librarians, engineers, accountants, and the like. Neo-Marxists generally emphasize the ownership or control of the means of production, but as Leo Panitch says, this century has seen the development of a stratum of employees without such ownership or control but who "nevertheless dispose of labour in terms of managing, supervising, and controlling the labour of others."[25]

To some extent, these two fractions of the middle class have considerably different economic interests and therefore different political demands. First, the members of the petite bourgeoisie are usually much wealthier than those of the new middle class and have many more tax breaks. Second, the petite bourgeoisie is made up largely of the self-employed and/or employers, while the new middle class is mostly composed of those who work for someone else. The new middle class largely works in the public sector, either directly for governments or in para-governmental institutions such as schools, universities, and hospitals. In the third place, this public-sector branch of the new middle class is increasingly organized into unions, such as government employee unions and nurses', teachers', and professors' associations. The petite bourgeoisie, on the other hand, normally abhors unions almost as much as does the economic elite.

While the middle class is therefore far from being a unified force, its members are normally well educated, and most are economically comfortable since they receive above-average levels of income. They own their homes and cars, and usually have assorted other material possessions. The middle class has benefited in recent years from structural changes in the economy; indeed, the categories of management, administration, and health are among the few that have grown in both number of jobs and proportion of total income. Some, especially the upper middle class, have also taken advantage of high interest rates to increase their investment income.[26]

Unlike the upper class, members of the middle class may not be sufficiently affluent to finance their own educational and medical needs, and usually demand and benefit from government programs in these fields. In addition, not all members of the middle class can take advantage of the clauses written into the tax laws to benefit the wealthy.[27] It does enjoy such tax shelters as RRSPs and certain investment incentives (see Figure 10.3). But the middle class pays a disproportionate amount of the taxes to finance government programs of all kinds. A study of federal tax changes between 1984 and 1988, for example, showed that while those earning under $13 000 and those over $117 000 gained, the hardest hit were middle-class families making between $29 000 and $43 000.[28] Thus it is on the "middle middle" and especially "lower middle" classes that the federal and provincial personal tax increases in recent years have fallen most heavily.

Figure 10.3   Distribution of RRSP Tax Breaks by Income

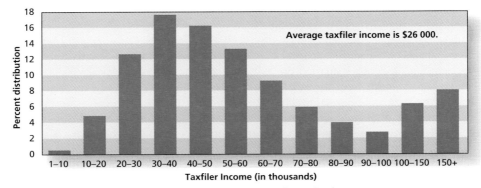

Source: Canadian Council on Social Development, Insight *(April 1995). Used with permission.*

   Many groups within the middle class are organized by profession, primarily at the provincial level. But there is no umbrella pressure group that transmits the class's demands collectively to the authorities. Some—especially those who are unionized—have been attracted by NDP promises to shift the tax burden to the corporate sector and upper classes, but most continue to support the Liberal and Conservative parties because of their lack of sympathy with the NDP's links to industrial labour unions. To some extent, therefore, even the new middle class confirms Marx's contention that the petite bourgeoisie functioned primarily as an ally of the economic elite.

THE WORKING CLASS

The working class is generally identified with manual or routine as opposed to intellectual work. Its members normally lack postsecondary education, but they are often qualified in a trade. They usually, but not always, receive less income than those in the middle class and are more frequently unionized. The typical member of the working class is engaged in resource exploitation, assembly line production, secretarial and clerical work, sales, and a variety of crafts and trades. (That portion of the working class living below the poverty line is discussed below in the section "The Poor.") While Marx categorized farmers as part of the petite bourgeoisie because of their ownership of land, most Canadian farmers have had to struggle for their existence. These less affluent farmers have sometimes cooperated with organized labour to support such organizations as the Cooperative Commonwealth Federation (CCF) and NDP.[29]

   The difference in economic status between unionized and nonunionized members of the working class is often profound, and the issue of unionization is a significant one for many members of the working class. Karl Marx's predictions of a violent proletarian revolt were dealt a blow when the Macdonald government legalized trade unions in Canada in 1890 and when the franchise was extended to the working class. Since then, the courts have decided that labour legislation falls primarily within provincial jurisdiction, and the impediments to unionization have varied across the country. Many provincial governments as well as many companies have been viciously hostile toward the formation of unions, and Canada has experienced a large number of violent strikes. Among the key labour struggles in Canadian history were the 1919 Winnipeg General Strike, the 1937 General Motors Strike in Oshawa, the 1945 Ford Strike in Windsor, the 1949 Asbestos Strike in Quebec, and the woodworkers strike in Newfoundland in 1959.[30] Labour legislation also deals with conciliation, mediation, arbitration, picketing, labour standards, occupational health and safety standards, and compensation for injury on the job. All of these usually provide minimal protection for the working class, as governments claim to be responding to labour demands, but still seek to avoid offending their own corporate supporters.

Others things being equal, it is in the interests of members of the working class to belong to a union: unionized employees almost always have higher wages (sometimes higher than the middle class), adequate benefits, better working conditions, and more protection against dismissal than those who do not engage in such collective bargaining. Nearly 80 percent of unionized workers have private pension coverage, for example, compared with only 30 percent of those who are not unionized.[31] In spite of these facts, the rate of unionization among "paid workers" is very low. Total union membership in 1992 was 3 866 100 or 34.9 percent of the 11 736 000 potential members in the country. This overall rate has ranged between 31 and 35 percent for over twenty years.[32]

Moreover, the number of blue-collar jobs is declining in such areas as resource industries, construction, and manufacturing where unionization was most common. New jobs in the "post-industrial" society are largely found in sales and services, especially in the private sector, and are traditionally part-time, poorly paid, and nonunionized. Between 1981 and 1994, the proportion of jobs in goods-producing industries fell from 34 to 26 percent, while that in the services sector increased from 66 to 74 percent.[33] Canada lost nearly 500 000 manufacturing jobs between 1989 and 1993.[34] Lacking a union, and given the nature of their job, those in sales and services occupations are not as likely to be class-conscious or to develop social democratic values as those who produce goods. The proportion of unionized workers in different sectors is shown in Table 10.5.

TABLE 10.5 Union Members as a Percent of Paid Workers, by Industry, 1992	
Agriculture	1.6
Other primary	33.9
Manufacturing	35.2
Construction	65.2
Transportation, communication, utilities	53.4
Trade	11.9
Finance	4.7
Services	35.7
Public administration	79.2

Source: Statistics Canada, CALURA, Trade Unions, Part II, 1992, cat. no. 71-202, May 1994. Reproduced with the permission of the Minister of Supply and Services Canada, 1995.

The composition of the unionized work force is changing in other ways as well. Once composed primarily of private-sector, male, manual workers, it is increasingly made up of public-sector unions, and women now constitute over 41 percent of union members.[35] Public-sector unions make up two of the six largest unions in the country, which are as follows: the Canadian Union of Public Employees (CUPE), 412 656; Canadian Auto Workers (CAW), 181 417; Food and Commercial Workers, 170 039; Public Service Alliance (PSAC), 141 513; United Steelworkers, 133 986; and the Communication, Energy, and Paperworkers (CEP), 133 664. Table 10.5 reveals that a higher proportion of public administration employees are unionized than any other sector.

The 1980s and 1990s have not been good years for the working class. High unemployment diminished the bargaining power of Canadian workers and forced them to concentrate on matters of job security rather than remuneration. On the other hand, high interest rates strengthened the resolve of employers to reduce costs in other areas including wages paid to employees.[36] Consequently, over the 1977–89 period, the contribution of labour income to total personal income fell from 71 to 64 percent.[37] Tax changes only exacerbated the situation, as did the recession of the early 1990s and government restraint programs across the country, so that the average family income fell from $46 250 in 1989 to $43 225 in 1993.

The principal federal interest in labour legislation is in the Unemployment Insurance program. This program was introduced in 1941 to tide workers over between jobs, but given the high national unemployment rates in the years since, and the even higher rates in certain regions in every year, UI is used much more heavily than was originally anticipated. With such large numbers of workers drawing on the fund, it has become both a vital source of individual and regional income and the subject of almost daily political controversy. How many weeks should one have to work in order to qualify? What proportion of a worker's previous wage level should be provided? Who should be included in its coverage? If there is a single national issue that clearly pits the working class against the middle and upper classes, it is probably this one.

The **Canadian Labour Congress** (CLC) is the lobbying body for over two million workers. The CLC has the largest membership of any pressure group in the country and represents the greatest number of voters. Its influence is diminished, however, by its divergent values and its outsider status, as well as by the fact that not all unions belong to it. Whether it increased or decreased its influence by affiliating with the NDP in 1961 is still an open question. Many unions have not joined any central organization, and others have formed such rival groups as the Canadian Federation of Labour (220 600 members) and the Confédération des syndicats nationaux (CSN, with 240 000 members). The historic factionalism within the Canadian union movement has not helped the cause of the working class.[38] Thus, out of a potential 11.7 million paid workers, only 3.9 million have joined a union, and only 2.2 million have affiliated with the largest central labour organization in the country.

······································

THE POOR

The poor can be defined as those living below the **poverty line**. Different organizations use slightly different definitions of poverty, and the lines vary according to location and size of family unit, but a wide consensus exists among them. The most common are those of Statistics Canada and the Canadian Council on Social Development.[39]

Statistics Canada uses the bureaucratic term "low-income cut-off," which is calculated as follows: any individual or family that spends more than 56.2 percent of their income on food, clothing and shelter, is considered to be living in poverty. The National Council of Welfare's (NCW) estimate for low-income cut-off for 1995 is shown in Table 10.6. The Canadian Council on Social Development (CCSD) uses a different standard for poverty: anyone living on less than 50 percent of the average disposable income for a family unit of equivalent size (without taking account of community size). Table 10.7 shows the proportion of the population below the Statistics Canada and CCSD poverty lines in selected years.

The extent of poverty in Canada has been revealed in the Canadian Council on Social Development's *The Canadian Fact Book on Poverty—1994* and the National Council of Welfare's

TABLE 10.6   Estimates of Statistics Canada's Low-Income Cut-offs (1986 Base) for 1995 and CCSD Poverty Lines, 1994

| | Community Size | | | | | |
Family Size	Cities of 500 000+	100 000– 499 999	30 000– 99 999	Less than 30 000	Rural Areas	CCSD Lines
1	$15 758	$13 841	$13 521	$12 326	$10 728	$13 770
2	21 359	18 762	18 328	16 706	14 543	22 950
3	27 150	23 848	23 296	21 235	18 484	27 540
4	31 261	27 454	26 822	24 451	21 281	32 720
5	34 154	29 997	29 305	26 714	23 252	36 720
6	37 075	32 559	31 808	28 996	25 238	41 310
7+	39 874	35 022	34 214	31 189	27 146	45 900

Source: *National Council of Welfare*, Poverty Profile 1993; *Canadian Council on Social Development*, The Canadian Fact Book on Poverty—1994. *Reproduced with permission.*

TABLE 10.7   Percent of Population below the Poverty Line in Selected Years

| | Below the NCW Line | | | | Below the CCSD Line | | | |
	1969	1979	1986	1993	1973	1979	1986	1991
Families	20.8	13.1	12.3	14.8	17.4	21.6	21.2	21.1
Unattached individuals	42.8	40.3	34.2	37.1	39.7	41.3	36.7	37.1
Total households	23.1	15.7	14.9	17.4	23.3	27.4	25.9	26.3

Sources: *National Council of Welfare*, Poverty Profile 1993; *Canadian Council on Social Development*, The Canadian Fact Book on Poverty—1994. *Reproduced with permission.*

Poverty Profile 1993. Depending on which poverty line is used, Canada had between 4 775 000 (NCW) and 6 054 000 (CCSD) people living in poverty in the 1991–93 period. The large group of near-poor that exists just above the arbitrary poverty line justifies the use of figures higher in this range, that is, over five million poor. According to the CCSD, the proportion of the population living below the poverty line remained fairly constant since 1973, but the absolute numbers have increased along with population growth. The NCW, on the other hand, cites a decline in the proportion of poor from 25 percent in 1969 to about 15 percent in 1986. Both organizations agree that during the 1990s the proportion of Canadians living in poverty has increased. Some of the highlights of both organizations' findings are reproduced below.

HIGHLIGHTS OF RECENT REPORTS ON POVERTY

- The number of children living in poverty is 1 415 000, or 20.8 percent of Canadian children (NCW); 1 786 000 or 26.9 percent (CCSD).
- Children from poor families have 2.5 times the high-school drop-out rate of children from nonpoor families, are 1.7 times more likely to have a psychiatric disorder, 1.8 times more likely to have an alcohol problem, and 1.4 times more likely to use drugs (CCSD).
- 752 000 poor children lived in two-parent families, and 595 000 poor children lived in lone-parent families headed by women.
- 59.8 percent of lone-parent mothers under 65 with children under 18 live in poverty, the highest poverty rate of any group (NCW); 66.3 percent, according to the CCSD.
- In March 1993, over half a million people received food from one of the 436 food banks in the country (CCSD).
- The number of seniors living in poverty is 636 000 or 20.5 percent of those aged 65 and over (NCW).
- In all categories, the poverty rates for women were higher than the rates for men (NCW).
- The earnings of wives in two-parent families significantly reduce the poverty rate in this category (NCW).
- The working poor were most prevalent in service industries (NCW).
- The higher the level of education, the lower the poverty rate (NCW).
- Poverty rates were higher for those who immigrated to Canada after 1979 than earlier (NCW).
- Quebec had the highest poverty rates for seniors, probably because it is the only large province without provincial income supplements for the elderly who are poor (NCW).
- Alberta had the highest increase in poverty rates between 1981 and 1991 (CCSD).

Those living in poverty can be subdivided into several main groups: women, children, aboriginals, people with disabilities, and the elderly. The aspect of poverty that is probably most heartbreaking and most intractable is the fact that 30 percent of the poor people in Canada are children. The child mortality rate is twice as high among families at the lowest income level than at the highest, and in 1986 the high-school drop-out rate among children from poor families was 2.2 times the rate of others. This tie between low income and low education is self-perpetuating, and ways must be found to encourage the children of poor families to pursue their education. The *Canadian Fact Book on Poverty* asserts that "the educational opportunities of children, whether at the primary, secondary or post-secondary level, must not be limited by the economic circumstances of their parents."[40] It also documents how children from low-income families stand out from their better-off peers:

> They are less healthy, have less access to skill-building activities, have more destructive habits and behaviours, live more stressful lives, and are subject to more humiliation. In short, they have less stable and less secure existences and as a result they are likely to be less secure as adults.[41]

As indicated above, while more than half of poor children live in two-parent families, over 40 percent of the children below the poverty line live with lone-parent mothers. Depending on which study is used, between 60 and 66 percent of such mothers exist in a state of poverty. In terms of depth of poverty, lone-parent mothers with children were also further below the poverty line than other groups.

Many poor people work full-time (27 percent of family heads and 19 percent of unattached individuals), and others part-time (40 percent and 54 percent, respectively), so that the poor can be about equally divided between those who work and those who are unemployed or unemployable.[42] The working poor try to scrape by on the minimum wage or have more than one low-paying job. Because the minimum wage is even lower than welfare benefits, many working poor choose to go on welfare because they are often better off that way. Rather than raise the minimum wage, however, many provincial governments have actually reduced welfare benefits in the 1990s. Even the combined incomes of two family members earning the minimum wage will not raise them above the poverty line.[43]

Unemployment insurance is of vital importance to the working poor.[44] The Mulroney government brought in sweeping changes to the UI program that required people to work longer and collect for a shorter period of time. While it estimated that about 160 000 people would get more from the program, almost one million would get less or be cut off entirely, with the lowest-income groups losing most. The government's rationale was to divert over one billion dollars into job training, but many doubted that this would result in subsequent employment in most of the hard-pressed parts of the country. The Chrétien Liberals cut the UI program even further.

When their UI runs out, the *working poor* become the *welfare poor*. Welfare benefits vary considerably from province to province, and even though they used to be partly financed by the federal government under the Canada Assistance Plan, they are not generous, contrary to the impression of many who have not had to rely on them. One of the chronic concerns about the welfare system across the country has been its disincentive effect for the welfare poor to seek employment. Earned income is usually deducted from welfare benefits, so that it is often not worth the effort to find a job. Figure 10.4 illustrates the increase in both welfare and unemployment insurance recipients after 1990, figures which do not include the working poor.

The poor are generally unorganized and collectively inarticulate in the political system. They lack the skills to organize effectively as pressure groups primarily because they do not

Figure 10.4 Welfare and Unemployment Insurance Recipients, 1976–1992

Source: Caledon Institute of Social Policy, reproduced in Canadian Council on Social Development: An Overview of Canadian Social Policy. 1993. Used with permission.

have the education, money, and time to develop such skills. Three main pressure groups attempt to include the voice of the poor in the political process. The first is the Canadian Council on Social Development, which represents middle-class, bureaucratic, and even some corporate concern with the state of social policy in the country. It has often provided the blueprint for social reform, even if it did not have the power to ensure that its recommendations were followed. Because the CCSD does not actually represent the poor as such, the government sponsored the creation of the National Council of Welfare in 1969 as an advisory group speaking on behalf of welfare clients themselves. Its members include welfare recipients, public housing tenants, and other low-income citizens as well as those involved in providing services to the poor. As this chapter has shown, both organizations produce studies of the poverty problem and other social issues; even though it is funded by the government, the NCW is usually more critical and radical than the CCSD. The third pressure group, the National Anti-Poverty Organization, was formed in 1971. It is an umbrella organization of various local and provincial poverty groups across the country, but typically lacks resources.

....

THE SOCIAL SECURITY SAFETY NET

Reflecting the influence of the affluent economic elite, the North American predilection for the "market ethos,"[45] and the assumption that jurisdiction over such matters rested primarily with the provinces, the federal government was slow to get involved in the provision of health and social service programs. By the early 1980s, however, Canada had become a "welfare state" in which federal, provincial, and municipal governments were engaged in a wide range of programs that contributed to a **social security safety net** protecting the weakest members of society, especially those unable or not expected to earn a living on their own. The principal federal measures can be divided into five basic fields—those relating to the young, the elderly, people with disabilities, the unemployed, and health insurance. These programs, together with their dates of adoption, are outlined in Table 10.8.

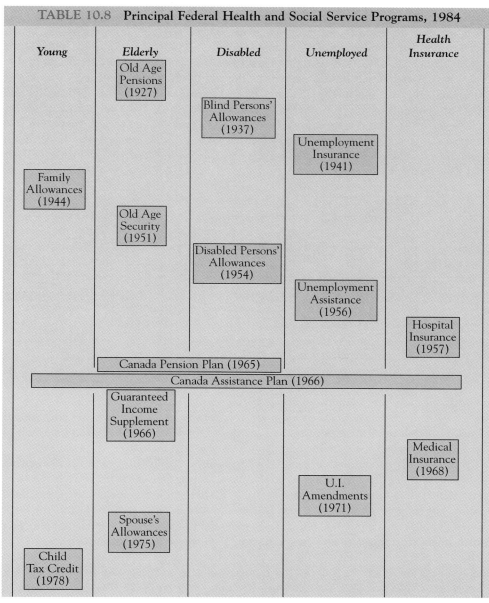

TABLE 10.8   Principal Federal Health and Social Service Programs, 1984

Young	Elderly	Disabled	Unemployed	Health Insurance
	Old Age Pensions (1927)			
		Blind Persons' Allowances (1937)		
			Unemployment Insurance (1941)	
Family Allowances (1944)				
	Old Age Security (1951)			
		Disabled Persons' Allowances (1954)		
			Unemployment Assistance (1956)	
				Hospital Insurance (1957)
	Canada Pension Plan (1965)			
	Canada Assistance Plan (1966)			
	Guaranteed Income Supplement (1966)			
				Medical Insurance (1968)
			U.I. Amendments (1971)	
	Spouse's Allowances (1975)			
Child Tax Credit (1978)				

Source: Devised by author.

Of these programs, only the Canada Assistance Plan, the Guaranteed Income Supplement, the Spouse's Allowance, and the Child Tax Credit were specifically designed to help the poor. Unemployment insurance, the Canada and Quebec Pension Plans, and health programs provide income or health insurance regardless of income, and the Old Age Security and Family Allowances were originally universal programs. Nevertheless, in a relative sense, they all benefit the poor more than the affluent.

Almost all of these measures faced much upper-class and corporate opposition before being adopted. Each one was passed when a Liberal government was in office, although it should be added that the first unemployment insurance legislation was introduced by the Conservative R.B. Bennett but thrown out by the courts, and the Diefenbaker government made incremental improvements to earlier Liberal measures. In the cases of hospital and medical insurance, the CCF pioneered the measures at the provincial level in Saskatchewan, and in several instances the Liberals introduced the federal programs when they were in a minority position in Parliament and depended on CCF or NDP support. The trade union movement, churches, and other progressive organizations like the Canadian Council on Social Development were also responsible for popularizing such programs and pressing the government to implement them.

Other aspects of the social security net include special federal programs for war veterans and Indians, and training schemes for the unemployed. Many provincial services supplement those outlined above. Primitive provincial welfare programs before the turn of the century gave way to mothers' allowances and family benefits after 1900, while child welfare programs, residential services, hospitals, workers' compensation, and student assistance can be found in every province. Some provide supplementary family allowances and assistance to the elderly; some include dental, drug, optical, and paramedical services under medicare; and most provide a variety of other public health, crisis intervention, rehabilitation, and information and referral services. Many of these programs are partially funded through federal–provincial shared-cost programs. Thus, in spite of the resistance of the upper classes and the economic elite, the lot of the working class and poor in Canada could be and has been worse.

In fact, it is actually becoming worse. Both federal and provincial governments in the 1990s are obsessed with their accumulated debts and current budgetary deficits, which they, along with business interests and conservative think-tanks, blame on over-spending on social programs. Although social programs loom large in both federal and provincial government budgets, Canada actually stands near the bottom of OECD countries in the proportion of gross domestic product spent on social programs, as seen in Table 10.9.

It is possible, therefore, that debts and deficits have been caused by under-taxation rather than by over-spending; indeed, on a comparative basis, Canada derives less tax revenue from corporations than all of its major allies. Canada is also one of the few major Western industrialized countries without a tax on wealth.[46] Linda McQuaig's book *Shooting the Hippo* blames the Bank of Canada's policy on maintaining high interest rates and a high Canadian dollar for promoting unemployment (and therefore social spending) and high payments on existing debts.[47]

Those in power in the 1990s so far have agreed that social spending must be chopped. By means of the "clawback," the Mulroney government effectively removed the universal aspect of family allowances and old age security but without redistributing such savings to the poor.

Reprinted with the permission of the Ottawa Sun.

In 1990 it reneged on its Canada Assistance Plan commitments with respect to providing half the costs of provincial and municipal social assistance in the three most prosperous provinces. In 1993, Ottawa reduced unemployment insurance entitlements to 57 percent of normal wages to a maximum of $425 a week, and replaced the Family Allowance Program with the refundable Child Tax Benefit. The latter move was designed to have a greater redistributive impact. The only social program the Mulroney government actually improved upon was the Spouse's Allowance, in 1985.

Source: Canadian Council on Social Development, An Overview of Canadian Social Policy (October 1993), based on Howard Oxley and John P. Martin, "Controlling Government Spending and Deficits: Trends in the 1980s and Prospects for the 1990s," OECD Economic Studies (Autumn 1991). Reproduced with permission.

Many observers saw Mulroney's package of economic policies—the Free Trade Agreement, privatization, deregulation, tax reform including the GST, reductions in transfers to the provinces, and the many cutbacks in social programs—as an integrated strategy. While the government claimed that these measures were introduced either to improve the economy or to cut the deficit, they had the collective effect of making the rich richer and reducing the standard of living of the poor and the working class. Several provinces, led by Alberta, made their own massive cuts in social spending and would have done so regardless of federal transfers.

When the Chrétien Liberals were elected in 1993, Human Resources Minister Lloyd Axworthy undertook a major review of social programs. He presented his conclusions in a green paper in 1994, but his proposals were immediately highjacked by Paul Martin's 1995 budget. Martin cut transfers to the provinces far beyond anything attempted by the Mulroney government, especially in health, postsecondary education and welfare: a decrease of $7 billion over the 1996–98 period. In cutting contributions for social assistance, Ottawa repealed the Canada Assistance Plan, removed the conditions under which provinces received such funding, and lumped the three programs together under the label "Canada Health and Social Transfer." In other words, provincial governments could now restrict social assistance eligibility and promote "workfare" schemes at will. On the other hand, in spite of reducing health care grants, the federal government tried to hang on to the existing conditions of the Canada Health Act by continuing to provide part of the transfer in the form of cash rather than tax transfers. Martin was expected to reduce unemployment insurance and old age pensions in 1996, even though UI is self-funded. Not everyone agrees, however, that social programs must be savaged.[48]

CONCLUSION

Whatever conception of class one wishes to employ, the existence of different classes in Canadian society cannot be denied. In this chapter, it was useful to divide the population into four classes: upper, middle, working, and poor. If such class cleavages do not usually result in political action, it must be that many Canadians are unaware of them or feel powerless to change them.

Ⓒ Of the approaches outlined in Chapter 1, class analysis is obviously the one most concerned with class cleavages. This approach is also concerned with the lack of class-consciousness among the working class and the poor. Neo-Marxists argue that the upper classes, the petite bourgeoisie, and even the new middle class have defined what is politically relevant in society in regional, ethnic and religious terms.[49] When politicians and political parties appeal to members of the working class as Albertans, French Canadians, or Protestants rather than as workers, the latter develop a perverted view of who is an enemy or a friend. Members of one union can be persuaded that they should be hostile to the demands of another, or that they should support coercive back-to-work legislation to end another union's strike. They can also be collectively hoodwinked into thinking that their wage demands fuel inflation and must be curtailed by programs of wage and price controls.

Given such a weak sense of class consciousness in the two lower classes, how do class analysts explain the social security safety net? They argue that some such measures directly benefit the corporate sector, and the rest serve to legitimate the capitalist system and ensure social peace.[50] After the vote was extended to the working class, some minimal response had to be made to address its political demands, but not so much as to interrupt the accumulation activity of the bourgeoisie.

PC Public choice theory requires that voters be rational, self-interested, and conscious of their group position, something that many Canadian workers apparently are not. Such workers therefore rarely constitute a strategic group at election time. Politicians often promise programs of interest to the working class, but do not fulfil them; sometimes they even completely reverse their electoral commitments, as in the case of Trudeau's flip-flop on wage and price controls in 1974. Once the Chrétien Liberals were elected in 1993, they dragged their feet in implementing their Red Book commitments with respect to job creation and social programs. On rare occasions, however, politicians strike a bargain with the working class in which the former promise social programs in return for votes.

SC State-centred theorists argue that because of the divisions within the working class and their low level of class consciousness, politicians and bureaucrats can ignore their demands more easily than in the case of regional–economic and ethnic demands. Moreover, since very few working-class politicians have ever been elected in Canada and most bureaucrats are of middle-class background, policies have been designed in the interests of those in power. It should also be noted, however, that bureaucrats sometimes take a wider view of the national interest. Those bureaucrats in such class-oriented departments as health, welfare, labour, and human resources, along with their provincial counterparts, have been known to join organizations like the CCSD and do what they can to persuade the politicians to adopt their recommendations.[51] On the other hand, they generally do not feel capable of initiating such policies on their own.[52]

P Finally, pluralists emphasize the role of the one main working-class pressure group, the Canadian Labour Congress, and other groups speaking for the lower classes. When faced with the resources available to business pressure groups, however, even the most sanguine pluralist could not expect any degree of equality in the struggle among different classes. Like the other segments of society, the labour movement has its own elite—the leaders of the largest unions in the country. But John Porter found that the composition of the labour elite is quite different from others. Lacking socioeconomic credentials, the labour elite has minimal links to the other elites, whether in terms of marriage, friendship, school ties, or politics.[53] What is even more striking is the absence of any group that could be said to represent the middle class. If policy is arrived at through pressure group interaction, it is the middle class whose unarticulated interests are ignored.

• • • • • • • • • • • • • • • • •

DISCUSSION QUESTIONS

1. To what class do you and your family belong? Assess your family's class consciousness.

2. To what extent do you agree with the neo-Marxist approach to the concept of class?

3. What is the best way to define and distinguish among social classes?

4. Do you feel that the economic elite owe their wealth and power primarily to their own honest, individual efforts or to forms of profit-making and manipulation of the political system? Explain.

5. Is the extent of corporate concentration in Canada a source of concern? Explain.

6. Why do so many Canadians conceive of Canada as a middle-class nation?

7. Given that unions are generally the best way of improving the lot of the working class, why are they not more popular?

8. Will the poor always be with us, or can poverty be eliminated? What is likely to happen as poverty rates increase and governments cut back on social programs?

9. How do you explain the existence of the social security safety net, given the lack of political power of the poor and working class?

10. To what extent do your answers to questions 2–9 follow logically from your answer to Question 1?

NOTES

1. Irving Abella, ed., *On Strike* (Toronto: James Lewis & Samuel, 1974).
2. Dennis Forcese, *The Canadian Class Structure* (Toronto: McGraw-Hill Ryerson, 1975), p. 14. Other basic books on class include Alfred A. Hunter, *Class Tells: On Social Inequality in Canada* (Toronto: Butterworths, 1981 and subsequent editions), and Henry Veltmeyer, *Canadian Class Structure* (Toronto: Garamond Press, 1986).
3. See, for example, Stephen Brooks and Andrew Stritch, *Business and Government in Canada* (Scarborough: Prentice-Hall Canada, 1991), p. 101; Economic Council of Canada, *Good Jobs, Bad Jobs: Employment in the Service Economy* (Ottawa: Supply and Services, 1990).
4. See, for example, Neil Nevitte, Herman Bakvis, and Roger Gibbins, "The Ideological Contours of 'New Politics' in Canada: Policy, Mobilization and Partisan Support," *Canadian Journal of Political Science* (September 1989), pp. 475–503.
5. Henry Veltmeyer's *Canadian Class Structure* (Toronto: Garamond Press, 1986) is the only attempt by a Canadian sociologist that I could find to estimate the actual number of people in each class. He does so for those in the labour force, and I have generally based Table 10.3 on his figures. But since I am more interested in numbers of *voters* in each class, I had to add spouses, children over 18, and retirees to his figures. I did so by applying an arbitrary factor of 0.5 to the number in each class in the labour force. Union membership in Canada is about 4 million, of whom I arbitrarily placed 1 million in the middle class (unionized teachers, civil servants, etc.). Paid workers number about 11 million, of whom I placed the one million mentioned above into the middle class, one million as working poor, and the other nine million as working class. Statistics show about 5 million below the poverty line, but about one-third of these are nonvoting children. My more detailed table follows:

	No. in Labour Force	Children >18, Retirees & Spouses Not in Labour Force	Total Voters	Percent of Electorate
Upper class	330 000[a]	165 000	500 000	2.5
Middle class	2 000 000[a]	1 000 000	3 000 000	15.0
Petite bourgeoisie	1 000 000[a]	500 000	1 500 000	7.5
New middle class	1 000 000[a]	500 000	1 500 000	7.5
Working class	9 000 000[a]	4 500 000	13 500 000	67.5
Unionized	3 000 000	1 500 000	4 500 000	22.5
Nonunionized	6 000 000	3 000 000	9 000 000	45.0
Poor	2 000 000	1 000 000	3 000 000	15.0
Working	1 000 000	500 000	1 500 000	7.5
Welfare	1 000 000	500 000	1 500 000	7.5

[a] *Roughly based on Veltmeyer,* Canadian Class Structure.

6. *The Financial Post Moneywise* (May 1989).
7. See also Peter C. Newman, *The Canadian Establishment, Volume Two: The Acquisitors* (Toronto: McClelland and Stewart, 1990); Diane Francis, *Controlling Interest: Who Owns Canada?* (Toronto: Macmillan, 1986); and John DeMont, *Citizen Irving and His Legacy* (Toronto: Doubleday, 1991).
8. Statistics Canada, *Inter-corporate Ownership*, cat. no. 61-517, April 1990; Royal Commission on Corporate Concentration, *Report* (Ottawa: Supply and Services, 1978); Brooks and Stritch, *Business and Government in Canada*, ch. 5. The 1994 edition of *Inter-Corporate Ownership* extends to 777 pages!
9. Statistics Canada, *CALURA, Financial Statistics for Enterprises, 1994*, cat. no. 61-219P, March 1995.
10. Statistics Canada, *CALURA, Part I—Corporations, Foreign Control in the Canadian Economy*, cat. no. 61-220, December 1993.

11. Wallace Clement, *The Canadian Corporate Elite* (Toronto: McClelland and Stewart, 1975), and his *Continental Corporate Power* (Toronto: McClelland and Stewart, 1977).

12. William Carroll argues that corporate power is held not so much by foreigners as by indigenous Canadian capitalists who have preserved and expanded their accumulation base while maintaining a dense network of intercorporate relations focused on Canadian-controlled financial and industrial companies. See his *Corporate Power and Canadian Capitalism* (Vancouver: University of British Columbia Press, 1986).

13. Brooks and Stritch, *Business and Government in Canada*, pp. 143–53.

14. This perspective is presented in the various works of R.T. Naylor, including *The History of Canadian Business* (Toronto: Lorimer, 1975).

15. Newman describes the new acquisitors as "strangers by birth and behaviour, to the traditional elite," in *The Acquisitors*, p. 12.

16. Linda McQuaig details "how the rich won control of Canada's tax system ... and ended up richer" in *Behind Closed Doors* (Toronto: Penguin, 1987). See also her *The Quick and the Dead* (Toronto: Penguin, 1991). Even Allan Gregg, the Tory pollster, gives the following examples of corporations that did not pay any taxes despite enormous profits—Bramalea ($33 million), Brascade ($64 million), Xerox ($74 million), and Tridel Enterprises ($72 million)—in *The Big Picture: What Canadians Think About Almost Everything* (Toronto: Macfarlane Walter & Ross, 1990), p. 55.

17. Newman, *The Acquisitors*, p. 569.

18. Colin Campbell, *The Canadian Senate: A Lobby from Within* (Toronto: Macmillan, 1978); John McMenemy, "The Senate as an Instrument of Business and Party," in Paul Fox and Graham White, eds., *Politics: Canada*, 7th ed. (Toronto: McGraw-Hill Ryerson, 1991).

19. *Toronto Star* (March 20, 1990), p. A23.

20. Newman, *The Acquisitors*, p. 13.

21. David Lewis, *Louder Voices: Corporate Welfare Bums* (Toronto: James Lewis & Samuel, 1972). R. Chodos and R. Murphy, eds., *Let Us Prey* (Toronto: Lorimer, 1974), take a similar perspective.

22. Alvin Finkel, *Business and Social Reform in the Thirties* (Toronto: Lorimer, 1979), p. 176.

23. Marsha Chandler, "State Enterprise and Partisanship in Provincial Politics," *Canadian Journal of Political Science* (December 1982), pp. 711–40.

24. Newman, *The Acquisitors*, p. 578.

25. Leo Panitch, "Elites, Classes, and Power," in Michael Whittington and Glen Williams, eds., *Canadian Politics in the 1990s*, 4th ed. (Scarborough: Nelson Canada, 1995), p. 168.

26. Economic Council of Canada, *Legacies, Twenty-Sixth Annual Review*, 1989, p. 40.

27. Linda McQuaig, *Behind Closed Doors*.

28. Allan Maslove, *Tax Reform in Canada: The Process and Impact* (Halifax: Institute for Research on Public Policy, 1989).

29. J.F. Conway, "Populism in the United States, Russia, and Canada: Explaining the Roots of Canada's Third Parties," *Canadian Journal of Political Science* (March 1978), pp. 99–124.

30. Abella, *On Strike*; Walter Stewart, *Strike!* (Toronto: McClelland and Stewart, 1977), ch. 4.

31. Economic Council of Canada, *Legacies*, p. 45.

32. Statistics Canada, *CALURA, Part II—Labour Unions, 1992*, cat. no. 71-202, March 1994. The unionized workers can be subdivided into international unions, 1 156 700; national unions, 2 160 700; and government unions, 548 700. The paid workers can be subdivided into incorporated self-employed, 692 000; private-sector employees, 8 905 000; and government employees, 2 139 000. The remainder are unincorporated self-employed, 1 359 000, and unpaid family workers, 59 000.

33. Economic Council of Canada, *Legacies*, p. 41; Statistics Canada, *CALURA Part II—Labour Unions, 1991*, cat. no. 71-202 (March 1994).

34. Canadian Labour Congress, *The Crisis of Canadian Manufacturing* (Ottawa, 1991); Statistics Canada, *The Labour Force*, cat. no. 71-001 (July 1989 and January 1993).

35. Statistics Canada, *CALURA, Part II—Labour Unions, 1988*.

36. Economic Council of Canada, *Legacies*, pp. 35, 40.

37. John Gaitley, *Earnings of Canadians* (Statistics Canada cat. no. 96-317), 1994.

38. On such factionalism, see, for example, Gad Horowitz, *Canadian Labour in Politics* (Toronto: University of Toronto Press, 1968).
39. Among others that should be mentioned is that of the late Senator David Croll, the chairman of the 1971 Special Senate Committee on Poverty, whose Report had a major effect on raising public consciousness of this issue.
40. Canadian Council on Social Development, *The Canadian Poverty Fact Book—1989*, p. 93.
41. Ibid., 1994, p. 2.
42. National Council of Welfare, *Poverty Profile 1993* (Ottawa: Supply and Services, 1995), p. 57.
43. Ibid., 1989, p. 91. As of July 1, 1995, here are the federal and provincial minimum wage levels, together with the year of their most recent revision: federal, $4.00 (1986); Alberta, $5.00 (1992); B.C., $6.50 (1995); Manitoba, $5.25 (1995); New Brunswick, $5.00 (1991); Newfoundland, $4.74 (1991); Nova Scotia, $5.15 (1993); Ontario, $6.85 (1995); P.E.I., $4.75 (1991); Quebec, $6.00 (1994); Saskatchewan, $5.35 (1992). Figures courtesy of the Bureau of Labour Information, Human Resources Development, Ottawa.
44. It was implemented shortly after the Depression, when unemployed men were placed in labour camps. When they began a trek from B.C. to Ottawa, they were blocked by police in the Regina Riot of July 1, 1935.
45. Kenneth Bryden, *Old Age Pensions and Policy-Making in Canada* (Montreal: McGill–Queen's University Press, 1974).
46. Roger S. Smith, *Personal Wealth Taxation* (Toronto: Canadian Tax Foundation, 1993), p. iii.
47. Linda McQuaig, *Shooting the Hippo: Death by Deficit and Other Canadian Myths* (Toronto: Viking, 1995).
48. See, for example, three National Council of Welfare publications: *A Blueprint for Social Security Reform* (Autumn 1994); *The Canada Assistance Plan: No Time For Cuts* (Winter 1991); and *Funding Health and Higher Education: Danger Looming* (Spring 1991); the Caledon Institute of Social Policy, "Green Light, Red Flat: Caledon Statement on the Social Security Review," 1994; and Steven Langdon et al., *In the Public Interest: The Value of Public Services* (Prescott: Voyageur Publishing, 1995).
49. Janine Brodie and Jane Jenson, *Crisis, Challenge and Change: Party and Class in Canada Revisited* (Ottawa: Carleton University Press, 1988).
50. Finkel, *Business and Social Reform in the Thirties.*
51. Richard Splane, "Social Policy-Making in the Government of Canada: Reflections of a Reformist Bureaucrat," in S.A. Yelaja, ed., *Canadian Social Policy* (Waterloo: Wilfrid Laurier University Press, 1978).
52. Rand Dyck, "The Canada Assistance Plan: The Ultimate in Cooperative Federalism," *Canadian Public Administration* (Winter 1976), pp. 587–602. Carl Cuneo and Leslie Pal engaged in an interesting intellectual dialogue on the question of the significance of class in the bureaucracy in the March 1986 issue of the *Canadian Journal of Political Science*, pp. 71–102.
53. John Porter, *The Vertical Mosaic* (Toronto: University of Toronto Press, 1965), chs. XI and XVII.

FURTHER READING

Abella, Irving, ed. *On Strike.* Toronto: James Lewis & Samuel, 1974.

Brodie, Janine, and Jane Jenson. *Crisis, Challenge and Change: Party and Class in Canada Revisited.* Ottawa: Carleton University Press, 1988.

Brooks, Stephen, and Andrew Stritch. *Business and Government in Canada.* Scarborough: Prentice-Hall Canada, 1991.

Clement, Wallace. *The Canadian Corporate Elite.* Toronto: McClelland and Stewart, 1975.

———. *Continental Corporate Power.* Toronto: McClelland and Stewart, 1977.

———. *The Challenge of Class Analysis.* Ottawa: Carleton University Press, 1988.

Clement, Wallace, and Daniel Drache. *A New Practical Guide to Canadian Political Economy* (Toronto: Lorimer, 1985).

Clement, Wallace, and Glen Williams, eds. *The New Canadian Political Economy*. Montreal: McGill–Queen's University Press, 1989.

Coleman, William. *Business and Politics: A Study of Collective Action*. Montreal: McGill-Queen's University Press, 1988.

Economic Council of Canada. *Legacies, 1989 Annual Review*. Ottawa: Supply and Services, 1989.

Fleming, James. *Circles of Power: The Most Influential People in Canada*. Toronto: Doubleday, 1991.

Forcese, Dennis. *The Canadian Class Structure*. Toronto: McGraw-Hill Ryerson, 1975.

Langdon, Steven, et al. *In the Public Interest: The Value of Public Services* (Prescott: Voyageur Publishing, 1995).

Lewis, David. *Louder Voices: The Corporate Welfare Bums*. Toronto: James Lewis & Samuel, 1972.

McQuaig, Linda. *Behind Closed Doors*. Toronto: Penguin, 1987.

———. *The Quick and the Dead*. Toronto: Penguin, 1991.

———. *Shooting the Hippo: Death by Deficit and Other Canadian Myths*. Toronto: Viking, 1995.

National Council of Welfare. *Poverty Profile 1993*. Ottawa, 1995.

Naylor, R.T. *The History of Canadian Business*. Toronto: Lorimer, 1975.

Palmer, Bryan. *Working-Class Experience: The Rise and Reconstitution of Canadian Labour, 1800–1980*. Toronto: Butterworth, 1983.

Panitch, Leo, ed. *The Canadian State: Political Economy and Political Power*. Toronto: University of Toronto Press, 1977.

Porter, John. *The Vertical Mosaic*. Toronto: University of Toronto Press, 1965.

Ross, David, and Richard Shillington. *The Canadian Fact Book on Poverty—1994*. Ottawa: Canadian Council on Social Development, 1994.

Special Senate Committee on Poverty. *Poverty in Canada*. Ottawa: 1971.

Stewart, Walter. *Strike!* Toronto: McClelland and Stewart, 1977.

Veltmeyer, Henry. *Canadian Class Structure*. Toronto: Garamond Press, 1986.

Chapter 11

The WOMEN'S MOVEMENT and gender issues

Feminists seek gender equality—in employment equity, pay equity, equity in law, equity in the various institutions of government, and equity in the family setting. Not all women are agreed on all these demands, however, and while a large proportion of men support most of them, many young men feel that employment equity makes it even more difficult for them to find a job. Sexual harassment and assault have become major societal concerns; so have abortion, divorce, child care, and many concerns related to reproduction. Gender issues have created considerable political controversy and are of increasing significance as women take a more equal part in the economic and political systems. Beyond the equality of women are other gender-related issues, specifically concerning the gay, lesbian, and bisexual communities.

This chapter begins by outlining the historical evolution of women's rights in Canada. It then examines the women's movement today, which has brought a whole new set of demands onto the political agenda. After discussing the contemporary manifestations of such issues, the chapter concludes with a brief overview of gay and lesbian concerns.

EVOLUTION OF WOMEN'S RIGHTS TO 1970

Men and male-oriented issues virtually monopolized Canadian politics before 1900. In those early years, when all women were expected to marry and then became chattels of their husbands, they first had to fight for educational and occupational rights, such as admission to universities and to the medical and legal professions.[1] This battle was led by the first prominent feminist, Dr. Emily Stowe, who in 1880 was the first female to practise medicine in Canada. The first female lawyer was admitted to the bar in 1897. Women later demanded the right to make contracts and to own property, and increasingly began to work in factories and offices, to become teachers and nurses, and to make major contributions "on the farm." At the turn of the century farm women in particular became active in reform organizations of many kinds, pressing for the prohibition of alcohol and the establishment of new public health facilities, better housing, and improved working conditions for women and children.

As influential as women were in promoting these causes, many began to feel that their impact would always be limited until they could vote. Thus, women demanded the franchise, although some were more insistent than others, and not all men opposed the idea. It was a conflict between those who saw women primarily as wives and mothers, whose influence could be best exercised within the home, and those who felt that women should be treated as equals of men in the wider society.

After the outbreak of the First World War, proponents of female suffrage had an additional argument—that women should be rewarded for their contribution to the war effort. Thus Manitoba, Alberta, and Saskatchewan, containing some of the most articulate women of the day, were the first provinces to extend the right to vote to women; Ontario and British Columbia did the same a year later, in 1917; and all the other provinces except Quebec followed shortly afterward. The first women legislators in the British Commonwealth, Louise McKinney and Roberta Macadams Price, were elected in Alberta in 1917; they were replaced in 1921 by Nellie McClung and Irene Parlby. Mary Ellen Smith was elected to the B.C. legislature in 1918 and became the first Canadian female cabinet minister in 1921.

At the federal level, the Borden government deliberately manipulated the franchise for the 1917 election, in part by giving the vote to women in the armed services (mostly nurses) and by allowing soldiers fighting abroad to appoint their nearest female relative at home— women who would likely support the war effort—to cast their vote by proxy. A year later the vote was extended to all women, and they had their first chance to exercise this new right in the 1921 election.

The reforms in social legislation that immediately followed the enfranchisement of women have been detailed as follows:

> By 1928, most provinces had introduced equal guardianship of children; mothers' allowances; the protection of labour, including child labour; protection for all children including adopted children, the children of unmarried mothers and juveniles appearing before the courts; and had raised the age for compulsory schooling and the age at which marriage could be solemnized within the province. At the federal level, the divorce law had been amended to establish "equality of cause" between wife and husband, and the Old Age Pensions Act had been passed.[2]

These reforms were achieved without the presence of women in the legislative bodies concerned, for while the right to vote entailed the right to hold office (except in New Brunswick where the latter was delayed until 1934), very few women were elected. In 1921 Agnes Macphail was the first woman elected to the House of Commons. She served alone until 1935, when a second woman was elected. Macphail stayed on until 1940 and then became the first woman elected to the Ontario legislature in 1943. A vigorous, articulate, and witty MP and MPP, Macphail promoted radical and progressive causes of many kinds, but she could only do so much by herself to advance women's issues in such an entrenched male bastion.³ The five most eastern provinces were slower to elect women, as Table 11.1 indicates. It was not until 1940 that Quebec women were enfranchised, largely as a result of the determined leadership of Thérèse Casgrain, and after 13 previous bills to this effect were defeated. Even worse, the legal status of married women under the Quebec Civil Code was such that until 1955 a woman could not seek a separation on the grounds of her husband's adultery and until 1964 had no right to carry on a trade without her husband's consent.⁴

TABLE 11.1 Women's Franchise and First Woman Elected

	Franchise	First Woman Elected
Canada	1917/1918	1921
Manitoba	1916	1920
Alberta	1916	1917
Saskatchewan	1916	1919
B.C.	1917	1918
Ontario	1917	1943
Nova Scotia	1918	1960
New Brunswick	1919	1967
P.E.I.	1922	1970
Newfoundland	1925	1975
Quebec	1940	1961

Source: Penney Kome, Women of Influence *(Toronto: University of Toronto Press, 1985); T.H. Qualter,* The Electoral Process in Canada *(Toronto: McGraw-Hill Ryerson, 1970). Reproduced with permission.*

The number of women who won seats in the House of Commons before 1970 was minuscule, as Table 11.2 demonstrates. Many of the pre-1970 female MPs were the widows or daughters of male members of Parliament. Female political participation was inhibited by many factors. First, both sexes were traditionally socialized into the view that politics was a masculine pursuit and that women should remain in the home. Such socialization patterns even affected those women who were not wives, mothers, and homemakers. Second, most women were constrained by the responsibilities of homemaking and child-rearing. Such roles had little prestige and prevented women from accumulating the money, contacts, and experience that political careers usually require. The long hours and unpredictable schedules of politicians conflicted with most women's family commitments and prevented them from being away from home for any length of time. Such factors at least delayed a woman's entry into active politics. Third, political parties discouraged female candidacies, however much they needed women at the constituency level to raise money and stuff envelopes. Most parties set up separate women's auxiliary organizations rather than encourage their participation in the mainstream of the party. When consciousness of the lack of female candidates increased, women were more frequently nominated, but usually as sacrificial lambs against a

TABLE 11.2 Number of Women Elected in Federal Elections, 1921–1968

Election	Women	Election	Women
1921	1	1953	4
1925	1	1957	2
1926	1	1958	2
1930	1	1962	4
1935	2	1963	4
1940	1	1965	3
1945	1	1968	1
1949	0		

Source: Penney Kome, Women of Influence.

strong male incumbent. This was especially evident in the two major parties, and led to the "law" that the closer a party is to power, the less likely it is to nominate women candidates.[5]

Until the late 1920s, no women had been appointed to the other house of Parliament, the Senate. When an enterprising group of Western women took this issue to court, the Supreme Court of Canada ruled in 1928 that in terms of the law respecting Senate appointments, women were not persons. In 1929 this decision was appealed to the Judicial Committee of the Privy Council, which in the **Persons case** overruled the Supreme Court and declared women to be "qualified persons" within the meaning of s. 24 of the 1867 Constitution Act and eligible to sit in the Senate. The women's movement continues to celebrate this decision to this day in the form of the "Person's Day Breakfast." Prime Minister Mackenzie King immediately appointed Cairine Wilson to the Senate, but even here progress was slow. The second woman was not appointed until 1935, and 18 years would pass before three more received the call.

It was not until 1957 that the first woman, Ellen Fairclough, was appointed to the federal cabinet, by John Diefenbaker; she was followed by Judy LaMarsh in 1963. The advance of women to the cabinet at the provincial level was also very slow: B.C. and Alberta, 1921; Quebec, 1962; Manitoba, 1966; and New Brunswick, 1970.

Because other cleavages overshadowed the gender cleavage for the first 100 years after Confederation,

> farm women, working women, French-Canadian women, Protestant women, western women, [and] city women had quite different collective identities following from the ways in which class, religion and place entwined in Canadian politics. There was no single identity, nor was there a single women's politics.[6]

Nevertheless, gradual improvements continued to be made in federal and provincial programs and legislation to benefit women. The federal Family Allowances Act of 1944, for example, provided a small monthly payment to each Canadian mother to help care for her children, and often represented the only independent income the woman possessed. In 1952

Ontario passed the first equal pay legislation, to be followed by federal legislation two years later. After the invention of the birth control pill in 1960, amendments to the Criminal Code in 1969 made it legal to advertise birth control devices in Canada, and a new Divorce Act made it easier for people to get out of an unfulfilling marriage. A summary of the milestones in the evolution of women's rights up to 1970 is provided below.

MILESTONES IN THE EVOLUTION OF WOMEN'S RIGHTS TO 1970

- 1875   First university degree awarded to a woman
- 1880   First woman doctor
- 1897   First woman lawyer
- 1916   Women obtain vote in first three provinces
- 1917   First woman MLA
- 1917/18   Women obtain federal vote
- 1921   First provincial woman cabinet minister
- 1921   First woman MP
- 1929   Persons case
- 1930   First woman senator
- 1940   Women obtain vote in Quebec
- 1944   Federal family allowances
- 1952   Ontario equal pay law
- 1956   Federal equal pay law
- 1957   First federal woman cabinet minister
- 1967   Appointment of Royal Commission on the Status of Women
- 1969   Legislation on birth control and divorce

Source: Status of Women Canada, "Towards Equality for Women—A Canadian Chronology," 1994.
Reproduced with the permission of the Minister of Supply and Services Canada, 1995.

THE WOMEN'S MOVEMENT AFTER 1970

Around 1970 attitudes toward women and their role in society had changed sufficiently that it was now possible to speak of a **women's movement**, and the word "feminist" became a common term. Such terms are used to describe those who seek to establish complete gender equality, to free men and women from restrictive gender roles, and to end the subordination of women. However, even within the women's movement a variety of perspectives exists, including socialist feminists, Marxist feminists, radical feminists, and liberal feminists.[7]

This second wave of feminism coincided with the **Royal Commission on the Status of Women**, appointed in 1967 and reporting in 1970. It "provided a solid statistical base and a framework for most of the feminist action that followed during the 1970s,"[8] and made 167 recommendations, not all of which have been implemented even 25 years later. Since that time gender issues have become an important, daily factor in Canadian politics, and most governments now designate a minister responsible for women's issues, starting at the federal level in 1971. In 1972 the federal government established the Office of Employment Opportunity, followed by the Canadian Advisory Council on the Status of Women in 1973; the first federal–provincial conference on women's issues convened in 1982.

Representation in Politics and Government

In the post-1970 era, women's participation in politics and government increased substantially. Table 11.3 shows the increase in the number and proportion of women in the House of Commons in this period. Many of the factors that inhibited women from becoming politicians before 1970 are still present, although in recent years most parties have created special funds to support female candidates.

At the cabinet level, Jeanne Sauvé was appointed in 1972, Monique Bégin and Iona Campagnolo in 1976, and Flora MacDonald in 1979, but by the 1980s, one or two token female ministers were clearly insufficient. Brian Mulroney usually appointed six women to his cabinets after 1984. The rest of the provinces eventually appointed women ministers: Ontario and Prince Edward Island in 1972, Newfoundland in 1979, Saskatchewan in 1982, and Nova Scotia in 1985. Bob Rae came close to gender equality in his 1990 Ontario NDP cabinet: 11 women out of 26.

In the post-1970 period Canada finally saw women elected as political party leaders. Alexa McDonough led the way in the NDP in Nova Scotia in 1980, to be followed by Sharon Carstairs (Liberal, Manitoba), Elizabeth Weir and Barbara Baird-Filliter (NDP and PC respectively, New Brunswick), Lynda Haverstock (Liberal, Saskatchewan), Lyn McLeod (Liberal, Ontario), Rita Johnston (Social Credit, B.C.), and Catherine Callbeck (Liberal, P.E.I.). After Rosemary Brown made a serious stab at the NDP national leadership in 1975 and Flora Macdonald for the PCs in 1976, it remained for Audrey McLaughlin to make history when she was elected leader of the federal New Democratic Party in 1989, the first woman to lead a major national party. Alexa McDonough succeeded her in 1995.

TABLE 11.3	Representation of Women in the House of Commons 1970–1993	
Election	Number Elected	Proportion of MPs (percent)
1972	4	2
1974	9	3
1979	11	4
1980	14	5
1984	27	10
1988	39	13
1993	53	18

Source: Status of Women Canada, "Towards Equality for Women—A Canadian Chronology," 1994. Reproduced with the permission of the Minister of Supply and Services Canada, 1995.

Two of these provincial leaders even served as premier. Rita Johnston inherited the B.C. premiership from her disgraced predecessor, Bill Vander Zalm, while Catherine Callbeck was the first woman to be elected to premiership in 1993. Somewhat similarly to Johnston, Kim Campbell took over the federal PC leadership and prime ministership in 1993, only to lose the subsequent election to Jean Chrétien.

Jeanne Sauvé pioneered women's political participation in several fields: she was the third federal woman cabinet minister, the first woman Speaker of the House of Commons, and the first woman governor general (1984). Meanwhile, Bertha Wilson became the first woman to sit on the Supreme Court of Canada in 1982. At one point there were three women on the Supreme Court (out of nine judges), but the number fell back to two after 1990. Nevertheless, women judges have been appointed at an ever-increasing rate in other courts, and in 1993, 123 or about 15 percent of federally appointed judges were women.

Within the federal bureaucracy, the first women joined the RCMP in 1974, and the first woman deputy minister (Sylvia Ostry) was appointed in 1975; women gradually became eligible for full combat roles in the armed forces, and the first woman general was named in 1988. In 1993, Jocelyne Bourgon became the first woman to hold the top public-service position in Ottawa, Secretary to the Cabinet and Clerk of the Privy Council.

Employment Issues

Since about 60 percent of women of working age are now in the labour force (up from 50 percent in 1980), and since women constitute about 45 percent of the labour force, one major feminist concern is employment.[9] Women have traditionally been paid less than men, underrepresented in managerial positions, and discouraged from undertaking nontraditional occupations. In 1985, full-time female workers earned on average 65.5 percent of what men earned, leading to demands for "equal pay for work of equal value" or "pay equity." The first jurisdictions to pass **pay equity** legislation were the federal government, Manitoba, Ontario, Quebec, New Brunswick, Nova Scotia, and P.E.I. By 1994, women's earnings had risen to an average of 72 percent of men's.[10]

Economists point out that while women who work for pay outside the home contribute to government revenues by paying income taxes, women who work in the home generally carry out a variety of functions, such as caring for the young and the elderly, that reduces the demand for public services. Unpaid work in the home makes a major contribution to the economy that does not show up in traditional statistics: nearly $300 billion, or 41 percent, of the gross domestic product. Women perform two-thirds of unpaid work, such as household maintenance, care giving, and volunteer work, which is worth some $16 580 per year on an individual basis. On average, women spend approximately 29 hours per week on housework, almost double that of men.

Beyond pay equity is the broader subject of **employment equity**, that is, the elimination of discrimination in hiring and promoting, which is sometimes combined with **affirmative action** programs to give preference to women and other groups in order to make up for past inequities. In 1980 the federal bureaucracy established a pilot project with respect to affirmative action in the hiring of women; in 1983 this was made mandatory in all federal government departments. The 1984 Royal Commission Report, *Equality in Employment*, written by Rosalie Abella, became the foundation of the 1986 Employment Equity Act. It extended employment equity requirements to all Crown corporations, all federally regulated companies with over 100 employees, and other large companies in receipt of major government contracts. Nevertheless, while they constituted 45 percent of the federal government work force in 1994, women occupied only 17 percent of managerial jobs. However, almost one-quarter of the total service at the most senior level of deputy minister or heads of agencies were women, including 14 of 110 heads of Canadian missions abroad.

Ontario passed an even more extensive Employment Equity Act in 1993, which was the subject of much controversy in the 1995 provincial election campaign. Because most businesses see employment equity as a drain on their bottom line, they oppose it. Indeed, the area in which women are most severely underrepresented is at the top of private corporations. In a 1993 survey of over 500 companies, the *Financial Post* found only seven women who held the position of chair, chief executive officer, or president, and only 1.6 percent of corporate vice-presidents were women. The two most prominent female CEOs in the mid-1990s were Maureen Kempston Darkes at General Motors of Canada and Peggy Witte of Royal Oak Mines.

Some 71 percent of women in 1991 were employed in just five traditional occupational groups: clerical (29 percent), service (17 percent), sales (10 percent), nursing and related health occupations (9 percent), and teaching (6 percent). In these fields, pay is generally low and opportunities are few. On the other hand, it should not be overlooked that women have made gains in several professional occupations. In 1991, women accounted for 27 percent of all doctors, dentists, and other health-diagnosing and -treating professionals, and 56 percent of pharmacists. Figure 11.1 compares the percentages of women in selected occupations between 1982 and 1993.

Figure 11.1 Women as a Percentage of People Employed in Selected Occupations

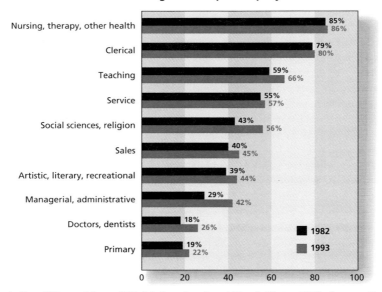

Source: Pamela Best, "Women, Men and Work," Canadian Social Trends *(Spring 1995), Statistics Canada, cat. no. 11-008. Reproduced with the permission of the Minister of Supply and Services Canada, 1995.*

Figure 11.2   Part-Time Workers, 1993

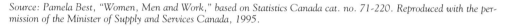

Source: Pamela Best, "Women, Men and Work," based on Statistics Canada cat. no. 71-220. Reproduced with the permission of the Minister of Supply and Services Canada, 1995.

Women make up 70 percent of the part-time work force, sometimes by choice, but often by necessity, and part-time workers generally have few benefits and little job security. In this era of global restructuring, companies are turning even more to part-time, contract work, and women are expected to suffer the most from such developments. Figure 11.2 compares the numbers of men and women who worked part-time in 1993 and outlines the major reasons for seeking such work.

Constitutional, Legal, and Aboriginal Women's Issues

A third category of post-1970 women's issues is related to the Constitution and the law. The first major issue was the question of equality rights in the 1982 Charter of Rights and Freedoms. This was especially important because the courts had made a mockery of the sexual equality provision in the 1960 Bill of Rights. As the Charter emerged from federal–provincial negotiations, gender equality was to be lumped into section 15 with such other factors as race, religion, and age, which governments would be allowed to override with the notwithstanding clause. Such treatment at the hands of 11 male first ministers galvanized the women's movement as never before; as a result of pressure from women's groups, section 28 was added to the final document to give gender equality a place of its own and protected from the notwithstanding clause.[11]

Women thus became part of the coalition including other Charter-based rights-bearers who used the Charter to advance their cause.[12] There followed a series of feminist challenges to laws that women felt discriminated against them. Women achieved the right to maternity leave under the Unemployment Insurance Act. The so-called "rape-shield law" restricted questions about past sexual history put to defendants in a case of sexual assault. The court, agreed that "no means no" with respect to a woman's consent to sexual relations. Battered wives have been excused for murdering their offending husbands, and gender discrimination in private employers' disability plans has been removed. The government itself encouraged such legal activity with the **Court Challenges Program** under which it subsidized the Legal Education and Action Fund (LEAF) in making such challenges. This was a continuation of Ottawa's attempt to strengthen the women's movement by funding advocacy groups.[13] When the Mulroney government cancelled the Court Challenges Program in 1992, women protested, and it was reinstated by the Chrétien government.

On the other hand, the Supreme Court did not advance the cause of women in decisions dealing with such issues as the deduction of child-care expenses from a self-employed woman's income tax (the 1993 Symes Case) and the taxation of support payments while men who made such payments deducted them from their income tax (the 1995 Thibaudeau case). In both of these decisions the female justices on the Court dissented. In addition, men actually made greater use of the equality provisions in section 15 than women, especially in child-custody cases.[14]

On the constitutional front, in the 1987–1990 period, the **National Action Committee on the Status of Women** (NAC) and certain subsidiary groups actively opposed the Meech Lake Accord. Having become part of the constitutional policy community in 1982, they demanded participation in any subsequent constitutional decisions and were concerned that the Accord, drawn up by 11 men, had nothing to say about women's rights. Certain anglophone women were afraid that their constitutional gains of 1982 might be diluted in Quebec by the Accord's "distinct society" clause for Quebec. Interestingly enough, their concerns were not shared by most feminists in that province. The NAC was also unhappy with the Charlottetown Accord, for even though it did reiterate the equality of men and women in the Canada clause, it was articulated in weaker language than that of other rights. Like the aboriginals, the official francophone minorities, people with disabilities, and other groups that achieved constitutional standing in 1982, women's groups were not satisfied with subsequent constitutional documents unless their status was further reinforced.[15]

Another longstanding legal issue was that of the equality of aboriginal women relative to aboriginal men. A provision in the Indian Act denied Indian status to Native women who married white men, but no such loss was involved when an Indian man married a white woman. After the *Lavell* case upheld this clause in the Indian Act, much pressure was brought to bear on the government, and in 1985 the provision was repealed. The Indian Act was amended to restore Indian status and the right to be considered for band membership to Indian women (and their children) who had lost such status through intermarriage. Their fate continued to rest, however, with the band membership. A year before, the Constitution itself was amended to recognize and affirm that aboriginal and treaty rights were guaranteed equally to male and female persons.

Reproductive, Sexual, Health, and Violence Issues

One of the main feminist rallying cries of the post-1970 period is that women must be able to control what happens to their own bodies. Many women's organizations supported Dr. Henry Morgentaler in his long fight (including several court cases, clinic raids, and jail terms) to reform the Criminal Code's provisions on abortion.[16] Although amendments were made in 1968, feminists did not regard these as sufficient, and the Supreme Court of Canada threw out the abortion law in the famous 1988 *Morgentaler* case. The Court also dismissed the *Borowski* case on fetal rights as well as the case against Chantal Daigle on father's rights.[17] Although the prospect of having no law at all restricting abortion was appealing to most feminists, a sizable proportion of public opinion disagreed; in 1990 the Mulroney government introduced a compromise abortion law, which was defeated in the Senate. The Mulroney government appointed a Royal Commission on New Reproductive Technologies, which was plagued by internal disputes and whose November 1993 report endorsed a cautious approach to this controversial subject.

Prostitution, pornography, sexual stereotyping, sexual harassment, and sexual assault are other major areas of concern to women's groups, although feminists are not totally united on the first two.[18] While they universally oppose practices that exploit or demean women, some women defend the "freedom of expression" argument in discussions of pornography, and some, the "right to work" defence of prostitution. The courts have also become engaged in these issues and ruled, in 1990, for example, that the existing law against soliciting was valid as a "reasonable limit" on freedom of speech. Women have repeatedly protested, with only limited results, sex-role stereotyping in educational materials and the media, in which women are portrayed in very traditional roles or as sexual objects.

Also of concern are the courts' treatment of sexual assault cases, sexual harassment in the workplace, and violence against women. One-half of all Canadian women report that they have experienced at least one incident of violence by a male since the age of 16. Nearly 40 percent report one incident of sexual assault. The federal government did embark on an initiative to combat family violence between 1988 and 1995, which among other things contributed to the creation of shelters for battered women, and which was supplemented by some provinces.[19]

While Canadian women clearly live longer than men (the average life expectancy of women being 81 years compared with 74 years for men), women are concerned about their own particular health issues. Probably the main concern is breast cancer, which one in nine women is expected to develop. Pressure is mounting on governments to take more initiative in this area, and some have responded. If breast cancer is something over which women have little control, however, many could do something about lung cancer, which is also a leading cause of death among Canadian women. Occupational health problems are also of increasing concern.

The Feminization of Poverty, and Child Care

Chapter 10 revealed the large extent to which Canada has experienced the **feminization of poverty**. As pointed out there, no less than 60 percent of sole-support mothers raise their children below the poverty line. With or without a male partner, large numbers of women with pre-school children find it necessary to work outside the home to support themselves and their families.[20] This has been the case even after the Child Tax Credit was added to the income tax system in 1978 to supplement and eventually replace the Family Allowance for low-income families. Such programs as pay equity, employment equity, higher minimum wages, increased unionization, and improved job training and literacy programs will help decrease the incidence of women living in poverty.

Reprinted with the permission of the Halifax Chronicle-Herald.

One of the major unresolved women's issues today is that of day care for children. Federal support for day care used to be available under the Canada Assistance Plan for those in need, and was supplemented by provincial and/or municipal funding. The level of funding, however, is inadequate for low-income women, and many middle-income women find it very difficult to find, let alone finance, day care for their children. The Mulroney government introduced legislation for a national day-care program in 1988, but when the bill failed to pass before the election, it fell victim to the budgetary restraints of 1989–92. Provincial programs in this area vary considerably, with only Quebec approaching an adequate standard. In 1991, there were 350 680 licensed full-time child-care spaces available, while some 2.2 million children 12 years of age or younger required such care.

Women's Centres and Women's Groups

Many women's centres were established across the country in the 1980s, financed by federal and/or provincial governments. While such centres primarily served as support and referral agencies for battered wives and others seeking help, they also promoted a variety of other women's causes such as abortion law reform. The Mulroney government cut the budget for such centres in 1989 and 1990, but then restored some of the funding after a vehement protest.

The National Council of Women of Canada (NCWC) was created in 1893 and still represents 750 000 women in autonomous provincial, regional, and municipal councils. The Voice of Women (VOW) was formed in 1960 around peace issues. The Canadian Advisory Council on the Status of Women (CACSW) was set up by the government in 1973 in response to the Royal Commission on the Status of Women. It is made up of government appointees who advise the responsible minister on women's concerns.

The number of women's groups has increased remarkably in recent years. The foremost women's pressure group today is the National Action Committee on the Status of Women (NAC). It was established in 1972, largely in response to government inaction on the Status of Women report. It functions as an umbrella lobbying group for over 250 local and national member groups representing over three million women. An indication of its importance and of politicians' consciousness of the female vote was the separate televised leaders' debate held on women's issues in 1984 sponsored by the NAC.

The Mulroney government was less sympathetic to the NAC and affiliated groups than the Trudeau government. It refused to attend NAC's annual meeting in 1989 and 1990, anticipating criticism of its cutbacks, and even began to fund the rival organization, REAL Women. REAL (Realistic, Equal, Active for Life) Women was founded in 1984 and opposes all feminist demands. The Catholic Women's League and various anti-abortion ("pro-life") groups have also played a major role on the abortion issue from the anti-feminist point of view. Thus, women themselves are divided on some or all of the issues raised, and this division gives male politicians and bureaucrats an excellent excuse to take no action.

OTHER GENDER ISSUES

A variety of political issues related to homosexuality have arisen in recent years, and these also figure prominently on the agenda of the 1990s. In most cases, politicians are reluctant to deal with demands coming from the gay, lesbian, and bisexual communities. These groups have thus often taken their concerns directly to the courts.

One of their first demands was protection from discrimination in human rights codes. Quebec was the first province to enact legislation prohibiting discrimination on the grounds of sexual orientation. By the mid-1990s, all provinces except Alberta, Newfoundland, and P.E.I. had implemented similar laws. When the Charter of Rights was adopted in 1982, section 15 prohibited discrimination by government or in law on the basis of sex. Although sexual orientation was not explicitly included, in a 1995 decision the Supreme Court of Canada ruled unanimously that the clause did indeed include sexual orientation. However, the court was split on whether such discrimination was involved in the case before them, which concerned the payment of the spouses' pension to same-sex couples.

Many employers in both the public and private sectors have extended employee benefits (health, dental, and retirement plans, and so on) to same-sex couples. No government has yet made this practice mandatory by law, and an attempt to do so was defeated in the Ontario legislature in 1994. In 1995, Justice Minister Allan Rock ran into considerable difficulty introducing a bill designed to increase sentences for those convicted of committing hate crimes (including crimes against homosexuals). Despite opposition within the Liberal caucus, the bill was eventually passed.

Given the reluctance of many politicians to amend the laws, some homosexual groups are taking other demands, such as adoption rights, to the courts. In 1995, an Ontario court took the position that a lesbian could legally adopt her partner's natural child, but this did not resolve the question of whether same-sex couples could adopt children together. At about the same time, another Ontario court ruled that the Criminal Code was discriminatory when it made it a crime to have anal sex with anyone under 18 while vaginal sex was legal at 14.

CONCLUSION

Although women's issues have been on the political agenda at least since the turn of the century, today's politicians must pay much more attention to gender questions than ever before. Increased participation by women in the work force and in society in general has created dramatic changes in the political system. This chapter has shown that, although the record is mixed in the post-1970 period, women have made immense progress. By the mid-1990s, the main obstacles to further progress include the fiscal restraint practised by all governments and a certain amount of backlash against employment equity programs. The increasing number and proportion of women in influential positions should, however, guarantee that advances will continue. At the same time, the gay and lesbian community has experienced advancements and setbacks in its struggle for equality. Most of their success so far has been achieved in the courts.

P| The pluralist approach is particularly appropriate in explaining gender politics. Pluralism emphasizes the vast increase in the number of women's groups in recent years and their increasing influence on public policy-making. It should also be emphasized that there is great ideological diversity within the women's movement, which is further divided by ethnic and regional factors.

(SC) The state-centred approach explains the period of inaction on women's issues (1920–70) by the fact that women were largely excluded from the cabinet and bureaucracy. Some have argued that when governments finally decided to act in this field, it was bureaucrats in status-of-women agencies who set the government agenda, bypassing women's groups and failing to reflect their predominant concerns.[21] Somewhat contrary to this perspective is that of Leslie Pal, who emphasizes the close links between the bureaucratic agencies established in this field and the women's groups that the government was itself helping to support financially.[22]

Women are still seriously underrepresented in all organs of government as well as in Parliament, but the proportion of women elected to Parliament increases with every federal election and their temporary one-third contingent on the Supreme Court was a promising precedent. Women can be appointed to some of these positions to increase their numbers, but greater female representation in the corridors of power will also require political parties and voters to elect more women to Parliament. Women are slowly rising to the top of some other institutions in society and are increasingly able to engage in processes of elite accommodation, but they remain almost invisible in the ranks of the influential corporate elite.

(C) Many radical, socialist, and neo-Marxist feminists take the view that women will never achieve full equality and emancipation in a capitalist system, which they claim depends on the exploitation of women. Some also point to the coercive aspect of the pre-1990 abortion laws, which were designed and passed primarily by men. Socialist feminists argue "that class and gender interact in the present system to produce women's inequality, and that significant transformations in both are necessary for women's emancipation."[23]

PC Public choice theory asks first about voting restrictions and then about the degree of gender consciousness among women voters. Women did not even have a vote for the first 50 years of Confederation, for example, and for a long time after that they seemed less concerned with gender than with other issues—ethnicity, location, and class. Since 1970, more women are conscious about "women's issues," and governments are paying more attention to them. But while women make up one-half of the electorate, they are not united on such issues, and this provides a good excuse for governments not to take action, such as the Mulroney government's abandonment of its promised national day-care program.

DISCUSSION QUESTIONS

1. Are you personally affected by the gender cleavages discussed in this chapter? If so, how?

2. Why was there a lull in women's political activities after they obtained the vote?

3. How do you explain the increase in women's collective self-consciousness over the past 25 years? Do you expect it to increase even more?

4. Do women party leaders have a more difficult time getting their parties elected? Explain.

5. To what extent should the private sector adopt employment equity programs?

6. How far should governments go in providing public day-care programs?

7. Has the abortion issue been laid to rest? Explain.

8. Why did feminists oppose the Meech Lake and Charlottetown Accords?

9. Compare the pluralist and state-centred approaches to the material in this chapter.

10. How do the other approaches outlined in Chapter 1 relate to the issues discussed in this chapter?

· · · · · · · · · · · · · · · · ·

NOTES

1. Early developments are outlined in a 1993 Status of Women Canada publication called *Toward Equality for Women—A Canadian Chronology*. Some other books on the subject include Jean Cochrane, *Women in Canadian Politics* (Toronto: Fitzhenry & Whiteside, 1977); Penney Kome, *Women of Influence* (Toronto: University of Toronto Press, 1985); Janine Brodie, *Women and Politics in Canada* (Toronto: McGraw-Hill Ryerson, 1985); Linda Kealey and Joan Sangster, eds., *Beyond the Vote: Canadian Women and Politics* (Toronto: University of Toronto Press, 1989); Sandra Burt et al., eds., *Changing Patterns: Women in Canada* (Toronto: McClelland and Stewart, 1988); Monique Bégin et al., *Some of Us: Women in Canadian Power and Politics* (Mississauga: Random House, 1991); and Sydney Sharpe, *The Gilded Ghetto: Women and Political Power in Canada* (Toronto: HarperCollins, 1994).

2. *Report of the Royal Commission on the Status of Women* (Ottawa: 1970), p. 338.

3. Doris Pennington, *Agnes Macphail, Reformer: Canada's First Female M.P.* (Toronto: Simon & Pierre, 1989); Terry Crowley, *Agnes Macphail and the Politics of Equality* (Toronto: Lorimer, 1990).

4. Micheline D. Johnson, "History of the Status of Women in the Province of Quebec," Background study for the Royal Commission on the Status of Women (Ottawa: 1968), p. 49.

5. Janine Brodie, *Women and Politics in Canada* (Toronto: McGraw-Hill Ryerson, 1985); Brodie, "Women and Political Leadership: A Case for Affirmative Action," in Maureen Mancuso et al., eds., *Leaders and Leadership in Canada* (Toronto: Oxford University Press, 1994).

6. Jane Jenson, "Wearing Your Adjectives Proudly: Citizenship and Gender in Turn-of-the Century Canada," Canadian Political Science Association, May 1990, p. 12.

7. Sandra Burt, "Rethinking Canadian Politics: The Impact of Gender," in Michael Whittington and Glen Williams, eds., *Canadian Politics in the 1990s*, 4th ed. (Scarborough: Nelson Canada, 1995).

8. Penney Kome, *Women of Influence*, p. 86.

9. Unless otherwise noted, the statistics in this section come from Status of Women Canada, *Women in Canada: A Statistical Profile*, September 1994. See also Statistics Canada, *Women in Canada: A Statistical Report*, 2nd ed., February 1990, cat. no. 89-503E (Ottawa).

10. Statistics Canada, *The Daily*, January 17, 1994, and *Earnings of Men and Women*, cat. no. 13-217 (February 1995). Other perspectives on female employment can be found in Status of Women Canada, *Economic Equality Workshop 1993, Summary of Proceedings*.

11. See Penney Kome, *The Taking of Twenty-Eight* (Toronto: Women's Educational Press, 1983), and *Women of Influence*, ch. 10.

12. Rainer Knopff and F.L. Morton, *Charter Politics* (Toronto: Nelson Canada, 1992).

13. Leslie Pal, *Interests of State: The Politics of Language, Multiculturalism and Feminism in Canada* (Montreal: McGill–Queen's University Press, 1993).

14. Burt, "Rethinking Canadian Politics: The Impact of Gender."
15. Alan Cairns is the main architect of this perspective. See his *Disruptions: Constitutional Struggles, from the Charter to Meech Lake* (Toronto: McClelland and Stewart, 1991).
16. Among the many sources on this subject, see Robert Campbell and Leslie Pal, *The Real Worlds of Canadian Politics*, 2nd ed. (Peterborough: Broadview Press, 1991).
17. *R. v. Morgentaler*, [1988] 1 S.C.R. 30; *Borowski v. Canada (Attorney General)*, [1989] 1 S.C.R. 342; *Tremblay v. Daigle*, [1989] 2 S.C.R. 530.
18. The 1989 first edition of Campbell and Pal's *The Real Worlds of Canadian Politics* contains a chapter on the pornography debate.
19. See articles on wife assault and shelters for abused women in Statistics Canada, *Canadian Social Trends* (Autumn 1994).
20. National Council of Welfare, *Poverty Profile 1994*; David Ross and Richard Shillington, *The Canadian Fact Book on Poverty—1994* (Ottawa: Canadian Council on Social Development, 1994).
21. Burt, "Rethinking Canadian Politics: the Impact of Gender," pp. 182–83.
22. Pal, *Interests of State*.
23. Burt, "Rethinking Canadian Politics: The Impact of Gender," p. 187.

FURTHER READING

Bashevkin, Sylvia. *Toeing the Lines*. Toronto: University of Toronto Press, 1985; 2nd ed., 1992.

Bégin, Monique, et al. *Some of Us: Women in Canadian Power and Politics*. Mississauga: Random House, 1991.

Best, Pamela. "Women, Men & Work." *Canadian Social Trends*. Ottawa: Statistics Canada, Spring 1995.

Brodie, Janine. *Women and Politics in Canada*. Toronto: McGraw-Hill Ryerson, 1985.

Brodie, Janine, et al. *The Politics of Abortion*. Toronto: Oxford University Press, 1992.

Burt, Sandra. "Women's Issues and the Women's Movement in Canada since 1970." In Alan Cairns and Cynthia Williams, eds., *The Politics of Gender, Ethnicity and Language in Canada*. Toronto: University of Toronto Press, 1986.

———. "Rethinking Canadian Politics: The Impact of Gender." In Michael Whittington and Glen Williams, eds. *Canadian Politics in the 1990s*, 4th ed. Scarborough: Nelson Canada, 1995.

Burt, Sandra, et al., eds. *Changing Patterns: Women in Canada*. Toronto: McClelland and Stewart, 1988; 2nd ed., 1993.

Campbell, Robert, and Leslie Pal. *The Real Worlds of Canadian Politics*. Peterborough: Broadview Press, 1989; 2nd ed., 1991.

Canada. *Report of the Royal Commission on the Status of Women*. Ottawa: Information Canada, 1970.

Cleverdon, Catherine L. *The Woman Suffrage Movement in Canada*. Toronto: University of Toronto Press, 1974.

Crowley, Terry. *Agnes Macphail and the Politics of Equality*. Toronto: Lorimer, 1990.

Gingras, François-Pierre. *Gender Politics*. Toronto: Oxford, 1995.

Kealey, Linda, and Joan Sangster, eds. *Beyond the Vote: Canadian Women and Politics*. Toronto: University of Toronto Press, 1989.

Kome, Penney. *The Taking of Twenty-Eight*. Toronto: Women's Educational Press, 1983.

———. *Women of Influence*. Toronto: Doubleday Canada, 1985.

MacIvor, H. *Women and Politics in Canada*. Peterborough: Broadview, 1994.

Megyery, K., ed. *Women in Canadian Politics: Toward Equity in Representation*. Research Studies, Vol. 6, Royal Commission on Electoral Reform and Party Financing, Ottawa, 1991.

Pal, Leslie. *Interests of State: The Politics of Language, Multiculturalism and Feminism in Canada*. Montreal: McGill–Queen's University Press, 1993.

Pennington, Doris. *Agnes Macphail, Reformer: Canada's First Female M.P.* Toronto: Simon & Pierre, 1989.

Sharpe, Sydney. *The Gilded Ghetto: Women and Political Power in Canada*. Toronto: HarperCollins, 1994.

Vickers, Jill, et al. *Politics as if Women Mattered: A Political Analysis of the National Action Committee on the Status of Women*. Toronto: University of Toronto Press, 1993.

Chapter 12

The EXTERNAL environment

The Canadian armed forces have participated in the Gulf War and many United Nations peacekeeping operations. The United States is a major market for Quebec electricity and Alberta petroleum. European and U.S. agricultural subsidies have nearly destroyed the Canadian grain industry. Canadians watch far more U.S. television than their own. Many companies operating in Canada have closed as a result of the combined forces of global restructuring, the early 1990s recession, and the Canada–U.S. Free Trade Agreement.

Canada obviously does not exist in a vacuum; instead, it is linked to the rest of the world by all sorts of political, economic, defensive, cultural, demographic, and individual ties. These links constitute the external environment of the Canadian political system; they have an ever-increasing impact upon it, causing Canadian governments more and more difficulty in pursuing their own policy preferences.

The country started as a combination of French and British colonies, with all basic decisions being made abroad. As Canada emerged into a sovereign state, however, the world was becoming increasingly interdependent, so that even though the country gained the legal powers to make decisions for itself, it faced a multitude of external influences. Given its location next to the most powerful country on earth, Canada has been particularly susceptible to influence from the United States in the second half of the twentieth century.

This chapter details Canada's slow but steady absorption into the U.S. sphere of influence. This chapter will discuss the demands and pressures that the United States makes on the Canadian political system, the effects of the U.S. presence on Canadian values and opinions, and the policies that have been adopted both to foster and resist such absorption. This influence can be seen most clearly in the areas of defence and foreign policy, economics, culture, and the free trade agreements, which are the major concerns of this chapter. Finally, the variety of other international, multinational, and supranational pressures to which the Canadian political system is subject will also be addressed.

AMERICAN INFLUENCE IN DEFENCE AND FOREIGN POLICY

Shortly after Confederation, Britain withdrew its garrisons from Canada and left the colony to fend for itself militarily. Canada's first military engagement after achieving full autonomy was the Second World War. The United States did not enter the war until the end of 1941, although for two years it cheered on the Allied forces from the sidelines. In 1940, Canada and the United States signed their first fateful defence pact, the Ogdensburg Agreement, which set up the Canada–United States Permanent Joint Board on Defence to study the common defence problems of the two countries and make recommendations to their governments. In 1941, the Hyde Park Declaration extended the planning of continental defence to cover the production of war materials.

After the war, the United States became increasingly obsessed with containing Soviet communism, and in 1949 persuaded Canada and most western European countries to form a new military alliance, the **North Atlantic Treaty Organization** (NATO). Commitments to NATO required a great increase in the size of the Canadian armed forces. U.S. attention was then drawn to the confrontation between North and South Korea, and the U.S. ambassador managed to get a resolution through the United Nations Security Council to provide assistance to the South. Thus the UN military intervention in the Korean War was effectively a U.S. effort, to which Canada made a significant military contribution and lost 1550 lives.

The next phase of the North Americanization of Canadian defence was the Pine Tree Line, a radar screen built across the United States and Canada between 1951 and 1954 to intercept anticipated Soviet bombers. This was supplemented in 1954 by an agreement to construct two more northerly lines, the Distant Early Warning (DEW) Line and the Mid-Canada Line, of which the former was to be installed and staffed by the United States.[1] These arrangements logically led to the North American Aerospace Defence Command (NORAD) of 1958, an agreement that had been worked out by the St. Laurent government before 1957. The agreement provided for a joint Canada–U.S. air defence system with headquarters in Colorado; an American was commander-in-chief and a Canadian was second in command. A Defence Production Sharing Program was established in 1959, the same year in which the Diefenbaker government cancelled the legendary Canadian airplane, the Avro Arrow. The advisability of this cancellation continues to be debated, but it meant the continued reliance on foreign-produced aircraft for Canadian air defence.[2]

Diefenbaker also encountered two serious missile crises in the 1957–63 period.[3] When U.S. President John Kennedy used the establishment of Soviet missile bases in Cuba as an excuse to announce a naval blockade of that country, the Canadian cabinet waited three days before putting its armed forces in a state of highest alert. Since the Americans expected this would be done automatically, the **Cuban missile crisis** soured relations between the two leaders, and this state was further compounded by American annoyance at Canada's stand with respect to **BOMARC missiles**. These had been established by the United States at two bases in Canada as part of the NORAD Agreement and were intended to be armed with nuclear warheads. Some cabinet ministers wished to take possession of the warheads as planned, but others argued that to place the warheads on Canadian soil would appear to proliferate the nuclear arms race. The Canadian–American defence relationship became a prominent issue in the 1962 and 1963 election campaigns. The Diefenbaker government eventually fell apart over the issue in 1963: it was defeated on a nonconfidence motion, and the Liberals won the resulting election under Lester Pearson. The new prime minister had the warheads installed as part of Canada's international commitments, but they were ultimately removed in 1971.

Pearson's successor, Pierre Trudeau, was more concerned with making the Canadian military bilingual than effective; spending was cut, and in a new emphasis on protecting domestic sovereignty, Canada's NATO contingent was halved in 1969. Nevertheless, the NORAD Agreement was repeatedly renewed, and another foreign plane, the F-18, was eventually bought to replace Canada's archaic military aircraft. The most prominent new issue had to do with allowing the United States to test yet another new weapon, the **Cruise missile**, over Canadian territory because of the resemblance of its terrain to that of the Soviet Union. In spite of considerable popular protest, the Trudeau government allowed the tests to take place starting in 1983, as did succeeding governments.[4]

Another problem was the refusal of the United States to recognize Canadian sovereignty over the Northwest Passage, the waters separating the Canadian Arctic islands. The Canadian government was helpless to prevent the U.S. supertanker *Manhattan* from travelling through the passage in 1969, just as it was with the U.S. Coast Guard icebreaker *Polar Sea* in 1985. In both cases, Canada tried to establish its sovereignty by granting authorization to the voyage even though no permission had been requested!

The Mulroney government promised to make defence a much higher priority than during the Trudeau years, and published a hawkish white paper on the subject in 1987. Partly due to public opposition, and partly to budgetary considerations, the paper was not implemented, a decision that was vindicated when the Cold War effectively ended a year or so later. The government also decided not to participate in U.S. President Ronald Reagan's science-fictional "Star Wars" plan. On the other hand, when Iraq invaded Kuwait in 1990, Canada readily agreed to participate in the U.S.-led coalition against Iraq, which was, like the Korean affair, theoretically a United Nations operation.

Thus it is clear that from 1945 to 1991 the United States exerted significant pressure on Canadian defence policy. Even though Canada did not always respond as energetically as the United States wished, such external demands influenced Canadian political outcomes, particularly helping to defeat the Diefenbaker government. Some Canadians were satisfied by the arrangement because the country was protected by the U.S. military arsenal and had to pay relatively little for its own defence. Others did not like the U.S. pressure and the loss of control of a vital aspect of public policy. Now that the end of the Cold War has removed the whole raison d'être of Western military alliances, U.S. arm-twisting should be less insistent.

To the extent that foreign policy can be distinguished from defence policy, the degree of U.S. influence in this field has also been a controversial question.[5] Canada sees itself as a "middle power" that has staked out an independent position on recognizing and/or trading with countries such as China, Cuba, and the Soviet Union. While Canada did not become directly involved in the Vietnam war, many Canadians would have preferred a foreign policy more critical of many U.S. military or diplomatic initiatives around the world, such as in Latin America, Korea, and Nicaragua. Nevertheless, the Canadian government was quick to respond to U.S. demands to contribute to its military efforts in Kuwait and its peacekeeping mission in Somalia, both ostensibly in the name of the United Nations. In the mid-1990s, long after the demise of the Soviet Union, the United States threatened to retaliate against Canada because of its trade with Cuba.

More independently, Canada responded to international pressure and made a major contribution in the Bosnian civil war, as well as in Rwanda. Such humanitarian interventions sparked debate within Canada, other countries, and the United Nations over the kind of rapid-reaction force most appropriate. Until Somalia, Canada had an impressive record as an international peacekeeper, but the behaviour of some members of the Airborne Regiment somewhat sullied this reputation.

AMERICAN ECONOMIC INFLUENCE ON CANADA

The U.S. economic influence on Canada is even more pervasive than its impact on defence and foreign policy. This influence is felt in almost every aspect of Canadian life, including investment, trade, interest rates, environment, energy, government borrowing, and labour unions. A later section of this chapter is devoted to the Canada–U.S. Free Trade and the North American Free Trade Agreements, whose effects go far beyond trade. In many ways, Canada constitutes a zone within the American economy rather than a distinctive national economy.[6]

Foreign Investment

A new country is not likely to produce enough domestic capital to finance all the development projects that appear desirable. Therefore, in the "British period" of Canadian history, a great deal of investment in Canada came from Britain. Some of this foreign capital was in the form of British companies operating in Canada such as the Hudson's Bay Co., but to a large extent it took the form of Canadian borrowing in the London bond market in what is called "portfolio investment" or "debt securities." Interest had to be paid on such loans, but ownership remained largely in Canadian hands.

When Canada entered the "American period" of its history, two significant factors changed. First, the source of foreign investment largely shifted from Britain to the United States; second, the form of investment switched from portfolio investment or loans to "direct" or "equity" investment, that is, control through the ownership of shares. Thus, to a large extent the Canadian economy has come to consist of branch plants of U.S. parent corporations. These companies typically operate in many other countries, too, and therefore gain the label of "multinational" or **transnational corporations**. Table 12.1 indicates the shift from British to U.S. investment in Canada between 1900 and 1967.

This pattern of economic development was fostered in the first instance by the National Policy of 1879, which put a tariff on imported manufactured goods. Rather than export to Canada from the United States and pay the tariff, U.S. companies set up branch plants within Canada behind the tariff wall. This was advantageous for the creation of employment in Canada and contributed to the general prosperity of the country. As time went on, however,

TABLE 12.1 **Percentage of British, U.S., and Other Foreign Investment in Canada, 1900–1967**

	1900	1914	1930	1939	1946	1950	1960	1967
U.S.	13.6	23.0	61.2	60.0	71.8	75.5	75.2	80.7
U.K.	85.2	72.4	36.3	35.8	23.2	20.1	15.1	10.3
Other	1.1	4.6	2.4	4.1	4.9	4.2	9.6	8.9

Source: Privy Council Office, Foreign Direct Investment in Canada (Gray Report, 1972), p. 15. Reproduced with the permission of the Minister of Supply and Services Canada, 1995.

considerable capital was generated within Canada, and the need for foreign investment declined. But partly because U.S. entrepreneurs were more inclined to take risks than Canadians and partly because Canadian banks were more willing to lend money to established foreign companies, the degree of foreign ownership continued to increase.

It was not only U.S. manufacturers that attracted favourable consideration from Canadian banks; so too did foreign companies that sought to exploit Canadian natural resources. "A large proportion of the investment in resource exploitation reflected the needs of the United States investors for raw materials for their processing and manufacturing plants in the United States." This integration often had the practical impact "of reducing the likelihood of further processing activity of Canadian natural resources in Canada."[7] Thus, along with many aspects of manufacturing, the mining, forestry, and petroleum industries came to be characterized by a high degree of foreign, mostly U.S., ownership. In fact, Canada has more foreign ownership than any other advanced industrial country.

The ten largest multinationals operating in Canada in 1994 are identified in Table 12.2. Other familiar corporate names that are foreign-owned include Mitsui, Honda, Cargill, A & P, Mobil Oil, Price Co., Kraft, Weyerhaeuser, Ultramar, DuPont, Fletcher Challenge, General Electric, McDonald's, Toyota, Digital Equipment, Pratt & Whitney, Mitsubishi, Suncor, Kmart, Chevron, Xerox, Stone-Consolidated, John Deere, Hewlett-Packard, Husky Oil, and Chevron. In total, 31 of the top 100 companies in Canada in terms of 1994 sales were foreign-owned.

Most advocates of the capitalist system such as "free market" economists are enthusiastic boosters of unlimited foreign investment. They claim that maximum efficiency results from capital being able to flow wherever it will yield the greatest returns. In this case, defenders of foreign investment argue that Canada still needs foreign capital and that such investment creates jobs, which in turn raise the Canadian standard of living. They also say that Canadians are too timid to take advantage of risky investment opportunities in their own country and that efficiency is enhanced when multinationals transfer "state-of-the-art" technology as well as well-trained managers and management techniques to their branch plants.

Others take the view that these advantages are short-term or short-sighted.[8] In the first place, more capital may eventually flow out of the country in interest and dividends than was originally brought in. Second, multinationals are likely to purchase supplies and component parts from the parent company or parent country, rather than buying them and creating

TABLE 12.2	Ten Largest Multinational Companies in Canada, 1994 Sales	
Company	Home Country	National Ranking
General Motors of Canada	U.S.	1
Ford Motor Co. of Canada	U.S.	3
Chrysler Canada	U.S.	4
IBM Canada	U.S.	9
Imperial Oil	U.S.	11
Shell Canada	Netherlands	23
Canada Safeway	U.S.	25
Amoco Canada Petroleum	U.S.	27
Sears Canada	U.S.	30
Total Petroleum (North America)	France	45

Source: The Financial Post 500, *Summer 1995. Reproduced with the permission of* The Financial Post.

employment in Canada. Third, such plants usually remain small and inefficient ("truncated") because they are designed to serve only the Canadian market rather than being encouraged to compete in export markets with the parent plant or branches set up in other countries. Critics also claim that a branch plant economy suffers because most of its R & D (research and development) is done in the parent plant. This limits the number of interesting and challenging jobs in science, engineering, and technology located in Canada. As convenient as it is to import such technology, this process hinders Canadian innovative efforts to develop distinctive export products, for almost all studies indicate that R & D is the secret of future economic success.

Critics of the situation also worry that decisions of multinational corporations, while based on the same profit motive as those of domestic firms, are less likely to conform to the Canadian national interest. If layoffs or shutdowns are necessary, for example, these are usually slated for branch plants first. Moreover, foreign firms may make less desirable kinds of investments than national firms, such as capital-intensive rather than labour-intensive, and resource-based rather than manufacturing. Such a high degree of U.S. ownership perpetuates the resource-export orientation of the Canadian economy and discourages Canadians from becoming more than "hewers of wood and drawers of water." The ultimate symbolic disadvantage of foreign-owned companies is that they may occasionally choose or be required to conform to the laws of the country in which their parent is located rather than those of Canada. The extension of U.S. laws to branch plants located in Canada is called **extra-territoriality**, and has regularly occurred, especially in the case of the Trading with the Enemy Act. When such branch plants in Canada have tried to do business with countries on the U.S. "enemy list," they have been told that they must follow U.S. law, thus reducing production and job opportunities in Canada. It is analogous to the Canadian air force taking orders from the NORAD commander in Colorado.

Official concern about the extent of foreign ownership in Canada was first expressed in the Gordon Royal Commission on Canada's Economic Prospects in 1958. Then, when Walter

Reproduced with permission.

Gordon became minister of finance in 1963, he experimented with measures to control the situation, but without much success. He at least left the legacy of the 1968 Watkins Report, *Foreign Ownership and the Structure of Canadian Industry*, which in turn led to the **Gray Report**, *Foreign Direct Investment in Canada*, of 1972. Named after Liberal cabinet minister Herb Gray, the Gray Report began with these words: "The degree of foreign ownership and control of economic activity is already substantially higher in Canada than in any other industrialized country and is continuing to increase."[9]

TABLE 12.3	Canadian and U.S. Ownership and Control of Canadian Industry (Excluding Agriculture and Finance), 1954–1967 (Percentage)			
	Canada		U.S.	
	Owned	Controlled	Owned	Controlled
1954	68	72	25	24
1960	66	67	27	26
1963	65	66	28	27
1967	65	65	29	28

Source: Privy Council Office, Foreign Direct Investment in Canada, p. 16. Reproduced with the permission of the Minister of Supply and Services Canada, 1995.

The Gray Report provided figures on the state of foreign investment in Canada, as shown in Table 12.3. They indicate that Canadian ownership and control of Canadian industry (excluding agriculture and finance) declined from about 70 percent to 65 percent over the 1954–67 period. One of the greatest concerns was that nearly 60 percent of all Canadian manufacturing industries were foreign-owned in 1967.

The principal government response to the Gray Report was the creation of the **Foreign Investment Review Agency** (FIRA) in the minority government period between 1972 and 1974. FIRA "screened" foreign takeovers of larger Canadian companies and new ventures by foreign firms in Canada in much the same way as took place in other countries, approving the deal if it involved "significant benefit to Canada." Perhaps its general effect was to allow foreign companies to prepare better takeover applications, for FIRA and the cabinet rarely disallowed any such initiatives and imposed minimal conditions. Although it had no jurisdiction at all over the expansion of existing foreign interests already in Canada and was not taken seriously by Canadian nationalists, FIRA became a major irritant to the United States, and the first act of the less nationalistic Mulroney government in 1984 was to replace FIRA with Investment Canada. In its recast form, the agency had the opposite objective of attracting increased foreign investment to Canada.

More recent statistics on the state of foreign investment in various Canadian industries are shown in Table 12.4. The proportion of foreign control began to increase again in 1984 after declining since 1971. In 1992, as measured by assets, foreigners controlled 20.8 percent of Canadian companies, of which exactly half were U.S.-controlled.

The policies that Canadian governments have adopted to counter this threat of U.S. or other foreign ownership and control of the Canadian economy can be divided into four main categories. First, Crown corporations have been established, partly to ensure that the company involved remains in Canadian hands. The Bank of Canada, Atomic Energy of Canada Ltd., and Petro-Canada were federal outputs in response to demands that a Canadian presence in strategic industries be retained. Second, while leaving other corporations to function privately, the federal government often created regulatory agencies. The National Energy

TABLE 12.4	Foreign-Controlled Shares of Assets in Various Canadian Industries, 1992 (Percentage)
Food, beverages, tobacco	29.5
Wood and paper	38.7
Energy	20.0
Chemicals, chemical products, textiles	66.0
Metallic minerals and metal products	28.0
Machinery and equipment	47.1
Transportation equipment	49.4
Electrical and electronic products	42.1
Construction and real estate	11.9
Transportation services	4.5
Communications	9.4
Services	15.8
Consumer goods and services	21.1
Finance and insurance industries	17.3

Source: Statistics Canada, CALURA—Part I—Corporations, 1992, cat. no. 61-220 (December 1993). Reproduced with the permission of the Minister of Supply and Services Canada, 1995.

Board, the Atomic Energy Control Board, the National Transportation Authority, and especially the Foreign Investment Review Agency were designed to protect the Canadian national interest in certain important respects. In the third place, ownership restrictions and tax incentives were introduced. Maximum foreign ownership limits exist in certain fields such as broadcasting, financial institutions, newspapers and publishing, and, before the Free Trade Agreement, banking. Incentives to Canadian ownership were exemplified by some of Walter Gordon's measures in the 1960s and the National Energy Program of 1980. The latter incentive (largely tax write-offs) was sufficient to persuade the Reichmann brothers to buy Gulf Canada from its American owners. Finally, the government established funding agencies such as the Federal Business Development Bank, whose mandate is to encourage Canadian entrepreneurship when the commercial banks are not interested. The Export Development Corporation could also be mentioned, but it does not limit its assistance to Canadian firms.

Many of these policies were half-hearted and others were later diluted under U.S. pressure. Many were weakened or withdrawn by the Mulroney government, both to increase foreign investment and to remove irritants in the Canada–U.S. relationship. Petro-Canada was semi-privatized, and recent foreign takeovers include Dome Petroleum by Amoco, de Havilland aircraft by Boeing (later re-Canadianized by Bombardier and the government of Ontario), Consolidated-Bathurst by Stone Containers, Cadillac-Fairview by JMB Reality, and Connaught BioSciences by Merieux of France. Thus, economic nationalists regard the situation as more critical than ever, especially in the light of the Free Trade Agreement.

Others remain indifferent or take the opposite side of this issue, seeing foreign investment as the source of badly needed jobs.

Trade

Because of geographic proximity, it is only logical that Canada and the United States be closely linked by trade. It is even more likely because of their complementary resources and industries—the abundance of primary resources in Canada and the amount of manufacturing in the United States. Thus, the extent of Canadian dependence on the United States as a market for its exports and as a source of its imports has gradually increased over time, as indicated in Table 12.5. Indeed, provinces trade more with neighbouring states than with each other, although much of this trade is of an intrafirm character rather than truly international.

Canadian exports to the United States exceeded those to the United Kingdom after 1921, have never fallen below 50 percent since 1950, and edged up to over 82 percent by 1994. Imports from the United States constituted nearly 50 percent of the Canadian total from the start, have never gone below that figure since 1900, and have risen to 75 percent in 1994.

Given the degree to which Canadian prosperity depends on export trade, it is advantageous to have ready access to the U.S. market; it is also convenient to have such a close supply of goods that are not produced in Canada. On the other hand, to have put so many eggs in one basket means that in times of U.S. recession, demand for Canadian goods falls off and the Canadian economy takes a nosedive too; and in prosperous periods, U.S. inflation also tends to increase prices in Canada. Furthermore, protectionist pressure in the United States for new or increased tariffs or quotas against Canadian exports can have a devastating effect on certain industries, as evidenced by the 10 percent surcharge imposed by U.S. President Richard Nixon in 1971. This problem could be dealt with by diversifying the Canadian export effort, as the Diefenbaker and Trudeau governments tried to do unsuccessfully in the case of Britain and Europe respectively, or by negotiating sectoral or comprehensive free trade agreements with the United States. While the Pearson government signed the sectoral **Auto Pact** with the United States to guarantee a balanced exchange of automobiles and parts, the Mulroney government chose to sign a comprehensive free trade deal and then to extend it to Mexico. Canada often has a positive balance with the United States in merchandise trade, but this is somewhat artificial, given the extent of imported parts within the exported goods; moreover, the nonmerchandise sector, which includes travel, services, and outflowing profits and dividends, usually results in an overall Canadian deficit in the total trade between the two countries.

In 1994, the European Union (EU) collectively constituted Canada's second-largest export market at 5.2 percent, and Japan was third at 4.3 percent. Similarly, on the import side, the collective EU was our second-largest supplier, at 8.0 percent, and Japan was third at 4.1 percent. Canadian trade with Mexico before the signing of NAFTA was negligible.[10]

TABLE 12.5	Canadian Exports to and Imports from the United States, Selected Years, 1886–1994 (Balance of Payments Basis, Percentage)	
	Exports to U.S.	Imports from U.S.
1886	44	44
1911	38	61
1921	46	69
1936	36	58
1946	38	73
1951	59	69
1960	56	67
1967	64	72
1977	70	70
1986	78	69
1987	77	69
1988	74	69
1989	75	69
1990	75	69
1991	75	69
1992	77	71
1993	80	73
1994	82	75

Source: Statistics Canada, Canada Year Book (to 1987) *and Statistics Canada*, Canada's Balance of International Payments, *cat. no. 67-001 (4th Quarter, 1994, March 1995) (after 1988). Reproduced with the permission of the Minister of Supply and Services Canada, 1995.*

Interest Rates

Once the Canadian and U.S. economies became closely intertwined by investment and trade, and given the ease with which capital could flow back and forth across the border, it became difficult for Canada to pursue an autonomous interest rate policy. Canadian interest rates are always set slightly higher than those south of the border for fear that if Canadian rates were lower a massive outflow of both Canadian and foreign capital would result. Indeed, increasing amounts of Canadian government and corporate bonds are held by foreigners, and both sectors would be in trouble if the money were withdrawn. Interest rates not only affect the propensity of consumers to take out mortgages and buy cars; more important, they determine whether large companies will expand their operations or new ones will get started. Thus, both consumer and corporate borrowing at low rates of interest has the effect of creating jobs. If Canada is hobbled from following the interest rate policy of its choice, the implications for unemployment can be very serious.

The Environment

Canadians have seriously damaged their own environment over the years, but the situation has been aggravated by proximity to the United States and by some of its even less restrictive anti-pollution laws. The largest transboundary environmental issue is that of acid rain. Studies of this problem have come to different conclusions, but Canadian research generally shows that about 50 percent of the acid rain falling north of the Canada–U.S. border is caused by U.S. sources. The primary cause is sulfur dioxide emitted from coal-burning hydroelectric plants in the Ohio Valley. These emissions flow northward and fall into Canadian lakes and rivers, killing plant and animal life, as well as damaging trees (especially for maple syrup), cars, and buildings. Thus, after waiting patiently and pressing the issue for many years, Canada welcomed President George Bush's Clean Air Act of 1990 as a major forward step in controlling North American air pollution.

The pollution of the Great Lakes is the other serious bilateral environmental problem. Here again, each side is to blame, but most of the responsibility rests with the chemicals discharged from the larger proportion of factories and waste dumps situated on the U.S. shores of the lakes. Phosphorous levels were reduced in the 1970s, but the Great Lakes are still in a critical state because of toxic pollution. The two countries try to improve the situation through the Boundary Waters Treaty.

Because of the peculiarities of the boundary between British Columbia and Alaska, Canada and the United States have had continuing differences over West Coast salmon: first, a boundary dispute, then a trade problem, and, in 1995, a conflict over conservation. Canadian salmon fishermen voluntarily reduced their catch because of dwindling stocks, but neither U.S. fishermen nor the U.S. government were prepared to follow suit. Another issue that originally arose in B.C. in the 1950s, but re-emerged in 1995, concerned the sale of downstream benefits under the Columbia River Treaty.

Energy

In the energy sector, the voracious U.S. industrial complex usually wants to import Canadian electric power and petroleum. Governments in Quebec, New Brunswick, Manitoba, and B.C. have been eager to export electricity, and those of Alberta, Saskatchewan, and B.C., to supply oil and natural gas. The federal government has normally approved these sales with little hesitation, although the **National Energy Board** is charged to ensure that long-term Canadian needs will not be compromised in the process. Native and environmental groups in some provinces have not been so favourably disposed to the hydro or nuclear plants necessary to produce the electricity, however, and Canadian nationalists worry about the future supply of petroleum for domestic purposes. Part of the controversy surrounding the Trans-Canada Pipeline project in 1956 derived from the involvement of U.S. firms and from the fact that the pipeline would serve the eastern United States as well as eastern Canada.

Canada–U.S. conflict has also centred on the question of transporting petroleum from Alaska and/or the Canadian North to supply the energy needs of the lower 48 states. Canada has been concerned about the dangers of carrying oil in tankers from Alaska through rocky, foggy Canadian straits to the Puget Sound area in the state of Washington, but was also hesitant to build pipelines across the fragile environment of the Canadian North as an alternative.

Finally, the degree of U.S. ownership of the Canadian petroleum industry has caused considerable conflict between the two countries. The National Energy Program (NEP) of 1980 set a target of 50 percent Canadian ownership of the oil and gas industry by 1990 and gave certain preferences to Petro-Canada and private Canadian firms. U.S. petroleum companies in Canada protested, and their government pressured Canada to remove these incentives to Canadianization. The Trudeau government made minor concessions, and the Mulroney cabinet dismantled the NEP entirely and began to privatize Petro-Canada.

Bond-Rating and Lending Agencies

In making public policy decisions, federal and provincial governments in Canada must increasingly defer to the dictates of bond-rating and lending agencies. This is because such agencies assign credit ratings, which in turn determine the interest rates at which governments borrow money to finance their deficits. Here it is important to note that Canadian federal and provincial governments do much of their borrowing in the United States, and it is often U.S. bond-rating and lending agencies that tell them how much they can spend. Premiers and prime ministers make regular forays to Wall Street to try to persuade such agencies that government finances are sound but that a little more credit is required.

Trade Unions

Historically, Canadian trade unions have been as closely allied with those in the United States as was the case in the corporate sector. Many unions in Canada, such as the United Steelworkers of America and the United Auto Workers, were part of "international unions" that had their headquarters in the United States. The Canadian union movement justified the relationship by arguing that as long as it had to bargain with multinational corporations, it needed the support of international unions, especially their larger strike funds. Membership in international unions peaked in 1965 at 67 percent of all union members in Canada. Since then, many of those involved in organized labour have felt uncomfortable with these arrangements. In recent years, therefore, a nationalist trend has been apparent in the Canadian labour movement, and several unions have either cut their ties with the international headquarters or defected to a different union. Bob White's creation of an autonomous **Canadian Auto Workers** union is the most striking example, but even some that remain part of international unions have successfully demanded greater autonomy than before. Thus, in 1992, 1 156 700 Canadians belonged to international unions out of a total union membership of 3 866 100, or 29.9 percent.[11] The largest remaining international unions in Canada are the Food and Commercial Workers, the Steelworkers, and the Teamsters. Figure 12.1 shows the change in the Canadian union movement from international to national and government between 1962 and 1992.

Figure 12.1   Diminution of International Control of Unions

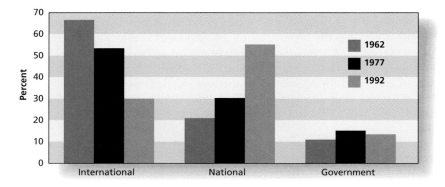

Source: *Statistics Canada, CALURA, Labour Unions, 1992. Reproduced with the permission of the Minister of Supply and Services Canada, 1995.*

AMERICAN INFLUENCE ON CANADIAN CULTURE

People around the world enjoy U.S. popular culture. Canadians are a particularly captive market, given their geographical proximity, their linguistic similarity, their small domestic market, their chronic feeling of dependence and inferiority, and the degree of economic integration between the two countries. The general public has little consciousness of the origin of most pop culture fare, and even less concern that so much of it originates in the United States. But many nationalists among the intellectual elite are disturbed by the high proportion of television, magazines, movies, books, newspapers, and music in Canada that emanates from the United States. They are concerned that this cultural invasion stifles the development of a distinctive Canadian national identity, worry about its influence on Canadian attitudes and values, and wonder how long a separate political system can be maintained in these circumstances.

AMERICAN INFLUENCE ON SPECIFIC CULTURAL INDUSTRIES

Television is the most significant cultural institution of the second half of the twentieth century, whether used for entertainment, information, or advertising. The average Canadian watches about 22.8 hours of television per week, and 63.5 percent of that is foreign (mostly American in the case of anglophones) programming.[12] Indeed, if a Canadian resident wanted to watch U.S. television 24 hours a day, it would be quite possible to do so. Broken down by language group, anglophones watch 74.5 percent foreign programs while francophones watch only 37.1 percent. Much of the population lives close enough to the U.S. border to receive U.S. channels through the air; failing that, Canadian stations broadcast a large proportion of U.S. programming. Then, about 75 percent of Canadian households have purchased cable television, which normally offers them all the U.S. networks and a few additional Canadian channels. Beyond cable, many Canadians have pay television, which extends the U.S. content, for example, to U.S. movies and "superstations." Finally, satellite dishes can pick up even more U.S. channels, and by late 1995 pizza-sized dishes brought direct-to-home satellite transmission.

Canadians watch their own news, public affairs, and sports programs quite conscientiously, but otherwise prefer U.S. programs. Indeed, U.S. public television stations near the border depend on Canadians to contribute funds to their operations. Canadian television has a higher reputation abroad than it does at home, and those few Canadian series that are produced are readily sold to foreign networks. Canada sold about $100 million worth of television productions abroad in 1992.

There are two main reasons why Canadian television networks broadcast so much U.S. programming. First, it is much cheaper to buy a U.S. show or series than to produce a Canadian one. Second, U.S. programs generally attract a larger audience, so that they command higher advertising rates than do Canadian ones. If profit is the name of the game (or minimizing its deficit in the case of the publicly owned CBC), then the best way to play is to provide U.S. fare. The Canadian network CTV contends that each hour of Canadian television represents over $5 million in lost annual profit margin.[13]

Magazines are perhaps the second most important vehicle of popular culture, and this Canadian industry is also permeated by U.S. content. The 1995 Task Force on the Canadian Magazine Industry spoke of the "massive penetration of the Canadian market by foreign magazines," and added that "the United States is a daily presence in the life of every Canadian, through television programming, sports and film. It is reasonable to expect that the content of American magazines will be of interest to Canadians."[14] While Canadian magazines lead foreign magazines in terms of subscriptions in Canada, foreign magazines account for 81 percent of English-language newsstand sales. Overall, Canadian magazines have increased from 23.3 percent in 1959 to 67.6 percent of the total circulation in 1992, but as with television, the picture is much more positive on the French side (95 percent) than the English (60.1 percent). The 1995 Task Force emphasized the significance of such circulation figures as follows: "the larger the circulation, the more advertising a magazine can attract; the greater the advertising revenue, the more it can afford to spend on editorial content; and the more it spends, the more likely it will be attractive to readers, with the result that circulation will grow."[15]

The Canadian motion picture industry is even weaker than television or magazines, and the average Canadian moviegoer has rarely if ever seen a Canadian feature film. About five percent of the screen time in Canadian movie theatres was devoted to Canadian films in 1992 (and most of that is in the large, sophisticated Toronto and Montreal markets),[16] a figure that remains depressingly static. U.S. movie producers make many feature films in Canada every year, taking advantage of the low Canadian dollar, its scenic locations, and its technical expertise, but these are always disguised as U.S. movies by the time they hit the screen. The problem has many causes, including the fact that the Famous Players theatre chain is U.S.-owned, that the Cineplex-Odeon chain has suffered many financial problems, and that the film distribution system is U.S.-controlled, in addition to the undeniable Canadian fascination with Hollywood, the small Canadian market, and a shortage of funds. Canadian productions do slightly better in the home video market, where Canadian-content films rose to 23 percent in 1992.

When it comes to books, the Canadian market is again dominated by U.S. content. About 299 Canadian-controlled publishing firms had sales of their own titles in 1992–93 of $374 373 000, but 24 foreign-owned publishers in Canada sold $223 977 000 of their own titles.[17] Both kinds of companies also sell foreign titles. Nelson Canada, the publisher of this book, and McClelland and Stewart are among the large Canadian firms. Branch-plant firms such as Prentice-Hall Canada or McGraw-Hill Ryerson do publish Canadian books but also distribute their U.S. titles. Books are like television shows: they are cheaper to import than to make domestically. The problem is aggravated by the lack of effort to sell Canadian books at Canadian bookstores. Paperback books at newsstands, drug stores, and supermarkets come almost entirely from the United States because the publisher-distributors who control the supply are U.S.-owned companies.

Sound recording is another vulnerable industry. Some 15 foreign-controlled record companies had 84.6 percent of sales in Canada, even though 172 Canadian-controlled companies were also in business. More significantly, sales with Canadian content constituted only about 12 percent of total sales, and as for new releases, 673 contained Canadian content, compared with 5602 that did not.[18]

The Canadian newspaper and radio industries are much more autonomous. Canadian newspaper and radio firms are required by law to remain in Canadian hands, and several aggressive Canadian chains are alive and well in both industries. Nevertheless, the influence of the United States can be detected in these industries, too: the ready availability in some centres of such U.S. papers as *USA Today* and U.S. radio stations; the reliance on U.S. news-gathering agencies abroad, such as American Press reports; the dependence on U.S. sources for comics, crossword puzzles, and personal advice columns; and the tendency to include a large proportion of news coverage of U.S. events.

Other cultural fields could be mentioned—theatre and art—as well as the wider realm of education (including universities), religion, and sports, but the basic situation there is much the same: most aspects of Canadian culture are heavily influenced by U.S. institutions and values, and most Canadians accept this state of affairs without complaint. To a large extent the Canadian presence in such industries is the result of demands made by the nationalist minority for protection from U.S. domination and for promotion of Canadian content, a concern first given official expression in the **Massey Royal Commission** Report on National Development in the Arts, Letters, and Sciences in 1951.

POLICIES TO PROTECT AND PROMOTE CANADIAN CULTURE

As in economic matters, the Crown corporation is one nationalistic instrument in the cultural field. The **Canadian Broadcasting Corporation** (CBC), in its radio and television networks, and Radio-Canada, its French-language equivalent, is perhaps the most crucial agent of Canadian cultural expression. The origins of the CBC in the mid-1930s were discussed in Chapter 6; today, CBC radio is commercial-free, has virtually 100 percent Canadian content, and can be heard in almost every part of the country. Programs like "Morningside," "As It Happens," and "Cross-Country Checkup" are widely regarded as crucial links in keeping the country together. CBC television is less successful, mainly because the television medium is so expensive. The Mulroney government slashed millions of dollars from the CBC's budget after 1984, making the Corporation's task even harder. The 1991 Task Force on the Economic Status of Canadian Television, like many similar earlier reports, lamented the fact that government budget cuts for the CBC forced it to rely more and more on advertising revenue, reducing the income potential of private television broadcasters and causing the CBC to deviate from the high-quality cultural programming Canadians rightfully expect from their public broadcaster.[19] All such reports have said that the CBC should receive adequate, ongoing, multiyear, and stable public funding to enable it to fulfil its mandate,[20] but the Chrétien government cut its budget even further. In spite of such cuts and severe layoffs, the CBC decided in 1995 to remove all foreign programs in prime time.

Another Crown corporation, the National Film Board, also has an illustrious history, making impressive Canadian films and winning many international awards. It has two serious disadvantages, however: insufficient funding to make feature films, with the result that it has concentrated on documentaries and short films; and no effective mechanism for making its films available to the general public.

A second policy instrument to protect and promote Canadian culture is the regulatory agency, the **Canadian Radio-television and Telecommunications Commission (CRTC)**.[21] This agency issues broadcasting licences and Canadian-content regulations. These rules are more stringent for the CBC than for private stations and networks, and currently require all television stations to provide at least 60 percent Canadian content over the year; in prime time, private broadcasters can go as low as 50 percent. News, public affairs, and sports take up most of this time, especially on the private networks, and very little Canadian drama is produced. The CRTC requires that AM and FM radio stations play 30 percent Canadian music, a regulation that was generally seen as the catalyst for the explosion of the Canadian musical industry over the past 20 years.[22]

The CRTC, under strong industry and popular pressure to allow more U.S. outlets in Canada, approved cable and pay television, which diluted the audiences of Canadian channels. Canadians must buy cable TV in order to obtain the parliamentary channel and the CBC all-news channel, Newsworld. When the United States protested the substitution of an American country-music channel in favour of a Canadian channel, the compromise arrived at was to allow the American channel to buy a portion of the Canadian one. Also in 1995, the CRTC authorized direct-to-home (DTH) satellite services, the so-called "death-stars." Many nationalists accuse the CRTC of selling out to Canadian cable and satellite companies in their saturation of the Canadian television audience with U.S. fare, and fear for the future of Canadian content when the largely American 500-channel universe is beamed directly into Canadian homes.

In another aspect of regulation, both Marcel Masse and Flora MacDonald, as ministers of communications, tried to reform the film distribution system so that theatres would screen more Canadian feature films. They were unsuccessful, however, because the system was controlled in the U.S. and President Reagan, a former actor, would not relent.[23] On the other hand, an income tax loophole allowed the wealthy to write off their investments in Canadian film productions.

Ownership restrictions and financial incentives are also designed to protect Canadian culture. Ownership restrictions in the cultural field apply to radio, television, and newspaper companies in Canada. In the publishing field, when the parent of a Canadian subsidiary is taken over by another U.S. firm, the Canadian branch is supposed to be sold to Canadians, although this has not always happened. Another example of preferential "ownership" concerns Canadian immigration regulations, which require that before hiring a non-Canadian, employers must demonstrate that no qualified Canadian is available. This applies in particular to university professors and the heads of cultural institutions such as the Stratford Festival and the Art Gallery of Ontario.

Related to the ownership issue are tax incentives. For example, Canadian firms can only deduct magazine or television advertising expenses from their income tax if those advertisements are placed in Canadian magazines or on Canadian TV channels. Moreover, tariff code 9958 prohibits the entry into Canada of split-run editions of foreign magazines containing advertisements directed at Canadians. A major controversy occurred when these measures were introduced in 1965. When the Pearson government tried to include *Time* and *Reader's Digest* in the legislation, the U.S. government threatened to withhold its assent to the Auto Pact. Canada was forced to exempt these magazines until the Trudeau government finally removed the concession in calmer circumstances in 1976. *Reader's Digest* eventually Canadianized itself, and *Time* immediately closed down its Canadian edition. In the 1990s, however, *Sports Illustrated* started to produce a so-called Canadian split-run edition that challenged the law because such editions could now be physically printed in Canada via satellite. The 1994 Task Force on the Canadian Magazine Industry found the existing policies to be vital to the domestic industry, and recommended a way in which they could be revalidated without violating the rules of international trading agreements that Canada signed.[24]

A fourth device to promote Canadian culture is the funding agency. The Massey Commission recommended public financial assistance to the arts, and in response the **Canada Council** was set up in 1957. It gives life-saving grants to hundreds of individual writers, artists, musicians, and playwrights as well as to almost every orchestra, theatre centre, art gallery, ballet and opera company in the country. The Social Sciences and Humanities Research Council of Canada (SSHRCC) has taken over the subsidization of academic research and writing, while Telefilm Canada (formerly the Canadian Film Development Corporation) subsidizes the production of feature films.

THE CANADA–U.S. FREE TRADE AGREEMENT AND NAFTA

The 1989 Free Trade Agreement between Canada and the United States was a wide-ranging pact covering almost every aspect of the relationship between the two countries.[25] A brief historical overview should probably precede an examination of its contents and implications.

Trade constitutes over 30 percent of Canada's national income and provides about three million jobs. At the same time as trying to maximize their exports, all countries seek to protect their domestic industry from foreign competition through the imposition of tariffs, quotas, customs duties, and the like. In 1947, however, Canada was among the signatories of the General Agreement on Tariffs and Trade (GATT) under which countries pledged to remove such trade restrictions on a multinational basis. GATT allows its members to go even further with bilateral agreements, as Canada and the United States did in defence production arrangements and the 1965 Auto Pact. One way or another, close to 80 percent of Canada–U.S. trade was tariff-free even before 1985.

Canadian policy-makers had been concerned for some time that the country was being left out of the various regional trading blocks being formed, especially the EEC (now the European Union). In these organizations, tariffs were removed among member countries, and in the case of the EEC, a common tariff was established for the rest of the world. Under the Trudeau government, Canada sought to negotiate "sectoral" free trade with the United States—that is, arrangements in specific industries like the Auto Pact—but the U.S. was not interested. In fact, a protectionist mood descended on the U.S. Congress in the early 1980s, and new barriers to many Canadian exports were imposed: on shakes and shingles, softwood lumber, potash, potatoes, fish, and specialty steel.

Canada possessed a Reciprocity Treaty with the United States between 1854 and 1866, under which goods flowed across the border free of tariffs. On a number of later occasions, especially in 1911, the Canadian government tried to negotiate a similar agreement. But modern pressure for a free trade agreement with the United States came largely from Western Canadian resource producers, especially former Alberta premier Peter Lougheed; the issue was popularized by various C.D. Howe Institute and Senate Committee reports. Brian Mulroney did not advocate such a system until after he became prime minister in 1984. He was apparently converted when U.S. protectionist measures began to be felt in Canada and when the Trudeau-appointed Macdonald Royal Commission on the Economic Union and Development Prospects for Canada recommended that the country take such a "leap of faith." Mulroney found an advocate of free trade in the White House, so he and Ronald Reagan set the negotiations in motion. After many ups and downs, the **Canada–U.S. Free Trade Agreement** was finalized in October 1987, given congressional and parliamentary approval in 1988 (being delayed by the Canadian Senate until after the 1988 election), and took effect January 1, 1989.

The agreement removed almost all barriers to the flow of goods and services between the two countries over a ten-year period. Each country could henceforth send its products to the other without tariffs, quotas, or other impediments, but each continued to apply its own tariffs to imports from other countries. Goods had to be at least 50 percent domestically produced in order to qualify.

Most services were also included, such as car rental agencies and computer, advertising, and accounting services, although nondiscriminatory regulation by either government was permitted. On financial services, a significant change was the elimination for U.S. investors of the 25 percent ceiling on foreign ownership of Canadian banks. As for other investment, U.S. businesses would now be able to start new operations in Canada without restriction (and vice versa); Investment Canada could only screen acquisitions of firms with a value over $150 million, and it could not impose any performance requirements. Thus, the situation resembled the pre-FIRA era.

Energy, agriculture, and the Auto Pact were three of the most controversial sections of the agreement. A North American energy pool was created in which prices could not be discriminatory (that is, Canada had to sell oil, gas, or electricity to the United States at the

Canadian domestic price), and if cutbacks were ever necessary, domestic sales had to be reduced by the same proportion as exports. On this point the agreement went beyond existing GATT requirements.[26] On agriculture, Canada had to remove import restrictions on chickens, turkeys, and eggs, as well as tariffs on processed food, and ultimately all subsidies that distort agricultural trade were to be eliminated. Marketing boards were left intact for the time being. The Auto Pact was also changed to some extent in order to incorporate U.S. concerns. Meanwhile, on government procurement policies, the agreement provided that every government contract over $25 000 had to be open to bids from either country.

The agreement excluded existing cultural programs.[27] However, any *new* government support of cultural industries could be met by retaliation of equivalent value by the other country. More safely intact were such cultural treasures as beer, bourbon, and rye, as well as metric measurement and bilingual labelling.

For any future conflicts in trade between the two countries, a complex **dispute-settlement mechanism** involving binational panels and binding arbitration was set up. If either country refuses to abide by the final decision of the arbitrators, however, the other could retaliate ("countervail"), as before.

Those Canadians who favoured the agreement argued that in the absence of the deal the United States would have continued to apply a series of protectionist measures, threatening more jobs.[28] Canadian firms would now have access to the huge unprotected U.S. market, allowing them to expand and create employment. Everyone agreed that if this expansion took place anywhere, it was likely to be in petrochemicals, gas, oil, uranium, electricity, potash, forest products, cattle, and fish. Supporters of the FTA admitted that many Canadian firms would go under and thousands of Canadian jobs would be lost because of the competition from larger American companies, but they claimed that such competition would force Canadian corporations to become stronger and more efficient and more capable of functioning in the global economy. Defenders also hailed the likelihood of increased U.S. investment in Canada, as well as higher levels of investment from other countries wishing to take advantage of Canadian access to the U.S. market. Some also expected lower consumer prices or at least a wider selection of goods and services. Many asked whether any practical alternative existed, although they wondered if the deal had to be so comprehensive. It was clearly designed, they said, to enshrine neoconservative values and corporate rights, and prevent the recurrence of such economic nationalistic measures as FIRA and NEP.[29]

While the Conservative government was strongly in favour of the Free Trade Agreement and found supporters especially among big business, Western resource industries, and the province of Quebec, the federal Liberal and New Democratic parties opposed it, along with the province of Ontario, organized labour, and nationalist groups.[30] Opponents argued that the deal would lead to a loss of jobs rather than an increase because the Canadian market would be inundated by U.S. exports, and small Canadian firms would not be able to compete. Massive layoffs and shutdowns were predicted, particularly in such industries as processed food, electrical goods, textiles, clothing, and footwear, where the labour force was largely female. Jobs would also be lost because U.S. branch plants would close, supplying the Canadian market instead from the parent plant south of the border, and some Canadian firms would move to the United States to take advantage of backward labour and environmental laws in certain states. Any increase in Canadian employment would be in resource industries, to place further dependence on those capital-intensive and economically erratic sectors. Nationalists also argued that the United States was a faltering industrial giant, with its large government and foreign trade deficits, and was not a reliable market. They felt that for reasons outlined earlier in this chapter, the existing degree of integration of the two countries' economies in terms of trade, investment, and interest rates was already detrimental to Canadian interests.

Some of the specific provisions that caused anxiety among opponents of the deal included the removal of most restrictions on U.S. investment, especially in banks; the energy section, which would no longer enable Canada to put its own interests first or take advantage of its natural resources by selling them at a premium price; and the small but possibly dangerous concessions in the already threatened cultural industries. Many were dissatisfied with the dispute-settlement mechanism, which would not ultimately prevent some of the incidents that inspired the deal in the first place.

The results have been mixed, but more significantly, the number of conflicts has been large. Some of the same issues that precipitated the Free Trade Agreement have continued to be problematic, especially Canadian exports of softwood lumber. Other areas of dispute include uranium, beer, government procurement, magnesium, steel, swine, wheat, sugar, peanut butter, tobacco, milk, meat, paper, salmon and herring, poultry products, magazine publishing, and country-music television.

Many opponents worry that the final definition of "unfair subsidy" would endanger agricultural marketing boards, regional development programs, and the Canadian social security safety net. They expected pressure for policy harmonization in every field: taxation, pollution control and product standards, and social programs. Sure enough, by 1995, some observers in both countries were calling for a common external tariff and a common North American currency. Opponents also saw threats to basic Canadian values, in which there would be pressure for less government, less caring and equality, more social Darwinism ("survival of the fittest"), and more obsession with profits. Finally, they felt that the Free Trade Agreement would reduce Canadian flexibility of action on the world stage and limit its ability to pursue an independent Canadian foreign policy.

The ink was hardly dry on the Canada–U.S. Free Trade Agreement when the Mulroney government began talks with the United States and Mexico to enter into a **North American Free Trade Agreement (NAFTA)**. This agreement essentially extended FTA to Mexico, and most provisions in the two agreements were identical. Canada entered the agreement mainly to preclude the other partners from endangering its position, although some corporations saw it as a means of enhancing the efficiency of their operations. Partly because of Canada's minuscule trade with Mexico, the Liberal Party did not oppose NAFTA in principle; it only sought to make marginal changes. Stronger opponents feared that companies would move from Canada to Mexico because of the low wages and environmental standards in that country; they also complained that Mexico was able to negotiate a stronger energy clause with the United States than had Canada under the FTA. Despite pre-election fanfare, the Chrétien government was content with minor changes in the pact once in office. It established the office of the environmental arm of the agreement in Montreal. Not long afterwards, negotiations began to add Chile to the trade agreement, although Prime Minister Chrétien also led major trade missions to the Far East and the rest of Latin America.

In the wake of these agreements, Canada signed the "Open Skies" agreement with the United States in 1995. It essentially deregulated the cross-border airline industry, giving U.S. and Canadian companies equal access to routes between the two countries.

OTHER EXTERNAL INFLUENCES

Even before the Free Trade Agreement, U.S. influence was established in such other fields as science, social policy, and general consumer behaviour. Although Canadians consider themselves ahead of Americans in social policy, for example, the U.S. New Deal in the 1930s and the U.S. War on Poverty in the 1960s inspired similar initiatives in Canada. Many social and political protest movements have also spilled over the border, including farmer movements and anti-poverty and aboriginal groups. Fraternal organizations like the Kiwanis and Masons also have their headquarters in the United States, and links are close in many religious organizations.

Although Canadian defence and foreign policies are influenced by its membership in NATO and NORAD, Canada is part of the British Commonwealth and the French equivalent, the Francophonie. These organizations provide some distinctive aspects to Canadian foreign policy. So, too, does Canadian membership in the United Nations, where we have often played a distinguished part. Canada's admission to the Organization of American States and the growing membership in NAFTA will provide a new Latin American dimension to Canadian foreign policy and make new demands on the Canadian political system. On the other hand, the 1995 "turbot war" with Spain revealed new tensions in Canada's relations with Europe.

As in foreign policy, Canadian economic and social policies are also subject to many contemporary supranational influences beyond those of the United States. The United Nations has criticized several domestic Canadian policies, including Quebec language legislation and federal or provincial laws on labour, aboriginals, and women, among others. The International Monetary Fund puts pressure on member countries with respect to the size of national deficits, and advised the Canadian government in 1991 not to raise public servants' salaries. Because Canadian governments borrow money from countries other than the United States, foreign bond-rating agencies and lending institutions influence government policies, as does Canada's membership in the G7 (the Group of Seven leading Western industrialized countries), as the leaders meet annually to try to come to a consensus on economic and other matters. The Organisation for Economic Cooperation and Development subtly influences member policies with its comparative statistics and recommendations, while the General Agreement on Tariffs and Trade, now renamed the World Trade Organization, can actually order its members to change their trading practices. For example, in the Uruguay Round of GATT talks, which concluded in 1993, Canada agreed to abandon its historic use of agricultural marketing boards.

Canada must also respond to all sorts of other transnational forces.[31] Money, banking, finance, and investment flow between countries almost at will, and the government must cope with questions of international exchange rates and the balance of payments. It is widely acknowledged that national governments anywhere in the world have difficulty in regulating or taxing transnational corporations. Indeed, the "globalization" that has characterized corporate behaviour in recent years has meant that more companies are outgrowing their domestic state, that they are introducing new forms of technology at an incredible rate, and that they are opening or closing operations strictly on the basis of economic efficiency. Such globalization has had many implications for the economy, mostly in the form of seeing transnational corporations closing their manufacturing plants in Canada. It is increasingly difficult for national or provincial governments to maintain distinctive labour, tax, or environmental laws because such companies regularly threaten to move to jurisdictions they find more congenial.

The policies and problems of other countries also have an increasing influence on Canadian domestic and foreign policies. These include OPEC oil prices, Japanese car exports, EU agricultural subsidies and the complete removal of all tariff and non-tariff barriers within the European Union, refugee problems around the world, Third World indebtedness and poverty, the liberation of Eastern Europe and South Africa, the disintegration of the Soviet Union and Yugoslavia, the Greenhouse effect and other environmental degradation, epidemics, international terrorism, Arab–Israeli conflict, Iraq's invasion of Kuwait, tribal warfare in Rwanda, the democratization of Haiti, and fighting among Somali warlords. Ironically, despite all this transnationalism, Canada's response is increasingly determined by its own domestic, economic interests, a case in point being assistance to Third World countries, which is provided regardless of human rights records, as long as it benefits Canada economically. The Chrétien government also announced that Canada would keep "trade before aid" in dealing with the Third World, as external policy was influenced by the government's internal budgetary situation.

CONCLUSION

Canada follows U.S. examples because of tradition, convenience, or economics; because the U.S. presence makes it necessary; and because of explicit U.S. government or corporate pressure. Most observers expect that, directly or indirectly, the free trade agreements will increase such U.S. influence on almost all aspects of Canadian policy. Thus, during the twentieth century, Canada has gone from being a British colony to a colony of the United States, or from colony to nation to colony.[32] The Mulroney government was particularly cooperative with the United States, while the Chrétien regime saw itself as friendly but more businesslike, ready to pursue Canadian interests where they differed from those of the United States. Furthermore, as political, economic, and environmental developments become common global problems, Canada must increasingly respond to transnational and supranational demands. As insistent as demands may be from forces in the domestic Canadian society, Canadian politicians must also pay greater attention to their external surroundings.

It is often contended in political science that a country's foreign policy is more state-centred than its domestic policy—that politicians and bureaucrats operate with greater autonomy in international affairs.[33] In Canada's case, the continentalism of postwar economic policies was largely the work of the American-born minister of trade and commerce, C.D. Howe, and others in the political and bureaucratic elites that shared his assumptions.[34] A more nationalistic elite briefly held sway in the late 1960s and 1970s, including Walter Gordon and Herb Gray. The concept of free trade emerged after Mulroney's election in 1984 even though it had not been mentioned during that election campaign and had not been preceded by widespread public demands.

The class-based or neo-Marxist approach also has much to say about the external environment.[35] Indeed, a large part of the capitalist domination of Canadian government and society consists of multinational firms. Such analysts are foremost among those who criticize the extent to which the Canadian government has supported, and Canadian companies have been part of, the U.S. military–industrial complex. They have also identified the role of the "comprador elite"—officials of American branch plants operating in Canada—who are likely to pursue the interests of their external parent corporations in dealing with Canadian governments. Multinational corporate links shape Canadian economic policy in many ways, including the reliance on resource exports, the weakness in manufacturing, and the virtual absence of research and development. Class-based analysis cites Brian Mulroney as an excellent example of the comprador elite, claiming that his upbringing in a U.S. company town in Quebec and his later stint as president of a U.S. subsidiary in that province left him with a markedly deferential approach to Canada–U.S. relations.[36] Analysts further decry the influx of foreign investment, the limited effort to diversify trade patterns, the inability to set distinctive interest rates, the international environmental devastation, and the limited control over national energy resources. As far as free trade is concerned, they note that many U.S. subsidiaries supported the Canadian Alliance for Trade and Job Opportunities, the ad hoc corporate group that pushed for free trade before and during the 1988 election campaign. Representatives of Canadian industry—both foreign and domestic—were part of the FTA negotiating process through Sectoral Advisory Groups on International Trade, but the Canadian Labour Congress was not involved. In addition, class analysts abhor the anticipated exploitation of Mexican labour under NAFTA, and are profoundly concerned about U.S. corporate influence on Canadian culture.

The other approaches outlined in Chapter 1 are less concerned about the external environment. Public choice theory might note that the 1988 election was almost a single-issue election and that different regional voting patterns emerged depending on whether voters felt that free trade was in their own interest. Finally, many Canadians lament the *lack* of pluralism in Canada's external environment.

DISCUSSION QUESTIONS

1. Why did Canada fall into the U.S. sphere of influence so soon after emerging from British domination?

2. Does Canada have any realistic alternative to military alliances with the United States?

3. What are the advantages and disadvantages of foreign investment in Canada? Of the other economic relationships between the two countries?

4. What are the advantages and disadvantages of the close cultural relationship between the two countries?

5. Is U.S. cultural domination of Canada inevitable, or could additional measures be taken to strengthen Canadian cultural industries?

6. What are the advantages and disadvantages of the Free Trade Agreement?

7. Was the Canada–U.S. Free Trade Agreement inevitable? What alternatives were available in the increasing regionalization of world trading patterns?

8. Give examples of U.S. influence on Canadian foreign policy and examples of an independent Canadian foreign policy.

9. What other international, multinational, and supranational influences affect the Canadian political system?

10. Is the state-centred or the class analysis approach most useful in explaining the material in this chapter?

NOTES

1. These radar lines were obsolete by the time construction was completed. See Edelgard Mahant and Graeme Mount, *An Introduction to Canadian-American Relations*, 2nd ed. (Scarborough: Nelson Canada, 1989), p. 196.
2. Knowlton Nash, *Kennedy and Diefenbaker* (Toronto: McClelland and Stewart, 1990); H.B. Robinson, *Diefenbaker's World* (Toronto: University of Toronto Press, 1989).
3. Nash, *Kennedy and Diefenbaker*; Robinson, *Diefenbaker's World*.
4. J.L. Granatstein and Robert Bothwell, *Pirouette: Pierre Trudeau and Canadian Foreign Policy* (Toronto: University of Toronto Press, 1990).
5. Among the many sources on this subject, see *Foreign Direct Investment in Canada* (Ottawa: Supply and Services, 1972), ch. 19; K.R. Nossal, *The Politics of Canadian Foreign Policy*, 2nd ed. (Scarborough: Prentice-Hall Canada, 1989); David Dewitt and John Kirton, *Canada as a Principal Power* (Toronto: Wiley, 1983); J.L. Granatstein, ed., *Canadian Foreign Policy: Historical Readings* (Toronto: Copp Clark Pitman, 1986); J.L. Granatstein and Robert Bothwell, *Pirouette*; and the annual series *Canada among Nations* produced since 1984 by the Carleton University School of International Affairs by Maureen Molot and others.
6. Glen Williams, "Regions within Region: Continentalism Ascendant," in M.S. Whittington and G. Williams, eds., *Canadian Politics in the 1990s*, 4th ed. (Scarborough: Nelson Canada, 1995).
7. Canada, *Foreign Direct Investment in Canada* (Ottawa: Supply and Services, 1972), p. 14; Stephen Brooks and Andrew Stritch, *Business and Government in Canada* (Scarborough: Prentice-Hall Canada, 1991).
8. The pioneer of this theme was Kari Levitt, *Silent Surrender: The Multinational Corporation in Canada* (Toronto: Macmillan, 1970).
9. *Foreign Direct Investment in Canada*, p. 5.
10. Imports and exports are measured in a variety of ways; I have tried to use the "balance of payments" method consistently.
11. Statistics Canada, *CALURA, Part II—Labour Unions*, cat. no. 71-202 (November 1994).

12. Statistics Canada, *Television Viewing 1993*, cat. no. 87-208 (December 1994).
13. Department of Communications, *Report of the Task Force on the Economic Status of Canadian Television* (Ottawa, 1991), p. 39.
14. Task Force on the Canadian Magazine Industry, *A Question of Balance* (Ottawa, 1994), p. 40; Department of Communications, *Vital Links* (Ottawa, April 1987), p. 36.
15. *A Question of Balance*, p. 40.
16. Statistics Canada, *Film and Video 1992–93*, cat. no. 87-204 (February 1995).
17. Statistics Canada, *Book Publishing 1992–93*, cat. no. 87-210 (February 1995).
18. Statistics Canada, *Sound Recording 1992–93*, cat. no. 87-202 (July 1994).
19. *The Economic Status of Canadian Television*, p. 9.
20. Ibid., 169.
21. For a scathing attack on the timidity of the CRTC, see Herschel Hardin, *Closed Circuits* (Vancouver: Douglas & McIntyre, 1985). For a more scholarly critique, see Marc Raboy, *Missed Opportunities: The Story of Canada's Broadcasting Policy* (Montreal: McGill–Queen's University Press, 1990). See also S.M. Crean, *Who's Afraid of Canadian Culture?* (Don Mills: General Publishing, 1976); Morris Wolfe, *Jolts: The TV Wasteland and the Canadian Oasis* (Toronto: Lorimer, 1985); and the *Report of the Task Force on Broadcasting Policy* (Ottawa: Supply and Services, 1986).
22. Considerable controversy surrounds the definition of Canadian content: if the music was composed by a Canadian, if the lyrics were written by a Canadian, if it is performed by a Canadian, if it was recorded in Canada, etc. The Bryan Adams hit "Everything I Do I Do for You" failed to meet this test.
23. Reagan was a Republican, but Hollywood also had a powerful Democrat, Jack Valenti, lobbying aggressively throughout the U.S. government on its behalf.
24. *A Question of Balance*.
25. Bruce Doern and Brian Tomlin, *Faith and Fear: The Free Trade Story* (Toronto: Stoddart, 1991); Brooks and Stritch, *Business and Government in Canada*, ch. 13; Robert Campbell and Leslie Pal, *The Real Worlds of Canadian Politics*, 2nd ed. (Peterborough: Broadview Press, 1991).
26. Brooks and Stritch, *Business and Government in Canada*, p. 396.
27. But see S.M. Crean, "Reading between the Lies: Culture and the Free Trade Agreement," in Duncan Cameron, ed., *The Free Trade Deal* (Toronto: Lorimer, 1988).
28. John Crispo, ed., *Free Trade: The Real Story* (Toronto: Gage, 1988).
29. Williams, "Regions within Region: Continentalism Ascendant."
30. Cameron, *The Free Trade Deal*; Marjory Bowker, *On Guard for Thee* (Hull: Voyageur, 1988); John Warnock, *Free Trade and the New Right Agenda* (Vancouver: New Star Books, 1988); Maude Barlow, *Parcel of Rogues* (Toronto: Key Porter Books, 1991); and Mel Hurtig, *The Betrayal of Canada* (Toronto: Stoddart, 1991).
31. David J. Elkins, *Beyond Sovereignty: Territory and Political Economy in the Twenty-First Century* (Toronto: University of Toronto Press, 1995) takes the position that the very concept of territory is increasingly outmoded.
32. Donald Creighton, *Canada's First Century* (Toronto: Macmillan, 1970), and George Grant, *Lament for a Nation: The Defeat of Canadian Nationalism* (Toronto: McClelland and Stewart, 1965). Northrop Frye notes that Canada passed from a pre-national to a post-national phase without ever having become a nation, in his Conclusion to Carl F. Klinck, ed., *The Literary History of Canada: Canadian Literature in English* (Toronto: University of Toronto Press, 1976).
33. Tom Keating, "The State, the Public and the Making of Canadian Foreign Policy," in Robert Jackson et al., eds., *Contemporary Canadian Politics: Readings and Notes* (Scarborough: Prentice-Hall Canada, 1987); Elizabeth Riddell-Dixon, "State Autonomy and Canadian Foreign Policy: The Case of Deep Seabed Mining," *Canadian Journal of Political Science* (June 1988), pp. 297–317.
34. Williams, "Regions within Region: Continentalism Ascendant."
35. For example, Wallace Clement, *Continental Corporate Power* (Toronto: McClelland and Stewart, 1977); Gordon Laxer, *Open for Business: The Roots of Foreign Ownership in Canada* (Don Mills: Oxford University Press, 1989); and Levitt, *Silent Surrender*.

36. As a boy, Mulroney ingratiated himself with the U.S. owner of the Tribune company, Col. Robert McCormick, and sang for him whenever he came to town. Some critics have said that Mulroney never shed this deferential attitude toward the United States. See L. Ian MacDonald, *Mulroney: The Making of the Prime Minister* (Toronto: McClelland and Stewart, 1984), p. 31, and John Sawatsky, *Mulroney: The Politics of Ambition* (Toronto: Macfarlane Walter & Ross, 1991), p. 13.

FURTHER READING

Barlow, Maude. *Parcel of Rogues*. Toronto: Key Porter Books, 1991.

Barlow, Maude, and Bruce Campbell. *Take Back the Nation*. Toronto: Key Porter Books, 1991.

Cameron, Duncan, ed. *The Free Trade Papers*. Toronto: Lorimer, 1986.

———. *The Free Trade Deal*. Toronto: Lorimer, 1988.

Campbell, Robert, and Leslie Pal. *The Real Worlds of Canadian Politics*, 2nd ed. Peterborough: Broadview Press, 1991.

Canada. *Foreign Direct Investment in Canada* (Gray Report). Ottawa: Supply and Services, 1972.

———. *Report of the Royal Commission on the Economic Union and Development Prospects for Canada*. Ottawa: Supply and Services, 1984.

Canada Among Nations. Annual. Toronto: Lorimer.

Chodos, R., et al. *Canada and the Global Economy*. Halifax: Lorimer, 1995.

Clarkson, Stephen. *Canada and the Reagan Challenge*, updated ed. Toronto: Lorimer, 1985.

Clement, Wallace. *Continental Corporate Power*. Toronto: McClelland and Stewart, 1977.

Crean, S.M. *Who's Afraid of Canadian Culture?* Don Mills: General Publishing, 1976.

Creighton, Donald. *Canada's First Century*. Toronto: Macmillan, 1970.

Crispo, John, ed. *Free Trade: The Real Story*. Toronto: Gage, 1988.

Dewitt, David, and John Kirton. *Canada as a Principal Power*. Toronto: Wiley, 1983.

Doern, Bruce, and Brian Tomlin. *Faith and Fear: The Free Trade Story*. Toronto: Stoddart, 1991.

Drache, Daniel, and Duncan Cameron. *The Other Macdonald Report*. Toronto: Lorimer, 1985.

Drache, Daniel, and Meric Gertler, eds. *The New Era of Global Competition: State Policy and Market Power*. Montreal: McGill–Queen's University Press, 1991.

Elkins, David J. *Beyond Sovereignty: Territory and Political Economy in the Twenty-First Century*. Toronto: University of Toronto Press, 1995.

Flaherty, David, and Frank E. Manning, eds. *The Beaver Bites Back? American Popular Culture in Canada*. Montreal: McGill–Queen's University Press, 1993.

Gordon, Walter. *A Choice for Canada*. Toronto: McClelland and Stewart, 1966.

Granatstein, J.L., and Robert Bothwell. *Pirouette: Pierre Trudeau and Canadian Foreign Policy*. Toronto: University of Toronto Press, 1990.

Granatstein, J.L., and Norman Hillmer. *For Better or Worse: Canada and the United States in the 1990s*. Mississauga: Copp Clark Pitman, 1991.

Grant, George. *Lament for a Nation: The Defeat of Canadian Nationalism*. Toronto: McClelland and Stewart, 1965.

Hardin, Herschel. *Closed Circuits*. Vancouver: Douglas & McIntyre, 1985.

Hart, Michael. *Decision at Midnight: Inside the Canada–U.S. Free Trade Negotiations*. Vancouver: University of British Columbia Press, 1995.

Laxer, Gordon. *Open for Business: The Roots of Foreign Ownership in Canada*. Don Mills: Oxford University Press, 1989.

McDonald, Marci. *Yankee Doodle Dandy*. Toronto: Stoddart, 1995.

Mahant, Edelgard, and Graeme Mount. *An Introduction to Canadian-American Relations*, 2nd ed. Scarborough: Nelson Canada, 1989.

Nossal, K.R. *The Politics of Canadian Foreign Policy*, 2nd ed. Scarborough: Prentice-Hall Canada, 1989.

Raboy, Marc. *Missed Opportunities: The Story of Canada's Broadcasting Policy*. Montreal: McGill–Queen's University Press, 1990.

Thomas, David, ed. *Canada and the United States: Differences That Count*. Peterborough: Broadview Press, 1993.

Warnock, John. *Free Trade and the New Right Agenda*. Vancouver: New Star Books, 1988.

Williams, Glen. *Not for Export: The International Competitiveness of Canadian Manufacturing*, 3rd ed. Toronto: McClelland and Stewart, 1994.

Wolfe, Morris. *Jolts: The TV Wasteland and the Canadian Oasis*. Toronto: Lorimer, 1985.

PART 4

Linking People to Government

Having established Canada's constitutional and societal environment, we are ready to examine Canadian politics as such. The three traditional elements of Canadian politics are the electoral system, political parties, and pressure groups, each of which, along with the election campaign, is discussed in its own chapter in the following section. But the context of values, attitudes, opinions (and how they are acquired), and patterns of political participation in which these three familiar institutions operate must also be examined. Moreover, no one can deny the ubiquitous importance of the mass media and public opinion polls in linking people to government. Thus we begin with chapters on the Canadian political culture, and political socialization, the mass media, and public opinion polls.

Chapter 13

The CANADIAN POLITICAL Culture

Most Canadians think they live in the best country on earth, but they do not get overly excited by national symbols like the flag or "O Canada." Others would prefer to live in an independent Quebec and some would not object to becoming part of the United States. Canadians have historically looked upon the state as a benevolent force, although recent surveys indicate widespread disrespect for all institutions in society, including government. The Meech Lake Accord was drawn up behind closed doors, and Canadians have since demanded more meaningful participation in the country's constitutional affairs.

All these phenomena and countless others are encompassed in the concept of **political culture**, which can be defined as the sum total of the political or politically relevant values, beliefs, attitudes, and orientations in a society. Vague and elusive as these values and attitudes may be, they are thought by most political scientists to influence what is done within a political system, and the discipline therefore does its best to identify them.

Political culture includes feelings people have toward the overall political community of Canada—reaction to national symbols (flag, anthem, Constitution) and feelings of patriotism, nationalism, and pride (or the lack thereof), including the question of how people feel toward their province as opposed to the whole country. A second aspect of political culture involves beliefs regarding the role of the state—how large a part Canadians want it to play in their lives and the kinds of policies it should adopt. Another variable consists of orientations to the decision-making apparatus. Are people aware of it, and to what extent do they want to control it? How do Canadians feel, in general, about the police, the bureaucracy, the courts, and the politicians? Do citizens trust them? Alternatively, do people feel that their participation in the political system can make any difference? That is, do Canadians have a sense of **political efficacy**? And to what extent do they participate? Patterns of actual participation can also be considered part of political culture.

Given the breadth of the political culture concept, political scientists use two principal methods of identifying its ingredients, both of which we will rely on here.[1] One is to survey individual Canadians and ask them about their attitudes and values. If and when such values and attitudes are widely shared by individuals, they can be said to constitute the collective political culture. A second approach is to develop an understanding of the political culture from observing the operation of the political system and society more generally. This can be achieved, for example, from a reading of history and literature and from a study of government decisions and political institutions.

This chapter will focus on the Canadian commitment to democracy, distinguish between Canadian and U.S. political values, attempt to identify other aspects of the Canadian national identity, discuss the concept of subcultures or "limited identities," and examine patterns of Canadian political participation. While political culture is usually considered to be fairly stable, it will also be necessary to sketch how in the Canadian case it seems to be changing.

THE TRADITIONAL CANADIAN POLITICAL CULTURE
Democracy

The first conclusion that emerges from a quest for Canadian political values is that almost all Canadians believe in **democracy**. The preamble to the Canadian Charter of Rights and Freedoms acknowledges democracy to be a foremost value in the country when it speaks of Canada as a "free and democratic society," but the Charter is not particularly enlightening about what this means. Definitions of democracy in the modern Western world usually include the elements of popular sovereignty, political equality, political freedom, and majority rule.[2]

POPULAR SOVEREIGNTY

Popular sovereignty means that the people have the final say, which in large, modern political systems usually takes the form of elections at certain specified intervals. At the federal and provincial levels in Canada, the Constitution requires that elections be held at least every five years, and tradition usually reduces this to four. For most Canadians, this is a sufficient opportunity for the exercise of popular sovereignty, although few would be content with anything less. Some states have a tradition of plebiscites or referenda, but they are largely foreign to the Canadian mentality. Only three national referenda have occurred since 1867, although the incidence is slightly higher at the provincial and municipal levels. At least in the past, Canadians cherished representative democracy in which elected officials and appointed authorities made decisions on their behalf.

Popular sovereignty is thus normally exercised in periodic elections, which are, more than anything, mere opportunities to select those who will be responsible for the big political decisions over the next four years or so on behalf of the whole population. As pointed out in Chapter 17, specific policy mandates are rare. Needless to say, it is an element of the law-abiding nature of most Canadians that everyone recognize the legitimacy of the election results and accept this expression of the popular will, however misguided it might seem. While Canadians allow many public officials like judges to be appointed, a consensus now exists that the Senate should become an elected body.

POLITICAL EQUALITY

Given the significance of elections as the means of implementing the principle of popular sovereignty, a second aspect of the Canadian conception of democracy is that everyone is equal on election day. In essence, this means that every person has one vote and no more than one vote, which is precisely what the Canada Elections Act provides and the Charter of Rights and Freedoms guarantees. It is only in relatively recent times, however, that Canada has met this ideal, and at one time or another in the past several groups were excluded: women, those without property, and various ethnic groups, including aboriginal Canadians.

The principle of one person–one vote is a minimal expression of **political equality**. A major deviation from the ideal occurs if constituencies are not divided among provinces on the basis of "representation by population." Chapter 15 reveals significant deviations in this respect. Another discrepancy occurs if constituencies are not of equal population size within a province, which is also a considerable problem because of Canada's huge uninhabited spaces. These are issues that concern political scientists more than the general public, but are of increasing interest to the courts as well.

It should also be said that even if every vote carried exactly equal weight, there is considerable room for political inequality in the electoral system. Political parties in Canada are to a large extent privately financed, and it may well be that those who contribute money to a party or candidate expect something in return. Thus, those who have the resources to help finance elections are likely to have more influence than those who merely vote. Beyond election day itself, tremendous inequalities in political influence begin to emerge, such as in pressure group activity. Such nonelectoral inequalities, however, are beyond the scope of political equality as a bare ingredient of the definition of democracy.

POLITICAL FREEDOM

Just as the 1982 Charter of Rights and Freedoms enhanced protection of aspects of popular sovereignty and political equality, it also provided an explicit constitutional statement of **political freedom** in Canada, as noted in Chapter 5:

> Everyone has the following fundamental freedoms:
> (a) freedom of conscience and religion;
> (b) freedom of thought, belief, opinion and expression, including freedom of the press and other media of communication;
> (c) freedom of peaceful assembly; and
> (d) freedom of association.

That document did not create these political freedoms, however; it basically provided a new means of enforcing them—using the courts to invalidate legislation that infringed civil liberties rather than having to persuade politicians to do so. Whether or not the Charter will significantly strengthen these freedoms, it is interesting to note to what extent they were respected or violated before its adoption.

That political freedoms were a longstanding part of the Canadian political culture, recognized by governmental authorities as well as by the general public, can be seen in the relatively small number of cases where they were seriously infringed. Three of these occurred at the federal level.[3] The first interference with freedom of speech or assembly had to do with section 98 of the Criminal Code prohibiting "unlawful associations." It was introduced after the 1919 Winnipeg General Strike and not repealed until 1936. The language of section 98 was sufficiently wide "to encompass the extravagant rhetoric of a trade-union meeting," and was used by the police to spy on unions, socialist and social democratic organizations, ethnic clubs and schools. The Communist Party was a particular target, and many party members were imprisoned or deported.[4] The second case involved the incarceration and/or deportation of Canadians of Japanese extraction during the Second World War, depriving this group of personal liberty, property, and livelihood, as well as freedom of expression.[5] The third example, the invocation of the War Measures Act in 1970, outlawed support for the FLQ, but was used to imprison over 400 nonviolent Quebec separatists who had no connection to that organization.[6]

The use of such measures on even three occasions raises the question of how committed the political authorities are to the principle of political freedom. Furthermore, the overwhelming popular support given to the implementation of such measures indicates a rather superficial commitment to political freedom on the part of the population at large. This relates to the strong Canadian feeling of deference to authority, which is discussed below. While Canadians normally believe in political freedom, therefore, they seem prepared to let the authorities restrain such individual or group liberty at the least threat of violence.

Violations of political freedom have been more common at the provincial level, especially during the authoritarian regime of Maurice Duplessis in Quebec and with the peculiarities of the Aberhart government in Alberta, as discussed in Chapter 5. The commitment to political freedom of more recent provincial authorities at first sight seems uncertain, when in 1981–82 certain premiers insisted that the "notwithstanding" clause be inserted into the Charter. Either federal or provincial governments can override the political freedoms guaranteed in the Charter merely by admitting that intention. On the other hand, some premiers felt that the traditional means of protecting civil liberties was superior to turning the function over to the courts. In the first 13 years after adoption of the Charter, the Quebec sign law provided the most controversial exercise of the notwithstanding clause, an indication either that the authorities are otherwise committed to political freedoms or else that they believe their electorates would not tolerate such infringements.

MAJORITY RULE

The Canadian conception of democracy also incorporates the notion of **majority rule**, that is, in case of dispute, the larger number takes precedence over the smaller number. This principle is generally accepted in elections and in legislatures that result from elections. On the other hand, it is sometimes felt necessary to protect certain minorities from the actions of the majority, so that specific minority rights are given constitutional protection. Roman Catholic and Protestant minority education rights were recognized in the Constitution Act, 1867, as were French- and English-minority language rights in the federal and Quebec legislatures and courts. Extension of these rights to Manitoba and their subsequent removal and resurrection were discussed in Chapter 8.

Over the past 13 years, Canada has extended minority rights in the Constitution to a considerable degree. The 1982 Charter of Rights guaranteed French and English language rights in all parts of the federal and New Brunswick governments, as well as French and English minority-language education in parts of all provinces where numbers warrant. The Charter also introduced the concept of constitutional equality rights for women (not actually a minority), and prohibited federal or provincial discrimination against minorities. The fact that the notwithstanding clause can be used to override minority rights other than those dealing with language or gender indicates that certain rights were considered to be more sacred than others, and that majority rule can still apply in certain cases. But women and Charter-based minorities—official language, other ethnic, and aboriginal minorities—have all used their new constitutional status to protect and promote their own interests.

Thus it is safe to say that almost every Canadian would claim democracy to be a fundamental political value of the country, and would support the four main ingredients identified. Canadian governments, both before and after 1982, have probably had as respectable records in refraining from the violation of democratic principles as any in the world. Nevertheless, given the fact that popular sovereignty is only exercised every four years or so, and given the limited scope of political equality, the apparent ease with which governments can violate fundamental freedoms, and the tension between majority rule and minority rights, the extent to which democracy is indeed a fundamental Canadian value should not be overstated.

Distinguishing between Canadian and American Values

Once beyond the consensus on democracy, it is difficult to find widespread agreement on other Canadian political values. One approach that bears promise, however, is to contrast widely held Canadian values with those of the United States. Of course, Canadian and American values are very much alike, and not all residents are conscious of them, whether similar or different. But a rich academic literature exists on this subject that is generally supported by public opinion polls when the attempt is made to survey the values of the mass population. The key proponent of this approach is the American sociologist, Seymour Martin Lipset, who has consolidated his thoughts on the subject in his book *Continental Divide*.[7] In Lipset's analysis, these differences have their foundation in the revolutionary origins of the United States and the "counter-revolutionary" (i.e., reaction against that revolution) origins of Canada.

Many have made the point that while the American Declaration of Independence lists the objectives of "life, liberty and the pursuit of happiness," Canada's 1867 Constitution Act talks about "peace, order and good government." Lipset goes on from this point to outline his basic distinction as follows: "Canada has been and is a more class-aware, elitist, law-abiding, statist, collectivity-oriented, and particularistic (group-oriented) society than the United

States."[8] Among Canadian commentators on the subject, Pierre Berton has noted that Canadians are law-abiding, peaceful, orderly, deferential toward authority, cautious, elitist, moralistic, tolerant, diffident, and unemotional.[9] For example, when U.S. President George Bush spoke of wanting to make the United States into a "kinder, gentler" society, many observers immediately thought of Canada. This approach leads us to identify five basic Canadian values that can be distinguished from those in the United States.

BALANCE BETWEEN INDIVIDUALISM AND COLLECTIVISM

If there is a value other than democracy to which most Canadians adhere, it is probably that of **individualism**, liberalism, or capitalism, often expressed as the sanctity of private enterprise or individual economic freedom. The general principle is widely shared that those with the greatest talent or those who work hardest should reap the benefits of their abilities and/or labour. Among these benefits are freedom of movement and freedom to spend the income accumulated as one wishes. The extent of such commitment can be best gauged, however, in comparison with the United States.

While both countries have "mixed economies" today—that is, a combination of private enterprise and government involvement—the United States remains the world's last stronghold of liberalism or individualism with a relatively smaller public sector than other modern states. This is only to be expected, given its revolutionary origins—revolting against an oppressive foreign government—and its self-proclaimed role in recent times as the leader of capitalist and anti-communist forces.[10] Canada, on the other hand, has been less hostile toward public intervention and more inclined to rely on government. This is partly because of the geographical environment of the Canadian political system, and the U.S. threat, as seen in Chapters 6 and 12, but it also stems from the basic Canadian value of **collectivism**, or community, a value derived in the first instance from the French feudal system and the arrival of the United Empire Loyalists. Both founding groups (to say nothing of a similar value shared by aboriginal Canadians) saw society not as a mass of grasping, ambitious individuals, but as an organic community in which all people—high and low—had their place and did their respective part to contribute to the welfare of the whole.

The balance between capitalism and collectivism in Canada can be seen in Table 13.1, which shows that the public-sector share of the Canadian gross domestic product is now about 49 percent in terms of expenditures and about 44 percent in terms of revenue. This is still relatively low in current global terms, but Canada is in an almost exactly intermediate position relative to the other Western democracies. The table also indicates that Canada occupies a similar ranking with respect to government employment as a percent of total labour force and government social expenditures as a percent of gross domestic product.

Thus, while Canadians might instinctively claim a commitment to capitalism and might still be less reliant on the state than many other countries, it would be more accurate to say that the accumulation of public demands has given Canada an economy almost evenly divided between private and public sectors. Chapter 10 noted certain exceptional cases where even capitalists demand government action, while the middle and working classes and the poor have also demanded much government intervention over the years.

TABLE 13.1 Government Employment as Percent of Total Labour Force, Government Social Expenditure as Percent of GDP, and Government Expenditure and Revenue as Percent of GDP

Govt. Employment as % of Total Labour Force, 1993		Govt. Social Expenditure as % of GDP, 1986		Govt. Expenditure & Revenue as % of GDP, 1993		
					Rev.	Exp.
Sweden	32.4	Belgium	34.9	Sweden	59.5	64.5
Denmark	31.1	France	34.2	Denmark	57.3	58.2
Norway	28.7	Denmark	33.9	Netherlands	54.1	55.3
Finland	24.8	Sweden	32.0	Finland	53.2	56.1
France	24.3	Netherlands	30.7	Norway	55.3	52.9
New Zealand	22.1	Austria	28.8	Belgium	49.7	54.6
Austria	21.0	Italy	26.4	Italy	46.2	52.6
Canada	**20.7**	Ireland	26.1	Luxembourg	52.9	45.0
Belgium	19.3	Germany	25.2	France	47.0	50.9
Iceland	18.5	Norway	24.8	Austria	48.6	48.4
Australia	17.3	Finland	23.8	**Canada**	**43.7**	**49.2**
Italy	16.1	**Canada**	**22.3**	Germany	45.5	45.5
Spain	15.0	New Zealand	21.0	Greece	39.9	47.1
Germany	14.9	U.K.	20.6	Ireland	39.8	41.4
U.S.	14.5	Switzerland	20.5	U.K.	37.9	42.0
Ireland	14.2	Greece	19.5	Portugal	37.6	39.3
Portugal	13.6	Australia	18.4	Spain	38.6	38.9
Netherlands	12.8	U.S.	18.2	Switzerland	36.0	36.7
Switzerland	12.0	Spain	17.0	Iceland	35.9	34.9
Luxembourg	10.8	Japan	16.0	Australia	33.1	36.9
Japan	5.9			U.S.	31.7	35.8
				Japan	34.0	25.9

Source: OECD in Figures (*1989 edition for column two*). © OECD, 1995. *Reproduced by the permission of the OECD.*

Canada is generally less collectivist than western Europe, and the difference between the two North American countries should not be overstated, but much concrete evidence of a significant variation exists. The extent of federal and provincial Crown corporations, including broadcasting, transportation, electricity and other resources, is unheard of south of the border; the Canadian public health insurance system stands out in great contrast to that of the United States; the Canadian social security system is considered much more adequate; and taxes are generally higher in order to finance such collective activity. In just about every policy field, in fact, the extent of government intervention is greater in Canada than in the United States—labour legislation, agricultural marketing boards, and environmental regulation being further examples.[11] Canada has been called a more caring society and a "public-enterprise" country.[12] Two other differences between the two countries are that individual property rights, so valued in the United States, are not guaranteed in the Canadian Constitution; and that while private American individuals and corporations are generous philanthropists, Canadians prefer to have the government fund charitable causes.[13]

PARTICULARISM AND TOLERANCE

A second difference in the basic values of the two countries has to do with the distinction between *universalism* and **particularism**, leading many to argue that pluralism is a more appropriate description of Canada than the United States. This distinction is commonly expressed in terms of the melting pot and the mosaic: immigrants to the United States are urged to become unhyphenated Americans, whereas Canada encourages the retention of cultural particularisms. Sometimes this Canadian heterogeneity is simply called tolerance, and sometimes it is linked to the recognition of group rights as opposed to individual rights. The distinctiveness of the French-Canadian Roman Catholic community was the original basis of this value, but it has now spread to policies of multiculturalism and recognition of other group rights even in the Constitution. As noted in Chapter 9, multiculturalism means encouraging the retention of ethnic cultures rather than trying to assimilate all newcomers into some kind of homogeneous Canadianism. This official policy is seen as a means of enriching and enlivening the country, encouraging new Canadians to feel at home, promoting tolerance and minimizing discrimination, and perhaps enhancing Canada's contribution to world harmony. Lipset notes, however, that an ethnic revival has occurred in many countries, including the United States, and even there the ideal of the melting pot is being replaced by that of the mosaic.[14] He is not the only one to suggest that the two countries no longer present sharp contrasts in this respect.[15]

Particularism might be extended to women in the sense that they, like minorities, generally benefit from more advanced legislation in Canada than in the United States. It could also be seen in terms of acknowledging the existence of social classes. Americans have even less class-consciousness than Canadians, being imbued with the belief that through hard work anyone can make it to the top, and far more Americans than Canadians feel they belong to the middle class. All of this affects the tolerance of unions, which is much greater in Canada, because middle-class America sees no need for them. Particularism also has a territorial dimension—the fact that Canadian provinces are much stronger than the American states. Decentralization in Canada is accompanied by stronger regional or provincial loyalties and identities, due again to the example set by Quebec. Finally, American universalism can also be seen in its foreign policy, which would brook no compromise with "evil empires," whereas Canada has often played a useful negotiating role on the international scene because of the lessons of compromise and tolerance learned at home.[16]

ELITISM, HIERARCHY, AND DEFERENCE TO AUTHORITY

In certain respects, Canada is a more *elitist* society than the United States. That is, Canadians recognize the general superiority of high-status people and their society is characterized more by *hierarchy*—descending levels of authority. Canada was much slower than the United States to extend the vote to all males regardless of property (although American blacks had trouble exercising their franchise over the next 100 years!); until recently Canada allowed British subjects who were not Canadian citizens to vote; and at least in the past, a smaller proportion of Canadians advanced to postsecondary education than in the United States.[17] Some argue that Canadian elitism and hierarchy come in part from the monarchical and feudal traditions, which contain the idea of an organic community made up of people of different status. These values were reinforced by the two dominant churches in Canadian history, Roman Catholic and Anglican, which recognize priests, bishops, archbishops (as well as cardinals and popes in the former case) in a great hierarchy between ordinary mortals and God. Americans, on the other hand, exalting the sovereignty of "We, the People," revolted against the monarchical system and, when it came to religion, turned to anti-elitist, Protestant sects where power resided in the local congregation.

Related to elitism and hierarchy is another fundamental difference between Canadian and American values: the much greater **deference to authority** in Canadian society.[18] Canadians demonstrate greater respect toward the law, judges, police, religious leaders, and many others with "legitimate power." Peace, order, and good government rather than individual liberty is the Canadian ideal, and many observers have noted that Canada is probably the only country where a police officer is a national symbol—certainly a contrast to the U.S. hero, Horatio Alger, the self-made man. Unlike Americans, it is not part of the Canadian psyche to be instinctively suspicious of the state; indeed, Canadians have not seen the government in terms of an alien imposition, but as the authorized agent to respond to their individual and collective demands. Such respect for authority and trust in government goes so far as to permit much greater government secrecy in Canada than in the United States, to be less concerned about the admissibility of evidence obtained illegally by the Crown,[19] and even to allow the RCMP to engage in a wide range of illegal activities such as opening mail. To recognize the pervasive presence of the state is to acknowledge, perhaps unconsciously, the significance of the bureaucracy.[20]

Deference is related to other values already mentioned. Americans are the epitome of the "Protestant ethic," that is, members of Protestant sects that emphasize that hard work in this life is the key to entering the next. But in their frenzy to get ahead at all costs, individualistic, competititive, and achievement-oriented Americans may find it necessary to bend or break the law. Canadians, less obsessed with material success, are more likely to obey a law even if they do not like it. Crime rates are considerably lower in Canada, gun control laws are stronger, and the drug problem is much less severe. Furthermore, the United States has many more lawyers per capita, and Americans are more litigious by nature, having a much greater propensity to take disputes to court.

Respect for authority and the law is related to the settlement of the western frontier. In the Canadian West, the law and enforcement of the law by the RCMP preceded settlement, whereas in the violent American frontier, settlers arrived ahead of the law. This state of affairs not only provided Canada with a more peaceful settlement of its frontier (and, believe it or not, better treatment of its aboriginals), but reinforced the previously established respect for law and order.

EGALITARIANISM

In his earlier writings, Lipset argued that because Canada was more elitist, the United States was more egalitarian—that is, Americans treated everyone more equally. In his more recent work he admits that elitism and equality are not necessarily opposites,[21] that both are elements of the Canadian political culture, and that in some ways Canada is more *egalitarian* than the United States. One striking example is in the constitutional equality of women. In the United States the proposed Equal Rights Amendment did not pass, whereas at about the same time, Canada adopted a strong guarantee of gender equality (including affirmative action) in the 1982 Canadian Charter of Rights and Freedoms. Somewhat similarly, the health and welfare programs that flow from Canadian collectivism ensure a greater degree of equality for the poor and working classes. Canada extends this redistributive egalitarianism to have-not regions as well as have-not individuals through equalization payments and regional economic development programs. Even in the realm of higher education, Canada now appears to be more egalitarian than the United States, as seen in Figure 13.1.

Canadian egalitarianism is related to the comparative strength of class-consciousness, trade unions, and social democratic parties in the two countries. It can also be seen in a strong cooperative movement, stretching from Prairie grain elevators to Quebec's caisses populaires. Perhaps it also results from the feeling of noblesse oblige among those in the upper echelons of the hierarchy, the feudal concept that the lord was responsible for the well-being of his serfs. In any case, Lipset now argues that Canadians are more committed to "redistributive egalitarianism, while Americans place more emphasis on meritocratic competition and equality of opportunity." He also admits that while a higher proportion of Americans have had postsecondary education in the past, the United States has a greater hierarchy of educational institutions than is found in Canada.[22]

CAUTION, DIFFIDENCE, NONVIOLENCE, AND COLONIAL MENTALITY

A final value difference to emerge from the Lipset analysis, one that is both difficult to label and hard to prove, relates to Canadian diffidence, sometimes called a national inferiority complex. It includes a historical dependence on other countries, the acceptance of mediocrity, the lack of will to be truly exceptional or to stand out from the crowd, or the absence of a spirit of innovation and risk taking.[23] Canadians delight in the security of savings and in understatement. Of course there have been many Canadian "winners" in all walks of life, in whose accomplishments Canadians vicariously share: Margaret Atwood, Glenn Gould, Wayne Gretzky, Karen Kain, Keanu Reeves, and Bryan Adams, for example, in addition to Nobel Prize winners Frederick Banting, Lester Pearson, John Polanyi, and others. Canadians also claim those who have been lost to other countries such as Joni Mitchell and John

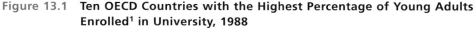

Figure 13.1   **Ten OECD Countries with the Highest Percentage of Young Adults Enrolled[1] in University, 1988**

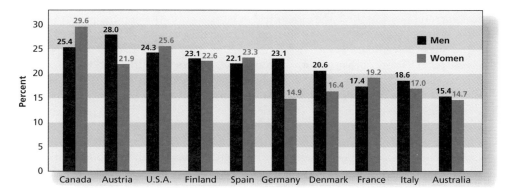

[1] Full-time and part-time enrolment converted to full-time equivalents. Population is those of theoretical university enrolment age (18–25 in Canada).
Source: OECD, 1992, from Statistics Canada, Canadian Social Trends *(Autumn 1993). Reproduced with the permission of the Minister of Supply and Services Canada, 1995.*

Kenneth Galbraith, and are proud of their exports to the U.S. media, including Robert MacNeil, Morley Safer, and Peter Jennings. But Canadians sometimes take satisfaction in being "beautiful losers"; they are obsessed with "survival" rather than success; they are especially good at deprecating themselves, and almost always think things American are superior. They are prudent and cautious, sober and solemn, as Pierre Berton says, and introverted, uncertain, and always questioning themselves. Most Canadians take quiet satisfaction in their accomplishments—a 1995 survey showed that 89 percent of Canadians felt proud when they saw the Canadian flag or heard the national anthem—but they are embarrassed to proclaim it aloud.[24]

Although Canada made major contributions to two world wars, Canadians are not a warlike people.[25] They abhor violence at home and abroad; they have no enemies, and their military establishment is minimal. Instead, they have tried to be peacemakers and peacekeepers in international relations, putting special emphasis on the United Nations (another "collective authority"), trying to reduce the militancy of the foreign policy of the United States in quiet, backroom diplomacy, and helping to remove the causes of war through assistance to the Third World.

Some observers take this point one step further and argue that it is primarily because of Canada's proximity to the United States and the "relentless American cultural penetration"[26] that the Canadian national identity is otherwise so fragile. Certainly, the Americanization of so much of Canadian society, partly the result of the Canadian colonial mentality, is a dominant characteristic of the country.

Other Basic Values

At least in the past, a set of four additional national characteristics based on geography, ethnicity, and political institutions have been considered part of the basic Canadian political value structure. Some of these were identified as basic constitutional principles in Chapter 2.

First, Canadians are a northern people, attached to the land.[27] To a large extent they enjoy the wilderness, relish four distinct seasons, including the cold, and are immensely proud of the beauty and variety of their natural surroundings, whether it is the Rocky Mountains, the Prairie wheatfields, the rugged Canadian Shield, or picturesque Atlantic fishing villages.[28]

Second, Canada is an officially bilingual country. French and English have been recognized as official languages, at least at the federal level, and since 1970 or so have become well established in national institutions. Governors general, prime ministers, ministers, Supreme Court judges, members of Parliament, and senior bureaucrats are increasingly expected to be able to function in both languages, and for those who arrive at such high office without such capability, second-language training is available at public expense. Federal publications, signs, services, and ceremonies all reflect this policy, and while many oppose it, others see it as a key feature distinguishing Canada from the United States.[29] The companion policy of official multiculturalism has already been covered in terms of particularism.

Third, Canada is a federation, with a division of powers between two levels of government such that neither is subordinate to the other. This characteristic of government was adapted from the United States, but Canadian federalism has developed its own unique features, seen in Chapter 4, especially an extremely decentralized character. This has resulted from Quebec's promotion of provincial autonomy, with the governments of the other large, wealthy provinces following suit.

Canada's adoption of the British parliamentary system is a fourth prominent national characteristic. As noted in Chapter 2, Canada was the first country to combine federalism with the parliamentary system. Thus, both federal and provincial governments operate with a strong executive, a relatively weak legislative branch, and, until 1982, a judiciary that had very limited powers of judicial review. The recent addition to the Constitution of a Charter of Rights and Freedoms granting authority to the courts to invalidate legislation conflicting with the Charter is a U.S. anomaly grafted onto the British institutional trunk. Other than the Charter and the French civil code used in Quebec, the whole Canadian legal system is based on that of Britain, including the British common law.

One place to look for basic Canadian political values would be in the Constitution. Unfortunately, the Canadian Constitution has never included a statement of basic values beyond that of "peace, order and good government," but the "Canada Clause" in the Charlottetown Accord made such an attempt, which more or less confirms the values identified above.

···

FUNDAMENTAL CHARACTERISTICS OF CANADA, ACCORDING TO THE "CANADA CLAUSE" OF THE CHARLOTTETOWN ACCORD

- Democracy
- Parliamentary system of government
- Federal system of government

- Aboriginal peoples constitute one of three orders of government
- Quebec constitutes a distinct society within Canada
- Official bilingualism (official language minorities)
- Racial, ethnic, and cultural equality and diversity
- Individual and collective human rights and freedoms
- Equality of men and women
- Equality of the provinces, but recognition of diversity

When pollster Allan Gregg asked ordinary Canadians in 1995 what they thought was distinctive about Canada and Canadians, he received much the same results as we discussed above: nonviolence, tolerance of minorities, humane treatment of poor and disadvantaged, official bilingualism, history and climate, and reluctance to boast.[30] In short, Canadians have traditionally seen themselves inhabiting a sprawling, decentralized country of great natural beauty and variety and an officially bilingual and multicultural society characterized by severe regional and ethnic strains, which fuses the British parliamentary system with American federalism. It has a restrained commitment to democracy combined with deferential and elitist traits, and prefers a strong government. This reflects the strength of social democratic sentiments and has resulted in redistributive egalitarianism. Moreover, in an international reflection of its domestic character, Canada is a peaceful, constructive member of the world community.

CANADA'S CHANGING POLITICAL CULTURE

As Canada approaches the turn of the century, many aspects of this traditional value structure seem to be changing. Different concepts of democracy are emerging, the distinction between Canadian and American values appears to be declining, and some of the other values identified above have diminishing support. Much of this transformation can be attributed to the presence of the United States, directly or indirectly; some of it is part of a worldwide change in political values; and some is not so easily explained.

As far as democracy is concerned, the 1990s saw an upsurge in interest in the means of more direct popular participation. The most common prescription in this regard is the referendum, in which legislators would be guided or bound by frequent referrals to the electorate as a whole. Quebec has used this device twice on the question of sovereignty; certain other provinces now require it for approval of constitutional amendments; and some have prescribed its use for other issues such as significant tax increases. Many observers believe that since the Charlottetown Accord was put to a popular vote in 1992 any other major constitutional changes will require a national referendum as well, even though this is not required by the constitutional amending formula.

Direct participation also includes the concept of the "initiative," in which legislators respond to demands expressed by voters in the form of a petition, although this device has not made much headway. The third aspect of this "new democracy" is the "recall," in which a certain proportion of electors in a constituency sign a petition forcing their member of Parliament to resign. This device seems to be gaining popularity, although at the time of writing, it has been legislated only in B.C.

Another aspect of dissatisfaction with the traditional notion of democracy is the now commonly argued idea that elected members of Parliament should vote on certain issues in accordance with the views of their constituents rather than follow the party line. Even assuming that it would be technically possible to discover the majority opinion in a legislator's constituency, however, this argument has not yet been advanced with sufficient strength to alter existing practices. This position does not always influence the legislative behaviour of even Reform Party MPs, but defections from the party line, even in the Liberal case, were more common after 1993 than ever before.

Several of the Canadian values described above emanate from British, United Empire Loyalist, or French feudal origins and may lose their salience as these influences fade into the past or are diluted by immigration from other parts of the world. The distinctions between Canadian and American values are also threatened in at least three ways by the influence of the United States on Canada. First, given the extent of U.S. control over Canada and Canadian exposure to the United States, values implicit in that country's popular culture, as transmitted by television, movies, books, magazines and music, in business, and the military, are likely to have some impact on those north of the border. It is debatable whether distinctive Canadian values can withstand the homogenizing force of modern technology, especially that originating from the south.[31] Second, Canadian nationalists see all these influences increasing under the Free Trade Agreement and NAFTA, and fear that the distinctiveness of their values will suffer as a result. Third, some observers such as Lipset feel that the adoption of a U.S.-style Charter of Rights and Freedoms will have a profound effect on diminishing distinctive Canadian values. The Charter places the power of the state under judicial restraint and "makes Canada a more individualistic and litigious culture."[32]

In a country that articulates its basic values so diffidently to start with, these powerful threats are not to be taken lightly. The situation is only exacerbated when a major party leader, Preston Manning, takes much of his script from south of the border. There are several recent indications that support for collectivism and feelings of deference in Canada are already on the decline, one of which was the refusal to endorse the Charlottetown Accord, a product of the political elite.[33] Although it cannot be blamed entirely on Americans, the new obsession with government debts and deficits at both federal and provincial levels has seriously eroded social programs and many other public interventions into the private sector. Privatization of Crown corporations and deregulation have become rampant. Canadians have also developed an increasingly negative attitude toward politicians and political parties, as can be seen in Figures 13.2 and 13.3.

Even the other distinctive Canadian values mentioned have recently been challenged.[34] Some commentators contend that Canadians have not really valued the land, but rather raped it; that bilingualism is not so much a source of pride as of discord; that Canadians do not show much tolerance toward racial minorities now that such groups are increasingly numerous and visible; that its governmental institutions have lost their capacity to make decisions quickly; that the Trudeau and Mulroney governments destroyed much of Canadians' respect for and trust in government authority; and that the ideological objectives of the Mulroney government weakened the public sector and rendered impotent the collectivist, social democratic streak of the Canadian character. As far as equality is concerned, Canadians still appear to treasure equal access to health care and perhaps public schools, but they show little concern when politicians reduce redistributive social programs.

Figure 13.2 **Trust in Politicians**

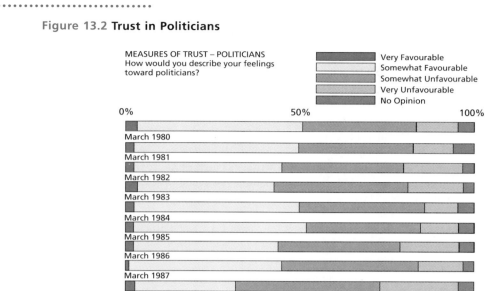

MEASURES OF TRUST – POLITICIANS
How would you describe your feelings
toward politicians?

- Very Favourable
- Somewhat Favourable
- Somewhat Unfavourable
- Very Unfavourable
- No Opinion

0%　　　　　　　50%　　　　　　　100%

March 1980
March 1981
March 1982
March 1983
March 1984
March 1985
March 1986
March 1987
March 1990

Source: The Big Picture: What Canadians Think About Almost Everything, *by Allan Gregg and Michael Posner, published by Macfarlane Walter and Ross, Toronto, 1990. Reproduced with permission.*

Figure 13.3 **Trust in Government**

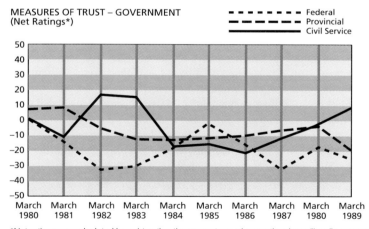

MEASURES OF TRUST – GOVERNMENT
(Net Ratings*)

- Federal
- Provincial
- Civil Service

| | March 1980 | March 1981 | March 1982 | March 1983 | March 1984 | March 1985 | March 1986 | March 1987 | March 1980 | March 1989 |

*Net ratings are calculated by subtracting the percentage who say they have "hardly any confidence" in those who run an institution from the percentage who say they have "a great deal" of confidence.

Source: The Big Picture: What Canadians Think About Almost Everything, *by Allan Gregg and Michael Posner, published by Macfarlane Walter and Ross, Toronto, 1990. Reproduced with permission.*

'LIMITED IDENTITIES': SUBCULTURES IN CANADA

Even before the recent pressures to change basic Canadian political values, the latter were submerged to some extent by regional, provincial, ethnic, and class variations. For generations, political scientists and historians in Canada have debated whether a pan-Canadian political culture really existed, or whether it made more sense to emphasize regional, provincial, ethnic, and class **subcultures** or **"limited identities."**[35] Subcultures are distinctive collections of values, beliefs, attitudes, and orientations held by smaller groups within the society. Given the strong influences of region, ethnicity, and class in Canadian society, it is not surprising that smaller clusters of values and attitudes based on these three factors would constitute subcultures supplementing the pan-Canadian values identified. In his study of the Canadian political culture, David Bell emphasizes that language and cultural divisions, regionalism, and class cleavages (as well as the omnipresence of the United States) are more than supplementary; they are dominant characteristics of the Canadian political culture and the "roots of disunity," retarding the development of more uniform values.[36]

Regional and Provincial Subcultures

Regional or provincial identities and loyalties, variations in attachment to national political values, variations in such attitudes as political efficacy and trust in government, and differences in party systems, political participation, and voting behaviour are all evidence of regional or provincial political subcultures.[37] Many of these subjects will be examined in later chapters, but a general description of each subculture can be provided now.

Canadians are frequently polled as to their respective federal and provincial loyalties. Table 13.2 indicates the results on this subject of a 1994 *Maclean's*/Decima poll. Ontarians were significantly more federally oriented than the residents of any other province or region, while Quebec and Newfoundland residents identified most with their province. In general, Western Canadians were more federally oriented than those in Atlantic provinces.

These figures can be taken to mean that Ontarians have the least defined concept of a provincial identity in Canada, and see themselves as Canadians who happen to be situated in Ontario. Quebeckers and Newfoundlanders have the strongest sense of being a "distinct society." The proud sense of history felt by the Maritime provinces is still evident, although it is restrained by a modern feeling of dependence on Ottawa and the rest of the country. The survey indicates that westerners are surprisingly federally oriented in spite of the fact that Alberta and British Columbia have increasingly strong self-images and that residents harbour feelings of **Western alienation**. Western alienation was defined in 1980 as follows:

> a regionally distinct political culture through and within which are expressed economic discontent, the rejection of a semi-colonial status within the Canadian state, antipathy towards Quebec and French-Canadian influence within the national government, the irritation of the West's partisan weakness within a succession of Liberal national governments, and the demand from provincial political elites for greater jurisdictional autonomy.[38]

TABLE 13.2 **Federal and Provincial Orientations of Canadians: "Do You Think of Yourself as a Canadian First or as a Citizen of Your Province?"**

	Canadian	*Provincial*
Newfoundland	39%	57%
Prince Edward Island	50%	44%
Nova Scotia	69%	27%
New Brunswick	64%	26%
Quebec	45%	49%
Ontario	90%	9%
Manitoba	77%	11%
Saskatchewan	82%	7%
Alberta	74%	16%
British Columbia	76%	17%
All Canada	72%	22%

Source: Maclean's, January 3, 1994. Used with permission.

Westerners also provide restrained support for the democratic principle of majority rule, which to them means that national policies are designed in the interests of central Canada. Many westerners also reject the existing decision-making structure in which the Senate does not give them sufficient voting strength to overcome Ontario's influence in other branches of government. Other studies of regional variations in Canadian political culture have shown that such differences are relatively pronounced on questions of federal party identification, but less marked in determining levels of political efficacy, participation, and ideological preferences on most policy issues.[39]

Ethnic Subcultures

French Canada provides the best example both of an ethnic subculture within Canada and the fact that values and attitudes can change over time. In the pre-1960 period, Quebec was extremely conservative in its attitudes and values, was heavily influenced by the Roman Catholic Church, had a low general level of education, and was less committed to the value of democracy than the rest of the country.[40] It was very inward-looking and obsessed with survival and with being left alone. Quebec remains a distinct ethnic subculture today, but its values have changed. It is still concerned with the preservation of the French language and culture, but no longer looks to the Church as a means of doing so. The Quebec provincial government has become the primary engine of French-Canadian "national" survival, and Quebeckers have become profoundly democratic. They now believe strongly in majority rule (at least within the province) and in political equality, for example, in regulating election contributions. French Canadians have become politically sophisticated, their culture has flourished, their attitudes have become more progressive than those of other Canadians on such issues as day care, abortion, and homosexuality, and they are becoming increasingly aggressive economically. A new francophone entrepreneurial elite is even confident of taking on the Americans under the Free Trade Agreement. For francophone Quebeckers, then, their distinctive provincial and ethnic subcultures coincide.[41] According to the 1995 *Maclean's* survey, however, 75 percent of Quebeckers reported feeling pride when they saw the Canadian flag or heard the national anthem.

New multicultural and aboriginal subcultures are also increasingly evident in Canada. Both groups have been passive until recently, neither articulating their demands strongly nor even participating actively as political candidates or voters. At the beginning of the 1990s, however, both subcultures suddenly became more self-confident and aggressive, demanding their place as party delegates, candidates, or participants in constitutional negotiations. Aboriginals have a distinct conception of their place in Canadian society and want to govern themselves, while the multicultural community wants to be a full participant in the overall political system.

Class Subcultures

Within the general Canadian political culture, different classes exhibit somewhat distinctive values, attitudes, and orientations, even where the individuals involved are lacking in class-consciousness. Attitudes of trust in government and feelings of political efficacy naturally decline from upper- to middle- to working-class groups and are lowest among the poor. It is also likely that the upper classes are less committed to communitarian and egalitarian values than the working classes and are more attached to elitism and hierarchy. In short, the upper classes have a political subculture distinguished by feelings of self-confidence, trust, participation and by demands for the retention of the status quo; the working classes have a political subculture characterized by alienation, lack of participation, and by demands for substantial economic reform. Most of the poor have dropped out of the political system entirely, evidence of a truly distinctive subculture.[42]

· ·

POLITICAL PARTICIPATION

Since many of the basic political values relate directly or indirectly to citizen participation in the political system, patterns of political participation can also be considered an aspect of political culture. *Political participation* consists of "those voluntary activities by citizens that are intended to influence the selection of government leaders or the decisions they make."[43] Numerous avenues of political participation exist, but actual participation takes effort, which not everyone is willing to exert, and which is partly related to the possession of political efficacy—a sense of political competence and a feeling that they can have some impact on the system. In a 1993 survey, for example, two-thirds of respondents complained that politics was too complicated for them to understand, that people like themselves had no say about what government did, and that government does not care about their opinions.[44] Participation also depends on the possession of such resources as time, money, and information. In the Canadian case, the opportunities for participation far exceed actual levels of involvement.

Electoral Participation

Voting on election day is a crucial aspect of democracy, as previously defined, and is the most common form of political participation in Canada. The voter turnout rate is also one of the few forms of participation that can be regularly and reliably measured. The overall average national turnout rate since 1900 has been 73 percent, or nearly three-quarters of those eligible to vote. The rate by province for each federal election between 1974 and 1993 is provided in Table 13.3. The 1993 rate appears to be lower than normal, perhaps due to the fact that a year-old voters' list—from the 1992 Referendum—was used. The number who voted is accurate, but the list of eligible voters was inflated because (1) an estimated 205 000 people on the 1992 list had died and (2) an estimated 1 617 384 people on the 1992 list had moved without asking to be deleted but had their names added under their new address. Thus, if these 1 822 384 people are subtracted from the 19 906 796 names of eligible voters in 1993, the real number would be 18 984 412, and the real turnout rate would be 73.0 percent—exactly the modern-day average.

Prince Edward Island stands out with an average turnout in recent federal elections of about 81 percent, while Saskatchewan, Ontario, and B.C. are in the 74–75 percent range. Quebec, Nova Scotia, and New Brunswick are slightly lower, at 73 percent, followed by Manitoba at 72 percent. Alberta, at 68 percent, the North at 62 percent, and Newfoundland, at 61 percent are substantially less participative. To some extent, these figures reflect varying degrees of interest in federal politics and loosely parallel the pattern of federal loyalties in Table 13.2 on the subject of regional subcultures. But these figures are also influenced by such factors as the degree of federal party competition within the province.

To see how voter turnout rates differ between federal and provincial elections, Table 13.4 reveals such rates in the elections in each province between 1970 and 1995. Here again, Prince Edward Island leads the nation, suggesting that in the small confines of that province, politics has a higher salience in residents' lives than elsewhere. Saskatchewan is second in provincial voter turnout too, again reflecting high degrees of party competition and public interest in politics. Quebeckers and Newfoundlanders turn out substantially more in provincial than federal elections, which is not surprising, given their greater interest in and loyalty to their respective provinces. Ontario stands out with a low provincial voter turnout, presumably because its residents are more federally oriented, as noted above. Conversely, Albertans turn out even less for provincial than federal elections. Alberta contains the only case in recent memory of a provincial election in which less than 50 percent of voters turned out at the polls, although this is common in municipal elections throughout the country.

TABLE 13.3 Percentage Voter Turnout, by Province, in Federal Elections, 1974–1993

Year	Ont.	Que.	N.S.	N.B.	Man.	B.C.	P.E.I	Sask.	Alta.	Nfld.	N.W.T.	Tot.
1974	74	67	74	71	70	72	80	72	67	57	64	71
1979	78	76	75	74	77	75	81	79	68	60	59	76
1980	72	68	72	71	69	71	79	71	61	59	40	69
1984	76	76	75	77	73	78	85	78	69	65	71	75
1988	75	75	75	76	75	79	85	78	75	67	73	75
1993	68	77	65	70	69	68	73	69	65	55	66	70
Average	74	73	73	73	72	74	81	75	68	61	62	73

Source: Reports of the Chief Electoral Officer. *Used with permission.*

TABLE 13.4 Percentage Voter Turnout Rate, by Province, in Provincial Elections, 1974–1994

											Average
P.E.I.	1974	82	1978	87	1982	78	1986	88	1989	83	1993	81	83.0
Sask.	1971	83	1975	80	1978	79	1982	84	1986	82	1991	83	81.8
Que.	1973	80	1976	85	1981	83	1985	76	1989	81	1994	82	81.2
N.B.	1970	81	1974	77	1978	76	1982	82	1987	82	1991	80	79.7
Nfld.	1975	73	1979	73	1982	78	1985	78	1989	81	1993	86	78.2
N.S.	1974	78	1978	78	1981	74	1984	68	1988	76	1993	75	74.8
B.C.	1972	69	1975	70	1979	69	1983	78	1986	77	1991	75	73.0
Man.	1973	78	1977	76	1981	72	1986	68	1988	74	1990	69	72.8
Ont.	1975	68	1977	66	1981	58	1985	62	1987	63	1990	64	63.5
Alta.	1975	60	1979	59	1982	66	1986	47	1989	54	1993	60	57.6

Source: Rand Dyck, Provincial Politics in Canada, *3rd ed. (Scarborough: Prentice-Hall Canada, 1995). Used with permission.*

In general terms, then, about 75 percent of Canadians vote in federal and provincial elections, with some significant provincial variations. The roughly 25 percent who do not vote have consistently been shown to be alienated from or uninformed about the political system; they are primarily made up of the poor and working classes. The 75 percent figure falls between the extremes of other countries, as revealed in Table 13.5. Canada is well above the United States in voter turnout, about the same as Britain, and behind many other states.

TABLE 13.5	Percentage Voter Turnout Rates in Eighteen Countries, 1980s		
Australia	94.3	Greece	82.0
Belgium	93.8	Ireland	74.2
Austria	91.5	United Kingdom	74.0
New Zealand	90.5	Spain	73.4
Italy	89.8	**Canada**	**73.3**
Sweden	89.1	Japan	71.4
France	86.2	India	62.0
Denmark	86.1	United States	54.3
Netherlands	83.4	Switzerland	47.5

Source: Royal Commission on Electoral Reform and Party Financing, Vol. I (Ottawa: Minister of Supply and Services Canada, 1991), pp. 52–53. Reproduced with permission of the Minister of Supply and Services Canada, 1995.

Within the 75 percent who do vote, we can distinguish other degrees possessed by the electoral involvement. As Chapter 17 indicates, the level of information of the typical voter should not be overestimated, and many who vote have paid little or no attention to the campaign. Even if around 80 percent claim to have exposed themselves to television or newspaper coverage of the election campaign, this figure falls to about 20 percent who closely follow politics on a daily basis between elections.[45]

A study of the 1984 election found that as a national average, voters could name 3.3 provincial premiers (out of ten) and 36 percent could define the concepts of left and right and place the NDP as the furthest left of the three main parties. The level of factual and conceptual knowledge increased with level of education and reading about politics in newspapers and magazines; significant regional variations were also evident, but viewing political programs on television was of negligible impact.[46]

Beyond those who cast an "informed vote," a smaller proportion of the electorate becomes actively involved in the election campaign. A small number attend all-candidates meetings; some work as enumerators, poll clerks, and deputy returning officers; some join a political party and vote at its local nomination meeting; some contribute money to political parties; some contribute time to a local candidate to do mailing, telephoning, or door-to-door canvassing; and a small number in each constituency become totally preoccupied with the local campaign. Members of this last group, including candidates themselves, are sometimes called "gladiators" as distinct from the great bulk of the population who are primarily "spectators."[47]

Table 13.6 indicates the number of individuals who contributed money to national parties and local candidates in 1993. Since some made contributions to both parties and candidates, a total of between 200 000 and 300 000 out of an electorate of 19 million, or between one and two percent, made financial contributions. This contrasts with the 13 percent who claim that they often or sometimes give money.[48]

TABLE 13.6 Numbers of Individuals Making Financial Contributions to National Parties and Local Candidates, 1993

	To Parties	To Candidates
PC	44 728	25 460
Liberal	41,058	32 907
NDP	65 301	12 367
Reform	49 488	25 211
BQ	29 084*	26 337
Total	229 659	122 282

*BQ figures include nonelection year 1994.

Sources: Report of the Chief Electoral Officer Respecting Election Expenses, *1993, and party returns; calculations by author. Used with permission.*

Nonelectoral Participation

The political participation of most Canadians peaks at election time, but many avenues are open between elections in which to make demands, demonstrate support, or otherwise become involved in the political process. Most Canadian political parties do not maintain reliable lists of party members, so it is impossible to say how many Canadians belong to a political party between elections. Ken Carty estimates this figure to be about 2.7 percent of the population,[49] and it is known that many people sign up before or during the campaign and then let their membership lapse.

Another means of political participation is to join a voluntary group, an action that some 60 percent of Canadians claim to do. As seen in Chapter 18, any group, whatever its primary orientation, can become a pressure group, so that membership in any group is potentially political. Even if the group itself takes a political turn, however, passive members rarely do more than send the occasional preprinted postcard to their MP or the prime minister. On the other hand, active executive and staff members of such groups may become highly involved in political campaigns. Even more initiative is required to form such a group, usually to protest against some political decision or lack of action at the municipal, provincial, or federal level.

Such group participation usually involves communicating with the authorities in routine ways, but occasionally it takes the form of peaceful demonstrations (locally or on Parliament Hill); sit-ins and other types of civil disobedience; and the rare case of violent protest. As noted above, Canadians are generally a peaceful lot, and instances of political violence are uncommon. The main historical incidents, all but one of which involved the loss of life, were the two Riel Rebellions of 1870 and 1885, the conscription riots in Quebec City in 1918, the Winnipeg General Strike of 1919, the Regina Riot of 1935, the various FLQ incidents of the 1960s culminating in the FLQ crisis of 1970, and the Mohawks' armed standoff at Oka in 1990.[50] In Table 13.7, an account of all such incidents between 1948 and 1982, indicates more widespread political violence in Canada, as would figures since 1982, especially those involving aboriginals.

Reprinted with permission.

Canadians can also participate politically between elections as individuals—writing or faxing letters to MPs or the prime minister, writing letters to the editors of newspapers, calling radio or television phone-in shows, signing petitions, or telephoning or meeting an MP. As with so many other aspects of political participation, however, it is difficult to obtain solid data on the degree of this category of individual involvement; one survey has reported two figures to be about 20 percent.[51] In general, few people take the initiative to do any of these things as individuals, so that upwards of 10 percent are completely disengaged politically and another 25 to 30 percent vote on election day and do nothing else.

TABLE 13.7	Instances of Political Violence in Canada, 1948–1982		
	Protest Demonstrations	*Riots*	*Deaths from Political Violence*
1948–67	27	29	8
1968–77	33	5	4
1978–82	13	0	0

Source: S.M. Lipset, Continental Divide *(New York: Routledge, 1990), p. 96. Used with permission.*

TABLE 13.8 Percentage Level of Participation in Selected Political Activities, 1993, by Occupation, Income, and Education

	Discuss Politics	Party Work	Sign Petition	March/ Rally	Sit-in
Occupation					
Blue Collar	75	4	71	26	9
White Collar	89	6	76	26	7
Professional/Managerial	86	9	78	37	10
Income					
Under $20 000	70	5	54	21	7
$20 000–39 999	80	5	69	24	8
$40 000–59 999	82	7	77	30	9
$60 000–69 999	87	9	76	27	10
$70 000 & over	87	12	79	30	7
Education					
Elementary or less	68	9	34	14	5
Some secondary	75	4	57	18	6
Complete secondary	82	8	69	19	6
Some university	82	7	78	32	10
University degree	86	7	86	45	13

Source: Mishler and Clarke, "Political Participation in Canada," p. 137. Used with permission.

One interesting question in this connection is the relationship between degree of participation and social status. Table 13.8 indicates five forms of participation broken down by level of income and education and occupational status. The table demonstrates that the degree of involvement increases with level of income and education and from blue-collar to white-collar to professional and managerial occupations. Possession of money provides the resources that facilitate high levels of participation. Such a pattern even exists for political protests, for students involved in such activities tend to be sons and daughters of the upper or upper-middle class. It should be added, however, that ethnicity, region, and religion do not usually seem to have a distinctive influence on political participation.[52] The middle-aged are somewhat more participatory than the younger or older groups, and while gender differences used to be significant at all levels, they remain primarily at the gladiator level, especially in the case of candidates.

CONCLUSION

Although the values and attitudes that constitute the political culture of any society are difficult to establish, certain Canadian political values can be identified. In many cases, it is clearest to see them in contrast to those of the United States. Canada has a more even balance between individualism and collectivism; it gives greater weight to particularism and is more tolerant, elitist, hierarchical, and deferential to authority; it is also more egalitarian, cautious, diffident, and dependent. Efforts to define such pan-Canadian values, attitudes, and identities are complicated by the existence of regional, ethnic, and class political subcultures. As for political participation in Canada, it "bears little similarity to the classical democratic ideal of widespread citizen involvement in all aspects of the political process."[53] Whether it is the low level of public information and participation that requires a reliance on elitist representative government to make public decisions, or the nature of representative government that encourages such low popular involvement is not entirely clear.[54]

(SC) The limited nature of Canadian democracy, combined with Canadian caution and diffidence, deference to authority, and a penchant for elitism and hierarchy, means that political authorities have considerable autonomy in making their decisions. This is just what the state-centred approach suggests. It would be too much to claim that the state is completely autonomous from the rest of society and from demands flowing from the public, but it now becomes clear why state authorities can to a large extent pursue their own conception of the national interest. Canadians are also highly respectful of those in positions of authority in other segments of society, and this chapter has identified the various regional/provincial, ethnic and class subcultures whose leaders come together in a process of elite accommodation. They devise compromise arrangements with which to satisfy the mass members of these groups.

In terms of participation, the authorities choose the most convenient date for the election and the message to be conveyed, and, content in the knowledge that few people know what is going on and even fewer can be bothered to do anything about it, carry on with their own agenda. Politicians may encourage popular participation when it serves their own purposes, but bureaucrats are notoriously suspicious of public involvement.

P Pluralists centre on the "limited identities" that characterize Canadians and the many subcultures that exist in the country, each one providing a shading to the national values identified. They also focus on the values of particularism and tolerance. Rather than emphasize the elite interaction that emanates from such subcultures, however, pluralists note that most of these interests are organized into pressure groups and that public policies are the outcome of a broader interplay among such groups. Pluralism emphasizes that individuals are free to join or form any group, and while over half of Canadian adults do so, the passivity of most members is somewhat at odds with the idealistic picture that pluralists usually paint.

PC This chapter also demonstrates that relatively few citizens are either well informed or participate beyond voting, surely a smaller number than the public choice approach would have anticipated. Whether such behaviour is based on a rational understanding that greater effort would not be worthwhile or on simple apathy and laziness, it is clear that the "public choice" is often not a well-informed one.

© Class analysts are generally critical of the Canadian values and attitudes identified in this chapter. In particular, they emphasize the narrow conception of democracy held by most Canadians, deriding the notion of one person–one vote as a genuine measure of political equality, the view that political freedom is meaningful in the absence of economic and social freedom, and the claim that an election every four years is an effective implementation of popular sovereignty. Neither are they satisfied with many of the other values noted. They contend, for example, that the capitalist ethic is still predominant among the political and economic elite and that much of the government intervention that has occurred has been welcomed rather than opposed by the bourgeoisie. They also urge Canadians to demand greater egalitarianism and slough off notions of elitism, hierarchy, and deference to authority. They put little stock in such "tory" ideas as trusting a concerned and paternalistic political or economic elite to advance the position of the working class. Such analysts emphasize class subcultures and view regional and ethnic subcultures largely in class terms. They argue, too, that Canadians have not respected their heritage of natural resources, that federalism has impaired Ottawa's capacity to ensure greater economic equality in the country, that the state has not been strong in improving the condition of the working class, and that the social democratic movement has not been particularly effective.

As for participation, class analysts claim that the bourgeoisie encourages the masses to vote, but only to choose between parties equally committed to the capitalist system. If political violence occurs, such as in the Winnipeg General Strike, the Regina Riot, or the Oka incident, the authorities move the police in quickly to quell it, frequently exacerbating the situation with such coercive measures.

. . . .

DISCUSSION QUESTIONS

1. Do you agree that periodic elections are a sufficient means of exercising the principle of popular sovereignty, and that the principle of one person–one vote is a sufficient mark of political equality? Explain your answer.

2. How deep is the Canadian commitment to political freedom? What situations do you think justify government restriction of such freedom?

3. What kinds of minority rights should be protected in the Constitution, and in what circumstances should Canada follow the principle of majority rule?

4. To what extent do you agree with the Lipset analysis of the differences between Canadian and American values? Which society do you feel is more egalitarian?

5. To what extent has the traditional Canadian political culture been transformed in recent years?

6. Do you think it is more productive to speak of the national Canadian political culture or only of various subcultures? Is the national political culture more than just a sum of the subcultures?

7. How do you account for the fairly consistent 75 percent voter turnout in Canadian elections?

8. What forms of political participation have you engaged in? Why haven't you and/or other Canadians participated more?

9. How high a level of political information and political participation does a democracy require?

10. How can the approaches outlined in Chapter 1 be applied to the material discussed in this chapter?

NOTES

1. See, for example, David V.J. Bell, "Political Culture in Canada," in Michael Whittington and Glen Williams, eds., *Canadian Politics in the 1990s*, 4th ed. (Scarborough: Nelson Canada, 1995).
2. Henry B. Mayo, *An Introduction to Democratic Theory* (New York: Oxford University Press, 1960), ch. 4.
3. Thomas R. Berger, *Fragile Freedoms* (Toronto: Clarke, Irwin & Co., rev. and updated, 1982).
4. Ibid., ch. 5.
5. Ibid., ch. 4.
6. Ibid., ch. 7.
7. Seymour Martin Lipset, *Continental Divide* (New York: Routledge, 1990). His approach is consistent with the Hartz, McRae, Horowitz, and Christian and Campbell approach, which is discussed in terms of party ideology in Chapter 16 of this book.
8. Ibid., p. 8.
9. Pierre Berton, *Why We Act Like Canadians* (Toronto: McClelland and Stewart, 1982).
10. George Grant, *Lament for a Nation* (Toronto: McClelland and Stewart, 1965).
11. Lipset argues that the United States has more government regulation, and uses Sylvia Ostry's, "Government Intervention: Canada and the United States Compared," *Policy Options*, March 1980, pp. 26–31, to support his argument. Ostry, however, refers specifically to consumer and anti-trust regulation. See also David Thomas, ed., *Canada and the United States: Differences That Count* (Peterborough: Broadview Press, 1993).
12. Herschel Hardin, *A Nation Unaware* (Vancouver: J.J. Douglas Ltd., 1974).
13. Allan Gregg and Michael Posner, *The Big Picture: What Canadians Think about Almost Everything* (Toronto: Macfarlane Walter & Ross, 1990), pp. 11–13, 29. According to Gregg, the enormous public-sector expansion of the early Trudeau era (especially in terms of government spending and the resulting deficit) led Canadians to look to private-sector solutions during the recession of the early 1980s and since (p.119).
14. Lipset, *Continental Divide*, ch. 10.
15. Howard Palmer, "Mosaic versus Melting Pot?: Immigration and Ethnicity in Canada and the United States," in Eli Mandel and David Taras, eds., *A Passion for Identity* (Toronto: Methuen, 1987).
16. Given evidence of intolerance at home, this self-defined Canadian international image is a touch moralistic and in part provides an alternative role to that of a U.S. toady!
17. Gregg and Posner, *The Big Picture*, p. 29.

18. Edgar Friedenberg, *Deference to Authority* (White Plains, NY: M.E. Sharpe, 1980); Judy M. Torrance, *Public Violence in Canada* (Montreal: McGill–Queen's University Press, 1986).

19. Section 24(2) of the Charter allows the admissibility of tainted evidence if it does not detract from the "repute" of the Court!

20. Dominique Clift, *The Secret Kingdom: Interpretations of the Canadian Character* (Toronto: McClelland and Stewart, 1989), p. 153.

21. Lipset, *Continental Divide*, p. 156.

22. Apart from all the methodological problems in *Maclean's* annual ranking of Canadian universities, the author wishes to point out that the whole operation is essentially American-inspired and irrelevant to Canada. All Canadian universities are respectable, and the qualitative differences between them are minimal, unlike the situation in the United States.

23. Margaret Atwood, *Survival* (Toronto: Anansi, 1972); W.L. Morton, *The Canadian National Identity* (Toronto: University of Toronto Press, 1961); Clift, *The Secret Kingdom*, p. 227.

24. Lipset, *Continental Divide*, ch. 4; *Maclean's*, July 1, 1995, p. 15.

25. While almost all recent U.S. presidents had distinguished military records, few Canadian prime ministers had any at all. John Diefenbaker and Lester Pearson were invalided home in the First World War after being hit respectively by an entrenching tool and a London bus, Pierre Trudeau avoided military service in the Second World War, motorcycling through the Quebec woods in a Nazi uniform! On the other hand, Canada has more cenotaphs than the United States, and Canadian seniors make greater use of military titles.

26. Bell, "Political Culture in Canada," p. 118, quoting ex-CBC president Albert Johnson.

27. W.L. Morton, *The Canadian Identity*, and articles by Carl Berger and Cole Harris in Peter Russell, ed., *Nationalism in Canada* (Toronto: McGraw-Hill, 1966).

28. Not all foreigners were equally impressed: one unkind Englishman said that "Canada is Montreal and Vancouver with bugger all in between," and Voltaire referred to Canada disparagingly as "quelques arpents de neige."

29. Gregg and Posner, *The Big Picture*, p. 23.

30. *Maclean's*, July 1, 1995, p. 15.

31. The Massey Commission asked this question just at the dawn of the television age. See Dominique Clift, *The Secret Kingdom*, p. 142, and George Grant, *Technology and Empire* (Toronto: Anansi, 1969).

32. Lipset, *Continental Divide*, p. 225.

33. Gregg and Posner, *The Big Picture*, pp. 11–13, 54–6, 65–8; 204–5; Alan Frizzell et al., *The Canadian General Election of 1988* (Ottawa: Carleton University Press, 1989), pp. 105, 112; Peter C. Newman, *The Canadian Revolution 1985–1995: From Deference to Defiance* (Toronto: Viking, 1995).

34. For example, William Thorsell, "Let Us Compare Methodologies," *Globe and Mail Report on Business*, May 1990. He challenges the myths of monarchy, linguistic duality, mixed economy, helpful fixer in international affairs, and kinder, gentler nation, adding that many Canadians are even questioning the ideal of democracy. See also Michael Valpy, "The Myth of Canadian Compassion," in *Family Security in Insecure Times* (Ottawa: Canadian Council on Social Development, 1993); and the forthcoming book by Neil Nevitte, *The Decline of Deference*.

35. J.M.S. Careless, "Limited Identities," *Canadian Historical Review* (March 1969), pp. 1–10.

36. David V.J. Bell, *The Roots of Disunity: A Study of Canadian Political Culture*, rev. ed. (Toronto: Oxford University Press, 1992).

37. Two pioneering studies of provincial political cultures were Richard Simeon and David Elkins, "Regional Political Cultures in Canada," *Canadian Journal of Political Science*, September 1974, pp. 397–437, along with their book, *Small Worlds* (Toronto: Methuen, 1980), and John Wilson, "The Canadian Political Cultures: Towards a Redefinition of the Nature of the Canadian Political System," *Canadian Journal of Political Science* (September 1974), pp. 438–83. See also Nelson Wiseman, "The Use, Misuse, and Abuse of the National Election Studies," *Journal of Canadian Studies*, Spring 1986, pp. 21–35.

38. Roger Gibbins, *Prairie Politics and Society* (Toronto: Butterworths, 1980), p. 191; Roger Gibbins and Sonia Arrison, *Western Canadian Nationalism*, forthcoming.

39. Michael Ornstein, Michael Stevenson, and Paul Williams, "Region, Class and Political Culture in Canada," *Canadian Journal of Political Science*, June 1980, pp. 227–71.

40. Pierre Elliott Trudeau, "Some Obstacles to Democracy in Quebec," in *Federalism and the French Canadians* (Toronto: Macmillan, 1968).

41. Ornstein, "Region, Class and Political Culture in Canada." Is there and English-Canadian subculture? See Philip Resnick, *Thinking English Canada* (Toronto: Stoddart, 1995), and Kenneth McRoberts, ed., *Beyond Quebec: Taking Stock of Canada* (Montreal: McGill–Queen's University Press, 1995).

42. Ibid.

43. William Mishler and Harold D. Clarke, "Political Participation in Canada," in Michael Whittington and Glen Williams, eds., *Canadian Politics in the 1990s*, 4th ed. (Scarborough: Nelson Canada, 1995), p. 130.

44. Ibid., p. 134.

45. Ibid., pp. 134, 143.

46. Ronald D. Lambert et al., "The Social Sources of Political Knowledge," *Canadian Journal of Political Science*, June 1988, pp. 359–74.

47. Lester Milbraith, *Political Participation* (Chicago: Rand McNally, 1965), and Richard Van Loon, "Political Participation in Canada," *Canadian Journal of Political Science*, September 1970, pp. 376–99.

48. Mishler and Clarke, "Political Participation in Canada"; W.T. Stanbury, "Financing Federal Political Parties in Canada, 1974–1986," in Alain Gagnon and Brian Tanguay, eds., *Canadian Parties in Transition* (Scarborough: Nelson Canada, 1989).

49. R. Kenneth Carty, *Canadian Political Parties in the Constituencies*. Royal Commission on Electoral Reform and Party Financing Research Studies, Vol. 23, cat. no. 21-1989/2-41-23E.

50. Judy Torrance, *Public Violence in Canada* (Montreal: McGill–Queen's University Press, 1986).

51. Mishler and Clarke, "Political Participation in Canada," p. 134.

52. Ibid., pp. 139–40.

53. Mishler, *Political Participation in Canada: Prospects for Democratic Citizenship* (Toronto: Macmillan, 1979), p. 36.

54. Jon Pammett, "Political Education and Democratic Participation," in Pammett and Jean-Luc Pépin, eds., *Political Education in Canada* (Halifax: Institute for Research on Public Policy, 1988), p. 210.

· ·

FURTHER READING

Bashevkin, Sylvia. *True Patriot Love: The Politics of Canadian Nationalism*. Don Mills: Oxford University Press, 1991.

Bell, David. *The Roots of Disunity: A Look at Canadian Political Culture*, rev. ed., Toronto: McClelland and Stewart, Oxford University Press, 1992.

———. "Political Culture in Canada." In Michael Whittington and Glen Williams, eds. *Canadian Politics in the 1990s*, 4th ed. Scarborough: Nelson Canada, 1995.

Berger, Thomas R. *Fragile Freedoms*. Toronto: Clarke, Irwin, revised and updated, 1982.

Berton, Pierre. *Why We Act Like Canadians*. Toronto: McClelland and Stewart, 1982.

Careless, J.M.S. "Limited Identities." *Canadian Historical Review* (March 1969), 1–10.

Clift, Dominique. *The Secret Kingdom: Interpretations of the Canadian Character*. Toronto: McClelland and Stewart, 1989.

Friedenberg, Edgar J. *Deference to Authority*. White Plains, NY: M.E. Sharpe, 1980.

Gregg, Allan, and Michael Posner. *The Big Picture: What Canadians Think about Almost Everything*. Toronto:

Macfarlane Walter & Ross, 1990.

Hardin, Herschel. *A Nation Unaware*. Vancouver: J.J. Douglas Ltd., 1974.

Lipset, Seymour Martin. *Continental Divide*. New York: Routledge, 1990.

Mishler, William. *Political Participation in Canada: Prospects for Democratic Citizenship*. Toronto: Macmillan, 1979.

Mishler, William, and Harold Clarke. "Political Participation in Canada." In Michael Whittington and Glen Williams, eds., *Canadian Politics in the 1990s*, 4th ed. Scarborough: Nelson Canada, 1995.

Morton, W.L. *The Canadian Identity*. Toronto: University of Toronto Press, 1961.

Newman, Peter C. *The Canadian Revolution 1985–1995: From Deference to Defiance*. Toronto: Viking, 1995.

Nevitte, Neil, and Roger Gibbins. *New Elites in Old States: Ideologies in the Anglo-American Democracies*. Toronto: Oxford University Press, 1991.

Ornstein, Michael, Michael Stevenson, and Paul Williams, "Region, Class and Political Culture in Canada." *Canadian Journal of Political Science* (June 1980), 227–71.

Ostry, Sylvia. "Government Intervention: Canada and the United States Compared." *Policy Options* (March 1980), 26–31.

Pocklington, T.C., ed. *Liberal Democracy in Canada and the United States*. Toronto: Holt, Rinehart and Winston, 1985.

Resnick, Philip. *Thinking English Canada*. Toronto: Stoddart, 1994.

Thomas, David, ed. *Canada and the United States: Differences That Count*. Peterborough: Broadview Press, 1993.

Torrance, Judy M. *Public Violence in Canada*. Montreal: McGill- Queen's University Press, 1986.

Trudeau, Pierre. *Federalism and the French Canadians*. Toronto: Macmillan, 1968.

Verney, Douglas V. *Three Civilizations, Two Cultures, One State: Canada's Political Traditions*. Durham, NC: Duke University Press, 1986.

Chapter 14

Political Socialization, MASS MEDIA, and Public Opinion Polls

Surveys indicate that many adults cannot identify their member of Parliament, and some show that more children can name American political officeholders than Canadian ones. The latter fact is often blamed on the inadequacies of the educational system or related to the high proportion of U.S. television to which Canadians are exposed. The highlight of each of the 1984 and 1988 election campaigns was a brief but endlessly replayed exchange between Brian Mulroney and John Turner in the televised leaders' debate. During election campaigns parties spend millions of dollars on media advertising and polling public opinion. Between elections, a large number of Canadians also watch coverage of political developments on television and/or read about them in a daily newspaper. The media also regularly report the findings of the latest public opinion poll.

The mass media—television, radio, and newspapers—are the primary source of most Canadians' knowledge and opinion about topical political issues and current personalities. At one time, politically aware citizens could gain their information and opinions from real, personal experience. But the expansion of the electorate coincided with a shift in the sources of political information and opinion to common "secondhand or vicarious experience"[1] in the mass circulation newspaper era of the turn of the century, followed by radio in the 1920s, and television since the 1950s. Another important link between people and government is the public opinion poll. Parties rely heavily on such polls immediately before and during election campaigns, but the media report the results of such polls almost daily, as governments and the media themselves seek to discover Canadians' opinions on every conceivable matter.

It is now commonly observed that the mass media and public opinion polls are two of the most important elements in the political system. In terms of the seven functions outlined in Chapter 1, the mass media and public opinion polls predominate in performing the function of "political communication" between public and government and among different branches of government. In addition, few of the other political functions could be performed without at least partial dependence on the media. This is especially true of political socialization, but it also holds for interest articulation and aggregation, political recruitment, rule making, rule application, and rule adjudication.

This chapter begins by outlining the various agents of political socialization, a principal one being the mass media. It then surveys the state of the media in Canada, including the question of ownership. It examines the relationship between the media and the public and between the media and the politicians, and concludes with a discussion of the role of public opinion polls.

POLITICAL SOCIALIZATION

Political socialization is the process by which individuals acquire their political values, attitudes, information, and opinions. Looked at in another way, it is the process by which society passes on its basic values or political culture from one generation to another. Political socialization is sometimes called political learning or education.

The process of political socialization consists in part of direct, individual observation of political phenomena, but is mostly performed by intermediaries or agents of socialization. It is relatively easy to identify the main agents of political socialization in Canada, but much more difficult to evaluate their relative impact. We begin with the four traditional agents—family, school, peers, and the media, family and peers sometimes being called "private" agents, and schools and media labelled "public" agents—and then examine other such influences.

PRINCIPAL AGENTS OF POLITICAL SOCIALIZATION

- Family
- School
- Interest groups
- Political parties
- Churches
- Mass media
- Government
- Peers
- Corporations

The Family

Despite many modern pressures—the increasing incidence of mothers working outside the home, the high divorce rate, and competing influences such as peers and the media—the family remains the basic cell of Canadian society. Parents, step-parents, or sometimes grandparents are the first major influence on a child's attitudes and values. At the very least, families provide children with certain circumstances of birth, especially their regional and ethnic origins and their class, all of which are bound to have some effect on their political attitudes and behaviour.[2] Next, most children absorb attitudes and values, some of which are of political significance, in a kind of osmosis from their family's talk and behaviour. Parents' casual comments about politics, politicians, parties, and police are good examples. In the third place, some parents deliberately try to indoctrinate their children with certain political values, such as supporting a particular political party or developing a sense of political efficacy. It seems, however, that what children pick up unconsciously and unintentionally is just as significant as what parents try to teach. For example, if parents talk about politics in the home, with or without attempting to guide their children's orientations, their children will usually become more politically interested later in life. If parents have a moderate or strong identification with a particular political party, children usually begin with the same party preference, whether or not parents insist on it, although they may change parties later as their experience grows and as they encounter other influences. Since the degree of party identification in Canada is relatively weak, as seen in Chapter 17, the influence of parents in this respect should not be over-estimated.[3] Nor should the more general political impact of the family in modern times, for political socialization is a process that continues throughout one's life.

The School

The school is the second main agent of political socialization. Although Canada has ten distinctive provincial educational systems, the school is a public institution providing a common experience for children so that its influence is relatively more uniform than that of the family. Moreover, with the decline of the family's influence, the school has probably increased in importance. Like the family, it is an early enough influence that it is likely to shape basic life-long values. All school systems in Canada and elsewhere deliberately attempt to inculcate certain basic values and attitudes, including some of a political nature such as a feeling of affection or support for the country, the governmental apparatus, the head of state, the police, the flag, and the national anthem. Some, even in Canada, go beyond this to dwell on the virtues of capitalism, cooperation, or other ideological, moral, religious, or political values.

Given the diversity of Canadian society, many questions arise about the role of the school in the political socialization process. Since the provinces have jurisdiction over education, do they deliberately contribute to distinctive provincial political cultures at the expense of overall country? The radically different accounts of certain historical events found in French and English textbooks are often cited as examples of the biased role of formal education in this process.[4] Louis Riel is portrayed either as a traitor or a hero, for example; Quebec's role in the Confederation Settlement, and interpretations of whether participation in two world wars was in the Canadian national interest vary widely. To what extent should history and political science be compulsory? Should aboriginal children be taught by white or aboriginal teachers? Should aboriginal and immigrant children be taught in English or French, or in their "heritage languages"? One point is clear: the forces of dualism, regionalism, and continentalism in Canadian society make it difficult for the school system to develop any pan-Canadian sense of national identity.[5]

Every educational system must also decide to what extent it should promote satisfaction with and support for existing political arrangements as opposed to advocating reform. Perhaps the best prescription on this point was articulated by A.B. Hodgetts, who wrote that the school should seek to produce an intelligent, knowledgeable affection for one's country along with a critically responsible interest in it.[6] Most observers feel, however, that the current state of Canadian political education is deficient and that students are not exposed to enough direct teaching about politics.[7]

When it comes to current events, for example, even high-school students usually demonstrate a deplorable lack of recognition of such figures as provincial premiers and federal cabinet ministers and a lack of knowledge about which political parties form federal and provincial governments.[8] Such gaps in political information reinforce the view that modern students are free spirits who do not always pay much attention to what teachers, textbooks, or school systems are trying to convey.

That is why the school's second type of influence may be of equal or greater importance. Just as happens in the family setting, students develop attitudes, values, and skills informally and unintentionally from the school. Such unconscious transmissions occur in teachers' remarks beyond the formal curriculum, in class discussions and excursions, and in extracurricular activities. The authority structure of the classroom or school can also be a factor. An authoritarian teacher or principal would likely promote different attitudes toward participation and dissent than would be acquired in a more democratic setting.

Peers

Peers are the third main agent of political socialization. Peers are simply friends, acquaintances, associates, cohorts, fellow students, workers, homemakers, and members of teams and clubs. The concept of "peer pressure" is probably most familiar at the adolescent level and is not usually concerned with political values, attitudes, and opinions; but we are all susceptible to peer influence at any stage of our lives. Wherever and whenever two or more people communicate, political issues of one kind or another may arise, and one person can influence the other. At this stage, given the likelihood that basic values have already been established, it is attitudes and opinions that are most open to persuasion. In any larger group setting, including peer group discussions that turn to politics, one person often becomes dominant, whether because of that person's knowledge, position, or strength of character.[9]

An excellent example of the use of peer group leaders occurs during election campaigns when the Canadian Labour Congress tries to persuade its members to vote for the New Democratic Party. Given their leadership status, it is expected that union stewards will be successful in their effort to "talk up" the NDP at coffee or lunch breaks. Since all union members are probably affected by government in a similar way, this a natural setting in which certain attitudes or opinions can be changed. Even in peer groups, therefore, the influence can be deliberate or indirect.

The Mass Media

The mass media are the fourth main agent of socialization. They are more often instruments of entertainment than enlightenment, however, and personal interaction with family members, teachers, or peers normally carries greater impact than passive, impersonal exposure to the media. Moreover, while the first three agents are more likely to influence lifelong values and attitudes, the media primarily transmit opinions on topical issues and personalities. Nevertheless, "there is evidence that Canadians do learn from this coverage, even though the average citizen has a limited grasp of the details of the political system or of the major issues of the day."[10] In addition, such short-term stimuli are becoming more important in determining how people vote.

Once again, media influence can be divided into that which is unconscious and that which is deliberate. In their editorials, newspapers explicitly attempt to influence opinions, while on the other pages of the paper, Canadians generally expect news coverage to be as unbiased and factual as possible. Whether newspapers can keep such a fine line between subjective editorials and objective reporting is an interesting question, and some have detected bias in the headlines, positioning, pictures, and selection of items to be included or excluded in various newspapers. Readers sometimes claim to find a pro-Conservative slant in the news coverage of the *Globe and Mail*, for example, or a preference for the Liberal party in the *Toronto Star*. To their credit, however, these two papers provide long, substantive accounts of major issues, considerable space for letters to the editor, and in the latter case in particular, opportunity for conflicting partisan points of view to be expressed.

Television does not usually have editorials, as such, but it actually has greater possibilities for presenting biased news coverage than do newspapers. That is partly because television has such a short time to deal with any one item that it cannot present the whole story, and such editing necessarily involves selection or bias on someone's part. Furthermore, television deals in images and impressions, which are subject to greater manipulation than the hard data that can be found in print; it also engages in "colour commentary," even on political events. Nevertheless, respectable television networks and stations probably strive to be as unbiased as possible, and periodic charges of pro- or anti-government bias of one kind or another on the publicly owned CBC are usually unfounded.[11] In some cases, too, the media broadcast political events live, in full, and without much commentary, so that the viewer is engaged in almost direct, personal observation.

Part of the problem with the media, of course, is the degree to which they transmit information and values of U.S. origin. Canadians may gain an inaccurate notion about how their legal system works from watching American police dramas, and adopt a view that the scope, urgency, and possible responses to U.S. problems are the same as their own. This and other aspects of the mass media will be dealt with in more detail in the following section.

Other Agents of Political Socialization

The family, school, peers, and media are probably the main agents of political socialization in Canada, but certainly not the only ones. Political parties, churches, groups of various kinds, corporations, and the government itself are secondary influences on political attitudes, values, information, and opinions.

Political parties practise the art of persuasion and seek to influence opinions and party preferences on a daily basis. Those who already identify with a particular party find that the simplest means of forming an opinion on any issue is to take their cue from the party leader. The more one identifies with a party or leader, and the less one is inclined to make the effort to research the issue for oneself, the greater the propensity to defer to the partisan perspective expressed.

While the power of religion in Canadian society is generally declining, churches have often influenced the political values, attitudes, and opinions of their members in the past, and their role in this connection remains significant. The classic case was the Roman Catholic Church in Quebec before 1960, when it had a close relationship with political authorities and did not hesitate to tell its members how to behave politically. That Church continues to take a strong stand across the country on the abortion issue, and frequently reminds its members that they are expected to follow suit. Other religious denominations are also involved in the abortion debate, while most churches articulate positions on other political issues from time to time, whether poverty, foreign policy, foreign aid, capital punishment, or sexual orientation.[12]

Over half the population belongs to a group of some kind, and although the orientation of such groups is primarily nonpolitical, all have the potential to influence their members' political views. Some, such as the Catholic Women's League, the Canadian Medical Association, or the Canadian Labour Congress, are quite determined to do so, as well as to extend their influence beyond their own members to the public at large. Others such as the Boy Scouts or Girl Guides try to instil in children an informed affection for the country. Some groups only get involved in political indoctrination on rare occasions when the interests of the group are threatened by government action, such as the funeral directors' association fighting against the Goods and Services Tax. As with parties and churches, taking one's opinions from the urging of a group one belongs to or respects will obviate the need to make further individual effort to understand the issue.

Like political parties, individual corporations are in the business of persuasion, trying to sell their own goods and services. Sometimes, however, companies will also try to influence political attitudes and opinions, an effort that is called **advocacy advertising**. Many such corporations were involved in the free trade debate, especially during the 1988 election campaign, expressing their support through "speeches, debates, letters, advertisements, information sessions with employees, and inserts in newspapers."[13] Others have used the media to try to influence Canadians' opinions on tax changes, nuclear energy, the National Energy Program, and the Meech Lake Accord. Sometimes employers also try to influence the opinions or voting preferences of their own employees with internal memos about how different parties or policies would affect the firm.

Finally, the government itself is often engaged in efforts to influence public views and behaviour. Sometimes this is done for what are widely recognized as legitimate purposes, such as encouraging physical fitness and discouraging smoking, impaired driving, racial discrimination, wife battery, and the use of drugs. Sometimes it is done for broadly acceptable political purposes, such as promoting vacations in Canada, the purchase of Canadian-made goods, or national unity. Governments are also expected to inform the public about new laws, regulations, and programs, through pamphlets and the mass media, but it is a fine line between simple information and extolling the virtues of such initiatives for partisan purposes. The Mulroney government, for example, spent large sums of public funds flaunting the merits of the Free Trade Agreement and the Goods and Services Tax in advertising campaigns that most observers felt were excessive and self-serving. In the latter case, the Speaker declared such advertising to be an affront to the House of Commons as it took place even before debate there had concluded. Governments often use public funds for "public education" purposes just before or during an election campaign, as they circumvent, at public expense, the spending ceilings of the Canada Elections Act.

How Canadians individually and collectively acquire their political values, attitudes and opinions is a complicated question. The whole process is so haphazard and complex and the stimuli in each person's own environment are so diverse that no deliberate effort is guaranteed to be successful. Instead, Canadians acquire many of their political values, attitudes and opinions in a totally unconscious way. Moreover, many Canadians are only semi-socialized: they simply do not have many political values, attitudes, and opinions or much political information. The general level of political awareness is not high, which in turn is reflected in patterns of political participation, as noted in Chapter 13.

THE MASS MEDIA
The State of the Media

In surveying the state of the newspaper, radio, and television industries in Canada today, we should first note that the privately owned media exist primarily to make a profit, and that whatever political functions they serve are incidental. Peter Trueman makes the point, for example, that major television newscasts in Canada are broadcast late at night so as not to deprive the networks of prime-time advertising revenues generated by larger audiences earlier in the evening.[14]

NEWSPAPERS

In 1995, 107 daily newspapers were published in Canada, 96 in English and 11 in French.[15] In 1994 Ken Thomson owned 39 of these papers, including the *Globe and Mail* and many less distinguished dailies like the *Sudbury Star* and the *St. John's Telegram*. The *Globe and Mail* calls itself "Canada's National Newspaper," and publishes a national edition transmitted by satellite to several printing locations so that it is available every morning in all major centres across the country. In 1995, however, Thomson sold 14 smaller dailies to Conrad Black. The Southam chain, increasingly controlled by the Desmarais and Black empires, owned 17 daily newspapers in Canada, including the *Calgary Herald, Edmonton Journal, Hamilton Spectator, Ottawa Citizen, Montreal Gazette*, and *Vancouver Province* and *Sun*. Conrad Black owned 12 daily papers, including three in French, before his acquisitions from Thomson in 1995. By buying the Maclean-Hunter empire, Ted Rogers became the owner of nine daily newspapers; Paul Desmarais owned four of the 11 French papers; K.C. Irving owned all four English dailies in New Brunswick; Pierre Péladeau's Quebecor also had four. If a "chain" is defined as a minimum of four papers, then 89 dailies out of 107 belong to chains, leaving only 18 daily newspapers in Canada that are independently owned and operated. Furthermore, the *Toronto Star* could be regarded as a chain because it publishes many suburban Toronto community weeklies. Thus, some of the wealthiest men in Canada control the country's newspaper industry, and the Thomson, Southam, and Black chains together produce about 60 percent of the daily newspaper circulation in English Canada. Moreover, one chain or another often has an overwhelming dominance in a single province, such as Irving in New Brunswick (100 percent English), Armadale

TABLE 14.1	Canadian Newspaper Ownership, 1995 (Ranked by Circulation)
Thomson	25
Southam	17
Black	26
Rogers	9
Smaller chains & independents	17
Toronto Star	1
Quebecor	4
Desmarais	4
Irving	4
Total	107

Source: Canadian Advertising Rates and Data *(August 1994), updated by author.*

in Saskatchewan (86 percent), and Thomson in Manitoba (75 percent) and Newfoundland (100 percent). Assuming that Desmarais and Black control Southam, those two moguls plus Péladeau control 97 percent of the daily newspaper circulation in Quebec.

A clear trend has developed toward increasingly concentrated chain ownership of Canadian daily newspapers. In 1970, for example, there were 45 independents out of 114; in 1995, less than 17 out of 107. Between 1970 and 1980, several major newspapers closed down, including the *Toronto Telegram*, the *Montreal Star*, the *Ottawa Journal*, the *Winnipeg Tribune*, and the *Quebec Chronicle-Telegraph*, while Thomson and Southam both expanded their holdings. In fact, Thomson closed the *Ottawa Journal*, giving Southam a monopoly in Ottawa, on the very same day that Southam shut the *Winnipeg Tribune*, leaving Thomson in a monopoly position in Winnipeg.

These actions prompted an investigation under the Combines Act and charges of collusion were laid. Nothing demonstrates the weakness of Canadian competition laws as much as the acquittal of Thomson and Southam chains on these charges.[16] An earlier case against Irving's monopoly in New Brunswick met the same fate in the courts.

Concentrated ownership of Canadian newspapers has always caused considerable concern in some quarters. Many fear that the owner of several papers will gain an unhealthy degree of influence over public opinion by establishing a common point of view for all papers in the chain. This anxiety deepened when there appeared to be collusion between the Southam and Thomson chains, prompting the Trudeau government to appoint the **Kent Royal Commission on Newspapers**. In response, the Commission said that the Thomson chain should divest itself of the *Globe and Mail* and future concentrations should be rigidly controlled. Thomas Worrall Kent also expressed concern in his report with the degree to which newspapers were involved in the ownership of radio and television stations, cable TV, and magazines, and recommended restrictions in multimedia holdings. He also sought to ensure that individual newspaper editors had complete autonomy so that they could not be told how to do their job by a common corporate owner.

The government's initial response to these recommendations consisted of introducing a bill to restrict any further concentration of media ownership in Canada, but not to disturb the status quo. Later, however, responding to strong corporate pressure, it abandoned the bill and took no action at all. It should be added that the Royal Commission did not actually find much evidence that any central owner had imposed a common editorial policy or standardized news coverage on all the newspapers; the most undesirable result was a reduction in the diversity of perspectives on national politics.[17] While chain ownership even has some advantages, the possibility of owners intervening in such undesirable ways continues to exist.

Since the Kent Report was published, four principal developments in the Canadian newspaper industry have occurred. The first is the expansion of populist morning tabloids. The *Sun* chain, which began in Toronto and Edmonton, took over the *Calgary Albertan*, and now publishes in Ottawa as well, tends to be more ideological and sensational than traditional Canadian fare, aiming for a less sophisticated audience that is more vulnerable to its right-wing and visceral approach.[18] It eventually came to be owned by Ted Rogers.[19] Other new morning tabloids include Quebecor's *Winnipeg Sun*, *Le Journal de Montréal*, and *Le Journal de Québec*, while several papers that previously came out in the afternoon have now switched to the morning. The second development is the takeover of the Maclean-Hunter chain by Ted Rogers. Although he was primarily interested in Maclean-Hunter's cable TV holdings, Rogers ended up with a significant newspaper chain as well. Third, Paul Desmarais and Conrad Black have taken over the Southam chain, and, fourth, Black purchased the 14 dailies and seven weeklies that Thomson put up for sale in 1995. Further, in early 1996 Black purchased Armadale and thus obtained a monopoly of dailies in Saskatchewan.

RADIO AND TELEVISION

The radio and television industries are distinct from newspapers in two respects: the degree of government regulation involved and the public ownership of English CBC and French Radio-Canada networks. The principles of the Canadian broadcasting system are listed below.

·······································

PRINCIPLES OF THE CANADIAN BROADCASTING SYSTEM

* Airwaves belong to the public, and the use of a frequency is a privilege to be exercised in the public interest.
* Canadians should own the system.
* Service should be extended to all Canadians.
* The system should depend for financial support on both public and private money.
* Programs should be Canadian and of high standard, but Canadians should also have access to quality programs from other sources.

Source: Industry Canada, Report of the Task Force on the Economic Status of Canadian Television, cat no. co22-107/1991, p. 13. Reproduced with permission of the Minister of Supply and Services Canada, 1995.

There are some 29 CBC AM and 35 CBC FM originating stations (English or French), and, through transmitter stations, coverage is almost nation-wide. In addition, 17 private radio stations are affiliated with the CBC. CBC radio has a relatively large and sophisticated audience and plays a major role in transmitting information and opinion in its extended newscasts and in such programs as "Morningside," "As It Happens," and "Cross-Country Check-Up."

Apart from CBC/Radio-Canada, the Canadian radio industry consists of nearly 500 local AM and FM stations, some of which put more effort than others into news-gathering and public affairs programming. These stations used to be independently owned, but are increasingly characterized by chain ownership, just as in the newspaper industry. Ownership changes quite frequently, but Table 14.2 shows that in 1994 over half of the radio market in Canada was controlled by the ten leading firms. Like newspapers, radio stations must be Canadian-owned, but the limited Canadian content on private radio stations has become a problem. Since they mainly transmit music, the CRTC has issued Canadian content rules, as noted in Chapter 12.

TABLE 14.2   **Top Ten Private Radio Station Ownership Groups in Canada, 1994, Ranked by Total Hours**

CHUM	9	Radiomutuel	4
Telemedia	9	Shaw Communications	4
Western International	8	Rawlinson Group	3
Standard Broadcasting	8	Maritime Broadcasting	2
Rogers Communications	8	Power Corp.	2

Source: BBM and CRTC. Used with permission.

Requiring Canadian television stations to be domestically owned or to telecast 50 percent or more Canadian content is virtually meaningless when almost all residents are within reach, directly or via cable, of a large assortment of U.S. television channels. On this point, Fletcher talks of "American images crowding out Canadian ones,"[20] and Black writes of the problem of trying to serve a small population in two language groups "who live in tempting, embarrassing, and almost smothering proximity to [ten times as many] Americans who speak the language of Canada's majority ... They also have the world's most penetrating and effective system for transmitting ideas en masse."[21] Trueman adds:

> I have felt for years that the greatest threat to Canada's integrity as a nation is not the crisis in Quebec ... but American television ... Think of the overwhelming preponderance of American programming, which in an unobtrusive way pumps us full of American values, American hopes, American history, even American patterns of speech.[22]

The publicly owned CBC/Radio-Canada television network has 19 stations across the country, 11 English and eight French. English production is centred in Toronto and French production in Montreal. These are supplemented by agreements with 22 English and five French privately owned affiliated stations, which agree to telecast a certain amount of CBC programming. This usually includes national news and public affairs, but not always drama or more sophisticated cultural programs.[23]

Twenty-eight privately owned stations comprise the CTV network, centred in CFTO in Toronto. CFTO and several other stations in the network are owned by the Eaton family under the Baton name and are run by Douglas Bassett. The Toronto-based Canwest Global system, owned by Izzy Asper of Winnipeg, serves most of Ontario. Asper also owns a number of other stations, and, with his loose affiliations with other independents in Western Canada, is trying to cobble together a third national English-language network. Most major cities also have an unaffiliated, independent private English station. On the French side, the equivalent of CTV is TVA, centred in Télé-Métropole in Montreal and consisting of nine other private stations; a second private French network is the seven-station Quatre Saisons.

Reprinted with permission.

CBC television has a strong commitment to Canadian programming, but suffers from a chronic shortage of funds. After severe bloodletting under the Mulroney government, the CBC had reason to expect better treatment under the Chrétien regime. Instead, that government slashed the CBC budget even further, precipitating the resignation of the Corporation's president. Ironically enough, the Liberals then replaced him with former Tory Communications minister Perrin Beatty, who proceeded with additional cuts.

The private stations and networks, on the other hand, are profit-oriented and realize that profits can be maximized by telecasting as much U.S. programming as the CRTC will allow. Nevertheless, the importance and popularity of CBC and CTV mid- to late-evening national newscasts, CBC's "The Morning News," "The Fifth Estate," and "Marketplace," Radio-Canada's "Téléjournal" and "Le Point," and CTV's "Canada AM" and "W5" should not be underestimated. Table 14.3 indicates that 24 percent of Canadian television viewing consists of news and public affairs, and that most of this is Canadian in origin. In 1993, the average Canadian watched 22.8 hours of television per week, higher in Atlantic Canada and French Quebec, and lower in Alberta and B.C. A considerable discrepancy existed between French and English Canadians in terms of the origin of programs watched, 65 percent Canadian in the former case, compared with 25.5 percent Canadian in the latter.

TABLE 14.3 Percentage Distribution of Viewing by Program Type and Canadian vs. Foreign Origin

Program Type	English-Language Canadian	Foreign	French-Language Canadian	Foreign	Total Canadian	Foreign
News & public affairs	15.0	7.9	25.0	1.4	17.9	6.1
Documentary	0.5	1.5	1.4	0.4	0.8	1.2
Instructional	0.9	1.8	2.7	0.3	1.4	1.4
Religion	0.2	0.1	0.3	0	0.2	0.1
Sports	5.2	2.7	5.7	0.7	5.4	2.1
Variety & games	0.7	6.2	5.7	1.9	4.8	5.0
Music & dance	0.4	1.0	1.0	0.2	0.6	0.7
Comedy	0.4	16.2	2.7	8.0	1.0	13.8
Drama	2.3	29.5	10.4	18.1	4.5	26.3
Other	0	7.7	0	4.2	0	6.9
Total	25.5	74.5	64.9	35.1	36.5	63.5

Source: Statistics Canada, "Television Viewing 1993," cat. no. 87-208 (December 1994). Reproduced with permission of the Minister of Supply and Services Canada, 1995.

Figure 14.1 illustrates the same basic information in graphic form. For example, in news and public affairs programs, English-language viewers prefer 68 percent Canadian content while French-language viewers watch 97 percent Canadian programs.

Another effort to strengthen Canadian television content was the establishment of CBC Newsworld in 1989. This all-news channel covers many political events live and more extensively than regular CBC, with which it works closely, and provides much regional coverage, documentaries, and in-depth interview programming. Newsworld is only available on cable, but while its audience is small, most members of the political elite tune in regularly. The CBC also operates the national parliamentary channel on cable; in some provinces another channel carries provincial legislative proceedings; and several provinces have educational television channels.

Figure 14.1 **Percentage of Television Viewing Time Spent Watching Canadian Content Programs, Anglophones and Francophones, 1991**

Source: Statistics Canada, Canadian Social Trends (Summer 1993), based on cat. no. 87-208. Reproduced with the permission of the Minister of Supply and Services Canada, 1995.

About 75 percent of Canadian homes subscribe to cable television, more than in any other country. Cable stations receive television signals from large satellite dishes and transmit them by means of cables to individual subscribers. To some extent the CRTC regulates which channels they carry, but in general, cable television is designed to bring the major U.S. networks, into almost every Canadian home. This gives most Canadians two chances to view popular U.S. shows—either on the originating network or on CBC, CTV, or Global, which bid for such programs. It also permits Canadians to watch U.S. news, public affairs, and sports programs, although Table 14.3 indicated strong Canadian preferences in all these areas. The Canadian cable industry is dominated by the giants of Canadian television and radio: Rogers Communications, Shaw Cablesystems, Vidéotron, Cogeco Inc., CFCF, and Moffat Communications. The variety of other channels on cable television, some of them of Canadian origin, is constantly increasing, but for some channels the subscriber must pay an additional fee. As mentioned in Chapter 12, popular and industry pressure forced the CRTC to allow such a wide range of U.S. channels to be available on Canadian cable and pay television. In 1994, the CRTC approved ten new "specialty services," Canadian or American, including "pay-per-view," and a year later authorized the first direct-to-home (DTH) satellite service. All of this served to dilute the audience of the conventional Canadian television stations.

A further word should be added on the extent of **cross-media ownership**. Maclean-Hunter used to be the largest general media corporation in Canada, with several radio and television stations in addition to its *Sun* and *Financial Post* newspapers, to say nothing of magazines and other interests. Ted Rogers, already a leader in cable television, took it over to create a megacompany in the Canadian communications field. In the wake of the Kent Report, the CRTC discouraged cross-media ownership, but these restrictions were later lifted.

The Media and the Public

PUBLIC PERCEPTIONS OF THE MEDIA

The influence of the mass media in the political system is profound and appears to be constantly increasing.[24] Most of the information Canadians receive about the political process comes from newspapers, radio, or television rather than from direct observation or other sources such as books or magazines, except perhaps for *Maclean's*. Some recipients may be able to separate this information from whatever commentary or biases accompany it, but many are also swayed by the particular perspective that the media give to the data they present.

Three different theories have arisen regarding the role of the media in this regard.[25] The first assumed that the media had a direct and crucial impact on virtually every individual in the community in terms of providing and interpreting information. When survey research showed this theory to be faulty, a second emerged to replace it. This was that the media primarily influence opinion leaders—those people who pay close attention to political developments and who then transmit this information and opinion to those around them in peer-group situations. There is probably much truth to this theory, but the current perspective on the role of the media is that their most important effect on the general public is in the realm of setting the political agenda for the country.[26] In other words, the media tell people what to think about, what the important issues are, and which political personalities are significant. *They help to define what is political.*[27] This is a function which the media share with political parties, and while parties may be more important as initiators of issues, these will not likely remain on the agenda without media attention.

The **parliamentary press gallery** is a key player in developing a consensus about what these issues are.[28] In part this reflects the influence of the daily Question Period in the House of Commons, which provides gallery reporters with short, superficial, and controversial issues that are well suited to media, especially television, coverage.

In addition to their representatives in the press gallery, all media outlets receive wire services. The most important is Canadian Press, an agency collectively owned by member newspapers, which hires several CP reporters in Ottawa and wires their stories to all outlets. Stories originating in other cities by reporters of individual papers are sent to Canadian Press, rewritten, and wired to all other members.[29] Canadian Press also has an electronic outlet, Broadcast News (BN).

The functions of the three principal media can be distinguished from each other as follows:

> To learn the bare facts of the most recent happenings, we look to radio news.
> To get a larger, detailed picture of the world's happenings over a longer period,
> we buy a daily newspaper. If we prefer to "see for ourselves" what a few of those
> events looked like, we turn to a favoured television newsreader for an impressionistic reconstruction on film.[30]

Public perception of the three media was surveyed for the Royal Commission on Newspapers in 1981. The Commission indicated that 42 percent of the population read one newspaper a day, 33 percent read two, 11 percent read three, 3 percent read four or more, while 11 percent did not read any, for an average of 6.4 issues per week. Such reading required nearly an hour per day.[31] This compared with an average of 191 minutes of television exposure per day (including 6.1 newscasts per week) and 185 minutes of radio exposure per day (including 3.6 newscasts per day). When asked about the political role of the three media, people invariably preferred television in almost every respect and newspapers second. Research done for the Commission found that television was preferred as the medium that best kept people up-to-date, was fairest, most influential, most believable, and best for both Canadian and international news. A poll taken five years later indicated that Canadians preferred television over newspapers even for coverage of local news, and the preference for television over newspapers further increased between 1986 and 1991, except for business and economic news.[32]

THE REALITY OF DIFFERENT MEDIA COVERAGE

These results are somewhat distressing to those who know the real advantages and disadvantages of the three media in question. Because of cost and time constraints, television must present a shorter and more superficial account of political events than either radio or newspapers. Everyone is familiar with the 60- to 90-second "news clip" with a 10-second "sound bite" of the voice of political leaders, in which how something is said is usually more important than what is said. The transcript of a 30-minute newscast would make up about one-third of a single newspaper page.[33] Moreover, because it is a visual medium, television must aim to show colourful, dramatic, emotional, conflictual, or entertaining pictures. Riots, demonstrations, and political conventions usually make good television, but the daily routine of politics does not lend itself as well to compelling visual coverage. (Witness the efforts taken by politicians and the media to find contrived and engaging settings in which to stage political happenings, make announcements, or tape interviews.) From Question Period to election campaigns, political events are now designed to appeal to television's definition of news.[34] Television portrays images and impressions, and is therefore much better at dealing with political leaders and personalities than with issues. When John Turner issued a 40-point policy manifesto just before the 1988 election, for example, "the electronic media, which have trouble transmitting more than a single idea in a 30-second clip, could not cope with such a cornucopia of ideas that had not been pre-digested into a simple theme wrapped around a few easily grasped issues."[35] These characteristics make television more open to distortion and exploitation, with the result that it may be the least believable and most biased of the three media.[36] Television meets the needs of the average citizen with a short attention span who is looking for visual stimulation and who does not wish to invest too much effort in understanding the political system. Black writes that television has replaced religion as the new "opiate of the masses."[37]

This situation is exacerbated by the increasing tendency of political parties and politicians to gear their activities to the demands of television. Press conferences are now dominated by television lights and cameras; leaders' tours during election campaigns are "photo opportunities"; party conventions and leaders' debates are scheduled for maximum air time; and governments convey public information via catchy, superficial television commercials rather than in detailed newspaper advertisements or pamphlets. The media nearly made a mockery of the 1989 NDP leadership convention by wiring selected delegates, including one candidate who forgot that his microphone was on. In addition, in preparing for elections, parties put greater effort into designing television commercials and trying them out before focus groups than in devising solutions to the country's problems; the leaders' debate has become the single most important event in an election campaign; and elections usually turn more on leader images than issues, policies, local candidates or other leading figures in the party. The appearance, style, and general image of the party leader, including his or her ability to perform on television, has become of crucial importance.[38] While Pierre Trudeau was naturally photogenic and graceful, the media made fun of the physical and vocal idiosyncrasies of Robert Stanfield and Joe Clark; Ed Broadbent saw fit to get his teeth straightened on becoming NDP leader; and John Turner had to learn how to breathe differently in order to overcome his staccato delivery.[39] This increasing emphasis on appearance, largely because of television, is often said to trivialize politics.

Newspapers generally offer more comprehensive coverage of political events, presenting both greater factual information and a wider range of interpretation. While the "average" Canadian relies on television for political information, those with political influence, whether in government, parties, pressure groups, or peer-group situations, depend on newspapers. In the survey cited above, for example, those who preferred newspapers over television had higher educations, higher incomes, were better informed, and tended to be middle-aged and live in urban areas. Furthermore, the broadcast media and opposition parties tend to take their cues from newspapers. In short, "the major daily newspapers remain the primary source of public affairs information not only for top decision-makers but also for the most politically attentive segment of the population at all levels, though television news has also become an important source."[40]

It should be added that the degree of political participation increases sharply with a person's level of newspaper consumption. In other words, those who make the effort to increase their political information by reading a newspaper are not only better informed, but are also most likely to go on to engage in some form of political participation, as shown in Table 14.4.

Among newspapers, the *Globe and Mail* is read by nearly three-quarters of Canada's top-level decision-makers across the country and more than 90 percent of media executives; it thus tends to set the agenda for other news organizations, including the Canadian Press.[41]

TABLE 14.4   Extent of Political Participation by Level of Newspaper Consumption

Activity	Low	Medium	High
Voting	79%	84%	90%
Campaigning	22%	38%	55%
Contacting MPs	17%	18%	34%
Community action	12%	19%	27%

Source: William Mishler, Political Participation in Canada, *p. 73. Used with permission.*

The independent but financially troubled *Le Devoir* occupies a somewhat similar position in French Canada. It is likely that few beyond the political elite read or are influenced by the editorials in such newspapers, however, and there is little evidence that editorial endorsement has much impact on the outcome of elections.[42]

The Media and the Politicians

Politicians and their bureaucratic advisers need publicity and therefore have a great interest in how the media cover their behaviour. Even though they have their own direct sources, these authorities also depend on the media to provide information they need about what is happening at home and abroad. The media, in turn, rely on the authorities for most of their information. A number of issues arise from this mutually dependent relationship.

POLITICIANS AND MEDIA OWNERS

In the newspaper era, when papers were individually owned by their editor, newspaper owners were generally on friendly terms with politicians, and regular confidential consultations took place. Several editors, including Joseph Howe and George Brown, were politicians themselves, and one politician, Henri Bourassa, founded a newspaper, *Le Devoir*. Most papers had a partisan perspective that was evident in their news columns and editorials. However, such factors as chain ownership, the quest for a mass audience, and the public expectation that partisanship be restricted to the editorial page have changed the relationship, between politicians and media owners. Indeed, to a large extent, the party press has been replaced by the critical press.[43] Some newspapers do retain partisan views, as was the case in the *Toronto Star*'s passionate editorial crusade against free trade and the Meech Lake Accord. The *Globe and Mail*'s support of these two initiatives was also evident beyond the editorial page.[44] Content analysis of the 1984 and 1988 election campaigns revealed that these two papers treated the leader of their choice more favourably than the others, but that in terms of overall space (or time) the major newspapers along with the three English-language television networks gave almost equal attention to the three main party leaders.[45] It has also been observed that French-Canadian journalists are allowed greater personal opinion in their reports, positive or negative, than in English Canada.[46]

POLITICIANS AND JOURNALISTS

A second issue is the relationship between working journalists and politicians. Both groups are essentially engaged in the same business, one needing publicity and the other, information. In principle, reporters should maintain enough distance from politicians in order to cover them objectively; on the other hand, it is often necessary to cultivate close relations in order to get the kind of information the media seek. Allan Fotheringham writes that "the narrowest line in journalism is the line between exploiting your sources (without ever destroying them) and being captured by them."[47] Journalists also worry that a critical account of a politician on one occasion may jeopardize a good story the next time around.[48] Furthermore, since politicians often confidentially seek out the opinions of reporters, the latter sometimes have to agonize over whether to reveal information that was given to them "off the record," that is, in the expectation that it will not be used.[49]

Another problem the media have to face is how much privacy to leave politicians. When do a politician's personal habits begin to interfere with his or her public functions, and when should they be revealed?[50] Beyond personal privacy is the question of whether the media should transmit information that it is not supposed to have, such as when Global Television came into advance possession of a summary of the 1988 budget.

These issues also relate to the complex legal question of libel, often defined as "a false statement about a person that is to his or her discredit."[51] In general, the media in Canada are cautious in what they write or broadcast, and the politicians are fairly thick-skinned, so that court cases involving libel are relatively rare. Three celebrated exceptions involved a CBC television show portraying former Alberta Premier Peter Lougheed in an unflattering light in negotiations over the tar sands project, a *Victoria Times* cartoon featuring Bill Vander Zalm, then the B.C. welfare minister, plucking the wings off a fly representing welfare recipients, and accounts in the *Ottawa Citizen* of Mulroney Defence Minister Robert Coates's night-time activities on an official trip to Germany.[52] Less serious instances of media bias or error are supposed to be handled by the CRTC or voluntary press councils.

NEWS MANAGEMENT

"News leaks" are yet another issue in the relations between media and politicians. When governments do not know what course to follow, they sometimes leak a proposal to the media as a "trial balloon," hoping for guidance from the kind of reaction received. Black points out that this practice is necessary because today's politicians usually have little time to respond to problems and little chance to sit back and give them comprehensive consideration.[53]

Leaks are a part of a broader problem of **news management** and manipulation, which appears to be increasingly common.[54] This relates especially to the timing and selective distribution of information; exaggerating the positive while keeping secret or past deadline time that which is negative; giving preference to friendly reporters over others; making prime ministerial requests for network television time for less than important announcements; or outright lying. News management also involves putting the best face on an unpopular government action or a politician's performance by having a partisan official tell the media how successful it actually was, in the hope that the media will transmit this evaluation to their audience. Those involved in such efforts are often called "media handlers" or **spin doctors**, because they try to put the best face, or "spin," on any event.

An even more serious aspect of news management, one that is sometimes justified, is censorship via the War Measures Act or Official Secrets Act. In 1970, for example, the media were prohibited from transmitting any stories that supported the FLQ. Short of actual censorship is the highly secretive tradition of Canadian governments. In 1982, however, the Access to Information Act made it somewhat easier for the media as well as other interested parties to obtain access to government information.

The ultimate problem in media–government relations is political interference with the "freedom of the press," or as the Charter of Rights puts it, "freedom of the press and other media of communication." This is one of the sacred principles of democracy as discussed in Chapter 13. The most blatant examples of such political interference have occurred at the provincial level. In Quebec, Maurice Duplessis kept the press under control by awarding advertising and printing contracts to newspaper owners and financial gifts to members of the press gallery.[55] In Alberta, the Social Credit government in the 1930s deliberately tried to force newspapers to retract any criticisms of the government. Occasional attempts have apparently been made by the Prime Minister's Office over the years to have the CBC take a certain perspective on a vital national issue. Much has been written—both claiming and refuting bias—about the CBC's coverage of the Meech Lake Accord.[56] Government pressure was also suspected in 1966 when the CBC cancelled the highly popular but critical public affairs program "This Hour Has Seven Days."[57] On the French side, the Trudeau government accused the Radio-Canada network of being riddled with separatists who gave a biased interpretation of federal–provincial relations. Although there was probably some truth to the charge, it smacked of political interference.

PUBLIC OPINION POLLS

Opinions are more specific, numerous, and changeable than values and attitudes. While very unstable, opinions about topical issues and current personalities often affect the political behaviour of individuals, especially in voting, and frequently influence the actions of government.

Measuring Public Opinion

The phrase **public opinion** is sometimes used to imply that all members of the public hold a unanimous, informed view on a particular issue. In actuality, many opinions are held on any issue, and each issue only interests a certain segment of the population. Furthermore, most political opinions are not well informed. They are based on little information, they are simplifications of complex issues, and they are often internally contradictory. Indeed, it is often the case that people form their opinions first and then look for information to confirm them; at the very least, they "seek out information that conforms to their predispositions ... and avoid or reinterpret any contrary and non-supportive messages."[58]

Given this great conglomeration of viewpoints, public opinion is very difficult to gauge. Haphazard methods such as reading editorials or letters to the editor or listening to open-line programs are obviously unreliable, but so are many amateur public opinion surveys. On the other hand, professional polling agencies claim to be able to select a representative sample of people, ask carefully worded questions, and report with a high degree of accuracy the opinions of the whole population. Such polls have assumed an immense importance in contemporary Canadian politics: "No political party plans campaign strategy without them, no government is prepared to risk major policy initiatives without gauging public opinion, and for major news organizations they are an indispensable reporting tool, both between and during elections."[59]

Beyond the now-common procedure for conducting a public opinion poll, two special techniques deserve mention. The first is "tracking," which entails telephoning samples of 100 to 500 people nightly during an election campaign in order to see how day-to-day developments are affecting them. The second is the "focus group," in which a small number of people are gathered together behind a one-way mirror with a group leader who encourages them to voice their "gut" reaction to various leaders, issues and slogans.[60]

Who are these professional pollsters?[61] The Canadian Institute for Public Opinion (CIPO) is the Canadian branch of the Gallup organization in the United States, the pioneer of public opinion measurement. It has operated in Canada since 1941 and is financed primarily by the newspapers in which its results appear. Gallup regularly asks the question "If an election were held today, which party's candidate do you think you would vote for?" Both the politicians and media anxiously await its monthly results. Other, newer pollsters generally look down on Gallup methodology, as well as the practice of private parties paying Gallup to attach supplementary questions to its survey. This technique has been frequently used by prospective leadership challengers when they want to show that more people would support the party if they became leader, as well as by single-interest pressure groups.

Another well-known pollster in Canada is Martin Goldfarb who was the official Liberal Party pollster from 1972 to the early 1990s and who worked closely with long-time party strategist Senator Keith Davey. Goldfarb also had corporate clients and did frequent and lucrative work for many federal government departments throughout the Trudeau regime. The Liberal Party began polling in earnest in 1961 and used U.S. pollsters before settling on Goldfarb.

The Conservatives originally employed U.S. polling firms, too, but around 1977 Allan Gregg and his Decima Research became the official party pollster. Like Goldfarb, Gregg had a corporate clientele and did polling for government departments when his party was in power. He later sold Decima Research to the lobby firm Hill and Knowlton, and after the disastrous 1993 PC campaign, severed his ties with both organizations, later emerging with a new polling company of his own.

Another major firm is Environics Research Group headed by Michael Adams and Donna Dasko. For some time Environics did quarterly public opinion surveys for the *Globe and Mail* and *Le Devoir*, but after 1990 the *Globe* teamed up with the CBC instead. Environics worked closely with the Quebec polling firm CROP, and the two firms became partners in 1988; the other major polling company in Quebec is Léger & Léger. In the 1993 election campaign the Reform Party used Environics surveys.

Angus Reid is another national polling firm. After doing work for the Liberals, the NDP, and various media outlets, Reid hoped to succeed Goldfarb as the official Liberal Party pollster. When the Liberals decided to stay with Goldfarb, Reid sold a 60 percent interest in his firm to Southam in 1989. Goldfarb was eventually replaced as the Liberal Party pollster by Michael Marzolini of Insight Canada, who had worked with CTV in the 1988 election.

Thus, more than half of the major public opinion polling operations in Canada are now attached to a political party or to a media outlet. They all have slightly different methodologies and are never hesitant to criticize each other, especially when the results of one survey differ from those of another. Indeed, considering their checkered track records, their contradictions and partisan ties, it is surprising how confident most of these pollsters are about their work.[62]

Exactly how accurate are they? The only way a survey's accuracy can be tested is through a comparison of its results immediately before an election with the electoral outcome itself. The immediate pre-election findings of most professional agencies have usually been within the range of accuracy the survey claimed, typically that the results were accurate within plus or minus four percent 19 times out of 20, although Gallup was quite wide of the mark in 1957 and 1980.

When two or more firms are seeking the same information but produce different results, doubts naturally arise about their methodology. The way a question is worded, the optional responses available, the sequence of the questions, the degree to which respondents are telling the truth, and many other variables can influence the result and account for such differences. Timing is also an important consideration, for results can sometimes be out-of-date by the time they are tabulated and reported.[63]

Impact of Polls on the Public

Perhaps the main issue that arises in the discussion of polls and pollsters is whether their pre-election predictions influence the actual election results. This question cannot be answered categorically, but it is unlikely that their direct effect is that great. First, most voters do not pay much attention to the poll results; second, not everyone believes them, and third, it is not important to everyone to vote for the winning side even if this is clear in advance. While some voters may want to jump on the victorious bandwagon—**bandwagon effect**—at least a few are likely to switch to the predicted loser—"the underdog effect"—either out of sympathy or to try to prevent an overwhelming victory for the prospective winner.[64]

On the other hand, polls may have a significant indirect effect on the election results. The media are as obsessed with the polls as the politicians are, and the survey results may well lead the media to concentrate on those parties and politicians who are in the lead or ignore those who are trailing. Furthermore, polls have a considerable effect on party morale. A positive poll usually generates greater enthusiasm and effort, better candidates, and larger financial contributions, while a negative poll saps the spirit of leaders, candidates, and footsoldiers alike. Both of these results undoubtedly affect the subtle "momentum" of the campaign.

Another issue can be addressed more categorically: polls definitely detract from the discussion of real issues in the election campaign.[65] The media are fascinated by polls primarily because they are good for business, and, given the media's ability to influence the political agenda even during election campaigns, they emphasize the **horse-race effect** of the contest. They tend to spend more time on who is ahead than on comparative analysis of party platforms, asking leaders to comment on the latest poll results, for example, rather than how the party would deal with a particular public problem. Now that the media actually hire or even own polling firms, survey results are becoming major news items themselves.

Many political losers have blamed their fate on the public opinion polls and some have called for the prohibition of polls during part or all of the campaign. Such bans do exist in many countries.[66] Whatever their faults, however, polls enliven the campaign and increase the information available, and many argue that to prohibit their publication in the media would not prevent parties, candidates, and others from conducting their own surveys. The main effect of a publication ban would be to give certain crucial information to those who could afford a survey and to deny it to the general public, a highly undemocratic suggestion. As Claire Hoy writes,

> to the extent that published polls do reflect public opinion, they infringe on the closeted wisdom of the power elite, giving the general public at least some information it wouldn't otherwise be privy to.... The strength of published public-opinion polls is that the knowledge they provide, however flawed, undercuts the exclusivity of the power elite.[67]

To overcome problems with polling, then, more details about the methodology of the survey should be revealed—how it was conducted, when the interviews took place, what the actual questions were, how large the sample was, what the margin of error is, and who paid for it. The media must also be more judicious in their interpretation and presentation of survey results. Instead of concentrating on the result of an individual poll and exaggerating small differences from one survey to another, the media and other commentators should emphasize the long-term trend.

One of the amendments to the Canada Elections Act made in the wake of the Royal Commission on Electoral Reform was to prohibit, in the final three days of the campaign, the broadcast, publication, or dissemination of the results of new or scientifically conducted opinion surveys that would identify a political party or candidate. This restriction was soon challenged by the Thomson and Southam newspaper chains as a violation of freedom of the press.

Impact of Polls on the Authorities

The other main question in the study of public opinion is the relationship between polls and the response of the authorities.[68] For nearly 100 years after Confederation, governments had to act in the absence of a reliable survey, but it now seems that they are reluctant to make any decision until it can be based on a poll. Even with such a poll, however, opinion is likely to be considerably divided, and clear-cut guidance cannot always be found.

Sometimes, even when public opinion is clearly in favour of a certain course of government action, the authorities may decide otherwise. This may be the consequence of the politicians' own convictions, the recommendations of the public service, the pressure of interest groups, or the rigidity of party discipline. Indeed, some hold the view that even in a democracy, politicians are not obliged to follow public opinion; they may also lead it.[69] This is especially the case, now that we realize how uninformed, superficial, and changeable most public opinions really are. While politicians and bureaucrats may be accused of acting in their own self-interest if they do not follow a clear-cut preference among the public, they may actually be relying on a deeper understanding of the issue, the greater information at their disposal, a more sophisticated analysis of its implications, a concern for minority rights, or a less prejudicial attitude. For example, capital punishment has been an issue on which public opinion was quite clear, but one on which the authorities repeatedly went their own way. Should Parliament reinstate capital punishment in response to overwhelming popular opinion based on a mistaken impression about rising crime rates, a desire for retribution, and an assumption of deterrence? Most political issues are even more complicated than capital punishment, and on most, public opinion is much more divided; thus the correlation between public opinion and public policy is not as strong as might be expected.

It is sometimes said that the Trudeau government ignored public opinion while the Mulroney administration pandered to it. In fact, although Trudeau may have imposed official bilingualism without regard to public reaction, on other issues he was guided by the polls as much as any modern government. Mulroney was personally more interested in polls, but adopted many policies such as the GST in defiance of public opinion. Both governments and most others nowadays spend huge sums of public funds on surveying public attitudes on various issues. In his book *Margin of Error*, Hoy reveals just how many public policies were adopted over the years and how many election dates were set on the basis of polls. He also shows how important they were in the 1988 election campaign. First, the Conservatives used many publicly funded polls to determine their election platform. Second, the Liberals surveyed public opinion in Quebec to see if a Senate veto of the Free Trade Agreement would detract from their support in that province. Third, the NDP avoided the free trade issue (and left the Liberals to capitalize on it) because party polling indicated that the NDP lacked public credibility on economic issues.[70] Indeed, the NDP used focus groups as early as 1984 to find that the phrase "ordinary Canadians" was preferable to "working Canadians" in its advertising.[71] When even the NDP starts to base its strategy on focus groups and public opinion polls, it is hard to overstate their present significance.

CONCLUSION

Students of political science and other readers of this book quite likely belong to the small proportion of the population for whom politics is a central concern and who are well informed about the subject. Such readers must be careful not to assume that the rest of the population is similarly inclined. In any case, this chapter has demonstrated the enormous significance of the media, especially television and mass circulation newspapers, and documented the increasing use in all branches of politics of public opinion polls and polling firms. Individually and combined, the electronic media and public opinion polls have completely transformed Canadian politics in the past 50 years.[72]

Ⓒ Of the approaches outlined in Chapter 1, class analysts have the most to say about the subject matter of this chapter. They emphasize the deliberate attempt of the bourgeoisie to socialize the masses into an acceptance of the status quo. They argue that the public agents of socialization, the school and the media, transmit messages to serve the interests of the economic elite, the school through elite control of the political system, and the media through outright elite ownership. Traditional political parties and pressure groups join in to help define politics in nonclass terms so that the lower classes are socialized into supporting a system that does not operate in their interests.[73] Socialization, in such observers' terms, is indoctrination into the virtues of capitalism.

Class analysts also have much to say about the political role of the media. First, there is nothing as elitist in Canadian society as the ownership of newspapers and private radio and television stations, and such owners have been known to issue orders regarding coverage of political events. Second, the media elite also includes a small number of influential journalists and columnists from whom most of their colleagues take their lead. The media and political elites share socioeconomic characteristics and meet at social gatherings.[74] Third, even when owners do not deliberately interfere in the editorial operations of their companies, the media transmit role models and images of an elite version of reality. As Fletcher says, "the media tend to reinforce the dominant institutional and cultural patterns of authority. By setting the limits for public debate, the media generally exclude serious challenges to the status quo, whether from the left or the right."[75] Edwin Black adds that the public generally acquiesces in decision-making by the elites so long as their decisions do not stray very far beyond society's broad set of fundamental values, and even those values are subject to some manipulation.[76]

Neo-Marxists go somewhat further, arguing that

> the media are an important part of an ideological system that effectively pro-
> motes the dominant ideology of society, providing a justification for the eco-
> nomic and political status quo, thus serving the interests of the rich and
> powerful. By establishing the limits of debate, the media screen out radical cri-
> tiques and reinforce existing values.... [They promote] consumerism ... the myth
> of "middle classness," [and] ... private ownership of property, [and are] a power-
> ful ideological weapon for holding the mass of people in voluntary submission
> to capitalism."[77]

The economic and political elites can use their control over the mass media to legitimate their power and reduce the extent to which they need to rely on coercion. Portraying pro-testers, radicals, and union leaders among others in an unfavourable light and trivializing political discourse help enormously to maintain the status quo. While the public is easily convinced of the dangers of public control of the media, it does not seem to be concerned about problems resulting from concentrated private ownership. It is even more difficult for the general public to see how state intervention, for example, regulating ownership, could protect the principle of freedom of the press.[78]

Wallace Clement and others point to the extent to which the richest and most powerful families in Canada either made their fortunes in the media business or else control media out-lets alongside other interests.[79] They say, along with the Kent Report, that "freedom of the press is not a property right of owners."[80] The costs of establishing a new media outlet of any kind are prohibitive except to the most wealthy individuals in the land, and this pattern of ownership allows them to shield their economic operations from media scrutiny. Moreover, among the leading business pressure groups are the Canadian Association of Broadcasters (CAB), representing private radio and television companies, and the Canadian Daily

Newspaper Publishers' Association (CDNPA). Through pressure on the CRTC and successive governments, the CAB has ensured its members a highly profitable position in the Canadian broadcasting system, while nothing so demonstrates the political dominance of the economic elite as the quick abandonment of the Kent Report due to pressure from the CDNPA.

As for public opinion polls, the corporate connections between media outlets and public opinion polls confirm the worst fears of class analysts. Only affluent interests can afford a proper national poll, and to the extent that they can keep it secret, they enhance their control over the masses.

P In contrast, the pluralist approach emphasizes the multitude of media outlets in the country, including the increasing number of cable television channels and the creation of several new morning tabloid newspapers. There are many sources of information to choose from and considerable competition between and among them. Pluralists must concede, however, that only a few large cities enjoy competitive daily newspapers. Pluralists also see nothing but good coming out of the frequent revelations of the views of the public in the form of public opinion polls.

PC Public choice theorists have identified a "media game" between the media and the politicians corresponding to the rational, self-seeking relationship between politicians and voters.[81] In this case, the two parties are engaged in an exchange in which each needs the other in order to maximize its self-interest. As for public opinion polls, the public choice approach is probably most relevant because polls are a principal means for the authorities to identify what the public wants from the government.[82] In this view, the authorities detect what policies would get them the most votes and promise such policies in the election campaign. As Taras writes, "polling tells the parties where the swing votes are—in which regions and among which income, ethnic, and age groups—and the messages that are most likely to move those votes."[83]

SC State-centred theorists begin by pointing out how the state can use the school system to encourage each new generation to feel satisfied with the status quo or helpless to change it. The authorities also engage in massive publicly financed advertising campaigns to persuade the electorate of the wisdom of their actions. The prime minister attempts to influence public opinion through press conferences and special televised statements, for example, and the bureaucrats use the media to foster favourable publicity about their program needs, especially when fighting for additional resources or against stringent cutbacks. Perhaps the main method of manipulation used by the bureaucracy is not so much in what information is disseminated, however, as in that which is withheld. The state-centred approach also points out that the amount of money spent by governments and even bureaucrats to do their own polling is quite staggering.

DISCUSSION QUESTIONS

1. Think about the relative importance of the agents of political socialization in your own life. Can you decipher your own socialization process?

2. What is the ideal role for the school in the political socialization process? Distinguish between legitimate government information services and partisan propaganda.

3. Does the fact that media companies have an impact on public opinion mean that concentrated ownership should be more restricted than in other industries?

4. What are the advantages and disadvantages of obtaining information from each of television, radio, and newspapers?

5. What problems can arise in the relationship between the working press and the authorities?

6. Which is a greater threat to manipulation of public opinion: public ownership of the CBC or concentrated private ownership of private radio, television, and newspapers?

7. Should the publication of public opinion polls be prohibited at some stage of an election campaign? Explain.

8. How seriously should the authorities take the results of public opinion polls?

9. Is the government justified in taking so many public opinion polls at public expense? Explain.

10. How do the approaches outlined in Chapter 1 relate to the material in this chapter?

....

NOTES

1. Edwin R. Black, *Politics and the News: The Political Functions of the Mass Media* (Toronto: Butterworths, 1982), pp. 6–7.
2. Ronald Landes, "Political Education and Political Socialization," in Jon Pammett and Jean-Luc Pépin, eds., *Political Education in Canada* (Halifax: Institute for Research on Public Policy, 1988), p. 17.
3. Jon Pammett, "The Development of Political Orientations in Canadian School Children," *Canadian Journal of Political Science* (March 1971), pp. 132–140.
4. Marcel Trudel and Genevieve Jain, *Canadian History Textbooks: A Comparative Study* (Ottawa: Royal Commission on Bilingualism and Biculturalism, 1970).
5. Landes, "Political Education and Political Socialization," p. 17.
6. A.B. Hodgetts, *What Culture? What Heritage?* (Toronto: Ontario Institute for Studies in Education, 1968), p. 76.
7. Pammett and Pépin, *Political Education in Canada*, p. xvii.
8. For example, John Ricker and Alan Skeoch, "The Contribution of Ontario's Schools to Political Education," in Pammett and Pépin, *Political Education in Canada*, p. 70.
9. E. Katz and P.F. Lazarsfeld, *Personal Influence: The Part Played by People in the Flow of Mass Communications* (Glencoe, IL: Free Press, 1955).
10. Frederick Fletcher, "The Mass Media and Political Education," in Pammett and Pépin, p. 92.

11. In another kind of bias, Pierre Trudeau had the CRTC commission a study of separatist influence in Radio-Canada, the Boyle Committee, after the PQ victory in Quebec in 1976.

12. The Canadian Conference of Catholic Bishops has extended traditional Catholic concerns and made passionate appeals on poverty, unemployment, housing, and other class issues.

13. Alan Frizzell et al., *The Canadian General Election of 1988* (Ottawa: Carleton University Press), p. 69.

14. Peter Trueman, *Smoke and Mirrors: The Inside Story of Television News in Canada* (Toronto: McClelland and Stewart, 1980), p. 188.

15. Based on the author's calculations, using the August 1994 edition of *Canadian Advertising Rates and Data* published by Maclean-Hunter.

16. Stephen Brooks and Andrew Stritch, *Business and Government in Canada* (Scarborough: Prentice-Hall Canada, 1991). The mutually advantageous simultaneous closings were deemed to be a coincidence and a normal part of doing business.

17. Frederick J. Fletcher, *The Newspaper and Public Affairs* (Ottawa: Royal Commission on Newspapers, 1981), pp. 29, 35, 87. The main exception was Paul Desmarais, who insisted that his newspapers in Quebec not support the "Yes" position in the 1980 Quebec referendum. See also the Royal Commission Report, pp. 163–67; David Taras, *The Newsmakers* (Scarborough: Nelson Canada, 1990), pp. 8–17; and Ronald Wagenberg and Walter Soderlund, "The Effects of Chain Ownership on Editorial Coverage: The Case of the 1974 Canadian General Election," *Canadian Journal of Political Science* (December 1976), pp. 682–89.

18. Fletcher calls them "populist, parochial, colloquial and entertainment-oriented," ibid., p. 43; "opinionated, populist and anti-government," in Penniman, *Canada at the Polls, 1984* (Durham, N.C.: Duke University Press, 1988), p. 164.

19. Peter Desbarats, *Guide to Canadian News Media* (Toronto: Harcourt Brace Jovanovich, 1990) updates the ownership situation to 1990.

20. Frederick J. Fletcher and Daphne Gottlieb Taras, "Images and Issues: The Mass Media and Politics in Canada," in Michael Whittington and Glen Williams, eds., *Canadian Politics in the 1990s*, 3rd ed. (Scarborough: Nelson Canada, 1990), p. 229.

21. Black, *Politics and the News*, p. 80.

22 Trueman, *Smoke and Mirrors*, p. 161.

23. Radio Canada International also broadcasts programming abroad by short and medium wave, while other countries use its transmitters in New Brunswick to broadcast to the western hemisphere.

24. The general thrust of David Taras in *The Newsmakers*. See Chapter 11 of his book for a discussion of how the media are performing functions previously the domain of political parties.

25. John McMenemy, "Getting to Know the Parties by the Company We Keep: Local Sources of Party Imagery," in Alain Gagnon and Brian Tanguay, *Canadian Parties in Transition* (Scarborough: Nelson Canada, 1989), pp. 309–10.

26. Taras, *The Newsmakers*, pp. 30–31; Walter C. Soderlund et al., "Regional and Linguistic Agenda Setting," in *Canadian Journal of Political Science* (December 1980), pp. 347–56; and Walter C. Soderlund et al., *Media and Elections in Canada* (Toronto: Holt, Rinehart and Winston, 1984).

27. Fletcher, p. 16; Fletcher and Taras, p. 222; Black, p. 183; Desbarats, p. 149; and Arthur Siegel, *Politics and the Media in Canada* (Toronto: McGraw-Hill Ryerson, 1983), p. 14.

28. Taras, *The Newsmakers*, ch. 3; and Allan Levine, *Scrum Wars: the Prime Ministers and the Media* (Toronto: Dundurn Press, 1993).

29. With the possible exception of other papers in the same city. Siegel, *Politics and the Media in Canada*, pp. 184–196; and Taras, *The Newsmakers*, p. 52.

30. Black, *Politics and the News*, p. 122.

31. Leonard Kubas, *Newspapers and Their Readers* (Ottawa: Royal Commission on Newspapers, 1981), pp. 11–12.

32. Environics Media Study (Environics Research Group, December 1986), cited by Desbarats, *Guide to Canadian News Media*, p. 28; and its *1991 Media Study*.

33. Taras, *The Newsmakers*, p. 102.

34. For example, in the GST debate, Jean Chrétien and his Liberal colleagues from the House of Commons marched to the doors of the Senate, and the senators "invited" television cameras onto the floor to substitute for the lack of coverage of the Senate debate on television. The Oka standoff involved concerted attempts by both sides to control the TV coverage.

35. Alan Frizzell et al., *The Canadian General Election of 1988* (Ottawa: Carleton University Press, 1989), p. 33.

36. Taras, *The Newsmakers*, ch. 4.

37. Black, *Politics and the News*, p. 90.

38. Taras, *The Newsmakers*, ch. 5; Penniman, *Canada at the Polls, 1984*, pp. 184 and 201; and Levine, *Scrum Wars*.

39. Allan Fotheringham, *Birds of a Feather: The Press and the Politicians* (Toronto: Key Porter Books, 1989), pp. 190–92.

40. Fletcher, *The Newspaper and Public Affairs*, p. 23.

41. Ibid., p. 30; Taras, *The Newsmakers*, pp. 87–89.

42. Fletcher, *The Newspaper and Public Affairs*, p. 11.

43. In contrast to Pierre Trudeau, who characteristically held the media in contempt while on occasion manipulating them masterfully (notably in the 1968 election and the 1970 October Crisis), Brian Mulroney, a media and telephone junkie, telephoned editors on occasion to canvass their opinion, but with no comparable mastery. Michel Gratton, *So, What Are the Boys Saying?* (Toronto: McGraw-Hill Ryerson, 1987); and Taras, *The Newsmakers*, pp. 139-140. Jean Chrétien is related to Paul Desmarais through the marriage of their children.

44. Allan Fotheringham claims that until his retirement in 1988, editor Beland Honderich ran the *Star* with an iron hand and manipulated the news in favour of his own political predilections. See *Birds of a Feather*, pp. 73, 94–95. The *Globe and Mail* found it necessary to reprint a collage of its pro–free trade editorials on the page opposite shortly before the election.

45. Frizzell, *The Canadian General Election of 1988*, p. 84; and *1984*, pp. 60–68. R.H. Wagenberg et al., "Campaigns, Images and Polls: Mass Media Coverage of the 1984 Canadian Election," *Canadian Journal of Political Science* (March 1988), pp. 117–29.

46. Taras, *The Newsmakers*, pp. 76–79.

47. Fotheringham, *Birds of a Feather*, p. 139.

48. Ibid., p. 33.

49. Taras, *The Newsmakers*, ch. 3.

50. Fotheringham, *Birds of a Feather*, p. 249.

51. Siegel, *Politics and the Media in Canada*, p. 80.

52. Ibid., pp. 79–82; Wilfred H. Kesterton, *The Law and the Press in Canada* (Toronto: McClelland and Stewart, 1976); The Royal Commission on Newspapers, pp. 47–53; and Desbarats, *Guide to Canadian News Media*, p. 157.

53. Black, *Politics and the News*, p. 12; Taras, *The Newsmakers*, p. 234.

54. See books by such press secretaries as Patrick Gossage, *Close to the Charisma: My Years between the Press and Pierre Elliott Trudeau* (Toronto: McClelland and Stewart, 1986), and Michel Gratton, *So, What Are the Boys Saying? An Inside Look at Brian Mulroney in Power* (Toronto: Paper Jacks, 1988); and Taras, *The Newsmakers*, pp. 125–130, 158, 172.

55. Pierre Laporte, *The True Face of Duplessis* (Montreal: Harvest House, 1960).

56. David Taras, "Television and Public Policy: The CBC's Coverage of the Meech Lake Accord," *Canadian Public Policy* (September 1989), pp. 322–34; Elly Alboim, "Inside the News Story: Meech Lake as Viewed by an Ottawa Bureau Chief," in Roger Gibbins et al., eds., *Meech Lake and Canada: Perspectives from the West* (Edmonton: Academic Printing and Publishing, 1988); and John Meisel, "Mirror? Searchlight? Interloper?—The Media and Meech," in David Smith, Peter MacKinnon, and John Courtney, eds., *After Meech Lake: Lessons for the Future* (Saskatoon: Fifth House Publishers, 1991).

57. Desbarats, *Guide to Canadian News Media*, p. 41.

58. Black, *Politics and the News*, p. 168. Frizzell and Westell are not overly concerned about the bias in any individual newspaper, for example, because "people are selective in what they read, have many

sources of information, and use information to some degree to reinforce their own opinions." Frizzell, *The Canadian General Election of 1988*, p. 88.

59. Frizzell, *1988*, p. 91.
60. Taras, *The Newsmakers*, pp. 182–186.
61. Ibid., ch. 7.
62. The height of arrogance is expressed by Goldfarb in Martin Goldfarb and Thomas Axworthy, *Marching to a Different Drummer* (Toronto: Stoddart, 1988).
63. Taras, *The Newsmakers*, pp. 187–92.
64. John Turner's election in Vancouver Quadra in 1984 is often cited as an example of the underdog effect, given that all polls in the constituency indicated that he would lose.
65. Taras, *The Newsmakers*, p. 187, 192–94; Desbarats, *Guide*, p. 138.
66. Claire Hoy, *Margin of Error* (Toronto: Key Porter Books, 1989), pp. 219–20; and Taras, *The Newsmakers*, p. 193.
67. Hoy, *Margin of Error*, p. 228. Hoy discusses the government's first poll on the conscription issue in 1942, which it wanted to keep secret, p. 14. See also Paul Fox, "The Danger Is Private Polling," in Paul Fox and Graham White, eds., *Politics: Canada*, 6th ed. (Toronto: McGraw-Hill Ryerson, 1987).
68. Richard Johnston, *Public Opinion and Public Policy in Canada* (Toronto: University of Toronto Press, 1986).
69. Hoy writes that in one view "the essence of parliamentary democracy is that we elect politicians to lead, to take risks, to stand for something more than the latest popular sentiment or the collective public wisdom, which may be based more on short-term emotion or outright ignorance than on anything else," p. 7.
70. Hoy, *Margin of Error*, pp. 1–5. In 1984, the NDP fired one pollster and hired an American replacement, Vic Fingerhut, over the issue of trying to change the negative public perception of its economic policies. See Howard K. Penniman, ed., *Canada at the Polls, 1984* (Durham NC: Duke University Press, 1988), p. 129.
71. Penniman, p. 131.
72. Taras, *The Newsmakers*, pp. 233–38.
73. Janine Brodie and Jane Jenson, *Crisis, Challenge and Change: Party and Class in Canada Revisited* (Ottawa: Carleton University Press, 1988).
74. Fotheringham describes one such event, a Barbara Frum party, in *Birds of a Feather*, pp. 146–50.
75. Fletcher, "Images and Issues," pp. 233–34.
76. Black, *Politics and the News*, pp. 188–89.
77. Fletcher and Taras, "Images and Issues," p. 223; Black, *Politics and the News*, pp. 43–44; John Porter, *The Vertical Mosaic* (Toronto: University of Toronto Press, 1965), ch. XV; and Ted Magder, "Taking Culture Seriously: A Political Economy of Communications," in Wallace Clement and Glen Williams, eds., *The New Canadian Political Economy* (Montreal: McGill–Queen's University Press, 1989). The "right-wing shift" at the *Globe and Mail* in 1989 could also be mentioned.
78. Desbarats, *Guide to Canadian News Media*, p. 69.
79. Wallace Clement, *The Canadian Corporate Elite* (Toronto: McClelland and Stewart, 1975), pp. 270–86.
80. Royal Commission on Newspapers, p. 1.
81. M.J. Trebilcock et al., *The Choice of Governing Instrument* (Ottawa: Supply and Services, 1982); and W.T. Stanbury, *Business–Government Relations in Canada* (Toronto: Methuen, 1986), pp. 147–48 and ch. 11.
82. Trebilcock et al., *The Choice of Governing Instrument*.
83. Taras, *The Newsmakers*, p. 186.

FURTHER READING

Babe, Robert E. *Telecommunications in Canada: Technology, Industry, and Government.* Toronto: University of Toronto Press, 1990.

Bird, Roger, ed. *Documents of Canadian Broadcasting*. Ottawa: Carleton University Press, 1988.

Black, E.R. *Politics and the News: The Political Functions of the Mass Media*. Toronto: Butterworths, 1982.

Comber, Mary Anne, and Robert S. Mayne. *The Newsmongers: How the Media Distort the Political News*. Toronto: McClelland and Stewart, 1986.

Desbarats, Peter. *Guide to Canadian News Media*. Toronto: Harcourt Brace Jovanovich, 1990.

Ericson, R.V., P.M. Baranek, and J.B.L. Chan. *Negotiating Control: A Study of News Sources*. Toronto: University of Toronto Press, 1989.

Fletcher, Frederick J. *The Newspaper and Public Affairs*. Ottawa: Royal Commission on Newspapers, 1981.

Fletcher, Frederick J., and Daphne Gottlieb Taras. "Images and Issues: The Mass Media and Politics in Canada." In Michael Whittington and Glen Williams, eds. *Canadian Politics in the 1990s*. Scarborough: Nelson Canada, 3rd ed., 1990; 4th ed., 1995.

Fotheringham, Allan. *Birds of a Feather: The Press and the Politicians*. Toronto: Key Porter Books, 1990.

Fox, Paul. "The Danger Is Private Polling." In Paul Fox and Graham White, eds. *Politics: Canada*. 6th ed. Toronto: McGraw-Hill Ryerson, 1987.

Frizzell, Alan, et al. *The Canadian General Election of 1984*. Ottawa: Carleton University Press, 1985.

———. *The Canadian General Election of 1988*. Ottawa: Carleton University Press, 1989.

———. *The Canadian General Election of 1993*. Ottawa: Carleton University Press, 1994.

Hodgetts, A.B. *What Culture? What Heritage? A Study of Civil Education in Canada*. Toronto: Ontario Institute for Studies in Education, 1968.

Holmes, Helen, and David Taras, eds. *In the Public Interest: Mass Media and Democracy in Canada*. Toronto: Holt, Rinehart and Winston, 1992.

Hoy, Claire. *Margin of Error*. Toronto: Key Porter Books, 1989.

Kubas, Leonard. *Newspapers and Their Readers*. Ottawa: Royal Commission on Newspapers, 1981.

Magder, Ted. "Taking Culture Seriously: A Political Economy of Communications." In Wallace Clement and Glen Williams, eds. *The New Canadian Political Economy*. Montreal: McGill–Queen's University Press, 1989.

Pammett, Jon, and Jean-Luc Pépin, eds. *Political Education in Canada*. Halifax: Institute for Research on Public Publicy, 1988.

Royal Commission on Newspapers. Ottawa: Supply and Services, 1981. See also its background research studies.

Sawatsky, John. *The Insiders: Government, Business and the Lobbyists*. Toronto: McClelland and Stewart, 1987.

Siegel, Arthur. *Politics and the Media in Canada*. Toronto: McGraw-Hill Ryerson, 1983.

Taras, David. *The Newsmakers*. Scarborough: Nelson Canada, 1990.

Trudel, Marcel and Genevieve Jain. *Canadian History Textbooks: A Comparative Study*. Ottawa: Royal Commission on Bilingualism and Biculturalism, 1970.

Trueman, Peter. *Smoke and Mirrors: The Inside Story of Television News in Canada*. Toronto: McClelland and Stewart, 1980.

Vipond, Mary. *The Mass Media in Canada*. Toronto: Lorimer, 1989.

Chapter 15

The
ELECTORAL
System

One of the most controversial clauses of the Charlottetown Accord would have given Quebec 25 percent of the seats in the House of Commons regardless of whether its future population merited such a number. Yet few people complain that Prince Edward Island has four seats when its population barely justifies two. Governing parties often claim a mandate to implement their election platform, yet rarely secure the support of a majority of those who vote and even more rarely a majority of the electorate as a whole. Opposition parties, on the other hand, are usually short-changed in the number of seats they obtain. Even greater controversy surrounds the question of party and election finance. If elections are a crucial component in the definition of a democracy, it is important that they be conducted in the fairest possible way.

This chapter examines the formal, legal, and official aspects of the electoral system, and has four parts: redistribution, or determining the number of seats each province is entitled to and drawing the electoral map; the official organization of elections; an evaluation of the electoral system and suggestions for reform; and party and election finance. The actual electoral contest between political parties and the questions of electoral behaviour and party support are discussed in Chapter 17.

THE REDISTRIBUTION PROCESS

Redistribution is the process of dividing the country into electoral districts or constituencies. It involves two stages: first, deciding how many seats in the House of Commons to allot to each province and territory, and second, actually drawing constituency boundaries within them.

Distribution of Seats among Provinces

The Constitution Act of 1867 requires that the readjustment process be repeated after each decennial census, for example, 1971, 1981, and 1991. Given the federal character of Canada with its strong provincial loyalties, the search for a fair means of distributing seats in the House of Commons among the provinces has been a long and unsatisfactory one. Four different formulas have been used over the years, but none has ever commanded unanimous support.[1] The formula used following the 1981 census and the one that resulted in the current 295 seats in the House of Commons after the 1988 and 1993 elections was adopted by means of the Representation Act, 1985. It involves the four following steps.

1. Starting with 282 seats, two seats are allocated to the Northwest Territories and one to the Yukon, leaving 279 seats.
2. The total population of the ten provinces is divided by 279 to obtain the electoral quota or quotient.
3. This electoral quota is divided into the population of each province to obtain the number of seats each is entitled to. (Remainders over 0.5 are rounded upward.)
4. If these provincial seat allocations result in any province having fewer seats than it has senators, then (under the "senatorial clause") it obtains such additional seats as to equal its number of senators, and if it results in any province having fewer seats than it had in 1985, then (under the "grandfather clause") such additional seats are also added.

Table 15.1 illustrates how such calculations were made. The grandfather clause, guaranteeing provinces at least as many seats as they had in 1985, was a political compromise arrived at to ensure that while no province would lose seats, those that were entitled to additional seats would only get about half as many as they were entitled to. As a result, Ontario, B.C., and Alberta have fewer seats than their populations justify, and all other provinces and territories are overrepresented. The Royal Commission on Electoral Reform recommended that Canada return to its original mechanism of distributing seats among provinces so that those with growing populations would not be penalized. When redistribution takes place, Ontario is entitled to four more seats and B.C. to two, for a total of 301.

Drawing Constituency Boundaries

The second phase of the redistribution process, drawing constituency boundaries within each province, was historically the prerogative of the politicians. They regularly engaged in the process of **gerrymandering**, that is, manipulating constituency boundaries so as to ensure as far as possible the re-election of the members of the government party.[2] In the absence of any written rules, some constituencies had huge populations while others were extremely small. A new system was adopted in the Electoral Boundaries Readjustment Act of 1964, however, so that beginning with the post-1961 redistribution, this task has been performed by inde-

TABLE 15.1 Calculation of Redistribution, 1986

Calculations

Province or Territory	No. of Seats Established in 1976 and Comprising 33rd Parliament	Population 1981	*Quotient	Seats	Applications of Senatorial and Grandfather Clauses	Total	Electoral Quotient
Ontario	95	8 625 107	87 005	99.133 (99)	—	99	87 122
Quebec	75	6 438 403	87 005	74.000 (74)	+1	75	85 845
Nova Scotia	11	847 442	87 005	9.740 (10)	+1	11	77 040
N.B.	10	696 403	87 005	8.004 (8)	+2	10	69 640
Manitoba	14	1 026 241	87 005	11.795 (12)	+2	14	73 303
B.C.	28	2 744 467	87 005	31.543 (32)	—	32	85 765
P.E.I.	4	122 506	87 005	1.408 (1)	+3	4	30 627
Saskatchewan	14	968 313	87 005	11.129 (11)	+3	14	69 165
Alberta	21	2 237 724	87 005	25.719 (26)	—	26	86 066
Newfoundland	7	567 681	87 005	6.525 (7)	—	7	81 097
N.W.T.	2	45 741	—	—	—	2	—
Yukon	1	23 153	—	—	—	1	—
Total	282	24 343 181				295	

Detailed Calculation
  1. Assign 2 seats to N.W.T. and one to Yukon (3 seats).
 *2. Use 279 seats and population (excluding N.W.T. and Yukon to establish quotient (24 274 287 ÷ 279 = 87 005).
  3. Calculate number of seats per province using quotient; remainder rounded up if higher than 0.50.
  4. Add seats to provinces pursuant to "senatorial clause" guarantee in the Constitution and new "grandfather clause" (based on 33rd Parliament).

Source: Reproduced with permission of the Chief Electoral Officer of Canada.

pendent commissions. An electoral boundaries commission is appointed for each province and one for the Northwest Territories, chaired by a judge designated by the chief justice of the province. The other two members of each commission are appointed by the Speaker of the House of Commons, typically including an academic and the provincial chief electoral officer or some other nonpartisan legislative official. All commissions draw extensively on the support and assistance of the chief electoral officer's staff.

The commissions swing into action as soon as the provincial population figures are available from the census. Theirs is a very delicate task of trying to arrive at a design that will provide constituencies of approximately equal population size throughout the province while also accounting for geographic characteristics, communities of interest, and other peculiarities. The most difficult problem is in dealing with sparsely populated rural or northern regions at the same time as concentrated urban centres. In recognition of this problem, the commissions in the 1960s and 1970s were allowed to deviate from the average population figure to a maximum tolerance of plus or minus 25 percent, but in the 1980s the law allowed them to exceed this limit "in circumstances viewed by the commission as being extraordinary" in order to arrive at a manageable geographic size for all districts. They must also consider the "community of interest or community of identity in or the historial pattern of an electoral district." Thus rural and northern constituencies tend to be under the provincial quotient and southern, urban ones slightly over it. In the 1985 operation, only five constituencies out of 295 exceeded the 25 percent limit (two in each of Newfoundland and Quebec and one in Ontario), while one-third were within plus or minus five percent and another one-third fell between plus or minus five and 10 percent.[3] The Royal Commission recommended a tolerance of 15 percent.

The publication of the map of proposed electoral boundaries is followed by a period of public hearings, which are normally held at several different locations in the province. During these hearings interested individuals, municipalities, groups, and MPs appear to express their views on the proposals. Then, within a year of the population data's becoming available, the commissions must complete their reports. They are sent through the chief electoral officer to the Speaker of the House of Commons, who must ensure that they are tabled and referred to the appropriate Commons committee. Written objections, signed by at least ten MPs may be filed with this committee, which has 30 days while the House is sitting to discuss and raise objections to the report. The committee's proceedings are sent back to the electoral boundaries commissions, which have the authority to alter their report or leave it as is. Thus, it is the independent commissions and not the politicans who have the final say.[4] Because of the time needed by the chief electoral officer, returning officers, and political parties to make adjustments in their operations, the new boundaries cannot be used at an election until at least one year after the date that the representation order encompassing the new boundaries is proclaimed. This is why the 1993 election was held on the basis of the 1981 census.

The effect of the provisions of both aspects of the redistribution process is to undermine the basic democratic principle of political equality or "one person, one vote." Since it takes a smaller number of votes in smaller provinces and in rural parts of all provinces to elect a member of Parliament, such votes are worth more than those in large provinces or in urban areas. John Courtney points out that the degree of intraprovincial similarity in constituency size is increasing, but that there is a widening disparity between the size of constituencies in different provinces.[5] In general, however, Canadians accept this deviation from the principle of representation by population or political equality out of charity, ignorance, or recognition of the fact that the Canadian population is peculiarly distributed. On the other hand, the democratic rights provision of the Charter of Rights and Freedoms opens up the possibility of a legal challenge on this subject.

The processes outlined above did not unfold as they were supposed to after the 1991 census. The electoral boundaries commissions drew new maps, which were ready shortly after the

1993 election, but many newly elected MPs were not happy with the results. A government bill would have abolished the boundaries commissions and suspended the Electoral Boundaries Readjustment Act for up to two years, possibly pre-empting a redistribution before the next election. The Tory majority in the Senate was unhappy with this apparent abuse of power by the Liberal majority in the Commons, and amended the bill to give the House time to make immediate changes to the act. The whole issue was sent to the Standing Committee on Procedure and House Affairs, which produced a new redistribution bill, unusual in that it was the product of a standing committee rather than being a government bill. The Senate was not entirely happy with the proposed changes, however, and delayed passage of the bill. Its main provisions are listed below.

MAIN PROVISIONS OF BILL C-69, THE PROPOSED NEW ELECTORAL BOUNDARIES ACT

* Redistribution of seats within a province would take place after each five-year census if there had been substantial population shifts.
* People could apply for positions on the electoral boundaries commissions; the House of Commons could veto the Speaker's appointments.
* Redistribution would not take place in those provinces that had no significant population shifts.
* There would be more opportunity for public input early in the process.
* Electoral boundaries commissions would prepare three alternative maps rather than one.
* Clearer guidelines would be issued to commissions regarding the use of community of interest and other factors.
* In extraordinary circumstances, constituencies could be less than 75 percent of the provincial quotient, but only if they were geographically isolated from the rest of the province or not readily accessible from it.
* A second set of hearings would be held after commissions release their final proposals if there are significant changes.
* The right of the House of Commons to review proposals of electoral boundaries commissions would be discontinued.
* New boundaries would come into force more quickly.

Meanwhile, as mentioned in Chapter 5, several provincial redistribution schemes have been challenged in the courts as violations of democratic rights in the Charter of Rights and Freedoms. Such a fate could also await a defective federal redistribution proposal.[6]

THE OFFICIAL ELECTION MACHINERY

Setting the Date

The prime minister normally has the prerogative to call the election within a five-year period from the previous trip to the polls. Largely based on the government party's standings in the public opinion polls, the election is typically called about four years after the previous campaign. Going into the fifth year, especially to the five-year limit, is usually seen as a sign of political weakness, and most governments that have waited that long have been defeated. Public opinion polls can be wrong, of course, or public opinion can change between the calling of the election and the actual voting day, so that the apparent advantage for the party in power in choosing the election date is not absolute, as John Turner discovered in 1984 when an 11-point lead in June dissolved into a 22-point lag in September. Many such reversals during the campaign period have also occurred at the provincial level, and Chapter 17 discusses the highly volatile nature of Canadian party preferences. Nevertheless, because of the potential unfairness of the existing system and because the uncertainty of the date causes inconvenience to many of those involved, some observers would prefer to establish fixed election dates. New Zealand has demonstrated that this can be done within the British parliamentary system.

The governor general must approve the prime minister's request to dissolve Parliament in order to call an election, but this is normally automatic. Only once in Canadian history (1926), in rather peculiar circumstances, did a governor general refuse such a request.[7] The defeat of a government in a nonconfidence vote in the House of Commons is the alternative precipitator of an election, in which case the prime minister's leeway is limited to choosing the exact date. The average time between elections since 1867 (reduced because of minority governments) has been about 41 months.

Election Officials

The **chief electoral officer** (CEO) is responsible for the overall administration of the election and must function with absolute impartiality. This post is therefore filled by a resolution of the whole House of Commons, rather than by a regular public servant hired by the government. On the other hand, *returning officers*, who organize the election in each of the 295 electoral districts (also called constituencies or ridings), are chosen by the cabinet, and are usually partisan appointees. Ironically, once appointed, they are expected to function in a completely nonpartisan fashion. Before the election call, each returning officer will have divided the constituency into polling divisions (or polls) of about 250 voters each, and a typical urban constituency will have about 250 polls. Because such preparations must be made beforehand, returning officers work part-time between elections and full-time during the campaign. They usually serve until a different party comes to power and replaces them with its own supporters. Many observers, including former CEO Jean-Marc Hamel, believe that this peculiar and paradoxical situation should be changed.[8]

The Voters List

In Canadian federal elections, the **voters list** is normally compiled from scratch after the election writ is issued. Since the reforms of 1993, the returning officer appoints two enumerators per poll in both urban and rural areas to go door to door and collect the names of eligible voters. The returning officer asks the two candidates who finished first and second on the previous occasion to nominate enumerators, and matches them in pairs so that they will not manipulate the voters list for partisan purposes. Once the enumerators type up the preliminary list for their poll, a card is sent to everyone included to confirm their enumeration and to provide details about when and where to vote. Those who were not enumerated have a chance to get their names included in the revision process. It used to be that only in rural polls could a ballot be issued to a person whose name was not on the voters' list, but the 1993 reforms extended this opportunity to valid voters in urban polls as well. It is largely because the voters list is compiled after the election is called that Canadian election campaigns are at least 47 days long; some kind of permanent voters list is often suggested so that campaigns could be shortened, and advances in computer technology will likely bring changes before long.

The 1993 reforms permitted the use of electoral lists prepared within the previous 12 months to substitute for a full-fledged enumeration. Since the 1992 Referendum was held almost exactly a year before the 1993 election, there was no 1993 enumeration except in Quebec (which had held its own simultaneous referendum). Even with ample provision for additions and revisions, this provision proved to generate considerable confusion.

Nomination

Once the enumeration process is on track, the returning officer is ready to receive official nominations. Most candidates are nominated by a political party, but they must submit formal **nomination** papers endorsed by 100 people on the local voters list accompanied by a $1000 deposit. Candidates receive one-half of this amount back if and when they file their financial statement, and those who received at least 15 percent of the vote are also reimbursed the other $500. Official candidates of registered parties must obtain the party leader's endorsement in order to use the party name on the ballot. This requirement was mainly adopted to pre-empt the possibility of local conflicts over who was the legitimate standard-bearer of the party, but it effectively gives the leader a veto over nominations—with many implications. In 1974, for example, Robert Stanfield denied the party label to Leonard Jones, who was nominated as the Conservative candidate in Moncton, because of Jones's outspoken opposition to official bilingualism, and Brian Mulroney refused to endorse discredited ex–cabinet minister Sinclair Stevens in 1988. When a number of Liberal backbenchers voted against government bills in mid-1995, Prime Minister Chrétien warned them that he might not sign their nomination papers in the next election.

Election Day

After nomination day, the returning officer arranges for the ballots to be printed and then allows people to vote in advance polls or by special ballot.[9] The 1993 reforms made voting much more convenient for those not at home on election day, including members of the armed forces and federal and provincial government officials posted outside the country; those absent from the country for less than five years who intend to return; and those who are unable to vote at the advance poll. By this time, the returning officer is also busy hiring and training deputy returning officers and poll clerks to look after each polling station on election day and finding appropriate polling stations, typically in schools, church basements, or community centres.

Canadian federal elections are held from 9 A.M. to 8 P.M. local time on Mondays. The 1993 reforms scrapped the clause whereby, if the Monday in question was a statutory holiday the election would be held on the next day. Voters are entitled to four consecutive hours in which to cast their ballot, so that those working normal hours are usually let off at 4 P.M. Polling stations must have level access, and mobile polls may also be established for the elderly or disabled. Other attempts to make the whole process more user-friendly allow the appointment of an interpreter and the use of a template for the visually impaired. Since 1993, the sale of liquor is no longer prohibited during polling hours. Many of these changes were adopted as a result of recommendations of the Royal Commission on Electoral Reform and Party Financing, but one suggestion that was not adopted was to have staggered voting hours for different time zones so that the polls would close at the same time all across the country and all the votes could be counted and the results announced simultaneously. This would have precluded the possibility of westerners feeling that the election had been won before their votes were even counted.

Voters mark their X in private on the ballots provided, and when the polls close the deputy returning officer and poll clerk count them, usually in the company of scrutineers from the various candidates who are allowed to challenge unorthodox markings on ballots and generally keep the whole process honest. Results are announced an hour or so after the polls close and the candidate with the most votes, the **first-past-the-post**, is declared elected. This means that the winner usually does not actually have a majority of the votes cast, only a plurality.

The Ballot

The secret ballot was introduced into federal elections in 1874, which means that in the first two elections after Confederation, people voted orally and were subject to bribery or intimidation, including the threat of physical assault if they voted the wrong way! Moreover, before 1874 Canada had "nonsimultaneous" elections in which different constituencies voted on different days. This practice allowed the government to call the election in its safest seats first, and then, having won them, hope that other constituencies would jump on the bandwagon. The candidates are listed in alphabetical order on the ballot, and, since 1970, the ballot has contained their party affiliation, if any. The chief electoral officer keeps a registry of political parties, and only registered parties (those that run at least 50 candidates) are allowed to use the party label on the ballot. Such parties must also register their national and constituency official agents and auditors for the purposes of keeping track of the party's and candidates' finances. Twelve parties were registered for the 1988 election, and 14 for 1993.[10]

The Franchise

The extension of the **franchise** beyond males with substantial property was mentioned in passing in Chapters 7 to 11. This evolution in Canada was complicated by the use of different provincial franchises in federal elections between 1867 and 1885 and between 1898 and 1917. A low property test for males was required of the federal franchise between 1885 and 1898, and gradually eliminated in most provinces about 1900.[11] In 1917 the franchise was manipulated so as to maximize support for the incumbent government. The vote was extended to women serving in the war as well as to female relatives of men overseas, but denied to Canadian citizens who had come from "enemy alien" countries. In 1918 all women were granted the vote, and since 1920 a uniform federal franchise has existed. Most Canadians of Asian ancestry (especially those from Japan, China, and India) were denied the right to vote in federal elections because the federal law disqualified anyone who for reasons of race was denied the vote under provincial electoral statutes. All such restrictions were removed by 1948. The vote was extended to the Inuit in 1953 and to Indians living on reserves in 1960. The voting age was reduced from 21 to 18 in 1970, and British subjects who were not Canadian citizens lost their vote in 1975.

By that time, the **Canada Elections Act** disqualified only the following individuals from voting: the chief and assistant chief electoral officers, returning officers (except in the case of a tie), federally appointed judges, prison inmates, those deprived of their liberty by reason of mental disease, and those convicted of corrupt or illegal electoral practices. In the course of the 1988 campaign, however, three of these disqualifications were challenged in the courts in terms of the Canadian Charter of Rights and Freedoms, which guarantees the vote to every Canadian citizen. In the case of judges and those in mental institutions, the provisions of the act were declared unconstitutional and the disqualifications removed. The courts made a number of contradictory decisions on whether prison inmates should be able to vote, and the 1993 amendments gave the vote to inmates serving sentences of less than two years and removed the other disqualifications (judges and the mentally disabled) determined by the courts.[12]

The other principal ingredients of the 1993 reforms were as follows: electors may now place their own ballots in the ballot box; candidates and canvassers are authorized to enter any apartment building; financial contributions are prohibited from outside the country; and the publication of public opinion polls is banned after midnight of the Friday before election day. Amendments with respect to "third-party" advertising are discussed in the section on electoral finance below.

EVALUATING THE ELECTORAL SYSTEM

In each constituency, the candidate with the most votes wins, even if this is less than 50 percent. Among the advantages of this electoral system are its simplicity, its quick calculation of results, and its provision for each constituency of a clear-cut representative. When all the local results are cumulated nationally, however, the proportion of seats a party wins does not necessarily bear much relationship to its overall share of the **popular vote**. Take as an extreme, hypothetical example a two-person race in each constituency in which the Liberal candidate beat the Conservative candidate by one vote in every case: the Liberal Party would then win 100 percent of the seats from just over 50 percent of the vote, and the Conservative

Party would have zero percent of the seats from just under 50 percent of the vote. In fact, this example is not so hypothetical: in the New Brunswick election of 1987, the Liberals won 100 percent of the seats with about 60 percent of the popular vote. Many political scientists are therefore concerned that such overall disparities can occur between percent of seats won and percent of popular vote.

Discrepancies between Seats and Votes: National Level

The actual disparities can be analyzed for both the national and provincial levels.[13] Overall, in 22 elections since 1921, the party with the largest popular vote won more seats than it deserved on 20 occasions, while the second party received at least as many seats as its popular vote justified in ten cases. On the other hand, third parties with broad national ("diffuse") support usually lost out, and the CCF/NDP regularly received only about half as many seats as its popular vote merited.

Some observers credit this electoral system with producing a majority government—the leading party obtaining more than 50 percent of the seats—even though a party rarely wins over 50 percent of the popular vote. Table 15.2 indicates that on three occasions (1940, 1958, and 1984) the winning party obtained at least 50 percent of the vote, and this automatically produced a majority government. On eight other occasions, a minority government resulted. But on 11 occasions out of 22 this electoral system manufactured a majority government in terms of seats, even though the leading party did not win a majority of the vote. Thus, this "first-past-the-post" system does have a tendency to produce a majority government, but, at the same time, it weakens the opposition. Moreover, on three occasions (1957, 1962, and 1979) the party with the second-largest popular vote ended up with more seats than the party that came first, and therefore went on to form the government.

In the 1993 context, it is worth noting that Reform, the NDP, and especially the PCs, deserved more seats in terms of their popular vote. Reform deserved to be the official opposition in the sense that it received more votes than the Bloc; the NDP deserved party status because 7 percent of the vote would theoretically produce about 20 seats; and the Conservatives ran a close third to Reform in popular vote and more than doubled the vote of the NDP but suffered from ridicule of its two-member caucus. That election also demonstrated the value of having a regionally concentrated minor party, especially in the case of the Bloc, but also of Reform.

Discrepancies between Seats and Votes: By Province

Another set of disparities between popular vote and seat figures exists on a province-by-province basis. In this case, Alan Cairns was particularly struck by the disparity between Conservative vote and seats in Quebec (1896–1984) and the disparity between Liberal vote and seats in Western Canada (since 1957). Table 15.3 shows the provincial breakdown of the seats–votes ratio for 1980 and is typical of election results over the preceding 20 years; while Tables 15.4 and 15.5 provide the figures for 1993.

TABLE 15.2	Comparison of Percentage of Popular Vote and Percentage of Seats by Party for Federal Elections, 1921–1993					
	Liberal		*Conservative*		*CCF/NDP*	
	% Vote	% Seats	% Vote	% Seats	% Vote	% Seats
1921	41	49	30	21	—	—
1925	40	40	46	47	—	—
1926	46	52	45	37	—	—
1930	45	37	49	56	—	—
1935	45	71	30	16	9	3
1940	52	74	31	16	9	3
1945	41	51	27	27	16	11
1949	49	74	30	16	13	5
1953	49	64	31	19	11	9
1957	41	40	39	42	11	9
1958	34	18	54	79	10	3
1962	37	38	37	44	14	7
1963	42	49	33	36	13	6
1965	40	49	33	36	18	8
1968	45	58	31	27	17	8
1972	38	41	35	40	18	12
1973	43	53	36	36	16	6
1979	40	40	36	48	18	9
1980	44	52	33	37	20	11
1984	28	14	50	75	19	11
1988	32	28	43	57	20	15

	Liberal	*PC*	*NDP*	*Reform*	*BQ*
1993 % Vote	41.3%	16.0%	6.9%	18.7%	13.5%
% Seats	60.0%	0.7%	3.1%	17.6%	18.3%

Source: Reports of the Chief Electoral Officer, *adapted by author. Used with permission.*

Cairns observed that such disparities affect parties in three principal ways: image, strategy, and policy. Each party's image is largely derived from attention given to its number of elected members in the House of Commons rather than from its popular vote. Thus, when the Conservatives had virtually no members from Quebec before 1984, they gained a non-French or anti-French image, even though they usually obtained at least 13 percent of the popular vote in that province. Similarly, the Liberals acquired an image of an anti-Western

TABLE 15.3 Comparison of Percentage of Seats and Votes in 1980 Election by Province

	Liberal		Conservative		NDP	
	% Vote	% Seats	% Vote	% Seats	% Vote	% Seats
Newfoundland	47	71	36	29	17	0
P.E.I.	47	50	46	50	6	0
Nova Scotia	40	45	39	55	21	0
New Brunswick	50	70	32	30	16	0
Quebec	68	99	13	1	9	0
Ontario	42	55	36	40	22	5
Manitoba	28	14	38	37	33	50
Saskatchewan	24	0	39	50	36	50
Alberta	22	0	65	100	10	0
B.C.	22	0	41	57	35	43
North	37	0	31	67	31	33

Source: Report of the Chief Electoral Officer, *adapted by author. Used with permission.*

TABLE 15.4 Results of 1993 Election—Seats Won by Party by Province

	Liberal	Reform	Bloc Québécois	PC	NDP	Ind.	TOTAL
Newfoundland	7	0	0	0	0	0	7
Prince Edward Island	4	0	0	0	0	0	4
Nova Scotia	11	0	0	0	0	0	11
New Brunswick	9	0	0	1	0	0	10
Quebec	19	0	54	1	0	1	75
Ontario	98	1	0	0	0	0	99
Manitoba	12	1	0	0	1	0	14
Saskatchewan	5	4	0	0	5	0	14
Alberta	4	22	0	0	0	0	26
British Columbia	6	24	0	0	2	0	32
Northwest Territories	2	0	0	0	0	0	2
Yukon	0	0	0	0	1	0	1
Total	177	52	54	2	9	1	295

Source: Report of the Chief Electoral Officer. *Used with permission.*

TABLE 15.5			Comparison of Percentage of Seats and Votes in 1993 Election by Province								
	Liberals		*Reform*		*Bloc Québécois*		*P.C.*		*NDP*	
	% V	% S	% V	% S	% V	% S	% V	% S	% V	% S
Newfoundland	67%	100%	1%	0%	0%	0%	27%	0%	4%	0%
P.E.I.	60%	100%	1%	0%	0%	0%	32%	0%	5%	0%
Nova Scotia	52%	100%	13%	0%	0%	0%	24%	0%	7%	0%
New Brunswick	56%	90%	9%	0%	0%	0%	28%	10%	5%	0%
Quebec	33%	25%	0%	0%	49%	72%	14%	1%	2%	0%
Ontario	53%	99%	20%	1%	0%	0%	18%	0%	6%	0%
Manitoba	45%	86%	22%	7%	0%	0%	12%	0%	17%	7%
Saskatchewan	32%	36%	27%	29%	0%	0%	11%	0%	27%	36%
Alberta	25%	15%	52%	85%	0%	0%	15%	0%	4%	0%
B.C.	28%	19%	36%	75%	0%	0%	14%	0%	16%	6%
N.W.T.	65%	100%	8%	0%	0%	0%	16%	0%	8%	0%
Yukon	23%	0%	13%	0%	0%	0%	18%	0%	43%	100%
Total	41.3%	60.0%	18.7%	17.6%	13.5%	18.3%	16.0%	0.7%	6.9%	3.1%

Source: Report of the Chief Electoral Officer, *adapted by author. Used with permission.*

party after 1957 because they rarely elected members west of Ontario, even though they normally received over 20 percent of the Western vote. The NDP had the image of a minor party because it elected only about half as many members as its popular vote actually justified. Historians and political scientists have even contributed to a misinterpretation of Canada's past by concentrating on seats rather than votes, such as in exaggerating the Liberal sweep in Quebec in 1896 (53 percent of the vote, 75 percent of the seats) and the national Liberal victory in 1935 (45 percent of the vote, 71 percent of the seats). In the 1993 context, on a provincial basis, Reform won 20 percent of the votes in Ontario but its Western seats (as well as the style of most of its members) contributed to a Western image. The Conservatives deserved to win seats in many provinces, and even the Liberals were stronger in Quebec than their image based on seats indicated.

As far as strategy is concerned, when Conservatives despaired of electing members from Quebec and felt they could form a government without much representation from that province, they ignored it, especially in 1957.[14] The Liberals have often similarly felt that campaigning in the West was a waste of time and money and therefore concentrated their effort elsewhere. These strategies are not good for keeping the country together, one of the functions that political parties and elections are supposed to perform.

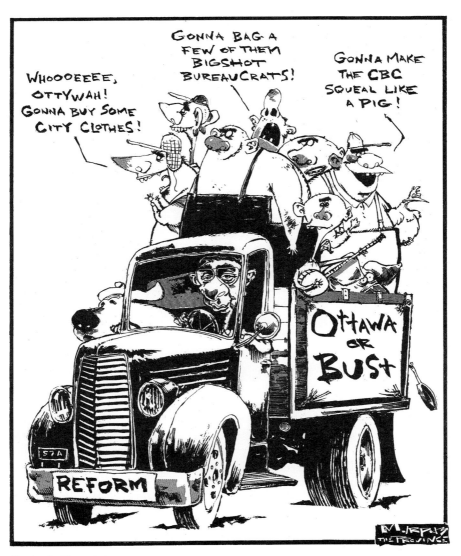

Reprinted with permission.

Finally, since the elected members of the party have a major role to play in the development of party policy, Conservative policy did not reflect the concerns of French Canada when the party lacked francophone and Quebec MPs, just as Liberal policy tended to ignore Western concerns because there were so few Liberals elected from Western Canada. This is especially serious for the party that forms the government, when it has few or no MPs from a province or region to put into the cabinet. Between 1962 and 1984 either Quebec or the West was effectively left out of national decision-making at the cabinet level. Residents of those provinces or regions that are omitted understandably feel that national policy does not reflect their interests and turn to provincial governments to defend these interests or start to think in separatist terms.

In 1984 and 1988 the Conservatives won a national victory, including a dramatic breakthrough in Quebec, largely by having chosen a fluently bilingual leader from that province; the Mulroney government could not be accused of ignoring Quebec in their policy or strategy afterwards. But the problem of provincial and regional distortions between popular vote and percentage of seats continued to haunt the Liberals and the NDP and generally exacerbated the regionalization of Canadian political parties. The Liberals achieved a fairly balanced national mandate in 1993, but more eastern Canadians in the Reform Party caucus might have an impact on its policies.

Remedies

Since Cairns first brought these problems to scholarly attention, reform of the electoral system has been frequently discussed. The most comprehensive reform proposal was prepared by William Irvine, who hoped to overcome the lack of representation of important segments of opinion in party caucuses and the cabinet, as well as to avoid the sense of regional–ethnic alienation that stems from this situation.[15] Irvine proposed a system somewhat akin to that in Germany in which about half of the MPs would be elected from constituencies, as they are now, and the others would be called "provincial MPs." These latter would be designated on the basis of popular vote by party in each province to bring each party's proportion of popular vote and percentage of seats into line. Irvine's proposal would result in an almost perfect relationship between a party's popular vote and its parliamentary representation, both in individual provinces and in the country as a whole. On the other hand, it would rarely produce a majority of seats for any party as long as at least three serious contenders existed.

That is why several authorities have suggested a smaller number of provincial MPs, say 50 or 60, who would overcome the worst problems of the existing system but still make majority government possible.[16] This system would start with the regularly elected constituency MPs who are necessary to ensure the representation of all parts of Canada. But some 50 supplementary MPs would be added, to be distributed on the basis of popular vote by party by province. They would correct the greatest discrepancies between the proportion of seats and votes, which in the pre-1984 period would mean rewarding the Liberals for their 20+ percent of the vote in the Western provinces and the Conservatives for their 13+ percent of the popular vote in Quebec. For the party in power, such supplementary MPs could provide provincial representation in the cabinet; for opposition parties, they would speak up for their provinces in the caucus and in Parliament. Representing an entire province, it is not likely that such provincial MPs would be underemployed, and would probably soon shed the status of "second-class" representatives. They could be drawn from the party's candidates in each province that were most narrowly defeated in the general election, and would seek re-election in a specific constituency the next time around.

Reform along these lines was first officially endorsed by the Pépin–Robarts Task Force on Canadian Unity in 1979 and the idea appealed to both Pierre Trudeau and Ed Broadbent as party leaders at the time. But while it would benefit all three parties in some ways, and perhaps the unity of the nation as a whole, its implementation appears unlikely. Some parties and politicians are concerned that it would benefit others more than themselves, while many are worried about the prevalence of minority government. Some feel it would give party organizers too much power in choosing and ranking candidates, and others argue that parties should have to fight for victory solely in individual constituencies. The Conservatives showed even less interest in electoral reform after their 1984 victory, but the problem resurfaced to some extent in 1993. The mandate of the Royal Commission on Electoral Reform specifically excluded consideration of this question.

FINANCING ELECTIONS[17]

Pre-1974

Before 1974 Canada had no effective laws with respect to party and election finance, and numerous irregularities and outright scandals occurred. The Liberal and Conservative parties relied almost completely on contributions from big business at the national level, which usually produced a surplus to be distributed to candidates' campaigns as well, and candidates were otherwise dependent on donations from local small firms. Both parties had fundraisers (sometimes called "bagmen")—often senators who could exploit their corporate connections and make use of their abundant spare time—assisted by corporate volunteers. Business also made contributions in kind, such as skilled human resources. Corporate contributions were supplemented by fundraising dinners, but party leaders themselves occasionally had to come to the party's rescue. This was especially the case in the Depression elections of 1930 and 1935 when the Conservatives were led by a multimillionaire, R.B. Bennett. The CCF/NDP depended primarily on individual membership fees supplemented by union contributions, but in this case the flow of funds was reversed, and the local candidates had to help finance the central campaign. Overall, the Liberals and Conservatives raised and spent far more than the CCF/NDP, both at the national and local levels.

The secrecy surrounding party and election finance before 1974 makes it difficult to know exactly how many irregularities and scandals actually took place. The first to come to light was the **Pacific scandal** of 1872, in which a group of businessmen eager to obtain the contract to build the CPR donated some $350 000 to John A. Macdonald's election campaign. When the scandal was revealed, Macdonald's government was defeated in the House of Commons, precipitating another election, which he lost. The second major scandal that came to public attention was the Beauharnois Scandal of 1930, in which a similar group gave $600 000 to the Liberal Party in hopes of obtaining the contract to build the Beauharnois Dam on the St. Lawrence River. By the time the deal was publicly exposed the Liberal Party was in opposition, and its leader, Mackenzie King, rather incredulously denied any knowledge of such a large contribution.[18] In the 1960s, the Rivard scandal involved drug trafficker

Lucien Rivard, who had been a regular contributor to the Liberal Party. He apparently felt that such donations, in addition to his attempted bribery of a government lawyer in a bail proceeding, should get him out of jail. These schemes did not work, but another, throwing a hose over the prison wall and escaping, turned out quite well!

This and other small-scale scandals in the 1960s, together with increasing public expectations of high political morality, caused the Pearson government to appoint a royal commission on the subject of party and election finance in 1964. But when its recommendations were published two years later, no action was taken. It required the heightened sense of public outrage at political immorality in the United States (the Watergate scandal), along with opposition pressure in the minority government period of 1972–74, to produce legislation more or less as recommended in 1966. Amendments to the Canada Elections Act were passed in 1974 but did not take effect until the election of 1979.

The Legislation of 1974

The legislation had five basic provisions. First, while no limit was placed on the size of contributions, a ceiling was imposed on both national party spending and on candidate expenditures.[19] Next, the disclosure provision required that the names of those contributing over $100 be filed with the chief electoral officer and such records be open to public inspection. A tax credit provision was added so that contributors with taxable incomes would receive a 75 percent income tax refund for contributions up to $100, a 50 percent tax credit for contributions between $100 and $550, and a 33 percent credit for contributions over $550, to a maximum tax credit of $500. Finally, candidates who received at least 15 percent of the vote would have a portion of their expenses subsidized by the public purse, the original formula being replaced by a flat 50 percent rate in amendments made in 1983. The same amendments altered the broadcasting provisions of the act, and instead of subsidizing parties for 50 percent of their broadcasting costs, parties would henceforth pay full price for such commercials and be subsidized for 22.5 percent of their total national expenditures if they spent at least 10 percent of their maximum.

· ·

MAIN PROVISIONS OF ELECTION FINANCE LAW

- Ceiling on candidate spending
- Ceiling on party spending
- Disclosure of contributions over $100
- Tax credit for contributions
- Public subsidy for candidates winning at least 15 percent of vote
- Public subsidy for major parties

The objectives of the legislation were thus to increase the equity, openness, and participatory nature of the electoral system. Equity was enhanced in limiting candidate and national party spending, as well as by the public subsidy provision; the disclosure clause would make it difficult in the future for large, secret contributions to be made in return for some favourable government decision, policy, or grant; and the tax credit would encourage individual contributions and reduce Liberal and Conservative dependence on corporations. For all the difficulties and loopholes remaining in the act, it has produced a more honest and equitable system of election finance.[20] At the same time, the need of political parties for more money to use mass marketing techniques in their electoral campaigns has driven them to become more reliant on subsidization by the state.

The Results of the 1974 Legislation

The figures in Tables 15.6 to 15.11 from the 1993 election reveal a great deal of change in Canadian election finance since 1974. They show that in a typical constituency in 1993, the three main parties spent approximately the same amount, but, combining all candidate spending and all party spending, the Conservatives and Liberals spent almost twice as much as the NDP. Some Liberal and Conservative candidates received more money than they were allowed to spend, but the number of individual contributors and total value of individual contributions was almost as great as that of corporate contributions to those two parties. The number and amount of individual contributions far exceeded that of union contributions in the case of the NDP; the Liberals and Conservatives received virtually no union contributions, while the NDP received almost no corporate contributions. The figures in Tables 15.8 and 15.9 do not include all contributions, only those from the three sources listed.

TABLE 15.6   Financial Statistics, Main Candidates in a Typical Constituency, 1993 Election (Sudbury, Ont.)

	Ceiling	Expenditures	Contributions	Public Subsidy
Liberal	$55 778	$37 453	$61 894	$19 196
Conservative	55 778	35 719	32 791	0
NDP	55 778	36 968	21 696	0
Reform	55 778	8 233	11 169	0

TABLE 15.7   Individual, Corporate, Union, and Other Contributions to Main Candidates in a Typical Constituency, 1993 Election (Sudbury, Ont.)

	Individual	Corporate	Union	Party/Political Organization
Liberal	147 ($18 305)	81 ($13 974)	0 (0)	3 ($29 615)
PC	144 ($17 770)	80 ($15 021)	0 (0)	0 (0)
NDP	107 ($11 914)	2 ($ 199)	3 ($1 500)	2 ($ 7 892)
Reform	47 ($ 4 934)	6 ($ 3 308)	0 (0)	2 ($ 2 723)

TABLE 15.8   Individual, Corporate, and Union Contributions to All Candidates and to Parties, 1993 Election

	All Candidates			Parties		
	Individual	*Corporate*	*Union*	*Individual*	*Corporate*	*Union*
Liberal	# 32 907	10 727	59	41 058	7 557	13
	$4 891 802	4 213 644	122 143	6 228 624	8 307 383	39 497
PC	# 25 460	9 881	3	44 728	8 898	0
	$4 390 856	4 059 623	1 335	9 060 423	13 215 683	0
NDP	# 12 367	332	842	65 301	458	885
	$1 411 528	104 860	799 421	5 215 018	147 332	3 182 396
Reform	# 25 211	3 439	1	49 488	1 230	0
	$3 361 694	1 219 368	200	5 077 291	1 021 634	0
BQ	# 26 337	27	0	29 084*	0	0
	$1 891 009	7 939	0	1 899 744*	0	0

*BQ figures include nonelection year 1994.

TABLE 15.9   Value and Percent of Individual, Corporate, and Union Contributions to All Candidates and Parties, 1993 Election

	Individual	*Corporate*	*Union*
Liberal	$11 120 426 (46.7%)	$12 521 027 (52.6%)	$ 161 640 (0.7%)
PC	13 451 279 (43.8%)	17 275 306 (56.2%)	1 335 (0%)
NDP	6 626 546 (61.0%)	252 192 (2.3%)	3 981 817 (36.7%)
Reform	8 438 985 (79.0%)	2 241 002 (21.0%)	200 (0%)
BQ			

TABLE 15.10   Total Election Expenses of Five Main Parties, 1993

	Candidates	*National*	*Total*
Liberal	$12 230 212	$ 9 913 190	$22 143 402
PC	$12 963 905	$10 398 901	$23 362 806
NDP	$ 4 871 183	$ 7 447 564	$12 318 747
Reform	$ 5 904 624	$ 1 465 380	$ 7 370 004
BQ	$ 2 713 778	$ 1 896 137	$ 4 609 915

TABLE 15.11   Public Subsidies to Parties and Candidates, 1993

	National Party	Candidates	No. of Subsidized Candidates	Total
Liberal	$2 076 624	$5 910 240	(285)	$7 986 864
PC	$2 339 753	$3 659 823	(146)	$5 999 576
NDP	$1 675 702	$1 123 130	(48)	$2 798 832
Reform	$ 329 710	$2 654 015	(153)	$2 983 725
BQ	$ 426 631	$1 415 227	(73)	$1 841 858

Source: (Tables 15.6–15.11) Chief Electoral Officer, Contributions and Expenses of Registered Political Parties and Candidates, 1993, *adapted by author. Used with permission.*

At least until 1993, the Conservatives were especially adept at using the 1974 legislation to their benefit. As Paltiel puts it:

> the PC Canada Fund, the party's fund-raising arm, pushed ahead with the electronically produced direct mail techniques.... [It] systematically canvassed the small business community, many of whom were disaffected with the Liberals. More important, the Conservatives discovered in the young, upwardly mobile, technobureaucratic cadres of private industry and the free professions—doctors, lawyers, accountants, engineers, and the knowledge industries—a major source of financial support that could be mobilized by employing properly segmented mailing lists developed for private commercial purposes and acquired from "quality" magazines and publications.[21]

Thus, while the Liberals and Conservatives now receive about half their contributions from individuals, some of the largest corporations in the country give the Liberal and Conservative parties an annual contribution of $50 000 or more. At election time, these contributions usually increase, as seen in the list of the largest donors in the 1993 campaign.

CORPORATE CONTRIBUTIONS OVER $50 000 TO LIBERAL AND CONSERVATIVE PARTIES, 1993 ELECTION

Conservatives		Liberals	
T'Ang Management	$216 000	ScotiaMcLeod	$108 382
ScotiaMcLeod	187 887	Coopers & Lybrand	107 862
Midland Walwyn	171 936	Wood Gundy	106 228
Coopers & Lybrand	164 646	Nesbitt Thomson	102 386
Richardson Greenshields	156 815	Midland Walwyn	100 415
Wood Gundy	156 206	Richardson Greenshields	99 359
			(continued)

Conservatives

RBC Dominion Securities	136 718
John Labatt	112 530
Imasco	112 500
Toronto-Dominion Bank	106 978
Nova Corp. of Alberta	103 500
Burns Fry	101 142
Hollywood Princess	100 000
Molson Companies	95 776
Bank of Montreal	94 172
Bank of Nova Scotia	93 503
Toronto Dominion Securities	93 500
Nesbitt Thomson	90 000
Royal Bank	85 391
CIBC	84 400
Westcoast Energy	84 000
Decima Research	83 206
Montreal Trust	83 010
Rogers Communications	81 681
Glaxo Canada	80 135
BCE	80 000
Ernst & Young	73 064
Bombardier	72 484
Gordon Capital	71 500
Magna	69 315
Brascan	66 899
Canadian Airlines Intl.	66 080
Peat Marwick Thorne	65 489
Repap Enterprises	63 764
Hollinger	62 500
Canadian Pacific	53 993
Yorkton Securities	53 950
American Barrick	53 744
Horsham Corp.	52 500
Northern Telecom	50 674
Banque Nationale	50 000
Skyline Aviation	50 000

Liberals

RBC Dominion Securities	99 018
Bank of Montreal	94 359
Royal Bank	88 718
CIBC	86 626
Toronto Dominion Securities	80 000
Toronto-Dominion Bank	77 649
Bank of Nova Scotia	76 825
Power Corporation	75 548
SNC Lavalin	73 249
Rogers Communications	69 965
Canadian Pacific	64 051
John Labatt	62 240
Molson Companies	53 922
BCE	52 819
Nova Corp. of Alberta	50 659
Banque Nationale	50 086

Source: Party Returns filed with Elections Canada, adapted by author. Used with permission.

In contrast, the Reform Party received only one corporate donation over $25 000, and only ten of $15 000 or more. The NDP does not attract large corporate contributions but gets a handful of union donations. Even though these typically increase at election time, they pale in comparison with the corporate contributions to the Liberal and Conservative parties, and a problem of inequity among the parties remains.

LARGEST REFORM CORPORATE CONTRIBUTIONS AND LARGEST NDP UNION CONTRIBUTIONS, 1993 ELECTION

Reform		NDP	
Sabre Energy	$75 000	CLC	$1 509 882
Canadian Pacific	25 000	Canadian Auto Workers	111 250
Burns Fry	25 000	USWA Headquarters	103 394
Hollinger	20 000	CUPE	63 576
Ocelot Energy	16 500	USWA District #6	55 802
TransCanada Pipelines	15 000	Ontario Federation of Labour	50 015
Tyoga Investments	15 000	SEIU	50 000
John Labatt	15 000	UFCW	41 500
135482 Canada	15 000	Newfoundland Federation of Labour	40 000
357814 BC	15 000	IWA	25 500

Source: Party returns filed with Elections Canada, adapted by author. Used with permission.

Third-Party Advertising

Another major problem in the realm of election finance is **third-party advertising**. The 1974 act had prohibited advocacy group spending during an election campaign that favoured or opposed a party or candidate, but exempted such spending that was related to an issue. The 1983 amendment removed that exemption and prohibited any election expense that was not channelled through a party or candidate campaign. It was argued that the only way party and candidate spending ceilings could be effective was if any spending on their behalf was included in the parties' budgets, such as in the case of Canadian Labour Congress spending to promote the NDP. But in the 1980s more and more groups began to advertise for or against various parties or candidates without having these expenses included in the parties' budgets. While such advertising was clearly a violation of the spirit of the act as well as its specific terms, the **National Citizens' Coalition** challenged subsections 70 and 72 of the act in the Alberta Court of Queen's Bench in 1984. That decision ruled the clauses unconstitutional as a violation of the freedom of expression provisions of the Charter of Rights and Freedoms. Technically the ruling applied only to federal elections in Alberta, but when the government did not appeal the ruling, the chief electoral officer decided not to prosecute any violations of these sections anywhere in Canada.

Third-party advertising increased enormously in the 1988 election campaign, especially in the case of the pro–free trade group, the Canadian Alliance for Trade and Job Opportunities. Receiving corporate contributions of as much as $250 000 from such companies as Canadian Pacific, Alcan Aluminum, and Shell; $200 000 from each of Noranda, Imperial Oil, and the Royal Bank; and at least $100 000 from each of Sun Life, Manufacturers' Life, Northern Telecom, IBM, INCO, Olympia & York, and Texaco, the group collected and spent over $5 million.[22] With only one political party in favour of free trade, namely the Conservatives, any advertising that promoted the Free Trade Agreement also promoted the Conservative Party. Thus the

Conservatives benefited from some $5 million in advertising by advocacy groups on top of its own national budget of nearly $8 million, with the same large corporations contributing to both causes. Such third-party advertising made a mockery of party spending ceilings and is widely thought to have helped the Conservatives achieve re-election by turning the momentum of the campaign back in their favour during the last two weeks, especially in Ontario.

The Royal Commission on Electoral Reform and Party Financing

In response to widespread public criticism of this problem and the retiring chief electoral officer's repeated recommendations for change in this and other aspects of the Canada Elections Act, the Mulroney government appointed a **Royal Commission on Electoral Reform and Party Financing** shortly after the 1988 election. It was headed by the former president of Provigo Inc., Pierre Lortie. That Commission identified several other concerns, held public hearings across the country, and commissioned extensive academic research. The Royal Commission recommended that spending during the election period by individuals or organizations other than candidates and political parties be restricted to $1000. The Commission argued that given the significance of the issue, to limit paid advertising of such advocacy groups during 50 days every four years was a "reasonable limit" on freedom of expression and would stand up to judicial scrutiny.

Among other issues that the Commission considered were whether a ceiling should be put on political contributions and whether such contributions should be limited to individuals, using the Quebec model of "financement populaire," rather than being made by corporations, unions, or other groups. It rejected such changes, but it did recommend extending the spending limit and tax credit provisions of the law to nomination meetings and leadership conventions. To restrict the expenditures of those seeking a party nomination was considered advantageous to potential women candidates in particular. The issue of regulating the financing of leadership campaigns arose when Jean Chrétien and Paul Martin each spent over $2 million in seeking the Liberal Party leadership in 1990, while Sheila Copps could not raise $1 million and Lloyd Axworthy declined to run for financial reasons. The Royal Commission also recommended the creation of a number of aboriginal constituencies and rewards for parties that elected a significant proportion of women MPs.

As mentioned, a number of relatively minor amendments were enacted just before the 1993 election, but nothing has come of the Commission's wider recommendations. The challenge to third-party advertising was upheld by the Alberta Court of Appeal, but many hoped that it would eventually get to the Supreme Court of Canada and be looked at from a different perspective.

CONCLUSION

If elections are crucial to the operation of Canadian democracy, it is unfortunate that the electoral system is so flawed. The principle of representation by population is widely breached, and while the actual operation of the system on election day is now basically satisfactory, the financing of elections is defective in many ways. The Royal Commission on Electoral Reform and Party Financing made many worthy recommendations for improvement, but only technical, administrative changes have been made.

Ⓒ Of the approaches outlined in Chapter 1, class analysts take the strongest exceptions to the revelations of this chapter, especially with respect to party and electoral finance. They emphasize that corporate contributions are made for a reason, and have little difficulty in finding the quid pro quo: tax concessions of all kinds, corporate loans and grants, government deficit reduction, free trade, and the GST. In addition, the Conservatives in particular extracted donations from individuals within corporate management, the small business community, and the self-employed upper middle class, and then adopted policies of interest to these groups.

PC The public choice model is interested in the mechanics of the electoral system insofar as they determine which groups within the electorate must be accommodated by political parties in order to achieve victory. An electoral system that overrepresents some interests and underrepresents others will affect the promises political parties make. Moreover, if the relationship between seats and votes is skewed, public choice theorists are the first to note that certain interests can be ignored. The way in which the mechanics of the electoral system traditionally gave the Liberals more seats than they deserved in Quebec and fewer in Western Canada (with the reverse for the Conservatives) meant that both parties put greatest effort into Ontario, which is where such effort would pay them dividends. Public choice also has things to say about how parties, once in office, can get around those planks of their election platforms that they never intended to implement.

P Pluralists rejoice at the greatest possible diversity of representation in the House of Commons, and are therefore probably not overly concerned with the strict numerical principle of representation by population. They would point out that it is often more important for a constituency to reflect a distinct "community of interest" than an exactly equal number of voters. They also applaud the elimination of restrictions to the franchise and the judicial elimination of restrictions on third-party advertising.

SC State-centred theorists and neo-institutionalists emphasize how the mechanics of the electoral system can affect the results and how most of these mechanics are beyond the interest or comprehension of the general electorate. Such concerns include the way in which the redistribution process is handled, the discrepancies between votes and seats, and the rules with respect to party and election finance. One of the most blatant is how established parties have rigged the rules to favour themselves in the distribution of broadcast time and in the subsidies for party advertising, as mentioned in Chapter 17.

DISCUSSION QUESTIONS

1. Given the peculiar distribution of the Canadian population, to what extent should we adhere to the principle of "representation by population"?

2. Once agreed on the principles involved, how should the redistribution process be carried out?

3. Is there a better way to prepare the voters' list? Should Canada move to a permanent voters' list?

4. Should the party leader have a veto on local nominations? Why or why not?

5. What are the principal discrepancies between parties' popular vote and percentage of seats at the national level?

6. What are the principal discrepancies between parties' popular vote and percentage of seats at the provincial level? What are the implications of such discrepancies?

7. Should the electoral system be reformed to bring about a closer relationship between percentage of votes and percentage of seats for each party? If so, how?

8. What changes should be made to the law governing party and election finance?

9. What are the arguments on each side of the debate over third-party advertising?

10. How do the approaches outlined in Chapter 1 apply to the material in this chapter?

NOTES

1. From 1867 to 1915, the basic procedure was to obtain a quota by giving Quebec 65 seats and dividing Quebec's population by 65. This quota would then be divided into each other province's population to determine its number of seats. The only exception was the "one-twentieth rule" under which no province could lose seats unless its share of the national population had decreased by at least one-twentieth between the last two censuses. In 1915 a second exception was added, the "senatorial clause," under which no province could have fewer seats in the House of Commons than it had in the Senate. The second formula was adopted in 1946. It provided for 255 (later 263) seats divided among the provinces in proportion to their share of the total population of the country. But after 1951 a "15 percent clause" was added, providing that no province could lose more than 15 percent of the number of seats to which it had been entitled at the last readjustment. The third formula, called the "amalgam" formula, was adopted in 1974 and guaranteed that no province could lose seats at all. Quebec was again used as the basic yardstick, and the other provinces were divided into large, intermediate, or small categories, with different calculations for each.

2. Elections Canada, *Representation in the Federal Parliament*, p. 9. For Sir John A. Macdonald's efforts, see R.M. Dawson, "The Gerrymander of 1881," *Canadian Journal of Economics and Political Science* (May 1935), pp. 197–221.

3. John C. Courtney, "Parliament and Representation: The Unfinished Agenda of Electoral Redistributions," *Canadian Journal of Political Science* (December 1988), pp. 675–90; and Andrew Sancton, "Eroding Representation-by-Population in the Canadian House of Commons: The Representation Act, 1985," *Canadian Journal of Political Science* (September 1990), pp. 441–57.

4. Jean-Marc Hamel argues that politicians should have only one chance to influence the commissions—at the stage of public hearings—not a second chance in parliamentary committees. *Report of the Chief Electoral Officer of Canada* (Ottawa: Supply and Services, 1989), p. 15. For revelations of other partisan influence, see *Maclean's* (January 25, 1988), p. 14.
5. Courtney, "Parliament and Representation," p. 689.
6. See Ch. 5; also John C. Courtney et al., eds., *Drawing Boundaries: Legislatures, Courts and Electoral Values* (Saskatoon: Fifth House Publishers, 1992).
7. See Chapter 20 on this subject.
8. *Report of the Chief Electoral Officer of Canada*, p. 46.
9. Advance polls are held on the ninth, seventh, and sixth days before election day. Proxy voting is permitted in the case of illness and physical incapacity, and for students and people in various mobile occupations; after completing the proper forms, they can appoint another qualified elector to vote in their place. Members of the Canadian public service and armed forces stationed overseas, along with their qualified spouses and dependents, can also vote by mail.
10. Progressive Conservative, Liberal, NDP, Social Credit, Communist, Libertarian, Rhinoceros, Green, Confederation of Regions, Commonwealth, Reform, and Christian Heritage.
11. T.H. Qualter, *The Election Process in Canada* (Toronto: McGraw-Hill Ryerson, 1970).
12. Chief Electoral Officer, *Towards the 35th General Election* (Ottawa: 1994), cat. no. SE 1-5/1993.
13. Alan C. Cairns, "The Electoral System and the Party System in Canada," *Canadian Journal of Political Science* (March 1968), pp. 55–80.
14. John Meisel, *The Canadian General Election of 1957* (Toronto: University of Toronto Press, 1962).
15. William Irvine, *Does Canada Need a New Electoral System?* (Kingston: Institute of Intergovernmental Relations, Queen's University, 1979).
16. Ibid., ch. 5.
17. K.Z. Paltiel, *Political Party Financing in Canada* (Toronto: McGraw-Hill Ryerson, 1970); Paltiel, "The 1984 Federal General Election and Developments in Canadian Party Finance," in Penniman, *Canada at the Polls, 1984*; Paltiel, "Political Marketing, Party Finance and the Decline of Canadian Parties," in Alain Gagnon and Brian Tanguay, eds., *Canadian Parties in Transition* (Scarborough: Nelson Canada, 1989); W.T. Stanbury, "Financing Federal Political Parties in Canada, 1974–1986," in Gagnon and Tanguay; Stanbury, *Business–Government Relations in Canada* (Toronto: Methuen, 1986), ch. 10; Joseph and Peter Wearing, "Mother's Milk Revisited: The Effect of Foreign Ownership on Political Contributions," *Canadian Journal of Political Science* (March 1990), pp. 115–23; and Stephen Brooks and Andrew Stritch, *Business and Government in Canada* (Scarborough: Prentice-Hall Canada, 1991), ch. 9.
18. T.D. Regehr, *The Beauharnois Scandal* (Toronto: University of Toronto Press, 1990).
19. The national party ceiling was based on 30 cents per name on the national voters' list, while the candidate ceiling was based on $1.00 per voter for the first 15 000 names on the local voters' list, 50 cents for each of the next 10 000 names on the list, and 25 cents for each of the names beyond the first 25 000. In subsequent elections an inflation factor was applied to these amounts, so that they were multiplied by 1.3 in 1984 and by 1.555 in 1988. Paltiel, "The 1984 Federal General Election."
20. Stanbury, "Financing Federal Political Parties."
21. Paltiel, "The 1984 Federal General Election," pp. 139–40.
22. *Toronto Star* (December 9, 1989), p. C1.

FURTHER READING

Cairns, Alan C. "The Electoral System and the Party System in Canada." *Canadian Journal of Political Science* (March 1968), pp. 55–80.

Courtney, John C. "Parliament and Representation: The Unfinished Agenda of Electoral Redistributions." *Canadian Journal of Political Science* (December 1988), pp. 675–90.

Courtney, John C., et al., eds. *Drawing Boundaries: Legislatures, Courts and Electoral Values*. Saskatoon: Fifth House Publishers, 1992.

Elections Canada. *Canada's Electoral System*.

————. *Reports of the Chief Electoral Officer of Canada*. For each federal election.

————. *Representation in the Federal Parliament*.

————. *Report of the Chief Electoral Officer Respecting Election Expenses*.

————. *Annual Reports of the Chief Electoral Officer*.

Irvine, William. *Does Canada Need a New Electoral System?* Kingston: Institute of Intergovernmental Relations, Queen's University, 1979.

Johnston, J. Paul, and Harvey Pasis. *Representation and Electoral Systems*. Scarborough: Prentice-Hall Canada, 1990.

Paltiel, K.Z. *Political Party Financing in Canada*. Toronto: McGraw-Hill Ryerson, 1970.

————. "Political Marketing, Party Finance and the Decline of Canadian Parties." In Alain Gagnon and Brian Tanguay, eds., *Canadian Parties in Transition*. Scarborough: Nelson Canada, 1989.

Qualter, T.H. *The Election Process in Canada*. Toronto: McGraw- Hill Ryerson, 1970.

Royal Commission on Electoral Reform and Party Financing. *Reforming Electoral Democracy*. Ottawa: Supply and Services, 1992.

Sancton, Andrew Sancton. "Eroding 'Rep-by-Pop' in the Canadian House of Commons: The Representation Act, 1985." *Canadian Political Science Association* (June 1989), pp. 441–51.

Stanbury, W.T. *Business–Government Relations in Canada*. Toronto: Methuen, 1986.

Tanguay, A.B., and A.-G. Gagnon, eds. *Canadian Parties in Transition*, 2nd ed. Scarborough: Nelson Canada, 1996.

Chapter 16

Political Parties
AND THE
Party System

The Liberal and Conservative parties have dominated the Canadian political scene since 1867. More recently, the New Democratic Party established itself as a third serious contender, while various smaller parties—the Progressives, CCF, Social Credit, Créditistes, and Union Nationale—have also come and gone, some of them forming governments at the provincial level. In the 1990s the Bloc Québécois and the Reform Party joined the fray, and the results of the 1993 election led observers to question the future of the PC and New Democratic Parties. Political parties are integral to the operation of almost every aspect of a modern political system, but Canadians are generally more attuned to their faults than to their virtues.

Political parties can be defined as organized groups that nominate candidates and contest elections in order to influence the personnel and policy of government. While some parties operate for long periods of time in the political wilderness and may be able to exert a certain amount of influence without being in power, every party ultimately hopes to form the government and make policy and personnel decisions on its own. More subtle differences between parties and other groups in society can also be noted. Whereas most other groups possess a fairly narrow focus and articulate a single interest, political parties are usually broader in scope and seek to aggregate, combine, consolidate, or appeal to many different interests or demands. In the process, parties reduce these interests and demands to a manageable quantity called "issues." In addition, while other groups provide "functional" representation—economic, occupational, cultural, religious—political parties are closely tied to the formal institutions of government including the electoral system and Parliament, all of which are based on territorial representation.

Another function of political parties is to recruit decision-makers, primarily by means of the electoral system. They usually choose as candidates people who have been party members for some time and who have been "groomed" or trained. The government party also appoints political officeholders, often from the ranks of its own supporters, a practice referred to as **political patronage**. In addition to recruitment, parties engage in political socialization and citizen education as they point out their own strengths and their opponents' weaknesses in the daily partisan battle in Parliament as well as on the election trail.

Parties are also integrally involved in the rule-making function, as they organize the legislative and executive operations of government. The formal and informal procedures of the House of Commons and Senate are completely imbued with partisan considerations, especially in the party discipline they display, while the Canadian cabinet tradition is that all ministers come from a single party so that they will be able to come to agreement more easily on government policy.

Beyond the list of functions mentioned in Chapter 1, parties may be engaged in formulating public policy. In theory, at least, each party develops a distinctive election platform; the successful party then proceeds to implement it, while the opposition parties continue to provide clear-cut policy alternatives. This chapter will show, however, that the policy-making role of political parties is often minimal, that parties do not always provide policy alternatives to the electorate, and that governments frequently obtain their policy ideas from other sources.

This chapter is divided into four main sections: the historical evolution of Canadian political parties; interpretations of the Canadian party system; party organization; and party ideology. Party and electoral finance were examined in Chapter 15, and the role of parties in the electoral campaign, including electoral behaviour and party support, is discussed in Chapter 17.

HISTORICAL EVOLUTION OF CANADIAN PARTIES

For those unfamiliar with the main lines of post-Confederation Canadian political history, a brief discussion of the historial evolution of Canadian political parties may be useful.[1] Such an outline can be structured around Table 16.1, which lists the prime ministers of Canada, their parties, and their dates of office.

The Conservative Party is usually said to have had its beginnings in 1854 when John A. Macdonald formed a coalition of four pre-Confederation groupings: Tories and Moderates from Upper Canada (Ontario), along with English businessmen and French Conservatives from Lower Canada (Quebec). Party lines for individual politicians were quite flexible in those days, and many MPs were called "ministerialists" because of their promise to support the ministry of the day in return for government favours. Alliances among groups were also unstable, but Macdonald's coalition gradually melded into an organized political party. The two main groups left out of this coalition—the French radicals in Quebec and the Clear Grits from Upper Canada—periodically joined forces in the pre-Confederation era, but it was not until much later that they became the nucleus around which an organized Liberal party took form. After Macdonald was disgraced by the Pacific scandal, the Liberals took office between 1873 and 1878 under Alexander Mackenzie, but his government reflected this early lack of cohesion. Macdonald returned to power in 1878 and the Conservatives demonstrated increasing party unity as time went on. After the execution of Louis Riel, however, French-Canadian support started to fall away from the Conservative Party, helped by the fact that an attractive French Canadian, Wilfrid Laurier, became leader of the Liberal Party shortly after-

TABLE 16.1   **Prime Ministers of Canada**

John A. Macdonald	Conservative	1867–1873
Alexander Mackenzie	Liberal	1873–1878
John A. Macdonald	Conservative	1878–1891
John Abbott	Conservative	1891–1892
John Thompson	Conservative	1892–1894
Mackenzie Bowell	Conservative	1894–1896
Charles Tupper	Conservative	1896
Wilfrid Laurier	Liberal	1896–1911
Robert Borden	Conservative	1911–1920
Arthur Meighen	Conservative	1920–1921
Mackenzie King	Liberal	1921–1926
Arthur Meighen	Conservative	1926
Mackenzie King	Liberal	1926–1930
R.B. Bennett	Conservative	1930–1935
Mackenzie King	Liberal	1935–1948
Louis St. Laurent	Liberal	1948–1957
John Diefenbaker	Progressive Conservative	1957–1963
Lester Pearson	Liberal	1963–1968
Pierre Elliott Trudeau	Liberal	1968–1979
Joe Clark	Progressive Conservative	1979–1980
Pierre Elliott Trudeau	Liberal	1980–1984
John Turner	Liberal	1984
Brian Mulroney	Progressive Conservative	1984–1993
Kim Campbell	Progressive Conservative	1993
Jean Chrétien	Liberal	1993–

wards. Macdonald died in 1891, and his party experienced a period of great instability as it went through four leaders in the subsequent five years. Thus, with the government party in decline and the Liberals finally showing the marks of a well-organized national party, it is not surprising that Laurier won the watershed election of 1896.[2] At that time Canada moved from a Conservative **one-party dominant** system to a classic **two-party system** in which Liberals and Conservatives competed on equal terms.

Laurier governed quite successfully until he was beaten in 1911 when the two main issues were reciprocity (free trade with the United States) and the naval question (whether Canada should establish its own navy or contribute to that of Britain). Robert Borden's Conservatives took over and were soon confronted with the monumental task of managing Canada's war effort. In 1917, after three years of war, Borden concluded that conscription would have to be adopted, but conscious of French-Canadian opposition, he proposed a coalition government with Laurier who still led the Liberals in opposition. Most English-speaking MPs agreed to join the Conservatives in a Union Government in 1917, but Laurier and the French-Canadian Liberals remained in opposition, leaving that party badly split. With conscription, the Conservatives almost totally alienated French Canada, at the same time as the policies of both Conservative and Liberal parties upset the farming community in English Canada, notably the West. Thus, while Mackenzie King succeeded Laurier as Liberal leader in 1919 and skilfully pursued party reconciliation, Arthur Meighen inherited an unpopular Conservative Party in 1920 when he took over from Borden. Although it seemed at first sight that conscription had damaged the Liberal Party, the Conservatives actually suffered most in the long run.

The 1921 election marked the end of the two-party system in Canada. On that occasion, farmers entered the contest with their own Progressive candidates and elected more members than the Conservatives,[3] and two Labour members were also successful. Farmers were particularly unhappy with conscription, tariff, agricultural and transportation policies, as well as prevailing political practices such as party patronage and rigid party discipline in the House of Commons. Nevertheless, Mackenzie King led his Liberals to victory in 1921, in 1925, and again in 1926 (after a brief Conservative interruption caused by the King–Byng dispute discussed in Chapter 20), and by the late 1920s most of the Progressive MPs had either become Liberals or had been defeated. A few of the more radical farmers joined with the Labour members to form the Ginger Group in Parliament, while the Liberals were defeated in 1930, primarily because of the onset of the Depression.

By this time the Conservatives were led by R.B. Bennett. Although he exercised vigorous leadership and even departed from orthodox Conservative policy to some extent, Bennett could not cope with the unemployment, poverty, and general devastation the Depression wrought. Along with almost every other government in office during this period, Bennett's Conservatives were defeated in 1935, and Mackenzie King's Liberals returned to power.

Besides contributing to this change of government, the Depression was the catalyst for the creation of several new political parties. The Cooperative Commonwealth Federation (CCF) was formed in Calgary in 1932, an amalgam of the parliamentary Ginger Group, the intellectual League for Social Reconstruction, largely centred in Toronto and Montreal, and various farmer and labour groups and scattered socialist and farmer–labour parties, primarily from the West. In 1933 the party adopted its radical platform, the Regina Manifesto, at its meeting in that city, and elected Labour member of Parliament, J.S. Woodsworth, as its leader. The party elected several MPs in 1935 and took office in Saskatchewan in 1944 under T.C. Douglas.[4]

The Social Credit Party was born in Alberta in 1935 around the charismatic evangelist William Aberhart. The party was originally concerned with the reform of the banking system as a means of dealing with the Depression, but it abandoned this platform when it proved to be both unworkable and unconstitutional. After Alberta became prosperous with the discovery of oil in the 1940s, Social Credit transformed itself into an orthodox conservative party under E.C. Manning. The party remained in power in Alberta for 36 years, came to power in British Columbia in 1952, and also elected several Western MPs.[5]

In Quebec, a group of disgruntled progressive Liberals defected from their provincial party in 1935 to join forces with the chronically unsuccessful provincial Conservative Party to form the Union Nationale. The leader, Maurice Duplessis, quickly discarded the comprehensive reform program on which the party was elected a year later and became ultra-conservative. Despite this shift in emphasis, the Union Nationale remained in power in Quebec until 1960 with only a four-year interruption between 1940 and 1944.[6]

None of these developments impeded the Liberal Party at the federal level; it continued to elect majority governments from 1935 to 1948 under Mackenzie King and then, until 1957, under his successor, Louis St. Laurent. King's conciliatory skills were severely tested during the Second World War (1939–45), but his government avoided a serious second conscription crisis. He also presided over the initiation of the Canadian welfare state. The St. Laurent period was one of great prosperity, largely financed by a tremendous inflow of American investment.[7]

The Conservative Party floundered for 20 years after 1935, having previously alienated French Canada, and having been blamed, however unfairly, for the Depression. It changed leaders repeatedly, changed party policy to some extent, and changed the party name to Progressive Conservative in 1942, all to no avail. The political climate was suddenly transformed with the choice of John Diefenbaker as party leader in 1956, partly due to the public's increasing resentment of Liberal arrogance (as demonstrated in the famous **pipeline debate**) and complacency. Diefenbaker led the Conservatives to a surprising minority government victory in 1957 and then to a record majority in 1958. His decline was almost as rapid as his ascent, however, as his government fell apart over defence policy. The party was reduced to a minority government position again in 1962 and defeated a year later, after which it engaged in a long period of bitter in-fighting over the leadership question.[8]

During the Diefenbaker period, significant developments in two minor parties took place. The CCF, which had seen its federal fortunes decline throughout the 1950s, decided to combine its efforts with those of the new national labour organization, the Canadian Labour Congress. The result was the creation of the New Democratic Party (NDP) in 1961. T.C. Douglas was persuaded to leave the premiership of Saskatchewan to become the first national NDP leader.[9] Then, out of the blue, a group of Social Credit or Créditiste MPs was elected from Quebec in 1962, just when the Western wing of the party was starting to decline.[10]

Lester Pearson's Liberals were elected in 1963 and re-elected in 1965, but the success of the Créditiste group in Quebec, NDP support in other parts of the country, and the continuing appeal of John Diefenbaker, especially in the West, denied Pearson a majority government. Nonetheless, in spite of his minority government status, Pearson tackled many controversial issues, particularly the new nationalism in Quebec, the Canada Pension Plan, medicare, and a new flag. One opposition party or another supported each of Pearson's measures so that he was able to continue in office until he retired in 1968.[11]

The Liberals then gained a majority government under their new leader Pierre Elliott Trudeau, but just narrowly defeated Robert Stanfield's Conservatives in 1972. In the resulting minority government, the Liberals worked closely with the NDP under David Lewis, but this support was withdrawn two years later. With Trudeau ridiculing Stanfield's proposal for **wage and price controls**, the Liberals were returned with a majority in 1974, only to turn around and implement such a policy themselves. By 1979 the Liberals had apparently accumulated other faults as well, for they were defeated by the Conservatives now led by Joe Clark. Nine months later, the Clark government fell with parliamentary rejection of its budget, and Trudeau hastily withdrew his resignation as Liberal leader to lead his party back to power in early 1980.[12]

The separatist Parti Québécois formed the government of Quebec between 1976 and 1984 under René Lévesque, and after persuading Quebeckers to give Canada one last chance in their May 1980 referendum, Trudeau patriated the Constitution, together with a Charter of Rights and Freedoms, and enacted the controversial National Energy Program.[13] He resigned in 1984, turning the reins over to John Turner, who was pitted against the new Conservative leader, Brian Mulroney. In the September 1984 election, the Conservatives won a landslide victory, including a startling majority of the seats in Quebec.[14] After the negotiation of the Canada–U.S. Free Trade Agreement and the Meech Lake Accord, Mulroney led his party to a second successive majority government in 1988, only to see Meech Lake fail to acquire the unanimous approval of new provincial governments in 1990.[15]

Because various minor parties made their presence felt but did not seriously challenge the dominance of the Liberals and Conservatives between 1921 and 1980, the Canadian party system during that period can be called a **two-plus** or **two-and-one-half party system**. The 1980s, on the other hand, might better be termed a **three-party** decade. While both western and eastern wings of Social Credit disappeared in the 1970s and 1980s respectively (except in the provincial government in British Columbia), the NDP became entrenched as the third major national party under Ed Broadbent's leadership between 1975 and 1989.

The Liberal Party's obsession with Quebec was the main reason that the West preferred the Conservatives after 1957. When Westerners perceived that federal Conservatives were likewise concerned primarily with holding on to their unprecedented Quebec support after 1984, however, several new parties emerged in the West, the most enduring being the Reform Party headed by Preston Manning, son of the former Social Credit premier of Alberta. Then, with the collapse of the Meech Lake Accord, sovereigntist sentiment increased in Quebec, and several Conservative and Liberal MPs defected to form a new federal separatist party, the Bloc Québécois. Thus, five parties of considerable strength contested the 1993 federal election, and produced a highly unusual result: the Liberals did well across the country, the Bloc Québécois displaced the Conservatives in Quebec, and the Reform Party displaced the Conservatives in the West. The PCs held on to 16 percent of the popular vote but only retained two seats, and the NDP did badly everywhere. Given that a minimum of 12 seats is required for official party standing in the House of Commons, only three parties came back as recognized parties, two of them new, and it seemed that a real and regionalized multiparty system had developed.[16]

EVOLUTION OF CANADIAN PARTY SYSTEM

Era	Major Parties	Minor Parties
1867–1896	Conservative	Liberal
1896–1921	Liberal, Conservative	
1921–1935	Liberal, Conservative	Progressive
1935–1961	Liberal, Conservative	CCF, Social Credit
1961–1980	Liberal, Conservative	NDP, Social Credit
1980–1993	Liberal, Conservative, NDP	Reform
1993–	Liberal	Reform, Conservative, Bloc Québécois, NDP

INTERPRETATIONS OF THE CANADIAN PARTY SYSTEM

Faced with the rather unusual party system—or succession of party systems—just outlined, several political scientists have proposed theories or interpretations in order to explain them.

The Broker System

The most traditional one is the **broker** or **brokerage** theory.[17] The essence of this interpretation is that, given the multiple cleavages in Canadian society and the function of parties to aggregate interests, political parties in Canada should be conciliators, mediators, or brokers among the cleavages already identified, that is, regions, ethnic and linguistic groups, classes, religions, ages, and genders. The theory suggests that maximizing their appeal to all such groups is not only the best way for parties to gain power, but in the fragmented Canadian society, this approach is also necessary in order to keep the country together. Thus, in their search for power, parties should act as agents of national integration and attempt to reconcile as many divergent interests as possible.

The interests to which parties give most attention are presumably those of greatest concern to the largest number of voters. In the past, religion was often prominent, while gender and age are emerging as increasingly important in the future. Throughout most of Canadian history, however, the two overriding cleavages that have concerned people as well as parties have been those of region and culture. While the class cleavage is the central focus of politics in most countries, it has usually attracted least attention in Canada. Whatever the reason—that Canadians genuinely feel that regional and linguistic concerns are more important than class interests, that Canadians have been conditioned to do so by the way political parties have defined what is political, or that the various cleavages are actually linked together[18]—the broker theory emphasizes the middle-class consciousness of most Canadians. The broker theory can thus be seen to argue that the Liberal and Conservative parties have no central ideological interests and merely promise to satisfy the most important interests felt by the voters at any point in time. Alternatively, they disguise their real ideological interests—

protecting the capitalist system—by emphasizing ethnic and regional concerns instead of class interests.[19] In any case, ideological differences between the two main parties are not profound. Defenders of the broker system argue that parties should not foment artificial class conflicts and ideological differences in a country that is already seriously divided; they should bring people together rather than drive them apart.

However appealing the broker system, its implications should not be overlooked. By concentrating on regional and ethnic cleavages, parties minimize the role of ideology in Canadian politics. Parties are opportunistic and pragmatic rather than offering the electorate a choice of principles and distinctive programs. Parties do not generate innovative policy approaches, but are content instead to respond to public opinion polls and interest group demands. What parties offer to the electorate in the place of alternative solutions to national problems are alternative slogans and leaders. In a television age, leaders have become the focus of elections in other countries, too, but probably nowhere else are such factors as a leader's personal appearance and deportment, regional origins, and fluency in two official languages of such paramount importance.

Not all Conservative and Liberal leaders have approached the task of seeking election in exactly the same way. David Smith emphasizes that Macdonald and Laurier sponsored great national projects on the one hand, while being masters of detailed constituency and patronage politics on the other. The King and St. Laurent periods were characterized by decentralized ministerial accommodation in which strong regional–ethnic cabinet ministers exercised a great deal of individual power and then spoke for their regions in the development of a national consensus. Smith contends that the Diefenbaker and Trudeau eras were marked by a more pan-Canadian approach, as each leader had a vision of the national interest that he sought to impose.[20] In this period television linked individual voters to these leaders without the need for regional or ethnic intermediaries.

Smith is undoubtedly correct in emphasizing such differences among prime ministers as they tried to contend with the cleavages in Canadian society. On the other hand, it would not be accurate to say that Macdonald or Laurier lacked regional ministers or that King or St. Laurent had no national projects or vision beyond accommodating different groups. Moreover, any praise of the pan-Canadianism of Diefenbaker and Trudeau must be offset by the serious flaws in their respective visions, as the former did not understand French Canada and the latter was concerned with little else. Ministerialism and pan-Canadianism can thus be seen as alternate ways of practising nonideological, brokerage politics, and can be distinguished from a more ideological approach.

Class-Based Parties

A second perspective on the Canadian party system, and a reaction to the broker approach, is the concept of a **class-based** party system.[21] Like the broker model, the class-based theory is partly an explanation of the existing system, but when it comes to prescribing an ideal situation, it rejects the status quo. Class-based analysts expect that in the pre-democratic period in a country such as Canada two parties will develop, both of which defend the capitalist system. When the vote is extended to the working class, however, a new working-class party will emerge that either joins the competition or displaces one of the existing parties, generally forcing politics to take on an ideological and class-based character. This evolution clearly occurred in Britain, for example, and can also be seen to some extent in the United States. In late nineteenth-century Canada, on the other hand, when the Liberal Party began to challenge the Conservatives, they both defended capitalism and differentiated themselves on ethnic and religious grounds as well as on minor policy differences such as the tariff. When the vote was extended to the working class at the turn of the century, some isolated labour, socialist, and communist political activity occurred, and by 1920 new class-based farmer and labour parties existed. But the newly enfranchised working class did not manage to create a successful class-based party, as the Liberals and Conservatives did everything in their power to discourage such a development, using both seductive and coercive techniques. Mackenzie King introduced policy innovations to attract farmer and labour voters and co-opted leaders of both farmer and labour movements into the Liberal cabinet, while the Conservatives used force to quell the Winnipeg General Strike and the 1935 On-to-Ottawa Trek of the unemployed.[22] Eventually, the farmers' intense interest in politics declined, and the working class continued to support the two old-line parties on ethnic/religious and regional grounds, rendered content by the occasional piece of social legislation.

The Depression represented the collapse of the capitalist system and might have been expected to give rise to new class-based parties, which to some extent it did. Of these, the CCF became the most sustained working class party, but most members of the working class continued to support the two traditional parties. Although unionization expanded significantly in the 1940s, the CCF's success was impeded by the Liberal Party's exploitation of divisions within the working class,[23] and by extremist anti-CCF propaganda sponsored by the business community. The CCF achieved its highest popular standing in the 1943–45 period, after which Liberal welfare initiatives helped to draw off working-class support. This decline led to the creation of the NDP in 1961 as a marriage of the CCF and the CLC, but even with the NDP's organic link to the labour movement, most working-class Canadians continued to vote Liberal or Conservative.

Reasons for the lack of class-consciousness among the Canadian working class have been noted earlier, but perhaps bear repetition.[24] Those who defend the lack of such consciousness argue that other divisions take precedence in Canada, that the system permits social mobility, that most people feel themselves to be middle class, that material benefits are widely shared, and that the Liberal and Conservative parties have accommodated working-class interests along with ethnic, religious, and regional interests in the broker system.[25] Those who decry the lack of working-class consciousness contend that the Liberals and Conservatives were firmly entrenched when the franchise was extended to the working class and had already defined politics around social differences other than class. These two parties either appealed to one or more ethnic/religious and regional groups or else developed pan-Canadian appeals that diverted attention from class-based issues. These parties persuaded most voters that they belonged to the middle class, and gave them the impression of inclusion and social mobility. Janine Brodie and Jane Jenson make the point that class-consciousness requires prior ideological and organizational activity by groups such as unions, farmers, cooperatives, and other reformers. They demonstrate that classes as active and self-conscious social actors have to be created, and that class-based organizations must precede the expectation of class-based voting.[26]

Thus, the attempts by farmers and unions to redefine Canadian politics in class terms were repelled by the traditional parties, their leaders were co-opted by the Liberal Party, and both organizations were internally divided. Moreover, many Canadian affiliates of American unions were encouraged to remain aloof from partisan politics. Some critics argue that the CCF/NDP did not try hard enough to redefine politics in class terms, and it has also been noted that people who are really destitute are inclined either to withdraw from politics or to support the status quo for fear that any change would make their situation even worse.

Advocates of a class-based party system thus point out that the existing system is partially class-based—the upper and middle classes are conscious of their class position and vote accordingly; it is just that the working class does not vote appropriately. They claim that a class-based system would provide ideological alternatives in elections that would make them more meaningful, and would more likely than at present offer innovative solutions to national problems.[27] Moreover, the broker system, with its emphasis on multiple cleavages, is dangerously destabilizing, for if the Liberals and Conservatives are unsuccessful as brokers, the separation of one or more ethnic–regional units is possible. In such circumstances, class could be the integrating ingredient: "a nation like Canada, which is in danger of falling apart on ethnic-regional lines, may be held together by a politics which unites the people of various regions and ethnic groups around the two poles of left and right."[28] Canadians would ideally be united by their common class position into two or three national class-based parties. Finally, it is said that class-based politics and parties are already the norm in Western Canadian provincial politics, so that this theory is quite a realistic proposition after all.

One-Party Dominance

The **one-party dominant** thesis is a third general theory regarding Canadian parties. H.G. Thorburn, for example, maintains that instead of looking at the Canadian party system as being made up of two major parties, it has really been dominated by one—the Liberals—since about 1900.[29] The Liberals are the *government party*, power-oriented rather than issue-oriented, attracting "winners" and "successes" as supporters and candidates, and maintaining themselves in office with the help of public-service expertise, public opinion polls, and the chance to choose election day. The Conservatives can be seen as the *opposition party*, ordinarily having to settle for the role of critics (from within the range of ideological conformity) but being elected to office only on those rare occasions when the people get thoroughly fed up with the Liberals. However, with their divisiveness, "opposition mentality," and lack of preparedness to govern, the Conservatives do not remain in power very long. Finally, the NDP can be termed the *innovative party*, never really having a chance to govern nationally, but being responsible for introducing new ideas from beyond the range of current ideological conformity, both at the federal and provincial levels. For a time in the 1980s, some observers thought that Thorburn's designations might be out-of-date, but sure enough, the Liberals returned to power in 1993.

The Decline of Parties

A final interpretation, coming from John Meisel, emphasizes the decline of political parties.[30] He suggests a number of reasons why this is the case and why their traditional functions have been taken over by other institutions. A decline in ideological differences among the parties has resulted in their being less capable of offering innovative solutions to national problems. People prefer to participate directly in specialized voluntary associations rather than take their concerns to an omnibus political party, with the result that the number and strength of interest groups has greatly increased. Such issue-oriented individuals anticipate more prompt and effective satisfaction of their demands by participating in group action, quite possibly by interacting with the bureaucracy, than by going through traditional political party channels. The quantity and complexity of information with which governments have to deal has come to mean that generalist politicians can no longer cope with it, leaving them increasingly dependent on the bureaucracy. This culminates in a situation in which interest groups confer with the bureaucrats and work out policies that the politicians can neither understand nor alter, further reducing the role of political parties in the policy-making process. Federal–provincial conferences and committees of all kinds have become the forum in which many public policies are ironed out, and once certain political and bureaucratic compromises have been made, there is little that other politicians or parties can do about them. Meisel also notes that parties now gear most of their activity to the demands of the media, and to the extent that elections are dominated by leader images and leader debates, the need for traditional party organizations diminishes. Similarly, public opinion polls provide better feedback to politicians than their traditional discussion with party activists. Investigative journalism has reduced the role of Opposition in Parliament; direct-mail appeals have replaced traditional forms of party fund-raising; and modern transnational corporations are beyond the control of any party or government. Other recent developments that have contributed to the decline of parties are the increasing power of the prime minister, the influence of election strategists and other specialist advisers, and the new role of the courts and the Charter of Rights and Freedoms. Parties are also having difficulty in incorporating the concerns of Natives, women, and new Canadians.

Meisel's critique of Canadian political parties has inspired other commentary that either defends them or suggests that rather than declining, they are in a state of transition.[31] Defenders of parties admit that certain traditional functions are being performed by interest groups, the media, public opinion polls, and the bureaucracy, but argue that others are simply being carried out by parties in different ways. Whether one prefers "decline" or "transition," Meisel makes many valid points.

Minor Parties

So much for theories that account for the overall party system in Canada. Because Canada has had more minor parties than any other similar political system, however, political scientists have also developed several theories to account specifically for them. Essentially, they can all be explained by the fact that at one time or another, ethnic, regional, or class grievances have gone unsatisfied by the broker parties. Moreover, new minor parties are only to be expected when individual voter identification with existing parties is generally so weak, and when ideological stagnation and opportunism characterize the broker system. In particular, if the working class never managed to establish a major party in Canada, it is not surprising that several minor working-class parties would be created. The principal factors responsible for the rise of the various minor parties in Canada involve region (including institutional malfunction), ethnicity, class or ideology, the poor economy, and charismatic leadership, as seen below.

FACTORS INVOLVED IN THE RISE OF MINOR PARTIES

	Region	Ethnicity	Class/Ideology	Economy	Leader
Progressives	*		*	*	
CCF			*	*	
Social Credit	*		*	*	*
Reconstruction			*	*	
Bloc Populaire	*	*			
NDP			*		
Créditistes	*	*	*	*	*
Libertarian			*		
Christian Heritage			*		
Green			*		
Confederation of Regions	*	*			
Reform	*	*	*		
Bloc Québécois	*	*			*

On a more theoretical note, it has also been argued that the rigid party discipline enforced in the Canadian Parliament has encouraged the development of minor protest parties.[32] When certain interests felt frustrated by the requirement of toeing the party line in Ottawa, they turned to form minor parties, usually at the provincial level, to vent their grievances. Some have gone so far as to suggest that the parliamentary system, with its rigid party discipline, is unsuitable for such a diverse country. S.M. Lipset applies his theory primarily to the Progressives and Social Credit, but it could equally apply to the Reform Party and perhaps to the Bloc Québécois.

Maurice Pinard's theory relates the rise of minor parties to a situation of one-party dominance, when dissatisfaction with the traditional party eventually sets in.[33] In these circumstances, voters see little use in supporting the weak existing opposition party, and instead, they turn to a new minor party, especially if it is headed by a strong, populist, charismatic leader. Pinard applies this hypothesis primarily to the strange eruption of Créditiste support in Quebec in 1962, when as a result of a downturn in the economy, many Quebeckers grew tired of supporting the Liberals, but preferred the fiery Réal Caouette to the traditional Conservative alternative.

Another prominent theory relating to minor parties is that of C.B. Macpherson in his explanation of the series of one-party-dominant eras in Alberta provincial politics. He labels this system, which included the nontraditional United Farmers and Social Credit, as a "quasi-party" system.[34] Macpherson applies a kind of Marxist theory to explain the situation by arguing that the province was characterized by a homogeneity of class interests—the predominance of small, independent producers—so that little internal class conflict could be detected. Instead, the whole Alberta society was held in a quasi-colonial relationship by Eastern Canada. The feeling of being exploited by the privileged classes in the East led Albertans to unite behind a dominant provincial party. Macpherson has been faulted for exaggerating the extent of one-party dominance in the province as well as overstating the proportion of farmers, but Albertans continued to act as if they were a homogeneous society exploited by the East for decades after he identified this phenomenon.

The rise of the CCF in Saskatchewan has also attracted specific explanations, including the collectivist streak in the Canadian political culture, which seems particularly strong in that province. Disagreeable weather, social isolation, and corporate and federal government exploitation all encouraged cooperative behaviour and organizations that eventually became transformed into a political party, the Cooperative Commonwealth Federation.[35]

PARTY ORGANIZATION

A political party has been defined as an organized group, but the structure of such a group requires clarification. Several different components of each party can be identified: the **parliamentary party** or caucus, that is, the party's elected representatives in Parliament; the **extra-parliamentary party** organization made up of party activists and executive members; the party headquarters, bureaucracy or staff; and ordinary party members.

When it comes to comparing party organizations, it is useful to apply two theoretical models, those of the **mass party** and the **cadre party**. These two models can be differentiated in five main ways: membership, leadership, finance, policy-making, and general structures and operations.

DISTINGUISHING BETWEEN MASS AND CADRE PARTIES

	Mass Party	**Cadre Party**
Membership	Has or aspires to have a large membership that possesses considerable power over the parliamentary wing, executive members, and party staffers.	Content to operate with a small elite, as long as workers, as distinct from members, materialize at election time.
Leadership	Chooses its leader at a convention or by giving every member a vote, and maintains some kind of control over the leader afterward.	Allows the parliamentary party to select the leader, who then operates without any formal accountability.

Finance	Financed by membership fees and other small contributions from its members.	Depends on a relatively small number of large contributions, usually corporate.
Policy-Making	Allows the membership to have a meaningful say in determining party policy.	Permits the parliamentary party, especially the leader and/or cabinet, to formulate party policy.
General Structures & Operations	Operates democratically, according to a written constitution, and throughout the year.	Run by an elite, pays little attention to its constitution, and barely exists except at election time.

While real-life parties should not be expected to fall perfectly into these theoretical categories and while every party may bear characteristics of both mass and cadre models, these ideal types are useful in comparing the main Canadian parties. The discussion of party and election finance in Chapter 15 showed that the Liberal and Conservative parties began as cadre parties dependent on large corporate contributions and then moved to an intermediate position in which they now receive about half their revenues from individual donations. The CCF/NDP, on the other hand, was always essentially a mass party with respect to party finance, which is more or less the case with the Reform and BQ parties too.

Party Membership

A significant difference among the parties can be seen in their provisions for membership. The NDP aspires to a large membership and its most active organizations operate an annual, year-round membership drive, even if the results are not always as "massive" as anticipated. New members must take an oath that they support the party's principles, and only those who have been members for at least 30 days and who live in the constituency are allowed to vote at nomination meetings. Constituency association representation at party conventions is based on the size of the local membership, and the party is unique in also having affiliated members, that is, members of unions that have voted to affiliate with the party. Like the NDP, the Reform Party has a 30-day membership qualification period, and convention representation is based on the number of local members.

Although they may conduct membership drives for a few weeks a year, the Liberals and Conservatives are normally more casual about the annual renewal of party memberships. For the most part their members sign up in connection with the meeting to nominate a candidate for the next election or to choose delegates to a national convention. In this case the Liberals are usually more restrictive than the Conservatives, such as requiring that at least 75 percent of those voting reside in the constituency and that all of those voting have signed up at least 72 hours ahead of time (or seven days, if the election has not yet been called). Even with such restrictions, it is typical for aspiring Liberal candidates or delegates to sign up large numbers of new members (often from ethnic groups in urban centres) just before the deadline. Some PC constituency associations have somewhat similar stipulations, but usually not. In the absence of such rules, those hoping to capture the party nomination or be chosen as delegates can pack the meeting with busloads of senior citizens or high-school students whose memberships are bought for them at the door. All parties have difficulty maintaining complete and current lists of their members, especially at provincial or national headquarters, but consistent with the mass–cadre categorizations made, the NDP, Reform and Bloc usually have a better grasp of their actual membership than the others and use their list repeatedly during the year for fund-raising purposes.

Party Leadership

There is probably less distinction among the parties when it comes to the question of leadership. The Liberals relied on the Parliamentary party to select its leaders before 1919 and the Conservatives did so until 1927, but federal parties currently choose their leaders at national conventions.[36] While leadership conventions are a more democratic means of choosing the party leader, the preference of party delegates does not always correspond to that of the parliamentary party, sometimes leading to considerable friction between the new leader and the caucus. The list of dates and winners of party leadership conventions is contained in Table 16.2.

It can be seen from Table 16.2 that Audrey McLaughlin was the first female national party leader in Canadian history, although Rosemary Brown (NDP), Flora MacDonald (PC), and Sheila Copps (Liberal) also gave male contenders a run for their money in 1975, 1976, and 1990 respectively. The Liberals have alternated anglophone and francophone leaders, partly by accident and partly by design, while the Conservatives never had a francophone leader before Jean Charest, Brian Mulroney being the first bilingual Quebecker to hold the post in that party. Most Liberal leaders have been Roman Catholics (King and Pearson excepted), while most PC leaders have been Protestants (with the exception of Clark, Mulroney, and Charest). All Liberal leaders have come from Ontario or Quebec, while the origin of most Conservative leaders was outside central Canada. Lawyers represent the most common occupational

TABLE 16.2 Dates and Victors of Party Leadership Conventions		
Liberals	*Conservatives*	*CCF/NDP*
1919 Mackenzie King	1927 R.B. Bennett	1932 J.S. Woodsworth
1948 Louis St. Laurent	1938 Robert Manion	1942 M.J. Coldwell
1958 Lester B. Pearson	1942 John Bracken	1960 Hazen Argue
1968 Pierre E. Trudeau	1948 George Drew	1961 T.C. Douglas
1984 John Turner	1956 John Diefenbaker	1971 David Lewis
1990 Jean Chrétien	1967 Robert Stanfield	1975 Ed Broadbent
	1976 Joe Clark	1989 Audrey McLaughlin
	1983 Brian Mulroney	1995 Alexa McDonough
	1993 Kim Campbell	
	1995 Jean Charest	

background (St. Laurent, Diefenbaker, Stanfield, Trudeau, Lewis, Turner, Mulroney, Charest, and Chrétien). With the exception of Brian Mulroney, all of the leaders have had some experience in the House of Commons or in provincial legislatures (Bracken, Drew, Stanfield, and McDonough), Douglas having been both a premier and an MP. What is more striking, however, is the brevity of their parliamentary experience. Most were relatively inexperienced in politics when they were chosen, and the Liberals' tendency to co-opt an extra-parliamentary notable for their leader has often been noted. Especially in a television age, a fresh face may be just as important as legislative experience in order to obtain the job, although it might not be so useful afterwards. Even in the case of Turner and Chrétien, a period out of the Commons' spotlight was apparently considered advantageous by the delegates who chose them.

Trick or Trick

Reprinted with permission.

An even more democratic procedure than the leadership convention has been proposed in recent years, that is, to allow every card-carrying member of the party to cast a vote for the leadership. Such a procedure avoids much of the cost of holding a national convention; it eliminates the unholy fight among various candidates for delegates at the constituency level; it ensures that the decision is not left to the more affluent members of the party who can afford the travel costs; and it removes the circus atmosphere of the convention. The Parti Québécois was the first Canadian party to move to a "one member–one vote" leadership selection process, and many provincial party leaders have now been elected on this basis. It has become popular to issue party members a PIN (personal identification number) and have them telephone in their choice rather than vote by ballot at the local level. Many partisans feel, however, that the loss of the publicity value of a nationally televised convention is too high a cost, and suggest that by imposing spending limits on candidates and subsidizing delegates' expenses, some of the worst features of conventions can be avoided. The Royal Commission on Electoral Reform and Party Financing recommended that legal spending limits and public tax credits be extended to leadership conventions. Preston Manning was elected at Reform's founding convention, but the Reform constitution provided that all members of the party would vote in any subsequent leadership contest, although exact procedures were not established.

Some parties try to combine the best of both worlds: giving every member a vote, but also having a leadership convention. After choosing Jean Chrétien in the traditional way in 1990, the Liberals adopted a new system in 1992 modelled on their provincial counterparts in Ontario. Every party member votes on the leadership candidates, as well as for delegates, and the latter are elected in proportion to the popular vote received by each leadership candidate. Similarly, when the NDP replaced Audrey McLaughlin in 1995, it wished to give the grassroots of the party a direct vote but still retain the drama of a convention. It sought to do so by providing for regional "primaries" in which all members could vote and that would determine which candidates would appear on the ballot at the actual convention.

The Conservatives had a problem when Kim Campbell resigned as leader after the 1993 election. For a number of reasons, the party was in no position to hold a full-fledged leadership convention, but the candidate who ran a close second in the last such convention was one of the two PC MPs elected. The national executive thus appointed Jean Charest as interim leader, to be confirmed by a vote at the next general meeting of the party. At that meeting, in April 1995, delegates were scheduled to vote on the question: "Do you wish a leadership convention?" The executive decided to add a supplementary question: "or do you wish to confirm Jean Charest as leader?" His position as leader was confirmed with 96 percent approval, but at the same time, the party adopted a new constitution that provides for the next leader to be chosen by a vote of all party members.

As suggested above, most parties also have **leadership review** mechanisms in their constitutions, although these vary in detail. The NDP opens nominations for the position of leader at their national convention every two years, so that at least in theory, the leader can be immediately replaced. However, in the absence of a concrete challenger, no vote is needed. Leadership review provisions were not added to the other parties' constitutions until after the Conservative civil war over John Diefenbaker's leadership between 1962 and 1967. From 1974 to 1983, that party took a vote at its national general meeting on three occasions on the question, "Are you in favour of holding a leadership convention?" This means that, to date, only Joe Clark's leadership has been so reviewed. In 1977, 93 percent rejected the idea of a leadership convention, and in 1981, 66 percent did so. Two years later, an almost identical 67 percent again opposed a leadership convention, but Clark decided to resign and call a leadership convention anyway. Running to succeed himself, he was defeated by Brian Mulroney. By this time the leadership review mechanism had caused so much turmoil in the party that it was changed in 1983 so that the question is put only at the first convention following an election that the party loses.

Seeking to avoid the Conservatives' difficulty, the Liberals added a leadership review clause in 1966 to the effect that at the first convention after each election (win or lose), delegates vote on whether they want a leadership convention to be called. Pierre Trudeau was backed by 89 percent in 1973 and 81 percent in 1975, while John Turner received the support of 76 percent in 1986 and then decided to resign before the scheduled 1990 convention. The Reform Party asks the question at every biennial national party assembly: "Do you want a leadership vote to be called?"

While it is obviously advantageous to have some means of getting rid of leaders who have outlived their usefulness, too much leadership accountability and review can also paralyze a party. Many Liberals and Conservatives have regretted the divisiveness and distraction caused by leadership review processes, and some prefer the NDP approach of having a real-life challenger on the ballot instead of voting hypothetically between the incumbent and some unblemished phantom.

Party Policy-Making

All political parties have difficulty designing their policy-making process. On the one hand, they want to give ordinary party members an opportunity to contribute to party policy (a mass characteristic), but at the same time, no party establishment wants to be saddled with unrealistic policy commitments (a cadre notion). Thus, they all struggle to combine these two forces in the most appropriate way.

Liberal and Conservative national conventions or general meetings usually include a policy session and sometimes focus primarily on policy. But even if specific resolutions are debated and passed, which is not always the case, party leaders or cabinets retain the right to determine official party policy. While parliamentary leaders may be influenced by such discussions to some extent, they are in no way bound by the policy resolutions of the party organization.

The Liberal Party did not even hold a national convention between 1919 and 1948, and instead mainly relied on the public service for policy advice. When the Liberals found themselves in opposition after 1957, however, and cut off from the public service, Lester Pearson was forced to turn to the party organization to help develop new policy proposals. A "thinkers' conference" held in Kingston in 1960 was followed by a national party policy rally in 1961, and once in power after 1963, the Pearson government quickly implemented most of the policies that had been adopted. Under Pierre Trudeau, the party went through a major policy generation effort consisting of a thinkers' conference in 1969, constituency association discussion of the ideas raised, and a national policy conference in 1970. Several party policy conferences were also held later in his term, but in contrast to Pearson, Trudeau did not pay much attention to the results.[37] Indeed, in 1986, the party eliminated from its constitution the "policy accountability" clause that required the parliamentary party to answer for deviations from resolutions passed at party conventions. Jean Chrétien tried to replicate the early 1960s experience with a policy conference in Aylmer in 1991, followed by the biennial party convention a year later, which debated such policy ideas. The Red Book used as the party platform in the 1993 election drew substantially upon these two party meetings. In 1994, the party held its next regular convention complete with policy workshops and a discussion of some 40 resolutions in a plenary session.

Like the Liberals, the Conservatives discussed policy to some extent at their many leadership conventions. But after the 1956 convention, Diefenbaker attempted to destroy all evidence of its policy proposals and governed for five years without any policy guidance from the party. When Robert Stanfield became leader in 1967, he was anxious to develop a stronger policy orientation, organizing a thinkers' conference in 1969, encouraging policy discussions at the grassroots level of the party, and then calling a national policy conference in 1971. Although he retained the right to make the final decisions, Stanfield took the results quite seriously, and possibly because he was able to use this party-generated policy in the 1972 election campaign, the Conservatives made major gains. Still finding themselves in opposition, however, both Stanfield and the party lost enthusiasm for policy. Joe Clark was not guided by the party very much in some of his more memorable (unimplemented) policies, and Brian Mulroney relied primarily on the public service, royal commissions, backroom advisers, and public opinion polls for his policies, although he held an unmemorable party policy conference in 1991. Recognizing past deficiencies, and as part of its rebuilding process after 1993, the PC Party is designing a new policy-making process combining greater membership input with expert advice. The party plans to move from "principles to policy to platform" with a major policy convention scheduled for August 1996, and hopes the process established will outlive the next election.

The NDP has always claimed to be particularly distinctive in the realm of party policy-making. It has regular policy sessions every two years, which are indeed the predominant item on the convention agenda. Grass-roots constituency associations are invited to submit resolutions in advance, and, most important, resolutions passed by the convention are considered to be official and binding on the leader and the parliamentary party. Giving such power to the rank-and-file membership, however, sometimes hobbles the leadership with policies that are embarrassing, unworkable, or at odds with its own views; there is often no connection between the hordes of resolutions passed; and occasionally problems erupt between the parliamentary caucus and the party organization. The party executive and council are thus allowed to submit resolutions of their own, and the council, which is subject to greater leadership manipulation than the convention, is given authority to "flesh out" the meaning of policies adopted. A good example concerned the NDP position on NATO just prior to the 1988 election. The post-1993 decimated NDP was not so sure that its traditional policy-making system was adequate, however, and revamped it in 1995. Instead of passing random policy resolutions at whim, riding associations would be expected to put more research into them in the first place, and such resolutions would then be vetted by the policy committee with its considerable resources before being transmitted to the council and on to the convention. This would no doubt leave the NDP with better policy, but make it less distinctive from other parties in its processes.

Wearing summarizes the policy-making process in the three traditional parties as follows:

It would be an over-simplification—though not so very far from the truth—to say that the Conservatives deal with this problem by not having policy conventions, the Liberals have policy conventions but forge the resolutions once the conventions are over, and the NDP leadership makes sure it gets the resolutions it wants.[38]

The Royal Commission on Electoral Reform recommended that political parties establish affiliated foundations that would strengthen their policy-making and public education functions, but as in the case of so many other recommendations, nothing happened.

As for the Reform Party, a certain tension exists in its policy-making process between its populist intentions and the leadership group around Preston Manning. It adopted a full-scale platform at its founding convention but has also established an elaborate policy-making process in which policy resolutions can originate at the constituency level, from caucus, from party task forces, and from the executive council. Such resolutions are collated by the resolutions committee, and an "exposure draft" is sent out to constituency associations for prioritization. The top 40 are then put on the agenda of the next national assembly. Changes to party policy must be approved by a majority of votes cast as well as a majority in a majority of provinces. In keeping with its populist approach, the executive council of the party can conduct an informal poll of the membership on an issue as well as hold a formal referendum.

General Structures and Operations

CONVENTIONS

All parties have constitutions that outline their objectives, structures, and procedures. In theory, at least, the ultimate power in each party is held by the party convention, which all now hold quite regularly at an average of about two-year intervals. The convention agenda normally includes the election of the party executive, constitutional amendments, policy discussions, and instruction in local election organization, but such conventions also serve important social and morale-building purposes. In the Liberal and Conservative cases each constituency association is entitled to an equal number of delegates, while in the NDP and Reform cases, representation is based on the size of the local membership. All parties include certain ex officio delegates such as MPs, and in some cases MPPs, MLAs, nominated or recently defeated candidates. In the NDP, affiliated labour unions also send delegates. The array of women's, youth, campus, Native, ethnic, and other associated groups is too complicated to fathom here, but party conventions, especially those of the Liberals and Conservatives, are not very representative of the electorate. Even at the level of party activists, most are of middle-class background. While women have traditionally done much menial work in these parties without being allowed to be part of the elite, most parties have deliberately boosted the effective participation of women within their ranks in recent years. Ethnic minorities have also begun to demand a more meaningful role.

PARTY EXECUTIVE

Each party has a national executive of some kind, including a president, vice-presidents, treasurer, and so on, and each establishes a number of executive committees. These officials usually perform such duties on a part-time basis, although it is helpful for the president to be close to Ottawa and readily available for meetings, campaign organization, and other functions. Both Liberals and Conservatives have sometimes elected a Senator as party president since such a person has considerable free time and is on the public payroll, saving the party the cost of a presidential salary. The party president usually has the confidence of the leader, and the contest for the presidency is sometimes a surrogate vote on the leadership. Dalton Camp was probably the most famous party president in Canadian history because of his feat in using that position to engineer the leadership convention that toppled John Diefenbaker. The Liberals and Conservatives have a two-tier executive structure, Reform's has only one, and the NDP has three, the third being a council that meets twice a year as a sort of mini-convention and is the governing body of the party between conventions.

NATIONAL STRUCTURES OF THE FOUR MAIN CANADIAN PARTIES (PARENTHESES REPRESENT APPROXIMATE SIZE)

Liberal
Management Committee (16)
National Executive (50)

NDP
Officers (10)
Executive (20)
Council (102)

PC
Management Committee (30)
National Council (350)

Reform
Executive Council (33)

PARTY HEADQUARTERS

Three parties maintain a headquarters in Ottawa, which is staffed by permanent party employees. This office is headed by the national director in the Liberal and Conservative cases, and the federal secretary in the NDP's. In each case, the size of the party staff varies considerably, depending on party finances and the imminence of an election. The PC and NDP offices were dramatically scaled down after the 1993 election, the latter having to sell its building and move into smaller rented space. In 1995, the Liberals maintained a staff of about 20, some of whom worked in the Federal Liberal Agency, the fund-raising branch of the office. The PC office, including the PC Fund, employed 14 people, with three additional organizers out in the field, while the NDP was slashed to a complement of six. The role of party headquarters during election campaigns is outlined in Chapter 17. Between elections, headquarters performs a variety of functions such as collecting money, ensuring local organizations are alive and well, arranging for speakers to local annual meetings, planning conventions, publishing newsletters, conducting surveys, and researching policy.

The Reform Party maintains a research and communications office in Ottawa, which, dealing largely with parliamentary work, is mostly funded by the public purse, while the official national office of the party is in Calgary. There it has a staff of about 20. This separation of the parliamentary and extra-parliamentary offices is consistent with its populist intentions and image but creates certain difficulties in coordination and communication. The party tries to overcome such problems with semi-annual joint caucus–executive meetings, quarterly strategic retreats (usually in Calgary), a weekly teleconference between officials in the two locations, and busy telephone and fax lines.

FEDERAL–PROVINCIAL PARTY LINKS

The federal nature of Canada and the existence of two levels of government at which political parties seek to influence policy and personnel raise the question of the relationship between national and provincial party organizations.[39] With ten provinces and two territories and so many parties, an amazing array of federal–provincial relationships exists. To oversimplify the situation, the Conservative Party could be said to have a "confederal" character—that is, the federal and provincial PC parties are essentially independent. There is virtually no formal organizational or financial link between the two wings of the party. Moreover, in British Columbia, the federal Conservative Party used to have stronger links with the provincial Social Credit Party than with its own fledgling organization, while there is no provincial Conservative Party at all in Quebec. Thus, federal and provincial party memberships are usually separate, and a complete set of federal riding associations and executives co-exists with provincial party organizations at the grass-roots level.

By contrast, the NDP could be called an "integrated" party because, with the exception of Quebec, one joins the NDP at the provincial level and automatically becomes a member of the national party, almost as if it were an afterthought. Only in areas of its strongest support does the party maintain full-fledged separate federal and provincial constituency associations, and provincial offices of the party theoretically serve the needs of both federal and provincial parties. To help overcome the provincial orientation of the party and to combat the dormancy of the federal party at the provincial and constituency levels between federal elections, the party created a Council of Federal Ridings in each province. The two levels of the party are integrated financially, such that the provincial parties must contribute 15 percent of their annual revenues to the federal party. In Quebec, however, federal and provincial wings of the party are quite separate. The 1995 Renewal Convention sought to change much of the relationship described above by severing many of the formal links between the federal and provincial branches of the party.

The Liberal Party is characterized by two different federal–provincial relationships. In Quebec, Ontario, Alberta, and British Columbia, the party is "split" into federal and provincial wings, each of which has separate finances, memberships, constituency associations, executives, conventions, and offices. In the other provinces and territories, the party is more "unitary." As in the case of the NDP, however, such an integrated relationship gives the party a provincial orientation; it is possible to join the federal party directly, but it is more common to join the provincial party and become an automatic member of the federal organization. The unitary relationship involves a complicated and troublesome financial connection in which the federal party picks up approximately one-half of the provincial party's budget.

In general, it would seem that the Conservative model of independent federal and provincial parties is most satisfactory. While the integration of federal and provincial wings in the Liberal and NDP cases can sometimes be advantageous to both levels, it just as often results in serious friction and endless haggling over finances.

The Bloc Québécois has no provincial counterpart as such, but the Parti Québécois more or less fulfills that function. The two parties were not as intimate as outsiders assumed, however, because they were led by two dominant leaders who disliked to share the limelight and because they prescribed slightly different versions of sovereignty. After it became apparent that Jacques Parizeau's concept of complete independence would not fly with the Quebec electorate, the two parties came together around the Bloc's idea of many continuing links between a "sovereign" Quebec and the "rest of Canada," and after the 1995 Quebec referendum Lucien Bouchard took over the PQ leadership.

Meanwhile, Preston Manning wanted to concentrate all of Reform's attention at the national level, and persuaded his members to back his objection to any provincial party branches. That did not completely end the discussion, however, for a provincial party in British Columbia had previously adopted the "Reform Party" label and continued to operate with a platform similar to Manning's, but without organic links to his federal party.

THE IRON LAW OF OLIGARCHY

To return to the concepts of mass and cadre parties, the relationships among the party membership, the executive, the parliamentary caucus, and the party leadership must be examined. As noted earlier, in a mass party, the membership, executive, and conventions have real power, whereas a cadre party is controlled by the leader and parliamentary wing. But Robert Michels, claiming that a tendency toward elitism was inevitable within all political parties, formulated his **iron law of oligarchy**.[40] Even in parties that seek or profess to belong to the mass category, a small elite invariably develops, such that rank-and-file party members have little real power.

One tendency is for party leaders, whether or not in government, to create a small coterie of advisers, who cut the leader off from party influence. This was particularly so in the Liberal Party during the tenure of Pierre Elliott Trudeau.[41] As party leader, Trudeau virtually ignored the party organization, paying little attention to its policy generation efforts, its increasing debt, its cynical electoral strategies, and participating in its unsavoury patronage practices. In fact, he left almost all such party and electoral matters in the hands of Jim Coutts in the Prime Minister's Office and Senator Keith Davey, neither of whom held any official position in the Liberal Party. Their style of operation and their ignoring the party organization led to the passage of an extremely critical resolution at the 1982 Liberal national convention, the election of a reform-minded president, and the creation of a reform committee. The general objective of these initiatives was to allow the party organization to take back control of the party policy, platform, appointments, and electoral strategy from this small group of back-room advisers. Certain minor changes followed, but in 1990 the party created another reform commission, evidence that little had changed. The commission was finally disbanded in 1992 after the constitution was considerably altered.

A second common development is that the parliamentary wing of the party claims precedence over the party organization. In terms of policy, for example, the caucus usually has more (publicly supported) research assistance than the party can afford, and such research may prescribe different policy approaches than come out of party policy discussions. Caucus members are usually more concerned about getting re-elected than other party members and may thus seek to tone down certain ideas emanating from the grass roots of the party. Moreover, when a party forms the government, it has the entire public service to advise it, and may find that the world looks somewhat different from the position of public responsibility than from the Opposition benches.

In the third place, even within the party organization, which has periodic elections, a small group of executive members often seek re-election for many terms and effectively maintain control. They use their experience, their access to party information, their connections, their control of party funds, and their influence over party policy to do so. Member apathy is also a factor, for the great bulk of party members are inactive and quite happy to have a handful of activists take charge.

Thus, we can conclude that the Liberals and Conservatives started out as cadre parties in the areas of membership, leadership, finance, policy-making, and general structures and operations but have moved some distance in the direction of the mass party model. The NDP is therefore less distinctive than it once was, but continues to be significantly closer to the mass party model than the other two. In some respects, Reform and the Bloc also approximate the mass party model, although both have been headed by dominant leaders who ensured that the membership did not get out of control.

A final word should be added on the efforts of the Conservative and New Democratic parties to rebuild their organizations after their disastrous fate in the 1993 election. Soon after he took over as party leader, Jean Charest announced a three-step plan to restore the PCs as a relevant political force. The "3 R" renewal plan consisted of restructuring the party, rebuilding its policy platform, and returning to government (election preparedness). He then appointed a national restructuring committee, which engaged in extensive consultation with party activists across the country and presented its report in March 1995. At the national meeting of the party held one month later, a new constitution was adopted, many of whose provisions have been outlined above: the new executive structure, the policy-making process, and the direct election of the next leader. It also included a new statement of the party's aims and principles.

If the PC constitution had not been seriously re-examined since 1956, this was almost as true in the case of the equally decimated NDP. It therefore engaged in a similar renewal process, with the results to be ratified at the October 1995 convention. In this case, changes were made in the executive structure, the policy-making process, and the leadership selection process. The NDP also reassessed its links with labour and other social movements, the federal–provincial relationship within the party (including its finances), and its principles and policies.

PARTY IDEOLOGY

Discussions of party ideology might be a relatively straightforward task in some political systems, but it is not so in Canada. Parties often play down their ideological differences in the search for votes, their positions change over time, and they are all internally divided to some extent. Moreover, it is difficult to know where to find evidence of party ideology and how to measure it, possible sources being election rhetoric, party policy resolutions, policies adopted when in office, government spending patterns, or surveys of the attitudes of party activists.

There are three different perspectives within the literature of Canadian political science with respect to party ideology. The first view is that no basic ideological differences exist between the Liberal and Conservative parties.[42] Either they are both pure broker parties with no ideology, responding pragmatically and opportunistically to public opinion polls in the pursuit of power, or else they are equally committed to the capitalist system but prepared to remedy its worst faults in order to maintain popular support.

The second interpretation of Canadian party ideology is that while no fundamental ideological differences exist between the Liberals and Conservatives, they have maintained certain consistent historic policy differences.[43] Failing that, they at least offer marginal policy differences at any point in time. Historians have generally observed, for example, that the Liberals were more continentalist or U.S.-oriented, while the Conservatives favoured the British connection; that the Liberals (at least since 1900) were more sympathetic to the concerns of Quebec and French Canada, while the Conservatives (at least since 1957) were more in tune with Western Canada; that the Liberals favoured lower tariffs, while the Conservatives stood for higher tariffs; and that the Liberals advocated provincial rights, while the Conservatives preferred a strong central government. Such policy differences were consistent for generations, but in recent times it appears that many of these stands have been reversed. So, while the parties continue to provide certain policy alternatives to the electorate, the contrast on free trade in 1988 being exceptional, voters must be forgiven if they are suspicious about how deeply held such differences are.

The third and most theoretical perspective is that genuine ideological differences do exist in Canada, and that such ideologies as liberalism, conservatism, and democratic socialism can be found to differentiate the three traditional parties to some extent. The ideological continuum can be sketched in diagrammatic form as in Figure 16.1.

This perspective is based on the writing of Louis Hartz, Kenneth MacRae, Gad Horowitz, and William Christian and Colin Campbell, among others.[44] It suggests that the basic ideology in Canada is **liberalism**, but that traces of **socialism** and **conservatism** also exist, and that each of the ideologies is represented by a corresponding party. Liberalism seeks to liberate the individual and maximize each individual's freedom and potential, something that almost all Canadians would support. Differences emerge, however, about how many individuals should be liberated, about what the inhibiting agent is, and about how to go about such liberation. Such differences primarily focus on the role of the state.

Figure 16.1   **The Ideological Continuum in Canada**

Democratic socialism seeks to liberate the individual from the inequalities and exploitation of the capitalist system; it believes in equality of condition, not merely equality of opportunity; and it prescribes a large element of state action or collectivism in order to achieve such liberation and equality. These views are generally referred to in discussions of political ideology as being on the **left**. In particular, democratic socialism emphasizes government planning, regulation, ownership of some of the major industries of the country, progressive taxation, and redistribution of income via social programs. Democratic socialists are sometimes subdivided between "socialists" and "social democrats," depending on the extent to which they wish the state to intervene and the extent of equality they wish to effect. The early CCF was certainly more socialistic than the current New Democratic Party, which is seen as containing both groups, but with its majority being of the social democratic persuasion. The CCF/NDP take credit for introducing public hospital and medical insurance when they formed the government of Saskatchewan, pressing for other social welfare programs, advocating a more progressive taxation system, creating a variety of Crown corporations in the provinces where they held power, and supporting the creation of several such government bodies in Ottawa.

Liberalism, too, has a dual personality and can be subdivided into welfare and business variants. Business liberals believe that the state inhibits individual self-fulfilment and that its role should therefore be minimized so that individualism can prevail. Welfare liberals, on the other hand, take the view that the state can be a positive agent in liberating individuals from the constraints of other forces including the private-enterprise economy. Welfare liberals therefore stand for a combination of individualism and collectivism and a combination of equality and inequality, which they usually label "equality of opportunity." In terms of the diagram in Figure 16.1, then, the Liberal Party is composed of business and welfare liberals, leaving it in the centre of the Canadian ideological continuum. While Liberals obviously hold the private-enterprise system in greater esteem than does the NDP, Liberal governments introduced old age pensions, family allowances, and many other social welfare programs over the years. Historians generally point out that the Liberal Party made an ideological shift about 1919 from a business–liberal to a welfare–liberal orientation. Some observers see a shift backwards after 1993.

Conservatism also has two variants. On the one hand, conservatives seek to liberate the individual from the restrictions of the state. Reducing the role of the state to a minimum and allowing capitalistic market forces to determine the distribution of power and wealth is often labelled "individualism." If this results in inequalities or elitism, conservatives are generally unconcerned; that is how it should be, because inequalities are both natural and deserved— some people are better and some work harder than others. These attitudes are labelled as being on the **right**, and these conservatives can be called "business liberals" in terms of the diagram. The second wing of the Canadian Progressive Conservative Party is the progressive element, people who are sometimes called **red tories**. These Conservatives combine beliefs in privilege and collectivism, seeing society as an organic whole, emphasizing community values as well as individualism, and standing for order, tradition, stability, and noblesse oblige. They believe in hierarchy and that everyone should occupy his or her place, but they also have a paternalistic concern with the condition of all the people. This aspect of conservatism is not unique to Canada, being found quite commonly in Britain and the rest of Europe; it stands out only in contrast to a lack of such sentiment within American conservatism. Thus, the ideology of the Canadian Conservative Party is not as clear-cut as the diagram indicates and is at least as divided as in the other two parties. Furthermore, the red tory element overlaps to some extent with welfare liberalism and even social democracy. While the Mulroney government pursued a fairly consistent business–liberal agenda—privatization, deregulation, deficit reduction, and cutting of social programs—its Conservative predecessors sometimes exhibited a strong red tory touch, such as in the creation of the RCMP, CBC, CNR, and the National Energy Board, the Bennett New Deal, and the Stanfield proposal for wage and price controls. An alternative diagram, Figure 16.2, clarifies the position of the red tory influence in the Conservative Party. It also indicates why it is sometimes difficult to distinguish among social democrats, welfare liberals, and red tories, and why some New Democrats feel closer to some Conservatives than to certain Liberals.[45]

If liberalism in the United States lacks the collectivist touch, how does one explain its presence in all three of the traditional Canadian party ideologies? One explanation focuses on the United Empire Loyalists, who removed most of the collectivist tendencies from the U.S. political culture when they migrated to Canada, and left behind almost undiluted business liberalism in that country. The United Empire Loyalists rendered ideological diversity legitimate in Canada and because of their early predominance, made collectivism a respectable and important element in the Canadian political culture. In fact, they added to the collectivist approach already found in the feudal background of French Canada, that is, the ideas of hierarchy, order, stability, and community. Collectivism was reinforced by subsequent waves of British immigration, whose intellectual baggage included both red tory and socialist views, along with the influence of the Social Gospel movement.[46] Such collectivist tendencies were discussed in Chapter 13.

Figure 16.2 **Canadian Party Ideology**

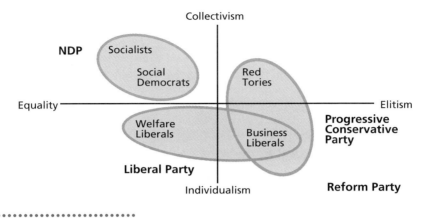

There is so much overlap in the ideological orientation of the Liberal and Conservative parties in particular that it is often difficult to detect the distinctions made above, and political scientists often ask the question: "Does party matter?"[47] Indeed, from about 1945 to 1980 or so the Liberal and Conservative parties shared a basic ideological approach that emphasized economic growth based on foreign investment, expanding the welfare state, and engaging in a certain amount of macroeconomic government regulation called Keynesian economics.[48] As time went on, however, this consensus broke down. The Liberals started to become concerned about the dangers of so much foreign investment, the Conservatives and some Liberals began to feel that the economy could not support any further social programs, and Keynesian economics did not seem to prevent the simultaneous occurrence of unemployment and inflation. Thus, especially after the Conservatives took office in 1984, policy and ideological differences between the two parties were much more obvious, with the Mulroney government pursuing a business–liberal or **neoconservative** agenda in which renewed reliance was placed on market forces and the extent of government intervention was actually reduced.

Indeed, over the past decade, the whole ideological spectrum has shifted to the right. For the first time in Canadian history, social programs are being cut back rather than expanded; Crown corporations are being privatized rather than created; regulations are being repealed rather than promulgated; public debts and deficits are being reduced rather than increased; and public servants are being fired rather than being hired. The phenomenon goes beyond one or two parties; it is happening around the world, and in Canada it has affected governing parties of all ideological persuasions: the NDP, especially in Saskatchewan, the Parti Québécois, and Liberal governments of the 1990s, such as Frank McKenna in New Brunswick, Clyde Wells in Newfoundland, and Jean Chrétien in Ottawa.

The Reform Party is very much part of this shift to the right, and has exerted great influence at both federal and provincial levels even though it has not formed the government. The leaders of this right-wing crusade, Ralph Klein in Alberta and Mike Harris in Ontario, are following the Reform program to a tee. Reform believes in reducing the role of government, reducing taxes, reducing regulation, privatizing Crown corporations, discontinuing government programs, laying off public servants, reducing the debt and the deficit, and cutting back on social programs. This is all consistent with a belief in individualism, which is unconcerned about whether it leads to socioeconomic inequalities. (Ironically, the Reform Party is a strong believer in treating everyone, including provinces, equally in *law*.) The only respect in which Reform is not completely right-wing is in its populist streak: it is against elitism and professes to value the wisdom of ordinary people. But even this is an Americanism as opposed to the traditional Canadian belief in British parliamentary democracy. It should be added that the other main concern of the Reform Party was a territorial rather than ideological issue—that the West was getting short-changed within Confederation. What distinguishes Reform from other Canadian parties is a complete absence of the collectivist value. In this respect, it is almost a clone of the U.S. Republican Party, with which it maintains contact.

The other new party, the Bloc Québécois, has one main objective: Quebec sovereignty. The question of nationalism generally overwhelms the left–right ideological approach in Quebec, but in some respects nationalism can be provided for within the format presented earlier. Nationalism is a kind of collectivism that usually involves a large role for the state, and at the pan-Canadian level—trying to make Canada more independent of Britain or the United States—has been a consistent mark of left-wing parties such as the NDP, as well as of red tories and left-wing Liberals. Although at the provincial level it is also possible for right-wingers to be nationalistic, the PQ has usually been placed on the left side of the continuum, somewhere between the Liberals and the NDP. The BQ does not have a comprehensive program apart from Quebec sovereignty and therefore no clear-cut left–right ideological stance, being made up of people who were previously members of all three other parties. Nevertheless, since its creation, it has usually adopted a slightly left-wing approach when required to take a stand on other issues.

To return to the shift to the right, the NDP is generally occupying the previous position of the Liberal Party. The Chrétien government is pursuing the same kind of leaner government that it previously condemned under Mulroney, and Finance Minister Paul Martin is forced to rationalize his dismemberment of the welfare state, which was largely the creation of his father Paul Martin, Sr., a Liberal cabinet minister in the 1940s, 1950s, and 1960s. As a result, a crush is occurring on the right-wing side of the spectrum. The Conservative Party is finding it difficult to identify its own ideological space between the Chrétien Liberals and Manning's Reform Party. The PCs claim to be more understanding of Quebec than Reform, of course, and therefore to be a "national" party; but it is hard to carve out a niche just slightly to the left of Reform, especially when so many provincial Conservatives are voting for that other federal party, and when Conservative governments in Alberta and Ontario are implementing Reform policies.

In these circumstances, in the mid-1990s, many observers wondered "what was left of the 'left'" or whether the "left" had a future. At that time, with an almost universal concern about government debts and deficits and when governments of every stripe were cutting back, it seemed unlikely that any advances to social programs would ever occur. Moreover, in an era of globalization, it also appeared that no single government could engage in personal or corporate taxation of a redistributive nature, regulation, or public ownership that was very much different from any other government around the world. On the other hand, those who held to the egalitarian ethic were not about to abandon it, and there was every likelihood that once governments got their finances under control and once the public came to the conclusion that the whole spectrum had moved too far to the right, support for social democratic policies would rise again.[49]

····················

CONCLUSION

However much Canadians tire of their endless bickering and lack of inspiration, political parties perform several crucial functions in the political system. In particular, they sort out the political issues, and in trying to bridge some of the many Canadian cleavages, make the political system more manageable. Many political observers are concerned about the danger of major political parties being outflanked by single-issue groups, whether as advocacy groups during and between election campaigns or as single-interest parties, in the representation of political interests and as the focus of political activity.[50] Such scholars argue that steps must be taken to strengthen mainline parties so that they can overcome their current lack of organizational depth and capacity to perform their representational and policy-making functions. Perhaps Canadians expect too much of their parties and place upon them too much of the burden of keeping the country together. Perhaps parties do not perform their functions well and are also dysfunctional in some respects. Perhaps their functions and methods of operation are in a state of change. Even so, or precisely because this is so, they must not be allowed to deteriorate further.

PC Since parties are so central to the operation of the political system, all of the approaches outlined in Chapter 1 have something to say about them. Parties are one of the main objects of the public choice approach, for example, and the efforts of political parties to bargain promises for votes can be seen in the attempt to develop attractive election platforms and in party policy-making processes. Politicians make such promises as will lead to their election, while rational, self-interested voters support the party whose policies are of greatest utility to themselves.[51] At least in the Liberal and Conservative parties, such promises and policies are not seriously limited by ideological consistency. As noted in Chapter 17, however, the alleged quid pro quo takes place in an environment of vague proposals, slogans, and leader images as far as the parties are concerned, and prejudices, ignorance, and family traditions on the part of many voters.

P The pluralist model, on the other hand, defends the broker system. In a country with many cleavages, it is not only desirable but necessary that political parties seek to accommodate the demands of all major groups. Unlike class analysts, pluralists do not see class divisions as taking priority over ethnic, religious, regional, or other concerns. They also note the increased role of women and new ethnic groups in party operations.

Ⓒ   The class analysis concern with corporate contributions to the Liberal and Conservative parties was addressed in Chapter 15. Here this approach can be seen in its critique of the broker system and in its alternative prescription for a class-based party system. In such analysts' eyes, the Liberal and Conservative parties (at least) are apologists for the capitalist system but have deliberately defined Canadian politics in terms of region and ethnicity in order to disguise their true motives. Both parties are so intermeshed with the capitalist system that any apparent choice they provide to the electorate is purely illusory. Other elite theorists observe that party activists overrepresent "elite" characteristics in society in terms of ethnicity and gender and emphasize the inevitable tendency toward oligarchy within all political parties, such that rank-and-file members have little real power.

ⓈⒸ   The state-centred approach is not overly interested in political parties and argues that it is largely irrelevant which party forms the government because the subsequent "government policy" is developed within the cabinet and bureaucracy. Such policy is more related to social and economic conditions and to the authorities' priorities than to election promises or party platforms. When parties neglect to develop policy within their ranks and fail to provide distinctive election platforms, they serve to confirm this contention. Even if they do put effort into the generation of party policy and even if they do propose specific policy positions in the campaign, government policies are rarely enacted without some evidence of bureaucratic modification. On the other hand, when a party comes to power fully committed to a new approach, the results are obvious. A Pearsonian commitment to social welfare programs, a Trudeauesque obsession with linguistic rights, or a Mulroneyite determination for free trade and deficit reduction (to say nothing of distinctive NDP, Social Credit, or Conservative approaches at the provincial level) all demonstrate that the state apparatus is not immune from party and societal influences.

DISCUSSION QUESTIONS

1. Why are political parties so prominent at the federal and provincial levels of government in Canada and so insignificant at the municipal level in most cases?

2. What historial events, political personalities, or other factors have been determining influences in the evolution of the Canadian party system?

3. Given the negative implications of the broker system (such as the emphasis on leadership and the lack of clear-cut policy alternatives in many cases), do you feel it would be advantageous to move to a class-based system? Why or why not?

4. Do you agree with the class-based theorists that the Liberals and Conservatives have defined Canadian politics in brokerage terms in order to disguise their own class-based interests?

5. What is the best method of choosing party leaders and the best approach to leadership accountability?

6. Is it possible in this complex, technological, information driven age for ordinary party members to make useful suggestions for national policies, or is it inevitable that the policy-making function will be turned over to party leaders and their advisers, bureaucrats, and pressure groups?

7. Is the NDP more of a mass party than the Liberals and Conservatives?

8. Is there a distinctive ideological base for the major parties in Canada? Is there at least a distinctive, consistent approach to policy questions?

9. What are the dangers of Canadian politics being taken over by special-interest advocacy groups and single-interest parties?

10. How do the approaches outlined in Chapter 1 relate to the material in this chapter?

NOTES

1. Conrad Winn and John McMenemy, *Political Parties in Canada* (Toronto: McGraw-Hill Ryerson, 1976), pp. 1–2, 10–11, 29–30.
2. J. Murray Beck, *Pendulum of Power* (Scarborough: Prentice-Hall Canada, 1968).
3. Ibid.; W.L. Morton, *The Progressive Party in Canada* (Toronto: University of Toronto Press, 1950).
4. Walter Young, *Anatomy of a Party: The National CCF 1932–1961* (Toronto: University of Toronto Press, 1969); Walter Young, *Democracy and Discontent* (Toronto: Ryerson Press, 1969); and S.M. Lipset, *Agrarian Socialism: The Cooperative Commonwealth Federation in Saskatchewan* (Los Angeles: University of California Press, 1950).
5. Alvin Finkel, *The Social Credit Phenomenon in Alberta* (Toronto: University of Toronto Press, 1989).
6. H.F. Quinn, *The Union Nationale* (Toronto: University of Toronto Press, 1963).
7. Reginald Whitaker, *The Government Party: Organizing and Financing the Liberal Party of Canada 1930–58* (Toronto: University of Toronto Press, 1977).
8. J.L. Granatstein, *The Politics of Survival: The Conservative Party of Canada, 1939–1945* (Toronto: University of Toronto Press, 1967); and George Perlin, *The Tory Syndrome: Leadership Politics in the Progressive Conservative Party* (Montreal: McGill–Queen's University Press, 1980).
9. Lynn McDonald, *The Party That Changed Canada: The New Democratic Party, Then and Now* (Toronto: McClelland and Stewart, 1987); Desmond Morton, *The New Democrats 1961–1986: The Politics of Change* (Toronto: Copp Clark Pitman, 1986); and Alan Whitehorn, *Canadian Socialism: Essays on the CCF and the NDP* (Toronto: Oxford University Press, 1992).
10. Maurice Pinard, *The Rise of a Third Party: A Study in Crisis Politics* (Scarborough: Prentice-Hall Canada, 1971); and Michael Stein, *The Dynamics of Right-Wing Protest: A Political Analysis of Social Credit in Quebec* (Toronto: University of Toronto Press, 1973).
11. Peter C. Newman, *The Distemper of Our Times* (Toronto: McClelland and Stewart, 1968).
12. Jeffrey Simpson, *Discipline of Power: The Conservative Interlude and the Liberal Restoration* (Toronto: Personal Library, 1980).
13. Christina McCall-Newman, *Grits: An Intimate Portrait of the Liberal Party* (Toronto: Macmillan, 1982); and Stephen Clarkson and Christina McCall, *Trudeau and Our Times* (Toronto: McClelland and Stewart, 1990).
14. Barry Kay et al., "The Character of Electoral Change: A Preliminary Report from the 1984 National Election Study," in Joseph Wearing, ed., *The Ballot and Its Message: Voting in Canada* (Toronto: Copp Clark Pitman, 1991).
15. Graham Fraser, *Playing for Keeps* (Toronto: McClelland and Stewart, 1989).

16. Alan Cairns, "An Election to Be Remembered: Canada 1993," *Canadian Public Policy* (September, 1994); Alan Frizzell et al., *The Canadian General Election of 1993* (Ottawa: Carleton University Press, 1994); Murray Dobbin, *Preston Manning and the Reform Party* (Toronto: Lorimer, 1991); Trevor Harrison, *Of Passionate Intensity: Right-Wing Populism and the Reform Party of Canada* (Toronto: University of Toronto Press, 1995); Preston Manning, *The New Canada* (Toronto: Macmillan Canada, 1992); Sydney Sharpe and Donald Braid, *Storming Babylon: Preston Manning and the Rise of the Reform Party* (Toronto: Key Porter Books, 1992); and Tom Flanagan, *Waiting for the Wave* (Toronto: Stoddart, 1995).

17. H.G. Thorburn, "Interpretations of the Canadian Party System," in H.G. Thorburn, ed., *Party Politics in Canada*, 6th ed. (Scarborough: Prentice-Hall Canada, 1991); R.M. Dawson, *The Government of Canada*, 4th ed. (Toronto: University of Toronto Press, 1963), ch. 21; J.A. Corry and J.E. Hodgetts, *Democratic Government and Politics*, 3rd rev. ed. (Toronto: University of Toronto Press, 1959), ch. VIII; and Paul Fox, "Middle-of-the Road Parties Are the Canadian Tradition," in his *Politics: Canada*, 6th ed. (Toronto: McGraw-Hill Ryerson, 1987).

18. Michael Ornstein et al., "Region, Class and Political Culture in Canada," *Canadian Journal of Political Science* (June 1980), pp. 227–71; and Elisabeth Gidengil, "Class and Region in Canadian Voting: A Dependency Interpretation," *Canadian Journal of Political Science* (September 1989), pp. 563–87.

19. Winn and McMenemy, *Political Parties*, pp. 19–26.

20. David E. Smith, "Canadian Political Parties and National Integration," in Alain Gagnon and Brian Tanguay, eds., *Canadian Parties in Transition* (Scarborough: Nelson Canda, 1989).

21. Janine Brodie and Jane Jenson, Crisis, *Challenge and Change: Party and Class in Canada Revisited* (Ottawa: Carleton University Press, 1988); Charles Taylor, *The Pattern of Politics* (Toronto: McClelland and Stewart, 1970); Gad Horowitz, "Toward the Democratic Class Struggle," in Trevor Lloyd and Jack McLeod, eds., *Agenda 1970* (Toronto: University of Toronto Press, 1968).

22. On seduction, see Whitaker, *The Government Party*, e.g., the co-opting of Saskatchewan farm leader C.A. Dunning and Humphrey Mitchell from the labour movement; on coercion, see Judy Torrance, *Public Violence in Canada* (Montreal: McGill–Queen's University Press, 1986).

23. The Liberals actually welcomed communist support if such working-class divisions would weaken the CCF. Gad Horowitz, *Canadian Labour in Politics* (Toronto: University of Toronto Press, 1968).

24. Jon Pammett, "Class Voting and Class Consciousness in Canada," *Canadian Review of Sociology and Anthropology* 24-2 (1987), pp. 269–90; and Keith Archer, "The Failure of the New Democratic Party: Unions, Unionists, and Politics in Canada," *Canadian Journal of Political Science* (June 1985), pp. 353–66.

25. Dawson, *The Government of Canada*; and Corry and Hodgetts, *Democratic Government and Politics*.

26. Brodie and Jenson, *Crisis, Challenge and Change*; Gagnon.

27. John Porter, *The Vertical Mosaic* (Toronto: University of Toronto Press, 1965).

28. Horowitz, "Towards the Democratic Class Struggle," p. 254.

29. Thorburn, "Interpretations of the Canadian Party System"; Whitaker, *The Government Party*; and Perlin, *The Tory Syndrome*.

30. John Meisel, "Decline of Party in Canada," in H.G. Thorburn, ed., *Party Politics in Canada*, 5th ed.; and John Meisel, "The Dysfunctions of Canadian Parties: An Exploratory Mapping," in Thorburn, 6th ed.

31. Gagnon and Tanguay, *Canadian Parties in Transition*.

32. S.M. Lipset, "Democracy in Alberta," *Canadian Forum* (November/December 1954); and Roger Gibbins, *Regionalism: Territorial Politics in Canada and the United States* (Toronto: Butterworths, 1982), ch. 5.

33. Pinard, *The Rise of a Third Party*; "Third Parties in Canada Revisited," *Canadian Journal of Political Science* (September 1973), pp. 439–60.

34. C.B. Macpherson, *Democracy in Alberta: Social Credit and the Party System* (Toronto: University of Toronto Press, 1953).

35. J.F. Conway, "Explaining the Roots of Canada's Third Parties," *Canadian Journal of Political Science* (1978), pp. 99–124.

36. John C. Courtney, *The Selection of National Party Leaders* (Toronto: Macmillan, 1973); Heather MacIvor, "The Leadership Convention: An Institution under Stress"; and Alan Whitehorn and Keith Archer, "Party Activists and Political Leadership: A Case Study of the NDP," in Maureen Mancuso et al., eds., *Leaders and Leadership in Canada* (Toronto: Oxford University Press, 1994).

37. Joseph Wearing, "Can an Old Dog Teach Itself New Tricks? The Liberal Party Attempts Reform," in Gagnon and Tanguay, *Canadian Parties in Transition.*

38. Joseph Wearing, *Strained Relations: Canadian Parties and Voters*, p. 195.

39. Donald Smiley, *Canada in Question: Federalism in the Eighties*, 3rd ed. (Toronto: McGraw-Hill Ryerson, 1980); and Rand Dyck, "Relations between Federal and Provincial Parties," in Gagnon and Tanguay, *Canadian Parties in Transition.*

40. Robert Michels, *Political Parties* (New York: Free Press, 1966).

41. Wearing, "Can an Old Dog Teach Itself New Tricks?"

42. Winn and McMenemy, *Political Parties in Canada*, pp. 4–5.

43. Dawson, *The Government of Canada*, pp. 466–72; and Mallory, *The Structure of Canadian Government* (Toronto: Macmillan, 1971), p. 197.

44. Louis Hartz, *The Founding of New Societies* (New York: Harcourt, Brace and World, 1964); Gad Horowitz, "Conservatism, Liberalism and Socialism in Canada: An Interpretation," *Canadian Journal of Economics and Political Science* (May 1966), pp. 143–71; Horowitz, "Notes on 'Conservatism, Liberalism and Socialism in Canada'," *Canadian Journal of Political Science* (June 1978), pp. 383–99; and William Christian and Colin Campbell, *Political Parties and Ideologies in Canada*, 3rd ed. (Toronto: McGraw-Hill Ryerson, 1990).

45. Neil Nevitte, Herman Bakvis, and Roger Gibbins, "The Ideological Contours of 'New Politics' in Canada: Policy, Mobilization and Partisan Support," *Canadian Journal of Political Science* (September 1989), pp. 475–503.

46. Horowitz, "Liberalism, Conservatism and Socialism in Canada."

47. James McAllister, "Do Parties Make a Difference?" in Gagnon and Tanguay, *Canadian Parties in Transition*; Winn and McMenemy, *Political Parties in Canada*. Leonard Pryra makes the case that a greater difference exists between the party in government and the party in opposition, in "Contending Approaches to the Study of Canadian Party Ideologies," Canadian Political Science Association (Kingston, June 1991).

48. Duncan Cameron, "Political Discourse in the Eighties," in Gagnon and Tanguay, *Canadian Parties in Transition.*

49. On this subject, see Anthony Westell, *Reinventing Canada* (Toronto: Dundurn Press, 1994); and Christopher Dunn, *Canadian Political Debates: Opposing Views on Issues That Divide Canadians* (Toronto: McClelland and Stewart, 1995), Part Six.

50. Pierre Lortie, "The Challenge of Electoral Reform: Combining Innovation with Continuity," Royal Commission on Electoral Reform and Party Financing, Winnipeg, 26 November, 1990.

51. W.T. Stanbury, *Business–Government Relations in Canada* (Toronto: Methuen, 1986), ch. 4.

· · · · · · · · · · · · · · · · · ·

FURTHER READING

Brodie, Janine, and Jane Jenson. *Crisis, Challenge and Change: Party and Class in Canada Revisited*. Ottawa: Carleton University Press, 1988.

Carrigan, D.O. *Canadian Party Platforms: 1867–1968*. Toronto: Copp-Clark, 1968.

Christian, William, and Colin Campbell. *Political Parties and Ideologies in Canada*. 3rd ed. Toronto: McGraw-Hill Ryerson, 1990.

Courtney, John. C. *Do Conventions Matter? Choosing National Party Leaders in Canada*. Montreal: McGill–Queen's University Press, 1995.

Forbes, H.D., ed. *Canadian Political Thought*. Toronto: Oxford University Press, 1985.

Horowitz, Gad. "Conservatism, Liberalism and Socialism in Canada: An Interpretation." *Canadian Journal of Political Science* (May 1966), pp. 143–71.

Marchak, Patricia. *Ideological Perspectives on Canada*, 3rd ed. Toronto: McGraw-Hill Ryerson, 1988.

Perlin, George. *Party Democracy in Canada*. Scarborough: Prentice-Hall Canada, 1988.

Simpson, Jeffrey. *Spoils of Power: The Politics of Patronage*. Toronto: Collins, 1988.

Tanguay, A.B., and A.-G. Gagnon, eds. *Canadian Parties in Transition*, 2nd ed. Scarborough: Nelson Canada, 1996.

Thorburn, H.G. *Party Politics in Canada*. Scarborough: Prentice-Hall Canada, 7 editions, incl. 1994.

Wearing, Joseph. *Strained Relations: Canadian Parties and Voters*. Toronto: McClelland and Stewart, 1988.

Winn, Conrad, and John McMenemy. *Political Parties in Canada*. Toronto: McGraw-Hill Ryerson, 1976.

Liberal Party

Goldfarb, Martin, and Thomas Axworthy. *Marching to a Different Drummer*. Toronto: Stoddart, 1988.

McCall-Newman, Christina. *Grits: An Intimate Portrait of the Liberal Party*. Toronto: Macmillan, 1982.

Wearing, Joseph. *The L-Shaped Party: The Liberal Party of Canada 1958–1980*. Toronto: McGraw-Hill Ryerson, 1981.

Whitaker, Reginald. *The Government Party: Organizing and Financing the Liberal Party of Canada 1930–58*. Toronto: University of Toronto Press, 1977.

Conservative Party

English, John. *The Decline of Politics: The Conservatives and the Party System 1901–20*. Toronto: University of Toronto Press, 1977.

Granatstein, J.L. *The Politics of Survival: The Conservative Party of Canada, 1939–1945*. Toronto: University of Toronto Press, 1967.

Martin, Patrick, Allan Gregg, and George Perlin. *Contenders: The Tory Quest for Power*. Scarborough: Prentice-Hall Canada, 1983.

McLaughlin, David. *Poisoned Chalice: The Last Campaign of the Progressive Conservative Party?* Toronto: Dundurn Press, 1994.

Perlin, George. *The Tory Syndrome: Leadership Politics in the Progressive Conservative Party*. Montreal: McGill–Queen's University Press, 1980.

Simpson, Jeffrey. *Discipline of Power: The Conservative Interlude and the Liberal Restoration*. Toronto: Personal Library, 1980.

Taylor, Charles. *Radical Tories*. Toronto: House of Anansi, 1982.

CCF/NDP

Avakumovic, Ivan. *Socialism in Canada*. Toronto: McClelland and Stewart, 1978.

Lipset, S.M. *Agrarian Socialism: The Cooperative Commonwealth Federation in Saskatchewan*. Los Angeles: University of California Press, 1950.

McDonald, Lynn. *The Party That Changed Canada: The New Democratic Party, Then and Now*. Toronto: McClelland and Stewart, 1987.

McLeod, Ian. *Under Siege: The Federal NDP in the Nineties*. Toronto: Lorimer, 1994.

Morton, Desmond. *The New Democrats 1961–1986: The Politics of Change*. Toronto: Copp Clark Pitman, 1986.

Whitehorn, Alan. *Canadian Socialism: Essays on the CCF and the NDP*. Toronto: Oxford University Press, 1992.

Young, Walter. *Anatomy of a Party: The National CCF 1932–1961*. Toronto: University of Toronto Press, 1969.

Social Credit
Finkel, Alvin. *The Social Credit Phenomenon in Alberta*. Toronto: University of Toronto Press, 1989.

Irving, J.A. *The Social Credit Movement in Alberta*. Toronto: University of Toronto Press, 1959.

Macpherson, C.B. *Democracy in Alberta: Social Credit and the Party System*. Toronto: University of Toronto Press, 1953.

Pinard, Maurice. *The Rise of a Third Party: A Study in Crisis Politics*. Scarborough: Prentice-Hall Canada, 1971.

Stein, Michael. *The Dynamics of Right-Wing Protest: A Political Analysis of Social Credit in Quebec*. Toronto: University of Toronto Press, 1973.

Reform Party
Dobbin, Murray. *Preston Manning and the Reform Party*. Toronto: Lorimer, 1991.

Flanagan, Tom. *Waiting for the Wave*. Toronto: Stoddart, 1995.

Harrison, Trevor. *Of Passionate Intensity: Right-Wing Populism and the Reform Party of Canada*. Toronto: University of Toronto Press, 1995.

Manning, Preston. *The New Canada*. Toronto: Macmillan, 1992.

Sharpe, Sydney, and Donald Braid. *Storming Babylon: Preston Manning and the Rise of the Reform Party*. Toronto: Key Porter Books, 1992).

Chapter 17

parties
AND THE ELECTION
campaign

Why did Jean Chrétien's Liberals defeat Kim Campbell's Conservatives in 1993? Were the local campaigns of Conservative and NDP incumbents of any significance? What did sections of the country find attractive about the Reform and Bloc Québécois parties? How seriously should we take the Liberals' famous election manifesto, the "Red Book"? How much do party standings in the public opinion polls change during the course of the campaign? To what extent does media coverage of the campaign influence the results?

Elections are not only the most colourful and exciting element in the Canadian political system; they are also in many ways the most important. Certain elections are great landmarks in a country's history and often change its course. Almost all the daily efforts of parties and politicians are ultimately geared toward maximizing their support in the next electoral contest. The election campaign constitutes the area in which political parties, the mass media, public opinion polls, and political participation all come together to play their most extensive role.

The primary function of elections is to allow the mass of citizens to choose their parliamentary representatives and, indirectly, their governmental leaders. In structural-functional terms, elections serve to recruit many of those who subsequently perform the rule-making function. Besides recruiting political leaders, elections serve to inform the public, which is part of the political socialization function. Moreover, both political parties and pressure groups take advantage of elections to articulate certain interests, and parties aggregate interests in trying to put forward a comprehensive, attractive election platform. Elections also serve the political communication function of transmitting information among the various participants within the system and between the system and its environment.

Beyond the functions as outlined by Almond in Chapter 1, elections serve a legitimation function. That is, by exercising their franchise, voters legitimize the power of those elected by agreeing to be bound by their decisions. This activity presumably also generates popular support for the political system as a whole. Elections similarly help to integrate the system by putting everyone in it through a common national experience. To the extent that policy concerns are central to the campaign, elections may also provide policy guidelines for the authorities and a feeling of political efficacy for the voters.

The official side of the electoral system having been examined in Chapter 15, this chapter explores the more colourful side of the campaign—that dominated by political parties, candidates, the media, and public opinion polls. The chapter has three main parts: the national party campaign; the local candidate campaign; and electoral behaviour and party support.

THE NATIONAL PARTY CAMPAIGN
Pre-Writ Preparations

At the national level, political parties usually begin to prepare for the next election about two years before they expect it to be called. This entails setting up a national campaign committee, which starts to think about such strategic matters as policy, image, and budget. Party headquarters conducts public opinion polls throughout the inter-election period in order to see how the voters perceive the various leaders, parties, and issues.[1] For the party in power such polls are central to deciding when to call the election in the first place, and for all major parties, polls serve to guide general strategy, media advertising, and the selection of priority ridings once the campaign begins. The Conservatives were able to afford daily tracking of public opinion in rolling polls during the 1984 and 1988 campaigns and changed strategy as required.[2]

Prime Minister Brian Mulroney named the co-managers of the next PC campaign in 1991, and a year later, a national platform planning committee began work on the party's election platform. Unfortunately for his successor, Kim Campbell, these committees were put on hold after the announcement of Mulroney's retirement, and the party went into the 1993 campaign without the usual preparedness.[3] Party headquarters organizes training sessions for campaign managers and candidates (right down to personal deportment), something the PCs were particularly good at in 1984 and 1988, and the headquarters of all parties produce mounds of election material for local candidates. In this respect, it was a sign of the PC disarray in 1993 that, having decided to rely completely on the appeal of the new leader, Kim Campbell, it lacked leader-oriented literature for the first month of the campaign.[4]

Election Strategy

To the extent that the PCs had a strategy in 1993, then, it was to emphasize the new leader (rather than the PC party), to distance itself from former leader Brian Mulroney, and to talk hopefully about the future rather than run on the Mulroney record. The party sent Campbell on a cross-country summertime tour in which people generally found her personality attractive, and were receptive to her call of "doing politics differently." Unfortunately, her early actions as prime minister did not establish the intended image of an agent of change. Although the media and opposition parties distorted some of her remarks about when the unemployment situation was likely to improve and how much analysis of social programs was possible during the heat of the election, Campbell's performance during the campaign left much to be desired, and it ended with an impression of "uncertainty, indecisiveness, and weakness."[5]

As for the Liberal strategy, Jean Chrétien often reminded voters that "I have the team, we have the plan, and we can make the difference." Chrétien's image at the start of the campaign was not one of the party's greatest assets, but as time went on he began to look better in comparison with his rivals. He was particularly adroit at exploiting Campbell's reported gaffes.

The NDP had been critical of Ed Broadbent's performance in 1988, especially the avoidance of free trade and other economic issues, and sought a campaign in which decision-making was more inclusive, more flexible, and in which it could take pride.[6] But the party suffered from an exodus of senior advisers in the period leading up to the campaign, especially as it dropped in the polls. It began by putting its main effort into 75 constituencies, but this number dwindled as time went on. When support completely collapsed, Audrey McLaughlin took a chance and publicly admitted that the Liberals would form a majority government. The party hoped that this would bring back NDP supporters who were planning to vote Liberal just to ensure the defeat of the PCs.

Being almost new on the scene, the Reform Party had used the referendum on the Charlottetown Accord as a test of its capacity to run a national campaign as well as of its grass-roots campaign organization. At the national level it was headed by a six-member Campaign Management Committee, which was centred in party headquarters in Calgary. As a reflection of its populist approach, during the first week of the campaign it claimed to be listening to the people rather than issuing a platform. Later it unveiled its economic strategy and became more emotional in its appeal toward the end. It did not run candidates in Quebec, even in largely anglophone ridings.[7]

In contrast, the Bloc Québécois nominated candidates only in Quebec constituencies and had the full support of its provincial counterpart, the Parti Québécois, whatever the differences in their respective versions of Quebec sovereignty.

Election Platform

One of the Liberals' great assets in the 1993 campaign was their "Red Book," *Creating Opportunity: The Liberal Plan for Canada*. This was basically the work of Chaviva Hosek, whom Chrétien brought in as director of party policy research, and his defeated rival Paul Martin; both functioned as co-chairs of the platform committee. To some extent the Red Book was based on a thinkers' conference in 1991 and policy debates at a party convention in 1992. It had something for almost everyone, including a $6 billion infrastructure program to address unemployment and a promise to reduce the deficit over three years to three percent of GNP. Chrétien claimed that, if elected, he would adhere to every word, and it provided a tremendous prop for a leader who was otherwise not policy-oriented in his public appearances.[8]

The other parties were not so comprehensive in their 1993 platforms. When the Conservatives found themselves without a response to the highly popular Red Book, they quickly put together "A Taxpayer's Agenda," but their campaign never had a policy focus. To the extent that the party had a platform, it consisted of promising jobs and economic development, improved quality of life, and deficit reduction. The NDP election platform committee combed through party convention resolutions to develop a coherent and appealing platform, which eventually emphasized their Jobs Plan. The party was determined to have an economic emphasis after much internal criticism of its lack thereof in 1988. The Reform Party had passed a variety of planks at its assemblies before the election, and these formed the basis for its election platform. They included economic reform through deficit reduction (to eliminate the deficit within three years), law and order, criminal justice, and parliamentary reform.

Candidate Search

Another national activity that begins before the calling of the election is the search for good candidates. The leader, regional lieutenants, and party organizers are always on the lookout for new blood, and while headquarters rarely imposes a candidate on an unwilling constituency association, it may try to parachute a few "star" candidates into safe seats. The Liberals, Conservatives, and NDP all ran a full slate of candidates up to and including 1993, so where local organizations were weak, the national level of the party sometimes had to take the initiative to find a candidate for them.[9] Because Liberal nominations were coveted by anti-abortionists and myriad ethnic groups, and to ensure a minimum number of candidates of cabinet calibre, Chrétien had the party give him, as leader, the power to appoint candidates in certain cases. These included seven women as well as Arthur Eggleton, Douglas Peters, Marcel Massé, and Michel Dupuy.

The NDP hoped to achieve gender parity in its 1993 candidates, but later was content with having nearly 50 percent women or visible minorities. This entailed considerable and sometimes difficult negotiation between headquarters and riding associations.

Because of its tendency to attract a certain number of racists and other extremists, the Reform Party constitution allows for the expulsion of members and elite approval of local nominations. Prospective candidates must complete a form detailing their background, and in cases when an "undesirable" person still manages to get nominated, the leadership may have to expel a candidate, as it did in one case in 1993.

Fund-Raising

National fund-raising is another activity that begins between elections, although it intensifies in the election period. Until 1993, the Conservatives possessed an impressive direct mail appeal to serve both financial and advertising purposes. With support so low in that election, however, both the PCs and NDP had to reduce their election budgets significantly during the course of the campaign. In contrast, contributions to the Reform Party increased during the campaign, and it ended with a surplus. Total amounts collected were revealed in Chapter 15.

The Leader's Tour

In addition to these activities, party headquarters organizes the leader's tour and national media campaign and gears up for the televised leaders' debate. The leader's tour consists of each party leader criss-crossing the country many times over the 50-day campaign period in an effort not only to attract attention in the areas visited, but also to generate one story every day for the national media. Such "free" coverage is eagerly sought, and parties spare no trouble or expense to obtain it.[10] Frizzell and Westell write that an effective media strategy has three main parts:

> Arrange events every day so that the TV crews, pressed by deadlines and demands from home stations for footage, will have little option but to picture the leader in a favourable setting ... ensure that in every speech or statement there is a phrase that sums up the message in a couple of seconds ... [and] keep the writing press as far away as possible from the leader.[11]

Almost like a royal tour, party "advance men" go ahead of the leader to make sure that every detail is in place. The leader is then accompanied by a horde of strategists and support staff, as well as by reporters who pay to travel aboard the party-chartered plane or bus. The Conservative tour in 1988 had a daily schedule of three events: a morning event to give the cameras some pictures to illustrate the day's theme; a luncheon speech to give thematic substance to the morning event; and an evening rally to illustrate enthusiasm and support for the leader and local candidate.[12] The NDP tour was designed so that Ed Broadbent would make an appearance in each region once a week in order to maintain local media coverage.[13] In 1993, the leader's tour was particularly important for the Reform Party. That party could not afford a national advertising campaign, and it had no other high-profile candidates. It therefore relied on free media coverage of Preston Manning's speeches, which were also a major source of fund-raising. At first the Reform tour travelled by bus, but, as money flowed in, it later chartered a plane.[14]

In general, national television newscasts contain one item per leader per day, and have provided almost equal time to the three main parties. A trend toward greater coverage of party strategy rather than policy has been detected, as has a greater degree of commentary in such coverage.[15] A content analysis of seven significant daily newspapers in 1993 revealed that less than one-third of the election coverage was of issues.[16] The quantity of newspaper election coverage declined from previous elections, possibly due to a shorter campaign period, the recession, which reduced the amount of news space available, a less newsworthy campaign, and less obsession with poll results.[17]

Although the space given by the media to the various party leaders was virtually equal in 1984 and 1988, the kind of treatment accorded to different leaders was not equitable; in 1984, for example, John Turner was plagued with unfavourable footage and commentary.[18] In 1993, Kim Campbell received more attention in the newspapers than her opponents, but the media distorted some of her spontaneous remarks.[19] In fact, all leaders received more unfavourable than favourable attention.

Reproduced with permission.

National Media Advertising

Each party turns its national paid media advertising over to one or more advertising agencies along with at least some indication of the party's campaign strategy.[20] As noted in Chapter 14, the most important part of the media campaign is television, and most parties spend huge amounts of money on the production of television commercials alone. Before the debates in 1988, for example, the Conservatives ran reassuring advertisements stressing the government's record and the prime minister's competence, but resorted afterwards to U.S.-style negative advertising attacking the personal credibility of John Turner. The Liberals, on the other hand, had a particularly effective television commercial showing a map with the Canada–U.S. border being erased under free trade. One of the most memorable, if short-lived negative commercials was that run by the Tories in 1993, which featured Jean Chrétien's face (the left side slightly paralyzed from a childhood disease) with such voice-over comments as

"I personally would be very embarrassed if he were to become prime minister of Canada" and "Is this a prime minister?" After an instantaneous public uproar, and Chrétien's response that "God gave me a physical defect and I've accepted that since I was a kid," Kim Campbell had it removed. [21]

Just before the 1993 election, the NDP paid for a one-hour television town hall special, which included a five-minute video. The video was soon criticized for having been made in the United States (it was actually only edited there), precipitating the resignation of the party's communications director. The NDP's early campaign commercials featured a cacophony of angry voters complaining about a variety of issues. Many felt the commercials were at best ineffective and may have driven people to vote for the Reform Party.

The purchase of broadcast time is closely regulated by the Elections Act. Representatives of registered parties meet with the broadcasting arbitrator before the election to try to agree on an allocation of broadcasting time. If they cannot agree, the arbitrator makes the allocation within the guidelines of the act. It requires each broadcaster to make available, for purchase by registered political parties, six and one-half hours of prime time during the last 39 days of the campaign. Such an allocation among parties is primarily based on the number of seats each held in the House of Commons and on popular vote received in the previous election, but no party can receive more than one-half of the total time. National parties cannot purchase more than these allotments, but candidates may purchase time for their own use outside these hours. Having been allotted over twice as much time as the Liberals and three times as much as the NDP, the Conservatives were allowed to saturate the airwaves in the last week of the 1988 campaign. In addition to purchasable time, parties are awarded free radio and television time in the same proportions.

Many observers, including supporters of minor parties, consider this distribution of paid and free broadcasting time to be extremely unfair, and the Royal Commission on Electoral Reform recommended a more equitable system. Part of the problem is that it is not known until midway through the campaign whether new parties will be able to nominate 50 candidates and therefore become registered. In 1992, the Reform Party went to court to challenge its original allotment of 11 minutes for the forthcoming election and was generally supported in the judicial decision. Since the broadcast arbitrator himself was dissatisfied with the distribution, he issued a revised allotment in August 1993, as seen in Table 17.1, which omits parties that ultimately failed to qualify.

TABLE 17.1	Allocation of Broadcast Time, August 1993, in Minutes		
Progressive Conservative Party	116	Green Party	15
Liberal Party	78	Commonwealth Party	14
NDP	55	Bloc Québécois	5
Reform Party	17	Marxist–Leninist Party	5
Christian Heritage Party	16	Nationalist Party of Quebec	5
Libertarian Party	16	Natural Law Party	5

Source: Report of the Broadcasting Arbitrator, included in the Report of the Chief Electoral Officer for the 1993 election. Used with permission.

In spite of its protests, the Reform Party could not afford a national advertising campaign in the end and relied instead on certain regional markets in Western Canada. It was also given nine minutes of free time. In total, the CBC and CTV networks were each obligated to provide 214 minutes of free time, and each of the three French-language networks, 62 minutes.

The Leaders' Debate

The other main aspect of the national campaign is the televised leaders' debate.[22] These have been held in 1968, 1979, 1984, 1988, and 1993 and are probably here to stay. Debates tend to benefit the Opposition party leaders because they otherwise have difficulty obtaining coverage, but it would be virtually impossible for the incumbent prime minister to refuse such a debate any more.[23] The debates have become crucial aspects of the campaign because of the combined importance of leaders and television, and because of the influence of American presidential politics.[24]

The debates are not mentioned in either the Canada Elections Act or the television broadcasting regulations, and the consortium of television stations that carry them essentially set the rules. The Royal Commission's recommendation that the debates become obligatory and regulated has not been implemented. The debates have to fit into the television networks' schedules and are held when least advertising revenue would be lost. In 1993, with a large number of parties in the race, the consortium agreed that only five parties would take part: those that were represented in Parliament and that had had a consistent impact in public debates and public opinion. Mel Hurtig, leader of the new National Party of Canada, went to court to try to force his way into the debate but did not succeed, even at the Supreme Court level.

Although the leaders are carefully trained and briefed (speech writers prepare opening and closing statements and one-liners), the leaders are in a much less controlled setting than they are used to. The debates are one of the few opportunities for the public to see them functioning on their own. Besides all the other qualities that they bring to such debates, Canadian leaders must now be fluently bilingual, which was to Mulroney's advantage, especially in 1984, and to Broadbent's detriment in 1988. As noted, each party immediately sends forth its "spin doctors" to persuade reporters that its leader won, but whether the public makes up its own mind on the winner or awaits the verdict of media commentators is not entirely certain.

About two-thirds of the electorate watched at least one debate in both 1984 and 1988, and nearly 60 percent in 1993.[25] Though 45 percent of respondents told a *Maclean's* poll that the 1988 debate, which ended with Turner at an advantage, had helped them decide how to vote,[26] much of this advantage had worn off by election day. The Conservatives had strategically insisted on having the debate early in the campaign in case they needed time to recover from just such an inferior performance.

The 1993 leaders' debates were less dramatic than in the two previous cases, but are interesting for several reasons. First, Kim Campbell's performance was probably hampered by her earlier refusal to engage in practice debates with her own party officials standing in for the other leaders. Second, Audrey McLaughlin was not helped by being seated at the far end of the row for both debates. Third, Preston Manning was not capable of participating in the French debate, but was allowed to read an opening and closing statement in English. In the English debate, his central physical position helped him to function almost as a moderator of the debate. Lucien Bouchard, however, participated in both English and French debates.[27] Finally, the debates may have had something to do with the fact that Campbell and Chrétien subsequently changed rankings in public opinion polls on the question of who would make the best prime minister.[28]

THE LOCAL CANDIDATE CAMPAIGN

Nomination

At the local level, each party's first priority is to nominate its candidate and to provide the returning officer with a list of names of party supporters who wish to be enumerators. In the case of incumbents, ambitious newcomers, and those who anticipate the date of the next election, the nomination meeting is often held before the election is called. This allows many preparations, such as the production of lawn signs, to be made ahead of time so that the campaign can get off to a strong and early start.

Given the explicit recruitment function of elections, it turns out that parties have nominated, and voters supported, a set of candidates unrepresentative of the general population. Nominated candidates overrepresent all the "elite" variables in Canadian society—class (upper-middle), ethnicity (anglophone), religion (prestige Protestant and Roman Catholic), and gender (male). Historically, the largest single category of candidates has been lawyers, although other professionals and businesspeople of the same socioeconomic status are now common as well.[29] Parties usually nominate francophones in French-Canadian constituencies, but not many non-British or non-French candidates appeared until recently. Besides the working class, women have been the most underrepresented of any demographic group, although the number of women candidates has increased significantly in the past few elections.

The Local Campaign

Once the nomination has taken place, a campaign committee headed by the campaign manager is established (see Figure 17.1). In most campaigns the other key official is the canvass organizer, who sets up the door-to-door "foot canvass" to distribute literature and/or a telephone canvass. Whether canvassers contact voters on the doorstep or on the phone, the object is only secondarily to spread the party's message. Canvassers primarily hope to discover which party or candidate prospective voters plan to support and to seek out their own supporters. Armed with a voters' list, they will put a positive, negative, or other distinguishing mark beside the names of all voters contacted. To cover an entire constituency in this fashion, especially if it is done two or three times as is often attempted by the NDP, requires a veritable army of volunteers and an elaborate hierarchical organization.[30] Since the campaign will need volunteers for many other tasks, and since few people relish door-to-door canvassing, the canvass organizer will probably not have enough workers and therefore have to concentrate efforts in priority polls, areas of the constituency where the party usually does well. If money is more plentiful than personnel, the local campaign may rely instead on media advertising. In recent elections, local polling was done in some constituencies, especially by Conservative candidates with the assistance of party headquarters. The Conservatives were also expert at computer-assisted mail and telephone campaigning directed at members of key groups in targeted constituencies. Such techniques gave the selected voters the impression they were being contacted by or on behalf of the prime minister.[31]

Figure 17.1 **Structure of a Typical Local Campaign Committee**

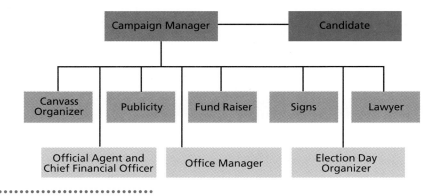

All this activity culminates on election day, when the organization tries to have party scrutineers placed in all the polls. Ideally, an inside scrutineer in each poll keeps track of which people on the list have cast their ballot, while an outside scrutineer periodically collects this information and then heads out to encourage all those previously identified as party supporters to get out to vote. In the past, much of this work was voluntary, but paid staff are increasingly engaged, sometimes consisting of "volunteers" paid by a business or union. The local campaign is thus a complex operation requiring more and more sophistication, staffing, and funding.

ELECTORAL BEHAVIOUR AND PARTY SUPPORT

Research by political scientists into electoral behaviour has shattered many myths. These include the myth of the rational, well-informed voter, the myth of the voter securely attached to a single party, the myth of the voter who weighs party positions on various issues before deciding how to cast his or her ballot, the myth that the voter identifies with the ideological position of a particular party, and the myth that most voters make up their minds long before the election is called.

Given the fact that the Liberals were so regularly victorious in Canadian federal elections between 1935 and 1984 and again in 1993, it is tempting to believe that a large proportion of voters have a strong identification with the Liberal Party and that any result other than a Liberal triumph is unlikely. Research shows, however, that more and more voters have no enduring party identification. Some of these "flexible partisans" possess a superficial party preference but they constitute a large pool of voters ready to be moved by the particular issues, candidates, and leaders in the campaign.[32] The overall aggregate stability, therefore, masked "the potential for significant variation in electoral outcomes,"[33] as became evident in the 1984 Conservative landslide. Other factors that add flexibility to the system are the group that votes in one election but not the next, as well as the newly eligible voters in each election, who generally seem to favour the incumbent government.[34] Table 17.2 summarizes the lack of consistency among the electorate between the 1988 and 1993 elections. Only 30.9 percent of 1993 voters voted the same as they did in 1988, and, counting only those who voted in both elections, the proportion of switchers rose to over 50 percent.

TABLE 17.2   1993 Voter Preference Compared with 1988

Voted same party	30.9%
Switched parties	40.6%
Previous voters not voting	7.6%
Previous non-voters voting	4.4%
Not voting either time	5.1%
New voters	10.7%

Source: Jon H. Pammett, "Tracking the Votes," in Alan Frizzell et al., The Canadian General Election of 1993. *Used with permission.*

In most other Western democracies the degree of voter identification with a specific party is much higher, and the flexibility of the Canadian electorate demands explanation. Jon Pammett accounts for this phenomenon as follows:

> The most basic [factor] is that Canadian political culture is relatively apolitical. While Canadians are moderately interested in politics, this interest does not translate for most into substantial political involvement. The amount of detailed political information possessed by the average Canadian is low. Studies of children's political learning, or socialization, show a relatively weak transference of preference for a political party from parent to child ... because these feelings may not be strongly or persistently held in the adult "socializer."[35]

Another factor is that a large proportion of voters feel negatively about almost everything associated with the political system and switch from party to party for negative rather than positive reasons.

Table 17.3 indicates the extent and direction of vote switching between 1988 and 1993, which is particularly interesting in the case of the Conservatives and the NDP. The Conservatives lost 26 percent of their 1988 vote to the Liberals, 24 percent to Reform, and 14 percent to the Bloc Québécois, while the NDP lost 27 percent to the Liberals, 14 percent to Reform, and 6 percent to the Bloc.

TABLE 17.3 Where the 1988 Vote Went in 1993			
	PC	Liberal	NDP
PC	22	5	8
Liberal	26	70	27
NDP	3	3	26
Reform	24	8	14
Bloc	14	6	6
Other	1	1	5
Did not vote	10	7	14

Source: Pammett, "Tracking the Votes." Used with permission.

The voting decision is an extremely complex and subtle one that is not easily explained. Nevertheless, voters are often asked what factor was most influential in helping them make up their mind—party, leader, issues, or local candidate. For "durable partisans" the party is most important, but for the "flexible partisans," it is usually the leader or issues. The local candidate is not normally a crucial factor.[36] Voters will often say that they were moved by the issues, but many have trouble identifying the issues that supposedly influenced them, or can only identify very general topics.[37] Pammett estimates that about half the flexible partisans have a high degree of political interest, and it is these voters who would be most likely moved by issues. The relative importance of issues and leaders also varies from one election to another. In the leader-dominated elections of 1958 and 1968, for example, the whole country voted positively for John Diefenbaker and Pierre Trudeau respectively, and in 1984, Quebeckers in particular were moved to vote for Brian Mulroney. In 1979 and 1980, on the other hand, voters felt negatively about Joe Clark and Pierre Trudeau, so that issues became more important. In 1988 the free trade question along with the lack of enthusiasm for all three leaders gave the election a much stronger issue orientation than usual. The 1993 campaign did not have a single dominant issue, in which case the importance of the party as a whole was more evident: when given these three options, party was mentioned by 57 percent, leaders by 22 percent, and local candidates by 21 percent.[38] When given an open-ended question in 1993, many respondents mentioned issues, as indicated in Table 17.4 by party preference. When the issues identified are examined in more detail, it appears that the Liberal job creation plan was a major reason for supporting that party, as was deficit reduction for voting Reform. As for BQ voters, 76 percent favoured Quebec independence, while others were more motivated by economic or other issues.

TABLE 17.4	**Reasons for Voting (Open-Ended Question), 1993**				
	Liberals	*PC*	*NDP*	*Reform*	*Bloc*
Issues	27%	20%	24%	26%	51%
Leadership	14%	10%	5%	6%	12%
Local candidate	7%	20%	21%	2%	5%
Party	52%	50%	50%	68%	33%

Source: Pammett, "Tracking the Votes." Used with permission.

In short, as Lawrence Leduc writes, "the Canadian electorate continues to be one with relatively weak long-term attachments to political parties, low ideological commitment, and high responsiveness to short-term forces such as leaders, issues, or political events."[39] Such flexibility means that over half of the electorate makes up its mind during the course of the campaign, that elections remain highly unpredictable, and that there are few **safe seats**. As a result, the turnover rate in the Canadian House of Commons far exceeds that of almost all other countries.

These revelations also cast doubt on the question of whether elections provide a policy mandate for the successful party—hence the concept, **absent mandate**. First, Canadian parties rarely present a comprehensive election platform. Next, government parties do not seem to feel bound by the specific policies they proposed in the campaign, such as the Liberal opposition to wage and price controls in 1974 and the Conservative promises in 1979 on moving the Canadian embassy in Israel and privatizing Petro-Canada. In the third place, the limited extent to which issues play a part in the campaign seriously detracts from the claim of any government that it has a mandate to pursue a particular policy. For example, free trade was never mentioned in the 1984 campaign and the GST was almost totally overlooked in 1988. Fourth, even on the rare occasion that a single issue figures prominently, the winning party almost never obtains a majority of the total votes cast, and certainly not a majority in all regions of the country, "so a *national* mandate is absent."[40] The free trade issue in 1988 provided the closest thing to a policy mandate for any Canadian government in recent times, yet the Conservatives received only 43 percent of the overall popular vote and less than 40 percent in six provinces and territories.[41] The Liberals made much of their Red Book during and immediately after the 1993 campaign, but as time went on strayed further and further from it.

The other aspect of electoral behaviour that has attracted much attention from political scientists is the relationship between voters' regional, cultural, and socioeconomic background and their party preference.[42] This relates to the cleavages discussed in Chapters 6 to 11. At least until the 1984 federal election, certain clear-cut patterns of socioeconomic support for the three main parties could be identified.

First, there were wide variations in regional support. The Liberals dominated Quebec, and the Conservatives excelled in the West, especially Alberta. While these respective patterns were not quite as dramatic in terms of popular vote as in the proportion of seats won, they were still significant. Liberal support in Quebec had been virtually unchanged since 1900, but the Conservative popularity in the West was primarily a legacy of John Diefenbaker in the 1950s and 1960s.[43] Such party strongholds resulted in the situation that election campaigns were most heatedly contested in Ontario, which could swing either way.

A second marked pattern in Canadian voting behaviour was religion. Roman Catholics have been strongly inclined to vote Liberal, whether they were French, English, or of other ethnic background, and regardless of where they lived in the country. This situation is especially striking when one considers that no serious religious issues divided the parties in Canadian federal politics for generations.[44]

Ethnicity was another significant factor in Canadian electoral behaviour. The French-Canadian preference for the Liberal Party is well known and exists outside as well as within Quebec. Among those of non-British and non-French origins, the Liberals also did best, especially among post–Second World War immigrants (largely of Mediterranean and Indian subcontinental origins), who apparently reacted with gratitude to the fact that the Liberal Party was in office when they arrived.

A final demographic factor is social class, the expectation being that upper-class citizens would vote Conservative, the middle class would support the Liberals, and the working and poorer classes would vote NDP. In most Western democracies such a pattern is quite significant, but it is not borne out well in Canada.[45] The Liberal Party has usually attracted nearly the same degree of support from all classes except farmers, who voted distinctively Conservative. As indicated in Chapter 10, only a small proportion of the working class vote for working-class parties. The NDP, for example, normally gets relatively more support from skilled and unskilled labour than from other groups, but it does not get as much from either group as does each of the other parties.

The low level of class-consciousness in Canada is quite striking. When voters were asked in 1979 if they thought of themselves as belonging to a social class, only 42 percent said yes, 25 percent identifying with the middle class and 10 percent with the working class. When forced to choose a class, 54 percent selected the middle class, compared with 33 percent for the working class, but three-fifths of this 33 percent reported themselves to be quite satisfied with their material standard of living. This leaves only about 13 percent who could be called a militant, dissatisfied core of the working class. Table 10.3 in Chapter 10 indicated that about two-thirds of voters actually belong to the working class, but without greater working-class consciousness, class-based voting can hardly be expected. In 1979, the NDP received the support of 11 percent of those not belonging to unions, 21 percent of union members, and 30 percent of those belonging to unions affiliated to the party. It also was supported by 25 percent of class-conscious skilled labourers (compared with 14 percent lacking class-consciousness).[46]

Many explanations have been offered for this low level of class-consciousness and class-based voting.[47] They include the fact that the Liberal and Conservative parties were well entrenched when the franchise was extended to the working class; the success of the Liberals and Conservatives in accommodating social protest, the degree of social mobility within the society, the failure of organized labour to develop a class-consciousness among its members and to persuade its locals to affiliate with the NDP; and the fact that voters feel other characteristics such as region, ethnicity, and religion have greater political salience. Moreover, NDP support actually increases as the level of voters' education rises, complicating its efforts to divide Canadians on class lines.[48]

Gender and age may also affect voting behaviour, and while not crucial factors, in some elections women and first-time voters have tended to prefer the Liberals, and the elderly, the Conservatives.[49]

The 1984 and 1988 elections ran counter to generations of traditional voting patterns, especially with Quebec French-Canadian Roman Catholics preferring the Conservatives over the Liberals. The 1993 election saw the West abandon the Conservatives for Reform, and Quebec switch to the Bloc Québécois. Thus, such socioeconomic patterns of party support as were once evident seem to have vanished.

CONCLUSION

While public opinion polls are increasingly common, elections remain the definitive measure of the public will. As such, elections leave much to be desired, because they do not often produce a victorious party with a specific policy mandate. Parties may offer only vague slogans like "national unity"; elections frequently turn on leader images; successful parties often renege on their policy promises once in office; and a large proportion of voters pay little attention to the campaign. As defective as elections are, however, caution should be exercised before jumping on populist bandwagons like referenda. In many cases, the electorate—having less incentive to be accommodating—takes policy positions that are more extreme and emotional and less well informed than those of political parties. Referenda are at odds with the virtues of representative democracy and may endanger the rights of certain ethnic, linguistic, religious, or ideological minorities.

PC Of the approaches outlined in Chapter 1, the public choice model is, at least at first sight, the one most relevant to elections. Extensive public opinion polling by political parties confirms the claims of this approach that parties make calculated promises in order to get elected, concentrating on strategically located groups. Parties tend to ignore their committed supporters as well as those who are hostile, and then, within a certain ideological range, promise whatever their polls tell them will maximize their electoral success. Nevertheless, the preceding account of voting behaviour puts into question some of the other claims of the public choice approach, at least with respect to its assumption of rational and well-informed voters. The average person spends more time researching the purchase of a television set or perusing the weekly supermarket fliers than in comparing party platforms. The successful party also emerges with a less specific policy mandate than the public choice model suggests.

© Class analysts add that the bargains struck between parties and voters during the campaign may not be honoured afterwards. Promises made to middle-income voters and the working class—for example, that social programs are a "sacred trust" or that wage controls will not be adopted—are often broken by the victorious party in record time. To a large extent, as discussed in Chapter 15, class analysts attribute this to the issue of party finance. That is, once in office, parties do what their financial supporters want them to do, which is often at odds with their promises. Non-Marxist elitist theorists argue that elections are held to produce a small group of authorities with a disproportionate amount of power. In this process, they add, parties nominate and voters support a set of candidates who bear little resemblance to the general population, overrepresenting all the "elite" variables in Canadian society.

P Pluralists emphasize the necessity of designing a party's election platform so that it appeals to many groups in society—all major ethnic categories, industries, regions, genders, and classes. Such platforms are usually classic brokerage documents. Election manifestos are increasingly based on what public opinion polls indicate the public wants or is willing to accept. Pluralists also point to the socioeconomic group preferences that have been evident in elections and the extent to which each party appeals to a coalition of certain groups. In addition, they note the increasing involvement of pressure groups in the election campaign.

SC Even this most "popular" aspect of the political system reveals the extent to which the state is relatively autonomous from the rest of society, as state-centred theorists contend. This is primarily because the focus of election campaigns is not usually on policy. If voters are uninformed about issues, if they make their decision on the basis of leader images, inexplicable party loyalty, or local candidate preferences, and if parties present only vague policy directions that few politicians or voters take seriously in any case, post-election policy innovation will stall or be dominated by the cabinet and bureaucracy. If the authorities decide to adopt policies that were not mentioned in the campaign or to leave unfulfilled promises that were made, they merely resort to publicly paid advertising campaigns to demonstrate the necessity of the statist decision.

DISCUSSION QUESTIONS

1. Is it fair to allow the prime minister to choose the date of the election? Why or why not?

2. What can be done to give more emphasis to the substance of each party's campaign (platform) and less to its presentation (personality, image, and advertising)?

3. Is the distribution of media time during election campaigns fair? If not, how could it be improved?

4. Should a televised leaders' debate be made mandatory? Is it fair to exclude minor party leaders?

5. How much difference does a well-organized local campaign make? What are the ingredients of such a local campaign?

6. To what extent do Canadians identify with a particular political party?

7. What are the main bases for such identification, and why does party identification seem to be declining?

8. How rational and well informed is the average voter?

9. If you voted recently, explain how you came to your decision.

10. How do the approaches outlined in Chapter 1 apply to the material in this chapter?

....

NOTES

1. Alan Frizzell, Jon Pammett, and Anthony Westell, *The Canadian General Election of 1988* (Ottawa: Carleton University Press, 1989), pp. 16–17, 45–46.
2. George Perlin, "Opportunity Regained: The Tory Victory in 1984," in Howard R. Penniman, ed., *Canada at the Polls, 1984* (Durham, NC: Duke University Press, 1988), p. 85.
3. Peter Woolstencroft, "'Doing Politics Differently': The Conservative Party and the Campaign of 1993," in Alan Frizzell et al., *The Canadian General Election of 1993* (Ottawa: Carleton University Press, 1994), pp. 12–13.
4. Ibid., p. 17.
5. Ibid., p. 23.
6. Alan Whitehorn, "The NDP's Quest for Survival," in Frizzell et al., *1993*, p. 44.
7. Faron Ellis and Keith Archer, "Reform: Electoral Breakthrough," in Frizzell et al., *1993*, ch. 5.
8. Stephen Clarkson, "Yesterday's Man and His Blue Grits: Backward into the Future," in Frizzell et al., *1993*, p. 33.
9. Perlin, "Opportunity Regained," p. 89.
10. John Meisel called the 1984 election "The Boob-Tube Election," in John Courtney, ed., *The Canadian House of Commons* (Calgary: University of Calgary, 1985).
11. Frizzell et al., *1988*, p. 75; David Taras, *The Newsmakers* (Scarborough: Nelson Canada, 1990), pp. 154–67.
12. Frizzell et al., *1988*, pp. 19–20.
13. Ibid., p. 49.
14. Ellis and Archer, "Reform," in Frizzell et al., *1993*, ch. 5.
15. Taras, *The Newsmakers*, ch. 8.
16. Alan Frizzell and Anthony Westell, "The Press and the Prime Minister," in Frizzell et al., *1993*, pp. 93–94.
17. Ibid., p. 91.
18. R.H. Wagenberg et al., "Campaigns, Images and Polls: Mass Media Coverage of the 1984 Canadian Election," *Canadian Journal of Political Science* (March 1988), pp. 117–29; Walter C. Soderlund et al., *Media and Elections in Canada* (Toronto: Holt, Rinehart and Winston, 1984); Taras, *The Newsmakers*, ch. 5.
19. Frederick Fletcher, "The Media and the 1984 Landslide," in Penniman, *Canada at the Polls*, pp. 168–70.
20. Lawrence LeDuc and Richard Price, "Great Debates: The Televised Leadership Debates of 1979," *Canadian Journal of Political Science* (March 1985), pp. 135–53; Barry Kay et al., "The Character of Electoral Change: A Preliminary Report from the 1984 National Election Study," in Joseph Wearing, ed., *The Ballot and Its Message* (Toronto: Copp Clark Pitman, 1991); David Lanoue, "Debates That Mattered: Voters' Reaction to the 1984 Canadian Leadership Debates," *Canadian Journal of Political Science* (March 1991), pp. 51–65; Lawrence LeDuc and Richard Price, "Campaign Debates and Party Leader Images: The "Encounter '88' Case," Canadian Political Science Association (Victoria, 1990); and Taras, *The Newsmakers*, pp. 167–75.
21. Woolstencroft, "Doing Politics Differently," p. 20; Lionel Lumb, "The Television of Inclusion," in Frizzell et al., *1993*, p. 122.

22. LeDuc and Price, "Campaign Debates."

23. Pierre Trudeau refused debates when he was ahead and sought them when he was behind. Lawrence LeDuc, "The Leaders' Debates: Critical Event or Non-Event?" in Frizzell et al., *1993*, p. 128.

24. Ibid., p. 127.

25. LeDuc and Price, "Campaign Debates."

26. Ibid.; Fletcher, "The Media and the 1984 Landslide," p. 181; and *Maclean's*, December 5, 1988.

27. LeDuc, "The Leaders' Debates," in Frizzell et al., *1993*.

28. Ibid., p. 137.

29. John Courtney, "Reinventing the Brokerage Wheel: The Tory Success in 1984," in Penniman, *Canada at the Polls, 1984*, p. 204.

30. Jerome H. Black, "Revisiting the Effects of Canvassing on Voting Behaviour," *Canadian Journal of Political Science* (June 1984), pp. 351–74; Tom Brook, *Getting Elected in Canada* (Stratford: Mercury Press, 1991); and Lynda Erickson and R.K. Carty, "Parties and Candidate Selection in the 1988 Canadian General Election," *Canadian Journal of Political Science* (June 1991), pp. 331–49.

31. Perlin, "Opportunity Regained," p. 85; Taras, *The Newsmakers*, pp. 186–87.

32. Lawrence LeDuc, "The Flexible Canadian Electorate," in Penniman, *Canada at the Polls, 1984*, p. 40.

33. Clarke, *Political Choice in Canada*, p. 204; Frizzell et al., *1988*, p. 109.

34. Pammett, "Elections," p. 277.

35. Jon H. Pammett, "Elections," in M. Whittington and G. Williams, eds., *Canadian Politics in the 1990s*, 4th ed. (Scarborough: Nelson Canada, 1995), p. 242.

36. William Irvine, "Does the Canadidate Make a Difference? The Macro-Politics and Micro-Politics of Getting Elected," *Canadian Journal of Political Science* (December 1982), pp. 755–82; Michael Krashinsky and William Milne, "Additional Evidence on the Effect of Incumbency in Canadian Elections," *CJPS* (March 1985), pp. 155–65; Krashinsky and Milne, "The Effect of Incumbency in the 1984 Federal and 1985 Ontario Elections," *CJPS* (June 1986), pp. 337–43; and Lynda Erickson and Ken Carty, "Parties and Canadian Selection in the 1988 Canadian General Election," *CJPS* (June 1991), pp. 331–50.

37. Typically, about 30 percent cannot name a single issue. Pammett explains that to affect an election outcome, an issue must meet three conditions: it must be salient, skewed, and linked to one party. These conditions further reduce the possibility that issues will affect the outcome. "The Liberal Party, however, has managed in this century to meet the three conditions on a set of Confederation issues, which include national unity, bilingualism, constitutional questions, and issues involving Quebec." "Elections," Whittington and Williams, 1991, p. 279.

38. Pammett, "Tracking the Votes," p. 148. I am personally unenthusiastic about how Pammett and company decide the importance of issues, which is why I prefer the open-ended responses in Table 17.4.

39. Leduc, "The Flexible Canadian Electorate," p. 51; LeDuc, "The Changeable Canadian Voter," in Frizzell et al., *1988*; Harold D. Clarke et al., *Absent Mandate* and Harold D. Clarke et al., *Political Choice in Canada*; and Leduc et al., "Partisan Instability in Canada: Evidence from a New Panel Study," in Wearing, *The Ballot and Its Message*.

40. Clarke, *Absent Mandate*, p. 182.

41. Surveys indicated that only about one-half claimed to make up their mind primarily on that basis, some on each side. Frizzell et al., *1993*, p. 125; and Richard Johnston et al., "Free Trade and the Dynamics of the 1988 Canadian Election," in Wearing, *The Ballot and Its Message*.

42. Elisabeth Gidengil, "Canada Votes: A Quarter Century of Canadian Election Studies," *Canadian Journal of Political Science* (June 1992).

43. Roger Gibbins, *Regionalism: Territorial Politics in Canada and the United States* (Toronto: Butterworths, 1982).

44. Richard Johnston, "The Reproduction of the Religious Cleavage in Canadian Elections," *Canadian Journal of Political Science* (March 1985), pp. 99–117; William Irvine, "Explaining the Religious Basis of the Canadian Partisan Identity: Success on the Third Try," *Canadian Journal of Political Science* (September 1974), pp. 560–63; and other articles in Wearing, *The Ballot and Its Message*.

45. Jon Pammett, "Class Voting and Class Consciousness in Canada," *Canadian Review of Sociology and Anthropology* 24-2 (1987), pp. 269–90; Keith Archer, "The Failure of the New Democratic Party:

Unions, Unionists, and Politics in Canada," *Canadian Journal of Political Science* (June 1985), pp. 353–66; other articles in Wearing, *The Ballot and Its Message;* Michael Ornstein et al., "Region, Class and Political Culture in Canada," *Canadian Journal of Political Science* (June 1980), pp. 227–71; Elisabeth Gidengil, "Class and Region in Canadian Voting: A Dependency Interpretation," *CJPS* (September 1989), pp. 563–87; Ronald D. Lambert et al., "Social Class and Voting," in James Curtis et al., eds., *Social Inequality in Canada* (Scarborough: Prentice-Hall Canada, 1988); and Keith Archer, *Political Choice and Electoral Consequences* (Montreal: McGill–Queen's University Press, 1990).

46. Pammett, "Class Voting," and Archer, "The Failure of the NDP."
47. Janine Brodie and Jane Jenson, *Crisis, Challenge and Change: Party and Class in Canada Revisited* (Ottawa: Carleton University Press, 1988); Dennis Forcese, *The Canadian Class Structure,* 3rd ed. (Toronto: McGraw-Hill Ryerson, 1986); Pammett, "Class Voting"; and Archer, "Failure of the NDP."
48. Joseph Fletcher and H.D. Forbes, "Class, Education and Vote in Canada, 1965–1984," Canadian Political Science Association (Quebec 1989).
49. Peter Wearing and Joseph Wearing, "Does Gender Make a Difference in Voting Behaviour?" in Wearing, *The Ballot and Its Message.*

FURTHER READING

Archer, Keith. "The Failure of the New Democratic Party: Unions, Unionists, and Politics in Canada." *Canadian Journal of Political Science* (June 1985), pp. 353–66.

————. *Political Choices and Electoral Consequences.* Montreal: McGill–Queen's University Press, 1990.

Bashevkin, Sylvia, ed. *Canadian Political Behaviour.* Toronto: Methuen, 1985.

Beck, J. Murray. *Pendulum of Power.* Scarborough: Prentice-Hall Canada, 1968.

Brodie, Janine, and Jane Jenson. *Crisis, Challenge and Change: Party and Class in Canada Revisited.* Ottawa: Carleton University Press, 1988.

Caplan, Gerald, Michael Kirby, and Hugh Segal. *Election: The Issues, the Strategies, the Aftermath.* Scarborough: Prentice-Hall Canada, 1989.

Clarke, Harold D., et al. *Political Choice in Canada.* Toronto: McGraw-Hill Ryerson, 1980.

————. *Absent Mandate.* Toronto: Gage, 1984.

————. *Absent Mandate: Interpreting Change in Canadian Elections.* 2nd ed. Toronto: Gage, 1991.

————. *Absent Mandate: Canadian Electoral Politics in an Era of Restructuring,* 3rd ed. Toronto: Gage, 1996.

Fraser, Graham. *Playing for Keeps: The Making of the Prime Minister, 1988.* Toronto: McClelland and Stewart, 1989.

Frizzell, Alan, and Anthony Westell. *The Canadian General Election of 1984.* Ottawa: Carleton University Press, 1985.

Frizzell, Alan, Jon H. Pammett, and Anthony Westell. *The Canadian General Election of 1988.* Ottawa: Carleton University Press, 1989.

————. *The Canadian General Election of 1993.* Ottawa: Carleton University Press, 1994.

Gidengil, Elisabeth. "Canada Votes: A Quarter Century of Canadian Election Studies." *Canadian Journal of Political Science* (June 1992).

Johnston, Richard, et al. *Letting the People Decide: Dynamics of a Canadian Election.* Montreal: McGill–Queen's University Press, 1992.

McLaughlin, David. *Poisoned Chalice: The Last Campaign of the Progressive Conservative Party?* Toronto: Dundurn Press, 1994.

Pammett, Jon. "Class Voting and Class Consciousness in Canada." *Canadian Review of Sociology and Anthropology* 24-2 (1987), pp. 269–90.

———. "Elections." In Michael Whittington and Glen Williams, eds. *Canadian Politics in the 1990s*, 4th ed. Scarborough: Nelson Canada, 1995.

Penniman, Howard R., ed. *Canada at the Polls*, 1984. Durham, NC: Duke University Press, 1988.

Tanguay, A.G., and A.-G. Gagnon, eds. *Canadian Parties in Transition*, 2nd ed. Scarborough: Nelson Canada, 1996.

Taras, David. *The Newsmakers.* Scarborough: Nelson Canada, 1990.

Wearing, Joseph, ed. *The Ballot and Its Message.* Toronto: Copp Clark Pitman, 1991.

Chapter 18

pressure GROUPS AND *lobbying*

The Pharmaceutical Manufacturers Association of Canada seeks legislative protection for the patents of its member companies against generic drug companies represented by the Canadian Drug Manufacturers' Association. The Brewers' Association of Canada puts pressure on the government to preserve the Canadian market for domestic beer. The Canadian Labour Congress protests against free trade, cutbacks to unemployment insurance, and back-to-work legislation. The Canadian Federation of Students and the Canadian Association of University Teachers demand that Ottawa continue to finance its share of postsecondary education. The Assembly of First Nations insists that the inherent right to aboriginal self-government be enshrined in the Constitution.

Pressure groups or interest groups such as these develop in almost every political system when individuals with common concerns band together in order to strengthen their cause. A **pressure group** or **interest group** (terms used interchangeably here) can therefore be defined as any group that seeks to influence government policy without contesting elections, that is, without putting forward its own candidates. Alternatively, they have been defined as "organizations whose members act together to influence public policy in order to promote their common interest."[1] Most such groups originally form for nonpolitical purposes and retain nonpolitical functions, but almost inevitably get drawn into political activity from time to time because of the pervasiveness of government.

The term **lobbying** is generally used to refer to any organized attempt to influence the authorities, an activity that is most commonly undertaken by pressure groups but could of course be done by individuals, companies, or other political actors. Increasingly, however, pressure groups have been joined by professional lobbying firms in this activity.

In the traditional discussion of functions performed in the political system, pressure groups are assigned the primary task of interest articulation. They normally have a narrow focus and are organized around a single, central interest that they try to impress upon those in authority. National pressure groups often experience internal regional, provincial, ethnic, and/or class tensions that must be bridged in constructing the message that they wish to articulate, so that such groups also play a limited part in the aggregation of interests. Because it is sometimes difficult to distinguish between interest articulation and interest aggregation, Paul Pross speaks of the "interest promotion" function of such groups.[2]

The party and electoral systems were originally assumed to be the principal means of accommodating various interests within the Canadian political system. Individuals would take their concerns to parties; parties would respond to any interest that appeared to be important; and regional, ethnic, religious, economic, professional, and other interests could be encompassed within the territorial representation provided by the electoral system. As society became more complex, however, Canadians increasingly demonstrated a preference to form or join more specialized, functional groups, rather than rely exclusively on the territorial representation of parties and elections. Thus, in the promotion of interests, pressure groups provide a supplementary kind of functional representation, especially between elections.[3]

Besides interest articulation and aggregation, pressure groups engage in political communication. They transmit demands from the people to the authorities as well as disseminate information in the other direction. In addition, groups may assist in the communication between different parts of government or between federal and provincial levels of government. They frequently communicate among themselves and build temporary alliances on common problems.

Pressure groups are also involved in the rule-making function. The enhanced complexity of society has meant that public issues now require information that is so technical and voluminous that politicians and parties, lacking both time and expertise, cannot handle it well. Consequently, pressure groups regularly interact with the bureaucracy to work out technical arrangements to their mutual satisfaction, and present these proposals to the politicians and parties as a fait accompli. Pressure groups are also increasingly involved in the rule-application function, that is, in the administration of government programs and even in regulation.

Pross goes beyond the functions listed in Chapter 1 by adding that of legitimation. When groups participate peacefully and cooperatively, they demonstrate support for the political system and confer legitimacy upon both it and those with whom they are interacting. Governments encourage groups to lend them such legitimacy and support by welcoming their advances, by "drawing them into a privileged advisory position," and sometimes by helping to create them. By keeping the authorities abreast of current demands and societal changes, pressure groups promote "general political stability."[4] If they can successfully achieve accommodations across regional and ethnic cleavages, they also become important unifying agents in Canadian society.

Having established their functions, this chapter proceeds to identify some of the leading Canadian pressure groups, to outline their targets and methods, to assess their resources, and to reveal the activity of professional lobbying firms.

THE ARRAY OF CANADIAN INTEREST GROUPS

The number of interest groups operating in Canada is in the thousands, so not all can be identified here. Instead, only some of the largest and most influential will be mentioned. Such a very selective list can be seen in Table 18.1.

TABLE 18.1	**Leading National Canadian Pressure Groups**[5]
Business	Canadian Manufacturers' Association
	Canadian Chamber of Commerce
	Business Council on National Issues
	Canadian Federation of Independent Business
	Retail Council of Canada
	Canadian Bankers' Association
	Air Transport Association of Canada
	Automotive Industries Association of Canada
	Brewers' Association of Canada
	Association of Canadian Distillers
	Canadian Association of Broadcasters
	Canadian Construction Association
	Canadian Forestry Association
	Canadian Life & Health Insurance Association Inc.
	Canadian Trucking Association
	Mining Association of Canada
	Pharmaceutical Manufacturers Association of Canada
	Canadian Pulp and Paper Association
	Canadian Petroleum Association
	Independent Petroleum Association of Canada
Agriculture	Canadian Federation of Agriculture
	National Farmers Union
Labour	Canadian Labour Congress
	Canadian Federation of Labour
Professions	Canadian Bar Association
	Canadian Medical Association
	Canadian Dental Association
	Canadian Nurses' Association
	Canadian Association of University Teachers
	Canadian Association of Chiefs of Police
	Canadian Teachers' Federation
	Canadian Council of Professional Engineers
	Canadian Federation of Students

Ethnic	Fédération des Francophones hors Québec
	Assembly of First Nations
	Canadian Ethnocultural Council
	National Congress of Italian Canadians
	German Canadian Congress
	National Association of Japanese Canadians
Religious	Canadian Council of Churches
	Canadian Conference of Catholic Bishops
	Catholic Women's League
	United Church of Canada
	Anglican Church of Canada
	Canadian Jewish Congress
Causes	John Howard Society
	Canadian Civil Liberties Association
	National Action Committee on the Status of Women
	Canadian Council on Social Development
	National Council of Welfare
	Pollution Probe
	Energy Probe
	Greenpeace
	Amnesty International
	Mothers Against Drunk Driving
	Non-Smokers' Rights Association
	National Anti-Poverty Organization
Other	Royal Canadian Legion
	Consumers' Association of Canada
	Federation of Canadian Municipalities

Business Groups[6]

In the case of business, nothing prevents individual companies from lobbying on their own for grants, subsidies, tariff changes, loan guarantees, tax write-offs, government contracts, or policy changes, and many firms do so on a regular basis. In addition, it is evident from the table that despite their supposed or real competition, the private firms within almost every industry have organized a common pressure group to promote the interests of the industry as a whole. Thus, to a large exent, the "system of business interest associations in Canada is highly fragmented, consisting of many small, narrowly focused organizations."[7] William Coleman counted about 600 business groups that were active in Canadian federal politics, about 40 percent of which were in the manufacturing sector. He summarizes the business pressure group scene as follows:

> a relatively small number of associations with members that are generally large firms, operating in large oligopolistic sectors. These associations spend in excess of $1 million annually, employ a minimum of 10 to 15 people, are institutionally bilingual, and have an officer, if not their head office, in Ottawa. Associations in this category are visible to the attentive public; their leaders are quoted frequently in the business press and move freely in government circles.... The several roles they play gives them a system of comprehensive political contacts, ranging from lower and middle technical levels of the bureaucracy to senior officials, MPs, and cabinet ministers.[8]

Superimposed upon these industrial groupings are such "peak" organizations as the **Canadian Manufacturers' Association**, the **Canadian Chamber of Commerce**, the **Business Council on National Issues**, and the **Canadian Federation of Independent Business**. The Canadian Manufacturers' Association, which goes back to 1874 and now represents some 2500 firms, can be seen as an aggregative organization, an umbrella under which many separate manufacturing groups gather. The Canadian Chamber of Commerce, formed in 1925, calls itself Canada's "largest and most successful business association." It represents about 170 000 business members. In recent years it successfully pursued changes to the GST, opposed a watchdog agency to monitor price increases, and, like the BCNI and CMA, engaged in a public education campaign about the dangers of the government deficit. The CFIB was founded in 1971 by John Bullock, and represents more than 50 000 small business members. The BCNI, led by Tom d'Aquino, was formed in 1976 and represents the chief executive officers of 150 of the largest firms in the country, which together have some 1.3 million employees. The BCNI sees itself as the "senior voice of Canadian business," and gives automatic membership on its board of directors to the heads of the CCC, the CMA, and the Conseil du Patronat du Québec. The organization was particularly influential with the Mulroney Conservative government; it fought hard for the Canada–U.S. Free Trade Agreement, and, having been successful in that enterprise, then sought, in its own words, "to broaden public understanding of the need for more responsible fiscal policies." While Canada thus lacks a single peak voice for the business community as a whole, that community may be even more influential for being represented by at least four national organizations.

On the agricultural side of business, Coleman found 95 active associations in 1980, the Canadian Federation of Agriculture tending to represent the more affluent farmers, while the National Farmers Union speaks for those who are not doing so well.[9] The CFA was formed in 1935 and now represents ten provincial farm organizations and eight national commodity organizations. Other specific commodity groups exist outside the aegis of the CFA, such as the Canadian Cattlemen's Association and the Canadian Grains Council.

Nonbusiness Groups

The Canadian Labour Congress functions more satisfactorily as a common voice for organized labour, but only about 58 percent of Canadian union members actually belong to unions affiliated with the CLC. About five percent belong to each of the breakaway Canadian Federation of Labour and the Quebec-based Conseil des Syndicats Nationaux (CSN), while unions representing the other 30 percent have not joined any central labour organization.[10] The CLC maintains a link to the New Democratic Party, as do many of its individual unions, which is unique among Canadian pressure groups.

Many of the ethnic groups in Canada have their own organized groups, such as the National Congress of Italian Canadians, the German Canadian Congress, the National Association of Japanese Canadians, the Chinese Canadian National Council, and the National Association of Canadians of Origins in India. Most of these have been brought together, with government support, in the peak organization, the Canadian Ethnocultural Council. The largest of several aboriginal groups is the Assembly of First Nations. The English and French, on the other hand, are only organized where they are minorities—the anglophone Alliance Quebec and the Fédération des Francophones hors Québec incorporating provincial units such as the Association canadienne-française de l'Ontario (ACFO). Most of the religious denominations in Canada function as pressure groups from time to time, with the Canadian Conference of Catholic Bishops, the United Church of Canada and the Canadian Jewish Congress probably being most influential. In recent years the Roman Catholic Church has joined the umbrella Christian group, the Canadian Council of Churches.

Most professions have organizations that speak for their members on relevant issues, the Canadian Medical and Bar Associations being two of the oldest and most important. The CMA was formed in 1867 and has about 46 000 members, about 80 percent of the country's doctors. In addition to serving the needs of its own members, the CMA advises the government on other health matters in the broader public interest. The Canadian Bar Association, incorporated in 1921, has a membership of over 35 000, which represents approximately two-thirds of all practising lawyers. Besides promoting the interests of the legal profession, as such, the CBA is integrally involved in improving the law and the administration of justice.

The Royal Canadian Legion is by far the largest veterans' organization, going back to 1926 and representing about 580 000 members who served in Canada's armed forces or who are associated with those who did. Besides working for better pensions and other benefits for its own members and a strong military establishment, the Legion is prominently involved in public service and charitable work.

The Consumers' Association of Canada has a near monopoly on representing the interests of consumers, while the Canadian Federation of Municipalities speaks for all the local governments in the country.

Other Categorizations of Pressure Groups

However much any of the above-mentioned groups claim to be pursuing the public interest, they can be generally categorized as "self-interested" or "material" groups because their principal concern is to improve their own economic position. The true "public interest" or "purposive" group exists to promote causes that it sees as beneficial to society as a whole and that do not directly benefit its own members: the John Howard Society (improving prison conditions and the lot of ex-inmates), the Canadian Council on Social Development (promoting better social policy), the Canadian Civil Liberties Association (protecting civil liberties from government infringement), and a variety of environmental groups, among others.

With the exception of some of the public interest and ethnic groups, those named above and many others are called **institutionalized groups** because they are permanent, well-established, formal organizations. Almost all maintain a head office in Ottawa with a full-time staff, a sizable budget, and a reasonably stable membership. Most have developed continuous links with the authorities, and represent their members' interests on a daily basis, year after year.

These characteristics are not possessed by all pressure groups, however, and other labels have been attached to them. Some groups spring up spontaneously around a specific issue, and once the issue is resolved, they fade away. Such **issue-oriented groups** lack the institutionalized groups' permanence, office, staff, budget, membership, and access to the authorities. Instead, they more likely resort to attracting public attention to their cause through media coverage of such actions as demonstrations. Since issue-oriented groups usually disappear when the issue has been resolved, they are not as familiar as institutionalized groups, but several famous examples can be cited. In the early 1970s the Stop Spadina group opposed extension of the Spadina Expressway in Toronto, the People or Planes group fought the proposed Pickering airport east of that city, and, more recently, "Bread Not Circuses" opposed Toronto's bid to host the 1996 Olympic Games. In the 1980s, when Finance Minister Michael Wilson attempted to de-index the old age pension, an ad hoc group of seniors organized across the country and forced him to back down. Another recent case is Rural Dignity, a spontaneous national group that sprang up to fight against the deterioration of rural and small-town life in general, and of its mail service in particular. If their issue is not resolved, or if they anticipate further challenges, such groups may become a more permanent fixture, gradually evolving from an issue-oriented group to a fledgling group, to a mature group, and perhaps ultimately to the institutionalized category.[11] The National Pensioners and Senior Citizens Federation, for example, remains intact.

Political scientists often find it useful to distinguish between pressure groups and social movements. Many of the issue-oriented groups referred to are, in fact, part of larger unstructured social movements, of which the environmental, women's, and peace movements have been most prominent. Other examples include the aboriginal, gay and lesbian, and animal rights movements. Social movements begin at the margins of the political system, possessing an alternate vision of "the good life," and usually consist of coalitions of small local groups that have not (yet) hardened into a cohesive national pressure group.[12] The umbrella women's group, the National Action Committee on the Status of Women, is a coalition of some 500 member groups, while the Canadian Environmental Network contains about 1800 groups. Such movements run into much bureaucratic and political party resistance, and often do not achieve immediate success. In the long run, however, they widen the scope of public discourse, and parties and other mainstream political institutions eventually respond. Take recent improvements in legislation with respect to women and the environment, for example, and changes in public attitudes toward war, aboriginals, homosexuals, and the treatment of animals.

Other categorizations are also sometimes useful in discussing pressure groups. Most groups are "autonomous" in the sense that they develop without government initiative, although they may later seek government financial support. The creation of *reverse groups*, on the other hand, involves politicians or bureaucrats. This may be for either personal gain or in the hope of promoting a certain public policy objective. In the late 1960s, for example, the federal government began to fund anti-poverty, women's, minority official language, aboriginal, and other ethnic groups,[13] and by 1987 it was handing out $185 million to interest groups in grants of over $50 000 (and much more in smaller grants). At that point, however, the Mulroney government began to cut back on grants to Native, women's, poor, and disabled people's groups, both for fiscal and ideological reasons, something the Trudeau government had also done on occasion when a particular group became too critical of the hand that fed it. Canada has been something of a world leader in government support of critical interest groups, and the Department of Regional Industrial Expansion even encouraged the establishment of industrial groups like the Canadian Ocean Industries Association and the Canadian Railway and Transit Manufacturers' Association.[14] Such grant reductions, however, demonstrate a lack of political sincerity as well as the dangers involved in a group's becoming too critical and too dependent.[15]

A distinction can also be made between "active" groups, which have a formal organization and a name, and "categoric" groups, which are simply a number of unorganized individuals who share a common characteristic. Categoric groups are potential pressure groups, since an issue could come along that would bring them to life, but if their numbers are sufficient the authorities may pay attention to them even in their latent state.

Pressure Group Structures

A word should be added about the structure of pressure groups. Issue-oriented groups may burst forth anywhere an issue arises—at the federal, provincial, or municipal level. Institutionalized groups, on the other hand, tend to be organized wherever government decisions regularly affect them. The federal nature of the country means that authoritative decisions are made at two (or even three) levels of government, and most institutionalized groups parallel the federal structure of government.[16] They find it advantageous to be organized at both levels because, as discussed in Chapter 4, the division of powers between the federal and provincial governments is so blurred. The Canadian Medical Association is composed of ten autonomous provincial divisions (such as the Ontario Medical Association), the Canadian Chamber of Commerce has strong provincial branches (such as the Ontario Chamber of Commerce), and so does the Canadian Labour Congress (the Ontario Federation of Labour). These latter two groups in particular also maintain municipal organizations—some 500 community chambers of commerce or boards of trade and 123 local labour councils across the country. The Canadian Manufacturers' Association lacks such a formal federal structure, but it does maintain eight provincial offices.

Many pressure groups, including teachers, nurses, students, and professors, are actually more strongly organized at the provincial level than in Ottawa. This is because they are affected by decisions of provincial governments more than by federal ones. Some, such as the medical and legal professions, are even delegated powers by provincial governments to regulate themselves.

By increasing the number of decision-making centres in the political system, federalism generally makes it easier for groups to block government action, but harder to initiate new programs. Sometimes the national organization requests assistance from the provincial wings in dealing with an issue in Ottawa, while at other times a provincial unit seeks support from the national organization. For example, the insurance industry and the medical profession first fought against medicare in Saskatchewan when it was introduced there, then transferred the fight to Ottawa to oppose a national program, and finally went back to individual provinces to try to persuade them stay out of the national scheme.[17] At other times, certain groups use their closer relations with provincial governments to transform provincial governments into allies in the group's attempt to pressure Ottawa, such as in the insurance industry's opposition to the Canada Pension Plan, the mining industry's fight against federal tax reform, or the petroleum industry's campaign against the National Energy Program.[18]

It should be added in this connection that many national groups are beset by regional and linguistic problems, and that the Quebec wing of many national organizations has a distinct status of one kind or another. Other groups seem to handle the cleavages fairly well, having a regular provincial branch in Quebec, attempting to operate on a bilingual basis at the national level, and striving to reconcile regional differences within the organization.

TARGETS AND METHODS OF PRESSURE GROUP ACTIVITY

Besides being affected by the federal system, Canadian interest groups are very much influenced in their operations by the fact that they exist in a parliamentary system. This, despite the name, places most of the decision-making power in the hands of the bureaucracy and the cabinet. Pressure groups that understand this basic truth direct most of their attention to these two branches of government.

In this connection Paul Pross's concept of **policy communities** should be mentioned.[19] This concept is based on the premise that each field of public policy is discrete and specialized, with its own constellation of participants. Each policy community consists of a grouping of government agencies, pressure groups, corporations, institutions, media people, and individuals including academics who have an interest in that particular policy field and attempt to influence it. Pross argues that every policy community is divided into two parts. The first, the "sub-government," includes a "lead government agency," other policy-making agencies, and a small group of interests with the right to be consulted on a daily basis; the second, the "attentive public," is composed of the other actors mentioned. These actors initially attempt to establish their legitimacy with the lead agency, and if they achieve such recognition and status, they may be appointed to advisory committees and be made part of the agency's information flow. Pross cites the examples of the Canadian Bankers' Association and the Canadian Tax Foundation as groups that have achieved such legitimacy, as opposed to the National Farmers Union, which has not. Once such groups are given the privilege of consultation and access to strategic information, they normally behave quite cooperatively, and the whole policy community becomes cohesive and mutually supportive. All the actors involved, including the lead agency, prefer to keep the issues that concern them within the community and have a strong incentive to resolve any problems there rather than open the issues up to cabinet discussion or, even worse, public debate and confrontation. More will be said about such policy communities in Chapter 19, but for now it is sufficient to emphasize the specialized nature of different policy fields and the varied configurations of actors they contain. Figure 18.1 provides a diagram of a typical policy community.

Figure 18.1 The Policy Community

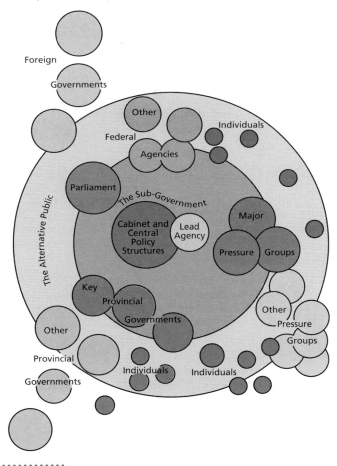

The Bureaucracy

As will be discussed in Chapter 21, the bureaucracy advises the cabinet on almost all of its decisions; it drafts legislation and regulations according to the cabinet's general instructions; it proposes budgets and spends government money; and it implements policies and programs once they have been given cabinet and/or legislative approval. All of these areas hold considerable scope for bureaucratic discretion, and Pross speaks of "bureaucratic pluralism," in which various government agencies and departments gain considerable autonomy.[20] It is for this reason that institutionalized groups in particular direct their messages at the bureaucratic target more than at any other institution of government.[21] Many pressure group demands involve technical matters that only the bureaucracy understands and that it may be able to satisfy without reference to the politicians. Although bureaucrats may initially consider meeting pressure groups as a waste of precious time and be suspicious of their motives,[22] such groups try to cultivate close relationships with the senior public servants so that they feel comfortable in contacting these officials on an informal, direct, day-to-day basis. This contact can take the form of telephone calls, meetings, letters, and business lunches. If a first-name relationship emerges, so much the better.[23]

A very close relationship often develops between a pressure group and its most relevant government department. This relationship may, however, be a reciprocal one, as desirable for the public service as it is for the group. In return for the various ways in which the bureaucracy can respond to group demands, the group may possess information the department needs or desires in order to understand certain situations with which it is trying to deal. As issues become too complex for politicians—ministers or MPs—to understand, and larger numbers of issues, constituents, and obligations eat up their time, legislation is increasingly drafted in skeletal form with the specifics delegated to the bureaucracy to be added later in the form of regulations or "delegated legislation." Bureaucrats regularly consult pressure groups as they draft such legislation, design new programs, and draw up regulations. As president of the Canadian Tobacco Manufacturers' Association, for example, Bill Neville managed to dilute the original regulations dealing with the anti-smoking message that the Health Department imposed on packages of cigarettes.[24] The group may also be a valuable ally in persuading other bureaucratic agencies or cabinet to do what the department wants, and in various "output" functions described below.

Thus, what is called a **clientele relationship** sometimes develops between such groups as the Royal Canadian Legion and the Department of Veterans' Affairs, between the Canadian Federation of Agriculture and the Department of Agriculture, between the Canadian Medical Association and the Department of Health, between the petroleum and mining associations and the Department of Natural Resources, and between business organizations and the Department of Finance. The relations between such an agency or department and its allied pressure groups may become so close that it is difficult to tell them apart. The agency or department almost becomes an extension of the pressure group, making policy in the interest of the group and promoting within the higher councils of government the interest they both represent. The minister, deputy minister, and department of Finance speak for the business community, while the minister, deputy minister, and department of Agriculture speak for the farming community, and so on.

Although pressure groups are usually seen in terms of their "input" function—making demands or "policy advocacy"—they may also perform various "policy participation" or "output" functions.[25] A group may be better equipped to inform its specialized membership or audience about new laws, regulations, or programs than a department that is restricted to the media or other regular channels of communication. Ethnic groups, for example, can help the Immigration Department in the dissemination of information about policy changes to a specialized audience. In addition, the cooperation of the group might be indispensable to the successful execution of a program, such as the role of the medical profession in the administration of medicare. In some cases, as noted, certain groups are even delegated powers of self-regulation, especially the medical and legal professions at the provincial level.

Besides such direct, personal, informal contact, interest groups interact with the bureaucracy through numerous permanent and ad hoc advisory committees. Most departments set up several advisory committees and offer representation on them to the pressure groups most affected. For example, the Canadian Federation of Agriculture is represented on the International Trade Advisory Committee Trade Policy Task Force and the Agriculture, Food and Beverage Sectoral Advisory Group on International Trade. The Canadian Medical Association is represented on the National Advisory Committee on Immunization, the Canadian Association of Chiefs of Police on the Federal Working Group on the Smuggling of Firearms, and the Canadian Construction Association on the Regulatory Advisory Committee to the Canadian Environmental Assessment Act and the Canadian Labour Force Development Board. The National Council of Welfare is a classic "reverse" group that was not only created by government to serve as an advisory committee directly representing poor people, but was originally even given a home and staff within the building housing the Welfare Department.

In addition, public servants themselves may be members of interest groups. For example, bureaucrats in welfare departments often belong to the Canadian Council on Social Development, a situation that naturally assists the group in maximizing its influence; medical bureaucrats may belong to the Canadian Medical Association, and legal bureaucrats to the Canadian Bar Association. In fact, considerable movement of personnel takes place between interest groups and the higher levels of the public service; officials often move from pressure group jobs to the bureaucracy or vice versa.

The Cabinet

The cabinet is the second branch of government that pressure groups frequently try to influence. This, of course, is because the cabinet makes the major governmental decisions in a parliamentary system, as discussed in Chapter 20. One traditional method that institutionalized groups utilized in the past was the omnibus annual brief to the whole cabinet. Such sessions are almost a thing of the past, however, since many decisions are now made by individual ministers or cabinet committees. It is probably more productive to submit single-issue representations to individual ministers, who indeed spend much of their time in meetings with such groups.[26] If a minister stays in one position long enough, a pressure group may be able to construct a more personal, informal relationship, as did the Canadian Federation of Agriculture with Jimmy Gardiner, who served as minister of Agriculture from 1935 to

1957.[27] The recent practice of shuffling ministers from one department to another every couple of years decreases the likelihood of developing such intimacy. The social scene in Ottawa should also be mentioned, for parties and receptions provide excellent opportunities for cabinet ministers, deputy ministers, and established pressure group representatives (especially corporate) to meet and mingle.

The Trudeau government established the precedent of encouraging various groups to meet with the minister of Finance before the preparation of the annual budget, a practice that was even more widespread under Mulroney's first Finance minister, Michael Wilson. But in 1990 Wilson evoked considerable protest when he told business, labour, and social groups that he was too busy to meet with them before the budget, inviting them to submit written advice instead.

Occasionally ministers are themselves members of the interest group, in which case this interlocking membership is probably an advantage to the group. Less institutionalized groups, on the other hand, may have to forego such close relationships with cabinet ministers in favour of letters, faxes, or other means of more formal or mass communication.

The concept of **elite accommodation**[28] is most relevant to this process. It claims that most public decisions in Canada emerge from the interaction of three agents: the cabinet, the senior public service, and pressure groups, especially in the business field. The individuals who occupy the top positions in these sectors are elites both in the sense of being small numbers of people with disproportionate amounts of power (compared with ordinary citizens) and in the sense of their exclusive socioeconomic backgrounds, coming from families of higher social class, higher incomes, and higher educations. Robert Presthus thus postulates that the common backgrounds and values of political, bureaucratic, and corporate leaders help to facilitate agreement among them. Commanding the heights of these sectors of society, they easily accommodate each other in the working out of public policies. Lobbyists from professional lobbying firms also fit perfectly into this arrangement.

Corporatism, on the other hand, is a concept that includes labour in the equation. Corporatism conceives of society as being divided into a relatively few functional sectors, such as business, labour, farmers, and professions, and prescribes some type of formal, functional representation in the making of general policies for society as a whole, especially in the interaction of large national groups like business, labour, and government. Corporatism is sometimes identified with the powers of self-regulation that are delegated to professional organizations, and Canadian farmers have sometimes argued that each sector of society should be self-governing and that functional representation should replace territorial representation in Parliament. But in the sense of multilateral negotiation among conflicting social interests in which the state is a major party, corporatism is much more prevalent in other countries than in Canada. That is largely because Canada does not have a single, authoritative peak organization that speaks for either business or labour, because labour is generally not given the same kind of attention that it is accorded elsewhere, and because of greater hostility between labour and business. The closest Canadian approximation to corporatism involved tripartite (business, labour, and government) schemes tried in the 1970s to develop general economic policies.[29] Elite accommodation is generally a more accurate depiction of the Canadian scene than corporatism, therefore, largely because the former virtually eliminates the labour component.

Parliament

The third main branch of the government is the legislature or Parliament, but as will be discussed in Chapter 22, it largely legitimizes decisions previously taken by the executive. That being the case, the House of Commons is not as often the target of interest group activity, but it does remain the object of considerable attention. One of the main reasons that a bill is usually sent to a legislative committee during its passage is to allow interest groups to make representations on it, and such committee scrutiny of bills often carries on for weeks. Especially in a majority government situation, however, ministers have traditionally been reluctant to accept amendments proposed at the legislative stage, so that groups were better advised to make their case at the executive level before the bill was made public. It has even been said that the sight of a pressure group at the legislative level in Canada is a sign that the group already failed at the level of the bureaucracy and the cabinet. Nevertheless, groups also converge on MPs in their offices or inundate them with letters, telegrams, or postcards from group members. For example, while not diminishing its influence at the levels of cabinet and bureaucracy, the Canadian Chamber of Commerce is particularly adept at applying pressure on MPs through its base in almost every constituency across the country. Groups also meet with individual party caucuses. Certain MPs may already belong to the interest group or may be persuaded to join, in which case they can be expected to speak on behalf of the group on a committee or in the Commons, in another aspect of interlocking membership between groups and authorities.

In tracing the evolution of power since Confederation, Pross sees a resurrection of Parliament over the past 25 years after 30 years of dominance by public service mandarins. This is because the increasing diffusion of power in Ottawa has enhanced the importance of the legitimation function of the House of Commons.[30] Many pressure group–inspired amendments to legislation have been accepted in recent years, perhaps most notably the changes made to the Charter of Rights before its final adoption in the early 1980s as a result of pressure from women's, aboriginal, disability, and ethnic groups. The Standing Committee on Finance, with its pre-budget hearings, is now integrated into the expenditure management system, to some extent replacing meetings with the minster.

The upper chamber of Parliament, the Senate, is probably even more involved in the lobbying process. Because so many senators have close corporate connections and function regularly as lobbyists for big business, the Senate has been called a *lobby from within*.[31] During passage in that chamber, much legislation is considered by the Senate Committee on Banking, Trade and Commerce, most of whose members hold directorships in Canadian banks and other large corporations. Such holdings have not deterred Committee members from active consideration of questions relating to financial institutions in what many observers see as a classic case of conflict of interest.

Other Targets

Interest groups have many targets beyond these three main branches of government. If they can find a legal or constitutional angle to their demand, for example, such groups may take cases to the courts. Corporations have sometimes challenged federal or provincial legislation in the courts as a violation of the division of powers; francophone groups have used the courts to uphold constitutionally guaranteed minority language rights when politicians were reluctant to do so; and aboriginal groups are increasingly using the courts to uphold or broaden the meaning of treaty and aboriginal rights. The Charter of Rights and Freedoms provides added potential for targeting the courts by actually inviting individuals and groups to challenge federal or provincial legislation they consider to be discriminatory.

As mentioned, only the Canadian Labour Congress has seen fit to attach itself formally to a political party. This strategy may have reduced the group's impact on Liberal and Conservative governments as it awaited an NDP victory, however, and other groups remain scrupulously nonpartisan so that they can exert equal influence on whichever party is in power. Another target of pressure group activity is the royal commission. These elaborate investigations of public problems normally invite pressure groups and experts to submit briefs in public hearings in order to supplement whatever original research the commission itself undertakes, as well as to generate support for its recommendations. Sometimes a pressure group is actually represented on the commission itself, as in the case of the Canadian Medical Association and the Hall Royal Commission on Medical Services in the 1960s.

Besides their direct representations to government, pressure groups increasingly try to influence public opinion in the hope that the authorities will respond to a clear message from the public. In what is called "advocacy advertising," corporations and groups use media advertising in an attempt to sway public opinion to their point of view.[32] In 1991, for example, both the Pharmaceutical Manufacturers Association and the rival Canadian Drug Manufacturers' Association took out media advertisements to make their case on the question of patent protection for new pharmaceuticals.

Many pressure groups increase their public profile once an election has been called. This phenomenon, discussed in Chapter 15, is usually called "third-party" or advocacy group advertising. Pressure groups often seek the response of parties and candidates to questions of concern to the group. They then indicate their support or opposition in media advertising which is contrary to the spirit of expenditure ceilings in the Canada Elections Act. Groups on either side of the abortion debate and the National Citizens' Coalition are regular examples, while the Canadian Alliance for Jobs and Trade Prospects and its anti–free trade counterpart, the Pro-Canada Network, were particularly visible in 1988. National or local pressure groups sometimes target particular politicians or ministers for defeat, as the anti-abortionists did in 1988 to then Justice minister (later governor general) Ray Hnatyshyn and as those opposed to a "fixed link" between PEI and New Brunswick did to then Environment minister Tom McMillan.

If all else fails, the group may resort to demonstrations, protest marches, tractor parades, sit-ins, and road and bridge blockades. Some of these are peaceful and legal, such as the orderly demonstrations that are an almost daily occurrence on Parliament Hill and that frequently greet prime ministers on their travels. But the frustration of aboriginal, environmentalist (e.g., Greenpeace), and other radical or issue-oriented groups increasingly takes the form of civil disobedience. The armed stand-off at Oka, Quebec, in 1990 was one of the rare occasions in which a group resorted to violence.

Pressure groups are not restricted to one target and method, of course, and groups may use a variety of methods directed at a number of different targets. The Canadian Labour Congress, for example, was so distraught over the wage and price control program in 1975 that beyond its direct daily contact with government officials, its annual brief to the cabinet, and its affiliation with the NDP, it challenged the legislation in the Supreme Court and organized a national day of protest. Five years later, the CLC held one of the largest demonstrations in Canadian history on Parliament Hill. After a few tense moments, it ended peacefully, much to the relief of the anxious House of Commons security guards.

GROUP RESOURCES AND DETERMINANTS OF SUCCESS

The fact that an institutionalized group like the CLC could fight an issue on so many fronts and still lose leads to the question: why are groups sometimes successful and sometimes not? A variety of factors is involved in accounting for such success and failure.[33]

INTEREST GROUP RESOURCES

* members
* cohesion
* tenor of message
* leadership
* prestige
* information
* absence of opposition
* money
* financial position of government

The size of the group is probably most important, considering that membership numbers represent votes. The authorities at least feel comfortable ignoring very small groups because the electoral consequences would be minimal. In this respect, the Canadian Labour Congress should be regularly successful in having the authorities respond to its demands because it is the largest pressure group in Canada with over two million members.

The fact that the CLC is not usually very influential points to the importance not just of a large membership, but of the cohesiveness of the organization. First of all, as mentioned, only about one-third of paid workers belong to unions and only 57 percent of Canadian union members belong to the CLC, so that the labour movement as a whole is not very cohesive. But even among those who are members of the CLC, unity, commitment, and militancy are notoriously lacking. In addition to the weak sense of class-consciousness in Canada, there is a lack of union-consciousness, an unwillingness of one union to support another. The CLC's ultimate threat to Liberal or Conservative governments is that the more unhappy the group is, the more likely its members are to vote NDP. But even on those occasions when the CLC "declared war" on the government, the bulk of its members continued to vote for the old-line parties. Liberal and Conservative governments apparently feel that the CLC is so incapable of mobilizing its members behind the demands issued by its leadership that it can often be ignored.

The CLC contrasts with such other groups as the Royal Canadian Legion or the Canadian Chamber of Commerce with respect to member cohesion.[34] Both of these, and many others, are able to mobilize their members to inundate the authorities with demands for concerted action. The CCC, for example, issues periodic action calls which tell its members to

> use the facts and arguments outlined in this bulletin [to] deliver the message in your own words on your own letterhead to your Member of Parliament by let-ter, phone, fax or in person. Make it clear that, in the next federal budget: debt and deficit reduction must be the goal; no tax increases will be acceptable; fed-eral program spending must be reduced or frozen, in current dollars, over the next two years. To have an impact on the makeup of the budget, early action is imperative. The content of the budget will be determined in the next 30 days. Send a copy of your message directly to the Minister of Finance and the Prime Minister.[35]

As in other aspects of politics and life in general, money is an important resource. In the case of pressure groups, money can buy staff, offices, organization, expertise, publicity, and other useful weapons with which to get the group's message across. For example, the Canadian Medical Association has a staff of about 100 and an annual budget of about $20 million; the Canadian Bar Association, a staff of 50 and a budget of about $10 million; and the Canadian Manufacturers' Association, a staff of 100 and a budget of about $5 million. The Business Council on National Issues and the Canadian Chamber of Commerce are also very well endowed financially, giving them the capacity both to generate the information to strengthen their case and to transmit it to relevant targets. Except for those representing big business or highly paid professions, however, most groups have financial problems. The Canadian Federation of Agriculture is typical of many groups with a staff of less than ten and a budget of less than $1 million; the Canadian Construction Association has a staff of 16 and a budget of less than $2 million. On rare occasions, on the other hand, the very poverty of the group may actually be an asset in seeking government assistance: it strengthens the case for public support.

Information is a fourth crucial resource in pressure group politics. Especially at the bureau-cratic level, where much of this politics takes place, any vital information that is lacking as the public service drafts technical laws and regulations will be eagerly accepted. Even at the political level, the group may be able to present data and alternative analyses of policy that will lead ministers to rethink their proposals. Closely associated with information is the pro-fessional expertise of the pressure group's staff, and in this connection, the large business groups are able to produce mounds of well-researched and glossy documents. The Canadian Bar Association makes frequent representations to parliamentary committees, royal commis-sions, and government departments, and because of its expertise in both the substance of many issues and in the drafting of legislation, is often asked for advice. The CBA and Canadian Chamber of Commerce are among many groups that monitor federal political issues and the passage of legislation and keep their members informed via monthly newsletters.

The quality of group leadership and the prestige of the group are other important factors. In recent years, for example, even the Canadian Labour Congress has quite deliberately sought to choose "smooth," articulate, attractive leaders to make its case. When dealing with a Liberal or Conservative government, however, organized labour probably does not rival doctors, lawyers, or businesspeople as far as prestige is concerned.

The tenor of the group's message is also important. If a basic correspondence exists between the demands of the group and the government's stated objectives or the prevailing values of society in general, the pressure group will have greater success than if there is a vast gap in ideological perspective. It is not surprising that the CLC would be virtually ignored by the business-oriented Mulroney government. Similarly, the minister responsible for the Status of Women in that cabinet repeatedly refused to meet the National Action Committee on the Status of Women because of its intense criticism. At the same time the government cut NAC's grant and gave the first federal grant to its rival, REAL Women (Realistic, Equal, Active for Life). Related to ideology is the sharing of a professional orientation between group leaders and authorities, especially in the bureaucracy. Many examples could be given of the success of a group because its officials shared the professional norms of the relevant public servants in their reciprocal, clientele relationship. A government or societal guilty conscience can sometimes also be helpful, such as in the provision of grants to aboriginal, Japanese-Canadian, or anti-poverty groups.

Since many pressure group demands relate to the spending of public money, the financial position of the government will often influence a group's success. In the prosperous and free-spending 1960s and 1970s, for example, requests for funds were more likely to be fulfilled than in the 1980s and 1990s, which constituted an era of government restraint.

Finally, a group will be more influential if it has no organized opposition. One of the reasons for the success of the Canadian Medical Association over the years, for example, was that it had medical politics almost all to itself.[36] Contrast that situation with the evenly divided forces on either side of the abortion debate. Alternatively, success can be influenced by whether or not a rival group expresses more or less the same point of view, such as in the competition between the Canadian Federation of Agriculture and the National Farmers Union or between the CLC and the Canadian Federation of Labour.

LOBBYING IN CANADA

The tendency of the rich and powerful, including big business, to benefit from pressure group politics and elite accommodation can only be enhanced by recent developments in the practice of lobbying in Canada. If lobbying is the activity of trying to influence the authorities, it is, of course, a perfectly legitimate activity for anyone to undertake in a democracy. Traditionally, individuals, companies, unions, and pressure groups of all kinds have done their own lobbying, but in recent years Canada has seen the mushrooming of professional lobbying, consultant, or government relations firms that lobby on behalf of an individual, company, or pressure group in return for a fee.

According to the 1989 **Lobbyists Registration Act**, a lobbyist is an individual who, for payment, on behalf of any person or organization ... undertakes to arrange a meeting with a public office holder or to communicate with a public office holder in an attempt to influence

(a) the development of a legislative proposal ...

(b) the introduction, passage, defeat or amendment of any bill or resolution ...

(c) the making or amending of any regulation ...

(d) the development or amendment of any policy or program ...

(e) the awarding of any monetary grant or contribution or other financial benefit ... or

(f) the awarding of any contract.

The law divides lobbyists into two categories: those who work for any client for a fee are classified as "Tier I" lobbyists, while "Tier II" lobbyists include those who engage in traditional pressure group or corporate lobbying—that is, in-house employees of an organization whose duties involve communicating with public officeholders on behalf of that organization. Both types of lobbyists must register their activities in the Registry of Lobbyists.

Those engaged in the new lobbying industry justify their existence largely in terms of the increasing size and complexity of government. The federal government grew enormously in the 1960s and 1970s, and the policy-making process was restructured so that corporations and interest groups could no longer find their way around Ottawa.[37] That the hostile budgets of 1980 (National Energy Program) and 1981 (corporate tax reform) caught the business community by surprise also contributed to the development of means through which the corporate sector could make its voice heard more effectively.

The early 1980s was a period in which new means of influence were being sought, and an expansion of such firms appeared to take place about the time the Mulroney government was elected in 1984. Many of the leading figures in the early establishment of professional lobby firms, such as Gerald and Fred Doucet, Gary Ouellet, Patrick MacAdam, Frank Moores, Bill Fox, Bill Neville, and David Angus, were cronies of the prime minister.[38] In addition, certain leading legal firms have also set up lobbying operations. The largest consultant lobbying firms and largest legal lobbying firms are listed below.

····································

LARGEST CONSULTANT LOBBYING FIRMS, 1995

	Clients	Registered Lobbyists
Capital Hill Group	74	11
Government Policy Consultants	69	23
Hill & Knowlton	65	14
S.A. Murray	55	11
Corporation House	40	12
Government Business Consultants	33	11
Earnscliffe Strategy Group	30	3
Public Sector Corporation	30	7

LARGEST LEGAL LOBBYING FIRMS

	Clients	Registered Lobbyists
Osler, Hoskin & Harcourt	60	28
Strikeman, Elliott	42	32
McCarthy Tétrault	22	20
McMillan Binch	22	10
Tory, Tory	21	11
Fraser & Beatty	20	17
Lang Michener	18	11

Source: John A. Chenier, ed., The Federal Lobbyists 1995 (Ottawa: ARC Publications, 1995). Used with permission.

A sample of the clients of some of the principal lobbying firms is listed below. It can be seen that some corporations hire more than one lobbying firm to make their case. In the case of the rivalry between the two major pharmaceutical groups, the head of the Canadian Drug Manufacturers' Association said: "The Pharmaceutical Manufacturers' Association of Canada had already tied up most of the firms in Ottawa, so we had to pick up what was left."[39]

A SAMPLE OF CLIENTS OF PRINCIPAL LOBBYING FIRMS

Capital Hill
Canadian Tire
Cineplex Odeon
Coopers & Lybrand
Spar Aerospace
Stentor

Corporation House
Avon Canada Inc.
Coca-Cola Ltd.
INCO Ltd.
John Deere Ltd.
P. Lawson Travel

Earnscliffe
Cameco Corporation
Canadian Airlines Intl.
CP Rail System
John Labatt Ltd.
Nova Corp. of Alberta
Unitel

Hill & Knowlton
Amex Canada Ltd.
British Aerospace
Cameco
CP Rail System
INCO Ltd.
Pepsi-Cola Ltd.
Shell Canada Ltd.

Osler, Hoskin, Harcourt
Amex Bank of Canada
Coca-Cola Ltd.
General Motors
Imasco Ltd.
Imperial Oil Ltd.
Nova Corp. of Alberta
Time Canada Ltd.

Strikeman Elliott
Canadian Tire
Chrysler Canada
Husky Oil Ltd.
Repap Enterprises
Texaco Inc.
Wal-Mart Canada
Westinghouse Inc.

GBC Group	GPC	S.A. Murray
American Airlines	3M Canada Inc.	CTV Television
Bombardier Inc.	Chrysler Canada Ltd.	Eli Lilly Canada
Brascan Ltd.	Great West Life Co.	Hudson's Bay Co.
Merck Frosst Canada	Hydro-Québec	Labatt Breweries
Noranda Inc.	Imasco Ltd.	Macmillan Bloedel
Royal Trustco Ltd.	London Life	Noranda Inc.

Source: Chenier, The Federal Lobbyists 1995. *Used with permission.*

Finally, some corporations and groups have in-house lobbyists (Tier II) but also make use of professional lobby firms (Tier I) to supplement their efforts. Contrasting examples follow. It should be noted, however, that in some cases, such as Abitibi, Imperial Oil, Ford, and GM, the large number of Tier II lobbyists includes technical people involved in safety and environmental regulation and procurement.

SELECTED CORPORATIONS AND GROUPS USING EITHER OR BOTH TIERS

	Tier I	Tier II
Abitibi-Price Inc.	0	26
Air Canada	5	8
Amex Canada Inc.	4	2
Bell Canada	1	2
Canadian Airlines International Ltd.	3	7
Canadian Bankers Association	1	10
Canadian Drug Manufacturers' Association	3	3
Canadian Life & Health Insurance Association	9	14
Ford Motor Co. of Canada	0	12
General Motors of Canada	2	13
Imperial Oil	4	28
INCO	2	7
Insurance Bureau of Canada	5	8
Pharmaceutical Manufacturers Association of Canada	4	10
Royal Bank of Canada	2	2

Source: Chenier, The Federal Lobbyists, *1995. Used with permission.*

Even during the Mulroney era, some groups felt it advantageous to take on prominent Liberal ex-politicians as well as Conservatives, while former Liberal cabinet minister Judy Erola became head of the Pharmaceutical Manufacturers Association. Given that the bureaucracy can satisfy many of the corporations' needs, many ex-bureaucrats such as Simon Reisman, former deputy minister of Finance and Canadian negotiator of the Free Trade Agreement, have also joined or formed lobbying firms in order to capitalize on their inside knowledge and connections. Federal conflict-of-interest guidelines preclude senior government employees from dealing with their former departments for one year after their departure from public employment, but these rules are sometimes broken, and, in any case, many critics doubt that it is sufficient time in which to be away.

After the emergence of such professional lobbying firms, a consensus developed among politicians that legislation, registration, and regulation were necessary. The registration idea was part of the Conservatives' ethics package unveiled after its early troubled record of cabinet resignations due to conflicts of interest and numerous legal charges against Tory backbenchers.[40] The legislation might never have come to pass without the consensus and determination of three key backbenchers, Albert Cooper (PC), Don Boudria (Liberal), and John Rodriguez (NDP),[41] but the government diluted their original draft.

The legislation acknowledged that lobbying public officeholders was a legitimate activity, but required lobbyists to register because it was desirable that officials and the public knew who was attempting to influence government and because paid lobbyists should not impede free and open access to government. It excluded representations made to parliamentary committees or oral or written submissions made to a public officeholder by an individual on behalf of any person or organization with respect to the enforcement, interpretation, or application of existing acts or regulations. Otherwise, lobbyists had to file a return including the name and address of the lobbyist and the lobbying firm, the name and address of the client, and the subject matter of the solicitation.

Reprinted with permission.

Many critics felt that the legislation was very weak and contrasted it with the U.S. law on this subject, which was adopted in 1946.[42] Some lobbyists did not register, and even when they did, the disclosure provisions in the Canadian law were quite minimal. In their report, lobbyists had to select from 52 general categories of subject matter (agriculture, energy, etc.) and seven general categories of objects (legislation, contract, etc.), such as "43-B." The law did not require revelation of the means of exerting pressure, the specific object of the representations, the fee, or the outcome of the effort. Furthermore, the act was almost totally lacking in an effective enforcement mechanism.

The whole procedure provided a lucrative living to those who could claim to be intimates of ministers or ministries, and favoured those who could afford to hire such professional lobbyists. In what John Sawatsky calls "one of the most odious lobby campaigns in the history of Canada," the fight of the Pharmaceutical Manufacturers Association to extend drug patent protection, "Gerry Doucet handled the PMAC file in GCI's (Government Consultants International) office; his brother Fred handled the issue in the Prime Minister's Office."[43] Such lobbying also gave individuals, companies, and traditional pressure groups the impression that they must hire someone to do their bidding for them rather than take their demands directly to the relevant authorities. They came to feel they had lost their democratic right to approach their own government and even their member of parliament. Moreover, as noted above, many traditional pressure groups even engaged the services of professional lobbyists to supplement their supplications to government. This is because Tier I lobbyists tend to be better strategists and to have better perspective, and can be used by pressure groups to build coalitions and share expenses on matters in which such cooperation is advantageous. In rare cases, academic expertise is also of value!

In the Mulroney era, ministers were allowed to set up large offices with which to provide stronger direction to the bureaucracy. As a result, lobbyists' efforts were often focused on ministers' offices, and partisan links were particularly important. Under Chrétien, ministers were forced to get by with a small number of partisan assistants, and the bureaucracy was allowed to operate with greater independence. Hence, the focus of lobbyists' efforts switched to the level of the senior bureaucracy. Having Liberal connections was still important for lobbyists, however, because a knowledge of cabinet thinking helped them influence decisions actually taken by the bureaucracy. Another distinctive mark of the Chrétien government was its massive consultation program; it sought the views of the stakeholders involved in so many issues that it almost overwhelmed both traditional pressure groups and Tier I lobbyists.

A parliamentary committee reviewed the Lobbyists Registration Act in 1993 and made many recommendations to strengthen the act. These recommendations were not implemented before the PCs were defeated, but the Liberal Party promised in the Red Book to take such action. Not surprisingly, the lobbyists lobbied ferociously against greater transparency in their operations, and the amendments that were finally adopted in 1995 were a pale imitation of what had been recommended by the committee and promised during the election campaign. Rather than do away with the distinction between Tier I and Tier II lobbyists, the new act recognized three categories: Tier I (consultant lobbyists who lobby for clients), and two types of Tier II lobbyists, in-house lobbyists (corporate), and in-house lobbyists (organization)—that is, employees of corporations or interest group organizations for whom lobbying was a significant part of their duties. Otherwise, the new legislation requires coalitions and grass-roots lobbying to be registered, and is slightly more rigorous in what else must be reported. Rather than just the general object of lobbying, the specific legislative proposal, bill, resolution, regulation, policy, program, or contract in question must be identified. So must the name of each department or other governmental institution lobbied. Contingency fees were not outlawed, but if contingency fees were involved they would have to be disclosed, as would the source and amount of any government funding of the client. As for enforcement, the registrar may audit information contained in any return or other document submitted and issue interpretative bulletins and advisory opinions. The six-month limitation of proceedings on contraventions was extended to two years. The ethics counsellor previously appointed by the Liberal government to administer the Conflict of Interest Code for ministers, parliamentary secretaries, and senior government officials was required to work with interested parties to develop a code of conduct for lobbyists. Lobbyists had a legal obligation to comply with the code. The ethics counsellor had to investigate and publicly report on breaches of the code, and could report publicly the fees, disbursements, and expenses paid to a lobbyist relating to any lobbying activity.

While this revised law was a slight improvement on the original, it remained highly defective. "By leaving vague the definitions of lobbying, and by excluding any lobbying associated with a consultative exercise, the government ... left much room for those sincerely wishing to avoid disclosing their activities or their aims to do so."[44] It did not require lobbyists to disclose positions currently or recently held in national political parties, ministers' offices, or the federal public service; it did not actually prohibit the use of contingency fees; and it did not require disclosure of the global cost of each lobbying campaign. It was not only lobbyists themselves who fought against a stronger law; it was also in the interests of bureaucrats and ministers that the lobbying activity be kept behind closed doors. Since the reports of the Lobbyists Registration Branch are not particularly revealing, it is fortunate that a private company, Advocacy Research Centre (ARC), fills the gap with a bi-weekly edition of the *Lobby Monitor*. This publication reveals the major lobbying efforts currently in progress, the techniques being used, and the people involved. The same company publishes an annual edition of *The Federal Lobbyists*, which gives a complete listing of lobbyist registrations for the year. Armed with these sources, the public can obtain a better understanding of the lobbying process, since the *Lobby Monitor* in particular is an investigative effort that reveals much more than is required under the law.

CONCLUSION

This discussion confirms the contention that pressure groups and lobbying are becoming increasingly important in the Canadian political system. The number and activity of such groups has grown over time, and however much they are an unintended appendage to the system, modern government could simply not do without them. Much has been said in academic circles in recent years of how pressure groups are displacing political parties, and a comparison of the budgets and staff of the leading parties and pressure groups only confirms the disparities in their resources. Because most lobbying takes place in the private offices of bureaucrats and politicians, parties and elections continue to be more visible to the general public. While media, opposition party reaction, academic exposure, and the ARC publications make pressure groups more noticeable all the time, the Lobbyists Registration Act needs to be further strengthened in order to keep pressure groups and lobbyists in proper perspective.

P Of the approaches outlined in Chapter 1, pluralism is most relevant to the subject of pressure groups. It argues that public policy emerges from the competiton and accommodation among organized groups. Pluralists argue that all interests in society are free to organize and participate in the group competition, as the array of pressure groups mentioned in this chapter at least partly confirms. They contend that the political system is not tightly controlled by any elite, business or otherwise; it contains much "slack," which any interest can fill by merely getting organized. Each policy field has its own specialized audience and participants, so that different groups are influential in different areas. Pluralists endorse public financial assistance to those interests that are truly lacking in organizational resources and advise issue-oriented groups to seek cheap media publicity if they do not have well-established links to the authorities or the capacity to impress them in the usual behind-the-scenes way.

SC Given the frequency and intensity with which the authorities are approached by pressure groups and other lobbyists, it would take a resolute government indeed to ignore such group reaction, as is argued by the state-centred approach. In discussing the autonomy of the state, therefore, the concept of policy communities and the close relationship between a government department and a principal client group commend themselves. As Coleman and Skogstad write, "sectoral state actors appear more able to control the policy agenda ... when they enjoy the support of well organized client interests. Close state-societal relations may augment the state's ability to proceed with its state-societal agenda."[45] The concept of policy communities, therefore, combines the pluralist and state-centred approaches. It also bears a certain resemblance to elite accommodation, which was discussed earlier in the chapter.

C Class analysts refute the pluralist claim that with a little effort any interest can organize itself into a group; doing so is beyond the capacity of many individuals and interests. Such analysts are among those most alarmed at the disparity in resources and consequent influence between affluent business groups and hard-pressed labour, farmer, consumer, aboriginal, women's, and anti-poverty groups. Many "have-not" groups depend heavily on government support for their very existence but then find it cut just when they are beginning to make themselves heard. Moreover, class analysts add, nearly half the population does not belong to any pressure group, the poorest and weakest part at that. Furthermore, businesses can lobby as individual firms, in functional pressure groups, or in peak business groups, so that they have more approaches from which to choose. The recent advent of expensive professional lobby firms, which only the corporate sector can afford, merely heightens the disparities between business and other groups.

Class analysts and others contend that the predominance of business groups is not only a matter of material resources; it also flows naturally from the marriage of a capitalist economy with a democracy and reflects the dominant ideology of the two parties that have alternated in government. Leo Panitch writes that "it is not that political and bureaucratic officials *decide* to favour capitalist interests in case after case; it is rather that it rarely even *occurs* to them that they might do other than favour such interests."[46] In the same vein, Ralph Miliband says that "it is easier for ministers to ditch their stocks and shares when appointed to public office than it is to ditch their basic sympathies and predispositions toward the business world."[47] Moreover, the state is dependent on businesses and business groups for the performance of the economy, so that the government takes seriously any promise to create jobs or any threat to contract employment.[48]

· · · · · · · · · · · · · · · · · ·

DISCUSSION QUESTIONS

1. Are you a member of any groups that at least occasionally try to influence government policy? Are you familiar with any local issue-oriented groups?

2. Why do business groups have more influence than other kinds of groups? Do they have too much?

3. How could the unorganized be helped to organize and how could weak groups be strengthened in order to offset the influence of business?

4. In what sense do pressure groups act as integrating agents in society? On balance, are they more divisive or integrative?

5. What factors led to the growth in the professional lobbying industry in Canada in recent years?

6. How could the Lobbyist Registration Act be strengthened to keep lobbying completely above-board?

7. In accounting for pressure group activity, do you find the pluralist or class analysis approach more convincing?

· · · · · · · · · · · · · · · · · ·

NOTES

1. Paul Pross, *Group Politics and Public Policy* (Toronto: Oxford University Press, 1986).
2. Ibid., p. 87.
3. Ibid., esp. ch. 11.
4. Ibid., pp. 92–93.
5. Many groups are sloppy about using an apostrophe in their name. I have tried to be faithful to their desires, even when it was grammatically incorrect!
6. William D. Coleman, *Business and Politics: A Study of Collective Action* (Montreal: McGill–Queen's University Press, 1988); Stephen Brooks and Andrew Stritch, *Business and Government in Canada* (Scarborough: Prentice-Hall Canada, 1991), ch. 7; and W.T. Stanbury, *Business–Government Relations in Canada* (Toronto: Methuen, 1986), esp. ch. 7.

7. Coleman, *Business and Politics*, p. 6.

8. Ibid., p. 45. In 1994 he counted over 600. See "One Step Ahead: Business in the Policy Process in Canada," in Mark Charlton and Paul Barker, eds. *Crosscurrents: Contemporary Political Issues*, 2nd ed. (Scarborough: Nelson Canada, 1994).

9. Grace Skogstad, *The Politics of Agricultural Policy-Making in Canada* (Toronto: University of Toronto Press, 1987); and Helen Jones Dawson, "An Interest Group: The Canadian Federation of Agriculture, *Canadian Public Administration* (June 1960), pp. 134–49; Coleman, *Business and Politics*, ch. 6.

10. Gad Horowitz, *Canadian Labour in Politics* (Toronto: University of Toronto Press, 1968); and David Kwavnick, *Organized Labour and Pressure Politics: The Canadian Labour Congress, 1956–1958* (Montreal: McGill–Queen's University Press, 1972).

11. A continuum of development suggested by Paul Pross, *Group Politics and Public Policy*, ch. 5.

12. Claude Galipeau, "Political Parties, Interest Groups, and New Social Movements," in Alain Gagnon and Brian Tanguay, eds., *Canadian Parties in Transition* (Scarborough: Nelson Canada, 1989).

13. Leslie Pal, *Interests of State: The Politics of Language, Multiculturalism, and Feminism in Canada* (Montreal: McGill–Queen's University Press, 1993).

14. Brooks and Stritch, *Business and Government in Canada*, p. 223.

15. See William Coleman and Grace Skogstad, eds., *Policy Communities and Public Policy in Canada* (Mississauga: Copp Clark Pitman, 1990), esp. chs. 1, 2, 7, 8, 9.

16. H.G. Thorburn, *Interest Groups in the Canadian Federal System* (Toronto: University of Toronto Press, 1985).

17. Malcolm Taylor, *Health Insurance and Canadian Public Policy* (Montreal: McGill–Queen's University Press, 1978).

18. M.W. Bucovetsky, "The Mining Industry and the Great Tax Reform Debate," in Paul Pross, ed., *Pressure Group Behaviour in Canadian Politics* (Toronto: McGraw-Hill Ryerson, 1975); Glyn Berry, "The Oil Lobby and the Energy Crisis," *Canadian Public Administration* (Winter 1974), pp. 600–35; and Glen Toner and Bruce Doern, "The Two Energy Crises and Canadian Oil and Gas Interest Groups," *Canadian Journal of Political Science* (September 1986), pp. 467–93.

19. Pross, *Group Politics and Public Policy*, ch. 6. Somewhat similarly, Coleman speaks of "policy networks" in *Business and Politics*, ch. 4.

20. Paul Pross, "Parliamentary Influence and the Diffusion of Power," *Canadian Journal of Political Science* (June 1985), pp. 235–66.

21. In its advice to lobbyists, Corpus Information Services, *The Government Relations Handbook* (Don Mills: Southam, 1989) suggests that contacts be made from the director level up, p. 1-1.

22. Ibid., p. 1-2.

23. Pross, *Group Politics and Public Policy*; Brooks and Stritch, *Business and Government in Canada*, ch. 7.; Coleman, *Business and Politics*; and Stanbury, *Business–Government Relations in Canada*, ch. 7.

24. Brooks and Stritch, *Business and Government in Canada*, pp. 237–38.

25. Coleman, *Business and Politics*, ch. 3.

26. Pross, "Parliamentary Influence and the Diffusion of Power."

27. Dawson, "An Interest Group: The Canadian Federation of Agriculture." John Munro, as minister of Indian Affairs, became so close to his clientele that aboriginal groups made controversial contributions to his Liberal leadership bid in 1984 that to some extent came out of government grants.

28. Robert Presthus, *Elite Accommodation in Canada* (Toronto: Macmillan, 1973).

29. Stephen McBride, "Public Policy as a Determinant of Interest Group Behaviour: The Canadian Labour Congress' Corporatist Initiative, 1976–1978," *Canadian Journal of Political Science* (September 1983), pp. 501–17.

30. Pross, "Parliamentary Influence and the Diffusion of Power."

31. Colin Campbell, *The Canadian Senate: A Lobby from Within* (Toronto: Methuen, 1983); and John McMenemy, "The Senate as an Instrument of Business and Party," in Paul Fox and Graham White, eds., *Politics: Canada*, 7th ed. (Toronto: McGraw-Hill Ryerson, 1991).

32. Brooks and Stritch, *Business and Government in Canada*, pp. 260–64; and Stanbury, *Business–Government Relations in Canada*, ch. 12.

33. Brooks and Stritch, *Business and Government in Canada*, ch. 7; Coleman, *Business and Politics*; and Stanbury, *Business–Government Relations in Canada*.

34. On the question of internal group dynamics, see R.A. Young and Shirley Forsyth, "Leaders' Communications in Public-Interest and Material-Interest Groups," *Canadian Journal of Political Science* (September 1991), pp. 525–40.

35. The Canadian Chamber of Commerce, "Action Call," 1990.

36. Malcolm Taylor, "The Role of the Medical Profession in the Formulation of Public Policy," *Canadian Journal of Economics and Political Science* (February, 1960), pp. 108–27.

37. Peter Aucoin, "Organizational Change in the Machinery of Canadian Government: From Rational Management to Brokerage Politics," *Canadian Journal of Political Science* (March 1986), pp. 3–27.

38. Brooks and Stritch, *Business and Government in Canada*, ch. 4.

39. John A. Chenier, ed., *The Federal Lobbyists 1995* (Ottawa: ARC Publications, 1995), p. 154.

40. Ian Greene, "Conflict of Interest and the Canadian Constitution: An Analysis of Conflict of Interest Rules for Canadian Cabinet Ministers," *Canadian Journal of Political Science* (June 1990), pp. 233–56.

41. John Sawatsky, *The Insiders: Government, Business, and the Lobbyists* (Toronto: McClelland and Stewart, 1987), ch. 20.

42. Brooks and Stritch, *Business and Government in Canada*, p. 240; and Sawatsky, *The Insiders*, Epilogue.

43. John Sawatsky, *The Insiders*, pp. 315–16.

44. Chenier, *The Federal Lobbyists*, p. ii.

45. Coleman and Skogstad, *Policy Communities and Public Policy in Canada*, p. 6.

46. Leo Panitch, ed., *The Canadian State: Political Economy and Political Power* (Toronto: University of Toronto Press, 1977), p. 14.

47. Ralph Miliband, *The State in Capitalist Society* (London: Quartet Books, 1973), p. 55.

48. Brooks and Stritch, *Business and Government in Canada*, ch. 1; and Coleman, *Business and Politics*, ch. 1.

....

FURTHER READING

Archibald, Clinton, and Gilles Paquet. "Lobbying in Canada." In Alain Gagnon and Brian Tanguay, eds. *Canadian Parties in Transition*. Scarborough: Nelson Canada, 1989.

Banting, Keith, ed. *The State and Economic Interests*. Toronto: University of Toronto Press, 1986.

Banting, Keith, and Richard Simeon. *And No One Cheered: Federalism, Democracy and the Constitution Act*. Toronto: Methuen, 1983.

Bon, D.L. *Lobbying: A Right? A Necessity? A Danger*. Ottawa: Conference Board of Canada, 1981.

Campbell, Colin. *The Canadian Senate: A Lobby from Within*. Toronto: Macmillan, 1978.

Chenier, John A., ed. *The Federal Lobbyists 1995*. Ottawa: ARC Publications, 1995.

Coleman, William. *Business and Politics*. Montreal: McGill–Queen's University Press, 1988.

Coleman, William, and Grace Skogstad. *Policy Communities and Public Policy in Canada*. Mississauga: Copp Clark Pitman, 1990.

Consumer and Corporate Affairs Canada. "Information on the Lobbyists Registration Act and Regulations." Ottawa: Supply and Services, 1989.

Corpus Information Services. *The Government Relations Handbook*. Don Mills: Southam, 1989.

Horowitz, Gad. *Canadian Labour in Politics*. Toronto: University of Toronto Press, 1968.

Islam, Nasir, and S.A. Ahmed. "Business Influence on Government: A Comparison of Public and Private Sector Perceptions." *Canadian Public Administration* (Spring 1984), pp. 87–102.

Kwavnick, David. *Organized Labor and Pressure Politics*. Montreal: McGill–Queen's University Press, 1972.

Laycock, David. "Representative Economic Democracy and the Problem of Policy Influence: The Case of Canadian Cooperatives." *Canadian Journal of Political Science* (December 1989), pp. 765–92.

The Lobby Monitor. Ottawa: ARC Publications, monthly.

Malvern, Paul. *Persuaders: Lobbying, Influence Peddling and Political Corruption in Canada*. Toronto: Methuen, 1985.

McBride, Stephen. "Public Policy as a Determinant of Interest Group Behaviour: The Canadian Labour Congress' Corporatist Initiative, 1976–1978." *Canadian Journal of Political Science* (September 1983), pp. 501–17.

Murray, V.V., and C.J. McMillan. "Business–Government Relations in Canada: A Conceptual Map." *Canadian Public Administration* (Winter 1983), pp. 591–609.

Pal, Leslie. *Interests of State: The Politics of Language, Multiculturalism, and Feminism in Canada*. Montreal: McGill–Queen's University Press, 1993.

Presthus, Robert. *Elite Accommodation in Canadian Politics*. Toronto: Macmillan, 1973.

Pross, Paul, ed. *Pressure Group Behaviour in Canadian Politics*. Toronto: McGraw-Hill Ryerson, 1975.

———. "Parliamentary Influence and the Diffusion of Power." *Canadian Journal of Political Science* (June 1985), pp. 235–66.

———. *Group Politics and Public Policy*. Toronto: Oxford University Press, 1986.

Sarpkaya, S. *Lobbying in Canada—Ways and Means*. Toronto: CCH, 1988.

Sawatsky, John. *The Insiders: Power, Money and Secrets in Ottawa*. Toronto: McClelland and Stewart, 1987.

Skogstad, Grace. "Interest Groups, Representation and Conflict Management in the Standing Committees of the House of Commons." *Canadian Journal of Political Science* (December 1985), pp. 739–72.

———. *The Politics of Agricultural Policy-Making in Canada*. Toronto: University of Toronto Press, 1987.

Stanbury, W.T. *Business–Government Relations in Canada*. Toronto: Methuen, 1986.

Tanguay, A.B., and A.-G. Gagnon, eds. *Canadian Parties in Transition*, 2nd ed. Scarborough: Nelson Canada, 1996.

Taylor, Malcolm. "The Role of the Medical Profession in the Formulation of Public Policy." *Canadian Journal of Economics and Political Science* (February 1960), pp. 108–27.

———. *Health Insurance and Canadian Public Policy*. Montreal: McGill-Queen's University Press, 1978.

Thorburn, H.G. *Interest Groups in the Canadian Federal System*. Toronto: University of Toronto Press, 1985.

Waterman, A.M.C. "The Catholic Bishops and Canadian Public Policy." *Canadian Public Policy* (September 1983), pp. 374–82.

PART 5

GOVERNING

Having examined the constitutional and societal contexts of the political system and the means of linking people to government, we now begin to focus on the authorities themselves or what might be termed "government." This section, therefore, examines the individual institutions of government in detail. These institutions include the executive, including the Crown, the prime minister and the cabinet; the bureaucracy; Parliament, including the House of Commons and the Senate; and the judiciary. The functions and operations of each branch of government are outlined, as are the kinds of outputs or authoritative decisions that each can make. Initially, however, Chapter 19 puts these institutions into the context of the policy-making process, which provides an overview of how they interact with each other in order to produce public policies. It also outlines the array of policy instruments from which the authorities choose.

the POLICY-MAKING PROCESS and policy instruments

To many citizens, Ottawa is one big blur; it is "the government." Some people with a little more sophistication disparage "the politicians," "the bureaucrats," or "the judges," but without much knowledge of who is really responsible for the decisions about which they are complaining. While the institutions of government interact in many and mysterious ways, it is the job of political science to distinguish one from the other and to analyze how they operate individually and collectively.

The discussion of the individual institutions of government that follows in subsequent chapters will be more meaningful if they are first put in the context of the policy-making process. This chapter provides an overview of that process, indicating in a general way how the various institutions interact with each other in the making of public policy. **Public policy** can be defined as "a course of action or inaction chosen by public authorities to address a given problem or interrelated set of problems."[1]

In Chapter 1 a model of the whole political system was presented; it included such components as demands, support, outputs, feedback, the authorities, and the environment. Now imagine focusing in more detail on the authorities part of that model. The result would be an enlargement of that part of the system directly involved in the policy-making process and would look something like the model shown in Figure 19.1. That general model is discussed in the first part of this chapter, followed by an elaboration of the concept of policy communities, which was first broached in Chapter 18. The chapter ends with an overview of policy instruments, that is, the various devices among which the authorities may choose to give effect to their decisions.

Figure 19.1   The Canadian Policy-Making Process

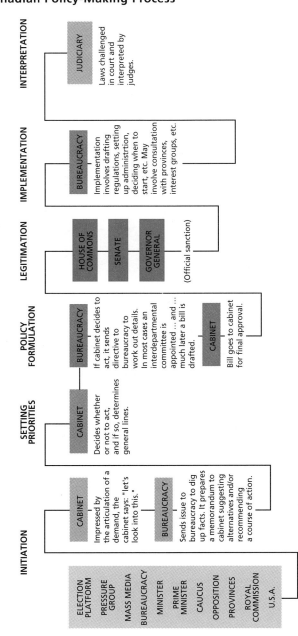

THE POLICY-MAKING PROCESS

As the model in Figure 19.1 suggests, the actual policy-making process can be divided into six phases: initiation, priority-setting, policy formulation, legitimation, implementation, and interpretation. Not all policies or decisions involve such an elaborate process including all the institutions of government; indeed, many can be made unilaterally by the prime minister, the cabinet, the bureaucracy, or the courts. But the model shows the policy-making process in its broadest form, that is, a policy that requires the passage of a new law or an amendment to an existing law and whose constitutionality is later challenged in the courts. Such a model does not necessarily imply that decision-makers within each phase function with complete rationality; they may equally well act out of expediency or habit.

Initiation

The authorities are bombarded daily with hundreds of demands. These demands emanate from many different sources: the provinces, opposition parties, the media, pressure groups, lobbyists, corporations, royal commissions, election promises, personal concerns of ministers or the prime minister, the government caucus, the bureaucracy, foreign countries (usually the United States), or other forces within the internal or external environments of the political system. The policy-making process is set in motion when the prime minister and cabinet, having been impressed with the articulation of a demand, decide to look into the matter further. On a smaller scale, a single minister may also make such a decision. It is at this point that a "demand" is sometimes said to become an "issue." An issue, therefore, is a demand that has made it onto the public agenda and that is under serious consideration by the authorities. In such a case, the cabinet ordinarily sends a directive to the bureaucracy to dig up more facts on the matter. The public service then prepares a Memorandum to Cabinet suggesting alternatives and/or recommending a course of action. Although this advice is normally confidential, such alternatives are sometimes published in "coloured papers" and made available to the public. A "green paper," for example, consists of an early consideration of an issue, with little indication of the direction of government policy.[2]

Priority-Setting

The second phase of the policy-making process involves the prime minister and cabinet again, this time in their Priority-Setting capacity. They decide which of the proposals they have previously selected for consideration are worthy of adoption. In other words, the prime minister and cabinet (or on lesser issues an individual minister) must decide whether or not to take action on the issue, and if they decide to act, they must determine the general lines of the new initiative. At this point the cabinet may choose which policy instrument will be most appropriate to achieve their objective. Here a major constraint is the cost of the proposal, since almost all such proposals face fierce competition with others for the scarce financial resources available.

Policy Formulation

The limited number of projects that have been given the green light by the cabinet in the priority-setting phase then enter the policy formulation phase. Once the cabinet has approved a proposal in principle, it usually sends another directive to the bureaucracy to work out the details. This is often a very time-consuming process that requires coordination among many federal government departments and may also involve consultation with provincial governments, interest groups, and others. Questions may be referred back to the cabinet for further direction. At this stage on major, complex policy initiatives, the cabinet sometimes issues a "white paper," which provides a clear indication of its intentions but still leaves room for public input with respect to details. Eventually a second Memorandum to Cabinet is submitted, which outlines the substance of policy.[3] If the proposal requires legislative action, the policy formulation stage culminates in a bill being drafted on the basis of the Memorandum to Cabinet. During this process, the minister will discuss the principles of the proposal with interested members of the government caucus.

Legitimation

The proposal then enters the legislative arena. The relevant minister may accept technical alterations to the bill as it proceeds through the House of Commons and the Senate, but the main intent or principle of the bill cannot be changed without being approved by the cabinet. The legislative stage is referred to as legitimizing the bill because it is put under the scrutiny of the democratically elected representatives of the people and made legitimate by their approval. The cabinet and members of Parliament contribute political expertise to the process, but given the shortage of time and limited technical expertise characteristic of the legislative branch, most such bills are passed in "skeletal" form; that is, a statute usually contains only the general principles or objectives that the authorities wish to achieve, and the act delegates authority to the relevant minister, on the advice of the bureaucracy, to issue regulations to flesh it out later in the process. The legitimation stage ends with the token approval of the governor general, which is the sign that the policy has been officially sanctioned. On occasion, public noncompliance with the law requires that a distinction be made between such formal, legal legitimation and popular legitimation.

Implementation

Royal assent is by no means the end of the policy-making process. Few laws attain any significance just by sitting on the statute books; they must be implemented in order to be made effective. Implementation almost always involves the drafting of detailed regulations by the bureaucracy, to add meat to the skeleton of the statute. Even though they have the same legal standing as if they were part of the enabling statute itself, the regulations that a law authorizes the executive to make are given only slight scrutiny by either ministers or Parliament, and thus are almost the exclusive preserve of the bureaucracy. Implementation normally requires the setting up of new administrative machinery—new staff, new agencies, new field offices, and new operational manuals among other things. It is therefore not surprising that most legislation does not automatically take effect upon royal assent; it is not "proclaimed" or made operational until the government is ready to implement it.

Interpretation

The policy-making process may well end, at least for the time being, with the implementation phase. But if new legislation is involved, its constitutionality may be challenged in the courts, especially if it appears to violate the Charter of Rights and Freedoms in any way. Thus, especially since 1982, it is appropriate to add a sixth phase to the policy-making process, that of judicial interpretation. If a statute is challenged in the courts, the judiciary must interpret the law and decide whether its provisions are contrary to the Charter or to the division of powers between federal and provincial governments.

POLICY COMMUNITIES REVISITED

Although this section of the book focuses on the operation of the authoritative policy-making institutions, it must be emphasized that they operate within a never-ending "political" environment. Indeed, if various interests know that the authorities have a problem under active consideration, they usually step up their attempts to influence the course of authoritative decision-making. It is in this context that the concept of the "policy community" should be mentioned again.[4]

While Figure 19.1 provides a framework in which to understand the policy-making process and the interaction of various government institutions in general, it must be emphasized that distinctive policy communities, participants, and processes are involved in different fields. Power is dispersed in many directions, and different politicians, bureaucrats, interest groups, and individuals participate in different sectors of public policy. The cabinet and central policy structures are at the core of the whole process regardless of subject matter, but each policy community has its own "lead government agency," normally a department or section of a department of government: Agriculture Canada for agricultural policy, Fisheries and Oceans for fisheries policy, and so on.

Each lead agency is surrounded by associated Crown corporations and regulatory agencies, such as the CBC and CRTC operating at arm's length from the Canadian Heritage department or the Canadian Wheat Board and the Farm Credit Corporation, which are linked to Agriculture Canada. Still within the "subgovernment" circle are the major pressure groups and corporations, key provincial governments, and parliamentary committees interested in respective policy fields. The wider "attentive public" consists of other pressure groups, other provincial governments, and other parliamentarians, corporations, and individuals interested in a particular policy field who are not part of the inner circle.[5]

Thus, in the initiation stage of the policy-making process, demands primarily arise from the responsible minister, lead agency officials, associated government agencies, pressure groups and corporations, interested parliamentarians, and individuals within each distinctive policy community. When a minister or the cabinet seek advice on whether or not to take action on a particular problem, they refer the problem to the lead agency in each field.

In the priority-setting phase, it may only take a single minister or sympathetic cabinet committee to make the decision to go forward. But on controversial issues or policies involving major expenditures, decisions are taken out of the specialized policy community and made subject to the critical review and/or veto of cabinet committees or the cabinet as a whole, acting on the advice of such central agencies as the Department of Finance, Treasury Board, or the Privy Council Office.

Once a policy initiative has survived the priority-setting barrier, however, the minister or cabinet refer the matter back to the lead agency to coordinate the efforts involved in policy formulation. An interdepartmental committee representing every government agency with an interest in the policy is usually appointed at this stage, and, as mentioned, if pressure groups and interested corporations are aware that a new policy is under consideration, they will do their best to get involved. Whether or not pressure groups, provincial governments, or other interested actors are formally consulted in this phase of the process, the officials in the lead agency are sure to be conscious of the views of their "attentive public" and take its past representations and anticipated reaction into account. Moreover, before the minister or cabinet give their final approval to a new policy or bill, these officials will likely have been subject to further pressure from within the policy community.

When legislation is required to implement the policy, the legitimation phase is dominated by parliamentarians with a particular interest in the subject and primarily attracts the attention of the major pressure groups, the key provincial governments, and the individuals within the general public who are part of the specialized policy community. If a bill goes to a parliamentary committee, for example, the committee is made up of interested MPs, before whom specialized bureaucrats, pressure groups, and other experts make representations.

Again at the next phase, the lead agency is primarily responsible for implementing the policy. But it often does so in close consultation with the pressure groups and provincial governments most intimately involved. They may be asked, for example, to comment on the first draft of the regulations.

Finally, if the legislation is challenged in court, the challenger is usually a corporation, pressure group, provincial government, or individual member of the "attentive public" whose views are not consistent with the final version of the policy. The government defends its legislation on the advice of the lead agency and the Department of Justice.

This discussion thus indicates that while a fairly uniform process exists for the making of Canadian public policy, regardless of subject matter, the specific individuals, corporations, groups, and lead agencies involved vary to a large extent from one policy field to another. The key players in each distinctive policy community are sometimes referred to as **stakeholders**.

POLICY INSTRUMENTS

Once the authorities decide to take action in response to a problem, they must choose the means of addressing the issue. The specific techniques or devices chosen are often called **policy instruments**. Such instruments constitute government intervention in the private sector of society and are commonly categorized according to the degree of intervention, intrusiveness, or coerciveness they represent.[6] Nicholas Baxter-Moore includes nine stages of intervention in his discussion of the subject, while other authorities present slightly different categorizations of such instruments.[7]

Privatization of Conflict

The full range of policy instruments theoretically encompasses the decision to take no action at all. It is very common for the government to decide to leave the problem to be handled entirely by the forces of the private sector. Baxter-Moore refers to such public inaction as the *privatization of conflict* and points out that it can assume two forms. The government can either completely ignore the problem or explictly decide to refer the question to some private sector authority. An example of the latter would be the self-regulation of professional bodies such as medical and legal associations.[8]

Symbolic Response

The second policy instrument is the *symbolic response*. This can take the form of a statement of government concern, consultation with those raising the problem, passive dissemination of information, appointment of a task force or royal commission, or setting up of a new government department. All of these, at least in the short run, are substitutes for any substantive government action. It is commonly held, for example, that a royal commission is appointed to take the heat off the government in connection with some problematic situation in the hope that by the time the commission's report is published, the problem will have evaporated.

Exhortation

The third degree of intervention is often called *exhortation*. This instrument goes one step further than the symbolic response because in this case the government urges the public to change its behaviour in some way. Exhortation uses persuasion in an attempt to secure voluntary compliance with government objectives without recourse to threats or rewards. "Participaction" commercials are one example, while others are pleas to restrain wage demands or to conserve the use of water or electricity (without any accompanying rate increases or regulations), or promotion of "blue box" programs or the use of condoms.

Tax Expenditures

Tax expenditures are the fourth category of policy instrument. These consist of tax credits and tax deductions that individuals or companies can claim by spending money in certain ways: contributing to political parties, making certain kinds of investments, donating to charities, and so on. Tax expenditures do not actually involve taxing or spending by government; rather, they are tax-based incentives to use individual or corporate income in particular ways.

Public Expenditures

The fifth policy instrument, one that is much more obvious, is *public expenditures*. Unlike tax expenditures, public spending involves the actual disbursement of funds acquired and controlled by the state. The size of modern government budgets is an indication of how frequently the authorities try to solve problems by spending public money. Governments provide transfer payments to individuals, such as in unemployment insurance, old age security, and social assistance programs; the federal government advances money to the provinces for health care, postsecondary education, regional economic development, and many other purposes; governments subsidize farmers, fishermen, painters, and orchestras, and give grants, loans, and loan guarantees to corporations. The "spending power" of the federal government—that is, its right to spend money for any purpose it chooses—is discussed in Chapter 4, although it should be added that governments avoid this policy instrument in this age of retrenchment.

Regulation

Government becomes more intrusive still when it chooses the instrument of *regulation*. Almost every aspect of our lives is now regulated by government, although we may not always be aware of it. Minimum wage laws; highway speed limits; restaurant and elevator inspections; gradations of eggs; building codes; consumer product safety; rent controls; pollution emissions; hunting, fishing, driver, and liquor licences; store hours; seat belts; Canadian content on radio and television; telephone rates; and bilingual labelling are examples that just scratch the surface. Government regulation interferes with individual or corporate freedom more than any instrument listed previously and is therefore more frequently criticized. But such regulations were obviously considered necessary by one government or another in order to promote some greater public purpose, such as public health, safety, or order; Canadianization; bilingualism; or protection from corporate exploitation. Many of these regulatory functions have been delegated to semi-independent regulatory agencies such as the CRTC, marketing boards, rent control tribunals, or liquor licensing boards rather than to regular government departments. Such agencies are discussed in more detail in Chapter 21. The neoconservatism of recent Canadian politics, however, has been characterized by a certain amount of deregulation.

Taxation

Taxation, the seventh type of policy instrument, is generally considered even more intrusive than regulation because, while it also has the effect of constraining behaviour, it actually takes something away from the individuals or corporations on whom it is imposed.[9] Previous chapters have provided some indication of the number and kinds of taxes levied by both federal and provincial governments. Personal and corporate income and general sales taxes are used by both levels of government, to say nothing of excise taxes; special taxes on alcohol, tobacco, amusement, and gasoline; natural resource levies; health insurance premiums; payroll taxes; and the property taxes used by municipal governments. Just as in the case of regulation, however, many people are not conscious of all the taxes they pay. Thus, the relative extent of the intrusiveness of taxation is somewhat subjective, depending on the awareness of and degree of constraint imposed by various taxes as well as on the level of consciousness and support of the public programs they are used to finance. The public became aroused over the very visible GST, for example, even though it largely replaced the invisible manufacturers' sales tax.

Public Ownership

The eighth policy instrument is **public ownership**, typically taking the form of a Crown corporation. Governments routinely regulate and tax private companies, of course, but to "nationalize" them, to take them into public ownership or to create Crown corporations, obviously represents a greater degree of government intervention. At both federal and provincial levels, the "collectivist" streak in the Canadian political culture has given rise to the existence of a large number of important state enterprises, including Canadian National, the Canadian Broadcasting Corporation, the Canada Mortgage and Housing Corporation, the Bank of Canada, the Farm Credit Corporation, Atomic Energy of Canada Ltd., the Cape Breton Development Corporation, and electric power corporations in most of the provinces. Research indicates, however, that governments usually resort to public enterprise only as a last resort, when taxation and regulation fail to meet their objectives.[10] The Mulroney government "privatized" several Crown corporations, including Air Canada, putting such organizations (back) into the private sector. Several provincial governments also privatized some of their Crown corporations in the wave of neoconservatism that swept the country in the late 1980s and 1990s.

State of Emergency

Baxter-Moore completes his catalogue of policy instruments with the **state of emergency**. In a situation of natural disasters, domestic insurrection, or external military threat, governments can usually invoke emergency powers. These powers give special coercive functions to the police and/or military to assist the government in achieving its policy objectives. The use of the War Measures Act in the First and Second World Wars is the best Canadian example.

Prime Minister Trudeau invoked the War Measures Act again in 1970 to deal with the FLQ crisis. Armed forces personnel suddenly appeared on the streets of Ottawa and Montreal, the police were given extraordinary powers, and certain civil liberties were suspended. Acknowledgment that the War Measures Act was inappropriate in these circumstances led to the creation of a less coercive Emergencies Act in 1988.

....

CONCLUSION

This discussion of the policy-making process and policy instruments is of necessity superficial. It does, however, provide a framework on which to hang the remaining chapters of the book, which deal in greater detail with the individual institutions of government, and it introduces the reader to the range of devices available to a government in order to achieve its objectives.

In terms of the approaches outlined in Chapter 1, public choice theory argues that in the initiation and priority-setting phases the cabinet will choose to look into and then act on those issues that provide benefits to marginal voters. In choosing policy instruments, the authorities will similarly be guided by the anticipated reaction of these same marginal groups.

The state-centred approach contends that the policy-making process functions without significant input from society as a whole. The initiation phase is dominated by "withinputs," that is, demands from politicians and bureaucrats themselves, and the authorities define as "issues" only those demands that are of interest to them. Most of the other phases of the policy-making process are carried out behind closed doors by bureaucrats and politicians, and when their actions are unveiled to the public in the legitimation phase, members of Parliament must toe the party line and are not allowed to respond to the demands of their constituencies. State-centred theorists also emphasize that the bureaucracy is present in more phases of the policy-making process than any other institution of government.

The class analysis model assumes that whatever the formal phases of the policy-making process, the political system ultimately responds to the demands of the bourgeoisie or corporate elite. This school of analysis emphasizes the connections between the state and corporate elites and, while discovering much evidence of such linkage, adds that "the economically powerful have not had to seek political office directly [for] their interests are usually served by those who are already there."[11]

Class analysis finds that the political, bureaucratic, and corporate elites share many characteristics and values.[12] At least until recently, the cabinet, higher public service, and pressure group leadership was made up of men who had family, corporate, educational, geographic, and/or social ties.[13]

Class analysts also have the most to say about the choice of policy instruments. They divide policy outputs between those that facilitate the *accumulation* of capital for the bourgeoisie, those that encourage the *legitimation* of the capitalist system by promoting social harmony, and those that provide for *coercion* if accumulation is seriously threatened by proletarian elements. Such analysts also distinguish between the transparency, intrusiveness, and coerciveness of various policy instruments in terms of the classes to whom they are applied.[14] The state will often disguise its activities on behalf of capital accumulation, using less visible instruments, while it will employ more obvious instruments when it seeks to legitimize its rule. The state will use less intrusive instruments against dominant-class interests (e.g., tax expenditures) and more intrusive policies against subordinate classes or groups (e.g., taxation). On the other hand, it will respond to corporate demands for government assistance with public expenditures, while it will offer only symbolic responses to working-class demands. Finally, if the state must take action against dominant-class interests, it will not attach significant coercive penalties to such instruments, but it tends "to enforce all instruments more coercively when they are targeted at labour and other subordinate groups."[15] In this instance, the small fines handed out to corporate polluters can be contrasted with the "heavier financial penalties for unions involved in unofficial strikes … and heavy police presence at sites of labour unrest."[16]

DISCUSSION QUESTIONS

1. Do all demands have an equal chance of coming to the attention of the prime minister and cabinet? Explain.

2. To what extent do the social background characteristics of cabinet ministers skew their choice of issues? To what extent are electoral considerations dominant in their choice?

3. To what extent does the bureaucracy put forward its own demands?

4. Is the proportion of new laws challenged in the courts sufficient to add the sixth "judicial interpretation" phase to the policy-making process?

5. Do you agree with the sequence of policy instruments outlined in the continuum of degree of government intrusiveness?

6. Do you agree with the class analysis view that the degree of intrusiveness and coerciveness of policy instruments varies according to the class that is subject to the intervention?

7. What other aspects of the approaches outlined in Chapter 1 are relevant to the material in this chapter?

NOTES

1. Leslie A. Pal, *Public Policy Analysis: An Introduction* (Toronto: Methuen, 1987), p. 4.
2. Kenneth Kernaghan and David Siegel, *Public Administration in Canada: A Text*, 2nd ed. (Scarborough: Nelson Canada, 1991; third edition, 1995), pp. 128–30.
3. Department of Justice, *The Federal Legislative Process in Canada* (Ottawa: Supply and Services, 1987).
4. This concept, based on Paul Pross's *Group Politics and Public Policy* (Toronto: Oxford University Press, 1986), especially ch. 6, was first discussed in this book in Ch. 18. See also William Coleman and Grace Skogstad, *Policy Communities and Public Policy in Canada* (Mississauga: Copp Clark Pitman, 1990).
5. For a discussion of the social policy community, see A.R. Dobell and S.H. Mansbridge, *The Social Policy Process in Canada* (Montreal: Institute for Research on Public Policy, 1986). Coleman and Skogstad outline this policy community as well as several others.
6. Canadian sources on this subject are included in the list of Further Readings.
7. For example, Michael Howlett and M. Ramesh, *Studying Public Policy* (Toronto: Oxford University Press, 1995), ch. 4.
8. Nicholas Baxter-Moore, "Policy Implementation and the Role of the State," in Robert Jackson et al., eds., *Contemporary Canadian Politics: Readings and Notes* (Scarborough: Prentice-Hall Canada, 1987), p. 340. This example was mentioned in Chapter 18 as one objective of professional pressure groups. Some authorities, however, prefer to put self-regulation in the regulation category.
9. There is some disagreement about these points in the literature; sometimes regulation is considered more intrusive than taxation, and at other times taxation is treated as a type of regulation.
10. Allan Tupper and Bruce Doern, *Public Corporations and Public Policy in Canada* (Montreal: Institute for Research on Public Policy, 1981).
11. Dennis Olsen, *The State Elite* (Toronto: McClelland and Stewart, 1980), p. 21; Wallace Clement, *The Canadian Corporate Elite: An Analysis of Economic Power* (Toronto: McClelland and Stewart, Carleton Library, 1975).
12. Clement, *The Canadian Corporate Elite*, p. 258; and Robert Presthus, *Elite Accommodation in Canada* (Toronto: Macmillan, 1973).
13. See, for example, John Porter, *The Vertical Mosaic* (Toronto: University of Toronto Press, 1965).
14. Baxter-Moore, "Policy Implementation and the Role of the State," pp. 346–48.
15. Ibid.
16. Ibid.

FURTHER READING

Baxter-Moore, Nicholas. "Policy Implementation and the Role of the State: A Revised Approach to the Study of Policy Instruments." In Robert Jackson et al., eds. *Contemporary Canadian Politics: Readings and Notes*. Scarborough: Prentice-Hall Canada, 1987.

Brooks, Stephen. *Public Policy in Canada: An Introduction*, 2nd ed. Toronto: McClelland and Stewart, 1993.

Department of Justice. *The Federal Legislative Process in Canada*. Ottawa: Supply and Services, 1987.

Dobell, A.R., and S.H. Mansbridge. *The Social Policy Process in Canada*. Montreal: Institute for Research on Public Policy, 1986.

Doern, Bruce, and Richard Phidd. *Canadian Public Policy: Ideas, Structure, Process*, 2nd ed. Toronto: Nelson Canada, 1992.

Kernaghan, Kenneth, and David Siegel. *Public Administration in Canada: A Text*, 3rd ed. Scarborough: Nelson Canada, 1995.

Olsen, Dennis. *The State Elite*. Toronto: McClelland and Stewart, 1980.

Pal, Leslie. *Public Policy Analysis: An Introduction*, 2nd ed. Scarborough: Nelson Canada, 1992.

Porter, John. *The Vertical Mosaic*. Toronto: University of Toronto Press, 1965.

Presthus, Robert. *Elite Accommodation in Canada*. Toronto: Macmillan, 1973.

Pross, Paul. *Group Politics and Public Policy*. Toronto: Oxford University Press, 1986.

Stanbury, W.T. *Business–Government Relations in Canada*. Toronto: Methuen, 1986.

Trebilcock, M.J., et al. *The Choice of Governing Instrument*. Ottawa: Economic Council of Canada, 1982.

Tupper, Allan, and Bruce Doern. *Public Corporations and Public Policy in Canada*. Montreal: Institute for Research on Public Policy, 1981.

Chapter 20

the executive: CROWN, PRIME MINISTER, *and cabinet*

When the Queen visits Canada, she is often mistakenly referred to as Queen of England rather than Queen of Canada. Some Canadians are very attached to the monarchy, but others cannot understand what all the fuss is about. Few events in Ottawa match the suspense and speculation of the naming of a new cabinet or a major cabinet shuffle. Almost every member of Parliament aspires to become a cabinet minister someday, and many ministers hope to become prime minister. These positions offer many perks and much prestige as well as the opportunity to influence the shape of public policy.

As seen in Chapter 19, the prime minister and cabinet are active in many phases of the Canadian policy-making process. Their decisions will sometimes be overturned by the courts and occasionally even by Parliament, and are usually based to a considerable extent on advice from the bureaucracy. But in the end, the prime minister and cabinet do make and are responsible for making the biggest political decisions in the country. This chapter begins with a discussion of the Crown, including the monarch and governor general, and then examines the political executive, the prime minister and cabinet.

THE CROWN

To classify Canada as a *constitutional monarchy* means that it is a democracy headed by a king or queen. In other words, the Queen is the Canadian *head of state*, but she reigns according to the Constitution. Canada is also said to have "dual executive"—the formal and largely symbolic executive powers are given to the Queen, but the effective executive is made up of the prime minister and cabinet.

The concept of the **Crown** revolves around the head of state and can be defined as the collectivity of executive powers exercised by or in the name of the monarch. Although the Crown is also largely irrelevant to the functions of government, as outlined in Chapter 1, rule-making, application, and adjudication are often performed in the name of the Queen or governor general. On the other hand, the Crown does perform useful functions in the Canadian political system that are largely of a symbolic and ceremonial nature.

The Crown is not only the collectivity of executive powers; it also represents the entire state and embodies what belongs to the people collectively. This can be seen in Crown corporations (state-owned corporations) or Crown lands (state-owned lands). The Crown is also central to the legal system: Crown attorneys, those who prosecute crimes on behalf of society; court cases initiated in the name of the Queen referred to as *R.* (for Regina) *v. John Doe* or court cases against the government (*Smith v. The Queen*); branches of the judiciary called the Court of Queen's Bench; and lawyers awarded the title of Queen's Counsel (Q.C.). The term "royal" is also widely used in Canada to refer to institutions that function for the advantage of all in the name of the Queen: royal commissions, which investigate problems for the general good, and the Royal Canadian Mounted Police, whose job is to capture violators of society's laws. Three important aspects of Parliament also reflect the existence of the monarchical system: Royal Assent, the Speech from the Throne, and Her Majesty's Loyal Opposition. "Loyal Opposition" demonstrates that criticism of the government has been legitimized and institutionalized in the name of the Queen.

The concept of the Crown is not widely understood by Canadians. For example, since the Queen represents the whole state and its people, oaths of allegiance to the Queen are really pledges of support for the Canadian political system, and saying or singing "God Save the Queen" really means "God help us to govern ourselves."[1] Putting the Queen's picture on stamps or coins, in classrooms or courtrooms, is not to glorify her personally, but to recognize her as a unifying symbol of the state. Similarly, in speaking of the powers of the Crown, it is best to see them as being in the possession of the Queen but exercised by the prime minister and cabinet. The monarch "holds the powers on behalf of the people," as a custodian or trustee.[2] She does not use them, but her presence keeps those who do wield them from becoming too powerful or irresponsible. It is an elegant fiction that the government of the day *advises* the Crown on the use of such powers. The Crown also "acts as the repository for the decorative and emotional functions which are inevitable in any state."[3] It is probably beneficial to divert favourable popular feelings to the harmless head of state because politicians might abuse such popularity. Another misconception is that the adoption of the Constitution Act, 1982, affected Canada's relationship with the Queen. That act allowed Canada to amend its own Constitution, but it left the Queen in place as the Canadian head of state.

The Governor General

The Queen of Canada, Elizabeth II, is also Queen of other countries, and normally resides in London, England. That means that she needs a local representative in Canada, the governor general, who may perform any of her functions and exercise any of her powers in her absence. Until 1926 the governor was a double agent: besides being the representative of the Queen, he was an agent of the British government, and as long as Canada was a British colony, the governor general exercised authority over Canada on behalf of the British cabinet. Today, the governor general is only the personal representative of the Queen and has no connection whatsoever to the British government. The Canadian prime minister actually chooses the governor general, who serves a term of approximately five years. Surprisingly, even though the Canadian government has made the selection since 1926, it continued to appoint British governors general until 1952, when Vincent Massey became the first Canadian-born person to hold the post. Since then, as indicated below, Canada has alternated anglophone and francophone appointments.

GOVERNORS GENERAL SINCE 1952

Vincent Massey	1952–59	Edward Schreyer	1979–84
Georges Vanier	1959–67	Jeanne Sauvé	1984–90
Roland Michener	1967–74	Ramon Hnatyshyn	1990–95
Jules Léger	1974–79	Romeo Leblanc	1995–

Sources of the Crown's Powers

The Queen of Canada and governor general derive their powers, all of which are exercised according to firmly established constitutional conventions, from three main sources: the Constitution Act, 1867, the Letters Patent, and the royal prerogative. Section 9 of the 1867 act declared that the "Executive Government and Authority of and over Canada is ... vested in the Queen," and section 15 made her Commander-in-Chief of Canada's military forces. Among the powers given explicitly to the Queen was the one to appoint extra senators, as was done by Brian Mulroney in 1990, although this must be done on the recommendation of the governor general. The 1867 act gave the governor general the power to appoint other senators and judges, to appoint the Speaker of the Senate, to give royal assent to legislation, and to recommend money bills to the House of Commons. In addition, it referred to the governor's power to summon and dissolve Parliament. The governor in council, meaning the cabinet operating in the name of the Crown, was given the power to appoint lieutenant governors and other officers. In fact, the act was somewhat sloppy in not carefully distinguishing between the governor general and the governor in council, which suggests that even as early as 1867 the governor was normally expected to act on the advice of the cabinet.

The Letters Patent is an obscure document that creates the office of governor general and accords it additional authority.[4] The Letters Patent confer upon the position all powers of the monarchy with respect to Canada, including the title of Commander-in-Chief and the power to appoint and remove ministers and judges, to summon, prorogue, and dissolve Parliament, and the power of pardon.

The royal prerogative or **prerogative powers** involve the residual authority of the Crown, which remains from the days when the monarch was almost absolute. These are customary, unwritten powers, although some of them, such as the right to summon and dissolve

Parliament, are mentioned in the Constitution Act, 1867, and in the Letters Patent. Being unwritten makes the prerogative powers vulnerable to parliamentary restriction. Many such powers have been taken away and given to the cabinet—such as the power to negotiate treaties, to declare war and peace, and to appoint ambassadors—and those which remain could be removed if Parliament chose to do so.

Discretionary Powers of the Crown

Despite the impressive theoretical list of powers possessed by the Queen and governor general, there is no doubt that in a democratic age almost all of them must be exercised on the advice of the government—the prime minister and cabinet—of the day. It would be totally unconstitutional, for example, for the governor to refuse to give assent to any piece of legislation. The Queen retains a minimal right to decide on certain honours herself, primarily within Britain, but the governor general was stripped of this power in the early years of this century. Canada created its own set of honours in 1967, the Order of Canada, and while such honours are presented by the governor general, they are decided by a nonpartisan committee consisting of the Chief Justice of Canada, the Clerk of the Privy Council, the Undersecretary of State, the Chair of the Canada Council, the President of the Royal Society of Canada, and the President of the Association of Universities and Colleges of Canada.

The most important prerogative power of the governor general is the appointment of the prime minister, but this must be performed on the basis of constitutional convention. In ensuring that the office of prime minister is never vacant, the governor general normally relies on the operation of political parties and elections, and does not have far to look. On two occasions in the 1890s, however, the governor had to help find a person to be prime minister. This action was necessitated by the sudden death of John A. Macdonald in 1891 and then of John Thompson in 1894, for in both cases the Conservative Party did not possess an obvious successor. Political parties are better organized today, and prefer to choose their own leader. Thus, if the position should suddenly become vacant, such as through the death of the prime minister, the cabinet and/or government caucus would usually name an acting leader pending a leadership convention.

The two most controversial acts of Canadian governors general took place in 1896 and 1926 when the men in question not only acted on their own initiative but refused the advice of the prime minister and cabinet. The first concerned the question of making government appointments. Many appointments such as senators and judges are announced by the governor general, even though they are decided by the cabinet. But the Charles Tupper government chose to retain office after it lost the 1896 election (awaiting defeat in the House of Commons), and during that interim period presented a list of several recommended appointments to the governor general which he refused to make. Lord Aberdeen felt that the newly elected Wilfrid Laurier, rather than the recently defeated Tupper, had the authority to make such appointments, and that he was actually upholding the Constitution by interceding.[5]

The second famous case of refusing government advice, the **King-Byng dispute**, had to do with the **dissolution of Parliament**. The governor general normally summons and dissolves Parliament on the advice of the prime minister, but in 1926 Lord Byng refused Mackenzie

King's request to dissolve Parliament and call an election. In this case, the governor general was primarily influenced by the fact that a motion of censure against the government regarding a scandal in the Customs Department was under debate in the House of Commons. The request for a dissolution appeared to be an attempt to curtail debate and avoid defeat in the Commons. In addition, the opposition Conservatives actually had more seats than the governing Liberals (who had been kept in power with the support of the Progressives), and an election had been held only eight months before. Thus, it seemed logical to Lord Byng to try to avoid an election when an alternative government might be available. As in 1896, the governor general felt that he was upholding the Constitution against unscrupulous behaviour by the government rather than subverting the democratic will. Most authorities agree that King's advice was inappropriate and that Byng was right in not automatically acceding to the advice.[6] On the other hand, many feel that Byng should not have refused until he had assured himself that another viable government could be found. When the Meighen government fell three days later and a dissolution was granted to King's successor, it appeared that the governor had acted in a partisan way. Byng's position was further weakened when the electorate returned King to office in the subsequent election. Although it should not be thought that the voters understood the subtleties of the situation or that they cast their ballots primarily on this issue, the impression that the election results repudiated the governor general's intervention has probably made subsequent governors more wary of using their prerogative powers.

The fourth potential prerogative power of the governor general is to dismiss a government. Constitutional convention allows a governor to do so if the government refuses to resign after an election defeat or refuses to resign or call an election after a clear vote of nonconfidence. This has never happened at the federal level in Canada, but the power was exercised as recently as 1975, amid great controversy, in Australia. Indeed, in the 1981–82 period in Canada, Governor General Edward Schreyer contemplated forcing an election (tantamount to dismissing a government) if the Trudeau government had not backed down from its threat to impose unilateral amendment of the Constitution and agreed to further negotiations with the provinces.

The great Canadian constitutional scholar, Eugene Forsey, staunchly defended Lord Byng's refusal in 1926, arguing that such intervention was valid as long as the governor general could find another government to take responsibility for his action. Indeed, Forsey found many other hypothetical situations in which he would approve of similar intervention.[7] Others find it impossible to specify the exact circumstances in which a governor general might refuse the advice of a prime minister. A third view is that in a democratic age, the governor general should leave even outrageous government behaviour to the will of the electorate.

Whether any discretionary action of the governor general is constitutional today or such action guards against unconstitutional behaviour by prime ministers and cabinets thus remains an open question. Everyone is agreed, however, that in normal circumstances governors general must act on the advice of the prime minister and cabinet. Before they invoke such emergency powers, "they must be sure they have reached the danger point, and that their actions will stand up to the subsequent judgement of other institutions and the people."[8] The governor general has been called an insurance policy against the unforeseeable,[9] or a "constitutional fire extinguisher" whose emergency powers can only be used "when normal controls cannot operate and a crisis gets out of hand."[10] Andrew Heard adds that "governors should intrude into the democratic process only to the minimum extent absolutely required for the basic functioning of Parliamentary government."[11] Since the governor general is to function as an impartial symbol of unity, any act that could remotely be interpreted as partisan must be avoided.

Other Functions of the Crown

Leaving aside these very rare occasions, the governor general primarily plays a ceremonial and symbolic role. The governor presides over the opening of Parliament, reading the government's Speech from the Throne, lays a wreath at the national war memorial on Remembrance Day, and leads Canada Day celebrations. The governor general is busy entertaining at Rideau Hall: visiting dignitaries must be wined and dined, honours and awards must be presented, and receptions of every kind must be held. Foreign diplomats present their credentials to, and take their leave of, the governor general acting as the Canadian head of state. Although extremely busy in Ottawa, the governor general is also expected to maintain a hectic travel schedule, promoting national unity, demonstrating moral leadership, encouraging good works as patron of many service organizations, and performing other ceremonial functions from coast to coast to coast. The Stanley and Grey Cups were both donated by governors general, and the Lady Byng trophy by Lord Byng's wife.

Between the drastic intervention of the emergency powers and the carefree ceremonial activities lies the traditional advisory role of the monarch: the right to be consulted, the right to encourage, and the right to warn the prime minister in the secrecy of their regular meetings.[12] Prime ministers often find it helpful to confide certain problems that cannot be discussed with anyone else, and on which the governor general might be able to offer sage advice. Due to the limited five-year term, the usefulness of the governor general to a Canadian prime minister cannot compare with the Queen's experience in advising a British prime minister in this respect, but many prime ministers have spoken warmly of these relationships.[13]

Advantages and Disadvantages of the Monarchy

The fact that the Queen of Canada is neither a resident nor even a citizen of Canada has given rise to considerable dissatisfaction with the position in some quarters and raised the question of abolishing the monarchy. The Queen's position as Canadian head of state is left over from the time Canada was a British colony. Some Canadians feel that this is inconsistent with their country's independent status and find that her British background and residence seriously detract from her ability to perform one of her main functions—to serve as a symbol of Canadian national unity—especially as far as Canadians of non-British background are concerned. Some take the view that most of the ceremonial functions of the head of state are foreign, archaic, and too expensive, while other critics argue that the monarchical system brings with it a whole set of undemocratic values and attitudes, including hierarchy, elitism, and privilege.

Supporters of the monarchy point out that the Crown played a part in allowing French-speaking Canadians to retain rights and privileges after the conquest,[14] and that the monarchy helps to legitimize the pluralism of society by attracting attention to groups and demands that might otherwise be overlooked. There are some worthy causes, the aboriginal question being one, that can benefit considerably from the impartial prestige and media power of the monarchy. It is also argued that Canada benefits from the worldwide celebrity status of the Queen and her capacity for pomp and ceremony. Most people like a little celebrity and spectacle in life, and a royal family is an appropriate group to provide it. Moreover, apart from paying the costs of a royal visit, Canada gets all the prestige of the monarchy free of charge. The monarchy also helps to distinguish Canada from the United States, and as head of the Commonwealth, the Queen provides a link between Canada and many other countries.

Supporters of the monarchy point out that the great advantage of dividing the head of state and head of government functions is to make the best use of the prime minister's time. The latter can concentrate on the serious business of governance, while the governor general or Queen tend to the ceremonial functions. It is difficult for a partisan prime minister to serve as a symbol of unity, but being above the partisan fray, it is theoretically possible for a governor general or Queen to do so.

Given the advantages and disadvantages of the monarchy, Canada has the choice of retaining the Queen as head of state or elevating the governor general to the position of a largely ceremonial president, as several other ex-British colonies have done, and as Australia is planning to do. Such a move would depart from historical tradition and cause some dislocation in renaming and reorienting all those public institutions that now bear the crown or royal label. On the other hand, as time diminishes Canada's historic ties to Britain and as immigration dilutes the proportion of the population with British connections, Canada will someday probably reconsider retaining the British royal family as its own. The Rae government in Ontario removed the Queen from the oath of allegiance for police officers in 1991, continuing earlier disengaging moves at the federal level and in Quebec. Canada could continue to be a leading member of the Commonwealth and to recognize the Queen as the head of that organization even if she were replaced by a ceremonial Canadian president.

THE PRIME MINISTER AND CABINET

The prime minister and cabinet perform the rule-making function in the political system. Within their deliberations, individual ministers also engage in a certain amount of interest articulation, and most of their decisions involve high-level interest aggregation. This section of the chapter is largely concerned with how they carry out these functions. It begins by examining the powers of the political executive in Canada and then discusses the pre-eminent position of the prime minister. The composition and operation of the cabinet, including cabinet committees, are addressed in the following sections, after which an outline of cabinet support agencies is provided along with two examples of how the political executive functions as a whole.

Powers of the Prime Minister and Cabinet

Given the importance of the prime minister and cabinet, it is ironic that they are not provided for in the written parts of the Constitution, their functions and powers resting instead on custom and convention.[15] What *is* provided for in the 1867 Constitution Act is a Privy Council to advise the governor general in the exercise of the powers of that office. As mentioned above, at other points the 1867 act refers to the governor in council, which essentially means the cabinet functioning as the Privy Council. In fact, the cabinet acts as a committee of the Privy Council, but rather than merely advising the governor general, it actually makes the decisions in question. With the rare exception of governors general intervening on their own discretion, the prime minister and cabinet exercise whatever powers are given to the Queen or the governor general in the Constitution.

Thus, after an election, the governor general calls on the leader of the party with the most members elected to the House of Commons to become prime minister and to form a government. If there is any doubt about who won the election, an incumbent prime minister has the right to remain in office until defeated in the House of Commons, but the transfer of power usually takes place within a few weeks of the election and before Parliament meets. The prime minister assumes the title "Right Honourable"[16] and selects the cabinet ministers, all of whom are sworn into the Privy Council. This allows them to use the title "Honourable" as well as the initials "P.C." (Privy Councillor, not to be confused with Progressive Conservative) behind their name. Since these are lifelong appointments and titles, members of former cabinets remain in the Privy Council, but only those in the cabinet of the day are invited to cabinet meetings, hence the concept of the cabinet as a committee of the Privy Council. From time to time other prominent people are appointed to the Privy Council as an honour, but they are not invited to cabinet meetings either. As of mid-1995, the Privy Council consisted of about 270 members, almost all of them current or former federal cabinet ministers. The title President of the Privy Council is often assumed by the prime minister, but it can also be bestowed upon another cabinet minister.

In normal circumstances, then, the prime minister and cabinet exercise the powers of the Crown. These powers include the summoning and dissolving of Parliament, the pardoning power, and the appointment of senators, judges, and other officials, including royal commissions. The prime minister and cabinet, rather than the governor general, really recommend money bills to Parliament, and all international acts and the general conduct of foreign relations are the prerogative of the cabinet, including declarations of war and peace, signing treaties, appointing ambassadors, and recognizing foreign governments. The cabinet may feel it politically advantageous to have Parliament debate declarations of war and may need to submit legislation to Parliament to make treaties effective, but unlike the system in the United States, such international acts are essentially within the purview of the executive, not the legislature.

Exercising the powers of the Crown is only a small part of the reason that the prime minister and cabinet are the centre of gravity in the Canadian political system, however. More important, they have the responsibility for providing political leadership and determining priorities for the country. That is, the prime minister and cabinet decide which problems to deal with, establish the general thrust and direction of new policies, and determine the spending priorities of the government. As noted in Chapter 19, the cabinet is bombarded by demands but chooses to look into only a few of them in the initiation phase of the policy-making process, and then gives the green light to even fewer, in the priority-setting phase. In the British and Canadian systems, the responsibility for initiating legislation rests primarily with the cabinet. As will be seen in Chapter 22, opportunities do exist for other members of Parliament to introduce bills, but most of the time of the House of Commons is set aside for government business. The Speech from the Throne provides the cabinet with an opportunity to outline its legislative program at the beginning of the session, while the Constitution requires that any bill to raise or spend money must also originate with the cabinet. The cabinet's virtual monopoly over the passage of legislation should ensure coordination among government policies, while its total monopoly over financial legislation is designed to guarantee a close relationship between policies adopted and the funds to make them effective. Such strong executive leadership, based on tradition, necessity, and the Constitution Act, has evolved over many centuries and has generally proven itself to be an effective way to run a country.

Beyond the powers of the Crown and this general leadership function, cabinet power is also derived from specific acts of Parliament. Almost every law delegates to a minister or the governor in council the power to make decisions of one kind or another. Among other things, these include the quasi-legislative power to issue regulations under a law, sometimes called delegated or subordinate legislation. The cabinet is given many quasi-judicial powers, such as hearing appeals from administrative agencies like the Canadian Radio-television and Telecommunications Commission (CRTC).

It is largely based on acts of Parliament as well that individual ministers are charged with supervising the administration of their departments. They provide direction and leadership, establish priorities, and transmit their personal, party, and cabinet perspectives, all in an effort to ensure that public servants remain accountable to democratically elected leaders and public opinion. Ministers are also given the power to flesh out the bare bones of the statute with all sorts of detailed stipulations that Parliament did not have the time or expertise to discuss. In addition, ministers are involved in Parliament, answering questions about the department's operations, defending departmental spending proposals, and piloting bills emanating from the department. The principle of ministerial responsibility—each minister being held responsible to Parliament for everything that goes on in his or her department—was once thought to entail a minister's resignation over errors of public servants, even those that the minister knew nothing about.[17] In an age of big government, however, the principle has lost most of its meaning. Ministers can still be criticized for departmental failures, and are expected to correct them, but they rarely resign except for serious personal mistakes and conflicts of interest. Much depends on the personal ethical code of the minister to do the "proper thing,"[18] and the sanction for error rests more with the prime minister (demotion or forced resignation) than with Parliament.

- Powers of the Crown
- Responsibility for political leadership and priority determination (based on tradition, necessity, and the Constitution)
- Acts of Parliament

Can a single minister possibly control several thousand public servants in the department, or do ministers merely rubber-stamp decisions already made by their officials? This is one of the key questions in all of political science, not only in Canada, and will be considered in more depth in Chapter 21. Suffice it to say at this point that a minister is entitled to bring along a small personal staff, and may be assisted by another member of parliament called a parliamentary secretary. The various executive and special assistants in the minister's office (corresponding to those in the Prime Minister's Office) are involved in offering partisan advice, writing the minister's speeches, taking care of media relations, responding to requests for information and favours from partisan supporters, keeping the minister in the public eye, and generally cultivating his or her chances for promotion. Although this entourage may help ministers impose their will on the department rather than have it function out of bureaucratic habit, deputy ministers sometimes resent the interference of what are often brash, young party hacks.[19] Jean Chrétien severely cut back on the size of ministerial offices from the excesses of the Mulroney regime.

Parliamentary secretaries have been a permanent fixture on the political scene since 1943 and have been provided for in legislation since 1959. They are members of Parliament who "assist the minister in such manner as the minister directs," which most often takes the form of making speeches on behalf of the minister, receiving deputations, sitting in for the minister in House debates, whether of government or private members' bills or on adjournment, defending the department's estimates, and maintaining liaison with other MPs.

The Prime Minister

The system of government that Canada inherited from Britain has traditionally been called **cabinet government**, but most observers argue that such a label does not do justice to the modern pre-eminence of the prime minister. Political scientists and practitioners disagree as to whether cabinet government has been completely transformed into a system of **prime ministerial government**"[20] but no one doubts that the prime minister has enormous power and should be singled out for special attention.

The prime minister has always lent his name and style to the government, such as the "Trudeau cabinet" or the "Mulroney government." Such leadership styles have varied enormously.[21] An interesting contrast has been made between the way in which Mackenzie King practised the politics of procrastination, compromise, and delegation, governing in response to public opinion, and the manner in which his less successful contemporary, Arthur Meighen, tried to lead the public by convincing it of the correctness of his principles.[22] The

St. Laurent government gained an efficient and highly bureaucratic image, the Diefenbaker cabinet reflected the dominance of a populist, somewhat unpredictable leader, and the Pearson government acquired a reputation for innovation, informality, and lack of discipline.

....

SOURCES OF THE PRIME MINISTER'S POWER

* Cabinet-maker
* Chair of cabinet meetings
* Party leader
* Chief policy-maker
* Dominates House of Commons
* Power of appointment
* Controls government organization
* Advises governor general
* Chief diplomat
* Public persuader

The pre-eminence of the prime minister over cabinet colleagues can be seen in ten of the PM's principal powers, rights, or responsibilities, some of which have always existed while others are of more recent origin. In many cases, these relate to the different arenas in which the prime minister must operate, such as cabinet, Parliament, party, media, federal–provincial relations, international diplomacy, and the economy.[23]

First, the prime minister is the cabinet-maker.[24] Prime ministers select their own ministers, subject to certain conventions discussed below, and decide what portfolios to assign them. Ministers thus owe allegiance to the prime minister, who may sometimes dictate to them the policies they must adopt. The prime minister also promotes and demotes ministers, asks for their resignation, and, if necessary, dismisses them. All of these possibilities tend to keep ministers submissive if and when there is any difference in their policy priorities. Prime ministers are usually reluctant to drop or demote ministers who have outlived their usefulness, although appointment to the Senate provides a valuable safety valve in this connection. Mackenzie King's skilled precipitation of the resignation of Defence Minister J.L. Ralston in 1944 is the classic case of a prime minister acting as a ruthless butcher.[25]

The prime minister's chairmanship of cabinet meetings is a second main source of power. To start with, the prime minister determines the agenda of such meetings. A former cabinet secretary wrote, for example, that for any reason the prime minister deems sufficient the order of business may be altered, and an agenda already settled may be set aside in favour of other subjects of greater importance and urgency. The PM may suspend meetings, summon additional meetings, dispense with or extend the normal record kept by the secretary, or modify or set aside the normal rules of procedure.[26] In addition to the usual advantages of a chairman, the prime minister benefits from the peculiar way in which cabinet decisions are arrived at. Rather than by motions and votes, the decision is reached when the PM summarizes the discussion and articulates the "consensus," which can actually come either from prime ministers extracting a consensus from the meeting or from imposing their own viewpoint. Ministers who do not agree with this interpretation either keep quiet or resign. Thomas Hockin writes that "in the process of getting the Cabinet to agree on a policy or a position, a Prime Minister may find that he must accept a collective cabinet decision at some distance from his original hopes, but in some cases if the Prime Minister can set the vocabulary, research and priorities in which the decision is to be made, Cabinet will not stray too far from his wishes."[27] Even though many decisions are now made by cabinet committees, the prime minister decides which committees will be struck, who will chair them, and who will sit on them, and which matters will be sent to them, so that this delegation of power from the full cabinet does not necessarily reduce the PM's control.

In the third place, the prime minister is the leader of the party, and the PM's pre-eminence has probably increased over the years as political parties have become more cohesive and as election campaigns have come to focus on party leaders.[28] In fact, many ministers may have been elected on the leader's coattails. Some prime ministers, like Pierre Trudeau, may ignore and neglect the party between elections, but others, like Brian Mulroney, seemed to be more clearly in personal control of the party machine. As leader, the prime minister can control party organization, personnel, strategy, and policy.[29] Moreover, unlike other ministers, some of whom may have specialized constituencies of support within the party, the PM has been chosen by the party as a whole, and can usually count on a broad base of support.

Fourth, the prime minister could be called chief policy-maker. The PM has the last word on party and government policy, whether in personal interaction with individual ministers, within the cabinet chamber, in Parliament, or in other forums such as the media. Modern government, of course, is too complex for political leaders to have an active role in formulating most policies, but the prime minister "can play a critical role in problem definition."[30] In two extreme examples, R.B. Bennett delivered a startling series of radio broadcasts in 1935 that committed his Conservative Party to a wide-ranging, radical "new deal," and Pierre Trudeau returned from a meeting with West German Chancellor Helmut Schmidt in 1975 to announce a major restraint program without even consulting his minister of Finance.[31] In any case of real or apparent policy conflict between the party organization and the government, between two ministers, or between a minister and the prime minister, the PM rules. Prime ministers are frequently asked whether an individual minister's remarks represented government policy, and Diefenbaker overruled his defence minister's "clarification" of government policy with respect to nuclear warheads in 1963.

In the fifth place, the prime minister is the central player in the House of Commons.[32] Some prime ministers have had greater control over the House and have been better performers there than others: Diefenbaker was always more comfortable in the Commons than Pearson, for example, and Meighen more than King. Even since prime ministers have delegated direction of the business of the House to a government House leader, they are still expected to be there for the oral Question Period every day, in contrast to Britain where the prime minister only appears twice a week.

A sixth source of prime ministerial pre-eminence is an enormous power of appointment. This includes the appointment of ministers, senators, Supreme Court judges, deputy ministers, and heads of a wide range of government agencies.[33] The appointment power can serve to keep those hopeful for appointment docile and supportive, as well as to impose the PM's ideological position on much of the government.

Given the extent and power of the bureaucracy today, the prime minister's control over government organization, the seventh power, is also significant. Subject to usually routine parliamentary approval, the PM can decide to create new departments and set out their mandates. Prime ministers can also reorganize government departments, such as Trudeau's amalgamation of Trade and Commerce and External Affairs to give the latter a more commercial orientation, or Mulroney's combination of Trade and Industry to bolster Canada's export potential. Today, it is more common to abolish departments or agencies that predecessors have established or to privatize Crown corporations.

In the eighth place, the prime minister personally advises the governor general on such matters as when to call the next election. This power is sometimes thought to be important in permitting prime ministers to get their own way in conflicts with ministers, government backbenchers, or the parliamentary opposition because none of these members want to risk their seats and the many benefits of public office.

Furthermore, in an era of summit diplomacy, the prime minister often overshadows the secretary of state for External Affairs on the world stage.[34] The prime minister doubled as secretary of state until 1946 and still functions as Canada's chief diplomat in annual bilateral meetings with the U.S. president, annual meetings of the Group of Seven leading industrial countries, Commonwealth conferences, meetings of the Francophonie, and occasional appearances at the United Nations.

The prime minister is also the chief "public relations officer" of the government or "public persuader."[35] Television has become the main instrument for transmitting the prime minister's message to his or her party, the government, and the public, and survival in the "battleground" of media relations "threatens to become the key determinant of prime ministerial success."[36] Trudeau and Mulroney used television to appeal to public opinion for support on such issues as wage and price controls or constitutional reform, for example. A crucial position in the Prime Minister's Office is the press secretary, who organizes the prime minister's media appearances and often speaks on the PM's behalf.[37]

In order to perform these ten varied and significant functions, the prime minister must be adequately advised. It is not surprising, therefore, that in recent years both Trudeau and Mulroney substantially enlarged their two principal sources of advice, the Prime Minister's Office (PMO) and the Privy Council Office (PCO). These two agencies will be examined in detail below.

Given all these powers as well as a deferential majority in the House of Commons, the PM can usually succeed in terms of controlling the policy and personnel of government. Richard Crossman and others trace the historical evolution of the centre of power in the British political system from monarch to Parliament, from Parliament to cabinet, from cabinet to public service, and from public service to prime minister.[38] In many respects, in fact, the Canadian prime minister is more powerful than the American president, except of course in terms of international clout. In order to get his agenda adopted, the latter must bargain with Congress, in which party discipline is not strong, whereas prime ministers can normally count on a disciplined majority to back their measures. The prime minister is probably also more elevated than first ministers in other dual executive systems because of the low profile of the Canadian head of state.[39] Indeed, the expansion of the PCO and PMO, the holding of prime ministerial news conferences, the making of televised addresses to the nation, luxurious travel arrangements, and other conspicuous trappings of power have led many observers to criticize the recent presidentialization of the office of prime minister.[40]

Others continue to emphasize the restraints on the power of the prime minister, such as financial constraints, opposition from the provinces, international influences, and the limits to which government policy of any kind can effect societal change.[41] The prime minister is often at the mercy of events, and despite trying to control them, they may cause the PM to fall in public support and in turn lose much of his or her overall influence. In 1896 Mackenzie Bowell's cabinet rebelled and forced him from office, but John Diefenbaker survived a cabinet

Reprinted with permission.

revolt in 1963 when he appealed over the heads of the cabinet to his supporters in the government caucus.[42] Generally speaking, however, prime ministers are almost as unmovable as American presidents, who have a fixed term of office and can only be removed by impeachment; opposition party leaders in Canada are much more vulnerable to attack from within their own ranks.

Out of 20 prime ministers between 1867 and 1996, eight held the position for less than two years, while 11 served at least a four-year term of office, as seen in the accompanying box. Of the 11 longest-serving PMs, eight were lawyers, seven were anglophone Protestants, three were francophone Catholics, and Brian Mulroney, a bilingual anglophone Catholic. Robert Borden came from the Atlantic region, four from Quebec, four from Ontario, and R.B. Bennett and John Diefenbaker spent their adult lives in the West. At least two (Bennett and Trudeau) were millionaires, and several others (St. Laurent, Turner, Mulroney, and King) had abundant corporate connections. Lester Pearson and Mackenzie King came from elitist academic–public service backgrounds.

PRIME MINISTERS OF CANADA, RANKED BY TENURE (YEARS)

Mackenzie King	22	Alexander Mackenzie	5
John A. Macdonald	19	Jean Chrétien	2+
Pierre Elliott Trudeau	15	John Thompson	2
Wilfrid Laurier	15	Arthur Meighen	2
Brian Mulroney	9	John Abbott	1
Robert L. Borden	9	Mackenzie Bowell	1
Louis St. Laurent	9	Joe Clark	9 mos.
John Diefenbaker	6	Kim Campbell	4 mos.
R.B. Bennett	5	John Turner	2 mos.
Lester Pearson	5	Charles Tupper	2 mos.

Composition of the Cabinet

In theory, all cabinet ministers are equal, although in practice this is far from being the case. While Pierre Trudeau periodically designated one minister as deputy prime minister, this title often seemed to carry more prestige than any real power. As deputy PM to Mulroney, however, Don Mazankowski exercised general administrative control of the government and a small deputy prime minister's office was created to support him. For a time Mazankowski also served as president of the Treasury Board and House Leader, then doubled as minister of Agriculture and, later, as minister of Finance. Mazankowski's appointment as deputy prime minister allowed Mulroney to travel, campaign, and think about the broader picture, but some observers began to wonder who was really running the country. Sheila Copps's appointment as Jean Chrétien's deputy prime minister seemed to be of much less significance; in fact, both Paul Martin and Herb Gray appeared to have more power than she did.

A forerunner to the deputy prime minister was the francophone "lieutenant" of various anglophone first ministers. Ernest Lapointe (1923–41) and Louis St. Laurent (1941–48), the Quebec lieutenants of Mackenzie King, were each given wide discretion to deal with issues from that province. Macdonald used George-Étienne Cartier in a similar role for a few years, and to some extent C.D. Howe was an anglophone lieutenant to Louis St. Laurent.[43]

Below the deputy PM are the regular departmental ministers, each normally in charge of a single department. An informal ranking of these departments may result in variations in influence among this group of ministers, with Finance, External Affairs, Justice, Trade, Treasury Board, Human Resources, and Transport usually being among the key portfolios. One rank lower than other departmental ministers were the ministers of state who were members of the cabinet from the early 1970s to the early 1990s. They were either junior ministers in charge of small agencies (e.g., Fitness and Amateur Sport), had responsibility for a particular constituency (e.g., women, youth, or seniors), or were assigned to assist a senior minister (e.g., Finance). In any case, somewhat similar to ministers without portfolio, they did not have regular departments to administer. The list is completed with the government leaders in the House of Commons and the Senate.

Since the cabinet occupies such a central position in the Canadian policy-making process, every interest in the country would like to be represented around the cabinet table.[44] This desire alone creates pressure to expand its size. In addition, until Jean Chrétien and unlike Britain, the Canadian tradition was that all ministers, even ministers of state, were included in the cabinet, so that every time a new junior minister was appointed, the cabinet grew. In general, the cabinet contained about 13 or 14 ministers before 1911, then rose to around 20 until about 1960, increased to the 30 mark under Trudeau, and to around 40 in the Mulroney period.[45] Chrétien's nine junior ministers, called secretaries of state, were part of the ministry but not invited to cabinet, which he reduced in size to 23 in 1993 and 25 in 1996. The secretaries of state each had a small staff and operating budget and received 75 percent of a cabinet minister's pay.

While the prime minister decides who will sit in the cabinet, several conventions have come to constrain the PM's prerogatives in the selection of ministers.[46] In the first place, reflecting the fact that Canada is a democracy and that the ministers represent the people, all cabinet ministers must have a seat in Parliament. Like Britain, and unlike the United States, ministers sit in the legislative branch of government at the same time as they form the executive.

A seat in Parliament would theoretically include a seat in the Senate. A number of senators sat in the early post-Confederation cabinets—indeed, senators Abbott and Bowell served briefly as prime minister in the 1890s—but the modern tradition is to include only one senator in the cabinet. This senator usually serves as government leader in that chamber and has no departmental responsibilities. The Diefenbaker cabinet functioned between 1958 and 1962 without a single senator, however, while Brian Mulroney gave Senator Lowell Murray important responsibilities as minister of Federal–Provincial Relations in the Meech Lake period.

Almost all ministers therefore have a seat in the House of Commons. It is possible for the prime minister to name someone to the cabinet who has not won election to the Commons, but convention dictates that such a person run in a by-election as soon as possible in order to obtain a seat. This sometimes happens when a PM chooses to appoint someone of unusual qualifications from outside parliamentary life, rather than a sitting backbencher, a practice that does not reflect well on the parliamentary caucus of the party and is usually resented by those who were passed over. In at least two cases such appointees lost the by-election in which they sought entry to the House and ultimately resigned from the cabinet, confirming the view that it is impossible to sit in the cabinet very long without a seat in Parliament.[47] Having been selected as Liberal leader in 1984 after an absence from politics, John Turner even served briefly as prime minister without a seat, but this was only temporarily legitimate.

A prime minister will usually feel compelled to appoint veteran MPs to the cabinet, including those who served in previous cabinets or those who ran for the party leadership. It is often thought safer to put leadership rivals into the cabinet, subject to all its constraints, than to leave them to continue their campaigns outside. As a result of this necessity, able newcomers are often overlooked. The prime minister will also be concerned with the ideological slant of the cabinet and seek either to balance various ideological factions within the party or else to ensure that a particular stream predominates.

The next constraint on the prime minister is the convention that each province be represented in the cabinet. This flows from the fact that Canada is a federation and that the Senate has never performed its intended role of representing provincial interests in Ottawa. Thus, with the occasional exception of Prince Edward Island, every province that has elected a member to the government side of the chamber has always been awarded a cabinet position. In both the Trudeau and Clark governments, the prime minister chose to appoint senators to the cabinet to represent provinces that had not elected any or enough government members (the three Western provinces in the former case and Quebec in the latter). That such a practice breaks the modern tradition of having only one senator in the cabinet attests to the importance of provincial representation. This convention usually results in some ministers being appointed only because their province needs cabinet representation, rather than on their merits, leaving worthy MPs from other locations excluded because their region is already adequately represented. Where an inner cabinet or Priorities and Planning Committee existed in the past, a similar concern occurred for provincial representation within that smaller group. Because of such representational imperatives, Brian Mulroney's Priorities and Planning Committee reached the almost unmanageable size of 24.

It is not only that residents of a province feel more secure if one of their number is in the cabinet; it is also useful for the cabinet itself to have such provincial representation.[48] In fact, ministers essentially wear two hats: they speak for their department as well as for their province. This arrangement is functional for patronage as well as policy purposes: those government appointments and contracts awarded on a partisan basis will be the responsibility of the relevant provincial minister, often called the "political minister" for that province. Two of the most famous cases of regional ministers were Allan MacEachen and Lloyd Axworthy, who succeeded in bringing public works of all kinds to eastern Nova Scotia and Winnipeg respectively.

Larger provinces are not content with a single minister, of course, and in a cabinet of 30 or 40 members, Ontario and Quebec have sometimes exceeded ten each. In such cases the ministers can be distributed so that each region within the province gains its own representative. Before 1984, however, Quebec was usually underrepresented in the cabinet when the Conservatives were in power, largely because not many PC members were elected from that province, while the West was inadequately represented in the Pearson and Trudeau cabinets.

Table 20.1 indicates the regional distribution of federal cabinet ministers when each new government took office.[49]

The next convention of Canadian cabinet-making is a recognition of the need for a balance of ethnic representatives. A proper balance of anglophone and francophone ministers—that is, about one-third francophone and two-thirds anglophone—may result almost automatically from the carefully constructed provincial representation. As indicated in Table 20.2, however, French Canadians were underrepresented even in Liberal governments before 1963, and often grossly underrepresented in Conservative cabinets. It was only in the Pearson, Trudeau, and Mulroney cabinets that francophone ministers achieved or exceeded the one-third benchmark. Those of other ethnic origins were not proportionately represented in Canadian cabinets until the Clark and Mulroney periods. Michael Starr, of Ukrainian background, was one of the first to be appointed, in 1957, but nontraditional representatives in recent years included Stanley Haidasz, Leonard Marchand, Norman Cafik, Lincoln Alexander, Don Mazankowski, Ray Hnatyshyn, Steve Paproski, Judy Erola, Charles Caccia, Otto Jelinek, and Sergio Marchi.

TABLE 20.1	Regional Distribution of Federal Cabinet Ministers at the Beginning of Each Ministry					
		Atlantic	*Quebec*	*Ontario*	*West*	*Total*
Macdonald	(1867)	4	4	5	—	13
Mackenzie	(1873)	5	3	6	—	14
Macdonald	(1878)	5	4	4	1	14
Laurier	(1896)	4	5	4	1	14
Borden	(1911)	4	5	7	2	18
Borden	(1917)	6	4	9	3	22
Meighen	(1920)	5	3	6	3	17
King	(1921)	4	6	6	3	19
Bennett	(1930)	4	5	7	3	19
King	(1935)	5	5	4	2	16
St. Laurent	(1948)	4	6	7	3	20
Diefenbaker	(1957)	8	3	6	4	21
Pearson	(1963)	4	7	11	4	26
Trudeau	(1968)	6	10	10	3	29
Clark	(1979)	5	5	11	9	30
Trudeau	(1980)	5	12	12	4	33
Turner	(1984)	5	10	12	2	29
Mulroney	(1984)	5	11	11	13	40
Chrétien	(1993)	3	5	10	5	23

Source: W.A. Matheson, The Prime Minister and the Cabinet, *updated by author.*

As for other social divisions, the religion factor was much more important in the pre-1900 period than it is today. Some early prime ministers were careful to balance representation among Protestant groups as well as between Protestants and Catholics. Ministers increasingly decline to declare a religious affiliation, however, and the Jewish community has usually claimed one or two spots since the appointment of Herb Gray in 1969. Prime ministers are now more concerned to appoint women to the cabinet. As noted in Chapter 11, the cabinet contained one woman between 1957 and 1968, between 1972 and 1976, and between 1979 and 1980; two between 1980 and 1984; three between 1976 and 1979; six out of 40 in 1984, four out of 23 in 1993, and six out of 25 in 1996. Since it was difficult to include representatives of all expectant groups in a cabinet of only 23, Chrétien tried to appease others in the appointment of his secretaries of state: three women, one minister from P.E.I., one aboriginal, and one Asian Canadian.

Matheson writes of a representative cabinet as follows:

> Adherence to the representation principle first introduced by Sir John A. Macdonald in 1867 has brought together the elites from the various subcultures and provided them with a means whereby they can work together to stabilize the Canadian political system. Thus in the Canadian context the cabinet has filled a dual role, for in addition to exercising the usual functions of executive leadership, the cabinet has provided an arena in which the elites may counter the dysfunctional and unstabilizing effects of cultural, regional, and religious fragmentation.[50]

Once the PM has chosen the people who will form the cabinet, they must be assigned portfolios, that is, departmental responsibilities. Certain traditions surround this task, too, such as that Finance usually goes to an anglophone in whom the business community has confidence; Fisheries and Oceans is normally given to someone from Atlantic Canada; and Agriculture has traditionally (but not always) gone to a Westerner. Justice was historically awarded to a Quebecker, primarily because of the dual system of law in that province, and Public Works and the Post Office were also often claimed by ministers from Quebec. It was sometimes argued that francophone ministers preferred cabinet posts that dispensed a great deal of patronage, while only anglophones were trusted with the big economic portfolios.[51] Whatever truth there might once have been in this portrait, it changed dramatically under Trudeau, as he appointed the first francophone ministers of Trade and Commerce and Finance.

It is not normally expected that ministers will be expert in the field to which they are appointed, partly because the electorate is not likely to furnish the prime minister with members of Parliament with such credentials. Indeed, an argument can be made that a semi-expert is more dangerous than a total amateur since the latter will have enough sense to listen to the real experts within the department, while the former might try to substitute his or her limited knowledge for theirs. Thus, apart from the minister of Justice's normally being a lawyer, there is no necessary relationship between ministers' training or pre-political occupation and their departmental assignment.

TABLE 20.2 Ethnic and Religious Distribution of Federal Cabinet Ministers at the Beginning of Each Ministry

		"English"	French	Protestant	Roman Catholic	Total
Macdonald	(1867)	10	3	9	4	13
Mackenzie	(1873)	11	3	10	4	14
Macdonald	(1878)	11	3	10	4	14
Laurier	(1896)	11	3	11	3	14
Borden	(1911)	15	3	14	4	18
Borden	(1917)	20	2	19	3	22
Meighen	(1920)	16	1	15	2	17
King	(1921)	14	5	12	7	19
Bennett	(1930)	16	3	14	5	19
King	(1935)	11	5	10	6	16
St. Laurent	(1948)	14	6	13	7	20
Diefenbaker	(1957)	19	2	16	4	21
Pearson	(1963)	17	9	13	12	26
Trudeau	(1968)	20	9	15	14	29
Clark	(1979)	26[1]	4	21	8	30
Trudeau	(1980)	19	14	10	21	33
Turner	(1984)	18	11	11	16	29
Mulroney	(1984)	31[1]	9	25[2]	14	40
Chrétien[3]	(1993)	18	5	11	11	23

[1]Includes 3 or 4 "other ethnics."
[2]Includes 3 or 4 who did not declare a religion.
[3]Includes 1 of Italian background under "English" and estimates of religion in several cases.

Where horizontal numbers do not total properly, omissions are usually caused by those of "other" religions.

Source: W.A. Matheson, The Prime Minister and the Cabinet, *updated by author.*

Operation of the Cabinet

CABINET SOLIDARITY, COLLECTIVE RESPONSIBILITY, AND SECRECY

The cabinet is usually considered to be a collective decision-making body. Exceptions to this notion include the prime minister's making some decisions single-handedly, and decisions taken by cabinet committees or by individual ministers. Regardless of which or how many ministers are involved in making such decisions, however, the cabinet operates on the principle of **cabinet solidarity**, which means that all ministers must publicly defend all cabinet policies or else resign. The most extreme manifestation of cabinet solidarity can be seen in terms of the annual **budget**, usually the most important government policy statement of the year. Only the Finance minister and PM know much about it until the budget is delivered in Parliament. Matheson writes:

> This procedure is unfortunate, in that it prevents the experience of the cabinet from being utilized in the preparation of the budget and makes a mockery of the idea of cabinet responsibility, since ministers must assume responsibility for something they have had little or no voice in preparing. It also illustrates the great influence of the civil servants who advise the Minister of Finance on this matter.[52]

Ministerial resignations because of policy differences are very rare in Canada, perhaps only 28 since 1867,[53] which suggests that the thought of giving up the perks of office engenders considerable flexibility in ministers' principles. Cabinet solidarity has only been suspended in the case of parliamentary debates and votes on capital punishment and abortion.

Cabinet solidarity is related to the principle of **collective responsibility** to Parliament: if the government loses the confidence of the legislature, it must resign or call an election. More will be said on this point in Chapter 22.

Cabinet solidarity and collective responsibility are also linked to a third principle, that of **cabinet secrecy** or confidentiality. Cabinet operations are shrouded in secrecy and ministers are not supposed to disclose information about its deliberations. Such confidentiality protects state secrets, protects the cabinet against opposition and media exploitation of ministerial discord, and protects senior civil servants from identification and public criticism. Cabinet secrecy is also justified as the only way in which ministers can engage in no-holds-barred discussion of crucial issues and in which public servants can render impartial advice. Cabinet documents are not normally made public for thirty years, and, as a result, we do not know as much about how the cabinet operates as about decision-making bodies that meet in public, a fact that particularly frustrates political scientists. On the other hand, clever ministers are conscious that information represents power and that a well-timed leak can sometimes benefit them when involved in a battle within cabinet. Prime Minister Pearson had much difficulty with ministers who regularly leaked confidential cabinet documents.

DEPARTMENTAL AND INSTITUTIONALIZED CABINETS

As mentioned, cabinet-level decisions can be made by the prime minister alone, by the cabinet collectively, by a cabinet committee, or by a single minister.[54] In this connection, Chapter 4 briefly referred to the distinction between a **departmental** and an **institutionalized** cabinet.[55] The former was characteristic of the Canadian cabinet before 1960 or so, perhaps especially in the Mackenzie King and St. Laurent eras, in which ministers and departments were largely autonomous. Each developed its own policies and programs with little regard for central coordination and with only minimal prime ministerial interference.[56] Strong ministers could make many decisions and policies without consulting their colleagues, and such ministers tended to remain in charge of a single department for long periods of time (e.g., Jimmy Gardiner as minister of Agriculture for 22 years) rather than being shuffled on a regular basis. Such autonomous departmental ministers often doubled as strong regional ministers, who were also allowed to handle regional responsibilities on their own.[57] In addition, senior appointed officials usually served their careers within a single department and became "carriers of the interests, traditions, skills and memories of these particularized bureaucratic organizations."[58] At the same time, however, prime ministers could make certain decisions unilaterally, and some interfered in the operations of various departments more than others. R.B. Bennett and John Diefenbaker gained a reputation for excessive interference, for example, while Louis St. Laurent was said to give too much authority to individual ministers.[59]

Despite what has been said above about the assumption of collective cabinet decision-making, the institutionalized or collegial cabinet is really a product of the period after 1960 and the enormous expansion of government activity in the past 35 years. As society and its problems became more complex, individual ministers and departments could no longer make decisions and policies in isolation. The policies of one department almost inevitably affected those of another. More consultation and coordination were called for, with the result that ministerial collegiality replaced departmental autonomy. To some extent the need for policy coordination coincided with the view that cabinet ministers should have greater control over the bureaucracy, while another stimulus was the development of techniques for more rational government decision-making. The Pearson era was transitional in this respect, and the institutionalized cabinet became fully developed in the Trudeau period. As Smiley puts it,

> Ministers became involved in the activities of departments other than their own through cabinet and ... cabinet committees. New central agencies with jurisdiction-wide responsibilities were established ... restricting departmental autonomy in the process. Super-ministries and ministries of state were developed whose major or exclusive role was the coordination of a comprehensive range of programs.[60]

Much has been written on the Trudeau approach to increasing the rationality of government policy-making, developed in consultation with his cabinet secretary, Michael Pitfield. The approach involved six main elements.[61] First, the priorities and planning committee of cabinet established the overall priorities of the government. Too often in the past, it was argued, policy-making started at the bottom instead of at the top, no one had a view of the whole picture, and policy-making had been ad hoc and incremental.

Second, the Prime Minister's Office and the Privy Council Office were expanded and strengthened so as to provide independent policy analysis to the prime minister and cabinet. The Department of Finance and the Treasury Board also became more effective central agencies, advising the cabinet on its financial decisions. When ministers presented their departmental proposals to cabinet in the past, the bureaucratic initiatives were often rubber-stamped because neither prime minister nor cabinet colleagues had the resources to challenge them. Trudeau wished to re-establish political direction to the public service.

Third, to avoid cabinet overload and to enhance specialization within it, most of the cabinet's work was done in committees. These included functional committees like that on social policy, and coordinating committees such as one on federal–provincial relations. Later, ministries of state for Social and Economic Development provided advice for the corresponding cabinet committees so that they could engage in effective policy coordination and analysis of expenditures in their respective fields.

Fourth, cabinet procedures were rigidly adhered to, including agendas, advance notice of issues, and advance circulation of background documents. In the fifth place, new techniques of policy analysis, especially at the bureaucratic levels, provided ministers with a more rational basis for their decisions. These included the Planning and Program Budgeting System, cost-benefit analysis, Management by Objectives, and policy evaluation. Finally, the attempt to go beyond traditional departmental thinking on problems led to the setting up of new ministries of state, task forces, and, occasionally, royal commissions. Public discussion of policy options was encouraged by means of publishing green papers and white papers on a subject before the cabinet had made up its mind.[62]

All of these measures tended to render cabinet decisions more coordinated, organized, disciplined, political, and rational, hence the term "institutionalized cabinet." Whatever the benefits of this approach, however, it also had negative implications. First, most ministers did not have the time or capacity to study all the background documents that were prepared for them. This often meant that departmental bureaucrats had become subordinate not to their ministers but to the new central agencies, the PCO, PMO, Treasury Board, and Department of Finance. Second, policies were often coordinated and analyzed to the point of paralysis.[63] They had to pass through so many time-consuming procedural barriers that they sometimes emerged irrelevant to the problem they were originally designed to address. Third, as was usually the case in previous governments, a small informal group of trusted ministers and intimate advisers emerged as a "supergroup" who made key decisions regardless of the authorized channels.[64] Fourth, since this decision-making model was generally replicated at the provincial level, it had particularly negative effects on federal–provincial relations, as discussed in Chapter 4.

Peter Aucoin has drawn an interesting contrast between the Trudeau and Mulroney approaches to political leadership. Trudeau's objective of "rational management" involved collegial argument such that cabinet meetings were an intellectual exercise featuring an interplay of ideas. The prime minister, as political philosopher, had his own policy goals in certain fields, but otherwise set up a system of checks and balances from which the best argument would eventually triumph. At least in his first term, Mulroney's main objectives were consensus and compromise. Unlike Trudeau, he excelled at people management, and therefore preferred to deal with ministers on a one-by-one basis rather than collectively. Mulroney continued where John Turner left off in dismantling much of the "rational" policy-making machinery, such as the ministries of state for Social and Economic Development, both of them feeling that it was too elaborate, complex, and slow. They also argued that the responsibility of individual ministers should be restored, and being distrustful of the bureaucracy, Mulroney relied excessively on the PMO and ministers' offices, and underutilized the PCO.[65]

Jean Chrétien reverted to the St. Laurent model of a departmental cabinet in which individual ministers and departments were allowed to look after their own affairs. The maze of cabinet committees was reduced, as was the scope of many other coordinating, central agencies. Departments were allowed more leeway in moving funds from one program to another as long as they did not exceed their overall allotment. Even in an era of government downsizing, however, many observers felt that the complexity of issues required greater coordination and consultation and that the 40-year-old model was no longer adequate. The Finance Department began to fill the gap, partly because the budget and the deficit were the driving forces of the day, but also because some kind of coordinating device was needed. Not everyone was satisfied that deficit reduction was a sufficient basis for policy coordination.

CABINET AND CABINET COMMITTEES

The cabinet as a whole normally meets for about three or four hours once a week. An agenda is prepared under the prime minister's supervision and circulated in advance, together with background documents and cabinet committee decisions and recommendations. The cabinet usually tackles four or five major issues and several minor matters at each session. Rather than resolving questions by a formal vote, the prime minister sums up the discussion on each item and articulates the consensus arrived at. A handful of senior officials is on hand to take note of the discussion and decisions, and then to circulate minutes afterwards. Given the demands on the time of those involved, meetings are conducted in a very businesslike manner.

Since the mid-1960s more and more of this work has been done by cabinet committees rather than by the full cabinet.[66] Each committee also normally meets once a week, and ministers are likely to be members of one or two committees. Unlike cabinet meetings as such, ministers may bring along advisers to cabinet committees, so they are less reliant on their own personal resources.

Between the Pearson and Mulroney regimes, the Priorities and Planning Committee was clearly the most important cabinet committee. Its special functions included setting priorities, allocating budgets, reviewing other committee decisions, making many important decisions itself, and supervising federal–provincial relations. Being chaired by the prime minister and containing the most important ministers (including the chairs of other cabinet committees) also added to its significance. On the other hand, Joe Clark pioneered the two-tier cabinet in Canada by explicitly naming an inner cabinet instead of Priorities and Planning. That brief period saw another major departure from the usual collective decision-making process because the full cabinet rarely met.

After Clark, Trudeau and Mulroney reverted to the Priorities and Planning Committee, along with other committees. Constant pressure to make P and P more representative had an unfortunate effect on the size and efficiency of this committee. So, with Priorities and Planning growing so large, Mulroney established a new Operations Committee of nine members that effectively became the gatekeeper for P and P. Another new committee was that on Expenditure Review, chaired by the PM himself.

Kim Campbell reduced the number of cabinet committees from 11 to five, and replaced Priorities and Planning with the Operations Committee. In 1993, Chrétien established only four cabinet committees: Economic Development Policy, Social Development Policy, Treasury Board, and the Special Committee of Council. The first, chaired by André Ouellet, had 13 members, and the second, chaired by Sheila Copps, had 11, with four ministers sitting on both. The Treasury Board was chaired by the president of the Treasury Board and the Finance minister served as vice-chair, with four other ministers also members. The Special Committee of Council, chaired by Herb Gray, was a group of six who handled routine legal matters.[67]

Cabinet Support Agencies

In addition to regular departments that advise individual ministers, the subject of Chapter 21, four main agencies exist to support the prime minister and/or the cabinet as a whole.[68] These four **central agencies**, already mentioned in passing, are the Prime Minister's Office, the Privy Council Office, the Finance Department, and the Treasury Board.

THE PRIME MINISTER'S OFFICE

The **Prime Minister's Office**, which was considerably expanded by both Trudeau and Mulroney, deals with such matters as the prime minister's correspondence, media relations, partisan appointments, public appearances, and speeches, and briefs the PM on legislative proceedings.[69] It monitors political developments and offers policy advice from a partisan point of view. Under Trudeau the PMO was headed by a series of principal secretaries, one of whom, Jim Coutts, delighted in engaging in "the politics of manipulation."[70] When Brian Mulroney first came to office, he put all his closest advisers into the PMO and expanded its influence even beyond the level it enjoyed under Trudeau. However, after a series of political mistakes and the government's sharp decline in the polls, most of these original advisers were let go and a new chief of staff brought order to the operation. Ironically, Mulroney seconded a career public servant, Derek Burney, rather than a partisan friend to transform this partisan office. After the 1988 election, the PMO was less influential, as Stanley Hartt and Norman Spector passed through the office of chief of staff until it was filled by the popular partisan, Hugh Segal.

Jean Chrétien's PMO of about 68 bodies was headed by chief of staff Jean Pelletier. Its other principal officials were Eddie Goldenberg, senior policy adviser; Chaviva Hosek, policy and research director; Peter Donolo, director of communications; and Jean Carle, director of operations. The PM usually meets daily with the head of the PMO to be briefed on developments from a partisan perspective.

THE PRIVY COUNCIL OFFICE

The **Privy Council Office** has served several unique purposes since it was recognized as the cabinet secretariat and since cabinet meetings became more businesslike in 1940 due to the pressures of war.[71] First, it provides logistical support for the cabinet—preparing agendas, organizing meetings, writing and distributing background material ("briefing notes"), taking and circulating minutes, and communicating cabinet decisions. In these ways the PCO is engaged in the coordination of overall government policy. It also performs the same services for cabinet committees; in fact, a branch of the PCO serves as a secretariat for each cabinet committee (except for Treasury Board, which is supported by the Treasury Board Secretariat). Other sections of the Privy Council Office have responsibility for the machinery of government and the appointment of senior public-service personnel, and in 1993 the Federal–Provincial

Relations Office was reintegrated with the PCO. The head of the PCO is called the **Secretary to the Cabinet and Clerk of the Privy Council** and is regarded as the government's highest-ranking public servant. The Clerk meets daily with the prime minister to review problems and render nonpartisan advice. Trudeau's original intention in expanding the Privy Council Office was to establish a source of policy advice for himself as prime minister, independent of regular departments, with which he could counter regular bureaucratic recommendations. While the Secretary to the Cabinet, the secretaries of cabinet committees, and other officials in the PCO still frequently advise on policy issues, this aspect of their work is probably not as prominent as it once was. The PCO grew from ten officer positions in 1945, to 68 in 1971, to 125 in 1975, to about 290 in 1991, with another 200 people providing administrative support.

The PCO under Jean Chrétien was headed by Jocelyne Bourgon, the first woman to occupy this prestigious post. She had deputies in charge of Operations, Plans and Consultation, Government Renewal, Intergovernmental Affairs, and Security and Intelligence, and among the assistant secretaries were those in charge of Priorities and Planning, Aboriginal Affairs, Policy Development and Constitutional Affairs, Foreign and Defence Policy, Economic and Regional Development Policy, Social Development, Machinery of Government, Unity Operations, Senior Personnel Management, and Legislation and House Planning. Such officials brief cabinet committee chairs and the prime minister even on the strategy of conducting their meetings, all of which helps the PCO obtain the kind of decisions it considers best. Another example of its influence is in its detailed strategy notes for the prime minister when meeting important people or making critical telephone calls.

THE FINANCE DEPARTMENT

The **Department of Finance** and the Treasury Board primarily supply financial information to the cabinet, and have historically exercised a cautioning, restraining influence on new program proposals. The role of the Finance Department is to look at the government's overall revenue and expenditure situation, including its accumulated debt and annual deficit, and to advise on allocations among departments. Under the powerful deputy minister, it is also the chief adviser on taxation policy and on transfer payments to the provinces. While reporting directly to the minister of Finance and in that sense an ordinary department of government, Finance has a special responsibility of advising the cabinet collectively on such matters, being incorporated into the process of developing memoranda to cabinet, as well as preparing the budget. In an age of government restraint and retrenchment, the influence of Finance necessarily increases, and in the Chrétien regime, that department was really determining the government's agenda. When Finance said that there was no more money available, for example, Red Book promises were ignored. To some extent it was the minister of Finance talking, but in large measure he was repeating what his senior officials told him to say.

THE TREASURY BOARD

The **Treasury Board** is a committee of cabinet chaired by the minister called President of the Treasury Board, who is in turn in charge of a full-fledged government department, the **Treasury**

Board Secretariat. This secretariat, under the Secretary of the Treasury Board and Comptroller General, has the overall responsibility for controlling regular departmental spending, being involved in the detailed development of departmental budgets, the Estimates (the government's spending proposal), and overseeing the actual expenditure of funds. The Treasury Board is also in charge of labour relations in the public service and issues policies on personnel, administration, and finance. In particular, Treasury Board approval is required for the hiring of any new personnel. Although its perspective is more detailed than that of Finance, the two agencies usually see things in a similar light, and Treasury Board's influence also increases when a government is obsessed with its deficit.

The Memorandum to Cabinet and Expenditure Management System

The two most significant decisions taken by the cabinet are the adoption of new policies and the design of the annual budget. These two aspects of the decision-making system can be profitably examined in order to witness the interaction of all the elements previously discussed, namely prime minister, cabinet, cabinet committees, minister, departments, and central agencies.

THE MEMORANDUM TO CABINET

A **Memorandum to Cabinet** (MC) is "the key instrument of written policy advice to Cabinet and, as the tool an individual Minister uses to obtain the support of Cabinet colleagues for a proposed course of action, it plays a pivotal role in the Cabinet decision-making process."[72] The MC starts in an individual department, which develops a policy proposal in consultation with other departments and agencies likely to have an interest, as well as with the PCO, Treasury Board Secretariat, and Finance. Once signed by a minister, the MC is sent to the PCO where it is printed, distributed, and placed on the agenda of the relevant cabinet committee. It is the prime minister's prerogative to determine to which committee each MC is referred. The PCO secretariat prepares briefing notes for the committee chair that outline the gist of the issue, include Treasury Board and Finance Department comments, and offer suggestions as to how the chair might best conduct the meeting.

In the committee, the sponsoring minister may make an oral presentation, occasionally involving audio-visual aids such as flip-charts and overheads. The cabinet committee's report on the MC is called a Committee Report (CR) and is referred either to the full cabinet for ratification or back to the sponsoring minister to be reworked. If the committee was unanimous, the CR is usually just appendixed to the agenda of the full cabinet, and when ratified, an RD (Record of Decision) is issued and referred to the relevant department for action. If a full-scale cabinet discussion is required, the PCO and PMO prepare briefings for the prime minister, which include advice on how best to approach the discussion in the meeting, such as where various ministers stand on the issue. Audio-visual presentations are occasionally used for the full cabinet as well.

Each Memorandum to Cabinet contains a Ministerial Recommendation and an Analysis. The former includes a one-sentence summation of the issue and the decision that the sponsoring minister seeks. If it involves the expenditure of funds or bureaucratic resources, it must contain information about costs, sources of funds, and person-years of work. For this reason, departments are advised to establish contact with both Finance and Treasury Board early in the drafting process and maintain contact with them throughout. The next section is the rationale, which may mention the key groups or interests affected. The problems and strategies section notes the positive or negative impacts on a province, region, or other sector of society. The section on political considerations describes consultations with caucus, past party commitments, etc., while the section on departmental positions outlines the positions taken by concerned departments, for or against. The analysis section has three parts: background, considerations, and options. It is supposed to provide ministers with an outline of the full range of realistic options, the advantages and disadvantages of each, and their financial and policy implications.

Each MC is accompanied by a Communications Plan that explains how the minister intends to present and explain a decision to the public. It normally assesses attention given to the issue in the House of Commons, in the media, in public opinion polls, and by lobbyists. It identifies the groups with an interest in the proposal, and explains how the department will deal with each one. In particular, it outlines the announcement-day media strategy, as well as follow-up activities to reinforce the message, including speaking tours.

THE EXPENDITURE MANAGEMENT SYSTEM

The government was not without a formalized system for determining its financial priorities and the distribution of funds long before 1979, but many observers considered it inadequate. New policies had been developed without much concern for their financial implications, and departmental budgeting had started from the bottom up. Thus it fell to Prime Minister Joe Clark to implement a more institutionalized procedure, the Program and Expenditure Management System (PEMS) or "Envelope System," designed by cabinet secretary Michael Pitfield. PEMS was heralded at the time for ensuring an integration of policy-making and financial planning because most cabinet committees would combine policy and expenditure decisions. The budgetary process would also start at the top, based on overall government priorities. Government operations were divided among ten (later eight) policy sectors, or "envelopes," and the Inner Cabinet, on the advice of Treasury Board, the Department of Finance, and the Privy Council Office, allocated a global amount of funding to each envelope. Then each relevant cabinet committee divided up this amount among the departments associated with that committee.[73] Although the new system seemed more logical, and was therefore retained by Pierre Trudeau after 1980, it was later left to disintegrate under Mulroney, divorcing the policy and expenditure functions of most cabinet committees. Instead, the Operations Committee and Treasury Board continued to make spending allocations (and the Expenditure Review Committee to reduce them), but the other cabinet committees dealt only with policy, not money. "PEMS" was replaced by "Ops and Chops."[74]

The new Liberal government reformed the expenditure management system once again, largely because of its commitment to reducing the deficit. The annual cycle of the new system, providing for input from departments, TBS, Commons committees, cabinet committees, ministers, PCO, the Finance Department, the minister of Finance, and the prime minister, is best observed in Figure 20.1.[75]

Figure 20.1 The Expenditure Management System

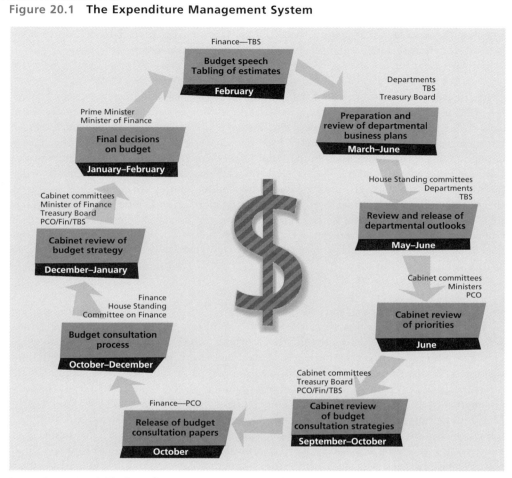

Source: Treasury Board, The Expenditure Management System of the Government of Canada, *1995, cat. no. BT22-37/ 1995. Reproduced with permission of the Minister of Supply and Services Canada, 1995.*

CONCLUSION

While it is increasingly anomalous for Canada to share its head of state with others, every country needs symbols of unity and colourful ceremonies. In this connection there are advantages in having a head of state separate from the head of government. In addition, the Crown helps to "keep the government honest." The governor general can intervene in rare emergency situations to ensure that the government of the day does not abuse its power. On a daily basis, however, few doubt that the political executive is the most significant part of the policy-making process. Individuals want to be appointed to the cabinet, and societal interests want to feel represented there. Given its importance, the composition of the cabinet and the manner in which it makes decisions are of great interest to political science. This chapter has shown how the composition of the cabinet and its decision-making process have changed over time.

(SC) Given the obvious power of the prime minister and cabinet, the state-centred theory has much to say about the political executive. Most prime ministers, even Mackenzie King, had *some* personal conception of the public interest that they sought to pursue, but some were more courageous than others about imposing their own agenda in the absence of public support. In promoting their personal ideas, the prime minister and cabinet must, of course, rely on advice from the bureaucracy. In fact, they often do little more than prioritize problems and then charge the public service with finding solutions to them. Trudeau's objective of rendering the whole decision-making process more rational reflected a dirigiste mentality—government directing society rather than responding to it. On the other hand, in emphasizing privatization, deregulation, and deficit reduction, Mulroney determined that government should not direct society to the same extent, ironically attempting to lead society to be less reliant on the state.

(C) Class analysts claim that the prime minister and cabinet either come from or respond to the whims of the bourgeoisie. Most cabinet ministers have been lawyers or business-people and are largely from the petite bourgeoisie or upper middle class rather than the corporate elite. Nevertheless, the big-business connections of cabinet ministers are quite striking.[76] At the time of Confederation, for example, many ministers were simultaneously directors of railway companies. Later examples of ministers who kept one foot in the business community were Sir Charles Tupper, Lomer Gouin, C.H. Cahan, C.D. Howe, and J.J. McCann. During the Borden period ministers were required to divorce themselves from their former business connections, but under King and St. Laurent some ministers maintained such relationships. It is only since about 1960 that ministers have been required to resign directorships and sever active business connections under various versions of conflict-of-interest guidelines. Most have done so, including former businessmen Walter Gordon, J.R. Nicholson, Robert Winters, C.M. Drury, Mitchell Sharp, Eric Kierans, James Richardson, John Crosbie, Michael Wilson, and Paul Martin, but Sinclair Stevens was forced to resign from the Mulroney cabinet for not having separated his private and personal affairs.

Class analysts maintain that even if ministers are required to resign corporate positions and to put their investments into some kind of trust, their previous corporate connections will never be far from their mind. Moreover, ministers will be contemplating their post-political existence. Significant numbers of ex-ministers have been appointed to corporate boards while others assumed active executive positions in the business or lobbying communities, including C.A. Dunning, Brooke Claxton, Walter Harris, Donald Fleming, William Hamilton, Walter Gordon, Robert Winters, Maurice Sauvé, Otto Lang, Barney Danson, Doug Frith, Judy Erola, and Brian Mulroney. Such evidence of the close connection between cabinet members and the business community bolsters the class analysis critique, especially when only two prominent labour leaders, Humphrey Mitchell and Jean Marchand, have ever been named to the cabinet. Class analysts such as John Porter found considerable intermarriage and other family connections among the political, bureaucratic, corporate, and intellectual elites.[77]

P Pluralists can hardly argue against the elitist nature of the cabinet, but they emphasize the conventions of provincial and regional representation therein and point out that the cabinet is becoming more diverse in social background over time. Even one of his critics acknowledged that of all political leaders of his generation, Mackenzie King alone really understood that "the essential task of Canadian statesmanship is to discover the terms on which as many as possible of the significant interest groups of our country can be induced to work together in a common policy."[78]

PC Mackenzie King was also perhaps the ultimate practitioner of "public choice" politics. He carefully calculated the electoral consequences of every decision, took whatever decisions were necessary to retain power, and felt that political security usually lay in inaction rather than action.[79] Much evidence of public choice can also be found in the records of other prime ministers and cabinets, even those of Trudeau and Mulroney, who claimed to be unconcerned with the electoral consequences of their policies. Consistent with the public choice approach, every cabinet document from both regimes contained a "communications strategy which spells out in considerable detail how policies should be sold."[80]

DISCUSSION QUESTIONS

1. Was Lord Byng justified in 1926 in refusing to grant Prime Minister Mackenzie King a dissolution of Parliament?

2. Do the monarchy and governor general perform a useful function in a democracy?

3. What would be the advantages and disadvantages of no longer recognizing the Queen as our head of state?

4. Do the prime minister and cabinet, backed up by a majority in the House of Commons, have too much power in the Canadian system of government?

5. Do you think "cabinet government" or "prime ministerial government" is a more accurate label for the Canadian system?

6. Is the prime ministership becoming increasingly presidentialized? In the absence of the American system of checks and balances between president and Congress, what constraints must the prime minister live with?

7. Should cabinet solidarity be relaxed? Should ministers have to defend a budget they had so little part in drafting?

8. Is a departmental or institutionalized cabinet more appropriate?

9. What were the advantages and disadvantages of the Trudeau effort to make cabinet decision-making more rational?

10. How do the approaches outlined in Chapter 1 apply to the material in this chapter?

· · · · · · · · · · · · · · · · ·

NOTES

1. Frank McKinnon, *The Crown in Canada* (Calgary: McClelland and Stewart West, 1976), p. 13.
2. Ibid., p. 15.
3. Ibid., p. 47. See also David E. Smith, *The Invisible Crown* (Toronto: University of Toronto Press, 1995).
4. For the new Letters Patent of 1947, see the *Canada Gazette*, Part I, October 11, 1947, pp. 3014–16. See also Andrew Heard, *Canadian Constitutional Conventions* (Toronto: Oxford University Press, 1991), p. 16.
5. J.T. Saywell, "The Crown and the Politicians: The Canadian Succession Question, 1891–1896," *Canadian Historical Review* (December 1956), pp. 309–37.
6. See, for example, MacKinnon, *The Crown in Canada*, pp. 127–132, and J.R. Mallory, *The Structure of Canadian Government*, rev. ed. (Toronto: Gage, 1984), pp. 51–57.
7. Forsey wrote widely on these subjects, but his famous defence of Lord Byng is contained in *The Royal Power of Dissolution of Parliament in the British Commonwealth* (Toronto: Oxford University Press, 1943; reprinted 1968). See such other articles as "Appointment of Extra Senators under Section 26 of the British North America Act," *Canadian Journal of Economics and Political Science* (May 1946), pp. 159–67; and "Mr. King and Parliamentary Government," *Canadian Journal of Economics and Political Science* (November 1951), pp. 451–67.
8. MacKinnon, *The Crown in Canada*, p. 124.
9. Heard, *Canadian Constitutional Conventions*, p. 47.
10. Ibid., p. 123.
11. Ibid., p. 47.
12. Walter Bagehot, *The English Constitution* (London: Collins, 1963), first published in 1867.
13. See, for example, MacKinnon, *The Crown in Canada*, pp. 56, 101, 103, and Vincent Massey, *What's Past Is Prologue* (Toronto: Macmillan, 1963).
14. W.L. Morton, *The Canadian Identity* (Toronto: University of Toronto Press, 1961).
15. Andrew Heard, *Canadian Constitutional Conventions* (Toronto: Oxford University Press, 1991), ch. 3.
16. This title was originally based on appointment to the British Privy Council, but Lester Pearson created "Right Honourable" as a Canadian title, which is bestowed upon the prime minister, governor general, and chief justice of the Supreme Court.
17. Kenneth Kernaghan and David Siegel, *Public Administration in Canada: A Text*, 2nd ed. (Scarborough: Nelson Canada, 1991), pp. 379–85.
18. Heard, *Canadian Constitutional Conventions*, pp. 52–56.
19. Blair Williams, "The Para-Political Bureaucracy in Ottawa," in Harold D. Clarke et al., eds., *Parliament, Policy and Representation* (Toronto: Methuen, 1980); Gerald Lenoski, "Ministers' Staffs and Leadership Politics," in Thomas A. Hockin, ed., *Apex of Power*, 2nd ed. (Scarborough: Prentice-Hall Canada, 1977); and Kernaghan and Siegel, *Public Administration in Canada*, pp. 370–72.
20. The concept was first popularized by Richard Crossman in Britain in his Introduction to Walter Bagehot, *The English Constitution* (London: Collins, 1963) and elaborated in *The Myths of Cabinet Government* (Cambridge, MA: Harvard University Press, 1972). See also Patrick Weller, *First among Equals: Prime Ministers in Westminster Systems* (London: Allen & Unwin, 1985).
21. Prime ministerial biographies are very useful on this point. See also Leslie Pal and David Taras, eds., *Prime Ministers and Premiers: Political Leadership and Public Policy in Canada* (Scarborough: Prentice-Hall Canada, 1988).

22. R.M. Dawson, *William Lyon Mackenzie King* (Toronto: University of Toronto Press, 1958), pp. 415–19, reprinted in Hockin, *Apex of Power*. For a synopsis of all prime ministers' styles, see W.A. Matheson, *The Prime Minister and the Cabinet* (Toronto: Methuen, 1976), chs. VI, VII, and VIII.

23. Pal and Taras, *Prime Ministers and Premiers*; and Peter Aucoin, "Prime Ministerial Leadership: Position, Power, and Politics," in Maureen Mancuso et al., *Leaders and Leadership in Canada* (Toronto: Oxford University Press, 1994).

24. On this subject, see Matheson, *The Prime Minister and the Cabinet*, ch. III, and R.M. Punnett, *The Prime Minister in Canadian Government and Politics* (Toronto: Macmillan, 1977), ch. 4.

25. R.M. Dawson, *The Conscription Crisis of 1944* (Toronto: University of Toronto Press, 1961). Other examples include Trudeau's dismissal of six ministers in 1974.

26. A.D.P. Heeney, "Cabinet Government in Canada: Developments in the Machinery of the Central Executive," *Canadian Journal of Economics and Political Science* (August 1946), pp. 282–301.

27. Hockin, *Apex of Power*, p. 14.

28. Leslie Pal, "Prime Ministers and Their Parties: The Cauldron of Leadership," in Pal and Taras, *Prime Ministers and Premiers*.

29. Matheson, *The Prime Minister and the Cabinet*, pp. 127–28.

30. Leslie Pal, "Hands at the Helm? Leadership and Public Policy," in Pal and Taras, *Prime Ministers and Premiers*, p. 25.

31. On this famous incident, see Christina McCall-Newman, *Grits* (Toronto: Macmillan, 1982), pp. 236–37; Richard Gwyn, *The Northern Magus* (Toronto: McClelland and Stewart, 1980), pp. 325–27; and Patrick Gossage, *Close to the Charisma* (Toronto: McClelland and Stewart, 1986), pp. 145–46.

32. On this role, see Punnett, *The Prime Minister in Canadian Government and Politics*, ch. 6, and Matheson, *The Prime Minister and the Cabinet*, ch. IX.

33. In this connection, a 1935 minute of the Privy Council is often cited. It can be found in A.D.P. Heeney, "Cabinet Government in Canada," and in Hockin, *Apex of Power*, pp. 29–30.

34. Kim Richard Nossal, "Political Leadership and Foreign Policy: Trudeau and Mulroney," in Pal and Taras, *Prime Ministers and Premiers*.

35. Frederick Fletcher, "The Prime Minister as Public Persuader," in Hockin, *Apex of Power*. See also Punnett, *The Prime Minister in Canadian Government and Politics*, p. 22.

36. David Taras, "Prime Ministers and the Media," in Pal and Taras, *Prime Ministers and Premiers*.

37. Gossage, *Close to the Charisma*; and Michel Gratton, *So, What Are the Boys Saying?* (Toronto: McGraw-Hill Ryerson, 1987).

38. See also Fred Schindeler, "The Prime Minister and the Cabinet: History and Development," in Hockin, *Apex of Power*, p. 22.

39. Punnett, *The Prime Minister in Canadian Government and Politics*, p. 51.

40. Denis Smith, "President and Parliament: The Transformation of Parliamentary Government in Canada," in Hockin, *Apex of Power*, p. 315.

41. For example, Hockin, "The Prime Minister and Political Leadership: An Introduction to Some Restraints and Imperatives," in *Apex of Power*. See also Punnett, p. 157, Matheson, pp. 170–76, and Pal and Taras, pp. 102–3.

42. Peter C. Newman, *Renegade in Power* (Toronto: McClelland and Stewart, 1963).

43. F.W. Gibson, *Cabinet Formation and Bicultural Relations* (Ottawa: Queen's Printer, 1970), ch. VIII; John English, "The 'French Lieutenant' in Ottawa," in R.K. Carty and W.P. Ward, eds., *National Politics and Community in Canada* (Vancouver: University of British Columbia Press, 1986); and Matheson, pp. 34–38.

44. Matheson, *The Prime Minister and the Cabinet*, chs. II and V.

45. Ibid., p. 32. The most convenient source of the current cabinet is the Wednesday edition of the House of Commons Debates, to which a list of the ministry is attached.

46. Heard, *Canadian Constitutional Conventions*.

47. General A.G.L. McNaughton served for over nine months as minister of Defence in 1944–45, suffering a by-election loss and a general election loss before finally resigning from the cabinet. Pierre Juneau resigned as secretary of state when he failed to win a by-election in 1975.

48. Herman Bakvis, *Regional Ministers* (Toronto: University of Toronto Press, 1991). Bakvis has other interesting things to say about ministerial quality in "Cabinet Ministers: Leaders or Followers" in Maureen Mancuso et al., eds., *Leaders and Leadership in Canada* (Toronto: Oxford University Press, 1994).

49. This table does not include all ministers because cabinets were shuffled after being formed. Nevertheless, it provides just as accurate a presentation of provincial representation as including all ministers, because the latter figures are skewed due to varied lengths of ministerial service.

50. Matheson, *The Prime Minister and the Cabinet*, pp. ix, 22–23.

51. On this subject, see the seven case studies in the study of the Royal Commission on Bilingualism and Biculturalism edited by Frederick W. Gibson, *Cabinet Formation and Bicultural Relations*. Gibson argues that francophones had no monopoly on the desire for patronage, p. 172.

52. Matheson, *The Prime Minister and the Cabinet*, pp. 90–91.

53. S.L. Sutherland, "Responsible Government and Ministerial Responsibility: Every Reform Is Its Own Problem," *Canadian Journal of Political Science* (March 1991), p. 101.

54. Punnett, *The Prime Minister in Canadian Government and Politics*, p. 86.

55. J. Stefan Dupré, "Reflections on the Workability of Executive Federalism," in Richard Simeon, ed., *Intergovernmental Relations* (Toronto: University of Toronto Press, 1985).

56. Pickersgill, *The Mackenzie King Record*, Vol. I, p. 7.

57. Bakvis, *Regional Ministers*.

58. Donald Smiley, *The Federal Condition in Canada* (Toronto: McGraw-Hill Ryerson, 1987), p. 88.

59. Matheson, *The Prime Minister and the Cabinet*, p. 178.

60. Smiley, *The Federal Condition in Canada*, p. 88.

61. This vast literature includes the following: Bruce Doern and Peter Aucoin, eds., *The Structures of Policy-Making in Canada* (Toronto: Macmillan, 1971) and *Public Policy in Canada* (Toronto: Macmillan, 1979); Colin Campbell and George Szablowski, *The Superbureaucrats* (Toronto: Macmillan, 1979); several articles in Hockin's *Apex of Power*; Peter Aucoin, "Organizational Change in the Machinery of Canadian Government: From Rational Management to Brokerage Politics," *Canadian Journal of Political Science* (March 1986), pp. 3–27; and Richard French, *How Ottawa Decides*, 2nd ed. (Toronto: Lorimer, 1984). The classic account of Pierre Trudeau as prime minister is undoubtedly the two-volume *Trudeau and Our Times* by Stephen Clarkson and Christina McCall (Toronto: McClelland and Stewart, 1990 and 1994).

62. Doern and Aucoin, *The Structures of Policy-Making in Canada*.

63. Peter Aucoin, "Organizational Change in the Machinery of Canadian Government."

64. Punnett, *The Prime Minister*, p. 110; Walter Stewart, *Shrug: Trudeau in Power* (Toronto: New Press, 1971), ch. 11. Stewart identified the group in 1971 as Marc Lalonde, Jean Marchand, Gérard Pelletier, and Gordon Robertson, but before long it became Lalonde, Michael Pitfield, Allan MacEachen, and Jim Coutts.

65. Aucoin, "Organizational Change in the Machinery of Canadian Government."

66. Earlier cabinet committees were primarily used in the First and Second World Wars. See descriptions in Punnett, pp. 72–74 and Matheson, pp. 83–87.

67. On the Campbell and Chrétien changes, see *The New Face of Government: A Guide to the New Federal Government Structure* (Ottawa: Canada Communication Group, 1993; 2nd ed., 1994).

68. See Doern and Aucoin, *The Structures of Policy-Making in Canada* and *Public Policy in Canada*; Campbell and Szablowski, *The Superbureaucrats*; and Kernaghan and Siegel, *Public Administration in Canada*.

69. Marc Lalonde, "The Changing Role of the Prime Minister's Office," *Canadian Public Administration* (Winter 1971), pp. 509–37; Gossage, *Close to the Charisma*; and Gratton, "So, What Are the Boys Saying?"

70. Christina McCall-Newman, *Grits*, Part 3. See also the article by Coutts's successor, Thomas Axworthy, "Of Secretaries to Princes," *Canadian Public Administration* (Summer 1988), pp. 247–64.

71. Heeney, *The Things That Are Caesar's* (Toronto: 1972); and Gordon Robertson, "The Changing Role of the Privy Council Office," *Canadian Public Administration* (Winter 1971), pp. 487–508. Mr. Robertson was Clerk of the Privy Council throughout much of the Pearson and Trudeau periods.

72. This whole section is based on the Privy Council Office's document, *Memorandum to Cabinet*, a public document brought to my attention by James Hurley of the PCO and supplemented by a delightful interview.
73. Among many accounts of PEMS, see Richard French, *How Ottawa Decides*, and Ian D. Clark, "Recent Changes in the Cabinet Decision-Making System in Ottawa," *Canadian Public Administration* (Summer 1985), pp. 185–201.
74. Richard Van Loon and Michael Whittington, "Kaleidoscope in Grey: The Policy Process in Ottawa," in Michael Whittington and Glen Williams, eds., *Canadian Politics in the 1990s* (Scarborough: Nelson Canada, 1990), pp. 453–54.
75. Treasury Board, *The Expenditure Management System of the Government of Canada* (Ottawa: Supply and Services, 1995).
76. Matheson, *The Prime Minister and the Cabinet*, pp. 121–25.
77. John Porter, *The Vertical Mosaic* (Toronto: University of Toronto Press, 1965), ch. XVII.
78. F.H. Underhill, *In Search of Canadian Liberalism*, quoted in Hockin, *Apex of Power*, p. 290.
79. "Mackenzie King genuinely believed and frequently said that the real secret of political leadership was more in what was prevented than in what was accomplished." J.W. Pickersgill, *The Mackenzie King Record*, Vol. 1 (Toronto: University of Toronto Press, 1960), p. 10.
80. David Taras, "Prime Ministers and the Media," in Pal and Taras, *Prime Ministers and Premiers*, p. 38.

FURTHER READING

Crown

Bagehot, Walter. *The English Constitution*. London: Collins, 1963.

Canada Gazette. Part I, October 11, 1947, pp. 3014–16.

Forsey, Eugene. *The Royal Power of Dissolution of Parliament in the British Commonwealth*. Toronto: Oxford University Press, 1943; reprinted 1968.

Heard, Andrew. *Canadian Constitutional Conventions*. Toronto: Oxford University Press, 1991.

Massey, Vincent. *What's Past Is Prologue*. Toronto: Macmillan, 1963.

McKinnon, Frank. *The Crown in Canada*. Calgary: McClelland and Stewart West, 1976.

McWhinney, Edward. "Prerogative Powers of the Head of State" *Canadian Bar Review* (January 1957), pp. 92–96.

Saywell, J.T. "The Crown and the Politicians: The Canadian Succession Question 1891–1896." *Canadian Historical Review* (December 1956), pp. 309–37.

Prime Minister and Cabinet

Aucoin, Peter. "Organizational Change in the Machinery of Canadian Government: From Rational Management to Brokerage Politics." *Canadian Journal of Political Science* (March, 1986), pp. 3–27.

Axworthy, Thomas. "Of Secretaries to Princes." *Canadian Public Administration* (Summer 1988), pp. 247–64.

Bakvis, Herman. *Regional Ministers*. Toronto: University of Toronto Press, 1991.

Campbell, Colin. *Governments under Stress*. Toronto: University of Toronto Press, 1983.

Campbell, Colin, and George Szablowski. *The Superbureaucrats*. Toronto: Macmillan, 1979.

Clark, Ian D. "Recent Changes in the Cabinet Decision-Making System in Ottawa." *Canadian Public Administration* (Summer 1985), pp. 185–201.

Clarkson, Stephen, and Christina McCall. *Trudeau and Our Times*. Toronto: McClelland and Stewart, 1990 and 1994.

Crossman, Richard. Introduction to Walter Bagehot, *The English Constitution*. London: Collins, 1963.

Dupré, J. Stefan. "Reflections on the Workability of Executive Federalism." In Richard Simeon, ed. *Intergovernmental Relations*. Toronto: University of Toronto Press, 1985.

English, John. "The French 'Lieutenant' in Ottawa." In R.K. Carty and W.P. Ward, eds. *National Politics and Community in Canada*. Vancouver: University of British Columbia Press, 1986.

Gossage, Patrick. *Close to the Charisma*. Toronto: McClelland and Stewart, 1986.

Gratton, Michel. *"So, What Are the Boys Saying?"* Toronto: McGraw-Hill Ryerson, 1987.

Hockin, Thomas, ed. *Apex of Power*, 2nd ed. Scarborough: Prentice-Hall Canada, 1977.

Lalonde, Marc. "The Changing Role of the Prime Minister's Office." *Canadian Public Administration* (Winter 1971), pp. 509–37.

Mancuso, Maureen, et al., eds. *Leaders and Leadership in Canada*. Toronto: Oxford University Press, 1994.

Matheson, W.A. *The Prime Minister and the Cabinet*. Toronto: Methuen, 1976.

Pal, Leslie, and David Taras, eds. *Prime Ministers and Premiers: Political Leadership and Public Policy in Canada*. Scarborough: Prentice-Hall Canada, 1988.

Punnett, R.M. *The Prime Minister in Canadian Government*. Toronto: Macmillan, 1977.

Robertson, Gordon. "The Changing Role of the Privy Council Office." *Canadian Public Administration* (Winter 1971), pp. 487–508.

Smith, David E. *The Invisible Crown*. Toronto: University of Toronto Press, 1995.

Smith, Denis. "President and Parliament: The Transformation of Parliamentary Government in Canada," in Hockin, *Apex of Power*.

Chapter 21

the BUREAUCRACY

Federal public servants deliver the mail, issue old age security cheques and passports, process income tax and GST forms, admit immigrants, approve new drugs and search for illicit ones, guard penitentiaries, negotiate treaties with domestic aboriginals as well as with foreign countries, and provide myriad other services that are often taken for granted by the general public. If any hitch occurs, however, Canadians are quick to condemn the "red tape" and "bureaucrats" in Ottawa. Perhaps now that the Chrétien government has begun a process of downsizing the bureaucracy, it will attract less criticism and greater public understanding.

Even though the *bureaucracy*, or public service, is generally not as visible as the other three branches of government, it is no less important. Most citizens encounter public servants in the provision of services, but the bureaucracy is probably even more significant in its advisory role. Modern government is so pervasive and complex that ministers hardly make a move without the advice of their permanent, expert staff. Most public servants work in various government departments, but these are supplemented by a vast array of Crown corporations, regulatory agencies, and other governmental organizations. In fact, the bureaucracy has become so large and indispensable that many observers wonder whether it can be kept under political control.

This chapter begins by examining the functions and powers of the bureaucracy. It then deals in turn with the three main kinds of bureaucratic organization: the government department, the Crown corporation, and the regulatory agency. The chapter concludes with a discussion of controlling the bureaucracy and recent attempts to reform it.

FUNCTIONS AND POWERS OF THE BUREAUCRACY

The traditional function of the bureaucracy is that of rule application; it is a neutral agent administering policies established by the cabinet and legislature. While this is still an important part of its work, the bureaucracy is also involved in the other output functions of rule making and rule adjudication. Besides advising the politicians in their capacity as rule makers, the bureaucracy is delegated wide "quasi-legislative" powers to make subordinate rules on its own. And while the courts are the foremost adjudicators of disputes in society, the bureaucracy has also encroached upon their territory such that many disputes are now resolved by "quasi-judicial" administrative tribunals. Less formally, the bureaucracy also engages in interest articulation, in the sense of various departments speaking up for their own concerns or helping to advance the demands of their principal clientele. Interdepartmental and central support agencies are involved in interest aggregation, the bureaucracy recruits large numbers of significant political actors, and it has an important role in political communication, listening to the public and transmitting the government's response.

If the significance of the bureaucracy can be seen in its performance of all seven traditional functions in the political system, this can also be demonstrated by examining its presence in the model of the policy-making process presented in Chapter 19. First, it plays a crucial part in the initiation phase. The bureaucracy may be a source of demands, whether these are self-interested or on behalf of its clientele, since administrators of a program may be among the first to recognize its inadequacies. Even if a demand reaches the cabinet from other sources, once the politicians decide to look into an issue further, the public service will usually be asked to provide them with additional information and advice.

If the cabinet decides to take additional action at the priority-setting stage, the bureaucracy is then centrally involved in the policy formulation phase. With its concentration of technical information and experience, the public service spends a great deal of its time in formulating policies, since the details of such policies are usually beyond the grasp of the politicians.

In analyses of the role of the bureaucracy in policy formulation, several distinct subtheories arise, the first of which is the **rational choice** model. It suggests that once a problem has been identified, the bureaucrats will seek the most rational means to solve it. Rather than pay much attention to its political ramifications, public servants go through a rational procedure of setting their goal, developing a full range of possible solutions, gathering material on the pros and cons of each such alternative, and then making the most rational choice. Given the tremendous informational resources of the bureaucracy in modern government, it is sometimes assumed that such rational decisions are actually possible.

Even if the bureaucracy does operate in this fashion, however, some observers are sceptical that the politicians would always overlook the political implications of their decisions. Other observers argue that the bureaucracy is more inclined toward **incrementalism**, claiming that bureaucrats are likely to make only marginal changes in existing policy at any one time. That is to say, the bureaucracy's analysis of options is not so comprehensive, and its decisions and recommendations are usually small-scale, incremental alterations to the status quo.

Once the policy, program, or law has received political authorization by Parliament in the legitimization phase, implementation is almost exclusively a bureaucratic responsibility. In today's complex society, the politicians are forced to leave wide discretionary powers to the public service to carry out their general, abstract goals.[1] A considerable lag often exists between the political approval of a law and its effective implementation, during which time the public service drafts regulations under the act, sets up new administrative machinery, and hires new personnel. Because of the time and informational constraints on Parliament, most bills are passed in rather general or skeletal form, and the real meat or substance of the law is expressed in the **regulations** issued under it. These are published through the authority of the minister or cabinet in the *Canada Gazette*. The implementation of a law may thus see the bureaucracy making decisions that constitute quasi-legislative outputs. The implementation phase may involve time-consuming negotiations with the provinces or with relevant interest groups. Once the date set for the start of a new program arrives, it is the bureaucracy again that actually provides the service, does the regulating, or performs whatever other rule application functions are involved. Implementation also requires disseminating information to the public about new policies or programs. Governments now spend great quantities of public funds advertising their programs on the grounds that this is essential if they are to be fully effective. A final aspect of implementation is program evaluation, that is, an assessment of the adequacies of a policy after a period of operation. Program evaluation is becoming a more regular and sophisticated addition to the field of policy analysis.[2]

Given its role in almost all phases of the policy-making process, reference to "bureaucratic power" in political science or contentions that the bureaucracy is more powerful than the legislature or even the prime minister and cabinet should not be surprising. While it is more conventional to say that the cabinet makes the most important decisions in the political system and that it theoretically controls the bureaucracy, this is not to deny the extent of bureaucratic power in the modern state. The accompanying chart shows that the number of people involved in the federal public service is close to 500 000, and breaks this number down into its component parts.

THE FEDERAL PUBLIC SERVICE, AS OF DECEMBER 1992

• Regular government departments	235 343
• Crown corporations	152 383
• Other government agencies	32 802
• Canadian forces	115 320
• RCMP	19 911
• Total	555 759

Source: Public Service Commission, 1992, Annual Report Statistics, cat. no. SCI-1992/2. Reproduced with permission of the Minister of Supply and Services Canada, 1995.

GOVERNMENT DEPARTMENTS
Number and Structure

The most common forms of bureaucratic operations are regular government **departments**, **Crown corporations**, and **regulatory agencies**. Government departments are created and reorganized by Acts of Parliament, which also set out the responsibilities of each. But the cabinet can determine the internal structure of the department and even has the power to transfer responsibilities from one department to another.[3]

A major consolidation of departments took place in 1993, reducing the overall number from 25 to 20. The following departments continued to operate much as before: Finance, Fisheries and Oceans, Indian Affairs and Northern Development, International Trade, Justice, and Transport. External Affairs became Foreign Affairs and Agriculture became

Agriculture and Agri-Food. Industry incorporated Science, Small Business, and Consumer and Corporate Affairs; Public Works and Government Services were combined; and Natural Resources was formed from Forestry and Energy, Mines and Resources. The most significant changes were the creation of Human Resources Development, which incorporated Employment, Welfare, and Labour; and Canadian Heritage, made up of Secretary of State, Multiculturalism, and Communications. Under Kim Campbell, Immigration was lumped with the Solicitor General into Public Security, but Jean Chrétien re-established these two separate departments.

· ·

GOVERNMENT DEPARTMENTS IN THE CHRÉTIEN ERA

- Agriculture and Agri-Food
- Canadian Heritage
- Citizenship and Immigration
- Environment
- Finance
- Fisheries and Oceans
- Foreign Affairs and International Trade[1]
- Health
- Human Resources Development
- Indian Affairs and Northern Development
- Industry
- Justice
- Labour
- National Defence
- National Revenue
- Natural Resources
- Public Works and Government Services
- Solicitor General
- Transport
- Treasury Board
- Veterans Affairs[2]

[1]One department, but two separate ministers.
[2]A separate department, but presided over by the Minister of National Defence along with a Secretary of State.

The government department assumes a pyramidal shape, with the minister at its apex having direct management and control. Since ministers in this system (unlike the United States) are chosen from among the politicians elected to Parliament, it is too much to hope that they will be experts in the work of the department. All that is expected is that they are individuals with intelligence, ideas, common sense, and an ability to relay government priorities and public opinion to departmental experts as well as to relate expert advice from the department to Parliament and the public. Ministers will naturally develop some expertise if they stay in one cabinet position for any length of time, but nowadays they are usually shuffled to another department just as they are getting the hang of it. Jean Chrétien reverted to the earlier practice of leaving ministers in place if moves could be avoided.

Ministers are responsible for their department in the sense that they are expected to provide day-to-day direction and must accept criticism for its faults. In other words, ministers take most of the credit or blame for what the department does, whether or not they know what is going on within it. As pointed out in Chapter 20, the principle of **ministerial responsibility** was once thought to mean that ministers had to resign for serious mistakes made by their public servants, even if unaware of them. Whether this theory was ever practised in Canada is questionable—there are no cases of such resignations since 1867—but certainly in this age of big government it is not a realistic proposition.[4] What does ministerial responsibility mean today? First, ministers occasionally resign over their personal mistakes, but not as routinely as in Britain. Second, they must take political responsibility and answer to Parliament for all the actions of their officials. The minister must explain and defend the actions of the department in Parliament, especially during Question Period, and when a bureaucratic error is made, the minister must apologize and promise to correct the mistake. Third, although ministers may discreetly discipline the offender, they should not violate the traditions of public-service anonymity.[5]

The more permanent head of the department is the **deputy minister**. Even though appointed by the prime minister (on the advice of the Secretary to the Cabinet), "deputies" or "DM"s are usually career public servants. Deputy ministers have two principal roles: they act as chief policy adviser to the minister and function as manager of the department. Such officials used to spend a lifetime working their way toward the top of a single department and became great experts in its subject matter. Since the 1962 Glassco Report, which recommended the adoption of private-sector managerial techniques in the public sector, emphasis in the appointment of deputy ministers has switched from expertise in the subject matter of the department to managerial skills that can be applied in any administrative setting. In recent years they, too, have been frequently shuffled from one department to another. Even so, the deputy minister is usually there longer than the minister and is thus likely to develop greater knowledge of the department's work. Deputy ministers also interact regularly with DMs in other federal departments, provincial DMs in corresponding departments, and the heads of pressure groups particularly interested in the department's work.

The relationship between the minister and the deputy minister is of great interest and concern to political science and public administration.[6] Ideally, the minister sets the priorities for the department while the DM provides a number of options among which the minister can choose. The deputy should give the minister advice that is based not only on administrative, technical, and financial considerations, but that is also sensitive to the political context. Evidence exists that the reality of the relationship sometimes approaches this theoretical ideal. On the other hand, weak ministers may be mere puppets of their bureaucratic advisers, and even strong ministers may encounter bureaucratic resistance to new initiatives such as in being denied relevant information, having it delayed, or in not having new policies implemented with enthusiasm.[7]

It is not easy for a single, solitary, temporary, amateur minister to impose his or her will on thousands of expert, permanent public servants who have established departmental attitudes, values, policies, and procedures. Of all departments, it appears that this is most difficult of all in the Department of National Defence, as was evident in various aspects of Canada's contribution to Somalia. The small personal staff that ministers are allowed to appoint may be of some assistance in this situation. On the other hand, the minister's staff is primarily engaged in promoting the image and reputation of the minister, and while they may provide partisan policy advice, any effort to interfere in the administration of the department will be strongly resented by the deputy minister. In the Mulroney regime, ministers set up large offices headed by a powerful chief of staff, and these were, among other things, the target of most lobbying efforts. As in other ways, Chrétien reverted to an earlier era by reducing the size and significance of ministerial offices and eliminating the chief of staff position. Ministers could hire a maximum of five officers and seven support staff, with a maximum salary budget of $550 000 and a maximum operating budget of $500 000. One sign of the lesser importance of such offices was that lobbyists transferred their attention to the bureaucracy.[8]

It is sometimes suggested that Canada should move to the American practice of replacing the whole top level of bureaucrats when the cabinet changes so that the leading officials in each department will be enthusiastically supportive of the new government. Given the minor ideological differences between the Canadian parties at the national level, however, few observers find this either necessary or desirable. Opposition parties often accuse the public service of becoming too sympathetic to a longstanding government party (e.g., in the 1935–57 and 1963–84 Liberal periods), but the Diefenbaker, Clark, and Mulroney cabinets did not rid themselves of more than one or two senior bureaucrats.

Below the deputy minister, the department is typically divided into several branches each headed by an assistant deputy minister (ADM); these in turn are divided into directorates each headed by a director general; and these are divided into divisions each headed by a director. Figure 21.1 illustrates this hierarchical structure. Those divisions of a department that actually carry out services and interact with the public are said to be performing "line" functions. Except for the top managerial posts, most of the line positions in any department will be located in the "field"—in local offices in communities across the country. But every department will also have "staff" divisions that serve such internal needs as policy development and research, personnel, financial, information, and legal divisions. These positions are normally located in Ottawa along with the heads of the line divisions.

The hundreds or thousands of public servants in the department are ranged in descending levels of authority under the deputy minister and share four basic characteristics: they are expert, permanent, impartial, and anonymous. First, they are chosen on their merits—ability, knowledge, training, and/or experience—for the duties their position entails. Second, they are career public servants, who normally remain within the public service until retirement. Third, they are nonpartisan and expected to serve whichever party comes to power with equal loyalty and enthusiasm. Fourth, bureaucrats are not normally identified in public; instead, the minister speaks for the department and takes the public and parliamentary responsibility for its performance. Even when public servants brief the media about new policies, for example, they are only referred to as "an official of the department."[9]

The federal public service is divided into six occupational categories, within which are some 72 more specific occupational groups and 106 subgroups. The six categories with examples of

Figure 21.1 **Top of a Hypothetical Department Organization Chart**

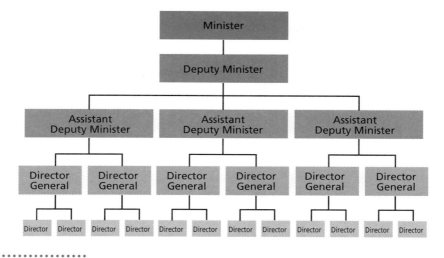

groups they contain are as follows: management (executive, senior management); scientific and professional (statistics, auditing); administrative and foreign service (personnel administration, program administration); technical (air traffic control, drafting); administrative support (clerical and regulatory, secretarial, stenographic and typing); and operational (correctional, firefighter). The first four categories are called "officer" categories, generally requiring postsecondary education, while the last two are called "support." Recent university graduates are normally hired in the administrative and foreign service or scientific and professional groups and work their way up from there, while it is rare for someone in administrative support to get promoted to these categories without a university degree. Within each group are many levels or steps—for example, within the clerk category are CR1, CR2, etc. which determine one's salary level. It is an extremely complex operation to draw up a job description for over 200 000 positions and to evaluate and classify them for purposes of determining necessary qualifications and salary.

Some public servants spend much of their time applying for positions higher in the scale and going to interviews in the hope of promotion. In order to make the appointment and promotion processes as equitable as possible, notice of vacancies must be given, and after the interviews are conducted and decisions made, there is provision for appeal, meaning that the whole operation is characterized by "long delays and procedural rigidities."[10] As in any such situation, it is difficult to make the interview fair and to prevent favouritism from intruding. Those who do stay in their jobs are subject to annual performance evaluation by their superiors that may also result in the filing of grievances and appeals.

Relations with Other Departments and Central Agencies

The operation of a government department is complicated by the necessity of interacting with other departments as well as by the authority of various central bureaucratic agencies to intervene in its affairs. Since almost any law, policy, or program affects a variety of departments, many permanent and ad hoc interdepartmental committees exist. Among the permanent ones is the Coordinating Committee of Deputy Ministers, and whenever a new policy is under active consideration, an ad hoc interdepartmental committee is appointed to look into it. Not only must the problem be examined from a number of departmental perspectives, but it is also subject to considerable bureaucratic "politics" and territorial claims.

The central agencies that complicate the life of a department include the Public Service Commission (PSC), the Treasury Board and Comptroller of the Treasury, the Privy Council Office, the Department of Finance, and the Prime Minister's Office, most of which were mentioned in Chapter 20.

The **Public Service Commission** is a three-member board headed by a chair of deputy minister status that is theoretically in charge of all hiring, promotions, and dismissals. In practice, however, the PSC delegates much of its authority to individual departments. It is primarily concerned to police the merit system, preventing appointments and promotions from being made on partisan or discriminatory grounds, and is consequently involved in the appeal process when claims of discrimination of any kind are made. It normally considers between 3000 and 5000 appeals and investigations per year. The PSC also offers staff development and training programs, including language training to about 5000 public servants per year, over half of them on a voluntary basis.

The Treasury Board as a cabinet committee was discussed in Chapter 20, but here the role of the Treasury Board Secretariat (TBS) as the staff of the president of the Treasury Board should be emphasized, especially in personnel, financial, and expenditure management. The TBS essentially determines the terms and conditions of employment for the public service. It must approve the creation of new positions as well as their classification or reclassification, and represents the employer in the collective bargaining process. On the financial management side, the TBS is responsible for the preparation of the Estimates, which normally involves cutting back on departmental spending proposals, especially when the government's priority is to reduce the deficit. It also issues all sorts of administrative policies such as on purchasing, contracts, and travel. The Comptroller of the Treasury is the branch of the Treasury Board that oversees the actual expenditure of public funds and tries to improve departmental management through such devices as program evaluation.

The Privy Council Office's relations with regular government departments primarily arise in connection with policy development and coordination, reallocation of programs between departments, the reorganization of departments, and senior management appointments. The Prime Minister's Office, on the other hand, does not interact frequently with departments except with respect to new policy initiatives or political problems engaging the prime minister. The Department of Finance (along with the Treasury Board) is usually an opponent of new departmental spending programs and an advocate of retrenchment. In addition, government-wide services, such as purchasing and accommodation, and regulations are provided by the newly combined Public Works and Supply and Services department.

The Merit Principle and a Representative Bureaucracy[11]

For about 40 years after Confederation, the Canadian public service operated on the **spoils system**, under which the party that won an election could replace those holding civil service positions with its own friends and supporters. One of the main motives for entering the political arena in that era was to reward family and friends with *political patronage*—government jobs and contracts.[12] Such partisan, amateur personnel proved to be increasingly inadequate as government operations grew more complex after the turn of the century. Hence the passage of the Civil Service Amendment Act in 1908, which created the Civil Service Commission (predecessor to the Public Service Commission). It meant that public servants in Ottawa were hired on the **merit system**, and after the 1918 Civil Service Act, field positions were also to be based on merit. Politicians, however, were reluctant to give up their traditional right to reward their supporters with government jobs, and it is difficult to say exactly when the merit system was finally entrenched. The foundations of the modern merit system in Ottawa were laid in the 1930s by O.D. Skelton, especially at External Affairs, Clifford Clark in Finance, and Graham Towers at the Bank of Canada.[13]

If patronage was virtually eliminated in the public service, however, there remained considerable scope for partisan appointments in other areas, to say nothing of contracts for corporate friends. Senators, the boards of regulatory agencies and Crown corporations, certain diplomatic posts, the PMO and ministers' offices, lieutenant governorships, citizenship judgeships (not real judges), and the occasional real judgeship were all positions in which partisan appointments still prevailed. The Liberals accused Brian Mulroney of excessive patronage, but in fact the Chrétien government had an undeserved reputation for being more restrained. The Liberals did, however, reduce the size of some of the boards of such agencies, not because of moral reservations, but as an economy move.

Almost as soon as the merit system was fully effective, the call began to be made that the bureaucracy should be more representative of the society it serves. Given the power of the public service and the assumption that its recommendations and decisions would reflect the origins and pre–public service values of its members, many critics argued that the public service could only be responsive to all parts of society if it included a proportional representation of various groups in the population. The senior levels of the public service had always overrepresented males, anglophones, the middle and upper classes, the well educated, and Ontarians.[14] Thus it was claimed that policy recommendations and implementation reflected an insensitivity to women, the working class and the poor, francophones and other ethnics, and to the peculiarities of hinterland regions and provinces.

The first main concerns in this connection were the small number of francophones in the higher reaches of the bureaucracy and the virtual absence of the use of the French language at the policy-making levels. The passage of the Official Languages Act of 1969 essentially bilingualized the executive branch of government. It gave both English- and French-speaking citizens the right to deal with head offices of government departments in either official language, as well as with local offices where numbers warranted. It also expanded language training programs started by the Pearson government in 1964, made recruitment and promotion of francophones a higher priority, and designated certain positions as bilingual. The Treasury Board was given authority to oversee the whole language policy program, and the position of Commissioner of

Official Languages was created to be responsible for assessing the implementation of the policy, dealing with complaints, and reporting back to Parliament. It was fortunate that the Quebec educational system had improved by this time so that the new policy involved little or no loss of quality in government appointments and promotions. It did, however, ignite a backlash against the preference given to French Canadians and to bilingualism. Nevertheless, the Official Languages Act was incorporated into the Charter of Rights and Freedoms in 1982. As of March 31, 1994, 29 percent of public service positions (64 080) had been designated as bilingual, 59 percent (129 876) as English essential, seven percent (14 230) as French essential, and five percent (10 314) as requiring either official language. Table 21.1 shows the language designation of actual public servants by category. The figures in the table bear a reasonably close approximation to census statistics (French mother tongue just under 25 percent), although francophones are overrepresented in the administrative and foreign service and administrative support categories.

TABLE 21.1 Language Designation of Public Servants by Category					
	Anglophone		Francophone		Total
	#	%	#	%	#
Management	2 660	77	794	23	3 454
Scientific & professional	19 269	77	5 756	23	25 025
Administrative & foreign service	47 279	70	20 263	30	67 542
Technical	20 563	79	5 466	21	26 029
Administrative support	43 347	67	21 350	33	64 697
Operational	24 767	78	6 986	22	31 753
Total	157 667	72	60 833	28	218 500

Source: Treasury Board, Official Languages in Federal Institutions, Annual Report 1993–1994 (Ottawa: Supply and Services, 1994). Reproduced with permission of the Minister of Supply and Servces Canada, 1995.

Women also began to be targeted for increased representation in the higher levels of the public service in the 1960s and 1970s.[15] In addition, the pay equity program of the 1980s and 1990s was primarily designed to ensure that women received equal pay for doing work that had the same value as that done by men. It is not easy to compare the value of dissimilar jobs, but many occupational groups made up largely of women have had their salaries increased as a result.

The next stage of making the public service more representative of society came in 1983 when an explicit **affirmative action** program was adopted for women, aboriginals, and people with disabilities, and two years later the list was expanded to include visible minorities. Once again, this did not necessarily result in a decline in the quality of appointments and promotions, but it sparked opposition from those who did not fall into the designated categories, such as able-bodied, anglophone, white, male university graduates. In defence of such a policy, it is pointed out that in an officially bilingual country, bilingual competence is an element of merit, and that within the target groups, people are still selected on the basis of their individual merits.[16]

TABLE 21.2 Public Service by Employment Equity Categories

	Women #	Women %	Aboriginals #	Aboriginals %	People with Disabilities #	People with Disabilities %	Visible Minorities #	Visible Minorities %	Total #
Management	708	18.3	44	1.1	77	2.0	88	2.3	3 878
Scientific & professional	7 410	28.9	328	1.3	472	1.8	2 131	8.3	25 598
Administrative & foreign service	35 518	47.9	1 515	2.0	2 482	3.4	2 807	3.8	74 073
Technical	4 855	18.5	296	1.1	494	1.9	602	2.3	26 275
Administrative support	52 904	83.6	1 495	2.4	2 396	3.8	2 242	3.8	63 282
Operational	4 226	13.4	814	2.6	702	2.2	514	1.6	31 534
Total	105 621	47.0	4 492	2.0	6 623	2.9	8 566	3.8	224 640

Source: Treasury Board, Employment Equity in the Public Service, Annual Report 1993–1994 *(Ottawa: Supply and Services, 1994). Reproduced with permission of the Minister of Supply and Services Canada, 1995.*

While the achievement of greater equity in educational attainment and recent affirmative action programs will probably reduce some of the elitist aspects of bureaucratic activity in the future, it should be added that two significant variables have been largely overlooked. The first is the geographic origins of senior public servants. Local people are naturally hired in field offices across the country, including Atlantic Canada and the West, but little effort has been made to bring people from these regions to the policy-making levels of the bureaucracy in Ottawa. Such levels have been dominated by those from families of professional bureaucrats in the Ottawa area. The higher bureaucracy is even less representative of the population in terms of class. Senior bureaucrats often have more than one university degree, and most come from middle-class backgrounds.

This whole discussion of a **representative bureaucracy** assumes that public servants will retain the geographic, ethnic, linguistic, class, and gender biases of their origins. Instead, some observers argue, they may become imbued with the values and attitudes of their new workplace, and end up as part of the amorphous, self-serving, middle-class, central Canadian, bilingual, bureaucratic elite.[17]

Political Activity

It is one thing to eliminate partisanship in appointments and promotions, but quite another to deny civil servants their basic democratic rights. Do these professional, permanent, impartial government employees have any political rights at all? The Public Service Employment Act of 1967 allowed most federal public servants to attend political meetings and make financial contributions to candidates or parties, and to take a leave of absence to stand for political office. But government employees were not permitted to work for or against a candidate or party in federal or provincial elections. When these restrictions were challenged in the Supreme Court, the Court ruled that they violated public servants' freedom of expression. They were "over-inclusive" and in many ways went "beyond what is necessary to achieve the objective of an impartial and loyal civil service."[18] Except for deputy ministers, therefore, restrictions on political activity have largely been eliminated.

Collective Bargaining

Until relatively recently, public servants did not belong to unions and had little input into determining their level of salary or other terms and conditions of employment. Employee influence in these matters gradually increased over time until they were granted collective bargaining rights in 1967 by means of the Public Service Staff Relations Act and the Public Service Employment Act. The 70 or so occupational groups mentioned above essentially constitute bargaining units whose representatives engage in negotiations with the Treasury Board, which acts as the employer. Given a total of 79 separate collective agreements represented by 16 different unions (the largest being the Public Service Alliance of Canada (PSAC), which represents about 165 000 employees), the collective bargaining process in the federal public service is extremely complex. When renegotiating their contract, the bargaining agent must specify in advance whether it wishes to have a possible impasse resolved by referral to binding arbitration or to a conciliation board, leading, if necessary, to a strike.

Certain subjects are recognized as rights of the employer and are not negotiable, and certain groups of public servants are excluded from the collective bargaining process. These include officers of Parliament, deputy ministers, casual and part-time employees, and personnel administrators. Furthermore, some groups such as federal hospital workers and correctional officers who are allowed to bargain are not allowed to strike. While most bargaining units choose the conciliation–strike option, public service strikes have occurred most frequently in connection with the post office, which was transformed into a Crown corporation in 1981. On several occasions, however, the government suspended collective bargaining on monetary matters and the right to strike. The first was in connection with the wage control program of 1974; the second was with the similar "6 and 5" program in 1982; and the third was the severe limitation on public-service salary increases announced in the 1991 budget. This resulted in a 33-day strike by the PSAC involving about 70 000 workers. All collective agreements were extended for 24 months from their expiry date, with pay increases of zero and three percent. The Conservatives passed legislation in early 1993 to extend the agreements for two additional years with no pay increases, but the Liberals extended the wage freeze until 1996–97 and froze increment increases as well, effectively suspending collective bargaining for most of the decade.

The Estimates System

As noted at several earlier points in the book, the authorities spend a great deal of their time discussing the expenditure of public funds. Members of Parliament want money allocated to their constituencies, premiers and federal ministers press to get funds allocated to their provinces, and bureaucrats seek funding for their programs and departments. In addition, much of the pressure on the authorities from interest groups and corporations consists of demands for federal funds. In earlier eras such spending was the prerogative of individual politicians or governing parties and was carried out on a patronage basis.[19] Nowadays, the spending process has been highly bureaucratized, and it is the function of the **Estimates** system to decide how such funds will be allocated in any fiscal year.[20]

The role of the cabinet in setting the overall parameters of the expenditure process was mentioned in Chapter 20. At that level various procedures have been used by different governments over the years, as illustrated by the adoption of the Program and Expenditure Management System by the Clark and Trudeau governments and its replacement by the Mulroney "Ops and Chops" system. In any case, the cabinet decides on the advice of the Finance Department, the Treasury Board, and the Privy Council Office what the government's financial priorities and overall level of government revenue and expenditure will be. New policy proposals and new spending initiatives must also be specifically approved at this level.

The whole budgetary process has recently been portrayed as a contest between "spenders" and "guardians."[21] The spenders are most of the ministers and departments in whose interest it is to increase their budgets. Spenders try to introduce new programs and expand existing ones in order to raise their prestige and enhance the support of their clientele. There are no incentives for spending ministers to restrain themselves. The guardians are essentially the minister of Finance and the president of the Treasury Board along with their respective departments. Ordinarily seen as villains by almost everyone else involved, they now receive some public praise if they manage to reduce the deficit.

Many government programs are automatically funded by the statutes that create them. The expenditures for these programs, called "statutory appropriations," cannot be changed without amending the relevant statutes; they are therefore more or less fixed and uncontrollable. Since these appropriations constitute over 60 percent of the total budget, they seriously limit the cabinet's discretion in altering the level or pattern of government expenditure.

The preparation of the Estimates involves projections of the cost of existing programs at the departmental level within the limits and guidelines laid down by higher authorities. Managerial personnel devote much of their time to such considerations. The preparation of the Estimates involves a great deal of interaction between each department and the Treasury Board Secretariat as deputy ministers and ministers try to maximize their departmental allocations while Treasury Board personnel engage in cutting them back. At the end of the process, the Estimates are consolidated for cabinet approval and introduced into Parliament by the President of the Treasury Board before the beginning of the next fiscal year. Once contained in a single, thick, blue volume, they now consist of a separate volume for each department and agency. Since the Estimates are prepared so far in advance of actual spending, several sets of supplementary Estimates are usually necessary to provide for unforeseen contingencies throughout the fiscal year.

Departmental Interaction with Provinces and Pressure Groups

Ministers and leading departmental officials do not interact only with other ministers and other officials within the federal government. Two other common forms of interaction are with the provinces and with pressure groups.

As noted in Chapter 4, much of the interaction between federal and provincial governments takes place at the bureaucratic level.[22] Because the division of powers between federal and provincial governments is often vague and because both levels usually try to maximize their jurisdiction, the two levels end up operating programs in the same fields. Limitations on provincial finances have also prompted the provinces to request federal financial assistance to which Ottawa has usually attached conditions, making it even more intertwined with provincial governments.

At the height of cooperative federalism, federal and provincial program administrators would interact harmoniously in the design and operation of such integrated programs. An excellent example was the Canada Assistance Plan in which cooperation was facilitated by personal friendships, frequent informal contact, and shared professional norms.[23] It is still the case that in almost every federal department line officials interact regularly with their provincial counterparts, often by letter, fax, or telephone, and sometimes more formally in federal–provincial conferences at the bureaucratic level. Nowadays, however, with public funding in short supply, they are less likely to be engaged in developing new initiatives and more likely be aiming to disengage so as to reduce duplication.

In addition to such vertical department-to-department interaction, each level of government has set up bureaucratic agencies to supervise federal–provincial relations. While these central agencies are necessary to keep track of the maze of such interaction and while they may facilitate federal–provincial bureaucratic cooperation in some instances, they often complicate the friendly relations that individual federal departments have established with their provincial counterparts.

The close relationship between pressure groups and the bureaucracy has already been discussed in Chapter 18. Groups that wish to influence either the formulation or implementation of policies and programs are active in taking their message to the relevant government department. Sometimes public servants resist the approach of self-seeking groups, but at other times the department may actually welcome it if the group has vital, reliable information that will lead to the development of a more effective program, if the group can help muster support for the departmental initiative among other key players in the policy-making process, or if it can serve as a channel of communication to that part of the public that is interested in the particular proposal.

These mutually advantageous contacts between a group and a department may become so close and congenial that a symbiotic, **clientele relationship** develops. The department gives official recognition to the group, regularly consults it on policy development and implementation, and gives it representation on advisory committees. It will generally be in the interest of both the department and the group to keep their relationship confidential so that they can present a united front in case central agencies and cabinet committees become involved. It is in this connection that Chapter 18 spoke of "policy communities" and of the interest articulation function of government departments. Where such a congenial, supportive group does not already exist, it may even be necessary for the department to create it.[24]

CROWN CORPORATIONS

The second most important form of bureaucratic organization is the Crown corporation.[25] These are government operations that assume a structure similar to a private corporation. Crown corporations may be private firms that have been nationalized by the government by buying their shares (CN and Petro-Canada), they may be transformed from regular departments (Canada Post), or, most typically in Canada, they may be created from scratch (Canada Mortgage and Housing Corporation). Probably more than 400 Crown corporations exist at the federal level, but some of the main ones are listed in the accompanying box. The largest in terms of employees in 1994 were Canada Post (43 699), Canadian National (34 707), CBC (9 117), VIA Rail (4 308), and Atomic Energy of Canada Ltd. (4 287), figures that represent significant declines since the mid-1980s.

MAJOR FEDERAL CROWN CORPORATIONS, 1995

- Atomic Energy of Canada Ltd.
- Bank of Canada
- Canada Mortgage and Housing Corporation
- Canada Ports Corporation
- Canada Post Corporation
- Canadian Broadcasting Corporation
- Canadian Museums Corporation
- Canadian National Railway Company
- Canadian Saltfish Corporation
- Canadian Wheat Board
- Cape Breton Development Corporation
- Export Development Corporation
- Farm Credit Corporation
- Federal Business Development Bank
- Marine Atlantic Inc.
- National Arts Centre Corporation
- National Capital Commission
- National Gallery of Canada
- Royal Canadian Mint
- St. Lawrence Seaway Authority
- VIA Rail Canada Inc.

The corporate structure referred to includes a board of directors, president, vice-presidents, and general manager. The cabinet appoints the board of directors, which theoretically sets the general policy of the corporation. However, the directors often lack credibility, normally being part-time, patronage appointees. The cabinet also appoints the president, but since this is a significant, full-time position whose performance reflects on the government, it is more often based on merit. If the 1992 Charlottetown Accord had been ratified, certain appointments such as the governor of the Bank of Canada would have required approval by the Senate. Thus one major difference between a Crown corporation and a regular government department can be seen in terms of structure.

A second distinguishing feature of the Crown corporation is that it is not subject to day-to-day political direction. The statute that creates the agency sets out its objectives to some extent and the cabinet may issue certain general policy guidelines, but the corporation otherwise operates more or less independently. The cabinet minister to whom the Crown corporation is attached largely acts as a channel of communication between it and Parliament, passing on answers to parliamentary inquiries but not being held responsible for them in the same way as for a regular department. On the other hand, because the government created the Crown corporation, appoints its leading personnel, and usually provides some of its funds, the minister and cabinet cannot totally avoid responsibility for its actions. Crown corporations must now submit an annual corporate plan to the minister as well as an annual year-end report. In some cases the cabinet can issue a directive to the corporation if informal persuasion to change its ways has not been effective, and a government obsessed with its deficit can make deep cuts in a Crown corporation's budget, as the CBC found throughout the Mulroney and Chrétien periods.

In the third place, Crown corporations are usually freer of bureaucratic controls than ordinary government departments. They are not usually subject to the same personnel supervision of the Public Service Commission, for example, or quite the same financial control of the Treasury Board. They can therefore operate more flexibly, especially if they are in competition with private firms. The Financial Administration Act contains different categories of Crown corporations, ranged in order of increasing independence from government control; as a general rule, the greater the financial self-sufficiency of the corporation, the greater its autonomy.

The reasons for government intervention at all are often related to national integration (CN, VIA Rail, and previously Air Canada), national identity (CBC and Canada Museums), economic development (Cape Breton Development Corporation), promotion of a particular industry (Canadian Wheat Board and Canadian Saltfish Corporation), and saving the jobs of a failing company (the temporary nationalization of Canadair and de Havilland Aircraft). But why establish a Crown corporation rather than an ordinary department, or why convert a department into a Crown corporation, as in the case of Canada Post? The Crown corporation is a logical structure for a governmental operation of a commercial or industrial nature; it may also be used in politically sensitive areas such as broadcasting; and the case for a crown corporation rather than a department is always stronger if the operation has private-sector competition. The unique blend of public and private corporations in such areas as air and rail transportation, broadcasting, and petroleum led one observer to refer to Canada's "public enterprise" political culture. He credited Crown corporations rather than private firms with the basic development of the country,[26] and regrets the recent wave of privatization.

Like other government operations, then, Crown corporations have a **public policy purpose**. They are created where, for one reason or another, the private sector has not met public needs, often because no profit would be feasible in serving the widely dispersed Canadian population. The basic objective of Crown corporations is to provide a public service, not to make a profit, but because most Crown corporations need annual public subsidies, they are often criticized for being inefficient. In fact, however, they are usually just as efficient as private companies; the subsidies are necessary to finance operations that are simply unprofitable by any standard.

....

MAJOR FEDERAL PRIVATIZATIONS, 1984–1994

* Air Canada
* Canada Development Corporation
* Canadair
* Canadian Arsenals Ltd.
* Co-Enerco Resources
* de Havilland Aircraft
* Eldorado Nuclear (Cameco)
* Fishery Products International
* Nordion International Inc.
* Northern Canada Power Commission
* Northern Transportation Company
* Petro-Canada
* Teleglobe Canada
* Telesat
* CN subsidiaries: CN Hotels
                   CPCN Telecommunications (CN half)
                   Northwestel Inc.
                   Terra Nova Telecommunications

The 1980s witnessed a worldwide trend toward the **privatization** of public enterprises, led by Margaret Thatcher in Britain, and the Mulroney government happily jumped on the privatization bandwagon. Such privatizations were made for largely ideological reasons;[27] the government had an instinctive preference for the private sector, and the sale of Crown corporation shares often helped to reduce the national deficit. Privatizers also argued that such Crown corporations no longer served a public policy purpose and that they would operate more efficiently as private companies. Moreover, the leading officials of Air Canada and Petro-Canada themselves urged the government to privatize them in order to allow them to compete more freely with other private companies. When shares are purchased by a broad cross-section of Canadians, the privatization has not been as controversial as when they are all sold to a single company (Teleglobe to Memotec) or when the corporation is sold to a foreign company (de Havilland to Boeing, before being resold to Bombardier). As of 1995, the federal government estimated that it had carried out at least 23 privatizations, which had raised some $4 billion and transferred 52 000 employees to the private sector.

By 1993 the new Liberal government claimed that privatization was no longer an ideological issue, and Finance Minister Paul Martin said: "If the government doesn't need to run something, it shouldn't. And in future, it won't." He argued that privatization freed up scarce resources for deficit reduction or new initiatives, that government was rethinking its role in society, that privatization reduced the scope of government to essentials, and that it improved service delivery, exposed government organizations to competitive business pressures, and broadened ownership of the Canadian economy. Against this background, the government announced that it would privatize the second-largest Crown corporation, the historic Canadian National Railway Company, and had many other cases under consideration.

REGULATORY AGENCIES

Regulatory agencies are the third basic form of bureaucratic organization.[28] Such agencies, generally less well known than government departments or Crown corporations, regulate many aspects of our daily lives. Some of the most important are listed below.

LEADING REGULATORY AGENCIES

- Atomic Energy Control Board
- Canadian Labour Relations Board
- Canadian Pension Commission
- Canadian Radio-television and Telecommunications Commission
- Immigration and Refugee Board
- Income Tax Appeal Board
- Investment Canada
- National Energy Board
- National Parole Board
- National Transportation Authority
- Tariff Board

In structure, regulatory agencies bear considerable resemblance to Crown corporations. They are made up of a chair and board appointed by the cabinet and advised by a permanent, expert staff. The incidence of partisanship in appointments to the chair and board is unfortunately quite large; indeed, regulatory agencies remain one of the last refuges of patronage in the political system. The 1992 Charlottetown Accord would have subjected some of these appointments to approval by the Senate. Regulatory agencies typically receive policy guidelines from the cabinet, but, as with Crown corporations, ministers are kept at arm's length from their day-to-day operations.

Regulatory agencies may make **quasi-legislative** rules and regulations, such as in the case of the Canadian content regulations of the Canadian Radio-television and Telecommunications Commission. A typical regulatory agency also makes **quasi-judicial** decisions based on the cabinet's policy guidelines and its own regulations. They issue radio and television licences (CRTC), approve long-distance telephone rates (CRTC), recognize unions (Canadian Labour Relations Board), approve foreign investment (Investment Canada), decide contentious immigration cases (Immigration and Refugee Board), and review transportation rates (National Transportation Authority).

These functions could presumably be performed by regular government departments, but they are given to semi-independent regulatory agencies in order to divorce them from political and especially partisan considerations. Such functions are usually of an adjudicative nature and could also be performed by the courts. But these kinds of decisions demand a technical expertise not expected in judges, and, given the backlog in the court system, it is hoped that the decisions of regulatory agencies will be made more quickly and more cheaply than those of the courts.

At the same time, however, regulatory agencies are expected to provide an impartial, courtlike hearing, and in many cases lawyers are present in the same capacity as in court. Decisions of such agencies are normally appealable to the courts on procedural grounds but not on the substance of the case. Some are appealable to the cabinet on the merits of the case (e.g., CRTC decisions on long-distance telephone rates), but the cabinet usually declines to overturn the agency's decision. It was therefore of some significance when the cabinet overturned a CRTC decision in 1995 with respect to direct-to-home satellite services, after Power Corporation of Montreal was unhappy with the regulatory body's ruling.

Two main criticisms of regulatory agencies have been made in recent years. On the one hand, it is argued that there are too many regulatory agencies with too much power. Hence, **deregulation** was a companion ingredient to privatization in the Anglo-American neo-conservatism of the 1980s. The Mulroney government issued a regulatory reform strategy in 1986 and proceeded to deregulate the transportation industry. On the other hand, an almost opposite criticism is that regulatory agencies become captives of the very industries they are supposed to be regulating. The agency and the industry operate as their own little policy community, divorced from other influences. In this connection it is often said that the consumer interest is overlooked as the regulatory agency falls victim to corporate pressure, with the CRTC being a good example. This problem is sometimes lessened by allowing consumer groups to intervene in the hearings of regulatory agencies or in government funding of intervener groups.

STRUCTURAL HERETICS

Not all government operations fall into the three categories discussed above. "Structural heretics"[29] include central agencies, royal commissions, task forces, advisory councils, funding bodies, and other one-of-a-kind agencies (the Chief Electoral Officer, the Public Archives, the RCMP, and the Canadian Security Intelligence Service).

Task forces are an informal means of quickly acquiring information and recommendations.[30] They may be composed of members of Parliament, ministers, public servants, outsiders, or some combination thereof. Task forces were used most extensively in the early Trudeau years when a new prime minister came to power with a desire to do things differently but without much knowledge of many issues and with typical suspicion of public service resistance to change. The most prominent were probably Paul Hellyer's Task Force on Housing and Urban Development and Herb Gray's Task Force on Foreign Investment.

Royal commissions are a much older instrument, about 450 having been appointed since 1867. Generally speaking, royal commissions are very formal, in-depth inquiries set up by the cabinet to investigate some difficult problem for which the resources of the regular public service are considered inadequate. Royal commissions may be made up of from one to ten commissioners, usually people of stature and expertise, and normally involve extensive public hearings and an elaborate research program. They are often regarded somewhat cynically because of the length of time it takes them to produce a report, and because they cost a great deal of money. The cynics also point out that governments have not had a good record of implementing royal commission recommendations, and that such commissions often appear to be appointed to take the heat off a particular issue. Sometimes they are also seen as devices with which to educate the public to the government's way of thinking or of generating support for a policy the government already had in mind. Nevertheless, many royal commissions have served a useful purpose, and many public policies such as equalization payments, medicare, bilingualism, and free trade owe their existence, at least in part, to royal commission reports. Whatever their formal name, they are often referred to by the name of their chair, such as Rowell–Sirois (Federal–Provincial Relations, 1940), Hall (Health Services, 1964–65), and Macdonald (Economic Prospects, 1985).

CONTROLLING THE BUREAUCRACY

Given the enormous influence and considerable power of the bureaucracy in the modern state, democracies are understandably concerned about keeping the public service under control. A number of means of doing so can be identified.

Ministers and Cabinet

In the first place, individual ministers and the cabinet as a whole are supposed to provide political control of the bureaucracy. The minister both gives direction to the public service and has the power to veto any of its proposals, at least in theory. Real ministers have provided varied accounts of what actually happens in practice: some argue that ministers can control their departments, while others feel that they were often manipulated by their public servants. Even where the minister in charge is weak or manipulated, however, the cabinet as a whole is likely to step in from time to time to reject bureaucratic advice and opt for an alternate proposal whose political implications are more favourable.

Bureaucrats Controlling Bureaucrats

In the second place, the power of some bureaucrats is controlled by other bureaucrats, such as the financial control of the Treasury Board and the Finance Department, the personnel control of the Public Service Commission, and the policy control of the Privy Council Office. To some extent the central agencies operate on the orders of the cabinet or cabinet committees, so that these agencies supplement the political control mentioned above.

House of Commons

The third line of defence against bureaucratic power is the House of Commons. While its operations will be examined in more detail in Chapter 22, one principle of parliamentary government relevant here is that the executive (cabinet or bureaucracy) is not allowed either to raise or spend money without parliamentary approval. In practice, proposals for tax changes as well as spending proposals all originate with the executive, they are rarely altered in the legislative process, and the taxing and spending usually begins before Parliament has given its consent. But ultimately Parliament must pass all such financial measures. The process of examining the Estimates gives the House of Commons an opportunity to question and criticize ministers and deputy ministers about all aspects of their departmental spending, programs, and policies. Furthermore, once the money has been spent, an official of Parliament, the **Auditor General**, inspects the Public Accounts and informs Parliament in an annual report of instances where funds were spent unlawfully or unwisely.[31] Considerable controversy raged in the 1980s over the size of the Auditor General's staff, their ability to gain access to cabinet documents, and whether they should function narrowly as auditors or make broader policy recommendations to individual departments. The **Public Accounts Committee** of the House (chaired by an opposition member) goes through the Auditor General's report and calls onto the carpet those ministers or deputy ministers who have committed the worst financial faults.

Another principal means used by the House of Commons to control the bureaucracy is the daily, oral Question Period. In this case, the Commons must act through the intermediary minister who is theoretically responsible for everything the department does. While the minister is expected to take the blame for bureaucratic errors, public servants seek to avoid bringing such embarrassment or disrepute upon their minister and department. In addition, members of Parliament receive requests on a daily basis from their constituents to intervene on their behalf to speed up or correct bureaucratic decisions. MPs and their staff normally handle such problems with a telephone call or a letter to the public servant or minister concerned. Another kind of parliamentary control of the bureaucracy is exercised by the Standing Joint Committee on the Scrutiny of Regulations, which attempts to review the reams of regulations that the bureaucracy produces annually.

The Judiciary

A fourth kind of control of the bureaucracy is provided by the judiciary.[32] The power of the courts to overturn decisions of bureaucrats in regular government departments is essentially restricted to cases of breaches of the law or actions taken beyond the public servant's jurisdiction. Such cases are rare, but the Charter of Rights and Freedoms provides more scope for this kind of judicial review of bureaucratic action than in the past. In the *Singh* case, for example, the Supreme Court ruled that the Immigration Department had to provide an oral hearing for refugee claimants. The Charter's effect on the bureaucracy primarily relates to police officers, a special kind of public servant, and to regulatory agencies. The latter are usually expected to operate in a courtlike manner, and their decisions can be overturned by the courts for procedural abuses as well as for exceeding their jurisdiction. The Federal Court of Canada, to be discussed in Chapter 23, specializes in hearing appeals from such regulatory agencies.

Ombudsmen

Every Canadian province except Prince Edward Island has supplemented these four means of controlling the bureaucracy with the appointment of an ombudsman, an official of the legislature to whom people can complain about bureaucratic decisions, mistakes, abuse, discrimination, or indecision. Ombudsmen try to correct such errors by persuasion, but if that fails, they can resort to the power of legislative and media publicity. Canada has no ombudsman at the federal level, but several ombudsman-like officials exist to deal with specialized complaints. The Correctional Investigator looks into complaints from inmates against prison authorities; the Commissioner of Official Languages investigates public or bureaucratic claims regarding infringement of the Official Languages Act; and the Privacy Commissioner investigates complaints from citizens who believe that their privacy rights have been invaded.

The Information Commissioner

Perhaps the most important of these watchdog agencies is the **Information Commissioner**.[33] Canadian governments have traditionally functioned under a thick cloak of secrecy at both the cabinet and bureaucratic levels. This tradition has prevented the opposition and the public from knowing what alternative policies were considered in the executive branch, what kind of public opinion polling was carried out, and what advice was actually offered by the bureaucracy to the cabinet. The Canadian **Access to Information Act** was passed in 1983 and considerably improved the situation, although the many exemptions in the Act mean that it is not entirely effective. If citizens, journalists, companies, or pressure groups are denied access to a desired piece of government information, they can appeal to the Information Commissioner, who can overrule the department in the matter, with a final to appeal to the Federal Court.

In his 1995 Report, the Information Commissioner complained about the addiction to secrecy on the part of many government officials and made a plea for greater openness from the prime minister's level. He noted some improvements, however, such as in the Privy Council Office and in the routine release of public opinion polls.

....

OBSERVATIONS OF THE INFORMATION COMMISSIONER, 1995

Nothing handicapped the access law more during its first 10 years than the disdain shown for it by some at the most senior levels of government, even in the office of the Prime Minister. A climate of obstruction, obfuscation and delay was created and tolerated in responding to Canadians seeking information from the government.... [In spite of the promise in the Liberal "Red Book" to do better], a year and a half has gone by and the Prime Minister has given no such public signal of his support for openness ... Suspicion of the access law as an alien (read American) importation, coupled with a somewhat paternalistic faith in the integrity of public officials, continues to have a foothold among some members of the new government and public service.

Source: Information Commissioner, Annual Report, 1994–1995. *Reproduced with permission of the Minister of Supply and Services Canada, 1995.*

....

DYSFUNCTIONS AND REFORM OF THE BUREAUCRACY

Apart from the problem of keeping the bureaucracy under some kind of democratic control, three other problems or dysfunctions are often identified. First, from the public's perspective, there is the constant accusation of "red tape." This generally includes a collection of sins that characterize the behaviour of all large organizations, not only governmental ones, including delays, a multitude of forms, excessive rules and regulations, difficulty of communicating with the official who could solve the problem, and lack of helpful, personal attention. If these dysfunctions are more characteristic of government than of large private firms, it is primarily because governments are required to function according to the law and the rules and regulations issued under the law. Private firms may be able to modify their rules (and prices) much more easily. Government must also treat everyone in exactly the same way, so unlike private firms, it cannot show favouritism or make individual deals. Delays are usually the result of public servants wanting to be certain that any decision is absolutely right, because mistakes may be criticized in Parliament or in the media. Of course public servants should be prompt and courteous—at least civil!—but the public environment in which they work requires an equality of treatment that many people are not accustomed to in the private sector.

A second general criticism of bureaucracy is that it is inefficient because it lacks the profit motive of the private sector. Officials in private firms are said to move more quickly because they are in greater danger of losing their jobs and because minimizing costs is a higher priority. To some extent this is true. The essential difference between the public and private sectors, however, is that the bureaucracy is charged with providing a public service, and it should be judged primarily on the adequacy of that service. Nevertheless, there is a widespread belief—

Reprinted with the permission of Doubleday Canada.

among the business community, politicians, and the public at large—that the inefficiency of the bureaucracy is a factor in increasing the public debt. This perception led both the Mulroney and Chrétien governments to impose severe financial restraints on government departments and some Crown corporations, leading them to make across-the-board cuts, terminate programs, lay off staff, freeze hiring, depend on volunteers, charge user fees, and contract-out certain services.[34]

From a management point of view, the main dysfunction of the public service is that deputy ministers and other managerial personnel are too hemmed in by rules and regulations and their authority is too limited by central agencies. In consequence, in 1986 the Mulroney government introduced the Increased Ministerial Authority and Accountability (IMAA) process. The objective of IMAA was to provide more autonomy and managerial flexibility to deputy ministers by relaxing some of the detailed rules and reporting requirements if they sign a Memorandum of Understanding (MOU) with the Treasury Board.

IMAA was followed up in 1989 by Public Service 2000, an initiative to "enable the Public Service to provide the best possible service to Canadians into the 21st century."[35] PS 2000 involved the creation of several task forces made up of senior public servants and dealing with such matters as classification, compensation, staffing, training and development, staff relations, budget controls, and service to the public. Although PS 2000 was designed to meet certain managerial objectives, it was also aimed at improving public service morale, which was at an all-time low due to the government's public-service restraint program.

The issues mentioned above were merely parts of a major transformation of the Canadian federal public service that has been under consideration for almost a decade and that has parallels around the world. In 1987, even before Public Service 2000, the Public Policy Forum was established. It was a collaborative effort between the government and over 90 private-sector groups, including the largest corporations in the country, whose objects were promoting better relations between the public and private sectors and identifying measures to improve the functioning of government. In 1993 it published its blueprint, *Making Government Work*, which called for significant reform along private-sector lines.

Then, in 1992, Prime Minister Mulroney asked Secretary of State Robert de Cotret to undertake a review of government operations with the advice of former cabinet secretary Gordon Osbaldeston and the then cabinet secretary Glen Shortliffe. The major restructuring of government departments that took place a year later and discussed earlier in the chapter reflected the recommendations of that report. Its personnel implications were felt most heavily at the assistant deputy minister level, with 53 ADMs laid off. The Liberals retained most of the changes and appointed Marcel Massé, another former cabinet secretary and now a Liberal MP, as the minister responsible for Public Service Renewal. Beyond these domestic concerns, more general factors leading to public-service reform included "debt and deficits (both public and private), changing public and private sector expectations, an altered international trading environment, new technologies, growing doubts about the capacity of state institutions to fulfil their mandates, and a multitude of [others]."[36] Many of the results of such pressure for public-sector reform have already been mentioned: consolidating government departments, giving managers more autonomy, privatizing Crown corporations, and commercializing certain government services. Two other initiatives that should be mentioned are *Special Operating Agencies* (SOAs) and the 1995 budget.

Special Operating Agencies are units that function with relative autonomy within government departments. In most cases they have the potential to become self-financing, and the basic objective is to deliver a service along private-sector lines, that is, in a manner that is more sensitive to client requirements, that promotes a more creative, entrepreneurial working environment, and that brings savings to government. These units have a minimal role in policy advice, and their autonomy is based on a framework agreement with the department and a departmentally approved business plan. The head of the unit reports to the deputy minister, and the departmental minister retains political responsibility. The Passport and Patent Offices are examples of the 15 SOAs created by 1995, but more are likely in the future.

In the 1995 budget the minister of Finance declared his intention to eliminate 45 000 public-service jobs by 1998, the first 20 000 in 1995–96. Some public servants would be eligible for buyouts and early retirement packages, and some would be able to swap jobs with those who wished to leave but whose job was secure. Eleven departments were targeted for the most drastic cuts—especially Transport, many of whose operations would be privatized—but the policy was service-wide. The announcement aroused great opposition from public-sector unions, especially the PSAC, which had even earlier suggested alternative ways of saving government money.

During the first half of the 1990s, then, politicians have made two rather drastic changes in the Canadian federal public service. These served primarily to help the government reduce its deficit. Desirable as these changes may have been, they no doubt damaged public services in other ways, and they do not exhaust the reforms that would make it a more effective public service for all concerned.[37]

CONCLUSION

The central question that arises in any discussion of the bureaucracy is whether it is out of control. This issue primarily relates to the delicate relationship between the public service and the politicians. Several means of control were discussed above, but the question remains.

(SC) Bureaucratic power is central to the state-centred approach, which generally contends that the bureaucracy is a world unto itself. Ministers are so busy with cabinet and cabinet committee meetings, parliamentary responsibilities, public-speaking engagements, listening to pressure group and other demands, and looking after their constituencies, that they have little or no time left to spend in their department. They have only the most superficial idea of what their department is doing; for the most part, it is a self-governing operation, subject only to the authority of other bureaucratic central agencies. Even the prime minister and cabinet as a whole can do little but take the advice of the secretary to the cabinet, the deputy minister of Finance, the secretary of the Treasury Board, the governor of the Bank of Canada, and a handful of other key officials. State-centred theorists do not necessarily argue that such officials act only in their own narrow self-interest, however; they may pursue the public interest as they see it. The period between 1935 and 1957, for example, is sometimes seen as the era of the powerful *mandarins*, who brought Keynesian economics to Canada and developed the government's whole postwar social and economic program.[38] While such a small group of mandarins may not have exercised the same kind of innovative influence during the past 30 years or so, the politicians have become even more dependent on the bureaucracy as a whole. In an example from the 1960s, federal welfare officials pushed the politicians for reforms that in their opinion would help the poor and working classes.[39]

[P] Pluralists are not alarmed at the extent of bureaucratic power because they see it limited by the power of the cabinet, the House of Commons, the courts, and other agencies. Furthermore, pluralists emphasize the rivalry and competition within the bureaucracy, which make it difficult for any single bureaucrat, department, or agency to become authoritarian. They also see the widespread interest group interaction with departments as a way of influencing the outputs of government. The concept of government as a plethora of specialized policy communities, each with its own minister, department, associated agencies, pressure groups, and interested individuals, is particularly appealing to the pluralist and brings this approach together with state-centred theorists.

PC The "bureaucratic game" is another aspect of bargaining that is central to public choice theory. In their rational, mutually self-seeking relationship with ministers, bureaucrats seek to increase their jurisdiction, their staff, their status, their budget, and their salary, and pursue or recommend policy options that are most convenient and congenial to themselves. Politicians are agreeable to these bureaucratic objectives as long as public servants help them stay in power by keeping them out of trouble and by pacifying electorally strategic special-interest groups. On the other hand, the uninformed, the unorganized, and "their committed opponents in never-to-be-won constituencies"[40] can be ignored.

© Class analysts argue that the bureaucracy primarily serves the interests of the corporate elite. This is largely the inevitable result of the government's and the state's eventually having to defer to corporate imperatives in a capitalist system.[41] It is also related to the commonalities in socioeconomic characteristics of the senior public service and the business community, and the elite accommodation that goes on between the bureaucracy, cabinet, and pressure groups.[42] It is in response to the revelations that the higher levels of the bureaucracy have traditionally been unrepresentative of the wider population in terms of ethnicity, geography, class, and gender, of course, that recent affirmative action programs have been instituted. Besides the bureaucratic deference to the value of capital accumulation, class analysts remind us not to overlook the most coercive agencies of the bureaucracy, the RCMP and the Canadian Security Intelligence Service.

Increasingly, public servants are applying a class analysis to their own employment situation. After years of pay freezes and with new and drastic cuts to public service jobs, they are beginning to feel exploited themselves. Many feel that public-sector restraint programs are simply designed "to advance business interests behind a facade of protecting the public." They point to "the frequent use of back-to-work legislation, the jailing of union leaders, and reducing the right to strike by designating an increasing number of public sector workers as essential."[43]

DISCUSSION QUESTIONS

1. Is there any alternative to the "amateur" minister in the Canadian cabinet system?

2. What is the ideal relationship between the minister and the deputy minister?

3. Should deputy ministers be replaced with partisan appointees?

4. Do central agencies interfere excessively with the deputy minister's responsibility to manage the department?

5. To what extent should Canada establish a "representative bureaucracy"?

6. What limits, if any, should be put on the political activity of public servants? On their right to strike?

7. Do pressure groups and corporations have too much influence over departments and regulatory agencies?

8. Given the necessity of the bureaucracy in the modern state, are the democratic controls on its power sufficient?

9. How do you feel about downsizing the public service, privatizing Crown corporations, deregulation, and other current reforms being undertaken?

10. How do the approaches outlined in Chapter 1 relate to the material in this chapter?

. . . .

NOTES

1. Kenneth Kernaghan and David Siegel, *Public Administration in Canada: A Text*, 2nd ed. (Scarborough: Nelson Canada, 1991), p. 137. A third edition was published in 1995.
2. R.V. Segsworth, "Policy and Program Evaluation in the Government of Canada," in Ray C. Rist, ed., *Program Evaluation and the Management of Government* (New Brunswick, NJ: Transaction Publishers, 1990).
3. Two regularly updated sources are CCH Canadian Ltd., *Canadian Government Programs and Services*, and Canada Communication Group, *Organization of the Government of Canada*. See also Timothy Plumptre, *Beyond the Bottom Line: Management in Government* (Halifax: Institute for Research on Public Policy, 1988).
4. S.L. Sutherland, "Responsible Government and Ministerial Responsibility: Every Reform Is Its Own Problem," *Canadian Journal of Political Science* (March 1991), pp. 91–120.
5. Kernaghan and Siegel, *Public Administration in Canada*, pp. 379–85; and S.L. Sutherland, "The Al-Mashat Affair: Administrative Responsibility in Parliamentary Institutions," *Canadian Public Administration* (Winter 1991), pp. 573–603.
6. Among all the writing on this subject, the most authoritative is Gordon Osbaldeston, *Keeping Deputy Ministers Accountable* (Toronto: McGraw-Hill Ryerson, 1990).
7. See the exchange between Flora MacDonald and Mitchell Sharp in Paul Fox and Graham White, eds., *Politics: Canada*, 7th ed. (Toronto: McGraw-Hill Ryerson, 1991), and between Flora MacDonald and Don Page in Mark Charlton and Paul Barker, eds., *Crosscurrents: Contemporary Political Issues*, 2nd ed. (Scarborough: Nelson Canada, 1994).
8. Interview with John Chenier, editor of *The Federal Lobbyists*.
9. On the other hand, *Ottawa's Senior Executives Guide*, published annually by INFO GLOBE, now provides a profile of all senior bureaucrats, together with a picture!
10. Kernaghan and Siegel, *Public Administration in Canada*, p. 519.
11. Robert Adie and Paul Thomas, *Canadian Public Administration*, 2nd ed. (Scarborough: Prentice-Hall Canada, 1987), ch. 3; Kernaghan and Siegel, ch. 24; and Roger Gibbins, *Regionalism* (Toronto: Butterworths, 1982), pp. 71–75.
12. On the question of patronage, see Jeffrey Simpson, *Spoils of Power* (Toronto: Collins, 1988), and S.J.R. Noel, "Leadership and Clientelism," in David Bellamy et al., eds., *The Provincial Political Systems* (Toronto: Methuen, 1976).
13. J.L. Granatstein, *The Ottawa Men: The Civil Service Mandarins 1935–1957* (Toronto: Oxford University Press, 1982).
14. John Porter, *The Vertical Mosaic* (Toronto: University of Toronto Press, 1965); Dennis Olsen, *The State Elite* (Toronto: McClelland and Stewart, 1980); and Kernaghan and Siegel, p. 329.
15. Kathleen Archibald, *Sex and the Public Service* (Ottawa: Queen's Printer, 1970); Task Force on Barriers to Women in the Public Service, *Beneath the Veneer*, Vol. 1 (Ottawa: Supply and Services, 1990).
16. Kernaghan and Siegel, *Public Administration in Canada*, pp. 534–35.
17. Adie and Thomas, *Canadian Public Administration*, pp. 121–26.
18. *Osborne v. Canada (Treasury Board)* [1991] 2 S.C.R. 69. See also *OPSEU v. Ontario (Attorney General)*, [1987] 2 S.C.R. 2.

19. Noel, "Leadership and Clientelism."
20. Donald Savoie, *The Politics of Public Spending in Canada* (Toronto: University of Toronto Press, 1990); Adie and Thomas, ch. 7; and Kernaghan and Siegel, chs. 26 and 27.
21. Savoie, *The Politics of Public Spending in Canada.*
22. Adie and Thomas, ch. 11; and Kernaghan and Siegel, ch. 19.
23. Rand Dyck, "The Canada Assistance Plan: The Ultimate in Cooperative Federalism," *Canadian Public Administration* (Winter 1976).
24. Paul Pross, *Group Politics and Public Policy* (Toronto: Oxford University Press, 1986); William D. Coleman and Grace Skogstad, eds., *Policy Communities and Public Policy in Canada* (Mississauga: Copp Clark Pitman, 1990).
25. On this subject, see Jeanne Laux and Maureen Molot, *State Capitalism: Public Enterprise in Canada* (Ithaca, NY: Cornell University Press, 1988); Robert Prichard, ed., *Crown Corporations in Canada* (Toronto: Butterworths, 1983); Allan Tupper and Bruce Doern, eds., *Public Corporations and Public Policy in Canada* (Montreal: Institute for Research on Public Policy, 1981); Adie and Thomas, ch. 10; and Kernaghan and Siegel, ch. 9.
26. Herschel Hardin, *A Nation Unaware: The Canadian Economic Culture* (Vancouver: J.S. Douglas, 1974).
27. Herschel Hardin, *The Privatization Putsch* (Halifax: Institute for Research on Public Policy, 1989).
28. On the subject of regulation, see Lloyd Brown-John, *Canadian Regulatory Agencies* (Toronto: Butterworths, 1981); Bruce Doern, ed., *The Regulatory Process in Canada* (Toronto: Macmillan, 1978); Adie and Thomas, ch. 9; and Kernaghan and Siegel, ch. 10.
29. J.E. Hodgetts, *The Canadian Public Service: A Physiology of Government, 1867–1970* (Toronto: University of Toronto Press, 1973).
30. Kernaghan and Seigel, pp. 255–63.
31. S.L. Sutherland, "On the Audit Trail of the Auditor General: Parliament's Servant, 1973–80," *Canadian Public Administration* (Winter 1980), pp. 616–44; and S.L. Sutherland, "The Politics of Audit: The Federal Office of the Auditor General in Comparative Perspective," *Canadian Public Administration* (Spring 1986), pp. 118–48.
32. Adie and Thomas, ch. 12; and Kernaghan and Siegel, ch. 18.
33. Adie and Thomas, ch. 13; and Kernaghan and Siegel, ch. 21.
34. Kernaghan and Siegel, *Public Administration in Canada*, pp. 498–502; and Lloyd Brown-John, "If You're So Damned Smart, Why Don't You Run Government Like a Business?" in Katherine Graham, ed., *How Ottawa Spends* 1990–91 (Ottawa: Carleton University Press, 1990).
35. *Public Service 2000: The Renewal of the Public Service of Canada* (Ottawa: Supply and Services, 1990); David Zussman, "Managing the Federal Public Service as the Knot Tightens," in Katherine Graham, ed., *How Ottawa Spends 1990–91*; and Kenneth Kernaghan, "Career Public Service 2000: Road to Renewal or Impractical Vision?" *Canadian Public Administration* (Winter 1991), pp. 551–72.
36. Brian O'Neil, "Reorganizing Government: New Approaches to Public Service Reform" (Ottawa: Library of Parliament, 1994).
37. Leslie A. Pal, "The Federal Bureaucracy: Reinventing the Links between State and Society," in Michael Whittington and Glen Williams, eds., *Canadian Politics in the 1990s*, 4th ed. (Scarborough: Nelson Canada, 1995); and Steven Langdon et al., *In the Public Interest; The Value of Public Services* (Prescott, ON: Voyageur Publishing, 1995).
38. J.L. Granatstein, *The Ottawa Men.*
39. Richard Splane, "Social Policy-Making in the Government of Canada: Reflections of a Reformist Bureaucrat," in S.A. Yelaja, ed., *Canadian Social Policy* (Waterloo: Wilfrid Laurier University Press, 1978).
40. Douglas Hartle, *The Expenditure Process of the Government of Canada: A Public Choice–Rent-Seeking Perspective* (Toronto: Canadian Tax Foundation, 1988).
41. Ralph Miliband, *The State in Capitalist Society* (London: Weidenfeld and Nicolson, 1969).
42. Robert Presthus, *Elite Accommodation in Canadian Politics* (Toronto: Macmillan, 1973).
43. Kernaghan and Siegel, *Public Administration in Canada*, 2nd ed., p. 558.

FURTHER READING

Adie, Robert, and Paul Thomas. *Canadian Public Administration*, 2nd ed. Scarborough: Prentice-Hall Canada, 1987.

Brown-John, Lloyd. *Canadian Regulatory Agencies*. Toronto: Butterworths, 1981.

Campbell, Colin. *Governments under Stress: Political Executives and Key Bureaucrats in Washington, London, and Ottawa*. Toronto: University of Toronto Press, 1983.

Campbell, Colin, and George Szablowski. *The Superbureaucrats*. Toronto: Macmillan, 1979.

Doern, Bruce, ed. *The Regulatory Process in Canada*. Toronto: Macmillan, 1978.

Doerr, Audrey. *The Machinery of Government in Canada*. Toronto: Methuen, 1981.

Dwivedi, O.P., ed. *The Administrative State in Canada*. Toronto: University of Toronto Press, 1982.

Graham, Katherine, ed. *How Ottawa Spends 1988–89*. Ottawa: Carleton University Press, 1988.

———. *How Ottawa Spends 1989–90*. Ottawa: Carleton University Press, 1989.

———. *How Ottawa Spends 1990–91*. Ottawa: Carleton University Press, 1990.

Granatstein, J.L. *The Ottawa Men: The Civil Service Mandarins 1935–1957*. Toronto: Oxford University Press, 1982.

Hardin, Herschel. *A Nation Unaware: The Canadian Economic Culture*. Vancouver: J.S. Douglas, 1974.

———. *The Privatization Putsch*. Halifax: Institute for Research on Public Policy, 1989.

Hodgetts, J.E. *The Canadian Public Service: A Physiology of Government, 1867–1970*. Toronto: University of Toronto Press, 1973.

Kernaghan, Kenneth, and David Siegel. *Public Administration in Canada: A Text*, 2nd ed. Scarborough: Nelson Canada, 1991; 3rd ed., 1995.

Laux, Jeanne, and Maureen Molot. *State Capitalism: Public Enterprise in Canada*. Ithaca, NY: Cornell University Press, 1988.

Maslove, Allan, ed. *How Ottawa Spends 1984*. Toronto: Methuen, 1984.

Osbaldeston, Gordon. *Keeping Deputy Ministers Accountable*. Toronto: McGraw-Hill Ryerson, 1989.

Prince, Michael J., ed. *How Ottawa Spends 1985*. Toronto: Methuen, 1985.

———. *How Ottawa Spends 1986–87*. Toronto: Methuen, 1987.

Savoie, Donald. *The Politics of Public Spending in Canada*. Toronto: University of Toronto Press, 1990.

Chapter 22

PARLIAMENT

Almost every day the elected representatives of the Canadian people meet in open, verbal combat in Question Period in the House of Commons. Members of Parliament on the opposition side of the House attack the prime minister and other ministers for acts of omission and commission, while the government responds with laudatory statements and statistics on its own performance. In these exchanges and other debates, politicians' reputations are often made and broken. The House of Commons is the central link between the public and the government in Canadian democracy, and as such, it is the furnace of national politics. Most interests in society are represented there in one way or another, and they clash on a daily basis. The Commons is the primary battleground for the hearts and minds of Canadian voters, and House debate is a "lead-up" to the subsequent election campaign. The Senate, on the other hand, is normally a much more peaceful place, and is viewed by many Canadians as a group of elderly party hacks who collect generous remuneration for doing little work. When its majority belongs to a different party from that in the Commons, however, as has recently been the case, the work of the Senate becomes much more interesting.

Every four or five years, voters in each of 295 local constituencies elect their representative in the House of Commons. Partly because they have a direct part in electing its members and partly because it operates publicly and they often see it in action, at least on television, the House of Commons is the political institution most familiar to Canadians. This familiarity has sometimes led such voters and viewers to think that the Commons has more power in the policy-making process than it actually does. While it is largely to enhance that power that the procedures of the House are regularly reformed, the institution has other functions and values that are probably not widely understood.

As well as the House of Commons, the **Parliament of Canada** includes the Queen and the Senate, and a law must be approved by all three parts. In this respect Canada is sometimes said to employ the "Westminster model" of government because it is based on the British system. As noted in Chapter 2, this model begins with a bicameral legislature—an elected lower house with primary legislative powers answerable to the polity through elections, and an upper house with limited legislative powers, in law or in fact. The executive is part of the lower house and through the cabinet drives or "energizes" the legislative process. The government or cabinet is in charge of and responsible for the conduct of parliamentary business, while an institutionalized opposition has the right to criticize the government and the ability to make that criticism felt. The Westminister model, therefore, promises potent government and political stability through the cabinet, along with political accountability through open debate.

In popular parlance, however, the word "Parliament" is often used synonymously with the Commons, which is by far its most important part. Hence members of the House of Commons are called members of Parliament or MPs. MPs can be largely divided into three main groups: those who also serve as cabinet ministers, those who support the cabinet (government **backbenchers**), and those who oppose the government (the **opposition**).

This chapter examines the House of Commons from a number of perspectives. These include its functions and powers, its composition, the parliamentary timetable, party discipline and the party caucus, stages and kinds of legislation, the organization and officers of the House, the committee system, members' services, the roles of MPs, the government–opposition balance, minority government, and reform of the institution. The chapter later explores the role of the Senate.

FUNCTIONS AND POWERS OF THE HOUSE OF COMMONS

Historically, a basic principle of Canadian government has been the **sovereignty or supremacy of Parliament**; that is, apart from interfering in provincial jurisdiction and with other minor exceptions, Parliament could pass laws of any kind that were virtually beyond review by any other organ of government, including the courts. This principle was considerably transformed in 1982, however, with the adoption of the Canadian Charter of Rights and Freedoms. The courts have now been given the power to review both federal and provincial legislation in terms of the Charter, and to invalidate such legislation to the extent of any contradiction. On the other hand, the courts have often suggested that the legislation be redrafted to fit within the boundaries of the Charter, and the "notwithstanding" clause allows for the reassertion of parliamentary sovereignty on many points.

In terms of the seven functions performed in the political system, the House of Commons (and Senate) fall best into the rule-making category, although as the previous two chapters have shown, the rules are actually formulated in the executive branch. MPs (and senators) articulate local and other interests and party caucuses try to come up with compromises in which diverse interests are aggregated. The Commons also engages in political recruitment and political communication, and these four functions may actually be more important than its legislative role. Another way to address the functions of the House of Commons is in its relationship to the cabinet. The House of Commons does not make policy or govern, but in the first instance, through motions of confidence and nonconfidence, it decides who will form the government; second, it provides that government, on behalf of the people, with the authority, funds, and other resources necessary for governing the country; third, it makes the government behave by acting as a constant critic and watchdog; and fourth, it provides an alternative government by enabling the opposition to present its case to the public and become a credible choice for replacing the party in power.[1]

In discussing the functions of the House of Commons it is also instructive to examine its role in the chart of the policy-making process outlined in Chapter 19. In the first place, Parliament may be involved in the initiation phase by raising issues in the daily Question Period and in general debates, in criticizing existing spending programs, or by means of private members' bills. It is then virtually nonexistent in the priority-setting and policy formulation phases. Where the Commons dominates the picture is in the legitimation stage. Whether or not bills are refined in the course of their passage through the House of Commons, what is most important is that they are legitimated. This means that cabinet proposals embodied in bills are made legitimate by their passage through the formal, authorized, democratic channels of the Commons. It may not make many significant changes, but the House does subject bills to extended debate and publicizes their advantages and disadvantages before converting them into laws or statutes. C.E.S. Franks calls this process the "mobilization of consent."[2] The legislative stage serves to inform the public of the content of new policies, and out of this "prolonged warfare," consent or acceptance is eventually obtained. This debate essentially prepares the electorate for its decision on how to vote in the next election. The House then has little say in the fifth and sixth phases, the implementation and interpretation of laws, including scant supervision of regulations issued by the executive.

The various ways of looking at the functions of the House of Commons noted above emphasize the role of the institution as a whole. Individual members have interest articulation, representational, and ombudsman functions, as they speak out for their constituencies and generally take care of their constituents.

COMPOSITION OF THE HOUSE OF COMMONS

The basic principle in establishing the House of Commons is that each province is represented in proportion to its population. Chapter 15 outlined how the 295 seats in the Commons are distributed among the provinces, with the following results: Ontario, 99; Quebec, 75; B.C., 32; Alberta, 26; Manitoba, 14; Saskatchewan, 14; Nova Scotia, 11; New Brunswick, 10; Newfoundland, 7; P.E.I., 4; N.W.T., 2; and Yukon, 1.

Even if members of Parliament other than cabinet ministers have only a limited role in the policy-making process, they are important enough to justify an inquiry into their social background characteristics.[3] Since they are elected to represent territorial units and usually live in or near their constituencies, MPs almost automatically become representative of the population in a geographic sense. Although it is not quite so inevitable that they will be representative in terms of ethnic background, this also turns out to be the case, at least for those of English and French origins. The Constitution Act, 1867, required from the beginning that all House documents be printed in English and French, but the absence of simultaneous interpretation until 1958 and the unilingualism of most MPs served to limit the interaction between the two linguistic groups within the institution.

On the other hand, members of Parliament do not reflect the population very well in terms of education, occupation, or class. Although not as exclusive in these respects as cabinet ministers, MPs have higher educational levels and higher-status occupations than the

TABLE 22.1	Occupational Distribution of MPs, 1993				
Business	55	Education	60	Farmer	20
Lawyer	50	Other Professional	60	Others	50

Source: Compiled from the Canadian Parliamentary Guide, *1994.*

general population. Historically the legal profession has furnished the largest single group in the Commons, but the number of MPs with a business background equalled or exceeded the number of lawyers in the 1984 and 1988 Conservative victories. An indication of the occupational distribution of members of Parliament after 1993 is provided in Table 22.1. It shows roughly 20 percent for each of business, law, education, and other professions.

Members are also unrepresentative of the population with respect to gender. Relatively few women are elected to the House of Commons, although the number is on the increase, reaching 39 out of 295 in 1988 and 54 in 1993. The increasing proportion of MPs without any previous service in elected office at the municipal or provincial levels should also be mentioned. A municipal or provincial political career in Canada is apparently quite distinct from one in federal politics.

What is probably most striking about Canadian members of Parliament, especially compared with other legislatures around the world, is their rapid turnover in office. The proportion of new members after each election averages 40 percent, and the average length of time in office is less than ten years.[4] This means that Canadian MPs are transient amateurs who engage in "avocational politics."[5] Few members remain in Parliament long enough to develop an understanding of the institution, to master their extra-parliamentary responsibilities, or to stand up to a long-serving prime minister. The 1993 turnover was over 75 percent, due to the decimation of the Conservatives and NDP.

THE PARLIAMENTARY TIMETABLE

Perhaps the best way to get an overview of the work of the House of Commons is by examining the parliamentary timetable—the agenda of a typical session and a typical week. The Constitution requires that Parliament meet at least once a year, but it is now almost continually in operation. It is most desirable to have a session of Parliament correspond to the calendar year, but a session has often spilled over to two or even three years.

The Typical Session

A session begins with the **speech from the throne**, prepared by the prime minister and read by the governor general. Its function is to outline the government's legislative plans for the session, although the speech is often worded so vaguely that it is not a reliable guide. That speech introduces the throne speech debate, a six-day debate in which MPs can talk about anything under the sun. Party leaders and cabinet ministers may use the occasion to articulate their priorities, while backbenchers often expound on the wonders or troubles of their constituency.

The second major event of the session is the budget and the budget debate. The budget itself is a statement delivered by the minister of Finance, chiefly concerned with tax changes (i.e., the revenue side of the government's books) but also dealing with government finances in general. Among other things, the budget usually fleshes out the vague promises of the speech from the throne. So that no one can take advantage of tax changes beforehand, the budget is shrouded in secrecy until its delivery, and real or apparent "budget leaks" always generate great controversy.[6] The budget sets the stage for a four-day freewheeling debate and provides the opposition with a second opportunity to try to defeat the government. Majority governments need not worry, but the Trudeau and Clark minority governments were defeated on their budgets in 1974 and 1979 respectively. Legislation incorporating the specific tax changes mentioned in the budget comes along later, although the changes usually take effect as of budget night.

The other side of the financial picture is the government's spending proposals for the next fiscal year, the **Estimates**. Their presentation is the third major item of business in the session. Once tabled, however, the Estimates are transmitted to standing committees of the House for scrutiny, so that they actually occupy little of the Commons time as a whole.

A fourth element of the session consists of the 20 **opposition days** when the opposition parties choose the subject of debate and the government in turn responds. These are divided among the opposition parties and distributed throughout the session at the rate of approximately one per week. The number can be raised or reduced, depending on the length of the session.

Other than these four components, the time of the House of Commons is essentially taken up with the discussion of bills, and most of that time with bills introduced by the government. Indeed, it is partly because of the volume of government legislation that some sessions of Parliament exceed a year in length, but the cycle of events just outlined should be repeated annually.

When the government wishes to take a break within a session, it *adjourns* the House; when it wants to bring a session to an end, it *prorogues* the Commons; and when the government decides to call an election, Parliament is *dissolved*. It is because any bills not passed by prorogation die and must start again from scratch in the next session that governments are tempted to allow sessions to continue beyond one year until all current legislation is disposed of. Changes introduced in April 1991 were designed to reduce the number of sitting days from about 175 to 135 per year, without significantly reducing its number of sitting hours.

The Typical Week

The 1982 reforms eliminated the traditional evening sittings in favour of meeting in the morning, now starting at 11 A.M. on Monday and 10 A.M. on the other four days. Also since 1982, 15 minutes have been set aside preceding Question Period each day for *members' statements*, during which MPs can get something off their chests in 60 seconds. The other items on the daily agenda are government orders (usually government bills), private members' business (usually private members' bills), and the adjournment proceedings. "Routine proceedings" include the tabling of documents, statements by ministers, presentation of petitions and committee reports, and introduction and first reading of bills. Wednesday mornings are reserved for party caucus meetings. The weekly schedule as of mid-1995 can be seen in Figure 22.1.

The highlight of the day is the 45-minute **Question Period**. It is this period which offers the opposition its best opportunity to criticize and embarrass the government as it grills cabinet ministers about their deficiencies and faults. Ministers are not given notice of such questions, but before going into the chamber they are briefed by aides who try to anticipate what

Figure 22.1 Weekly Order of Business

HOURS	MONDAY	TUESDAY	WEDNESDAY	THURSDAY	FRIDAY	HOURS
10:00–11:00		Routine Proceedings		Routine Proceedings	Government Orders	10:00–11:00
11:00–11:15	Private Members' Business (3)				Members' Statements	11:00–11:15
11:15–12:00					Oral Questions	11:15–12:00
12:00–1:00					Routine Proceedings (1)	12:00–1:00
1:00–1:30	Government Orders	Government Orders (2)	Review of Delegated Legislation (4)	Government Orders (2)	Government Orders (2)	1:00–1:30
1:30–2:00					Private Members' Business	1:30–2:00
2:00–2:15	Members' Statements	Members' Statements	Members' Statements	Members' Statements		2:00–2:15
2:15–2:30	Oral Questions	Oral Questions	Oral Questions	Oral Questions		2:15–2:30
2:30–3:00						2:30–3:00
3:00–5:30	Routine Proceedings (1) Government Orders (2)	(1) Government Orders (2)	Routine Proceedings (1) Notices of Motions for the Production of Papers Government Orders (2)	(1) Government Orders (2)		3:00–5:30
5:30–6:30		Private Members' Business (3)	Private Members' Business (3)	Private Members' Business (3)		5:30–6:30
6:30–7:00	Adjournment Proceedings (2)	Adjournment Proceedings (2)	Adjournment Proceedings (2)	Adjournment Proceedings (2)		6:30–7:00

(1) Possible extension of Routine Proceedings to complete Introduction of Government Bills pursuant to Standing Order 30(4).
(2) Possible extension or delay pursuant to Standing Order 33(2) respecting Ministerial Statements.
(3) Possible delay or rescheduling pursuant to Standing Order 30(7) to compensate for a delay or an interruption of more than 30 minutes, and pursuant to Standing order 33(2) respecting Ministerial Statements.
(4) If required, House to sit at 1:00 p.m. for the review of Delegated Legislation pursuant to Standing Order 128(1).

questions might be asked. Even greater daily effort goes into the preparation and rehearsal of questions by opposition party leaders and their staff. The **Leader of the Opposition** and the leader of any other recognized party begin the attack, and the Speaker of the House distributes questions to various opposition parties in a rough proportion to their numbers. Government backbenchers are also allowed to participate, but they usually ask "planted" questions to which ministers give prepared and self-serving replies. Since ministers often respond in a deliberately vague manner, several supplementary questions are allowed to those initially posed, but the objective of the opposition is not so much to elicit information as to portray the government in a negative light. Such exchanges, along with corridor interviews and hallway "scrums" based on Question Period, find their way onto the television news and form the backbone of all media reporting on the House. Exciting as it is, many observers regret that Question Period gets so much attention and other aspects of Commons activity receive so little. Provision is also made for written questions from MPs genuinely concerned with seeking information.

After Question Period, unless the House is involved in one of the special events—the throne speech or budget debates or an opposition day—the regular business is the discussion of *government orders*, usually government bills. These debates are the basic routine of Commons life. At this point in the day most of the press gallery and MPs leave the chamber in search of more pressing or more interesting activity. The speeches in these debates, even with the 20-minute time limit imposed in 1982, are generally dull; the public and media can hardly be blamed for paying so little attention to them when MPs themselves rarely listen to each other. The few members assigned to make up quorum on any day are more likely to be answering their mail or reading the newspaper. The length of many speeches was further reduced to ten minutes in 1991.

Only five hours a week are reserved for **private members' bills** and motions, at the normal rate of one hour per bill. These bills and motions, introduced either by government supporters not in the cabinet or by opposition members, are usually even more uninteresting than government bills, and are virtually assured of being dropped to the bottom of the pile when their hour on the stage has elapsed. As mentioned below, however, they have attracted a little more attention in recent years.

Finally, the *adjournment proceeding* is a half-hour opportunity at the end of the daily sitting (6:30 to 7:00 P.M.) four times a week to pursue issues that MPs feel were inadequately answered in the Question Period. Five members have four minutes each to restate their question, and a parliamentary secretary representing the minister has two minutes to respond.

Given the sharply adversarial nature of Question Period and the dullness of the rest of the parliamentary day, television coverage of the House of Commons does little to enhance the public's support of the government or politicians in general. Television coverage may help explain why only one government has won back-to-back majorities since 1953 and may explain the public's attraction to parties and politicians yet unsullied by parliamentary exposure. On the other hand, "the all-consuming ritual of adversarial combat completely dominated by political parties" has its defenders. It serves the functions of keeping government conduct under constant surveillance and of providing an alternative,[7] and it presents a clear-cut picture to the electorate of which party is responsible for everything that has been done.[8]

PARTY DISCIPLINE

Probably the most significant aspect of the operation of the House of Commons is that everything is organized along party lines and that **party discipline** is so rigid. Almost all members belong to one party or another, and with rare exceptions, the MPs of each party vote together. Why is it that members of Parliament so consistently toe the party line?

The most obvious reason for party discipline, at least on the government side of the House, is the system of **responsible government**. It is generally believed, both inside and outside Parliament, that if the cabinet is defeated on a major measure, it must resign or call an election; therefore, its backbenchers must always ensure that cabinet proposals are passed.[9] Until such time as the principle of responsible government is interpreted more flexibly—by regarding a limited number of nonconfidence motions as really critical and then allowing the cabinet to carry on in spite of the occasional defeat of a piece of legislation—government supporters will always have to put party loyalty ahead of the consideration of their own views or those of their constituents.

Apart from the fact that some degree of party discipline is a corollary of the principle of responsible government, several reasons can be cited to explain why MPs of any party stick together in parliamentary votes. One is the tendency of people who belong to a political party to see things in a similar light—a natural cohesiveness common to most organized groups. Related to this cohesiveness is an equally natural deference to the leadership of the party and a desire to present an image of party unity to the public. In addition, MPs are encouraged to support the party line because of the prospects of promotion. Government backbenchers who are well behaved can become committee chairs, parliamentary secretaries, or cabinet ministers, while even in opposition parties one can be moved up to more important responsibilities.[10] Members also want to participate in the distribution of perks available in parliamentary life, especially opportunities to travel at public expense, which are generally in the control of the party whips. Those who demonstrate greatest party loyalty can be rewarded with such favours as inclusion in the Canadian delegation to the United Nations or in many other parliamentary junkets. Another inducement is to receive full support of the party organization in the next election, including campaign funds and a visit by the party leader. Moreover, many MPs depend on the government to provide them with employment if they suffer defeat, and are not unmindful of this dependence while serving in the House. The ultimate sanctions for disloyal behaviour are expulsion from the party caucus, involving relegation to the unpleasant status of an independent, and denial of the party label in the next election. In recent years, three Conservative MPs were expelled from the caucus (Alex Kindy, David Kilgour, and Suzanne Blais-Grenier) and two (Leonard Jones and Sinclair Stevens) were denied the party's candidacy.[11] For all these reasons, parties vote as blocs, and a government with a majority of seats in the Commons has always felt confident that it could get parliamentary approval for almost anything it wanted.

The British House of Commons is the model for the Canadian House in many ways, but party discipline is looser there and government legislation is frequently defeated without entailing the resignation of the government.[12] Franks attributes this significant difference in the operation of the two chambers to several factors: the larger number of members in Britain means that discipline is harder to enforce; incumbent British MPs can be sure of renomination, regardless of their degree of party loyalty; and the large proportion of safe seats results in fewer members being dependent on party patronage for their post-parliamentary livelihood. Moreover, long-serving British MPs co-exist with short-term prime ministers (with the exception of Margaret Thatcher) and are not so obsessed with promotion to the cabinet. They are more content than their Canadian counterparts to remain on the backbenches or act as committee chairs, combining outside interests with their parliamentary responsibilities.[13] Franks does not expect any dramatic change in the operation of the Canadian House of Commons to come from technical procedural reform; party discipline will predominate until such time as a sizable proportion of government backbenchers feel secure enough to act independently and force the cabinet to change its attitude about giving them more flexibility. Less media alarm about such dissent would also help.

It is fashionable to advocate more **free votes** and greater opportunity for MPs to represent the interests of their constituencies rather than slavishly follow the dictates of the party. The "free vote" on capital punishment in 1987 was a rare event, and featured a dramatic split among Tory MPs. A series of free votes on alternative ways of dealing with abortion in 1988 failed to produce a consensus, and the Mulroney government's "compromise" abortion bill of 1990 was defeated in a free vote in the Senate. Few would argue against a little more autonomy and freedom for the individual MP, but free-vote advocates sometimes fail to appreciate the merits of an executive-centred system. Forcing MPs to toe the party line has allowed the executive to pursue a collectivist public interest beyond the narrow interests of constituencies, provinces, parties, pressure groups, and lobbyists, and has permitted Canadian governments to be more activist and welfare-oriented than legislature-centred systems such as the United States.[14] Party discipline protects MPs individually and collectively from the blandishments and threats of single-interest pressure groups, whose presence is increasing, and promotes the accountability of the government party to the electorate. It also frees the prime minister from time-consuming negotiations with individual MPs.

Despite concessions made to Liberal dissenters and other opponents of the Chrétien government's 1995 gun control bill, many backbenchers absented themselves from the vote and three voted against it. The PM quickly retaliated by removing them from their committee assignments. When veteran MP and former minister Warren Allmand voted against the 1995 budget, because it dismantled historic Liberal social programs, the prime minister's attempt to remove him as a committee chair was delayed by Reformers who disagreed with what he said but defended his right to dissent from the Liberal line. The prime minister even threatened not to sign the nomination papers of Liberal candidates in the next election if they voted against government measures.

CAUCUS MEETINGS

The other side of this public display of party discipline is that MPs are allowed to speak their mind in the secrecy of the **party caucus**.[15] The caucus consists of all the elected members of each party (and such senators who choose to attend) who meet separately behind closed doors on Wednesday mornings. As in the case of cabinet secrecy, however, members occasionally "leak" caucus information for their own benefit. Provincial and regional caucus meetings of each party are held before the general caucus meeting, and caucus committees are often appointed. In the case of the government party, the prime minister and cabinet ministers attend such meetings, unlike the practice in Britain.

Reprinted with permission.

Some prime ministers and cabinets use caucus primarily to inform their backbenchers of government plans, others are reasonably receptive to backbench arguments and suggested alternatives, and some do both. Ministers may discuss the principles of a new policy with interested backbenchers in the course of its development, but it would breach the tradition of the House to show the caucus an actual bill before it is introduced in the Commons. Although no votes are taken, sufficient backbench dissatisfaction may occasionally carry the day. It is generally believed, for example, that backbench pressure had an influence on cabinet policy on electronic eavesdropping, immigration, and unemployment insurance in the 1974–79 period, on two railway bills and the Canada Health Act between 1980 and 1984; and on amendments to the Official Languages Act, gun control legislation, and the hiring of homosexuals in the armed forces between 1984 and 1993. The aforementioned Mulroney compromise abortion bill was probably unique in actually being written by a committee of four ministers and eight backbenchers.[16] In the early years of the Chrétien government, the caucus was successful in amending gun control legislation and delaying the inclusion of sexual orientation in the Canadian Human Rights Act.

STAGES AND KINDS OF LEGISLATION

The great bulk of legislation introduced takes the form of **public bills**. These are general bills, such as the Income Tax Act or the Unemployment Insurance Act, that affect all Canadians. Most public bills (and all that involve the raising or spending of money) are sponsored by the government and introduced by a cabinet minister, thereby being titled **government bills**.[17] As noted earlier, most of the weekly and yearly agenda is taken up with such government business. However, a certain amount of time (now normally five hours per week) is set aside for members who are not in the cabinet to introduce legislation and motions of their own. Since these MPs (on whichever side of the House) are private members, their proposals are called **private members' bills**. These bills are still of a general nature, such as Stanley Knowles's many attempts to abolish the Senate, or others to restore capital punishment, but they almost never reach the statute books because the government arranges to have them "talked out." That is, the cabinet ensures that a government backbencher is still talking when the time for their consideration expires and they therefore do not come to a vote. Historically, the most private members could hope for was that the cabinet might incorporate their ideas into a government bill. Since 1986, however, the situation has improved, and since 1992 provision has been given for a more in-depth examination of 30 private members' bills and motions drawn from a hat. A committee decides which ones are "votable" and up to ten of these get expanded debate and can come to a vote. Then, if successful, they could continue in the regular legislative channels. Lynn McDonald's 1988 private member's bill on nonsmokers' rights was a rare example of one that made it to the statute books; others included the bill to change the name of Trans-Canada Airlines to Air Canada and the act that recognized the beaver as a symbol of Canadian sovereignty.[18]

Private bills, on the other hand, refer to a specific person or corporation. Certain divorces used to be effected by Acts of Parliament and took the form of private bills, while today this category mostly consists of bills incorporating companies. Private bills now originate in the Senate and occupy very little of the Commons' time.

Turning to the stages of the legislative process, the first requirement is for three readings in each chamber. Most government bills originate in the Commons, although with the exception of money bills, they may be first introduced in the Senate. *First reading* simply means that a bill has been introduced—it is tabled, printed, and made public—and may be briefly explained. Some days later, the bill comes up for *second reading*. This stage involves a debate on the principle of the bill and may last several days, or even weeks if it is controversial. A favourable vote at the end of the second reading debate therefore means that the bill has been approved in principle.

Even if the opposition has little hope of defeating a bill, it may expect that prolonged exposure of the flaws in the legislation will persuade the government to amend it. Failing that, public opinion can be aroused via television or other media coverage to the extent that the electorate will remember the incident when the next election occurs. Excessive opposition debate is called **filibustering**, but government and opposition rarely agree on what is excessive. In 1913, during protracted opposition to the government's Naval Bill, the Borden government introduced **closure**, a rule allowing a majority government to cut off debate. This device was used with discretion until the famous **pipeline debate** of 1956, and it is widely believed that the abusive resort to closure helped to defeat the government a year later.[19] Although the closure rule is still on the books and is used more routinely in recent years, it is more civilized to negotiate with the opposition over the time to be allocated to debating various issues. Standing Order 78 provides for three kinds of time allocation motions depending on how much opposition consent can be acquired.

It is partly because of the length of debates that government legislation deliberately leaves wide discretion to the executive to issue regulations so that acts will not have to come back to the House for frequent amendments. Similarly, the government often introduces *omnibus bills* that deal with several different issues simultaneously because a number of individual bills would take longer to pass.

After second reading, a bill goes to committee where it is examined in detail. In the small, informal confines of a Commons committee, the bill is scrutinized and voted on clause by clause, and ministers, public servants, interest groups, and other experts may be called on for explanations or criticisms. After being approved, sometimes with amendments, the bill is reported back to the House in what is called the *report stage*. This phase gives all members of the House, not just those on the committee, an opportunity to move amendments. Once the bill is concurred in here, it goes to *third reading* for a final, overall appraisal.

Assuming that the bill started in the Commons, it must then go through the same procedure in the Senate, but there it is usually disposed of in much faster order.[20] In the rare case that the Senate amends a bill already approved by the Commons, the bill will have to go back to that house to see if it is acceptable in its amended form. Once a bill is passed in identical form by both houses, it is given royal assent by the governor general or a Supreme Court judge acting as "deputy governor general" and then becomes a law or statute, although it may not be immediately proclaimed.

Although this may seem like an overly complicated process, each stage has a distinctive purpose and most bills must be debated for some time before the media and public begin to pay attention to them. Besides being necessary to engender eventual public knowledge of and consent to the law, reasonably lengthy consideration of the merits and faults of the bill is required in the formulation of public opinion. It serves to help the electorate gradually make up its mind about whether to re-elect the government that introduced such legislation or to opt for an opposition party that criticized it effectively.

In 1994, the House adopted rule changes that allowed a bill to go to committee after first reading, before it had been approved in principle. Such a procedure considerably widens the scope of committee influence, but it only applies to government legislation and can only be used with the minister's consent. According to another procedure, a committee can be directed to study an issue and prepare a bill. This was done in the case of the post-1991 census redistribution process, but the Senate was not happy with the result and delayed the bill's adoption. These cases illustrate a slight loosening up of the cabinet's dominance of the legislative process.

ORGANIZATION AND OFFICERS OF THE COMMONS
The Speaker

The leading official of the House of Commons is the presiding officer, the **Speaker**, for whom one deputy and three acting speakers can substitute in the chair. In addition to ceremonial and administrative functions, the Speaker interprets and enforces the written rules of the Commons, which are called the **Standing Orders**,[21] plus unwritten traditions, practices, conventions, and usages. Given the powers of the Speakership—recognizing which member can speak, and ruling on whether motions are in order, whether debate is relevant, whether questions are urgent, and whether an unruly MP should be expelled—it is important for the person selected to be competent as well as totally impartial. In the past, many Speakers have lacked one or both of these qualities. Speakers were historically chosen by prime ministers from among their party's MPs and thus carried the suspicion of being biased in favour of the government. In seeking eventual reward beyond the Speakership such as promotion to the cabinet, some also feared displeasing the prime minister, the dispenser of such rewards.

In this connection, two promising precedents were set in the 1960s and 1970s. Once selected from the Liberal ranks as Speaker in 1965, Lucien Lamoureux sought re-election as an independent candidate and was twice re-appointed Speaker on that basis. In 1979, Jim Jerome, originally a Liberal appointee, was asked to continue as Speaker when the Conservative Joe Clark government came to power. Then, after a number of more partisan appointments, a major change was adopted that allowed MPs to choose their own Speaker by secret ballot for the first time in 1986, rather than merely ratifying the nomination of the prime minister. The first elected Speaker, John Fraser, was re-elected when the procedure was repeated after the 1988 election. At the same time, the Speaker was given new authority to "name" (i.e., suspend) a member for the rest of the day and for a period of five days for a second breach of the rules. Gilbert Parent was elected Speaker in 1994.

Many Canadians are upset at the rowdy behaviour of members of Parliament, and it is true that the British chamber is more sedate. This contrast is partly explained by the fact that opposition members in Britain expect to be on the government side some day, whereas in Canada, with long periods of one-party dominance, many MPs serve their entire parliamentary career in opposition. Never given the chance to govern, and rarely having the opportunity to amend legislation, they see victory in catcalls and obstruction. On the other hand, the rules demand a certain amount of civility, such as prohibiting name-calling or accusations of lying, and require MPs to speak to each other through the Chair and to refer to each other by the name of their constituency, as the "Honourable Member for ..."

Speakers can only vote in the case of a tie and cannot articulate the needs of their constituency or constituents in the Commons as such. In compensation, ministers and bureaucrats are especially sensitive to the concerns that the Speaker discusses with them outside the chamber.

House Leaders, Party Whips, and Clerk

From within their ranks, each party selects a **House leader** and a **party whip**. The government House leader is a cabinet minister who manages the government's business in the Commons. This minister seeks to work out an agenda for House business with the opposition House leaders, who function as procedural strategists for their parties and often speak for their parties if their leaders are absent. Party whips, on the other hand, are responsible for ensuring that their members are present for important votes and that their members vote the right way.[22] Whips must therefore know the whereabouts of all their members at all times. They also distribute members' offices, assign members to parliamentary committees, and line up the order of party speakers in Question Period and debates. It is largely through the whips, therefore, that party leaders impose discipline on their members. Members' opportunities to speak, to serve on the committee of their choice, and to travel as part of parliamentary delegations are largely influenced by their degree of party loyalty. In return, whips seek out backbench opinion on various matters and transmit it to the party leadership. Given the power of the party whips and party House leaders to organize its business, independent MPs find little opportunity to participate, even those who belong to a party with fewer than 12 members.

The chief permanent official of the Commons is the Clerk of the House. This position is analogous to a deputy minister in a government department. As chief procedural adviser to the Speaker and manager of the support staff attached to the Commons, the Clerk is also required to act in a totally nonpartisan manner. The Clerk is assisted at the table by the deputy clerk and several principal clerks. Figure 22.2 shows the layout of the Commons chamber.

Voting

Turning to the voting procedure in the Commons, decisions are in the first instance taken orally when the Speaker invites members to say "aye" or "nay." In declaring which side won, the Speaker is guided by the numbers rather than the volume on each side, and on a routine

Figure 22.2 **The House of Commons**

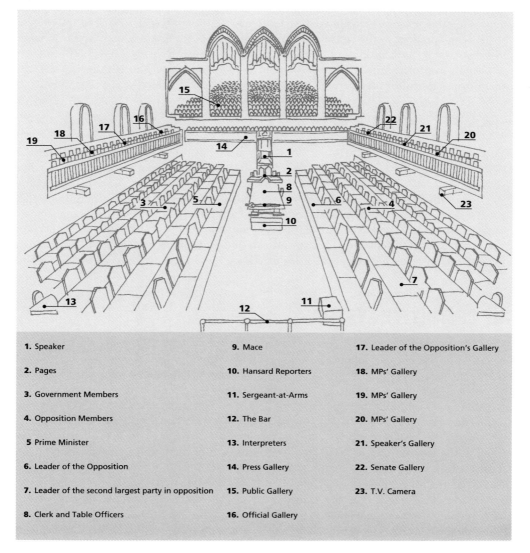

1. Speaker	**9.** Mace	**17.** Leader of the Opposition's Gallery
2. Pages	**10.** Hansard Reporters	**18.** MPs' Gallery
3. Government Members	**11.** Sergeant-at-Arms	**19.** MPs' Gallery
4. Opposition Members	**12.** The Bar	**20.** MPs' Gallery
5 Prime Minister	**13.** Interpreters	**21.** Speaker's Gallery
6. Leader of the Opposition	**14.** Press Gallery	**22.** Senate Gallery
7. Leader of the second largest party in opposition	**15.** Public Gallery	**23.** T.V. Camera
8. Clerk and Table Officers	**16.** Official Gallery	

matter in a majority situation, this will probably suffice. When either side wants a formal recorded vote it will request a **division**. In this case the division bells ring until the government and Official Opposition party whips agree that all their available members have arrived, at which time a standing vote is conducted. It used to be that if either whip refused to give the go-ahead, the bells could ring indefinitely, but after the two-week "bell-ringing incident" of

1982, a 30-minute limit was adopted in 1986. A new procedure in 1994 allowed for deferred divisions with all-party consent. Until the early 1980s, MPs sometimes engaged in the practice of **pairing**, in which two members on opposite sides would make arrangements so that if one was legitimately absent for a vote, the other would not vote either. Indeed, in 1926, a "broken pair" resulted in the defeat of the government.[23] After being discontinued for about ten years, a more limited kind of pairing appeared again in the early 1990s and has been increasingly institutionalized. Party whips are involved in putting members' names in the registry of pairs, and paired members are listed at the end of the division list printed in Hansard.

Speeches

The length of speeches that MPs are allowed to make has been severely curtailed over the past 15 or so years. The 1982 reforms generally shortened them from 40 minutes to 20, but this depends on who is speaking, in what debate, and at what stage of the debate. In many cases, especially as a debate drags on, the maximum length is reduced to ten minutes.

What is said in such speeches is also of interest. Of all the rights and **privileges** of members of Parliament, individual and collective, the most important is the protection from libel action for anything said in the chamber. Occasionally MPs take advantage of their privileged position in this respect by declining to repeat outside the House certain remarks they have made within.

THE COMMITTEE SYSTEM

Much of the important legislative work of the House takes place outside the Commons chamber in a variety of committees. These include standing, special, and legislative committees of the Commons, as well as joint standing and special committees of the Commons and Senate combined. Committees allow a small number of people to develop expertise in a particular field and to examine proposals in depth; moreover, if several committees operate simultaneously, a greater volume of business can be accomplished. In the parliamentary context, committees could allow private members to make constructive contributions to the governing of the country and to do so in a consensual rather than an adversarial atmosphere. Unfortunately, the Canadian Commons committee system did not function well during the first 100 years after Confederation. Committees were not used in a systematic way, and membership was so unstable that they failed to develop expertise. Repeated reforms of the Commons committee system since 1968 have made it more significant.

Standing committees are set up more or less permanently in most of the substantive areas of government policy, such as Agriculture and Transport. They have two principal functions: to examine the Estimates, that is, the government's spending proposals, and to examine legislation at the committee stage. The Estimates of the Department of Agriculture, for example, are scrutinized by the Standing Committee on Agriculture, and such an examination can now go beyond the spending plans of the current year. In examining bills, clause-by-clause, after second reading, committees question ministers, public servants, pressure groups, and other expert witnesses, who try either to convince committee members to approve the bill as introduced or else to effect changes. As a result of the 1986 changes, standing committees have new functions and resources. Since they largely parallel government departments, they are authorized to investigate any aspect of the department with which they are associated, including a review of nonjudicial government appointments. They also have a budget to hire a clerk, supporting staff, and researchers, and thus to develop independent expertise. The Standing Committee on Finance is perhaps most important, and now engages in pre-budget consultations, as outlined in Chapter 20.

Standing committees had 20 or 30 members in the past, but in 1984 their size was reduced to 10 or 15 members, and after 1986, to between seven and 15. This smaller, more stable, and more expert membership has served to increase the effectiveness of their deliberations. Because they often have a number of different issues on their agenda, it is now common for standing committees to set up subcommittees. Representation on all committees is proportional to party standings in the House. Committee chairs are elected by committee members, but in the case of standing and special committees at least, they are usually pre-selected by the PMO. Thus, in a majority situation, the government will have a majority on each committee and its own designated choice as chair. In Britain, committees have always had a more autonomous position, including the choice of their own chair, and many members have found career satisfaction at this level rather than yearning for appointment to the cabinet. The one exception to this government control in Canada is the **Public Accounts Committee**, which normally has a government majority but has been chaired by an opposition MP since 1958. It has the important function of examining the report of the auditor general, an official of Parliament who audits the government's accounts.

Special committees, which may be set up temporarily for some specific, special purpose, are now used more widely than in the past. They usually have an investigatory function—to examine an issue before the government has made up its mind on how to deal with it. Such committees may therefore be an important part of the initiation phase of the legislative process and have sometimes been called legislative task forces.

In addition to the standing and special committees of the House of Commons alone, the Commons and Senate sometimes work together in **joint committees**. Joint committees obviously avoid duplication and also give senators a chance to get involved at an earlier stage of the process than is usually the case. An important joint special committee was involved in the development of the Constitution Act, 1982, and the most permanent joint standing committee is that on the **Scrutiny of Regulations**. It has the vital but unenviable responsibility of scrutinizing the mounds of regulations and other subordinate legislation issued by the executive branch each year, and has been given the power to recommend rescission of offensive delegated legislation.

Between 1986 and 1994, a new breed of *legislative committee* was introduced. These were designed to replace standing committees for the clause-by-clause examination of legislation, and for a time, a legislative committee was set up for each bill passed at the second reading stage. In 1994, this function reverted to standing committees, because they had already developed the expertise required to study the bill.

Finally, there is the *committee of the whole*. This is simply the entire Commons membership sitting in the chamber as a committee. In such a case, the Speaker is replaced in the chair by the deputy speaker, and the rules are somewhat relaxed. This committee is only used to debate appropriation bills (once the Estimates have been approved) and certain noncontroversial bills, preference otherwise being given to smaller ones that can meet simultaneously in committee rooms outside the Commons chamber.

It is primarily the transformation of the committee system in recent years that has enhanced the position of MPs in the legislative process. As committees have become smaller, more stable in their membership, and more expert in their field, and as their members developed greater collegiality, they have shed a good deal of their partisanship. Since 1986, for example, many of these standing and legislative committees developed a consensus on the issues before them that cut cross party lines. Examples include constitutional affairs and official languages, environmental legislation, the Public Accounts, and Scrutiny of Regulations committees, and the final stages of the PC gun control legislation. Such committees have become newly independent sources of power in the legislative system, and this has led, among other things, to the acceptance of an unprecedented number of committee amendments to government bills.

One advantage of all committees that meet outside the Commons chamber is that they can listen to representations from interest groups, bureaucrats, and other experts.[24] It was traditionally said that pressure groups did not make much use of the legislative branch of government because the crucial decisions had previously been made in the executive. Paul Pross argues, however, that it is a sign of the increasing autonomy and cross-party cohesiveness of Commons committees that pressure groups are giving them more attention than in the past.[25] One example of a committee that made substantial changes to government proposals as a result of group pressure was that reviewing the Constitution Act, 1982.

MEMBERS' SERVICES[26]

How much to pay members of Parliament is an intractable problem. To pay considerably more than the average industrial wage is to ensure much public criticism, but as a general rule, the higher the level of remuneration, the better the quality of person that will be attracted to parliamentary life. The peculiar insecurity of political office in Canada must also be taken into account.

As of 1995, ordinary MPs received $64 400 in salary plus $21 300 in a tax-free expense allowance (for which they did not have to submit receipts). Since the equivalent taxable value of the expense allowance would be about double, the total remuneration package is worth approximately $100 000. Because of the typical public uproar over increasing this amount, the government has appointed a succession of external, independent committees to review such levels of remuneration. On top of this basic income, a large number of MPs received additional payments for supplementary responsibilities. These supplementary payments, in effect till the end of 1997, are as follows:

- Prime minister — $69 920
- Other ministers, Speaker, Opposition leader — 49 100
- Cabinet minister — 46 645
- Secretary of State — 34 983
- Other recognized party leader — 29 500
- Deputy speaker — 25 700
- Opposition house leader — 23 800
- Chief government whip and chief opposition whip — 13 200
- Asst. deputy speakers and parliamentary secretaries — 10 500
- Other party house leader — 10 100
- Deputy government and opposition party whips — 7 500

In addition to this basic pay, backbench MPs received many other benefits and services at public expense. For example, those who live at least 100 km from Ottawa may claim an additional expense allowance of $6000 per year. More controversial is the MPs' pension plan. Although contributory, many observers felt that it was too generous because it was indexed to the cost of living and because, regardless of age, members became eligible for the pension immediately upon leaving the Commons after six years of service. Moreover, those subsequently appointed to a government position continued to receive the pension on top of their new salary. In 1995, the Liberals removed some of these provisions for newly elected MPs: they would have to wait to age 55 to collect, they could not "double-dip," and they could opt out entirely. Allowances for office, staff, and travel expenses are as follows.

- Parliamentary office (including all equipment and supplies
- Constituency office (including all equipment and supplies)
- Staff: approximately $170 000 staff allowance
- Travel: 64 return trips between Ottawa and constituency by any means, with partial provision for family and staff, and travel within constituency
- Telephone: unlimited
- Mail: unlimited

Parliamentary parties received funds for research purposes of $1 349 000 (Liberal), $851 000 (Bloc Québécois), and $826 000 (Reform), and additional funds were provided for the operation of the offices of opposition leaders, whips, House leaders, and caucus chairs. Such funding is only provided to recognized parties in the House, that is, groups of at least 12 members, a major blow to the Conservatives and NDP after the 1993 election.

The lot of backbench members of Parliament is obviously much improved over the situation in the pre-1960 period in which they were not considered to occupy full-time positions, and their every need is now provided for. While their remuneration and services might seem excessive to many reporters[27] and members of the general public, the expenses of serving nearly 100 000 constituents and the insecurity of parliamentary life should not be underestimated. If their expenses were not completely covered, only wealthy individuals could seek federal political office.

ROLES OF MEMBERS OF PARLIAMENT

The roles that members of Parliament perform can be seen in two different lights. First, in terms of how they vote, MPs can be classified as trustees, constituency delegates, or party delegates. *Trustees* would be MPs who felt obliged to vote according to their own conscience, their own understanding of the issue in question, or their own conception of the national interest. Alternatively, *constituency delegates* would be MPs who voted the way they thought a majority of their constituents would want them to vote or in their conception of the best interests of their constituency. In other words, in situations where the two did not coincide, trustees would place their own views above those of their constituents, while constituency delegates would do the reverse. However much MPs may claim to fall into either of these categories, in practice they rarely deviate from the party line. In fact, then, they could all be labelled *party delegates*. If the party caucus determines a position that conflicts either with their own views or those of their constituents, MPs are almost always obliged to put the party position first. The reasons for such rigid party discipline were discussed earlier in the chapter. Public pressure for more free votes seems to be increasing, however, and, such discipline may also be in decline at the committee stage.

The other way to examine the roles of MPs is in terms of how they spend their time or what their priorities are. The first role in this respect is the *law-maker*, consisting of MPs who devote most of their attention to the legislative process, introducing, amending, and debating legislation. MPs are supported in these tasks by the Research Branch of the Library of Parliament,[28] but since this role is almost completely irrelevant to their constituents, not many MPs fall into this category. Another group sees its role primarily as being a *propagandist* for one or more causes. These MPs use every opportunity available—Question Period, general debates, and even public speeches outside of Parliament—to press for certain reforms they believe in. Determined crusaders against the metric system or in favour of capital punishment would be good examples. Then there are MPs whose main goal is to promote their constituency and bring back public favours, that could be called a *representational* role. These members lobby ministers and public servants for new public buildings, roads, wharves, and other facilities so that they will have something "concrete" to show for themselves by the time of the next election. Finally, many MPs function most frequently as *ombudsmen* or social workers for their individual constituents, intervening with ministers or public servants to hasten administrative decisions, to correct bureaucratic errors, and to repair governmental injustices. There will always be constituents with passport, immigration, UI, pension, and many other kinds of problems, and some MPs specialize in trying to resolve them. This "case-load" of MPs is now so heavy that they are provided with considerable administrative assistance both in their Ottawa and constituency offices so that they will have some time available for their other duties.

In any case, the life of an MP is extremely busy, being constantly engaged in meetings and talking with individual and groups of constituents, organized interest groups, the media, bureaucrats, party officials, staff, and other parliamentarians. Besides assuming heavy responsibilities in Ottawa, they are expected to be seen frequently in the constituency, both in their offices and at myriad social events, usually on weekends or when Parliament is recessed. All this activity interferes with a normal family life, whether those with spouses and/or children move their families to Ottawa or leave them at home to be visited when time permits.

THE GOVERNMENT–OPPOSITION BALANCE

An objective look at Parliament reveals a basic dilemma: the government wants to get legislation passed expeditiously, but the opposition must have time to articulate constituency needs as well as a chance to criticize government proposals in order to make the public aware of their defects. One manner of addressing this conflict is to summarize the ways in which the cabinet controls the Commons and then the ways in which the Commons controls the cabinet.

The cabinet, through the governor general, summons, prorogues, and dissolves Parliament, and basically determines the agenda of Parliamentary business. The cabinet has an absolute monopoly on the introduction of financial legislation and a virtual monopoly on the legislation that actually gets passed. Through the whip, the cabinet controls almost all parliamentary committee work and also has the power to introduce closure to cut off debate or time allocation motions to curtail it. Backing up all these specific devices of cabinet dominance are two other general powers. The cabinet continually enforces party discipline on its MPs in order to achieve its ends and has at its disposal the vast informational resources of the public service. Thus it is sometimes said that the cabinet operates as a virtual dictatorship until it has to face the electorate again some four or five years down the road.

Parliamentary control over the cabinet, on the other hand, refers mainly to opportunities to criticize and to delay, rather than any real power to alter the cabinet's proposals or to throw the government out. MPs, especially on the opposition side, have the chance daily to ask oral questions of ministers, in addition to the 15 minutes set aside for members' statements, and 30 minutes for adjournment proceedings four times per week. They can also submit written questions seeking detailed information. MPs have the throne speech and budget debates in which to criticize the government generally or raise their own alternatives, as well as 20 days per session to select the topic of debate. Limited research funds and the services of the Library of Parliament are made available in an attempt to begin to restore the balance in advisory and informational resources, and MPs can introduce legislation in the form of private members' bills. MPs can criticize specific cabinet measures at the second reading stage, introduce amendments at the committee and report stages, and have a chance to scrutinize the government's spending proposals. Opposition MPs may at least delay the adoption of government measures by prolonging debates and by raising procedural points. But when all is said and done, the cabinet almost always gets its way.

MINORITY GOVERNMENT

The foregoing account assumes that the government is in a majority position in the Commons. A **minority government** situation—in which the government is outnumbered by opposition members—is slightly better balanced. The government may have to negotiate with opposition parties to some extent, such as to amend its proposals, abandon them, or even accept opposition initiatives. Many observers who deplore the normal arrogance of a majority government and who regret that so much opposition talent and so many opposition ideas ordinarily go to waste actually prefer the minority government situation.

Eugene Forsey has reminded us that minority government is not exceptional, is not necessarily weak and indecisive, and does not have to be short-lived.[29] Between 1867 and 1996 there were nine minority governments in Canada: 1921–25 (King); 1925–26 (King); 1926 (Meighen); 1957–58 (Diefenbaker); 1962–63 (Diefenbaker); 1963–65 (Pearson); 1965–68 (Pearson); 1972–74 (Trudeau); and 1979–80 (Clark). Few of these governments could have been called weak and indecisive because of their minority position; many, such as the 1957–58 Diefenbaker government, were more active and courageous than the majority governments that preceded or followed them. Some were exceptionally bold and decisive, especially the Pearson governments and the Trudeau minority, the latter being particularly sensitive to opposition demands. While minority governments admittedly did not last as long as majority governments, not all of them ended by being defeated. The first Diefenbaker government and the two Pearson governments, for example, ended when the prime minister himself decided to call an election.

In a minority government situation, much is made of one or more opposition parties holding the balance of power. On occasion, for example, this position has allowed the CCF or NDP to force a Liberal minority to adopt some of its policies. But holding the balance of power is not normally an enviable position, especially if the opposition cannot amend or defeat a government measure without throwing out the whole government. If any such defeat were taken as a vote of nonconfidence in the government, it would precipitate another election. Such an opposition party may not have the finances to engage in a quick succession of election campaigns, and is sometimes thought to suffer at the hands of an electorate that blames it for the inconvenience and expense of another vote.

This leads to a discussion of the principle of responsible government—that the cabinet must have the confidence of the Commons or else call an election or resign. It is not always clear whether the cabinet is required to take such drastic action. In a majority situation the problem is most unlikely to arise, but when the government is in a minority position does it have to resign or call an election over any and every defeat? If there was any doubt about this point, it was probably resolved by the 1968 incident in which the Pearson government was defeated on a piece of financial legislation. Pearson argued that the defeat was a fluke and that his government should be able to carry on. In that case the matter was decided when the cabinet subsequently survived an explicit **nonconfidence motion**. Any other case of dispute about whether or not a government has been defeated should probably be settled in the same manner.[30] Alternatively, the government and opposition could agree that the defeat of individual government measures did not entail a loss of confidence in the government as a whole, as was done in the 1985 Liberal–NDP accord in Ontario.[31] If such an understanding were extended to majority situations as well, government backbenchers would have more freedom to vote according to the interests of their constituencies. Another alternative would be to adopt fixed election dates, subject to a government defeat on a motion of nonconfidence, as New Zealand has done.

REFORM OF THE HOUSE OF COMMONS

The imbalance between government and opposition is so great and the legislative role of ordinary MPs has been so ineffective that Parliamentary reform is never far from the minds of political scientists and politicians alike. Reform proposals are designed to remedy excessive partisanship, cabinet domination, and the lack of influence of the private member, and those adopted are summarized below.

RECENT PROCEDURAL CHANGES IN THE HOUSE OF COMMONS

1960s Reform of committee system, including Estimates and Supply
      Time allocation provisions
      Elimination of appeals of Speaker's decisions
      Research funds for parliamentary parties

1970s Improvement in members' services
      Televised proceedings

1982 Elimination of night sittings
      Adoption of year-long parliamentary calendar
      Speeches limited to 20 minutes
      Members' statements before Question Period

1986 Committees reduced in size and allowed to examine any aspect of government policy
      New "legislative committees"
      Committees allowed to hire staff
      Committees allowed to review order-in-council appointments
      Increased committee scrutiny of regulations
      20 private members' bills looked at seriously and six voted on
      Additional disciplinary authority for the Speaker
      30-minute maximum on ringing of division bells
      Speaker elected by secret ballot

1991 More hours per week but sitting days per year reduced to 135 from 175
      Annual calendar of sitting days adopted in advance
      Reduction in length of throne speech and budget debates
      Most speeches limited to ten minutes
      Opposition days reduced to 20
      Complete revamping of committee system into envelopes

1994 Revamping of committee system
      Bills normally go to standing committees after second reading, but some after first reading
      Deferred divisions
      Pre-budget consultations by Finance Committee

At the end of the 1960s changes in the committee system, provision for timetabling the business of the House, and funding of parliamentary parties for research purposes "inaugurated the modern era of parliamentary government."[32] Then in the 1970s, MPs saw considerable improvement in their services, especially in Parliamentary and constituency offices and staff. In addition, the proceedings of the Commons began to be televised in 1977. One of the ways in which television changed members' behaviour was that they began to applaud instead of pounding on their desks to indicate approval.[33] In 1982 a severe altercation occurred between the Trudeau government and the Conservative opposition over the form and substance of the National Energy Program, such that the opposition left the division bells ringing for 15 days. This incident led all concerned to strive to improve Commons procedures, and the recommendations of the Lefebvre Committee on procedural reform were implemented promptly. This momentum for reform survived the 1984 election, and as a result of the McGrath Committee, further reforms were made in 1986.[34] All of these procedural changes had the general objective of improving the lot of the backbench MP and were based on a consensus of the House. In 1991, responding to the low esteem in which politicians were held by the public, the Mulroney government introduced further changes. While the changes were aimed to accomplish as much parliamentary work in less time, to give MPs more time in their constituencies, and to make the committee system more effective, they were not the result of all-party agreement and opposition parties were not completely satisfied.

Despite these impressive changes, several recommendations of the 1985–86 Special Committee on Reform of the House of Commons were not immediately implemented. Chief among them was any loosening of party discipline or alteration in the concept of "confidence" in the government on individual pieces of legislation. Such a change could take the form of relaxing party discipline somewhat, accepting more opposition amendments to government initiatives, or even allowing the occasional defeat of a government scheme without entailing the government's resignation. As mentioned earlier, a small start has been made in the last few years in giving committees more latitude, but the cabinet, perhaps not surprisingly, was unwilling to go so far as to reduce its crushing monopoly on the legislative process.[35]

Such changes would enhance the legislative role of backbenchers, but Franks argues that this would be at the expense of the advantages of an executive-centred system. He feels that reform should be advocated with caution and that "Parliament is more in need of understanding than change."[36] He recommends that salaries be raised to attract a better calibre of member (and therefore cabinet minister), and that the Commons be enlarged so that more members are available to take care of legislative and constituency business.

Beyond changes in the existing operation of the Commons, some reformers advocate the adoption of such populist devices as the recall, the initiative, and the referendum. The recall would allow a certain proportion of the electorate to petition a sitting legislator to resign; the initiative would require the legislature to respond to a policy initiative endorsed by a certain proportion of the electorate; and the referendum would submit certain public policy proposals to the electorate. Such devices were widely advocated in the 1920s in Western Canada and have recently re-emerged on the political agenda, largely thanks to the Reform Party. More radical than the idea of loosening party discipline, these techniques are subject to even greater reservations in terms of an executive-centred system.

PURPOSES AND POWERS OF THE SENATE

The ideal of democracy was still not enthusiastically accepted in the 1860s and the Fathers of Confederation felt it advisable to provide for an appointed body that would exercise "sober second thought" with respect to measures emanating from the popularly elected House of Commons. Thus the Senate was to be the equivalent of the British House of Lords, an older, conservative influence, with a minimum age of 30, appointment for life, and a relatively high property qualification ($4000 over and above all debts). Sir John A. Macdonald argued that the Senate should protect minorities and the rich were always fewer in number than the poor![37]

In the second place, the smaller provinces would only agree to join Confederation and accept representation by population in the House of Commons if they were overrepresented in the Senate. The Fathers settled on a Senate that would be based on equal regional representation, a compromise between equal provincial representation (as in the United States and as since demanded by Triple-E advocates) and the principle of representation by population. Such a system gave the Maritimes and Quebec a limited amount of protection against the voting power of Ontario in the House of Commons. It followed that senators were supposed to represent their regions and provinces within the national policy-making system.

A third function of the Senate, not explicitly provided for in 1867 but that can also be seen as part of the concept of sober second thought, is to improve legislation from a technical point of view. This function—to act as a nonideological, routine revising chamber that picks up on flaws in legislation that have not been noticed during its passage through the busy Commons—has become one of the Senate's most important roles over the years.

As far as powers were concerned, the Senate was given a veto over all legislation, a power that was not restricted as in the case of the British House of Lords. The only point of Senate inferiority to the Commons was that "money bills," that is, legislation involving the raising or spending of money, had to be introduced in the lower chamber. Nothing in law prevented the Senate from delaying, amending, or vetoing any bills, whether or not they involved money. It was only the Standing Orders of the House of Commons that claimed the Senate could not amend money bills, an assertion never accepted by the Senate.[38]

It was not until 1982 that the Senate's power was in any way reduced, and that had to do only with constitutional amendments, not ordinary legislation. According to the Constitution Act, 1982, the Senate can only delay a constitutional amendment for 180 days. If the Senate has not approved such an amendment by then, it can be repassed by the Commons, and bypasses the Senate in the process of ratification. If the 1992 constitutional accord had been ratified, the range of ordinary legislation over which the Senate retained an absolute veto would have been severely restricted.

COMPOSITION OF THE SENATE

The basic structural principle of the Senate agreed to at the time of Confederation was equal regional representation. Thus Ontario, Quebec, and the Maritimes received 24 senators each. In the case of Quebec, the province was divided into 24 senatorial regions so that an appropriate balance of anglophone and francophone representatives would be chosen. Otherwise, senators do not officially represent a specific region of their province. When Prince Edward Island joined Confederation, it received four of the 24 Maritime senators, reducing Nova Scotia and New Brunswick to ten each. In a general reform in 1915 the West was designated as a senatorial region with 24 senators, preserving the principle of equal regional representation, with six being allocated to each Western province. In 1949, Newfoundland was awarded six senators in addition to the 96 already allotted, so as to leave the Maritime contingent intact. Finally, in 1975, the Yukon and Northwest Territories were given one senator each, so that the total became 104 (4 × 24 + 6 + 2), with only slight deviations from the principle of equal regional representation.

Section 24 of the 1867 Constitution Act gives the governor general the power to appoint senators, but by convention this is done on the advice of the prime minister. Prime ministers have almost always chosen partisan supporters such as MPs seeking a safe haven, defeated MPs or candidates, those who have served the party organization well, retired premiers or other ex-provincial politicians, and especially federal cabinet ministers who have outlived their usefulness. Rewarding party services, regenerating the cabinet, and maintaining party unity were the main considerations in the prime minister's mind. Hence, almost all of those appointed could be called "party hacks," and the image of the Senate was set: a home for the aged, a pension scheme for retired party warriors, and a reward for businessmen's contributions to the party war chest.[39]

In addition to rewarding faithful service to the party in the past, many appointments were made on the assumption that the new senator would continue to promote the party in the future. Such senators carried on as party fundraisers ("bagmen"), party presidents, party organizers, election campaign strategists or managers, or in other partisan capacities. Since Canadian parties are usually short of funds, it saved the party salary money if some of its officials could work out of the Senate at public expense. Pierre Trudeau was the only prime minister to make more than the occasional nonpartisan or cross-party appointment. On six occasions, for example, he deliberately replaced a Tory with a Tory, a practice adopted because the Senate was already overwhelmingly stacked with Liberals.

Senators have traditionally been English or French male lawyers or businessmen, and have maintained active business connections after their appointment.[40] Most saw nothing wrong with carrying on as directors of various corporations or even being appointed to new ones at the same time as they held public office.[41] They always had spare time, they welcomed the supplementary income, and they could be useful links between the corporate and political worlds. Because of ideological opposition to the whole concept of an appointed chamber, left-wing groups have refused the occasional offer of appointment, leaving labour and working-class representation in the Senate virtually nonexistent.

The Constitution Act, 1867, speaks of "qualified persons" being eligible for appointment to the Senate, and this was originally understood to include only men. In one of the most famous court cases in Canadian history, however, an enterprising group of women challenged this interpretation of the meaning of "persons," and in 1929 the Judicial Committee of the Privy Council decided that "persons" did include women![42] Henceforth women were eligible to sit in the Senate, although relatively few have been appointed (18 of 102 in 1995). In addition, ethnic and religious considerations have often played a part in Senate appointments. From the Diefenbaker period onward, prime ministers sought to diversify Senate membership in ethnic terms, and senators have been appointed as representatives of the aboriginal, Ukrainian, Italian, Greek, Icelandic, and black communities, among others.

Senators originally served for life, and many lived to the ripe old age of 80, 90, or 100 before they died. Lester Pearson had a constitutional amendment passed in 1965 to the effect that incumbent senators could stay until death or retire at 75 with a pension, but all subsequent appointees would have to retire at 75. In normal circumstances only one senator sits in the cabinet (the government leader in the Senate). But both Joe Clark (1979–80) and Pierre Trudeau (1980–84) had three or four senators in their cabinets to fill in gaps in their provincial representation.

OPERATION OF THE SENATE

In the light of its intended functions, what can be said about the actual operations of the Senate? First, as for acting as a conservative influence on legislation and representing the interests of property, two examples stand out: the Senate's defeat of the first Old Age Pensions bill in 1925, and its repeated refusal to repeal the notorious section 98 of the Criminal Code that had been passed at the height of the Winnipeg General Strike in 1919.[43] After an election in which Mackenzie King was deemed to receive a mandate for the Old Age Pensions legislation, the Senate passed the bill a year later, but section 98 was not repealed until 1936. It is not so much with reference to other social legislation that this conservative role is most obvious, but in relation to bills affecting the corporate community, discussed below.

Second, it must be concluded that the Senate has never effectively represented provincial and regional interests in the national policy-making process.[44] This is not particularly surprising when senators owe their appointment to the federal prime minister and not to any provincial or regional constituency. As a result, this function was soon undertaken by the Judicial Committee of the Privy Council, regional ministers in the federal cabinet, and provincial premiers in federal–provincial conferences.

Of its original purposes, then, the first has been rendered archaic and the second has been assumed by other agencies. Today's senators therefore try to justify their existence primarily in terms of the third function mentioned, routine revision of bills. R.A. MacKay argues that the nonpartisan, noncontroversial revising function of the Senate is virtually indispensable, and F.A. Kunz calls it one of great usefulness.[45] In addition to routine revision of government bills, the Senate sometimes undertakes detailed and protracted examination of complex legislation, such as the Bankruptcy Act or the Criminal Code. Similarly, a bill will sometimes be introduced simultaneously in both chambers so that the Senate can engage in an unhurried "pre-study" of the bill rather than wait until it has passed three readings in the Commons.

Senators also seek to emphasize other important aspects of their work. One is the Senate's consideration of private bills. These concern individuals, companies, churches, professional associations, and other institutions, and are a nuisance to the busy House of Commons, which is often backlogged with public bills. Since 1934, almost all private bills have been introduced in the Senate where the background work can be done so that the Commons can approve them routinely at a later date. This practice does help the Commons, but private bills are not numerous and do not absorb much of anyone's time.

For a period the Senate functioned more or less as a divorce court for Quebec and Newfoundland, when religious opposition to divorce in those two provinces pre-empted turning this responsibility over to their courts. Divorces were a special kind of private bill, and between 1964 and 1968 (when they finally became a judicial matter in those two provinces) divorces were disposed of by the Senate without reference to the Commons.

Another kind of work not originally provided for is the study of various public problems by Senate committees in what Colin Campbell calls "social investigations." Senators often have the expertise and certainly the time to conduct inquiries that relieve the pressure on the House of Commons and are cheaper than royal commissions. Among the issues investigated by the Senate over the years were poverty, aging, unemployment, the mass media, science policy, land use, national defence, Canadian–American relations, and the Canadian Security Intelligence Service.

Finally, the Senate reviews regulations issued by various government departments. The Standing Joint Committee on the Scrutiny of Regulations has the responsibility of reviewing the great quantity of subordinate legislation issued every year. Although this is a joint Commons–Senate committee, the senators who sit on it have more time to devote to its tedious work and perhaps more independence of mind in approaching it.

Worthy as all these functions are, even collectively they do not justify the expense of the Senate, especially given its lack of a popular base. Much of the problem is that almost no one who accepts appointment to the Senate expects to work very hard, and almost all who go there have other interests on the side. Lacking even minimal popular accountability, it is possible for some senators to do absolutely nothing and still collect their paycheques until the age of 75. As of January 1996, senators were paid $64 400 plus a nontaxable expense account of $10 000, for a total value of approximately $80 000.[46] The Senate timetable is very lax, and a small group of 15 or 20 does most of its work. Prime ministers and cabinets have often been disrespectful of the institution, leaving many vacancies for long periods of time and expecting it to pass large quantities of legislation quickly at the end of a session.

In the harshest criticism of the operation of the Senate, it is sometimes accused of systemic corruption. This accusation is particularly levelled at the Senate Committee on Banking, Trade and Commerce, which reviews a great deal of legislation at the committee stage, regardless of its subject matter. Colin Campbell has detailed and condemned these corporate connections in his book *The Canadian Senate: A Lobby from Within*. He writes of the Senate's adopted function of "business review," as its members "bargain and negotiate on business's behalf for amendments which are essential for a favourable financial and commercial climate." Campbell reveals the "one-sided review which takes place in a legislature created by a political system which bends over backwards to ensure that business has preferential access to the policy process."[47] Unrestrained by any conflict-of-interest legislation (except for the formal abstention from voting), members of the Senate's Banking Committee energetically engage in debating legislation dealing with companies on whose boards of directors they sit. Many senators also act as lobby-ists for business beyond the confines of the Senate chamber. Thus, "senators' lobbying activities are paid for by the people of Canada and not by the business firms and groups whose interests they advance." Even worse, some senators (usually lawyers) have received payment for acting as business lobbyists even after the Lobbyists Registration Act purported to make this illegal.[48]

Over the years, the Senate consistently challenged, delayed, and amended legislative pro-visions that might endanger major business or financial concerns. Examples include protect-ing the existing commercial banks, on which many senators were directors, in both the 1960s and 1970s; delaying and gutting the Hazardous Products bill in 1968–69; delaying and dilut-ing the Investment Companies bill in 1969; and amending the Income Tax Act in 1973.[49]

The Senate's exercise of its power to amend or veto legislation must be put into the con-text that an appointed legislative chamber lost much of its legitimacy with the spread of democratic sentiment shortly after Confederation. Thus, the Senate did not usually feel jus-tified in defying the will of the popularly elected House of Commons.[50] Moreover, given the partisan nature of Senate appointments, the majority in that chamber usually corresponded to the partisan complexion of the Commons. Both had a Conservative majority for about the first 30 years and both usually had a Liberal majority since 1900.

As for amendments, Kunz calculates that between 1923 and 1963 the Senate made amend-ments to about 15 percent of the bills coming from the Commons, while MacKay finds about 20 percent between 1867 and 1960.[51] Andrew Heard shows, however, that between 1957 and 1986 this figure fell to about four percent.[52] It must be said that in many cases such amendments were introduced by the cabinet reflecting its second thoughts on the matter after it had been approved by the Commons, and most of the others were of a technical nature. To reinforce this point, in accounting for the incidence of Senate amendments to Commons bills, it made little difference whether or not the majority in both chambers belonged to the same party.

On the other hand, partisanship is most striking when one considers the Senate's vetoing of Commons legislation. In almost all such cases, a Liberal majority in the Senate has obstructed a Conservative majority in the Commons, or vice versa. According to MacKay, of approximately 4200 public bills passed by the Commons between 1867 and 1960, about 100 failed to pass the Senate, although many of these were withdrawn voluntarily by the gov-ernment. Kunz found 18 vetoes of 1918 bills between 1926 and 1963. Rather than concen-trate on total numbers, it is more useful to list the 14 most controversial Senate vetoes (see accompanying list). MacKay argues that in these and other cases the Senate has never defeated the real will of the people when clearly expressed.[53]

THE FOURTEEN MOST CONTROVERSIAL SENATE VETOES

1. 1875   rejection of a bill for the construction of the Esquimalt–Nanaimo railway
2. 1899–1900   rejection of a bill to readjust representation in the House of Commons for Ontario
3. 1912   amendment of Highways bill that government rejected

4. 1912   amendment of Tariff Commission bill that government rejected

5. 1913   rejection of Borden's Naval bill

6. 1914   rejection of amendment of the BNA Act re: provincial representation in the Senate

7. 1914   rejection of Farmers Bank Depositors' Relief bill

8. 1923   rejection of bill for construction of CNR branch lines

9. 1926   rejection of Old Age Pensions bill

10. 1926, 1927, 1928, 1929   rejection of repeal of s. 98 of Criminal Code

11. 1936   rejection of amendment of the BNA Act re: allowing provinces to levy sales taxes

12. 1937   rejection of bill expanding jurisdiction of Board of Transport Commissioners

13. 1961   rejection of amendment to the Customs Act

14. 1990   rejection of Abortion bill

Brian Mulroney had considerable difficulty with the Senate, when, between 1984 and 1991, a Liberal majority in that chamber coincided with a Conservative majority in the Commons. The Senate delayed a government borrowing bill in 1984; it tried to amend a government measure on mandatory supervision of parolees; it repeatedly passed amendments to the government's drug patent bill, only retreating at the last minute; and it delayed amendments to copyright, immigration, and income tax acts.[54] The Senate also tried to alter the Meech Lake Accord, and its amendments had to be overridden by the Commons after the expiry of the 180-day limit on constitutional amendments. Then, in mid-1988, at John Turner's direction, the Liberal majority in the Senate held up the Canada–U.S. Free Trade Agreement until the electorate had a chance to express its will on such an important measure. After the 1988 election, the Senate bowed to the popular will and passed the Free Trade Agreement but later dug in its heels on unemployment insurance amendments, cutbacks to social programs, and especially the Goods and Services Tax (GST).

It is unlikely that the GST would have passed if Prime Minister Mulroney had not invoked an obscure clause in the 1867 Constitution Act, section 26, which allowed him to appoint eight additional senators (two for each of the four senatorial regions) to tip the balance in favour of the Conservatives.[55] After the GST passed in an atmosphere of great bitterness on both sides, the Senate went ahead and defeated the government's compromise abortion bill (on a tie vote). This became the first measure in 30 years that the Senate actually defeated, but it was a peculiar case in that the government allowed a "free vote" and some cabinet ministers were probably secretly relieved that the Senate had exercised such a rare veto.

Besides the intense partisan confrontation between the two chambers, the Mulroney period was exceptional for two reasons: first, the new government had embarked on a new, neoconservative ideological tangent; and second, the Liberal ex-ministers in the Senate had a difficult time accepting the fact that they were no longer in power. In most of these cases, ironically, the House of Commons was acting in a more conservative manner than the Senate, which suddenly saw itself protecting the little people!

By the time the Liberals came to power in 1993, the Conservatives had established a clear majority in the Senate, so positions were reversed, and the Liberals began to pay for their intransigence of a few years earlier. The Conservative majority in the Senate was particularly incensed about the Liberal bill cancelling privatization of the Toronto Pearson Airport, which had been done amid charges of patronage and profiteering at public expense. The PC-controlled Senate was also reluctant to agree to the bill designed to redistribute seats in the House of Commons even after forcing the Liberals to abandon their objective of postponing the whole operation.

Andrew Heard argues that a modern convention has developed such that the Senate can make purely technical amendments or others that it knows will be acceptable to the Commons and to the government. While it should not act to frustrate the general thrust of Commons legislation put before it, the Senate can on rare occasions make substantive amendments "when the government has no clear support from the majority of Canadians to implement a policy that adversely affects some individuals or groups." If repassed by the Commons, however, the Senate should give way.[56]

SENATE REFORM

Given the limited value of the Senate as it currently operates, its reform is high on the political agenda. All sorts of proposals have been made, ranging from abolition to election, to having provinces choose some or all of its members. The CCF/NDP has always favoured abolition because of the undemocratic nature of the Senate and its close links to the business community. Campbell also recommended abolition because of the Senate's illegitimate defence of corporate interests and the impossibility of making the institution more effective and more democratic without interfering with the will of the House of Commons.

Many reformers have advocated reactivating the Senate's role of representing regional and provincial interests at the federal level because the existing mechanisms of "intrastate federalism" have been flawed. The Trudeau government first attempted to make the Senate a House of the Federation in 1978 with half its members selected by the provinces. However, the Supreme Court held that such changes to the structure of the Senate required provincial approval.[57] To legitimize its existence in a democratic age, there is an increasing consensus that the Senate should also be elected.

To ensure that provinces other than Quebec could get something out of the 1987 Meech Lake Accord, three points regarding the Senate were agreed on in that document.[58] First, no changes could be made to the Senate without unanimous provincial consent; second, Senate reform would be the next topic of constitutional change; and third, until such time as the selection process was changed, the prime minister would appoint senators from lists provided by the provinces. By the time the Meech Lake Accord died and these interim measures with it, Brian Mulroney had only appointed a handful of senators from provincial lists.

Meanwhile, Alberta began pushing its Triple-E proposal for Senate reform: elected, effective, and equal.[59] Triple-E advocates were not entirely clear on what powers they saw as necessary to make the Senate "effective," but since they generally felt that laws currently emanating from the House of Commons were designed in the interests of central Canada, such proponents were not overly concerned about deadlock between their revamped Senate and the lower house.

The government of Alberta felt so strongly about an elected Senate that it held a "senatorial election" in 1989 when a vacancy occurred during the period in which Mulroney asked for a list of provincial nominees. The Reform Party candidate won the province-wide contest (coinciding with municipal elections), and Premier Don Getty forwarded his name to the prime minister. Although Mulroney preferred to choose from a *list* of provincial nominees, rather than being presented with a single name, and was certainly not happy to appoint a Reform Party senator, he eventually gave in. No other province has yet followed this precedent, but Senate reform was a prominent part of the 1992 Charlottetown Accord.

That Accord would have provided for a new 62-member Senate, with six representatives from each province and one from each territory. They would be popularly elected at the same time as MPs, except in Quebec where they would be chosen by the National Assembly. To reinforce their new role as independent, provincial representatives in Ottawa, they would not be eligible to sit in the cabinet. Defeat of a government bill in the Senate would not be considered a vote of nonconfidence; instead, when the Senate rejected a Commons bill, a joint sitting of both houses would be held and a combined vote taken in which the Commons would outnumber the Senate 337 to 62. However, legislation dealing with the taxation of natural resources, as in the case of the National Energy Program, could be killed by a simple majority in the Senate. It could also veto government appointments to national institutions such as the governor of the Bank of Canada. Bills dealing with the French language and culture would have to be approved by a majority of francophone senators as well as by the Senate as a whole. Any kind of legislation except government money (supply) bills could be initiated in the Senate, but a Senate vote against a supply bill could be simply overridden by reintroducing it in the Commons.

Such a system was not exactly the **Triple-E Senate**, but it was close enough to satisfy Premier Getty and different enough not to offend other participants in the conference. Ontario and Quebec were willing to give up 18 senators each in return for 18 additional seats in the House of Commons, while Nova Scotia and New Brunswick surrendered four Senate seats each. Some provinces indicated an interest in guaranteeing gender equality among their six Senate members. However, when the Accord went down to popular defeat, the Senate remained unreformed, and little on the subject has been heard since.

. . . .

CONCLUSION

This chapter demonstrates that apart from MPs who double as cabinet ministers, the role of the House of Commons in the policy-making process is not impressive, and that of the Senate even less so. On the other hand, the Commons at least does have significant functions—in debating public issues, in keeping the government honest, and in educating the electorate. The cabinet can win almost every "battle" with Parliament, but may still lose the next electoral "war" if the opposition has alerted the public to its faults via the media. There are advantages to concentrating the responsibility for public policy in the hands of the cabinet, but these could still be achieved if better use were made of the talent in the House of Commons.

P Pluralists have a positive view of the House of Commons. They note the diversity in the social background of MPs, such as the rising numbers of other ethnics and women, and emphasize the opportunities available to MPs to articulate a variety of interests. Pluralists also point to the participation of parliamentary committees and individual MPs in various policy communities, and see pressure groups interacting more regularly with MPs than in the past. On the other hand, pluralists question whether the rigid party discipline in the Canadian House of Commons is appropriate for such a pluralistic society. Such rigidity has forced various regional, ethnic, and class interests to form their own political parties when they felt unable to make themselves heard within traditional national parties. It has also led many people to look to provincial governments and premiers to articulate regional concerns. As for the Senate, pluralists emphasize its increasingly diversified membership and the wide range of its social investigations. While it was once the preserve of French and English males, the Senate now contains about 15 percent women and conventional representation of a variety of ethnic groups. Rather surprisingly, most of its committee inquiries have recommended changes that were at odds with the business sector, such as improving the lot of the poor and the aged and providing greater regulation of the mass media.

PC Public choice theory sees the House of Commons as the focal point of party conflict between elections in order to influence the electorate in its next trip to the polls. Much of the activity in the Commons is designed to manipulate public opinion, as all parties try to present themselves in the best possible light and have nothing but condemnation for their opponents. This chapter has shown the many opportunities available in the Commons to pursue this intensely adversarial activity. Since media coverage of the Commons is usually dominated by opposition criticism, however, the cabinet does its best to ignore the House and to interact directly with the public.

© Class analysts find that the "Commons" is still an elitist institution. Very few of its members come from manual occupations, for example, and a high proportion have post-secondary education. Even more telling are the results of a survey that indicated MPs overestimate the economic well-being of the other members of society.[60] At the very least, such analysts advocate more working-class representation in Parliament. But that in itself would be of limited value since MPs are largely impotent as representatives of the general public and the cabinet generally acts at the command of the corporate elite.

Class analysts find that the Senate performs one principal role: the systematic review of legislation from the standpoint of the interests of business.[61] As mentioned, a large proportion of senators at any given time simultaneously sit on various corporate boards and lobby fellow senators, MPs, bureaucrats, and cabinet ministers on behalf of individual corporations or the general capitalist cause, whether in respect to legislation, regulations, or grants. Campbell quotes one senator as follows: "without us the Cabinet and the bureaucracy would never get the type of cooperation out of the private sector which is needed to make the system run."[62] Class analysts argue that "technical review" is in reality "business review" and, at least until the Mulroney period, senatorial vetoes were usually in the corporate interest. The "social investigators" are a small minority within the Senate whose broader concerns mask the behind-the-scenes efforts of the majority who unashamedly pursue corporate goals.

Elite theorists point out other aspects of the unrepresentative nature of the Senate. Over the years it has greatly overrepresented men, those over 60 years of age, wealthy businesspeople and professionals, and the two charter ethnic groups. The only justification for such disparity between the socioeconomic background of members of the Senate and the general population would have been the effective engagement of the institution in elite accommodation as an integrating process in Canadian society. This, indeed, was the very task it was intended to perform, but one in which the Senate has rarely proved to be useful.

(SC) State-centred theorists also minimize the role of the House of Commons in the policy-making process and argue that MPs who do try to represent constituency and societal concerns are voices in the wilderness. The cabinet and bureaucracy decide what they want to do and, via orders-in-council and regulations, avoid the House of Commons as much as possible. Only when absolutely necessary do they go to Parliament for legitimation of their initiatives; otherwise MPs are kept busy with constituency work and content with generous salaries and services. The advantage of such a state-centred system is that special interests are subordinated to the collective public interest. State-centred theorists find that rather than represent societal interests within the government, the Senate is a useful mechanism through which the authorities—prime minister, cabinet, bureaucracy, and government party—can pursue their own objectives. Prime ministers make senatorial appointments primarily for partisan rather than policy purposes, but these usually guarantee that the institution will rubber-stamp government legislation, as carefully prepared by the bureaucracy. In 1990, Prime Minister Mulroney deliberately appointed senators and even "extra" senators who would support his highly unpopular GST bill. State-centred theorists argue that senators do not undertake studies because society demands them, but only to pre-empt public cries for abolition of the chamber. Moreover, Senators have virtually unrestricted access to the public trough, deciding almost unilaterally how much pay and what additional benefits to give themselves.

DISCUSSION QUESTIONS

1. If Parliament does not play a significant part in the policy-making process, what are its basic functions?

2. What are the advantages and disadvantages of rigid party discipline in the House of Commons?

3. What are the real reasons for such rigid party discipline?

4. Should the concept of "confidence" be limited to nonconfidence votes rather than be applied to every government bill?

5. What other aspects of the House of Commons, if any, should be reformed?

6. What are the advantages and disadvantages of the initiative, the referendum, and the recall?

7. Does the Senate do enough to justify its existence, or should it be abolished?

8. What are the pros and cons of the Triple-E Senate?

9. If elected, to what extent should the Senate be able to interfere with the will of the cabinet and the House of Commons?

10. How can the approaches outlined in Chapter 1 be applied to the material in this chapter?

NOTES

1. C.E.S. Franks, *The Parliament of Canada* (Toronto: University of Toronto Press, 1987), p. 5. In his book *The Canadian House of Commons: Procedure and Reform* (Montreal: McGill–Queen's University Press, 1977), John Stewart lists essentially the same functions: "first, to support a government; second, to prevent clandestine governing; third, to test the government's administrative policies and legislative proposals; fourth, to constrain the ministers; and fifth, to educate the electorate," p. 30.

2. Franks, *The Parliament of Canada*, p. 216.

3. These can best be deciphered from the annual *Canadian Parliamentary Guide*, edited by P.G. Normandin (Toronto: INFO GLOBE), or from Munroe Eagles et al., *The Almanac of Canadian Politics* (Toronto: Oxford University Press, 1995).

4. Franks, *The Parliament of Canada*, p. 73.

5. John Porter, *The Vertical Mosaic* (Toronto: University of Toronto Press, 1965), p. 402.

6. See, for example, the budgets of 1963 and 1990.

7. Franks, *The Parliament of Canada*, p. 142.

8. Stewart, *The Canadian House of Commons*, pp. 29–30.

9. Eugene Forsey and Graham Eglington, "Twenty-Five Fairy Tales about Parliamentary Government," in Paul Fox and Graham White, eds., *Politics: Canada*, 7th ed. (Toronto: McGraw-Hill Ryerson, 1991) argue that this is a mistaken belief.

10. Sometimes the concept of a "shadow cabinet" is used by opposition leaders.

11. Andrew Heard, *Canadian Constitutional Conventions* (Toronto: Oxford University Press, 1991), pp. 83–84.

12. Ibid., p. 80.

13. Franks, *The Parliament of Canada*, p. 110.

14. Ibid., pp. 6, 29, 96, 268.

15. Paul Thomas, "Parliamentary Reform through Political Parties," in John Courtney, ed., *The Canadian House of Commons: Essays in Honour of Norman Ward* (Calgary: University of Calgary Press, 1985); and Paul Thomas, "The Role of National Party Caucuses," in Peter Aucoin, ed., *Party Government and Regional Representation in Canada* (Toronto: University of Toronto Press, 1985).

16. Thomas, "The Role of the National Party Caucuses."

17. Government bills introduced in the House of Commons are numbered from C-1 to C-200; those introduced in the Senate have an S designation; and private members' bills in the Commons are numbered over C-200.

18. Most of the others that passed dealt with changes to the name of an MP's constituency. Heard, *Constitutional Conventions in Canada*, p. 78.

19. The government's resort to closure on every stage of the bill was seen as the work of Trade and Commerce Minister C.D. Howe, who was obsessed with getting the construction of the pipeline started.

20. The exceptional delays of the 1984–90 and 1994–95 periods are discussed below.
21. For compilation of and/or commentary on the rules, see *Standing Orders of the House of Commons* (September 1994) and *Précis of Procedure*, 4th ed. (1991), both published by the House of Commons, and Alistair Fraser, W.F. Dawson, and John Holtby, eds., *Beauchesne's Rules and Forms of the House of Commons of Canada*, 6th ed. (Toronto: Carswell, 1989).
22. Martin Westmacott, "Whips and Party Cohesion," *Canadian Parliamentary Review* (Autumn 1988). Conservative and Liberal whips are chosen by the party leader, but the NDP caucus elects its whip.
23. W.F. Dawson, *Procedure in the Canadian House of Commons*. Toronto: University of Toronto Press, 1962, pp. 188–90.
24. Grace Skogstad, "Interest Groups, Representation and Conflict Management in the Standing Committees of the House of Commons," *Canadian Journal of Political Science* (December 1985), pp. 739–72.
25. Paul Pross, "Parliamentary Influence and the Diffusion of Power," *Canadian Journal of Political Science* (June 1985).
26. This subject has been well documented in the works of R.J. Fleming, including *Canadian Legislatures 1987–88* (Ottawa: Ampersand Communications Services, 1988), and *Canadian Legislatures 1992: Issues, Structures and Costs* (Toronto: Global Press, 1992).
27. Robert Fife and John Warren, *A Capital Scandal* (Toronto: Key Porter Books, 1991).
28. The Research Branch of the Library of Parliament regularly publishes excellent summaries of topical political issues for the benefit of MPs and senators. These summaries are also very useful for students of political science. They are sent to most university libraries and can be found under the titles *Background Papers* and *Current Issue Review*.
29. Eugene Forsey, "The Problem of 'Minority Government' in Canada," *Canadian Journal of Economics and Political Science* (February 1964).
30. According to Franks, the Trudeau minority was actually defeated on 18 of 81 votes between 1972 and 1974 but only chose to resign on the defeat of the 1974 budget, while the Pearson government had suffered two other defeats without much fanfare. Franks, *The Parliament of Canada*, p. 139.
31. Bob Rae, "Changing the Confidence Convention in Ontario," *Canadian Parliamentary Review* (Winter 1985–86).
32. Franks, *The Parliament of Canada*, p. 132; and John Stewart, "Commons Procedure in the Trudeau Era," in John Courtney, ed., *The Canadian House of Commons: Essays in Honour of Norman Ward* (Calgary: University of Calgary Press, 1985).
33. One of the more controversial aspects of television was the rule that the camera could only focus on the person recognized by the Speaker, rather than show what else was going on in the chamber.
34. *Report of the Special Committee on Reform of the House of Commons* (Ottawa: House of Commons, 1985).
35. Paul Thomas argues that attitudinal change on the part of political parties in Parliament is just as important as technical procedural changes in enhancing its role in the policy-making process in "Parliamentary Reform through Political Parties," in Courtney, *The Canadian House of Commons*.
36. Franks, *The Parliament of Canada*, pp. 9, 261.
37. Quoted in R.A. MacKay, *The Unreformed Senate of Canada*, rev. ed. (Toronto: McClelland and Stewart, 1967), pp. 47–48.
38. MacKay, *The Unreformed Senate*, pp. 91-95; and Kunz, *The Modern Senate*, pp. 337–47. Andrew Heard argues that a constitutional convention is emerging that the Senate may not insist on altering the financial provisions of money bills. *Canadian Constitutional Conventions* (Toronto: Oxford University Press, 1991), p. 94.
39. MacKay, *The Unreformed Senate*, p. 9.
40. MacKay (ch. 9) and Kunz (ch. 2) both discuss socioeconomic backgrounds up to 1960 and 1963 respectively.
41. Even MacKay sees nothing wrong with it in *The Unreformed Senate*, p. 141.
42. Kunz discusses this issue on pp. 53–56. The case was officially referred to as *Edwards v. Att. Gen. of Can.* [1930] AC 124.
43. MacKay, *The Unreformed Senate*, p. 124.

44. Both MacKay and Kunz address this point. The former finds the record ambiguous (pp. 112–23), while the latter argues that the Senate was a supplementary line of defence of sectional interests (p. 336).

45. MacKay, *The Unreformed Senate*, p. 110; and Kunz, *The Modern Senate*, p. 186.

46. Senators also receive free transportation to and from Parliament, of course, but unlike MPs, they keep their "frequent flyer" points, even though these trips have been paid for by the public purse.

47. Colin Campbell, *The Canadian Senate: A Lobby from Within* (Toronto: Macmillan, 1978), pp. 10–11.

48. McMenemy, "The Senate as an Instrument of Business and Party," in Paul Fox and Graham White, eds., *Politics: Canada*, 7th ed. (Toronto: McGraw-Hill Ryerson, 1991), p. 455.

49. Campbell, *The Canadian Senate*, pp. 12–19; 147.

50. MacKay writes that it is an "institutional survival of a pre-democratic age, (p. 10) and that "in a democratic age an appointed upper house labours under the handicap that it has no political foundation" (p. 62).

51. MacKay, p. 87; and Kunz, pp. 116–17.

52. Heard, *Canadian Constitutional Conventions*, p. 89.

53. MacKay, *The Unreformed Senate*, pp. 96–112.

54. See the justification offered by Senator Lorna Marsden in "Doing Its Thing—Providing Sober Second Thought: The Canadian Senate, 1984–1990," in Fox and White, *Politics: Canada*, 7th ed. (1991).

55. In 1873 Alexander Mackenzie had asked the British government to summon additional senators but was refused on the ground that it was not necessary at the time.

56. Heard, *Canadian Constitutional Conventions*, p. 95.

57. *Reference Re Legislative Authority of Parliament to Alter or Replace the Senate*, [1980] 1 S.C.R. 54.

58. Gordon Robertson, *A House Divided: Meech Lake, Senate Reform, and the Canadian Union* (Halifax: Institute for Research on Public Policy, 1989).

59. See, for example, Peter McCormick, "Canada Needs a Triple E Senate," in Fox and White, eds., *Politics: Canada*, 7th ed. (1991); and H. McConnell, "The Case for a 'Triple E' Senate, *Queen's Quarterly* (Autumn 1988).

60. Franks, *The Parliament of Canada*, p. 69.

61. Campbell, *The Canadian Senate: A Lobby from Within*, p. 9.

62. Ibid., p. 71.

FURTHER READING

House of Commons:

Canadian Parliamentary Review. Quarterly publication of the Canadian Region of the Commonwealth Parliamentary Association.

Courtney, John, ed. *The Canadian House of Commons: Essays in Honour of Norman Ward.* Calgary: University of Calgary Press, 1985.

Dawson, W.F. *Procedure in the Canadian House of Commons.* Toronto: University of Toronto Press, 1962.

Eagles, Munroe, et al. *The Almanac of Canadian Politics*, 2nd ed. Toronto: Oxford University Press, 1995.

Fleming, R.J. *Canadian Legislatures 1987–1988.* Ottawa: Ampersand Communications Services, 1988.

———. *Canadian Legislatures 1992: Issues, Structures and Costs.* Toronto: Global Press, 1992.

Forsey, Eugene. "The Problem of 'Minority Government' in Canada." *Canadian Journal of Economics and Political Science* (February 1964).

Franks, C.E.S. *The Parliament of Canada.* Toronto: University of Toronto Press, 1987.

Fraser, Alistair, W.F. Dawson, and John Holtby, eds. *Beauchesne's Rules and Forms of the House of Commons of Canada*, 6th ed. Toronto: Carswell, 1989.

Heard, Andrew. *Canadian Constitutional Conventions*. Toronto: Oxford University Press, 1991.

House of Commons. *Précis of Procedure*, 4th ed., 1991.

———. *Standing Orders of the House of Commons*. September 1994.

Jackson, Robert, and Michael Atkinson. *The Canadian Legislative System*, 2nd rev. ed. Toronto: Macmillan, 1980.

Jerome, Jim. *Mr. Speaker*. Toronto: McClelland and Stewart, 1986.

Normandin, P.G., ed. *The Canadian Parliamentary Guide, 1994*. Toronto: INFO GLOBE, 1994 (annual).

Parliamentary Government (quarterly).

Pross, Paul. "Parliamentary Influence and the Diffusion of Power." *Canadian Journal of Political Science* (June 1985).

Rae, Bob. "Changing the Confidence Convention in Ontario." *Canadian Parliamentary Review* (Winter 1985–86).

Stewart, John. *The Canadian House of Commons: Procedure and Reform*. Montreal: McGill–Queen's University Press, 1977.

Thomas, Paul. "Parliamentary Reform through Political Parties" In John Courtney, ed. *The Canadian House of Commons*. Calgary: University of Calgary Press, 1985.

———. "The Role of National Party Caucuses." In Peter Aucoin, ed. *Party Government and Regional Representation in Canada*. Toronto: University of Toronto Press, 1985.

Westmacott, Martin. "Whips and Party Cohesion." *Canadian Parliamentary Review* (Autumn 1988).

White, Graham. "Recent Reforms of the House of Commons." In Paul Fox and Graham White, eds. *Politics: Canada*, 6th ed. Toronto: McGraw-Hill Ryerson, 1987.

———. "Functions of the House of Commons." In Paul Fox and Graham White, eds. *Politics: Canada*, 7th ed. Toronto: McGraw-Hill Ryerson, 1991.

Senate

Campbell, Colin. *The Canadian Senate: A Lobby from Within*. Toronto: Macmillan, 1978.

Forsey, Eugene. "No—More Than a Triple E Senate Is Needed." In Robert J. Fleming, ed. *Canadian Legislatures 1987–1988*. Ottawa: Ampersand Communications, 1988.

Government of Canada. *Reform of the Senate: A Discussion Paper*. Ottawa: Supply and Services, 1983.

Kunz, F.A. *The Modern Senate of Canada 1925–1963: A Re-Appraisal*. Toronto: University of Toronto Press, 1965.

McConnell, H. "The Case for a 'Triple E' Senate." *Queen's Quarterly* (Autumn 1988).

McCormick, Peter. "Canada Needs a Triple E Senate." In Paul Fox and Graham White, eds. *Politics: Canada*, 7th ed. Toronto: McGraw-Hill Ryerson, 1991.

Mackay, R.A. *The Unreformed Senate of Canada*, rev. ed. Toronto: McClelland and Stewart, 1967.

McMenemy, John. "The Senate as an Instrument of Business and Party." In Paul Fox and Graham White, eds. *Politics: Canada*, 7th ed. Toronto: McGraw-Hill Ryerson, 1991.

Marsden, Lorna. "Doing Its Thing—Providing 'Sober Second Thought': The Canadian Senate, 1984–1990." In Paul Fox and Graham White, eds. *Politics: Canada*, 7th ed. Toronto: McGraw-Hill Ryerson, 1991.

Special Joint Committee on Senate Reform. *Report*. Ottawa: Supply and Services, 1984.

White, R. *Voice of Region: The Long Journey to Senate Reform in Canada*. Toronto: Dundurn Press, 1990.

the JUDICIARY

The Federal Court of Canada quashes a decision of the Immigration and Refugee Board. The Supreme Court strikes down the Quebec sign law and throws out the abortion provision of the Criminal Code. It decides that Sue Rodriguez cannot avail herself of assisted suicide, but extreme drunkenness can sometimes excuse rape or murder. Women's and ethnic groups criticize the white, male dominance of judges across the country, and Natives demand a parallel aboriginal justice system. The public is appalled at residual patronage appointments to the bench, and troubled by cutbacks to legal aid plans.

Canadian political science was traditionally interested in the judiciary or court system primarily in terms of its interpretation of federal and provincial powers. Now that the Charter of Rights and Freedoms has catapulted the courts into the middle of many heated political issues, however, political scientists are giving this fourth branch of government much more attention.

This chapter examines the judiciary as an institution of government, discussing the function of adjudication, categories of laws, the structure of the courts, the functions of the Supreme Court of Canada, and the appointment, retirement, removal, and independence of judges. Chapter 5 considered the role of the courts in interpreting the Charter of Rights and Freedoms.

THE FUNCTION OF ADJUDICATION

The judiciary has always been associated with the **rule adjudication** function in the political system, although other institutions may perform part of this function, too. Adjudication can be defined as interpreting the law in cases of dispute, of settling disputes by applying the law to them, or making a judgment based on the law. Peter Russell defines the term as follows: "providing authoritative settlements in disputes about the law."[1]

In the authoritative resolution of legal disputes, judges only decide disputes about the law. But many legal disputes are resolved without going to court or before going through the entire judicial process. Such an "out-of-court" settlement, especially that between individuals or between governments, is likely to be some sort of personal or political compromise. It is only when an accommodation satisfactory to both sides cannot be reached that the formal adjudicatory process is pursued.

The function of the judiciary therefore is to render formal, impartial, authoritative judgments in the case of legal disputes between two parties that cannot be settled otherwise. It is a process that generally relies on the adversarial system, with lawyers representing each side. The judge, clothed with the coercive powers of the state, acts as an independent referee and decides which of the disputants is legally right. As a result, the process usually culminates in the designation of a winner and a loser, rather than in the achievement of some acceptable middle ground.

Other governmental structures also engage in rule adjudication, especially a great variety of administrative tribunals, as discussed in Chapter 21, and the distinction between them and real courts is often very subtle. On the other hand, the judiciary also has certain nonadjudicative functions. Because of their prestige and impartiality, for example, judges have frequently been appointed to head royal commissions or other commissions of inquiry. The nature of many such commissions has unfortunately been more political than judicial, and most observers feel that this is an inappropriate use of judicial personnel, especially given increasing backlogs in their regular adjudicative work.

Apart from the civil law system in Quebec, Canadian federal and provincial legal systems operate in the tradition of the English **common law**. The basis of that system is the accumulation over the centuries of judicial precedents, both in England and more recently in Canada. Thus, in a typical court case, the two sides seek to find precedents—previous court decisions—favouring their respective points of view. The judge (and sometimes the jury) have to decide which precedents most closely resemble the case currently before the court. The principle that precedents are binding on successive decisions is called **stare decisis**.

If the law were always comprehensive and crystal clear, and if the situations to which it applied were always simple and straightforward, rule adjudication would be fairly routine and the judiciary would not have much discretion in performing this function. The real world is more complex, and the law may not be clear on all points or provide for every conceivable situation. Russell refers to the "inescapable generality of the law" such that, while judges theoretically settle disputes according to pre-existing law, they actually shape and develop the law in the very process of settling disputes about it. At the very least, judges must establish priorities among competing legal rules and principles, and in this process they "put flesh on the bare skeleton of the law and shape its substance."[2]

The judiciary and the function of judicial interpretation were included in the chart of the policy-making process in Chapter 19. Rather than taking place subsequent to policy-making, where it once was placed, rule adjudication can now be considered as part of the policy-making process. Unlike Americans, Canadian observers have not given much recognition to the concept of judicial involvement in this process. But Russell argues that this Canadian approach "wrongly assumes that all important public policies are expressed in statutes passed by legislatures ... and overlooks the extent to which [such] policies ... are shaped through the process of being applied in particular cases by judges and administrators."[3] He cites such examples as the large element of discretion left to judges in the sentencing process, the decision of the Canadian courts to give little weight to the Canadian Bill of Rights, and the increasing judicial supervision of the operation of administrative agencies. Russell also refers specifically to the judicial interpretation of anti-monopoly laws that "decisively shaped industrial policy by making it nearly impossible to convict corporations for monopolistic practices."[4] Successive ministers of Consumer and Corporate Affairs found it difficult to overcome the effect of judicial decision-making in this field. In the course of adjudicating disputes, the courts are inherently involved in policy-making, hence the sixth phase of the Canadian policy-making process, that of judicial interpretation.

Related to this point, but taking it one step farther, is the explicit power of **judicial review**. Rather than merely interpret laws with discretion, judicial review is the power of the courts to declare them invalid. The original Constitution Act of 1867 did not contain any such provision, although the courts soon appropriated this power in one respect. Chapter 4 detailed the extent to which the courts invalidated federal and provincial legislation as violations of the division of powers between the two levels of government. In rendering federal or provincial legislation void if either encroached on the jurisdiction of the other level of government, the decisions of the courts had a significant effect on the shape of Canadian federalism. The court's power of judicial review was greatly enhanced with the adoption of the Canadian Charter of Rights and Freedoms in 1982, and the effects of the first 13 years of that review were discussed in Chapter 5. Peter McCormick writes in this connection:

> we should recognize that judges have always had power, have always affected our society by the decisions they make (and by the way they decide to decide and how to decide). The Charter has simply made a longstanding reality more immediately visible and directed us belatedly to an assessment of the implications of judicial power.[5]

CATEGORIES OF LAWS

The law can be defined as "society's system of binding rules."[6] Laws are commonly divided into different categories, primarily "civil" and "criminal." A **civil law** regulates relationships between two private parties such as individuals or corporations, and if private agreement cannot be reached in the case of dispute, one party may take the other to court. Most aspects of civil law in Canada are within provincial jurisdiction, largely because of the provincial power over property and civil rights. Civil cases often involve disputes over commercial contracts or property, and such cases are normally resolved by the court's ordering one party to pay damages to the other. Civil cases are decided on the basis of the "balance of probabilities" of the merits of each side.

Criminal law, on the other hand, is primarily a federal responsibility; it is thus more or less uniform throughout the country and has been consolidated in the **Criminal Code**. In this case, the commission of a crime such as murder, sexual assault, or theft is considered to be a wrong against society as a whole, and the state takes the initiative to bring the suspect to justice by means of the police and crown attorneys. In criminal cases, judges may impose fines or prison sentences if the accused is found guilty, such guilt having been proven "beyond a reasonable doubt."

One of the peculiarities of Canadian federalism is that while criminal law is within federal jurisdiction, it is usually the provincial attorneys general and their agents, the Crown attorneys, who are responsible for initiating proceedings against the person who is charged. This situation has come about because the provinces have jurisdiction over the administration of justice. Sometimes a case contains both civil and criminal elements, such as a drunken driver who does damage to another person's car. The state pursues the violation of the Criminal Code, but the victim's insurance company would have to take the initiative to sue for property damage.

Reprinted with permission.

Instead of this basic division between civil and criminal law, a distinction is sometimes made between public and private law.[7] Private law is essentially the same thing as civil law described above, that is, law in which private interests are primarily involved. Beyond the contracts and property mentioned, however, private law includes torts, wills, company law, and family law. Public law, primarily involving the public interest or the government, goes beyond criminal law to include constitutional law, administrative law, and taxation law. Constitutional law has traditionally involved questions about federal or provincial jurisdiction, and governments themselves have often been the parties to a constitutional case. With the adoption of the Charter of Rights and Freedoms, a whole new aspect of constitutional law in Canada has emerged. Administrative law concerns the operation of government departments and agencies, and as government activity has expanded over the years, this branch of law has also increased in significance.

By giving the provinces jurisdiction over property and civil rights, the Fathers of Confederation allowed the province of Quebec to retain its distinctive private or civil law system based on the French Napoleonic Code and called the **Code Civil du Québec**. The private law system in the other provinces is based on the English common law tradition. The theoretical distinction between the two systems in terms of form is that while the common law consists of a hodge-podge of judicial precedents, the Code Civil is a single comprehensive document. As Gall puts it, "in a common law system, the courts extract existing principles of law from decisions of previous cases, while in the civil law system, the courts look to the civil code to determine a given principle and they then apply the facts of an instant case to that principle."[8] The state has far greater ability to assert its authority and power through the written code than in the common law tradition where the law is written in more general terms and is susceptible to interpretation and application by judges and juries. There are also certain differences in substance, but while much attention is given to this distinction in Canadian legal and political life, the actual difference between the two systems is probably not as great as is often assumed. Lawyers and judges in the civil law system cannot help but pay some attention to precedents within that system, and cannot but be influenced by the common law system surrounding them.

STRUCTURE OF THE COURTS

Because the provinces that formed Confederation in 1867 already possessed a court system, and because the Judicial Committee of the Privy Council continued to function as a court of appeal for the whole British Empire, it was not necessary to devote much attention to the judiciary in the Constitution Act, 1867. The new federal government was allowed to establish a general court of appeal and any additional courts, but the provinces were otherwise given responsibility for the administration of justice, which included the establishment of a provincial court system. McCormick describes the logic of the court structure as follows:

First: Identify the more routine cases and those that involve less serious possible outcomes and assign them to an accessible high-volume, low-delay court, preferably one that sits in many different centres.

Second: Assign the less routine and more serious cases to a lower-volume court that can devote more time and more focused attention to each individual case.

Third: Establish a court of appeal to correct simple errors and to promote uniformity in the application of the law within each province.

Fourth: Establish a "general court of appeal" to promote uniformity in the application of the law within the country as a whole and to provide judicial leadership.

Fifth: Create a system of federal courts for cases directly involving the federal government as a party or raising issues concerning the administrative law applied by federal departments.[9]

As seen in Figure 23.1, the court systems within each province developed into a reasonably uniform three-level hierarchy. At the top are two "superior" courts—the superior trial court and the court of appeal, although they go by different names from province to province. At the bottom are provincial courts. Most provinces set up district and/or county courts between these two levels, but over the 1975–95 period they abolished this intermediate tier and integrated it with their superior courts.[10]

Because of the assumption that provinces could not be trusted to make worthy appointments to superior, district, and county courts, the Fathers of Confederation provided that the judges of these courts would be appointed by the governor general, conventionally meaning the federal cabinet. Such judges were also paid by the federal government. Thus, in another peculiarity of Canadian federalism, each province determines how many superior court judges it needs, but they are appointed and paid by Ottawa.[11] Since these courts were provided for in section 96 of the 1867 document, they are often called "section 96 courts" and

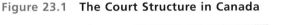

Figure 23.1   The Court Structure in Canada

their judges, "section 96 judges." Below the level of section 96 courts, each province established various "provincial courts" to which provincial cabinets appointed the judges. A brief discussion of each level of the judicial hierarchy follows.

Provincial Courts

Whatever their structure or name, provincial courts generally have the following functions:

1. summary offences including less serious crimes, provincial and municipal offences
2. most aspects of indictable offences, some mandatory and others optional
3. preliminary hearings for most serious crimes
4. bail hearings
5. Young Offenders Act offences
6. family law, except divorce and proceedings flowing from divorce
7. small civil cases

Provincial courts have a monopoly on summary offences except where even lower tribunals such as justices of the peace in some provinces have been given responsibility. More serious crimes, called indictable offences, can be subdivided into three categories. Some, like murder, are reserved for superior courts; some, like theft, are assigned to provincial courts; and those in an intermediate category can be tried in either section 96 or provincial courts. The federal Young Offenders Act covers offences committed by those aged 12 to 18. This is a complex area of federal–provincial interaction, but as far as courts are concerned, the offences are tried in provincial courts or special youth courts established in some provinces.

Family law is another area of great federal–provincial complexity. Since divorce is a federal responsibility, divorces are dealt with in section 96 courts, and any proceedings flowing from the divorce must also be dealt with there. On the other hand, as long as divorce is not involved, such matters as custody, access, maintenance, alimony, adoption, guardianship, and protection of children are handled in provincial courts. Some provinces have set up special family courts for this purpose. The fragmentation of family law presents one of the most serious problems of the Canadian court structure, not only because parts of it must be handled by section 96 courts and other aspects fall into the jurisdiction of provincial courts, but also because some problems, such as support payments, often involve both levels of courts.[12] Several provinces have tried to overcome the latter problem by experimenting with a "unified family court" presided over by a section 96 judge, but most authorities would prefer to unify family law jurisdiction at the provincial court level.[13]

Provincial courts, sometimes in a civil division, also have jurisdiction over disputes involving small amounts of money, although some provinces have established small claims courts for this purpose. Each province determines the monetary limit for cases that can be considered at that level, with disputes involving larger sums being initiated at the section 96 court level. Some provinces have also tried to remove the adversarial nature of small claims disputes by instituting various mediation services.

The Superior Trial Court

The functions of the superior trial court in the province, whatever its name, are as follows:

1. some mandatory and other elective indictable offences
2. civil matters over a given monetary amount
3. divorces and proceedings flowing therefrom
4. appeals from lower courts re summary convictions, juvenile and family cases
5. administrative law cases

In the superior trial court, the accused often has the option of trial by judge alone or trial by judge and jury. The former is increasingly the preferred option, and the latter has been curtailed to some extent by legislation. In the famous trials concerning Dr. Henry Morgentaler on charges of performing illegal abortions, juries repeatedly found him not guilty, although they were overruled on occasion by appeal courts. The jury had less trouble establishing the guilt of Paul Bernardo.

Many people cannot afford to hire a lawyer to defend themselves in a criminal (or even civil) case, yet the objective of the court system must be the search for truth and the obtention of justice, goals that have traditionally rested on the adversarial system. To ensure that those without the financial resources have a fairer chance to achieve justice, legal aid programs financed jointly by the federal and provincial governments have been established. Although these vary in detail from one province to another and do not cover every kind of legal work, they go some way to meet the fairness objective. Community legal clinics serve a similar function.

A related means of reducing the costs of the administration of justice as a whole are the practices of plea bargaining and pre-trial conferences. Plea bargaining involves discussions between defence and Crown attorneys with the aim of achieving agreement on charges to be pursued, typically by having the accused agree to plead guilty to one charge and the Crown agree to drop other charges. This practice is routine at the provincial court level and avoids a lengthy, costly trial. In the higher trial courts it is increasingly common for the judge to hold a pre-trial conference with the lawyers for each side. Such conferences can result in a negotiated settlement or at least a time-saving clarification of the issues involved. They have also proven useful at the level of family and small claims courts. While plea bargaining and pre-trial conferences must not be allowed to subvert justice, they are valuable devices to cut costs for everyone involved (including the public), and to reduce the workload of the usually congested court system. In the controversial case of Karla Homolka, the objectives were to avoid publicity that could jeopardize the trial of Paul Bernardo and to obtain evidence against him before the videotapes were found.

Provincial Courts of Appeal

Provincial courts of appeal hear criminal, civil, and other appeals, some of which have already been appealed from a lower court to a section 96 trial court. Although some of its judgments can be appealed to the Supreme Court of Canada, the decision of the provincial court of appeal is usually final, which adds to the significance of this level of court.[14] The basic function of an appeal court is to correct errors or injustices that one side claims were made in a lower court, but an appeal court is primarily interested in legal rather than factual issues. The second function of the appeal court is to render an opinion in a reference case, that is, on a constitutional issue referred to it by the provincial cabinet. Russell thus speaks of the "law-making" role of appeal courts because their legal interpretations have a "creative legislative dimension."[15] Decisions of the provincial court of appeal are binding on all courts below it in the same province and are "strongly persuasive" for trial courts in other provinces. Courts of appeal normally sit in banks of three judges, but the size of these panels can be increased to five for very important cases. Each side of a case submits a brief or "factum" in advance summarizing its arguments, and lawyers then engage in oral argument.

The Federal Court of Canada

The **Federal Court of Canada** was established in 1971 to replace the Exchequer Court created in 1875. Unlike its predecessor, the Federal Court has trial and appeal divisions. It was intended to relieve the Supreme Court of hearing routine appeals from certain federal administrative tribunals and to strengthen judicial review of federal administration by developing a more unified and cohesive body of federal administrative law.[16] Between its two divisions, the Federal Court has the following functions:

1. cases involving admiralty law, and copyright, trademark, and patent disputes
2. citizenship and immigration appeals
3. appeals from other federal administrative tribunals
4. civil cases involving the federal government
5. cases involving bills of exchange, promissory notes, aeronautics, and interprovincial works and undertakings
6. appeals from boards of referees under the Unemployment Insurance Act
7. prerogative writs (e.g., injunctions) applying to agencies of the federal government
8. appeals re Access to Information and Privacy Acts
9. issuance of Canadian Security Intelligence Service warrants

These functions reveal that while it is not well known to the public, the Federal Court has significant powers over the operation of the federal government. Federal administrative activities have been subject to much more frequent and consistent judicial review since the creation of the Federal Court. The court has wider authority to review decisions of judicial and quasi-judicial tribunals than of administrative agencies, but this distinction is difficult to draw in the field of administrative law. In the former case, the court may review a tribunal's decision on the basis that it breached the principles of natural justice, that it acted beyond its jurisdiction, or that it made errors in law, but purely administrative agencies must also act fairly. During its first twenty years, the jurisdiction of the Federal Court was restricted in several Supreme Court decisions, but amendments passed by Parliament in 1990 straightened out these problems.[17]

The work of the Federal Court is dominated by cases involving the Immigration Act and Immigration and Refugee Board, Unemployment Insurance, penitentiaries and the Parole

Board, the Public Service Commission and Public Service Staff Relations Board, and the Ministry of National Revenue. It has recently seen a growth in aboriginal cases, dealing with monetary and constitutional issues, land entitlements, and natural resources. Of great interest to political science, the Federal Court also hears appeals regarding the Access to Information Act and the Privacy Act and decides on requests for warrants from the Canadian Security Intelligence Service in order to plant bugs, open mail, and engage in other surreptitious activities.

The Federal Court consists of a chief justice and ten other judges on its appeal division and the associate chief justice and 19 other full-time and assorted part-time judges on its trial division. The appeal division judges sit in panels of at least three members.

The Tax Court of Canada is not so much a court as a judicialization of its predecessor, the Tax Review Board. It provides an easily accessible and independent tribunal for the disposition of tax disputes between citizens and the federal government. It deals primarily with matters arising under the Income Tax Act, the Unemployment Insurance Act, and the Excise Tax Act. Headed by a chief judge, it consists of 21 other full-time and assorted part-time judges, who hear cases across the country.

....

THE SUPREME COURT OF CANADA

The Supreme Court of Canada sits at the apex of the Canadian court system. It hears appeals from the provincial courts of appeal in civil and criminal cases and from the appeals division of the Federal Court of Canada in administrative law matters. That part of its work of most interest to political science involves constitutional law, whether in terms of the division of powers between federal and provincial governments or of interpretations of the Charter of Rights and Freedoms. Besides hearing actual appeal cases from lower courts, the Supreme Court can be asked by the federal cabinet to give opinions, usually on constitutional matters, in what are called **reference cases**. While the Supreme Court hears fewer cases per year than any lower court, it is interested almost exclusively in questions of law. Thus of all courts, it is the most heavily engaged in a "law-making" role, and its decisions are binding on all lower courts.

Until 1949, the Supreme Court was a seriously deficient institution. First, its decisions could be appealed to Canada's pre-1949 final court of appeal, the Judicial Committee of the Privy Council (JCPC) located in London, and it was bound by JCPC precedents. But even more humiliating, appeals could also go directly to that Empire court from provincial appeal courts, completely bypassing the Supreme Court of Canada. This weakness in authority was enhanced by the relatively poor quality of judges appointed to it in that earlier period, apart from such individuals as Lyman Duff and Ivan Rand.[18]

Canada could have cut off appeals to the Judicial Committee after obtaining complete independence in 1931, and pressure mounted to do so after the unpopular "New Deal" decisions of 1935 that were mentioned in Chapter 4. But the Second World War intervened, and it was unclear whether the provinces would have to agree to this measure since their appeals could already go directly to the JCPC. If so, there was some question of whether the provinces would agree to it, since they had been so well served by the Judicial Committee over the years. In 1947 it was determined that Ottawa could unilaterally curtail all such appeals, and it promptly did so. The Supreme Court of Canada has not been formally bound by Judicial Committee decisions since 1949 and has explicitly overruled them on occasion.

Until 1974, the Supreme Court had little discretion in deciding which cases it heard, but since then it has basically been in control of its own agenda. Today, only two categories of cases have an automatic right of appeal to the Supreme Court: provincial reference cases, and murder cases in which the provincial court of appeal was split on a question of law. Applications for leave to appeal discretionary cases are normally handled in writing by a panel of three judges, but sometimes the panel hears them live, giving lawyers 15 minutes to make their case, via two-way satellite television if they choose. Public law cases, especially criminal and constitutional, now clearly predominate over private law disputes on the Supreme Court docket. Such discretion considerably enhances the stature of the institution. Figure 23.2 outlines the Supreme Court appeal process.

Although an increasingly important institution of government, the Supreme Court rests primarily on the **Supreme Court Act** rather than being embedded in any constitution act as such.[19] The Supreme Court Act now provides for a nine-member court (six from 1875 to 1927 and seven from 1927 to 1949). Three of the nine must come from Quebec with its distinctive civil law system, while convention dictates that the other six be selected from a variety of locations, normally three from Ontario, two from the West, and one from Atlantic Canada. The act requires that at least five judges constitute a quorum, with the result that civil law cases from Quebec can be heard by a five-member panel including a majority (three) from the civil law system. The position of chief justice normally alternates between francophone and anglophone members, simultaneous interpretation is available, and Supreme Court judges are now expected to be at least functionally bilingual. Among other provisions of the Supreme Court Act are those that lay out the grounds for appeal and reference cases and those that stipulate that judges hold office during good behaviour until the age of 75. One of the merits of the Meech Lake and Charlottetown Accords would have been to "constitutionalize" the Supreme Court in order to give it a firmer foundation and to clarify how it could be changed.

The Court holds three sessions of about two months each per year and then adjourns to write up its decisions. Justices usually wear black silk robes at sittings of the Court, but have ceremonial robes of bright scarlet trimmed with Canadian white mink for special occasions. As much as possible, the Court tries to hear cases with a full complement of nine. Judges study the lower court proceedings and judgments in advance, along with the written arguments of the lawyers for each side. Oral arguments normally last only two hours, during which time the judges often ask trenchant questions. In some instances the Court also grants "intervenor status" to provincial governments and interest groups that are concerned about a case but not directly party to it. Once the arguments are completed, the judges usually "reserve judgment" and meet in private conference to discuss the case. Each gives his or her tentative decision, and it is decided how many draft opinions will be necessary and who will prepare them. These are later circulated and evoke comments before being revised. As in the case of most provincial courts of appeal, each Supreme Court judge is assisted by a number of outstanding new law school graduates called law clerks. They help the busy judges search for and sift through

Figure 23.2 Supreme Court Appeal Process

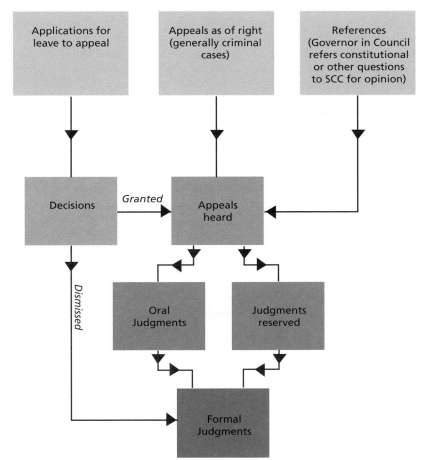

precedents and other relevant material on the issues involved. So much effort is put into the process of preparing their opinions that a decision is typically not issued until about six months after the Court hears the case, and it has occasionally taken over a year for all members of the Court to make up their minds, write their opinion, or concur with a colleague. The Court tries to issue a unanimous decision, sometimes anonymously, but if this is not possible, then one or more opinions on the majority side will be issued along with one or more dissenting opinions. Decisions are usually released in written form by depositing them with the Registrar, but the Court can pronounce formal judgments in the courtroom. Membership of the Supreme Court of Canada in recent years can be seen below.

MEMBERSHIP IN THE SUPREME COURT OF CANADA (1984–95)

Appointment	Name	Retirement (Death)
1973	Brian Dickson	1990 CJ:[1] 1984–1990
1974	Jean Beetz	1988
1977	William Estey	1988
1979	William McIntyre	1989
1979	Jean Chouinard	(1987)
1980	Antonio Lamer	CJ: 1990–
1982	Bertha Wilson	1990
1984	Gerald Le Dain	1988
1985	Gerald LaForest	
1987	Claire L'Heureux-Dubé	
1988	John Sopinka	
1989	Peter Cory	
1989	Charles Gonthier	
1989	Beverley McLachlin	
1990	William Stevenson	
1990	Frank Iacobucci	

[1] Chief Justice

This discussion of the structure of Canadian courts reveals an essentially integrated, vertical court system rather than two parallel systems of federal and provincial courts. With the exception of some federal matters that must be initiated in the Federal Court of Canada, the provincial court systems and the Supreme Court of Canada hear cases dealing with both federal and provincial laws. The judicial system is further integrated with provincial governments prosecuting federal crimes and with the federal cabinet appointing judges to section 96 courts within the provinces. Some aspects of the federal–provincial judicial integration could be improved, such as in the areas of Young Offenders and Family Law, the jurisdiction of the Federal Court, and the appointment of section 96 and Supreme Court of Canada judges. If the Meech Lake and Charlottetown Accords had been ratified, the federal government would have appointed judges to the highest court from lists of nominees submitted by the provinces. In addition, some federal–provincial conflict has arisen over provincial attempts to enhance the powers of their provincial courts and administrative tribunals at the expense of section 96 courts.[20] However, most authorities argue strenuously in favour of maintaining such an integrated system.[21]

While supporting such integration, Russell objects to the hierarchical nature of the Canadian courts with the implication that some judges are better than others and that some courts administer a higher standard of justice. He would prefer the ultimate integration of provincial courts and section 96 courts, as was once proposed in Ontario. Russell recommends specialized divisions—criminal, civil, family, etc.—within a single-level provincial court system with some mechanism for joint federal–provincial appointment and with a full range of legal aid, mediation, counselling, and other social services attached, preferably located in "community trial centres."

THE APPOINTMENT OF JUDGES

As has already been established, Supreme and Federal Court of Canada judges, as well as judges of provincial superior, district, and county courts are appointed by the federal cabinet, while provincial court judges are appointed by provincial cabinets. The former number about 750, and the latter, about 1250. All of the first group must be qualified lawyers of at least ten years' standing, as must provincial court judges in Ontario and Quebec. Elsewhere, provincial court judges have to be members of the bar for a minimum of five years.

In a high proportion of cases over the years Canadian cabinets at both federal and provincial levels have used judicial appointments to reward faithful party supporters, often defeated candidates.[22] Legal knowledge was also taken into account in some cases, but it was rarely the primary criterion. The prospect of a judgeship accounts in part for the active involvement of lawyers in many party organizations, while the promise of government legal business explains another part. Patronage raises three main problems in this area: unsuitable individuals are appointed because of their partisan connections; well-qualified candidates are overlooked because of their lack of service to the party in power; and partisan judges may favour their former political colleagues.[23] This patronage system of appointing judges is still alive, although it is on the decline.

At the federal level, Pierre Trudeau as minister of justice in 1967 instituted an informal practice of submitting names of potential judicial appointments to the National Committee on the Judiciary of the Canadian Bar Association. To his credit, the next justice minister, John Turner, appointed several prominent judges of non-Liberal backgrounds. Trudeau sullied his own government's record in this field with the appointment of six high-profile Liberal partisans in 1984, including the minister of justice himself and another minister who was not even assessed by the CBA committee. After an even more partisan record of judicial appointments during its first term,[24] the Mulroney government established a somewhat more satisfactory appointment system in 1988 for all "federal" judges except those on the Supreme Court of Canada, and modified it slightly in 1991. An independent **Commissioner for Federal Judicial Affairs** now maintains a record of those interested in federal judicial appointments. This official then submits such names to a seven-member committee set up in each province, which includes a section 96 judge; one nominee of each of the provincial law society, the provincial branch of the CBA, and the provincial attorney general; and three nominees of the federal minister of justice. This committee ranks each candidate as "highly recommended," "recommended," or "not able to recommend," and the minister makes the final decision, still being entitled to choose from the list of nonqualified candidates.[25] The minister may also consult senior members of the judiciary and the bar and the provincial attorney general.

The prime minister chooses the chief justices in each province, almost always from the existing bench, as well as new members of the Supreme Court of Canada. Patronage has not been much of a problem on the Supreme Court since the appointment of Finance minister Douglas Abbott in 1954. Prime ministers consult widely before making such appointments, have managed to overcome their penchant for partisanship in this one area, and are pleased to be evaluated on the quality of their choices. Chief Justices Bora Laskin and Brian Dickson and the first female appointee, Bertha Wilson, are outstanding examples.

At the provincial court level, it is now usually the case that the attorney general consults with the provincial judicial council or equivalent in making such appointments. For example, a central nonpartisan nominating commission consisting largely of nonlawyers was established in Ontario in 1988, originally headed by political scientist Peter Russell. It screens judicial applicants on their merits and leaves the attorney general little or no discretion. On the other hand, party service or legislative experience should not automatically disqualify a worthy candidate from a judicial appointment.[26]

Another controversial aspect of judicial appointments concerns the Supreme Court of Canada alone. Because this court must adjudicate federal–provincial disputes, concern has been expressed in some quarters that all of its members are federally appointed. In theory, once appointed, judges act with total impartiality, and their independence is protected in various ways. Nevertheless, it may not *appear* as if justice has been done. As early as 1971, federal–provincial agreement was achieved on provincial consultation in the appointment of Supreme Court judges, but such agreement was never implemented. Later, the Meech Lake and Charlottetown Accords provided for Ottawa to make Supreme Court of Canada appointments from lists provided by the provinces, but this too was ultimately abandoned. The 1992 document went beyond that of 1987 to outline a procedure to be used in case of federal–provincial deadlock. It also proposed federal and provincial consultation with aboriginal peoples in the appointment process. Some mechanism for federal–provincial consultation in this area is bound to be adopted in the future. On the other hand, to begin to regard Supreme Court judges as provincial representatives would do great disservice to the principle of judicial independence.

If a proper geographic balance is characteristic of Canadian judges, what can be said of their other socioeconomic characteristics? Partly as a consequence of geography, judicial appointments have also balanced francophone and anglophone origins at both federal and provincial court levels, especially in recent years as provinces have made more French-language court services available. Those of other origins have generally been excluded, but names such as Laskin (Jewish), Sopinka (Ukrainian), and Iacobuccci (Italian) are now appearing on the Supreme Court of Canada and increasingly on lower courts as well. Thus the most serious aspects of judicial underrepresentation relate to women and the working class.[27] In this connection, Paul Weiler writes:

> It is very natural that well-to-do families of the founding races and religions in Canada, especially those with a background of professional and/or public involvement, will produce the sons who will get the right kind of education, and thus the entrée into the kind of practice or position which produces a likely candidate for the Court.[28]

Just as in the case of "other ethnics," however, more female and working-class law school graduates are becoming available for judicial appointments, and governments have at least begun to recognize the necessity of appointing greater numbers of female judges. The

Supreme Court finally saw its first woman member in 1982, and for a time had a total of three women out of nine. Such female judges have sometimes used their position to point out the male bias in legislatures, judiciaries, and laws.[29]

As noted in Chapter 7, aboriginal Canadians have even more serious reservations about the Canadian judicial system, feeling that it discriminates against them at every turn. They argue that an increase in the number of Native judges would not substantially improve this situation, and therefore advocate the establishment of a parallel justice system (at least where they did no harm to nonaboriginals) that would reflect their own distinctive concepts of guilt and punishment.

Given the significant law-making potential of higher-level judges, another dimension of the appointment process is a consideration of candidates' views on other issues. Chapter 5 noted that the decisions rendered by the Supreme Court of Canada depended to some extent on the makeup of the panel considering the case. That being so, those who appoint judges are able to take into account the predilections of candidates with respect to being hawks or doves on criminal matters or Charter enthusiasts as opposed to legislative deferentialists.[30] To some extent, such preferences are reflected in the success rate of different categories of litigants, which for the Supreme Court of Canada in the 1982–93 period was as follows: Crown, 66 percent; provincial government, 57 percent; federal government, 56 percent; big business, 55 percent; smaller business, 46 percent; municipal government, 45 percent; unions, 42 percent; and individuals, 41 percent.[31] This issue prompts some authorities to recommend public hearings to fathom the views of judicial nominees.

RETIREMENT, REMOVAL, AND INDEPENDENCE OF JUDGES

Whatever the process involved in making judicial appointments, and whatever biases exist in the composition of the courts, judges are expected to abide by the principle of **judicial independence** or impartiality once they are on the bench. They are supposed to adjudicate without fear or favour with respect to private or political interests, and especially without any incentive to give preference to the government side where it is involved.

The independence of judges is primarily based on security of tenure, and it is difficult for the government to remove them before their scheduled date of retirement. Judges on the Supreme and Federal Courts of Canada and provincial superior courts have a mandatory retirement age of 75 years, and provincial court judges of 65 or 70. The general rule for all federally appointed judges and most provincial court judges is that they serve on "good behaviour"—that is, they do not serve at the pleasure of the government and cannot be removed unless they have been guilty of misbehaviour. While the meaning of these terms has never been definitively established, judges are certainly removable for serious criminal acts and possibly for reasons of infirmity or incapacity, failure to execute their duties, or bringing the judicial system into disrepute.[32] On the other hand, they cannot be removed merely because the government regards their decisions as erroneous or contrary to government policy, nor because they ruled against the Crown.

The process of removing a judge varies with the level of the position, and the degree of difficulty increases with the judge's rank in the hierarchy. Except in Ontario, where legislation is required, provincial court judges can be removed by an order-in-council of the provincial cabinet but only after an inquiry has been conducted by one of the judge's peers or by the provincial judicial council. County and district judges were removable by federal order-in-council but only after an inquiry by the new Canadian Judicial Council. It is even more difficult to remove judges of the provincial superior courts and the federal courts. In that situation, the Canadian Judicial Council conducts an inquiry and reports to the minister of Justice, after which the passage of a joint address of both houses of Parliament is required.

The **Canadian Judicial Council**, created in 1971, consists of all the chief justices and associate chief justices of courts staffed by federally appointed judges, and is chaired by the chief justice of the Canadian Supreme Court. Like the provincial judicial councils, its primary purpose is to deal with complaints raised against individual judges, but it also has a role in the continuing education of judges, provides a forum for developing consensus among its members, and makes representations to government with respect to judicial salaries and benefits.

While a number of judges have been reprimanded by judicial councils, the issue of judicial removal has rarely arisen. Several provincial court judges have been removed over the years, a practice that is increasingly common as the public becomes less tolerant of their faults. But only four county and district judges have met this fate since 1867, and not a single superior court judge has been removed from office. Such proceedings were initiated in four cases, but judges either died or resigned during the removal process.[33]

Besides security of tenure, judicial independence involves financial, administrative, and political independence.[34] Salaries and pensions are fixed in such a way that neither individually nor collectively can judges be intimidated by government threats to reduce them, although some judges went to court to challenge freezes or reductions in their salaries as part of provincial government restraint programs. In addition, judges are increasingly in control of the administration of the court system. Judges must also be able to function without political pressure—from cabinet ministers, legislators, bureaucrats, or other judges—whether in public or in private. At both federal and provincial levels, many cases have occurred of cabinet ministers contacting judges, but however innocent their questions might seem, this must not be done.[35]

It is sometimes thought that the prospect of promotion from one court to another might bias a judge's decisions, but no evidence has been found to justify this fear. Judges are rarely promoted from "provincial" to "federal" courts, but appeal court judges usually have previous judicial experience.[36] In 1988 it was also felt (by fellow judges) that to deny judges a vote in federal elections was not necessary to guarantee their independence. On the other hand, judges are not supposed to make public speeches that could compromise their impartiality. For example, when Tom Berger of the B.C. Supreme Court publicly criticized the 1982 Constitution Act for its omission of Quebec and virtual neglect of aboriginals, his actions were investigated by the Canadian Judicial Council. Although its recommendation was not to dismiss him, he felt enough pressure to resign.[37]

CONCLUSION

Rule adjudication remains the basic function of the judiciary, one that is becoming increasingly important in the political system. Judges also engage in pre-trial mediation of one kind or another and are occasionally called on to head commissions of inquiry. Other branches of government, especially administrative tribunals, also exercise the rule adjudication function to some extent, but this function can be generally equated with the courts.

In looking at the judiciary, class analysts begin with the argument that entry into law school has traditionally been restricted to the middle and upper classes, and then note the powers of the legal profession to govern itself. Moreover, federal or provincial authorities who make judicial appointments are usually lawyers themselves, and consultation with the Canadian Bar Association or judicial councils on new appointments gives the legal profession yet another avenue of influence in the selection of judges. Indeed, a disproportionate number of judges have previously served on the CBA executive.[38] "Appointing judges is part of the process of recruiting a society's governing elite," and with cabinets looking "for someone very much like themselves," the result is a judiciary that bears little resemblance to the general population in socioeconomic background.[39] The elitist nature of the judiciary in terms of gender and ethnicity was noted above, while of the first 50 judges of the Supreme Court only two came from working-class origins, as did only one among senior judges between 1961 and 1973.[40] Although it does not concern him, even Russell admits that

> as long as judges are recruited entirely from the ranks of successful lawyers ...
> the bourgeois orientation of the Canadian judiciary is unavoidable. This may
> very well mean that when class issues are clearly at stake in adjudication, the
> Canadian judiciary is not impartial.[41]

The elitist origins of judges, combined with the expense involved in going to court, leads class analysts to talk about a class system of justice. Michael Mandel notes that in a typical trial, "in terms of social class, the crown attorney, defence counsel, and judge have far more in common with each other than they have with either the victim or the criminal and vice versa."[42]

This school of thought dismisses notions of judicial impartiality and independence "as rhetorical facades behind which judges are free to exercise raw political power on behalf of themselves or their 'political masters,' or against their political or economic opponents."[43] Class analysts remember how often the courts, on the altar of section 92, responded to corporate claims in invalidating federal legislation that might have benefited the working class and point to the judicial emasculation of laws prohibiting corporate monopolies. Olsen mentions the high proportion of cases before the courts dealing with the protection of property, the high rate of incarceration of those accused who do not own property, the inadequacies of legal aid schemes, and the limited provision for "class action" suits in Canada in which small consumers can collectively take on giant corporations. He concludes that the judiciary provides legitimacy for the established social order, arguing that the chief function of the higher judiciary is to rationalize formal arrangements for the elites and the privileged classes and, by articulating these as principles and precedents, impose norms and values downward on the lower courts and hence on the behaviour of the lower classes. In this task they are most heartily joined by the various political elites who passed the controlling legislation in the first place.[44]

McCormick adds that "to make the courts more representative of women, of Canadians other than French and English, of visible minorities, and so on perhaps simply disguises, and may well reinforce, the extent to which they continue to be unrepresentative on a class basis."[45] Moreover, as mentioned earlier, big business had a significantly higher success rate in the Supreme Court of Canada from 1982–93 than individuals and unions.

(SC) State-centred theorists argue that the judiciary is part of the state apparatus and is not as independent of other institutions of government as is commonly assumed. Judges are appointed, promoted, and occasionally dismissed by politicians; judges are called upon to assist politicians in conducting inquiries; judges are of the same elitist origins as politicians and bureaucrats and move in many of the same social and professional circles, even after their appointment. Many provincial authorities have felt, rightly or wrongly, that the Supreme Court of Canada was an agent of the federal government, rather than a totally impartial referee of federal–provincial disputes, and others could argue that the Canadian Judicial Council is too eager to reprimand a judge who has criticized government policy.[46] Then, although some judicial decisions can be modified or overturned by subsequent legislation, state-centred theorists point out that the judiciary is the branch of government most insulated from public opinion. However "objective" its decisions, it has sometimes aided and abetted government policy that was at odds with public sentiment, such as in the Supreme Court's series of decisions with respect to official bilingualism.

[P] Pluralists, on the other hand, argue that the judiciary adds a relatively independent point of authoritative decision-making to the political system and counterbalances the other institutions of government. In Russell's words, "to liberals who are distrustful of an excessive concentration of power in the hands of any group or bureaucrats, the political pluralism fostered by a judiciary enjoying a high degree of independence is fundamental to maintaining political liberty."[47] Public opinion polls have repeatedly indicated greater confidence in judges than in politicians and a preference for courts rather than legislatures to have the final say in the interpretation of the Charter of Rights.[48] Pluralists also note the division of appointing power between federal and provincial governments, the different procedures involved, and the increasing proportion of female and other ethnic appointments. They are encouraged by the number of suits launched by interest groups and by the practice of allowing such groups to become interveners in constitutional cases. McCormick concludes that despite all the undemocratic aspects of the judiciary, "the law and the courts are nothing more than the continuation of politics by other means,"[49] and are likely to be a more prominent part in the future.

DISCUSSION QUESTIONS

1. Should the provincial courts be integrated with the provincial superior courts? If so, how could this be done?

2. Why should the Supreme Court of Canada be constitutionalized?

3. Should other jurisdictions follow Ontario's lead and remove all vestiges of patronage from the appointment of judges, or have existing reforms in this area gone far enough?

4. Should the provinces be involved in the appointment of provincial superior court judges? of judges of the Supreme Court of Canada? If so, how?

5. What should be the criteria for reprimanding or removing a judge? Should Mr. Justice Tom Berger have been able to criticize the 1982 Constitution Act?

6. How can justice be ensured for women involved in the courts?

7. How can justice be ensured for the working class?

8. Should Canada establish a parallel aboriginal justice system?

NOTES

1. Peter Russell, *The Judiciary in Canada: The Third Branch of Government* (Toronto: McGraw-Hill Ryerson, 1987), p. 5.
2. Ibid., p. 14.
3. Peter Russell, "The Effect of a Charter of Rights on the Policy-Making Role of the Canadian Courts," *Canadian Public Administration* (Spring 1982), p. 2.
4. Ibid., p. 12.
5. Peter McCormick, *Canada's Courts* (Toronto: Lorimer, 1994), p. 3.
6. Russell, *The Judiciary in Canada*, p. 6.
7. See, for example, Gerald L. Gall, *The Canadian Legal System*, 3rd ed. (Toronto: Carswell, 1990), p. 23–28.
8. Ibid., p. 30.
9. McCormick, *Canada's Courts*, p. 23.
10. Gall outlines this integration on pp. 157–59.
11. Occasional federal–provincial disputes have occurred over this point. See Russell, *The Judiciary in Canada*, pp. 122–23.
12. Russell says, for example, that the "judges who order the support have no role in overseeing its enforcement, and the judges responsible for enforcing the order play no role in either determining or modifying the level of support," p. 228.
13. Ibid, pp. 229–35; Peter Hogg, *Constitutional Law of Canada*, 2nd ed. (Toronto: Carswell, 1985), pp. 546–49.
14. McCormick, *Canada's Courts*, p. 56.
15. Russell, *The Judiciary in Canada*, p. 290.

16. Ibid., p. 313.
17. Ibid, pp. 319–27; and Peter Hogg, *Constitutional Law of Canada*, pp. 142–48.
18. James G. Snell and Frederick Vaughan, *The Supreme Court of Canada: History of the Institution* (Toronto: The Osgoode Society, 1985); and Russell, *The Judiciary in Canada*, p. 337.
19. Peter Russell, "Constitutional Reform of the Judicial Branch: Symbolic vs. Operational Considerations," *Canadian Journal of Political Science* (June 1984).
20. In 1981, for example, the Supreme Court ruled that Ontario legislation had given Residential Tenancy Commissions powers that could only reside in the courts.
21. Russell, *The Judiciary in Canada*, pp. 49–54, 327–29; and Hogg, *Constitutional Law in Canada*, ch. 7.
22. Carl Baar quotes an oft-repeated maxim that "to become a judge in the United States, you must be elected; to become a judge in Canada, you must be defeated," in "The Structure and Personnel of the Canadian Judiciary," in Paul Fox and Graham White, eds., *Politics: Canada*, 7th ed. (Toronto: McGraw-Hill Ryerson, 1991), p. 513.
23. Andrew Heard, *Canadian Constitutional Conventions* (Toronto: Oxford University Press, 1991), p. 135.
24. One study of the first-term record of the Mulroney government revealed that 48 percent of all judges appointed were known Conservative supporters compared with 7 percent who supported opposition parties. Peter Russell and Jacob Ziegel, "Federal Judicial Appointments: An Appraisal of the First Mulroney Government's Appointments and the New Judiciary Advisory Committees," *University of Toronto Law Journal* 41 (1991).
25. The new procedure is outlined in two documents published by the Commissioner for Federal Judicial Affairs: *Judicial Appointments: Information Guide* and *A New Judicial Appointments Process* (Ottawa: Supply and Services, 1988).
26. McCormick, *Canada's Courts*, p. 112.
27. Dennis Olsen, *The State Elite* (Toronto: McClelland and Stewart, 1980), ch. 3; and Russell, *The Judiciary in Canada*, pp. 164–65.
28. Quoted in Olsen, *The State Elite*, p. 47.
29. Bertha Wilson said that men didn't understand abortion in the Morgentaler case, but Peter McCormick (*Canada's Courts*, p. 115) discounts the distinctiveness of the judgments of women or visible minorities.
30. Ibid., p. 108.
31. Ibid., p. 165.
32. All the authorities mention the ambiguity on this point. See Heard, *Canadian Constitutional Conventions*, p. 124; Russell, *The Judiciary in Canada*, p. 176; and Gall, *The Canadian Legal System*, pp. 227–39.
33. The most famous case concerned Leo Landreville of the Supreme Court of Ontario. See Gall, *The Canadian Legal System*, pp. 231, 238–39, and Russell, *The Judiciary in Canada*, pp. 176–79.
34. The classic statement on this question was made by Mr. Justice LeDain in *Valente v. the Queen* [1985] 2 SCR 673. On the whole question of judicial administration, see Perry S. Millar and Carl Baar, *Judicial Administration in Canada* (Montreal: McGill–Queen's University Press, 1981).
35. See Heard, *Canadian Constitutional Conventions*, p. 128, and Russell, *The Judiciary in Canada*, pp. 78–81, especially regarding the "Judges Affair."
36. On the other hand, former party ties count in promotions. See Russell and Ziegel, "Federal Judicial Appointments."
37. Heard, *Canadian Constitutional Conventions*, p. 131; Russell, *The Canadian Judiciary*, pp. 85–89; Gall, *The Canadian Legal System*, pp. 236–38; and McCormick, *Canada's Courts*, pp. 130–31.
38. Russell, *The Judiciary in Canada*, p. 163; Olsen, *The State Elite*, p. 48; and Russell and Ziegel, "Federal Judicial Appointments."
39. Russell, *The Judiciary in Canada*, p. 107; and Olsen, *The State Elite*, p. 46.
40. Russell, *The Judiciary in Canada*, p. 164; and Olsen, *The State Elite*, p. 51.
41. Russell, *The Judiciary in Canada*, p. 165.
42. Michael Mandel, *The Charter of Rights and the Legalization of Politics in Canada* (Toronto: Wall and Thompson, 1989), p. 135.
43. Russell, *The Judiciary in Canada*, p. 4.

44. Olsen, *The State Elite*, p. 58.
45. McCormick, *Canada's Courts*, p. 115.
46. Despite all of his magnificent work on the Supreme Court, there was some suggestion that Chief Justice Bora Laskin was too close to Prime Minister Trudeau in some of his judgments and in his eagerness to reprimand Tom Berger. Michael Mandel, *The Charter of Rights and the Legalization of Politics in Canada*, pp. 17, 20, 22, 111.
47. Russell, *The Judiciary in Canada*, p. 24.
48. Russell, *The Judiciary in Canada*, p. 35; and Heard, *Canadian Constitutional Conventions*, p. 138.
49. McCormick, *Canada's Courts*, ch. 12.

· · · · · · · · · · · · · · · · · ·

FURTHER READING

Baar, Carl. "The Structure and Personnel of the Canadian Judiciary." In Paul Fox and Graham White, eds. *Politics: Canada*, 7th ed. Toronto: McGraw-Hill Ryerson, 1991.

Canadian Bar Foundation. *The Appointment of Judges in Canada*. Ottawa: Canadian Bar Association, 1985.

————. *The Independence of the Judiciary in Canada*. Ottawa: Canadian Bar Association, 1985.

Commissioner for Federal Judicial Affairs. *A New Judicial Appointments Process*. Ottawa: Supply and Services, 1988.

————. *Judicial Appointments: Information Guide*. Ottawa: Supply and Services, 1988.

The Federal Court of Canada—An Evaluation. Papers presented at the 20th Anniversary Symposium, June 26, 1991.

Gall, Gerald. *The Canadian Legal System*, 3rd ed. Toronto: Carswell, 1990.

Heard, Andrew. *Canadian Constitutional Conventions*. Toronto: Oxford University Press, 1991.

Hogg, Peter. *Constitutional Law of Canada*, 2nd ed. Toronto: Carswell, 1985.

Linden, A.M., ed. *The Canadian Judiciary*. Toronto: Osgoode Hall Law School, 1976.

McCormick, Peter. *Canada's Courts*. Toronto: Lorimer, 1994.

McCormick, Peter, and Ian Greene. *Judges and Judging: Inside the Canadian Judicial System*. Toronto: Lorimer, 1990.

Mandel, Michael. *The Charter of Rights and the Legalization of Politics in Canada*. Toronto: Wall and Thompson, 1989.

Millar, Perry S., and Carl Baar. *Judicial Administration in Canada*. Montreal: McGill–Queen's University Press, 1981.

Morton, F.L., ed. *Law, Politics and the Judicial Process in Canada*. Calgary: University of Calgary Press, 1984.

Olsen, Dennis. *The State Elite*. Toronto: McClelland and Stewart, 1980.

Russell, Peter. "The Effect of a Charter of Rights on the Policy-Making Role of the Canadian Courts." *Canadian Public Administration* (Spring 1982).

————. "Constitutional Reform of the Judicial Branch: Symbolic vs. Operational Considerations." *Canadian Journal of Political Science* (June 1984).

————. *The Judiciary in Canada: The Third Branch of Government*. Toronto: McGraw-Hill Ryerson, 1987.

Russell, Peter, and Jacob Ziegel. "Federal Judicial Appointments: An Appraisal of the First Mulroney Government's Appointments." *University of Toronto Law Journal* 41 (1991).

Snell, James G., and Frederick Vaughan. *The Supreme Court of Canada: History of the Institution*. Toronto: The Osgoode Society, 1985.

PART 6

Conclusion

The Conclusion is composed of three parts. The first part is a brief chapter that highlights some of the main points made in the course of the other five parts of the book and presents several critical, realistic reforms. The second part is a Glossary of key terms used in previous chapters. The third is a selection of Canadian constitutional documents, included in the Appendix.

Chapter 24

CONCLUSION

As Canada approaches the turn of the century, it faces a long list of political problems. The first and perennial one is the role of Quebec and French Canada generally within the Canadian federation. The results of the 1995 referendum on Quebec sovereignty did not make this problem any easier to resolve.

The second historic problem, involving fewer people but not necessarily less territory, is improving the condition of aboriginal life in the country. This issue is finally on the political agenda, although that is only the starting point.

Other ethnic/cultural/linguistic and regional issues also exist and are of intense concern to those involved. The problem of Western alienation having subsided to some extent, these other issues pale in comparison to the two mentioned above, both in terms of longevity and overall significance.

Another continuing problem is the difficulty of maintaining a distinctive culture in the shadow of the United States. For better or worse, Canada has tied its economic future to that country in terms of the wide-ranging Free Trade Agreement, and the character of the global economy makes it hard for any state to pursue economic sovereignty in the future. "Advances" in telecommunications technology mean that even more streams of American culture will be flooding the Canadian market and the Canadian living room, and the government may be powerless to stop them. Severely weakening the Canadian Broadcasting Corporation hardly seems the way to begin.

The topic of minority rights has been in the forefront of political discourse in recent years—official language minorities, ethnic and cultural minorities (apart from aboriginal Canadians), the gay and lesbian community, and women. These groups have all made substantial gains in public policy since 1970, although a backlash in public opinion was detectable in the 1990s. As has often been pointed out throughout this book, however, these groups have the Charter of Rights and Freedoms as a tool for further advancement, regardless of any negative prospects in dealing with the regular political process.

The other main question on the political agenda of the 1990s is that of government deficits and debts. Once the obsession of only neoconservatives, government parties of all stripes are now determined to balance their budgets. Few deny that they should do so; even Keynesian economics argued that governments should run a surplus in good years to pay off debts accumulated in economic recessions. But the speed and the method of dealing with this problem have angered many observers.

If government expenditures exceed revenues, there are two ways to make them balance. Most of the emphasis in recent years has been on reducing expenditures, but some analysts argue that the imbalance between expenditures and revenues is not so much caused by overspending as by forgoing billions of dollars in tax credits and tax deductions.

If expenditures must be reduced, it is also worth asking if social programs must be the main target for such cuts. The 1990s backlash against immigrants, other ethnic groups, bilingualism, and other minorities identified above has expanded to include the poor, the unemployed, those on social assistance, and those on unemployment insurance; governments now get elected on a promise of making it harder for such groups to obtain public support. Reducing government spending on education and health care threatens the once-heralded universal and egalitarian nature of such programs.

CRITICAL, REALISTIC REFORMS

Although Canada is not an easy country to govern, political behaviour and institutions can be altered in a variety of ways to render its governance more satisfactory. In the preceding chapters many defects in the machinery of Canadian politics and government have been identified, and among these at least eight critical but fairly straightforward and realistic reforms can be reiterated here. In outlining such areas for reform, it will sometimes be useful to refer to the experience of other political systems.

Reducing the Incidence of Partisanship, Patronage, and Corruption

One of the main complaints about politicians is the excessive partisanship that characterizes their activities. An adversarial system has its merits, primarily in ensuring that issues are thoroughly debated and that the public has a chance to see how different parties deal with each problem. But no one can blame the public for its disgust at much of the partisan confrontation they see in the House of Commons and the Senate. The British House of Commons, by contrast, demonstrates that parliamentary behaviour can be civilized and adversarial at the same time.

Another practice that stems from excessive partisanship is the widespread incidence of party patronage. It is an escapable reality that many people who join or volunteer to help political parties or agree to become candidates expect some tangible reward, especially if and when that party forms the government. The Senate, the judiciary, and especially the regulatory agencies have been filled with people of one kind or another who had few credentials other than past party service. Once again, the British system shows that patronage does not need to infiltrate every nook and cranny of the political system; indeed, in that country political patronage barely exists in the very areas where it is most predominant in Canada. Instead, political rewards take the form of a system of innocuous national honours, but even they are distributed on a multipartisan basis.

Canadians were led to believe that the Chrétien Liberals would be less patronage-oriented than the Mulroney Conservatives. But the Liberals have made patronage appointments to ambassadorships, Crown corporations, citizenship courts, and regulatory agencies, rendering their record no better than that of their widely discredited predecessors.

A step beyond patronage is political corruption, and while this occurs in every political system to some extent, it seemed to have become much too common during the Mulroney regime. The widespread incidence of corruption of individual Conservative ministers and MPs tended to reduce the image of all politicians in the eyes of Canadians. Although Chrétien has appointed an Ethics Commissioner, the Canadian system continues to lack meaningful conflict of interest rules for members of Parliament and senators.

Loosening Party Discipline in the House of Commons

One of the most disconcerting aspects of Canadian politics to the average voter is the rigidity of party discipline in the House of Commons. People generally believe that MPs should vote according to the wishes of their constituents rather than obey the edicts of the party leadership. Loosening the constraints of party discipline in the daily work of the Commons and instead making periodic confidence votes crucial to a government's survival would give voters the feeling that their MPs were really representing them. It would also reduce the momentum for greater use of referenda, which sound reasonable in theory but raise many problems in practice.

Once again, the British system provides a useful model. During the Thatcher years, for example, some 120 legislative amendments were carried against the government's wishes and 17 government bills were defeated; sanctions against the dissidents were minimal, and such gaps in discipline no longer attract particular attention.

The famous Liberal Red Book specifically promised some kind of relaxation of party discipline, but when the party line was threatened on gun control and other issues, Chrétien would not budge. He imposed what most observers felt were unnecessarily harsh sanctions on the dissenters. At the same time, he did not make a strong case for the virtues of party discipline.

The Need for Stronger Politicians

The problems of patronage and party discipline are related to the generally weak contingent of politicians who obtain office in Canada. Many only intend to stay for a short stint, practising "avocational politics," and others are cut off by electoral defeat. It often seems that the public prefers a fresh face over political experience. This is not the case in the United States, however, where incumbents are almost never defeated. Because the turnover in the Canadian House of Commons is very high, and because they are looking for an eventual patronage position when they leave, MPs are weak in relation to their own party leaders. (That is not to say that party leaders are particularly strong in Canada, either, many of them coming to the job with minimal political experience.) In addition, there is little "bench strength" when it comes to forming a cabinet or choosing a party leader, and ministers are not strong in interacting with their bureaucrats. Canada needs politicians of higher quality and greater experience. In Britain, prospective party candidates are thoroughly screened for intelligence, aptitude, and literary ability, and then usually work themselves up through two or three elections to a safe seat. Once elected to the government side, MPs serve a few years as a backbencher, then as a parliamentary secretary, and then as a minister not in the cabinet, until they become a cabinet minister with an average of about 11 years of Commons' experience.

Electoral Reform

Chapter 15 showed how the existing Canadian electoral system exacerbates regional–ethnic divisions because it awards seats to individual winning candidates with no concern about a party's popular vote within a province or at the national level. Parties have often attracted as much as 20 to 25 percent of the vote in a province without winning any seats. This becomes especially serious when a party forms the government and it has no MPs from a province or region to put into the cabinet. Such provinces and regions feel left out of the policy-making process and start to think in separatist terms. Chapter 15 also demonstrated how this problem could be overcome by awarding some 50 supplementary seats on the basis of popular vote per party per province, drawing to some extent on the German system. If such a relatively minor innovation would help to strengthen Canada's fragile state, it deserves more consideration than it has so far received.

The 1993 election produced a Liberal majority government with seats in every province, so that party was not particularly affected by the problem identified here. But this electoral system also rewards regionally concentrated third-party support, as in the case of Reform in the West and the Bloc Québécois in Quebec, while at the same time seriously depriving the Conservative party of significant national support. After the 1993 election, the House of Commons had no national opposition party, which has proved to be almost as harmful as not having a national party on the government side.

Reforming the Senate

Assessments of the present Senate range from the view that it is harmless or useless to the opinion that it is positively corrupt. If the troubled Canadian political system is to have a second chamber, that institution must obviously play a more important part than at present. Given that second chambers traditionally represent regions at the centre and that such representation is currently perceived to be lacking in Canada, the Senate must be reformed in order to perform this function. Being the site of the most blatant patronage in the whole system, it must also become an elected rather than an appointed body. On the other hand, to avoid paralyzing the operation of government, the Senate should be given only a suspensive veto over the House of Commons. Being popularly elected or chosen by provincial legislatures, senators would likely better represent provincial and regional interests. Election would also likely change the character of Senate members, reducing their links to the corporate elite and the backrooms of political parties.

Restricting Corporate Funding of Political Parties

Even though they have made strides to reduce their dependence on corporate contributions and to attract donations from individuals, the Liberal and Conservative parties continue to rely to a large extent on corporate funding. Small financial contributions to political parties usually have no strings attached, but no corporation makes a donation of $50 000 or $100 000 without expecting something in return. Is it any coincidence that the major banks, which give some of the largest annual and electoral contributions to the Liberal and Conservative parties, are allowed to accumulate the largest profits of any corporate sector? To enhance the democratic character of Canadian parties and elections, contributions should ideally be restricted to individuals; if corporations and unions are allowed to contribute on the grounds that Canadian parties should be strengthened rather than weakened, then a meaningful ceiling should be put on the size of such contributions. Among many others, the political donations and lobbying efforts of Curragh Resources, owners of the Westray coal mine, demonstrate that the Royal Commission on Electoral Reform was mistaken in not making such a recommendation.

Strengthening Political Parties

Chapter 16 noted that, for one reason or another, many alternative institutions, especially pressure groups, are assuming the traditional functions of political parties. This is unfortunate because political parties are one of the few national institutions that try to bridge all the divisions within Canadian society. Perhaps too much is expected of parties in this connection, but the least that can be done is to strengthen them so that they can better perform such functions as interest aggregation. This can be done by further public funding of political parties. It is inappropriate that a self-interested pressure group has a budget and staff several times the size of a national political party. The activities of pressure groups should also be restricted to some extent, especially during election campaigns. Uninhibited "third-party" advertising during elections not only makes a mockery of the concept of a fair election, but it also diverts attention from the real contestants in the race.

Strengthening the Lobbyists Registration and Access to Information Acts

Chapters 18 and 21 respectively noted that the Lobbyists Registration Act and the Access to Information Act were not particularly effective. The former act has not prevented unseemly acts of lobbying, provides only minimal information on the process, and is virtually unenforceable. If, in the interests of maintaining a degree of political equality, the use of paid, professional lobbyists is to be kept under any kind of control, then the act must be strengthened. The Access to Information Act has opened up access to government documents to a considerable extent, but still contains many exceptions. In order to promote an informed citizenry, the loopholes in this act should be narrowed.

The Liberal Red Book made promises in both of these directions. The Chrétien government did amend the Lobbyists Registration Act, but not to the extent promised, and the Information Commissioner complained in his 1995 report that the prime minister showed no leadership in getting ministers and bureaucrats to be more forthcoming with government information.

Canadian politicians have many faults. So do the media, the electoral system, political parties, pressure groups, the Constitution, and all the institutions of government. However, the Canadian electorate also has its faults, especially the fact that it does not put much effort into improving its knowledge of the country and its politics. This is not an easy country to govern, but the better Canadian citizens understand it, the less difficult that task will be.

Glossary

Aboriginal self-government. A demand by aboriginal groups that they be able to govern themselves.

Aboriginal title. The aboriginal claim to land on the basis of traditional occupancy and use rather than treaty, as recognized in the 1973 *Calder* case.

Absent mandate. The notion that governments come to power without a clear-cut policy mandate.

Access to Information Act. The 1983 act that gave citizens, journalists, and others the right to gain access to government documents, with certain exceptions, and established the office of Information Commissioner.

Act of Union. The 1840 act that united the colonies of Upper and Lower Canada into the colony of Canada; partly designed to assimilate the French.

Advocacy advertising. Advertising that advocates a political point of view, rather than trying to sell a good or service.

Affirmative action. A law or program that provides preference to individuals with certain characteristics in the hiring or promotion process.

Allaire Report. The 1991 Report of the Quebec Liberal Party in response to the rejection of the Meech Lake Accord that advocated a wholesale transfer of federal powers to Quebec.

Assembly of First Nations. The largest interest group representing status Indians, who now prefer to be called First Nation peoples.

Atlantic Canada Opportunities Agency. The federal agency that seeks to reduce regional economic disparities in the Atlantic region primarily through grants and loans to private firms.

Auditor General. The official of Parliament whose staff audit the expenditures of government departments and who provides an annual report on instances of funds being unlawfully or unwisely spent.

Auto Pact. The 1965 bilateral Canada–U.S. agreement under which automobiles and auto parts flowed across the border duty-free as long as the value of purchases equalled that of production in each country.

Backbenchers. Members of Parliament on the government side who sit on the backbenches and are not in the cabinet, or those similarly distant from important posts in opposition parties.

Bandwagon effect. The notion that, if and when they know which party or candidate is going to win the election, voters will move en masse in that direction.

Bélanger–Campeau Committee. The all-party committee appointed in Quebec after the rejection of the Meech Lake Accord to consider the province's future options.

Bill 22. The 1974 language law passed by Quebec that sought to enhance the status of the French language in that province and, among other things, required that immigrant children go to French schools unless they could already speak English.

Bill 86. The 1993 language law, passed by Quebec when Bill 178 expired, that permitted bilingual signs outside as well as inside and made other modifications to Bill 101.

Bill 101. The 1977 Quebec language law that sought to make French the official language of Quebec and put restrictions on the use of English in the courts, schools, and private sector. For example, all commercial signs had to be in French only.

Bill 178. The 1988 language law, passed by Quebec under the notwithstanding clause, that continued to require unilingual French signs on the outside of stores but permitted bilingual signs inside.

Block grant. A federal–provincial grant that is given for a specific purpose such as postsecondary education or health but does not contain rigid conditions or standards.

BOMARC missiles. A U.S. nuclear-tipped missile system without the nuclear warheads that was placed on Canadian soil in the 1950s and pointed at the Soviet Union.

Bourgeoisie. A Marxist term referring to those who own the means of production, otherwise known as the corporate elite.

British North America Act. The 1867 Act of the British Parliament that created Canada by combining Ontario, Quebec, Nova Scotia, and New Brunswick and that also provided some of the essential elements of the new country's Constitution. Renamed the Constitution Act, 1867, in 1982.

Broker or Brokerage. A kind of party system in which political parties try to appeal to many different interests and "broker" compromises among them, rather than having any distinct ideology.

Budget. The annual financial statement of the government issued in the spring by the minister of Finance that introduces tax changes and gives an overview of government spending for the next fiscal year.

Business Council on National Issues. The most powerful peak business interest group in Canada representing the 150 largest firms in the country.

Cabinet government. A system of government in which the major political decisions are made by the cabinet as a whole, as opposed to one in which the prime minister acts with considerable autonomy.

Cabinet secrecy. A convention that cabinet and cabinet committee meetings are held behind closed doors and that all documents and discussions relating thereto are strictly confidential. Only final, official decisions are made public, while documents remained locked up for 30 years.

Cabinet solidarity. A convention that all cabinet ministers publicly support whatever decisions the cabinet has taken, whatever their personal views.

Cadre party. A kind of political party that is run by a small elite, a few national and local notables, who do not share power with a wider party membership.

Canada Act. The 1982 act passed by Britain that terminated all British authority over Canada and under which Canada passed the Constitution Act, 1982, with a domestic constitutional amending formula.

Canada Assistance Plan. The 1966 act, the last of the major conditional grant programs, under which Ottawa shared the cost of provincial and municipal social assistance and welfare service programs; repealed in 1995.

Canada clause. The clause in the 1992 Charlottetown Accord that attempted to define the fundamental characteristics of Canada.

Canada Council. The government agency established in 1957 to provide financial support to all aspects of the artistic community.

Canada Elections Act. The act that governs all aspects of federal elections.

Canada Health Act. The 1984 act that reimposed conditions on federal block grants to the provinces for health programs, especially to prevent extra-billing or other moves toward a two-tier health system.

Canada–U.S. Free Trade Agreement. The agreement signed by Canada and the United States that came into effect in 1989 and that gradually eliminated tariffs between the two countries and otherwise prohibited governments from interfering in the private marketplace.

Canadian Auto Workers. One of Canada's largest private-sector unions whose leader, Bob White, divorced it from its U.S. parent in the first major wave of nationalism to hit the Canadian union movement.

Canadian Bill of Rights. An act of the Canadian Parliament passed in 1960 that outlined the basic civil liberties of Canadians but whose defects caused judicial confusion and limited the bill's effectiveness.

Canadian Broadcasting Corporation (CBC). The large national crown corporation (including its French equivalent, Radio-Canada) with radio and television arms whose mandate is to promote meaningful communication among all parts of the country.

Canadian Chamber of Commerce. A large, national peak business interest group with strong provincial and local bases.

Canadian Federation of Independent Business. A large interest group representing small business operations.

Canadian Judicial Council. An agency composed of the federal and provincial chief justices that disciplines federally appointed judges and otherwise provides leadership and coordination among federal and provincial judicial systems.

Canadian Labour Congress. The largest labour interest group in Canada; the political voice of over two million members.

Canadian Manufacturers' Association. A large and powerful business interest group representing a wide range of Canadian manufacturers.

Canadian Radio-television and Telecommunications Commission (CRTC). The regulatory agency established to police the communications industry, including radio, television, telephones, and telecommunications.

Canadian Wheat Board. A federal Crown corporation established to help grain farmers market their product in an aggressive way and to provide equitable returns to producers.

Central agencies. Government agencies such as the PMO, the PCO, the Treasury Board, and the Finance Department that have certain coordinating functions across the whole federal public service and that prevent individual departments from acting with too much autonomy.

Charter of Rights and Freedoms. The 1992 document added to the Canadian Constitution that guaranteed fundamental freedoms and rights (legal democratic, linguistic, mobility, egalitarian, limited aboriginal) to individual Canadian citizens.

Chief electoral officer. The independent and impartial official who is in charge of the operation of the whole electoral system.

Citizens' Forum. An operation headed by Keith Spicer in 1991–92 to hear what ordinary Canadians felt about constitutional issues after charges that they had not been able to contribute to the recently rejected Meech Lake Accord.

Civil law. A branch of the law dealing with relations between private parties, such as individuals and corporations, that do not involve government.

Civil liberties. Liberties or freedoms, including the fundamental freedoms of speech, press, religion, and assembly, that citizens enjoy and that cannot be infringed or encroached on by government.

Class-based parties. Political parties that appeal to one socioeconomic class or another; when all parties do so, they constitute a class-based party system.

Classical federalism. A variant of Canadian federalism in which the federal and provincial governments were not subordinate to each other and operated independently of each other.

Clientele relationship. The intimate and mutually advantageous relationship that sometimes develops between a government department or agency and the interest group with which it most frequently interacts.

Closure. A rule in the House of Commons in which a cabinet minister introduces a motion to cut off debate.

Code Civil du Québec. The unique system of civil law used in Quebec and based on the Napoleonic Code.

Coercion. Power based on authorized physical force (including police, armed forces, jails, etc.) on which government has a near monopoly. Also used by class analysts as a term for what government does (at the behest of the corporate elite) when the state cannot otherwise get the public to accept its decisions.

Collective responsibility. A convention holding that all cabinet ministers are collectively responsible for government policy and under which the whole cabinet must resign if defeated on a motion of nonconfidence.

Collectivism. An ideology holding that the public interest is enhanced by substantial collective action, normally via government, as opposed to individualism, which minimizes the role of government.

Commissioner for Federal Judicial Affairs. The official in charge of coordinating the process for the appointment of those judges who fall under the appointing power of the federal minister of Justice.

Common law. The basis of the British and Canadian legal systems, apart from the civil law system in Quebec, that consists of the accumulation of judicial precedents and seeks out the previous decisions in cases most closely resembling the one at hand.

Comprehensive claims. Aboriginal land claims based on aboriginal title—that is, traditional use and occupancy—rather than on treaties or other legal documents.

Concurrent powers. Powers officially shared by the federal and provincial governments, which in the Constitution Act, 1867, were agriculture, immigration, and, later, old age pensions.

Conditional grant. A federal grant to the provinces, usually in support of a subject within provincial jurisdiction, to which Ottawa attaches conditions or standards before the province receives the money.

Confederation Settlement. The deal made among the Fathers of Confederation that entailed setting up a new federal system of government with a division of powers, a division of financial powers, federal controls over the provinces, provincial representation in federal institutions, and certain cultural guarantees.

Conscription crises. Two political crises in Canada, one in each world war, in which the population and government were divided, largely on ethnic lines, over the necessity of compulsory military service.

Conservatism. A political ideology generally characterized by a belief in individualism and a minimum of government intervention in the economy and society, as well as by tradition, elitism, and opposition to change.

Constitution. The whole body of rules and principles according to which the state is governed that, in the Canadian case, consists of a conglomeration of documents and conventions.

Constitutional Act of 1791. The British law that divided Canada into two separate colonies, Upper and Lower Canada, each with a Governor, Executive and Legislative Councils, and an Assembly.

Constitution Act, 1867. The new name (changed in 1982) for the British North America Act, 1867.

Constitutional amending formula. The process for amending the Constitution.

Constitutional conventions. Unwritten rules of constitutional behaviour that are considered to be binding by and upon those who operate the Constitution, but that are not enforceable by the courts.

Cooperative federalism. A variant of Canadian federalism, in place in the post-1945 and especially post-1960 period, in which neither level of government is subordinate to the other and in which there is an extensive degree of interaction between them.

Corporate elite. A synonym for "big business" or the bourgeoisie—that is, the collection of individuals who own or manage the largest corporations in the country.

Corporatism. A notion that society can be divided into relatively few functional sectors, such as business, labour, farmers, and professions, that can either be self-governing or with whom the government can interact to make general policies.

Court Challenges Program. A program established after the adoption of the Charter of Rights and Freedoms in which the federal government helped to finance those who challenged laws on the basis of the Charter, on the assumption that the costs involved would otherwise be prohibitive.

Criminal Code. A federal document that codifies most of the criminal law in the country.

Criminal law. That branch of the law dealing with wrongs committed against others that are considered to be offensive to society as a whole, for which the state takes the initiative to investigate, and for which perpetrators can be fined or jailed.

Cross-media ownership. The ownership of different forms of mass media—newspaper, radio, or television—by the same individual or company.

Crown. The collectivity of executive powers exercised by or in the name of the monarch.

Crown corporations. Corporations owned by the government that assume a structure similar to a private company and that operate semi-independently of the cabinet.

Crow rate. A subsidized rail freight rate for Western goods, named after the Crow's Nest Pass, that was established in 1897, reduced in the 1970s, and eliminated in 1995.

Cruise missile. A type of missile that the United States tested over Canada because of the similarity of topography between Canada and the Soviet Union.

Cuban missile crisis. A worldwide crisis in the early 1960s precipitated by the stationing of Soviet missiles in Cuba pointing toward the United States; had negative implications for Canada–U.S. relations.

Declaratory power. The power in section 92(10c) of the Constitution Act, 1867, under which Ottawa can declare any local work or undertaking to be for the general advantage of Canada and thereby place it under federal jurisdiction.

Deference to authority. A value considered to be part of the Canadian political culture in which citizens are respectful of government authority and accept its word and orders with little question.

Democracy. A political system characterized by popular sovereignty, political equality, political freedom, and majority rule.

Democratic Rights. A section of the Charter of Rights and Freedoms that, among other things, guarantees the vote to every Canadian citizen.

Department of Finance. The government department that has overall responsibility for the government's finances and its role in the economy; has a powerful influence on all government policy.

Departmental cabinet. A cabinet characterized by ministers and departments that operate with substantial autonomy from other ministers and departments.

Departments. A kind of government organization headed by a minister who is politically accountable for its operations and a deputy minister who is in charge of its hierarchical administrative apparatus.

Deputy minister. The public servant who heads each government department, manages the department, and advises the minister.

Deregulation. A government policy that removes previous regulations, especially those affecting the corporate sector.

Direct taxes. A category of taxation that can be used by either level of government to extract money from the very person or corporation that is intended to pay it.

Disallowance. A power given to the federal government in the Constitution Act, 1867, but long since dormant, under which the cabinet can disallow any provincial law.

Dispute-settlement mechanism. A clause in the Canada–U.S. Free Trade Agreement designed to settle such trade disputes as might arise under the treaty by means of binational panels.

Dissolution of Parliament. The ending of a Parliament, usually after four or more years, by calling an election, an act normally in the hands of the prime minister but that formally requires the approval of the governor general.

Distinct society clause. A controversial clause in the Meech Lake Accord, and slightly modified in the Charlottetown Accord, claiming that Quebec constituted, within Canada, a distinct society.

Division. A formal standing, roll-call vote in the House of Commons in which members' names are recorded in Hansard.

Division of powers. The distribution of legislative powers between the federal and provincial governments, largely contained in sections 91 and 92 of the Constitution Act, 1867.

Durham Report. The 1839 report by Lord Durham that recommended the union of Upper and Lower Canada and the granting of responsible government to the colony of Canada.

Elite. A small group of people with a disproportionate amount of power; hence, *elitist*, an acceptance of making decisions in that manner.

Elite accommodation. The notion that public policies emerge from the interaction of various elites in society, who, sharing many socioeconomic characteristics and values, find it relatively easy to come to agreement.

Embedded state. The notion that the operations of the state are so extensive that they are connected to virtually every aspect of society, and that government therefore cannot act independently of societal forces.

Emergency doctrine. A constitutional doctrine invented by the Judicial Committee of the Privy Council that in times of national emergency, the Peace, Order and Good Government clause of the 1867 Constitution Act became an emergency clause.

Emergency federalism. The highly centralized variant of Canadian federalism that characterized the period of the two world wars.

Employment equity. A policy that seeks to guarantee complete fairness in hiring, promotion, or remuneration, regardless of gender, ethnicity, etc., and that may or may not incorporate affirmative action.

Enumerated powers. The powers of the federal and provincial governments explicitly listed in sections 91 and 92 of the Constitution Act, 1867.

Equality rights. A section of the Charter of Rights and Freedoms that prohibits governments from discriminating against certain categories of people.

Equalization payments. A large annual cash payment made by the federal government to have-not provinces to help them provide a satisfactory level of public services.

Established Programs Financing Act. An act passed in 1977 that altered the basis for federal–provincial grants, making health insurance a block grant rather than a conditional grant program.

Estimates. The annual spending plans of government departments and agencies for the following fiscal year, arrived at after gruelling negotiation with the Treasury Board Secretariat.

Executive federalism. A variant of cooperative federalism characterized by extensive federal–provincial interaction at the level of first ministers, departmental ministers, and deputy ministers, such as the process that produced the Meech Lake Accord.

Extra-parliamentary party. That part of a political party beyond its members of Parliament, that is, party members, local and national executives, and party headquarters.

Extra-territoriality. The ability of a state to pass laws having authority beyond its borders, especially related to the United States telling Canadian branches of U.S.-based transnational corporations with whom they can trade.

Federal Court of Canada. A court established by the federal government dealing with cases involving that level of government and other specialized subjects within federal jurisdiction.

Federalism (federation). A system of government characterized by two levels of authority (federal and provincial) and a division of powers such that neither is subordinate to the other.

Federal–provincial conferences. Periodic meetings of federal and provincial officials, especially first ministers or departmental ministers, characteristic of cooperative federalism, often making decisions that legislatures are not allowed to change.

Feminists. People who believe in removing barriers to the full equality of men and women.

Feminization of poverty. The notion that a high proportion of people living below the poverty line are women, usually sole-parent women with children.

Filibuster. An organized attempt by the opposition in the House of Commons to prolong debate and delay adoption of government measures.

First Ministers' Conference. A federal–provincial conference consisting of the prime minister and provincial premiers (and sometimes territorial and aboriginal leaders).

First Nations. The new term preferred by aboriginal Canadians to describe themselves, especially status Indians and those based on reserves.

First-past-the-post. The kind of electoral system used in Canada in which the candidate with the most votes wins, regardless if it is over 50 percent.

Foreign Investment Review Agency (FIRA). The agency established in the early 1970s to screen foreign investment in Canada and approve of foreign takeovers of Canadian firms; discontinued by the Mulroney government.

Francophonie. The international organization of French-speaking countries.

Franchise. The right to vote.

Free vote. A rare vote in the House of Commons (or Senate) in which members are not required to abide by the party line.

Front de Libération du Québec (FLQ). The terrorist wing of the Quebec separatist movement in the 1960s and 1970s.

Fundamental freedoms. Political freedoms—of speech, religion, press, assembly, association, etc.—that governments are not supposed to encroach on and that are guaranteed by the Charter of Rights and Freedoms.

Gerrymandering. An attempt to design constituency boundaries in the interests of the government party of the day in order to maximize the number of that party's seats and minimize the seats won by the opposition.

Government bills. Bills introduced by a cabinet minister on behalf of the whole government, the kind of bills dominating discussion in the House of Commons.

Gray Report. The government report authored by Herb Gray in 1972 expressing concern about the extent of foreign investment in Canada and recommending a screening agency.

Horse-race effect. The notion that election campaigns have degenerated into a "horse-race" where everyone, especially the media, are concerned with which party is ahead, not with how parties would tackle serious public issues.

House leader. The person appointed by each party in the House of Commons to deal with counterparts in other parties with respect to scheduling Commons business and to speak for the party if the leader is absent.

Immigration Act. The law that regulates the immigration process and determines the qualifications, categories, and, to some extent, the origins of immigrants.

Implied bill of rights. The notion that even before the enactment of the Canadian Bill of Rights or the Charter of Rights, the Constitution, especially in its preamble, contained an implied bill that protected civil liberties to some extent.

Incrementalism. The notion that, when confronted with a problem, governments—politicians and/or bureaucrats—prefer to make minor adjustments in existing policy rather than engage in a consideration of all possible alternative approaches.

Indian Act. The act that governed almost all aspects of Indian life in Canada since the 1870s, giving extensive authority to government bureaucrats and minimal discretion to Indians themselves.

Indirect taxes. A category of taxation, especially a tariff or customs duty, restricted to the federal government, in which the party that pays the tax is assumed to pass it along to some other customer.

Individualism. An ideology that individuals should have maximum freedom or liberty to do as they please, especially in economic terms, and that governments should not get involved in taxation, regulation, redistribution, or ownership.

Information Commissioner. The official of Parliament who encourages government to operate on a more open basis and makes judgments in cases where departments withhold information under the Access to Information Act.

Inherent right of aboriginal self-government. Aboriginal Canadians not only seek the right to govern themselves, but also the recognition that that right is inherent (in their having been here first) and is not a gift of the current occupants of their land.

Institutionalized Cabinet. A cabinet characterized by collective ministerial decision-making and strong central agencies that support collective cabinet operations.

Institutionalized pressure groups. A kind of pressure group characterized by permanence, resources, governmental recognition and acceptance, and well-developed links with the authorities.

Interest groups/pressure groups. Any group seeking to influence government policy without contesting elections; organizations whose members act together to influence public policy in order to promote their common interest.

Iron law of oligarchy. An observation about political parties that they almost always come to be controlled by a small group of permanent professional politicians and officials who are in charge of policy, finance, and strategy.

Issue-oriented groups. A kind of pressure group that springs up around an issue and disappears once that issue has been resolved.

James Bay and Northern Quebec Agreement. The deal signed in 1975 by the government of Quebec and its northern aboriginal residents that gave the latter land, cash, and hunting rights in return for surrendering land for the James Bay hydroelectric project.

Japanese Redress Agreement. The deal signed by the Mulroney government in 1988 to compensate Japanese Canadians for their internment and the confiscation of their property during the Second World War.

Joint committees. Parliamentary committees containing members from both the House of Commons and the Senate.

Judicial Committee of the Privy Council (JCPC). A committee of the British Parliament that functioned as Canada's final court of appeal until 1949.

Judicial discretion. The leeway inevitably bestowed on the courts when they interpret laws, even when they do not, or have no power to, overturn them.

Judicial independence. The constitutional principle that the courts should function independently of the rest of the government apparatus—that is, the politicians and bureaucrats—with implications for security of tenure and remuneration.

Judicial review. The power of the courts to overturn legislation.

Kent Royal Commission on Newspapers. The royal commission established in 1980 to investigate the newspaper industry after a rash of takeovers and closures in the 1970s.

Keynesian economics. An economic theory first enunciated by John Maynard Keynes that to promote general economic stability, government should counterbalance the private sector, spending (running deficit budgets) in periods of unemployment when the private sector doesn't spend, and taxing in periods of inflation when the private sector is spending too much.

King–Byng dispute. The dispute in 1926 between Prime Minister Mackenzie King and Governor General Lord Byng over King's request for a dissolution of Parliament, which Byng denied.

Leader of the Opposition. The leader of the main opposition party in the House of Commons, normally the party with the second-largest number of seats.

Leadership review. A clause in the constitutions of some political parties that allows party members to review the leader's performance and to vote on whether they want a leadership convention.

Left. That part of the ideological spectrum that believes in equality in society and the intervention of government via such collectivist measures as taxation, regulation, redistribution, and public ownership to effect such equality.

Legal rights. The rights of a person suspected or accused of committing a crime, now listed in the Charter of Rights and Freedoms.

Liberalism. An ideology based on a belief in the rationality of the individual and on maximizing individual freedom, liberty, and self-fulfilment. Before 1900 this was assumed to entail a minimal role for government, but post-1900 liberalism usually advocated a larger role for the state and therefore was placed on the left of the spectrum.

Limited identities. The notion that while the Canadian national identity is elusive, Canadian society is made up of all sorts of more limited identities or subcultures—regional, ethnic, linguistic, etc.

Lobbying. Any organized attempt to influence the authorities, now often performed by professional lobbyist firms.

Lobbyists Registration Act. The law passed in 1989 that sought to have lobbyists register with a government agency and submit a minimal amount of information about what they were doing to influence government.

Majority government. A situation in which the party in power has over 50 percent of the seats in the House of Commons.

Majority rule. An element in the definition of democracy that in any decision-making setting involving a difference of opinion, the larger number should carry the day.

Mandarins. A term applied to senior bureaucrats who are known to have great influence in government policy-making.

Mass party. A kind of political party in which the membership plays a meaningful role in such operations as financing, choosing and reviewing the leadership, and determining party policy.

Massey Royal Commission. A 1951 royal commission that expressed concern about the future prospects of Canadian culture and recommended ways to promote and protect it.

Meech Lake Accord. The 1987 package of constitutional amendments intended to bring Quebec back into the constitutional fold.

Memorandum to Cabinet. The formal written document that a minister submits to the whole cabinet seeking to initiate or change a government policy.

Merit system. A system of hiring or promoting public servants on the basis of their merits (education, training, experience, etc.) rather than on party preference or other considerations.

Ministerial responsibility. The principle that cabinet ministers are individually responsible to the House of Commons for everything that happens in their department.

Minority government. A situation in which the government party has less than 50 percent of the seats in the House of Commons.

Minority language education rights. Rights established by the 1982 Charter of Rights and Freedoms whereby French-speaking Canadians have the right to send their children to French-language schools, wherever their numbers warrant, a principle extended to English-speaking Canadians as well.

Mobility Rights. A category of rights in the Charter of Rights and Freedoms guaranteeing the freedom to move from one province to another and seek employment there.

Multiculturalism. A policy of encouraging ethnic and cultural groups to maintain their customs and traditions, often with public financial assistance.

National Action Committee on the Status of Women. The largest and most vocal women's interest group.

National Citizens' Coalition. A right-wing pressure group that successfully challenged limitations on third-party advertising during election campaigns.

National Energy Board. A regulatory agency that makes decisions relating to exports of electricity and petroleum.

National Energy Program. A 1980 initiative associated with Pierre Trudeau designed to skim off more petroleum tax revenue for Ottawa, keep the price of petroleum below world levels, encourage conservation, and Canadianize the industry; met with great opposition in Western Canada.

National Policy. A broad nation-building policy of John A. Macdonald unveiled in 1879 that included tariff protection for central Canadian manufacturing, massive immigration, and the construction of a national transportation system.

Neoconservative. An ideological term characterizing parties or politicians in the 1980s who not only advocated an end to government expansion, but believed in reducing its role via privatization, deregulation, deficit-cutting, and elimination of social programs.

New middle class. A term from class analysis describing salaried professionals such as teachers, public servants, nurses, and so on.

News management. A variety of techniques used by politicians and governments to ensure positive media coverage.

Nomination. The act of becoming a candidate in an election, normally entailing being selected to represent a party at a nomination meeting and then completing official nomination forms.

Nonconfidence motion. A periodic motion in the House of Commons, moved by the opposition, inviting the House to demonstrate its lack of confidence in the government; if successful, such a motion would require the cabinet's resignation or the calling of an election.

North American Free Trade Agreement (NAFTA). The 1994 extension of the Canada–U.S. Free Trade Agreement to Mexico, with provision for other Latin American countries to join.

North Atlantic Treaty Organization (NATO). A military alliance established by Canada, the United States, and their western European allies in 1949; originally designed to contain Soviet expansion.

Notwithstanding clause. Section 33 of the Charter of Rights and Freedoms, which allows federal or provincial governments to pass laws that violate certain sections of the Charter.

Nunavut. The eastern half of the Northwest Territories, which will be established as a separate, Inuit territory in 1999.

Oakes test. The strategy outlined in the *Oakes* case for interpreting the reasonable limits clause of the Charter of Rights and Freedoms.

Official Languages Act. A law passed in 1969 giving citizens the right to deal with head offices as well as certain local offices of the federal government in either official language; necessitated the hiring and promotion of francophone public servants.

One-party dominance. A party system characterized by the dominance of a single party, usually related to Conservative Party dominance before 1900 and Liberal Party dominance since.

Opposition. Those members of Parliament who do not support the government of the day.

Opposition days. Twenty days per session of Parliament set aside for the opposition to determine the topic of debate and for the government to respond.

Pacific scandal. A party finance scandal involving John A. Macdonald's Conservative Party and a group of businessmen who sought the contract to build the Canadian Pacific Railway.

Padlock Law. An infamous law passed by Premier Maurice Duplessis in Quebec in the late 1930s that allowed him to place a padlock on any building that was being used for purposes of opposing the government.

Pairing. A practice in the House of Commons whereby two MPs from opposite sides agree that if either is legitimately away for a vote the other will not vote either.

Parliamentary party. That wing of a political party made up of its elected members, that is, its MPs or its parliamentary caucus.

Parliament of Canada. The Queen, the House of Commons, and the Senate functioning collectively, such as in the approval of legislation.

Parliamentary press gallery. Those members of the media who are registered to sit in the press gallery in the House of Commons and who report on its proceedings or on government in general.

Parliamentary privileges. Historic privileges that adhere to a member of Parliament, the most important residual one being the freedom from prosecution for anything said in the Commons chamber.

Parliamentary secretaries. Government MPs who have been given additional responsibilities to assist a cabinet minister.

Particularism. A value identified as part of the Canadian political culture that encourages diversity rather than uniformity; most commonly takes the form of a mosaic of ethnic diversity and multiculturalism, in contrast to the U.S. melting pot.

Party caucus. The whole body of MPs of any party, who hold a regular weekly meeting, together with such senators as choose to attend, to discuss parliamentary strategy, party policy, and so on.

Party discipline. The convention that all MPs within any party vote together on every occasion, as predetermined in the party caucus meeting and as enforced by the party whip.

Party whip. An official of each party in the House of Commons whose function is to enforce party discipline, in part by drawing up speaking lists, committee assignments, office allocations, and official parliamentary travel plans.

Pay equity. An element of employment equity programs designed to ensure that all employees are paid equally for work of equal value and are not discriminated against on the basis of gender or other factors.

Peace, Order, and Good Government clause (POGG). The opening words of section 91 of the Constitution Act, 1867, describing the residual powers of the federal government (as well as the essence of the Canadian political culture), but often misinterpreted by the courts as an emergency power only.

Persons case. The decision by the Judicial Committee of the Privy Council that determined that women were persons for the purposes of appointment to the Senate.

Petite bourgeoisie. A Marxist term to describe self-employed professionals, affluent farmers, and those operating small businesses.

Pipeline debate. The heated House of Commons debate in the mid-1950s regarding the construction of the Trans-Canada Pipeline in which the Liberals treated Parliament in a particularly arrogant way.

Policy communities. The notion that government policy is made in a series of discrete and specialized clusters of government departments and agencies, interest groups, politicians, corporations, and interested individuals.

Policy instruments. The devices chosen by the government to effect public policy that are commonly arrayed in terms of degree of intrusion in society and the economy.

Political culture. The sum total of the political or politically relevant values, attitudes, beliefs, and orientations in any political system.

Political efficacy. The feeling that one has political influence, amd that one's political participation can make an impact.

Political equality. An element in the definition of democracy that entails the principle of "one person–one vote"—every citizen has a vote and each counts equally.

Political freedom. An element in the definition of democracy that entails freedom of speech, press, assembly, association, etc., such that people can organize and advocate in order to influence election results and public policy.

Political party. An organized group that makes nominations and contests elections in the hope of influencing the personnel and policy of government.

Political patronage. Making appointments to public offices or awarding government contracts on a partisan basis.

Political socialization. The process whereby individuals acquire their political values, attitudes, beliefs, and orientations.

Popular sovereignty. An element in the definition of democracy that entails periodically allowing the public at large to exert its will—to have the final say—normally through general elections.

Popular vote. The percent of all votes cast won by a candidate or party, regardless of who was elected.

Poverty line. An amount of income such that anyone who received less would be living in poverty.

Prerogative powers. That small residual of powers of the Crown—the Queen or governor general—that remain from the era of an all-powerful monarch and that the Crown can still exercise at its own discretion.

Prime ministerial government. The notion that the prime minister is now so pre-eminent that the label "cabinet government" no longer accurately describes how decisions are made in the political executive.

Prime Minister's Office (PMO). The office that supports and advises the prime minister in partisan terms.

Private bills. Bills introduced in Parliament that only affect a specific individual, company, organization, or group.

Private Members' bills. Public bills introduced in the House of Commons or Senate by members who are not in the cabinet.

Private sector. That part of the economy operated by individuals, corporations, and other non-governmental groups.

Privatization. Transferring a government program, agency, or Crown corporation to the private sector, such as by selling shares in a Crown corporation to the public at large or to a private firm.

Privy Council Office. The office that supports and advises the prime minister, cabinet, and cabinet committees in nonpartisan terms on such matters as overall government policy, the machinery of government, and senior bureaucratic appointments.

Proletariat. A Marxist term referring to those who sell their labour for an undervalued price to the bourgeoisie; the working class.

Public Accounts Committee. The House of Commons committee that examines the Public Accounts and the Auditor General's Report and criticizes government officials for illegal or unwise expenditures.

Public bills. Those bills introduced in Parliament that affect society in general.

Public opinion. The sum total of opinions held by members of the public on any subject.

Public ownership. A policy instrument involving government purchase ("nationalization") of a private corporation or the creation of a Crown corporation.

Public policy. A course of action or inaction chosen by public authorities to address a given problem or interrelated set of problems.

Public policy purpose. The point of creating a Crown corporation or other government program or agency—that is, to achieve the objectives of a public policy or to serve some public interest.

Public sector. That part of the economy operated or financed by government.

Public Service Commission. The central personnel agency of government designed to police the merit system and ensure that partisanship is kept out of the regular public service.

Quasi-federalism. That phase of Canadian federalism (1867–1896) in which the federal government was predominant over the provinces, just as John A. Macdonald intended.

Quasi-judicial. Courtlike functions, powers, and procedures often possessed by regulatory agencies (e.g., CRTC licence-issuing powers).

Quasi-legislative. Functions and powers of regulatory agencies to make lawlike regulations (e.g., CRTC Canadian-content regulations).

Quebec Act. The British law passed in 1774 that provided for a system of government for the colony of Quebec (Canada) and that provided certain privileges to the French-speaking majority.

Question Period. The daily 45-minute period in the House of Commons in which opposition members spar with the prime minister and cabinet ministers.

Quiet Revolution. The dramatic change of values and attitudes, especially toward the state, the new collective self-confidence, and the new brand of nationalism characterizing Quebec in the 1960s.

Rational choice. A model of the public policy–making process that prescribes consideration of the positive and negative implications of all policy alternatives until the most rational alternative is ultimately identified.

Reasonable limits clause. Section 1 of the Charter of Rights and Freedoms, which allows the courts to find that even though a law violates a Charter right, it is a reasonable limit on such and is therefore allowed to stand.

Red tories. A minority faction within the Canadian Conservative Party that has collectivist leanings akin to many British and European conservatives, stressing order, tradition, stability, and a paternalistic concern for the condition of the working class.

Redistribution. The process of reallocating seats in the House of Commons among the provinces after each decennial census and then redrawing constituency boundaries within each province.

Reference cases. Cases referred to the courts by provincial or federal cabinets in order to obtain a ruling on their constitutionality.

Regional economic development programs. Government programs designed to improve employment prospects in have-not parts of the country, usually by means of giving loans or grants to companies to establish or expand operations in such areas.

Regulations. The detailed rules drafted by the bureaucracy under the authority of laws passed by Parliament that are too voluminous and technical to put into the legislation itself.

Regulatory agencies. Government agencies established to regulate an area of public policy, such as transportation or communications, that operate at arm's length from the cabinet and often have quasi-legislative and/or quasi-judicial powers.

Representative bureaucracy. A public service that reflects the composition of the population, with the most usual concerns being gender, ethnicity, or region.

Representative government. A form of government including an assembly elected by the citizens, but one that does not necessarily incorporate the principle of responsible government.

Reservation. An obsolete power of the federally appointed lieutenant governor of each province to refrain from giving royal assent to provincial legislation and to send it instead to the federal cabinet for its consideration.

Residual powers. Those powers not explicitly given to the provinces in the Constitution Act, 1867, that were assigned to the federal government under the opening words of section 91.

Responsible government. A form of government in which the political executive must retain the confidence of the elected legislature or assembly and that must resign or call an election if and when it is defeated on a vote of nonconfidence.

Right. That part of the ideological spectrum that cherishes individualism and believes in leaving the private sector to operate with minimal government intervention.

Rowell–Sirois Commission. The royal commission appointed in 1937 to examine federal–provincial relations and whose 1940 report eventually led to many changes in the federal–provincial financial relationship.

Royal commission. An elaborate investigation set up by the cabinet to research significant policy problems, to listen to and educate the public, and to make recommendations to the government.

Royal Commission on Aboriginal Peoples. The royal commission appointed in the wake of the defeat of the Meech Lake Accord and the Oka stand-off to provide a blueprint for addressing the longstanding needs of the aboriginal community.

Royal Commission on Bilingualism and Biculturalism. The royal commission established in reaction to the Quiet Revolution in Quebec in the 1960s that recommended official bilingualism as a way of keeping the country together.

Royal Commission on Electoral Reform and Party Financing. The royal commission established in the wake of the controversial 1988 federal election, with the objective of enhancing the democratic character of Canadian elections.

Royal Commission on the Status of Women. The royal commission that reported in 1970 and helped to inspire the women's movement in its demands for policy changes over the following decades.

Royal Proclamation of 1763. The British policy enunciated after Britain won Quebec from France that in a large area called Indian Territory the purchase or settlement of land was forbidden without a treaty between the Crown and the Indian people concerned.

Rule adjudication. The process of providing authoritative settlements in disputes about the law, normally performed by the courts.

Rule of law. The constitutional principle that all government action must be based on law and that governments and government officials must obey the law.

Safe seats. Constituencies that a single party can be assured of winning election after election; the small number of these in the Canadian House of Commons results in a high MP turnover rate.

Scrutiny of Regulations. The joint parliamentary committee that is appointed to wade through the voluminous regulations issued by government departments under the authority of legislation and that has the power to recommend rescinding such regulations.

Secretary to the Cabinet and Clerk of the Privy Council. The head of the Privy Council Office and head of the federal public service; the chief nonpartisan adviser to the prime minister and cabinet.

Shared-cost programs. Government programs whose cost is shared by the federal and provincial governments.

Socialism. A leftist political ideology that emphasizes the principle of equality and usually prescribes a large role for government to intervene in society and the economy via taxation, regulation, redistribution, and public ownership.

Social security safety net. The conglomeration of social programs developed over the years by federal and provincial governments, individually and jointly, and designed to help those who could not otherwise care for their own basic needs or those of their family.

Sovereignty. Ultimate control or independence, whether in terms of Canadian national sovereignty vis-à-vis other countries or of Quebec sovereignty vis-à-vis the federal government.

Sovereignty-association. The Parti Québécois proposal in which Quebec would be sovereign while maintaining an economic association with the rest of Canada.

Speaker. The presiding officer of the House of Commons whose additional administrative responsibility includes the operation of the staff of the chamber.

Special committees. Committees of the House of Commons appointed for special, temporary purposes, such as to investigate a problem before the government has prepared legislation on the subject.

Specific claims. Aboriginal land claims arising from the alleged nonfulfilment of Indian treaties and other lawful obligations, as opposed to those based on traditional occupancy and use.

Speech from the Throne. The document prepared by the cabinet and read by the governor general at the opening of each session of Parliament outlining the government's legislative proposals for the session to follow.

Spending power. The unofficial power of the federal government to spend money on any subject, including those within provincial jurisdiction, and even to attach conditions to such grants to the provinces.

Spin doctors. Party officials and ministerial aides who talk to the media and try to influence media coverage by putting the best face on an event from their party's point of view.

Spoils system. Hiring public servants on the basis of political partisanship.

Stakeholders. Those individuals, groups, corporations, or other organizations who have a stake in any issue; the principal players involved in any policy community.

Standing committees. Those committees of the House of Commons that are set up semi-permanently and parallel government departments.

Standing Orders. The written rules of the House of Commons.

Staples theory. The notion that Canadian economic development has gone through a series of stages based on the exploitation of one natural resource or another and the export of such resources without the development of a secondary or tertiary sector.

Stare decisis. The legal principle that precedents are binding on similar subsequent cases; forms the basis of the common law system.

State of emergency. A policy instrument that involves the greatest degree of intrusion and coercion on the part of the state, now based on the Emergencies Act rather than the War Measures Act.

Status Indians. Those aboriginal Canadians registered with the federal government according to the terms of the Indian Act who have not had their status removed for any reason or those who have regained it.

Statute of Westminster. The 1931 British law that declared Canada and the other Dominions to be fully independent.

Subcultures. Clusters of people who share basic political values and attitudes based on common regional, ethnic, class, or other characteristics.

Supremacy of Parliament. The principle that no other organ of government can overrule Parliament or its laws; a principle modified to some extent in 1982 with an expanded power of judicial review incorporated in the Canadian Charter of Rights.

Supreme Court Act. The 1875 law of the Canadian Parliament that provided for the Supreme Court of Canada and that serves as a legal base for the institution in the absence of further constitutional entrenchment.

Tariff. A federal tax placed on imports that raises revenue for Ottawa and protects domestic manufacturers by making imported goods more expensive to buy.

Task forces. Informal devices set up by the cabinet, made up of bureaucrats, MPs, outside experts, or some combination thereof, to study an issue and make recommendations quickly.

Taxation agreements. Federal–provincial agreements, especially with respect to personal and corporate income taxes since 1945, under which Ottawa collects the taxes if provinces use a similar base for calculating their portion of the tax.

Tax expenditures. A policy instrument that provides a tax credit or tax deduction if taxpayers spend money in a desired way.

Third-party advertising. Advertising by advocacy groups, as opposed to political parties, during an election campaign.

Three-party system. A party system characterized by three main parties, all with approximately similar levels of support, as in Canada during the 1980s.

Trade and Commerce power. Subsection 2 of section 91 of the Constitution Act, 1867, which was intended to provide a broad base for federal jurisdiction in this field but which was whittled away by judicial interpretation.

Transnational corporations. Corporations operating simultaneously in many countries throughout the world that often take orders from company headquarters and that individual states find difficult to control.

Treasury Board. A cabinet committee whose primary responsibility is to restrain government spending.

Treasury Board Secretariat. The government department that advises the Treasury Board in its deliberations and that functions as a restraining influence on departmental spending.

Treaty power. Section 132 of the Constitution Act, 1867, which speaks of Empire treaties and was intended to provide the federal government with a broad power to sign and implement treaties, but whose scope was limited by judicial interpretation.

Triple-E Senate. A proposal for Senate reform in which each province would have an equal number of senators, who would be elected, and who would be given effective powers.

Two-party system. A type of party system in which two main parties are of approximately equal strength and alternate in office, as in Canada between 1896 and 1921.

Two-plus, or two-and-one-half, party system. A type of party system in which two main parties are of approximately equal strength and alternate in office, but which are accompanied by one or more minor parties of significant strength, as in Canada between 1921 and 1980.

Union government. The coalition government from 1917 to the end of the First World War made up of Conservatives and English-speaking Liberals whose aim was to enforce conscription and conduct the war in a vigorous manner.

Victoria Charter. The 1970 package of constitutional amendments including an amending formula, a charter of rights, and provisions designed to respond to demands emanating from the Quiet Revolution in Quebec.

Visible minorities. Members of ethnic groups, other than aboriginals, whose skin colour is not white.

Voters list. The list of eligible voters that is prepared from scratch via door-to-door enumeration once the election is called.

Wage and price controls. A controversial proposal put forward by the Conservatives in the 1974 election campaign to put a cap on wage and price increases.

War Measures Act. The law invoked during both world wars and during the 1970 FLQ crisis under which the federal cabinet is given emergency powers to deal with a crisis; later replaced by the Emergencies Act.

Western alienation. The feeling shared by many Western Canadians that their interests were not taken seriously in the national policy-making process.

Western Economic Diversification. The federal regional economic development program for the Western provinces.

Westminster model. The model of government developed in Britain in which the political executive is given extensive power to provide effective leadership.

White Paper on Indians. The 1969 Trudeau–Chrétien policy proposal to do away with the Indian Act and fully integrate aboriginals into Canadian society.

Women's movement. The collection of women's groups that mushroomed across the country starting about 1970 demanding complete equality for women.

Constitution Act, 1867 (excerpts)

VI. DISTRIBUTION OF LEGISLATIVE POWERS

Powers of the Parliament

Legislative Authority of Parliament of Canada

91. It shall be lawful for the Queen, by and with the Advice and Consent of the Senate and House of Commons, to make Laws for the Peace, Order, and good Government of Canada, in relation to all Matters not coming within the Classes of Subjects by this Act assigned exclusively to the Legislatures of the Provinces; and for greater Certainty, but not so as to restrict the Generality of the foregoing Terms of this Section, it is hereby declared that (notwithstanding anything in this Act) the exclusive Legislative Authority of the Parliament of Canada extends to all Matters coming within the Classes of Subjects next hereinafter enumerated; that is to say,—

1. Repealed.

1A. The Public Debt and Property.

2. The Regulation of Trade and Commerce.

2A. Unemployment insurance.

3. The raising of Money by any Mode or System of Taxation.

4. The borrowing of Money on the Public Credit.

5. Postal Service.

6. The Census and Statistics.

7. Militia, Military and Naval Service, and Defence.

8. The fixing of and providing for the Salaries and Allowances of Civil and other Officers of the Government of Canada.

9. Beacons, Buoys, Lighthouses, and Sable Island.

10. Navigation and Shipping.

11. Quarantine and the Establishment and Maintenance of Marine Hospitals.

12. Sea Coast and Inland Fisheries.

13. Ferries between a Province and any British or Foreign Country or between Two Provinces.
14. Currency and Coinage.
15. Banking, Incorporation of Banks, and the Issue of Paper Money.
16. Savings Banks.
17. Weights and Measures.
18. Bills of Exchange and Promissory Notes.
19. Interest.
20. Legal Tender.
21. Bankruptcy and Insolvency.
22. Patents of Invention and Discovery.
23. Copyrights.
24. Indians, and Lands reserved for the Indians.
25. Naturalization and Aliens.
26. Marriage and Divorce.
27. The Criminal Law, except the Constitution of Courts of Criminal Jurisdiction, but including the Procedure in Criminal Matters.
28. The Establishment, Maintenance, and Management of Penitentiaries.
29. Such Classes of Subjects as are expressly excepted in the Enumeration of the Classes of Subjects by this Act assigned exclusively to the Legislatures of the Provinces.

And any Matter coming within any of the Classes of Subjects enumerated in this Section shall not be deemed to come within the Class of Matters of a local or private Nature comprised in the Enumeration of the Classes of Subjects by this Act assigned exclusively to the Legislatures of the Provinces.

Exclusive Powers of Provincial Legislatures

92. In each Province the Legislature may exclusively make Laws in relation to Matters coming within the Classes of Subjects next hereinafter enumerated; that is to say,— *Subjects of exclusive Provincial Legislation*

1. Repealed.
2. Direct Taxation within the Province in order to the raising of a Revenue for Provincial Purposes.
3. The borrowing of Money on the sole Credit of the Province.
4. The Establishment and Tenure of Provincial Offices and the Appointment and Payment of Provincial Officers.
5. The Management and Sale of the Public Lands belonging to the Province and of the Timber and Wood thereon.
6. The Establishment, Maintenance, and Management of Public and Reformatory Prisons in and for the Province.
7. The Establishment, Maintenance, and Management of Hospitals, Asylums, Charities, and Eleemosynary Institutions in and for the Province, other than Marine Hospitals.
8. Municipal Institutions in the Province.
9. Shop, Saloon, Tavern, Auctioneer, and other Licences in order to the raising of a Revenue for Provincial, Local, or Municipal Purposes.

10. Local Works and Undertakings other than such as are of the following Classes:—
    (a) Lines of Steam or other Ships, Railways, Canals, Telegraphs, and other Works and Undertakings connecting the Province with any other or others of the Provinces, or extending beyond the Limits of the Province;
    (b) Lines of Steam Ships between the Province and any British or Foreign Country;
    (c) Such Works as, although wholly situate within the Province, are before or after their Execution declared by the Parliament of Canada to be for the general Advantage of Canada or for the Advantage of Two or more of the Provinces.
11. The Incorporation of Companies with Provincial Objects.
12. The Solemnization of Marriage in the Province.
13. Property and Civil Rights in the Province.
14. The Administration of Justice in the Province, including the Constitution, Maintenance, and Organization of Provincial Courts, both of Civil and of Criminal Jurisdiction, and including Procedure in Civil Matters in those Courts.
15. The Imposition of Punishment by Fine, Penalty, or Imprisonment for enforcing any Law of the Province made in relation to any Matter coming within any of the Classes of Subjects enumerated in this Section.
16. Generally all Matters of a merely local or private Nature in the Province.

Non-Renewable Natural Resources, Forestry Resources and Electrical Energy

92A. (1) In each province, the legislature may exclusively make laws in relation to
    (a) exploration for non-renewable natural resources in the province;
    (b) development, conservation and management of non-renewable natural resources and forestry resources in the province, including laws in relation to the rate of primary production therefrom; and
    (c) development, conservation and management of sites and facilities in the province for the generation and production of electrical energy.
(2) In each province, the legislature may make laws in relation to the export from the province to another part of Canada of the primary production from non-renewable natural resources and forestry resources in the province and the production from facilities in the province for the generation of electrical energy, but such laws may not authorize or provide for discrimination in prices or in supplies exported to another part of Canada.
(3) Nothing in subsection (2) derogates from the authority of Parliament to enact laws in relation to the matters referred to in that subsection and, where such a law of Parliament and a law of a province conflict, the law of Parliament prevails to the extent of the conflict.
(4) In each province, the legislature may make laws in relation to the raising of money by any mode or system of taxation in respect of
    (a) non-renewable natural resources and forestry resources in the province and the primary production therefrom, and

[margin notes: s respecting -renewable ral resources, stry resources electrical gy]

[margin notes: ort from ince of rces]

[margin notes: 1ority of ament]

[margin notes: tion of rces]

(b) sites and facilities in the province for the generation of electrical energy and the production therefrom,

whether or not such production is exported in whole or in part from the province, but such laws may not authorize or provide for taxation that differentiates between production exported to another part of Canada and production not exported from the province.

(5) The expression "primary production" has the meaning assigned by the Sixth Schedule.

(6) Nothing in subsections (1) to (5) derogates from any powers or rights that a legislature or government of a province had immediately before the coming into force of this section.

Education

93. In and for each Province the Legislature may exclusively make Laws in relation to Education, subject and according to the following Provisions:—

(1) Nothing in any such Law shall prejudicially affect any Right or Privilege with respect to Denominational Schools which any Class of Persons have by Law in the Province at the Union:

(2) All the Powers, Privileges, and Duties at the Union by Law conferred and imposed in Upper Canada on the Separate Schools and School Trustees of the Queen's Roman Catholic Subjects shall be and the same are hereby extended to the Dissentient Schools of the Queen's Protestant and Roman Catholic Subjects in Quebec:

(3) Where in any Province a System of Separate or Dissentient Schools exists by Law at the Union or is thereafter established by the Legislature of the Province, an Appeal shall lie to the Governor General in Council from any Act or Decision of any Provincial Authority affecting any Right or Privilege of the Protestant or Roman Catholic Minority of the Queen's Subjects in relation to Education:

(4) In case any such Provincial Law as from Time to Time seems to the Governor General in Council requisite for the due Execution of the Provisions of this Section is not made, or in case any Decision of the Governor General in Council on any appeal under this Section is not duly executed by the proper Provincial Authority in that Behalf, then and in every such Case, and as far only as the Circumstances of each Case require, the Parliament of Canada may make remedial Laws for the due Execution of the Provisions of this Section and of any Decision of the Governor General in Council under this Section.

Uniformity of Laws in Ontario, Nova Scotia and New Brunswick

94. Notwithstanding anything in this Act, the Parliament of Canada may make Provision for the Uniformity of all or any of the Laws relative to Property and Civil Rights in Ontario, Nova Scotia, and New Brunswick, and of the Procedure of all or any of the Courts in Those Three Provinces, and from and after the passing of any Act in that Behalf the Power of the Parliament of Canada to make Laws in relation to any Matter comprised in any such Act shall, notwithstanding anything in this Act, be unrestricted; but any Act of the Parliament of Canada making Provision for such Uniformity shall not have effect in any Province unless and until it is adopted and enacted as Law by the Legislature thereof.

Old Age Pensions

94A. The Parliament of Canada may make laws in relation to old age pensions and supplementary benefits, including survivors' and disability benefits irrespective of age, but no such law shall affect the operation of any law present or future of a provincial legislature in relation to any such matter.

Agriculture and Immigration

95. In each Province the Legislature may make Laws in relation to Agriculture in the Province, and to Immigration into the Province; and it is hereby declared that the Parliament of Canada may from Time to Time make Laws in relation to Agriculture in all or any of the Provinces, and to Immigration into all or any of the Provinces; and any Law of the Legislature of a Province relative to Agriculture or to Immigration shall have effect in and for the Province as long and as far only as it is not repugnant to any Act of the Parliament of Canada.

VII. JUDICATURE

96. The Governor General shall appoint the Judges of the Superior, District, and County Courts in each Province, except those of the Courts of Probate in Nova Scotia and New Brunswick.

97. Until the Laws relative to Property and Civil Rights in Ontario, Nova Scotia, and New Brunswick, and the Procedure of the Courts in those Provinces, are made uniform, the Judges of the Courts of those Provinces appointed by the Governor General shall be selected from the respective Bars of those Provinces.

98. The Judges of the Courts of Quebec shall be selected from the Bar of that Province.

99. (1) Subject to subsection two of this section, the Judges of the Superior Courts shall hold office during good behaviour, but shall be removable by the Governor General on Address of the Senate and House of Commons.

(2) A Judge of a Superior Court, whether appointed before or after the coming into force of this section, shall cease to hold office upon attaining the age of seventy-five years, or upon the coming into force of this section if at that time he has already attained that age.

100. The Salaries, Allowances, and Pensions of the Judges of the Superior, District, and County Courts (except the Courts of Probate in Nova Scotia and New Brunswick), and of the Admiralty Courts in Cases where the Judges thereof are for the Time being paid by Salary, shall be fixed and provided by the Parliament of Canada.

Marginal notes:

Legislation respecting old age pensions and supplementary benefits

Concurrent Powers of Legislation respecting Agriculture, etc.

Appointment of Judges

Selection of Judges in Ontario, etc.

Selection of Judges in Quebec

Tenure of office of Judges

Termination at age 75

Salaries, etc., of Judges

101. The Parliament of Canada may, notwithstanding anything in this Act, from Time to Time provide for the Constitution, Maintenance, and Organization of a General Court of Appeal for Canada, and for the Establishment of any additional Courts for the better Administration of the Laws of Canada.

132. The Parliament and Government of Canada shall have all Powers necessary or proper for performing the Obligations of Canada or of any Province thereof, as Part of the British Empire, towards Foreign Countries, arising under Treaties between the Empire and such Foreign Countries.

133. Either the English or the French Language may be used by any Person in the Debates of the Houses of the Parliament of Canada and of the Houses of the Legislature of Quebec; and both those Languages shall be used in the respective Records and Journals of those Houses; and either of those Languages may be used by any Person or in any Pleading or Process in or issuing from any Court of Canada established under this Act, and in or from all or any of the Courts of Quebec.

The Acts of the Parliament of Canada and of the Legislature of Quebec shall be printed and published in both those Languages.

Appendix B

Constitution Act, 1982

SCHEDULE B

PART I
CANADIAN CHARTER OF RIGHTS AND FREEDOMS

Whereas Canada is founded upon principles that recognize the supremacy of God and the rule of law:

Guarantee of Rights and Freedoms

1. The *Canadian Charter of Rights and Freedoms* guarantees the rights and freedoms set out in it subject only to such reasonable limits prescribed by law as can be demonstrably justified in a free and democratic society.

Fundamental Freedoms

2. Everyone has the following fundamental freedoms:
(a) freedom of conscience and religion;
(b) freedom of thought, belief, opinion and expression, including freedom of the press and other media of communication;
(c) freedom of peaceful assembly; and
(d) freedom of association.

Democratic Rights

3. Every citizen of Canada has the right to vote in an election of members of the House of Commons or of a legislative assembly and to be qualified for membership therein.

4. (1) No House of Commons and no legislative assembly shall continue for longer than five years from the date fixed for the return of the writs at a general election of its members.

(2) In time of real or apprehended war, invasion or insurrection, a House of Commons may be continued by Parliament and a legislative assembly may be continued by the legislature beyond five years if such continuation is not opposed by the votes of more than one-third of the members of the House of Commons or the legislative assembly, as the case may be.

5. There shall be a sitting of Parliament and of each legislature at least once every twelve months.

Mobility Rights

6. (1) Every citizen of Canada has the right to enter, remain in and leave Canada.

(2) Every citizen of Canada and every person who has the status of a permanent resident of Canada has the right
    (a) to move to and take up residence in any province; and
    (b) to pursue the gaining of a livelihood in any province

(3) The rights specified in subsection (2) are subject to
    (a) any laws or practices of general application in force in a province other than those that discriminate among persons primarily on the basis of province of present or previous residence; and
    (b) any laws providing for reasonable residency requirements as a qualification for the receipt of publicly provided social services.

(4) Subsections (2) and (3) do not preclude any law, program or activity that has as its object the amelioration in a province of conditions of individuals in that province who are socially or economically disadvantaged if the rate of employment in that province is below the rate of employment in Canada.

Legal Rights

7. Everyone has the right to life, liberty and security of the person and the right not to be deprived thereof except in accordance with the principles of fundamental justice.

8. Everyone has the right to be secure against unreasonable search or seizure.

9. Everyone has the right not to be arbitrarily detained or imprisoned.

10. Everyone has the right on arrest or detention
    (a) to be informed promptly of the reasons therefor;
    (b) to retain and instruct counsel without delay and to be informed of that right; and
    (c) to have the validity of the detention determined by way of *habeas corpus* and to be released if the detention is not lawful.

11. Any person charged with an offence has the right
    (a) to be informed without unreasonable delay of the specific offence;
    (b) to be tried within a reasonable time;

Marginal notes:
Maximum duration of legislative bodies
Continuation in special circumstances
Annual sitting of legislative bodies
Mobility of citizens
Rights to move and gain livelihood
Limitation
Affirmative action programs
Life, liberty and security of person
Search or seizure
Detention or imprisonment
Arrest or detention
Proceedings in criminal and penal matters

(c) not to be compelled to be a witness in proceedings against that person in respect of the offence;

(d) to be presumed innocent until proven guilty according to law in a fair and public hearing by an independent and impartial tribunal;

(e) not to be denied reasonable bail without just cause;

(f) except in the case of an offence under military law tried before a military tribunal, to the benefit of trial by jury where the maximum punishment for the offence is imprisonment for five years or a more severe punishment;

(g) not to be found guilty on account of any act or omission unless, at the time of the act or omission, it constituted an offence under Canadian or international law or was criminal according to the general principles of law recognized by the community of nations;

(h) if finally acquitted of the offence, not to be tried for it again and, if finally found guilty and punished for the offence, not to be tried or punished for it again; and

(i) if found guilty of the offence and if the punishment for the offence has been varied between the time of commission and the time of sentencing, to the benefit of the lesser punishment.

eatment or pun-
ment

12. Everyone has the right not to be subjected to any cruel and unusual treatment or punishment.

lf-crimination

13. A witness who testifies in any proceedings has the right not to have any incriminating evidence so given used to incriminate that witness in any other proceedings, except in a prosecution for perjury or for the giving of contradictory evidence.

terpreter

14. A party or witness in any proceedings who does not understand or speak the language in which the proceedings are conducted or who is deaf has the right to the assistance of an interpreter.

Equality Rights

uality before
d under law and
ual protection
d benefit of law

15. (1) Every individual is equal before and under the law and has the right to the equal protection and equal benefit of the law without discrimination and, in particular, without discrimination based on race, national or ethnic origin, colour, religion, sex, age or mental or physical disability.

firmative action
ograms

(2) Subsection (1) does not preclude any law, program or activity that has as its object the amelioration of conditions of disadvantaged individuals or groups including those that are disadvantaged because of race, national or ethnic origin, colour, religion, sex, age or mental or physical disability.

Official Languages of Canada

ficial languages
Canada

16. (1) English and French are the official languages of Canada and have equality of status and equal rights and privileges as to their use in all institutions of the Parliament and government of Canada.

(2) English and French are the official languages of New Brunswick and have equality of status and equal rights and privileges as to their use in all institutions of the legislature and government of New Brunswick.

Official languages of New Brunswick

(3) Nothing in this Charter limits the authority of Parliament or a legislature to advance the equality of status or use of English and French.

Advancement of status and use

17. (1) Everyone has the right to use English or French in any debates and other proceedings of Parliament.

Proceedings of Parliament

(2) Everyone has the right to use English or French in any debates and other proceedings of the legislature of New Brunswick.

Proceedings of New Brunswick legislature

18. (1) The statutes, records and journals of Parliament shall be printed and published in English and French and both language versions are equally authoritative.

Parliamentary statutes and record

(2) The statutes, records and journals of the legislature of New Brunswick shall be printed and published in English and French and both language versions are equally authoritative.

New Brunswick statutes and record

19. (1) Either English or French may be used by any person in, or in any pleading in or process issuing from, any court established by Parliament.

Proceedings in courts established by Parliament

(2) Either English or French may be used by any person in, or in any pleading in or process issuing from, any court of New Brunswick.

Proceedings in New Brunswick courts

20. (1) Any member of the public in Canada has the right to communicate with, and to receive available services from, any head or central office of an institution of the Parliament or government of Canada in English or French, and has the same right with respect to any other office of any such institution where

Communications by public with federal institutions

(a) there is a significant demand for communications with and services from that office in such language; or

(b) due to the nature of the office, it is reasonable that communications with and services from that office be available in both English and French.

(2) Any member of the public in New Brunswick has the right to communicate with, and to receive available services from, any office of an institution of the legislature or government of New Brunswick in English or French.

Communications by public with New Brunswick institutions

21. Nothing in sections 16 to 20 abrogates or derogates from any right, privilege or obligation with respect to the English and French languages, or either of them, that exists or is continued by virtue of any other provision of the Constitution of Canada.

Continuation of existing constitutional provisions

22. Nothing in sections 16 to 20 abrogates or derogates from any legal or customary right or privilege acquired or enjoyed either before or after the coming into force of this Charter with respect to any language that is not English or French.

Rights and privileges preserved

Minority Language Educational Rights

23. (1) Citizens of Canada

Language of instruction

(a) whose first language learned and still understood is that of the English or French linguistic minority population of the province in which they reside, or

(b) who have received their primary school instruction in Canada in English or French and reside in a province where the language in which they received that instruction is the language of the English or French linguistic minority population of the province, have the right to have their children receive primary and secondary school instruction in that language in that province.

(2) Citizens of Canada of whom any child has received or is receiving primary or secondary school instruction in English or French in Canada, have the right to have all their children receive primary and secondary school instruction in the same language.

(3) The right of citizens of Canada under subsections (1) and (2) to have their children receive primary and secondary school instruction in the language of the English or French linguistic minority population of a province

 (a) applies wherever in the province the number of children of citizens who have such a right is sufficient to warrant the provision to them out of public funds of minority language instruction; and

 (b) includes, where the number of those children so warrants, the right to have them receive that instruction in minority language educational facilities provided out of public funds.

Enforcement

24. (1) Anyone whose rights or freedoms, as guaranteed by this Charter, have been infringed or denied may apply to a court of competent jurisdiction to obtain such remedy as the court considers appropriate and just in the circumstances.

(2) Where, in proceedings under subsection (1), a court concludes that evidence was obtained in a manner that infringed or denied any rights or freedoms guaranteed by this Charter, the evidence shall be excluded if it is established that, having regard to all the circumstances, the admission of it in the proceedings would bring the administration of justice into disrepute.

General

25. The guarantee in this Charter of certain rights and freedoms shall not be construed so as to abrogate or derogate from any aboriginal, treaty or other rights or freedoms that pertain to the aboriginal peoples of Canada including

 (a) any rights or freedoms that have been recognized by the Royal Proclamation of October 7, 1763; and

 (b) any rights or freedoms that now exist by way of land claims settlement.

26. The guarantee in this Charter of certain rights and freedoms shall not be construed as denying the existence of any other rights or freedoms that exist in Canada.

27. This Charter shall be interpreted in a manner consistent with the preservation and enhancement of the multicultural heritage of Canadians.

28. Notwithstanding anything in this Charter, the rights and freedoms referred to in it are guaranteed equally to male and female persons.

29. Nothing in this Charter abrogates or derogates from any rights or privileges guaranteed by or under the Constitution of Canada in respect of denominational, separate or dissentient schools.

30. A reference in this Charter to a Province or to the legislative assembly or legislature of a province shall be deemed to include a reference to the Yukon Territory and the Northwest Territories, or to the appropriate legislative authority thereof, as the case may be.

31. Nothing in this Charter extends the legislative powers of any body or authority.

Application of Charter

32. (1) This Charter applies

   (a) to the Parliament and government of Canada in respect of all matters within the authority of Parliament including all matters relating to the Yukon Territory and Northwest Territories; and

   (b) to the legislature and government of each province in respect of all matters within the authority of the legislature of each province.

(2) Notwithstanding subsection (1), section 15 shall not have effect until three years after this section comes into force.

33. (1) Parliament or the legislature of a province may expressly declare in an Act of Parliament or of the legislature, as the case may be, that the Act or a provision thereof shall operate notwithstanding a provision included in section 2 or sections 7 to 15 of this Charter.

(2) An Act or a provision of an Act in respect of which a declaration made under this section is in effect shall have such operation as it would have but for the provision of this Charter referred to in the declaration.

(3) A declaration made under subsection (1) shall cease to have effect five years after it comes into force or on such earlier date as may be specified in the declaration.

(4) Parliament or the legislature of a province may re-enact a declaration made under subsection (1).

(5) Subsection (3) applies in respect of a re-enactment made under subsection (4).

Citation

34. This Part may be cited as the *Canadian Charter of Rights and Freedoms*.

· ·

PART II
RIGHTS OF THE ABORIGINAL PEOPLES OF CANADA

35. (1) The existing aboriginal and treaty rights of the aboriginal peoples of Canada are hereby recognized and affirmed.

(2) In this Act, "aboriginal peoples of Canada" includes the Indian, Inuit and Métis peoples of Canada.

(3) For greater certainty, in subsection (1) "treaty rights" includes rights that now exist by way of land claims agreements or may be so acquired.

(4) Notwithstanding any other provision of this Act, the aboriginal and treaty rights referred to in subsection (1) are guaranteed equally to male and female persons.

PART III
EQUALIZATION AND REGIONAL DISPARITIES

36. (1) Without altering the legislative authority of Parliament or of the provincial legislatures, or the rights of any of them with respect to the exercise of their legislative authority, Parliament and the legislatures, together with the government of Canada and the provincial governments, are committed to

    (a) promoting equal opportunities for the well-being of Canadians;

    (b) furthering economic development to reduce disparity in opportunities; and

    (c) providing essential public services of reasonable quality to all Canadians.

(2) Parliament and the government of Canada are committed to the principle of making equalization payments to ensure that provincial governments have sufficient revenues to provide reasonably comparable levels of public services at reasonably comparable levels of taxation.

PART IV
CONSTITUTIONAL CONFERENCE

37. (1) A constitutional conference composed of the Prime Minister of Canada and the first ministers of the provinces shall be convened by the Prime Minister of Canada within one year after this Part comes into force.

(2) The conference convened under subsection (1) shall have included in its agenda an item respecting constitutional matters that directly affect the aboriginal peoples of Canada, including the identification and definition of the rights of those peoples to be included in the Constitution of Canada, and the Prime Minister of Canada shall invite representatives of those peoples to participate in the discussions on that item.

(3) The Prime Minister of Canada shall invite elected representatives of the governments of the Yukon Territory and the Northwest Territories to participate in the discussions on any item on the agenda of the conference convened under subsection (1) that, in the opinion of the Prime Minister, directly affects the Yukon Territory and the Northwest Territories.

PART V
PROCEDURE FOR AMENDING CONSTITUTION OF CANADA

38. (1) An amendment to the Constitution of Canada may be made by proclamation issued by the Governor General under the Great Seal of Canada where so authorized by

General procedure for amending Constitution of Canada

    (a) resolutions of the Senate and House of Commons; and

    (b) resolutions of the legislative assemblies of at least two-thirds of the provinces that have, in the aggregate, according to the then latest general census, at least fifty per cent of the population of all the provinces.

(2) An amendment made under subsection (1) that derogates from the legislative powers, the proprietary rights or any other rights or privileges of the legislature or government of a province shall require a resolution supported by a majority of the members of each of the Senate, the House of Commons and the legislative assemblies required under subsection (1).

Majority of members

(3) An amendment referred to in subsection (2) shall not have effect in a province the legislative assembly of which has expressed its dissent thereto by resolution supported by a majority of its members prior to the issue of the proclamation to which the amendment relates unless that legislative assembly, subsequently, by resolution supported by a majority of its members, revokes its dissent and authorizes the amendment.

Expression of dissent

(4) A resolution of dissent made for the purposes of subsection (3) may be revoked at any time before or after the issue of the proclamation to which it relates.

Revocation of proclamation

39. (1) A proclamation shall not be issued under subsection 38(1) before the expiration of one year from the adoption of the resolution initiating the amendment procedure thereunder, unless the legislative assembly of each province has previously adopted a resolution of assent or dissent.

Restriction on proclamation

(2) A proclamation shall not be issued under subsection 38(1) after the expiration of three years from the adoption of the resolution initiating the amendment procedure thereunder.

Idem

40. Where an amendment is made under subsection 38(1) that transfers provincial legislative powers relating to education or other cultural matters from provincial legislatures to Parliament, Canada shall provide reasonable compensation to any province to which the amendment does not apply.

Compensation

41. An amendment to the Constitution of Canada in relation to the following matters may be made by proclamation issued by the Governor General under the Great Seal of Canada only where authorized by resolutions of the Senate and House of Commons and of the legislative assembly of each province:

Amendment by unanimous consent

    (a) the office of the Queen, the Governor General and the Lieutenant Governor of a province;

    (b) the right of a province to a number of members in the House of Commons not less than the number of Senators by which the province is entitled to be represented at the time this Part comes into force;

    (c) subject to section 43, the use of the English or the French language;

(d) the composition of the Supreme Court of Canada; and

(e) an amendment to this Part.

42. (1) An amendment to the Constitution of Canada in relation to the following matters may be made only in accordance with subsection 38(1):

(a) the principle of proportionate representation of the provinces in the House of Commons prescribed by the Constitution of Canada;

(b) the powers of the Senate and the method of selecting Senators;

(c) the number of members by which a province is entitled to be represented in the Senate and the residence qualifications of Senators;

(d) subject to paragraph 41(d), the Supreme Court of Canada;

(e) the extension of existing provinces into the territories; and

(f) notwithstanding any other law or practice, the establishment of new provinces.

(2) Subsections 38(2) to (4) do not apply in respect of amendments in relation to matters referred to in subsection (1).

43. An amendment to the Constitution of Canada in relation to any provision that applies to one or more, but not all, provinces, including

(a) any alteration to boundaries between provinces, and

(b) any amendment to any provision that relates to the use of the English or the French language within a province,

may be made by proclamation issued by the Governor General under the Great Seal of Canada only where so authorized by resolutions of the Senate and House of Commons and of the legislative assembly of each province to which the amendment applies.

44. Subject to sections 41 and 42, Parliament may exclusively make laws amending the Constitution of Canada in relation to the executive government of Canada or the Senate and House of Commons.

45. Subject to section 41, the legislature of each province may exclusively make laws amending the constitution of the province.

46. (1) The procedures for amendment under sections 38, 41, 42 and 43 may be initiated either by the Senate or the House of Commons or by the legislative assembly of a province.

(2) A resolution of assent made for the purposes of this Part may be revoked at any time before the issue of a proclamation authorized by it.

47. (1) An amendment to the Constitution of Canada made by proclamation under section 38, 41, 42 or 43 may be made without a resolution of the Senate authorizing the issue of the proclamation if, within one hundred and eighty days after the adoption by the House of Commons of a resolution authorizing its issue, the Senate has not adopted such a resolution and if, at any time after the expiration of that period, the House of Commons again adopts the resolution.

(2) Any period when Parliament is prorogued or dissolved shall not be counted in computing the one hundred and eighty day period referred to in subsection (1).

48. The Queen's Privy Council for Canada shall advise the Governor General to issue a proclamation under this Part forthwith on the adoption of the resolutions required for an amendment made by proclamation under this Part.

49. A constitutional conference composed of the Prime Minister of Canada and the first ministers of the provinces shall be convened by the Prime Minister of Canada within fifteen years after this Part comes into force to review the provisions of this Part.

....

PART VI
AMENDMENT TO THE CONSTITUTION ACT, 1867

50. [See section 92A of the Constitution Act, 1867]
51. (Schedule to section 92A).

....

PART VII
GENERAL

52. (1) The Constitution of Canada is the supreme law of Canada, and any law that is inconsistent with the provisions of the Constitution is, to the extent of the inconsistency, of no force or effect.

    (2) The Constitution of Canada includes
        (a) the *Canada Act 1982*, including this Act;
        (b) the Acts and orders referred to in the schedule; and
        (c) any amendment to any Act or order referred to in paragraph (a) or (b).

    (3) Amendments to the Constitution of Canada shall be made only in accordance with the authority contained in the Constitution of Canada.

53. (1) The enactments referred to in Column I of the schedule are hereby repealed or amended to the extent indicated in Column II thereof and, unless repealed, shall continue as law in Canada under the names set out in Column III thereof.

    (2) Every enactment, except the *Canada Act 1982*, that refers to an enactment referred to in the schedule by the name in Column I thereof is hereby amended by substituting for that name the corresponding name in Column III thereof, and any British North America Act not referred to in the schedule may be cited as the *Constitution Act* followed by the year and number, if any, of its enactment.

54. Part IV is repealed on the day that is one year after this Part comes into force and this section may be repealed and this Act renumbered, consequentially upon the repeal of Part IV and this section, by proclamation issued by the Governor General under the Great Seal of Canada.

55. A French version of the portions of the Constitution of Canada referred to in the schedule shall be prepared by the Minister of Justice of Canada as expeditiously as possible and, when any portion thereof sufficient to warrant action being taken has been so prepared, it shall be put forward for enactment by proclamation issued by the Governor General under the Great Seal of Canada pursuant to the procedure then applicable to an amendment of the same provisions of the Constitution of Canada.

56. Where any portion of the Constitution of Canada has been or is enacted in English and French or where a French version of any portion of the Constitution is enacted pursuant to section 55, the English and French versions of that portion of the Constitution are equally authoritative.

57. The English and French versions of this Act are equally authoritative.

58. Subject to section 59, this Act shall come into force on a day to be fixed by proclamation issued by the Queen or the Governor General under the Great Seal of Canada.

59. (1) Paragraph 23(1)(a) shall come into force in respect of Quebec on a day to be fixed by proclamation issued by the Queen or the Governor General under the Great Seal of Canada.

(2) A proclamation under subsection (1) shall be issued only where authorized by the legislative assembly or government of Quebec.

(3) This section may be repealed on the day paragraph 23(1)(a) comes into force in respect of Quebec and this Act amended and renumbered, consequentially upon the repeal of this section, by proclamation issued by the Queen or the Governor General under the Great Seal of Canada.

60. This Act may be cited as the *Constitution Act, 1982,* and the Constitution Acts 1867 to 1975 (No. 2) and this Act may be cited together as the *Constitution Acts, 1867 to 1982.*

The Meech Lake *Accord*

1. The *Constitution Act, 1867* is amended by adding thereto, immediately after section 1 thereof, the following section:

2. (1) The Constitution of Canada shall be interpreted in a manner consistent with

    (a) the recognition that the existence of French-speaking Canadians, centred in Quebec but also present elsewhere in Canada, and English-speaking Canadians, concentrated outside Quebec but also present in Quebec, constitutes a fundamental characteristic of Canada; and

    (b) the recognition that Quebec constitutes within Canada a distinct society.

Interpretation

(2) The role of the Parliament of Canada and the provincial legislatures to preserve the fundamental characteristics of Canada referred to in paragraph (1)(a) is affirmed.

Role of Parliament and legislatures

(3) The role of the legislature and Government of Quebec to preserve and promote the distinct identity of Quebec referred to in paragraph (1)(b) is affirmed.

Role of legislature and Government of Quebec

(4) Nothing in this section derogates from the powers, rights or privileges of Parliament or the Government of Canada, or of the legislatures or governments of the provinces, including any powers, rights or privileges relating to language.

Rights of legislatures and governments preserved

2. The said Act is further amended by adding thereto, immediately after section 24 thereof, the following section:

25. (1) Where a vacancy occurs in the Senate, the government of the province to which the vacancy relates may, in relation to that vacancy, submit to the Queen's Privy Council for Canada the names of persons who may be summoned to the Senate.

Names to be submitted

(2) Until an amendment to the Constitution of Canada is made in relation to the Senate pursuant to section 41 of the *Constitution Act, 1982*, the person summoned to fill a vacancy in the Senate shall be chosen from among persons whose names have been submitted under subsection (1) by the government of the province to which the vacancy relates and must be acceptable to the Queen's Privy Council for Canada.

Choice of Senator from names submitted

3. The said Act is further amended by adding thereto, immediately after section 95 thereof, the following heading and sections:

Agreements on Immigration and Aliens

95A. The Government of Canada shall, at the request of the government of any province, negotiate with the government of that province for the purpose of concluding an agreement relating to immigration or the temporary admission of aliens into that province that is appropriate to the needs and circumstances of that province.

95B. (1) Any agreement concluded between Canada and a province in relation to immigration or the temporary admission of aliens into that province has the force of law from the time it is declared to do so in accordance with subsection 95C(1) and shall from that time have effect notwithstanding class 25 of section 91 or section 95.

(2) An agreement that has the force of law under subsection (1) shall have effect only so long and so far as it is not repugnant to any provision of an Act of the Parliament of Canada that sets national standards and objectives relating to immigration or aliens, including any provision that establishes general classes of immigrants or relates to levels of immigration for Canada or that prescribes classes of individuals who are inadmissible into Canada.

(3) The *Canadian Charter of Rights and Freedoms* applies in respect of any agreement that has the force of law under subsection (1) and in respect of anything done by the Parliament or Government of Canada, or the legislature or government of a province, pursuant to any such agreement.

95C. (1) A declaration that an agreement referred to in subsection 95B (1) has the force of law may be made by proclamation issued by the Governor General under the Great Seal of Canada only where so authorized by resolutions of the Senate and House of Commons and of the legislative assembly of the province that is a party to the agreement.

(2) An amendment to an agreement referred to in subsection 95B(1) may be made by proclamation issued by the Governor General under the Great Seal of Canada only where so authorized

(a) by resolutions of the Senate and House of Commons and of the legislative assembly of the province that is a party to the agreement; or

(b) in such other manner as is set out in the agreement.

95D. Sections 46 to 48 of the *Constitution Act, 1982* apply, with such modifications as the circumstances require, in respect of any declaration made pursuant to subsection 95C(1), any amendment to an agreement made pursuant to subsection 95C(2) or any amendment made pursuant to section 95E.

95E. An amendment to sections 95A to 95D or this section may be made in accordance with the procedure set out in subsection 38(1) of the *Constitution Act, 1982*, but only if the amendment is authorized by resolutions of the legislative assemblies of all the provinces that are, at the time of the amendment, parties to an agreement that has the force of law under subsection 95B(1).

4. The said Act is further amended by adding thereto, immediately preceding section 96 thereof, the following heading:

Marginal notes: Commitment to negotiate; Agreements; Limitation; Application of Charter; Proclamation relating to agreements; Amendment of agreements; Application of sections 46 to 48 of Constitution Act, 1982; Amendments to sections 95A to 95D or this section

General

5. The said Act is further amended by adding thereto, immediately preceding section 101 thereof, the following heading:

Courts Established by the Parliament of Canada

6. The said Act is further amended by adding thereto, immediately after section 101 thereof, the following heading and sections:

Supreme Court of Canada

101A. (1) The court existing under the name of the Supreme Court of Canada is hereby continued as the general court of appeal for Canada, and as an additional court for the better administration of the laws of Canada, and shall continue to be a superior court of record.

(2) The Supreme Court of Canada shall consist of a chief justice to be called the Chief Justice of Canada and eight other judges, who shall be appointed by the Governor General in Council by letters patent under the Great Seal.

101B. (1) Any person may be appointed a judge of the Supreme Court of Canada who, after being admitted to the bar of any province or territory, has, for a total of at least ten years, been a judge of any court in Canada or a member of the bar of any province or territory.

(2) At least three judges of the Supreme Court of Canada shall be appointed from among persons who, after having been admitted to the bar of Quebec, have, for a total of at least ten years, been judges of any court of Quebec or of any court established by the Parliament of Canada, or members of the bar of Quebec.

101C. (1) Where a vacancy occurs in the Supreme Court of Canada, the government of each province may, in relation to that vacancy, submit to the Minister of Justice of Canada the names of any persons who have been admitted to the bar of that province and are qualified under section 101B for appointment to that court.

(2) Where an appointment is made to the Supreme Court of Canada, the Governor General in Council shall, except where the Chief Justice is appointed from among members of the Court, appoint a person whose name has been submitted under subsection (1) and who is acceptable to the Queen's Privy Council for Canada.

(3) Where an appointment is made in accordance with subsection (2) of any of the three judges necessary to meet the requirements as set out in subsection 101B(2), the Governor General in Council shall appoint a person whose name has been submitted by the Government of Quebec.

(4) Where an appointment is made in accordance with subsection(2) otherwise than is required under subsection (3), the Governor General in Council shall appoint a person whose name has been submitted by the government of a province other than Quebec.

101D. Sections 99 and 100 apply in respect of the judges of the Supreme Court of Canada.

Supreme Court
continued

Constitution of
court

Who may be
appointed judges

Three judges from
Quebec

Names may be
submitted

Appointment from
names submitted

Appointment from
Quebec

Appointment from
other provinces

Tenure, salaries,

101E. (1) Sections 101A to 101D shall not be construed as abrogating or derogating from the powers of the Parliament of Canada to make laws under section 101 except to the extent that such laws are inconsistent with those sections.

(2) For greater certainty, section 101A shall not be construed as abrogating or derogating from the powers of the Parliament of Canada to make laws relating to the reference of questions of law or fact, or any other matters, to the Supreme Court of Canada.

7. The said Act is further amended by adding thereto, immediately after section 106 thereof, the following section:

106A. (1) The Government of Canada shall provide reasonable compensation to the government of a province that chooses not to participate in a national shared-cost program that is established by the Government of Canada after the coming into force of this section in an area of exclusive provincial jurisdiction, if the province carries on a program or initiative that is compatible with the national objectives.

(2) Nothing in this section extends the legislative powers of the Parliament of Canada or of the legislatures of the provinces.

8. The said Act is further amended by adding thereto the following heading and sections:

XII—CONFERENCES ON THE ECONOMY AND OTHER MATTERS

148. A conference composed of the Prime Minister of Canada and the first ministers of the provinces shall be convened by the Prime Minister of Canada at least once each year to discuss the state of the Canadian economy and such other matters as may be appropriate.

XIII—REFERENCES

149. A reference to this Act shall be deemed to include a reference to any amendments thereto.

CONSTITUTION ACT, 1982

9. Sections 40 to 42 of the *Constitution Act, 1982* are repealed and the following substituted therefor:

40. Where an amendment is made under subsection 38(1) that transfers legislative powers from provincial legislatures to Parliament, Canada shall provide reasonable compensation to any province to which the amendment does not apply.

41. An amendment to the Constitution of Canada in relation to the following matters may be made by proclamation issued by the Governor General under the Great Seal of Canada

Margin notes (left column):

lationship to
tion 101

ferences to the
preme Court of
nada

ared-cost
gram

gislative power
extended

nferences on
economy and
er matters

erence includes
endments

npensation

endment by
nimous con-
t

only where authorized by resolutions of the Senate and House of Commons and of the legislative assembly of each province:

(a) the office of the Queen, the Governor General and the Lieutenant Governor of a province;

(b) the powers of the Senate and the method of selecting Senators;

(c) the number of members by which a province is entitled to be represented in the Senate and the residence qualifications of Senators;

(d) the right of a province to a number of members in the House of Commons not less than the number of Senators by which the province was entitled to be represented on April 17, 1982;

(e) the principle of proportionate representation of the provinces in the House of Commons prescribed by the Constitution of Canada;

(f) subject to section 43, the use of the English or the French language;

(g) the Supreme Court of Canada;

(h) the extension of existing provinces into the territories;

(i) notwithstanding any other law or practice, the establishment of new provinces; and

(j) an amendment to this Part.

10. Section 44 of the said Act is repealed and the following substituted therefor:

44. Subject to section 41, Parliament may exclusively make laws amending the Constitution of Canada in relation to the executive government of Canada or the Senate and House of Commons.

Amendments by Parliament

11. Subsection 46(1) of the said Act is repealed and the following substituted therefor:

46. (1) The procedures for amendment under sections 38, 41 and 43 may be initiated either by the Senate or the House of Commons or by the legislative assembly of a province.

Initiation of amendment procedures

12. Subsection 47(1) of the said Act is repealed and the following substituted therefor:

47. (1) An amendment to the Constitution of Canada made by proclamation under section 38, 41 or 43 may be made without a resolution of the Senate authorizing the issue of the proclamation if, within one hundred and eighty days after the adoption by the House of Commons of a resolution authorizing its issue, the Senate has not adopted such a resolution and if, at any time after the expiration of that period, the House of Commons again adopts the resolution.

Amendments without Senate resolution

13. Part VI of the said Act is repealed and the following substituted therefor:

PART VI
CONSTITUTIONAL CONFERENCES

50. (1) A constitutional conference composed of the Prime Minister of Canada and the first ministers of the provinces shall be convened by the Prime Minister of Canada at least once each year, commencing in 1988.

Constitutional conference

(2) The conferences convened under subsection (1) shall have included on their agenda the following matters:
> (a) Senate reform, including the role and functions of the Senate, its powers, the method of selecting Senators and representation in the Senate;
> (b) roles and responsibilities in relation to fisheries; and
> (c) such other matters as are agreed upon.

14. Subsection 52(2) of the said Act is amended by striking out the word "and" at the end of paragraph (b) thereof, by adding the word "and" at the end of paragraph (c) thereof and by adding thereto the following paragraph:
> (d) any other amendment to the Constitution of Canada.

15. Section 61 of the said Act is repealed and the following substituted therefor:
61. A reference to the *Constitution Act, 1982* or a reference to the *Constitution Acts 1867* to *1982*, shall be deemed to include a reference to any amendments thereto.

General

16. Nothing in section 2 of the *Constitution Act, 1867* affects section 25 or 27 of the *Canadian Charter of Rights and Freedoms*, section 35 of the *Constitution Act, 1982* or class 24 of section 91 of the *Constitution Act, 1867*.

Citation

17. This amendment may be cited as the *Constitution Amendment, 1987*.

Canada Clause from the CHARLOTTETOWN *Accord, 1992*

1. The *Constitution Act, 1867* is amended by adding thereto, immediately after section 1 thereof, the following section:

   "**2.** (1) The Constitution of Canada, including the *Canadian Charter of Rights and Freedoms*, shall be interpreted in a manner consistent with the following fundamental characteristics:

Canada Clause

   (a) Canada is a democracy committed to a parliamentary and federal system of government and to the rule of law;

   (b) the Aboriginal peoples of Canada, being the first peoples to govern this land, have the right to promote their languages, cultures and traditions and to ensure the integrity of their societies, and their governments constitute one of three orders of government in Canada;

   (c) Quebec constitutes within Canada a distinct society, which includes a French-speaking majority, a unique culture and a civil law tradition;

   (d) Canadians and their governments are committed to the vitality and development of official language minority communities throughout Canada;

   (e) Canadians are committed to racial and ethnic equality in a society that includes citizens from many lands who have contributed, and continue to contribute, to the building of a strong Canada that reflects its cultural and racial diversity;

   (f) Canadians are committed to a respect for individual and collective human rights and freedoms of all people;

   (g) Canadians are committed to the equality of female and male persons; and

   (h) Canadians confirm the principle of the equality of the provinces at the same time as recognizing their diverse characteristics.

   (2) The role of the legislature and Government of Quebec to preserve and promote the distinct society of Quebec is affirmed.

Role of legislatu[re] and Governmen[t] of Quebec

   (3) Nothing in this section derogates from the powers, rights or privileges of the Parliament or the Government of Canada, or of the legislatures or governments of the

Powers, rights a[nd] privileges preser[ved]

provinces, or of the legislative bodies or governments of the Aboriginal peoples of Canada, including any powers, rights or privileges relating to language.

original and aty rights

(4) For greater certainty, nothing in this section abrogates or derogates from the aboriginal and treaty rights of the Aboriginal peoples of Canada."

Index

Bill of Rights, 47, 51, 100–3, 241, 576
Bills, 479, 547–48, 552–53, 557, 559
 government, 460, 479, 541, 543,
  547, 557, 563, 565–66, 568
 money (supply), 478–79, 547, 557,
  561, 568
 private, 547, 563–64
 private members', 543, 547, 557, 559
Black, Conrad, 210, 317–19
Blacks, 101, 191–92, 195, 200
Bloc Québécois (BQ), 5, 63–64, 182, 350,
 359, 374, 380, 382, 391–92, 397, 407,
 416, 419, 555, 604
Bond-rating agencies, 263, 272
Books, 266, 268, 324
Borden, R.L., 35, 37, 176, 234, 371–72,
 485, 500
Bosnia, 254, 273
Bouchard, Lucien, 63–64, 182, 391, 413
Bourassa, Robert, 53, 55, 59, 113, 179–81,
 186
Bowell, Mackenzie, 484, 486
British Columbia, 35, 46, 60, 62, 83, 101,
 126, 131, 135, 138, 140, 142, 145,
 154–55, 161, 163, 170, 192–93,
 195–96, 234, 262, 296, 342, 372, 391
British North America Act (BNA Act).
 See Constitution Act, 1867
British parliamentary system. *See*
 Westminster model
Broadbent, Ed, 326, 356, 374, 383, 407,
 409, 412
Brokerage, 11–12, 375–76, 378, 380, 393,
 398, 420
Bronfman family, 209–10
Budget, 491, 496–97, 541, 557
Bureaucracy, 4, 13, 17–21, 29, 85, 87–92,
 105, 113, 115, 134, 148, 164, 169, 178,
 187, 197–98, 201, 212, 227–28,
 238–40, 247, 273, 289, 292, 305, 327,
 332, 335, 379, 386, 392, 396, 399, 420,
 426, 432–33, 435–38, 441–42, 445–48,
 459–62, 466, 471, 479–80, 484,

492–93, 496, 500, 507–33, 548, 552,
 570
Bush, George, 262, 286
Business Council on National Issues, 214,
 427, 429, 441
Business influence, 14–16, 33–35, 93, 116,
 149, 170, 174, 212–14, 274, 365, 399,
 420–21, 427–29, 437, 449–50, 466,
 500, 533, 564–65, 569, 590, 605

C

Cabinet, 17, 20, 29–30, 44, 48, 60, 71, 83,
 87, 92, 115, 148–49, 174, 187, 201,
 234, 237, 247, 258, 355, 370, 399, 420,
 433, 435–38, 459–62, 466, 471–501,
 507–9, 519, 522, 524–26, 532, 538,
 545, 554, 557–60, 563, 565, 568–70,
 580, 588, 604. *See also* Ministers and
 Prime Ministers.
 Cabinet committees, 491–92,
  494–95, 499
 Departmental and institutionalized
  cabinets, 87, 436, 462, 482,
  491–95
Caisse de Dépôt et Placement du Quebec,
 137
Callbeck, Catherine, 238–39
Camp, Dalton, 389
Campbell, Kim, 239, 383, 385, 406–7,
 409, 411–13, 494, 510
Canada Act, 46
Canada Assistance Plan (CAP), 78–81,
 88, 221, 224–26, 244, 520
Canada clause, 60, 242, 292–93
Canada Council, 268
Canada Health Act, 79–80, 88, 226, 547
Canada Health and Social Transfer,
 80–81, 226
Canada–U.S. Free Trade Agreement, 88,
 140, 143, 214, 226, 251, 259, 268–71,
 273, 294, 298, 316, 362, 374, 417, 429,
 439, 526, 566, 601

section 33 (notwithstanding clause), 103, 112–13, 241, 284

Chief Electoral Officer, 343, 346, 363

Children and child care, 220–21, 223, 225, 234, 242, 244–45, 298, 312–14, 316

Chrétien, Jean, 55, 63, 88, 128, 130, 141, 180, 182, 186, 199, 213, 221, 226–27, 242, 267, 271–73, 321, 347, 363, 383–84, 386, 396–97, 407–8, 410–11, 413, 447, 480, 486, 493–96, 507, 510–12, 515, 545, 603, 606

Churches. *See* Religion; Roman Catholic Church

Churchill Falls, 144

Citizens' Forum, 52, 59, 64, 199

Civil law (Quebec), 26, 31, 72, 174, 182, 235, 489, 576–79, 585

Civil liberties, 32, 46–48, 51, 99–117, 283, 285

Clark, Joe, 59, 326, 374, 383, 385, 387, 416, 487–88, 494, 498, 512, 519, 541, 549

Class analysis, 10, 12, 14–16, 19–20, 37, 65, 93, 114, 116–17, 137, 149, 170, 178, 188, 202, 205–28, 247, 274, 288, 296, 298, 304, 306, 333–35, 364, 375–79, 381, 399, 413, 418–19, 449–50, 466–67, 500–1, 517, 533, 539, 569–70, 592. *See also* Middle class; Poor and poverty; Upper class; Working class

Class consciousness, 14, 188, 205, 217, 227, 236, 288, 290, 298, 312, 375, 377–78, 418, 440, 533

Cleavages, 7–8, 375–76, 417, 489, 604

Clientele relationship, 435, 442, 520

Coalition Government. *See* Union Government

Coercion, 4, 15–7, 20, 164, 188, 205, 227, 284, 306, 334, 377, 465–67, 533

Collective bargaining, 514, 518. *See also* Labour; Unions; Strikes

Collectivism, 114, 117, 154, 181, 285–88,

290–91, 294, 381, 394–97, 465, 545, 570

Common Law, 100, 576, 579

Commonwealth, 35–36, 272, 477, 483

Communications, 130–31, 137, 264–68

Communist Party, 51, 284

Confederation, 27–28, 31, 70, 76, 83

Confederation of Regions Party (COR), 184, 186, 380

Confederation of Tomorrow Conference, 52–53

Conscription, 176–77, 302, 372–73

Conservative Party. *See* Progressive Conservative Party

Conservatism, 393–98

Constitution, 32–34, 43–48, 64, 88

Constitution Act, 1867, 28, 34, 44, 70, 72, 101, 154–55, 160, 174–75, 236, 473, 478, 566, 577, 579, 581

Constitution Act, 1982, 45–48, 50–51, 53–55, 146, 179, 183, 374, 472, 561. *See also* Charter of Rights and Freedoms

Constitutional Act (1791), 26, 174

Constitutional amending formula, 45–46, 48–51, 53, 55–56, 59, 61, 63–64, 72, 167, 181–82, 293, 561

Constitutional amendments, 36, 45–46, 49, 72

Constitutional conventions, 48–49, 54, 83, 85, 473–75, 478, 481, 487, 567

Cooperation and cooperatives, 290, 377

Cooperative Commonwealth Federation (CCF), 78, 216, 224, 356, 372–73, 377–78, 380–81, 394, 558, 567

Cooperative federalism, 85–88, 520

Copps, Sheila, 363, 383, 485, 494

Core-Periphery Analysis, 131, 139, 142

Corporations, 5–7, 11–12, 14–16, 19, 21, 31, 37, 75–76, 92–93, 107–8, 114–15, 126, 130–31, 141, 147, 149, 163, 169–70, 186, 188, 202, 210–21, 214, 216, 224, 227, 240, 254–56, 258,

To the owner of this book

We hope that you have enjoyed *Canadian Politics*, Second Edition, and we would like to know as much about your experiences with this text as you would care to offer. Only through your comments and those of others can we learn how to make this a better text for future readers.

School _____ Your instructor's name _____

Course _____ Was the text required? _____ Recommended? _____

1. What did you like the most about *Canadian Politics?*

_____

_____

_____

2. How useful was this text for your course?

_____

_____

_____

3. Do you have any recommendations for ways to improve the next edition of this text?

_____

_____

_____

4. In the space below or in a separate letter, please write any other comments you have about the book. (For example, please feel free to comment on reading level, writing style, terminology, design features, and learning aids.)

_____

_____

_____

_____

Optional

Your name _____ Date _____

May Nelson Canada quote you, either in promotion for *Canadian Politics* or in future publishing ventures?

Yes _____ No _____

Thanks!

PLEASE TAPE SHUT. DO NOT STAPLE.

TAPE SHUT

TAPE SHUT

FOLD HERE

Nelson

MAIL ⟩ POSTE
Canada Post Corporation
Société canadienne des postes
Postage paid   Port payé
if mailed in Canada si posté au Canada
Business Reply   **Réponse d'affaires**
0066102399   01

TAPE SHUT

TAPE SHUT

0066102399-M1K5G4-BR01

NELSON CANADA
Market and Product Development
PO BOX 60225 STN BRM B
TORONTO ON M7Y 2H1